The **Rough Guide** to

Mallorca and Menorca

written and researched by
Phil Lee

with additional research by
Jeffrey Kennedy

ROUGH GUIDES

NEW YORK • LONDON • DELHI
www.roughguides.com

△ Old town, Palma

Introduction to

Mallorca and Menorca

Few Mediterranean holiday spots are as often and as unfairly maligned as Mallorca. The largest of the Balearic Islands, an archipelago to the east of the Spanish mainland comprising four main islands – Mallorca, Menorca, Ibiza and Formentera – Mallorca is commonly perceived as little more than sun, sex, booze and high-rise hotels. Indeed, there's a long-standing Spanish joke about a mythical fifth Balearic island called "Majorca" (the English spelling), visited by an estimated eight million tourists a year – tourists who know little and care less about their island surroundings.

This negative image was spawned by the helter-skelter development of the 1960s, which submerged tracts of the coastline beneath hotels, villas and apartment blocks. In reality, however, the concrete sprawl is largely confined to the Bay of Palma and a handful of mega-resorts notching the east coast,

iii

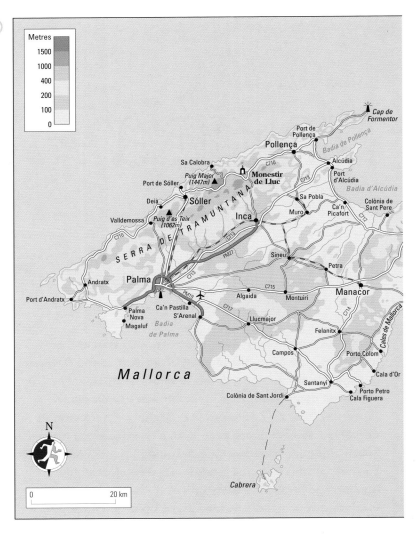

and for the most part Mallorca remains – to the surprise of many first-time visitors – often beautiful and frequently fascinating, from the craggy mountains and medieval monasteries of its north coast through to the antique towns of the central plain. Indeed, there's a startling variety and physical beauty to the island, which, along with the mildness of the climate, has drawn well-heeled expatriates to settle here since the nineteenth century, from Habsburg dukes to artists, actors and writers of many descriptions, including Robert Graves, Michael Douglas and Roger McGough.

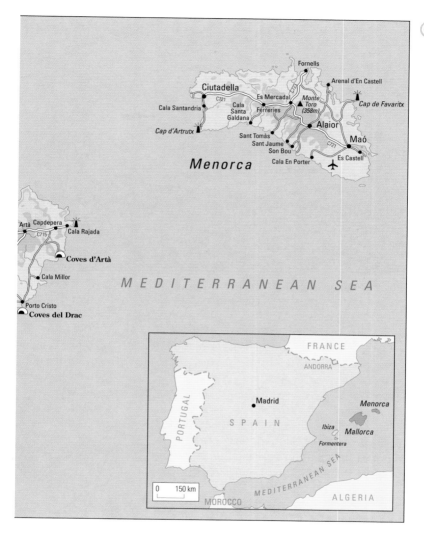

Straddling the sailing routes between the east and west Mediterranean, Mallorca was an important and prosperous trading station throughout the medieval period, but it was left behind in the Spanish dash to exploit the Americas from the early sixteenth century onwards. Neglected, Mallorca turned in on itself, becoming a deeply hierarchical and profoundly Catholic backwater dominated by a conservative landed gentry, who ruled the economic and political roost from their large estates on the fertile central plain, Es Pla. Since the 1960s, however, **mass tourism** has literally

▽ Serra de Tramuntana

stood things on its head. Agriculture, once the mainstay of the local economy, faded into the background, and the island's former poverty was all but washed away: Mallorca's population of 640,000 now enjoy the highest per capita level of disposable income in Spain.

To the east of Mallorca lies **Menorca**, the second largest and most agricultural island in the Balearic archipelago, with a population of just 66,000. Menorca's rolling fields, wooded ravines and humpy hills fill out the interior in between its two main – but still small – towns of Maó, the island's capital, and Ciutadella. Much of Menorca's landscape looks pretty much as it did at the turn of the twentieth century, though many of the fields are no longer cultivated, and only on the edge of the island (and then only in parts) have its rocky coves been colonized by sprawling villa complexes. Nor is the development likely to spread: the resorts have been kept at a discreet distance from the two main towns, and this is how the Menorcans like it. In addition, the islanders are also pushing ahead with a variety of environmental schemes, the most prominent being the creation of a chain of conservation areas that will eventually protect about half of the island, including the pristine coves that are one of its real delights.

▽ Boats, Port de Pollença

Where to go

In **Mallorca**, the obvious place to begin is **Palma**, the island capital, which arches around the shores of its bay just a few kilometres from its busy international airport. Palma is the Balearics' one real city, a bustling, historic place whose grandee mansions and magnificent Gothic cathedral serve as a fine backdrop to an excellent café and restaurant scene. Add to this lots of good hotels and you've got a city that deserves at least a couple of days. Indeed, many visitors spend their entire holiday here, day-tripping out into the rest of the island as the mood (and weather) takes them – an easy proposition given that it's only a couple of hours drive from one end of Mallorca to the other. To the east of Palma stretches **Es Pla**, an agricultural plain that fills out the centre of the island, sprinkled with ancient and seldom-visited country towns, the most interesting of which are **Binissalem**, **Sineu** and **Petra**. On either side of the plain are coastal mountains. To the north, the wild and wonderful **Serra de Tramuntana** rolls along the entire coastline, punctuated by deep sheltered valleys and beautiful cove **beaches**, notably Cala de Deià and Platja de Formentor. Tucked away here too is **Sóller**, a delightful market town of old stone merchant houses that is best reached from Palma on the antique **railway**, an extraordinarily scenic journey. The mountains also hide a string of picturesque villages, most memorably **Banyalbufar**, **Deià**, the long-time haunt of Robert Graves, and **Fornalutx**, as well as a pair of intriguing monasteries at **Valldemossa**, where Chopin and George Sand famously wintered, and **Lluc**, home to a much-venerated statue of the

Catalan and Castilian

Catalan (*Català*) is spoken by over six million people spread across the Balearics, parts of eastern Spain, Andorra and the French Pyrenees. It is a Romance language, stemming from Latin via medieval Provençal, though despite its ancient origins, Spaniards in the rest of the country often belittle it, saying that to get a Catalan word you just cut a Castilian (Spanish) one in half. When Franco came to power in 1939, Catalan publishing houses, bookshops and libraries were raided and books destroyed, and throughout his dictatorship he excluded Catalan from the media and, most importantly, the schools, which is why many older people cannot read or write Catalan, even if they speak it all the time.

Since the death of Franco in 1975 and the subsequent federalization of Spain, the Balearics have reasserted the primacy of Catalan. The most obvious sign of this linguistic renaissance is the replacement of Castilian street names by their Catalan equivalents. Despite the resurgence of Catalan, however, the emigration of thousands of mainland Spaniards to the islands means that Castilian is now the dominant language in around forty percent of Balearic households.

Madonna. The range is also criss-crossed with footpaths and makes for ideal **hiking**, particularly in the cooler spring and autumn. Beyond Lluc, the mountains roll down to a coastal plain that holds the lovely little town of **Pollença** and one of the island's most appealing medium-sized resorts, **Port de Pollença**, which is itself just along the bay from the sprawling but well-kept resort of **Port d'Al-cúdia**. In the north, Mallorca finishes with a final scenic flourish in the rearing cliffs of the **Península de Formentor**, where the final cape draws hundreds of seabirds.

Mallorca's second mountain range, the gentler, greener **Serres de Llevant** shadows the coves of the southeast coast and culminates in the pine-clad headlands and medieval hill towns of the island's northeast corner. Many of the east-coast resorts are rather overblown – the pick are **Cala Rajada**, close to several fine beaches, and **Porto Petro**. There are also a couple of easily visited cave systems – the most diverting is the **Coves del Drac** – and the comely hilltop town of **Artà**, close to the substantial prehistoric remains of **Ses Paisses**.

Smaller, flatter **Menorca**, the most easterly of the Balearics, boasts two attractive towns, the island capital of **Maó**, just 5km from the airport, and **Ciutadella**, 45km away to the west. Both towns have preserved much of their eighteenth- and early nineteenth-century appearance, though Ciutadella has the aesthetic edge, the mazy lanes and alleys of its antique centre shadowed by fine old mansions and monasteries, plus a set of

▽ Olive trees

△ Cala San Vicenç

charming Gothic churches. Linking the two is the island's one and only main road, the **C721**, which slips across the rural interior, passing by the pleasant market towns of **Alaior**, **Es Mercadal** and **Ferreries**. A series of side roads connects the C721 with the island's **resorts**, the best appointed of which are **Cala Santa Galdana** and the one-time fishing village of **Fornells**, as well as

Life's a beach

For all their diverse charms, the main Balearic activity – or lack of it – is sunbathing on the beach. Some resorts, like S'Arenal, attract a crowd for whom time on the beach is a serious beauty business, as borne out by all the flat-pack stomachs and glistening pecs. At others, like Port de Pollença, it's a family affair, involving a bit of sandcastle building here and a bit of swimming and pedalo-pedalling there. On Mallorca, the finest sandy beaches are in the north fringing Port d'Alcúdia; at Cala Millor on the east coast; and, most fashionably – or, in terms of costume, most skimpily – at the Platja de Palma, just to the east of Palma at S'Arenal. All three of these beaches are flanked by a veritable army of hotels, whereas Es Trenc, another long sandy strand on the south coast, is comparatively undeveloped.

The rockier northern coast from Port d'Alcúdia to Port d'Andratx is home to a string of cove beaches, almost invariably made up of shingle and pebble – two of the most scenic are Cala Deià and Cala Estellencs. On Menorca, there are wide sandy beaches on the south coast at Sant Jaume and Son Bou and a battery of lovely sandy cove beaches, like those at Cala Turqueta and Cala d'Algaiarens.

wind-battered headlands and remote **cove beaches**, where there's not a concrete block in sight. The highway also squeezes past **Monte Toro**, Menorca's highest peak and the site of a quaint little convent, from where there are superlative island-wide views. Menorca's other claim to fame is its liberal smattering of prehistoric remains – two of the most substantial are the **Talatí de Dalt**, outside Maó, and **Torre d'en Gaumés**.

△ Palma Old Town

When to go

There's little difference between the **climates** of Mallorca and Menorca. Spring and autumn are the ideal times for a visit, when the weather is comfortably warm, with none of the oven-like temperatures which bake the islands in July and August. It's well worth considering a winter break too: even in January temperatures are usually

Talayots and taulas

Mallorca and, more especially, Menorca are dotted with an extraordinary number of prehistoric remains, mostly dating from the so-called Talayotic period (roughly 1400–800 BC), named after the distinctive conical rock mounds – *talayots* – found on Menorca. *Talayots* are often found next to *taulas*, T-shaped structures formed from two large stones and usually standing around four metres high. Both represent a distinctively Menorcan form of megalithic ruin: *taulas* are unique to the island, while the nearest equivalent to *talayots* are the Nuragh towers of Sardinia.

There are scores of *taulas* and *talayots* scattered across Menorca, but despite the quantity of the remains, their original purpose continues to perplex archeologists. *Talayots* have been variously claimed to have served as watchtowers, burial sites or storehouses, whilst the enigmatic *taulas* have provoked an even wilder range of hypotheses – one over-imaginative nineteenth-century writer claimed they were tables used for human sacrifice, though a more convincing explanation suggests that they represent the stylised head of a bull at a time when the worship of the bull was common across much of the Mediterranean.

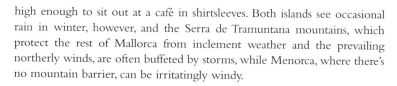

high enough to sit out at a café in shirtsleeves. Both islands see occasional rain in winter, however, and the Serra de Tramuntana mountains, which protect the rest of Mallorca from inclement weather and the prevailing northerly winds, are often buffeted by storms, while Menorca, where there's no mountain barrier, can be irritatingly windy.

Palma climate table

	Jan	Feb	Mar	Apr	May	June	July	Aug	Sept	Oct	Nov	Dec
Highest recorded temp °C												
	22	23	24	26	31	37	39	37	35	31	26	24
Average daily max temp °C												
	14	15	17	19	22	26	29	29	27	23	18	15
Average daily min temp °C												
	6	6	8	10	13	17	20	20	18	14	10	8
Lowest recorded temp °C												
	-3	-4	-1	1	5	8	12	11	4	1	1	-1
Average hours of sunshine per day												
	5	6	6	7	9	10	11	11	8	6	5	4
Average number of days with rain												
	8	6	8	6	5	3	1	3	5	9	8	9

things not to miss

What follows is a selective taste of the country's highlights – magnificent scenery, beautiful beaches, outstanding places to eat – arranged in five colour-coded categories. All highlights have a page reference to take you straight into the guide, where you can find out more.

01 Deià Page **120** • The coastal village of Deià is an enchanting huddle of ancient stone buildings set against a handsome mountain backdrop – no wonder Robert Graves made his home here.

02 Valldemossa Page **125** • Sitting pretty in the hills, the ancient town of Valldemossa is home to a fascinating monastery whose echoing cloisters and ancient cells once accommodated Chopin and George Sand.

04 Ciutadella Page **251** • The prettiest town on Menorca, with an antique centre full of mazy lanes shadowed by fine old mansions and monasteries, plus charming Gothic churches.

03 Eating in Palma Page **86** • Palma has the liveliest café and restaurant scene in the Balearics, with a hat full of excellent tapas bars.

05 Palma-Sóller train Page **108** • The antique train that weaves its way over the mountains from Palma to Sóller provides wonderful views and serves as a fine introduction to the island's varied landscapes.

06 Península de Formentor Page **160** • The knobbly peaks and sheer cliffs of this spectacular peninsula backdrop one of the island's best beaches and finest hotels.

08 **Platja de Palma, S'Arenal** Page **95** • Mallorca's most self-conscious beach, the Platja de Palma's miles of white sand are a magnet to the bronzed and the beautiful.

07 **Modernista architecture** Page **82** • The distinctive Catalan version of Art Nouveau, characterized by flowing organic lines, graceful balconies and brilliantly coloured ceramics.

09 **Jardins d'Alfabia** Page **114** • The lush, oasis-like Jardins d'Alfabia are the finest gardens on Mallorca, their watered trellises and terraces dating back to the time of the Moors.

10 **Cap de Favaritx** Page **234** • This windswept cape, with its bare, lunar-like rocks, is a highlight of Menorca's north coast.

11 Cabrera island Page **204** • This austere, scrub-covered islet is home to a fourteenth-century castle, plentiful bird life and the rare Lilfords wall lizard.

12 Fornells Page **235** • The stylish little resort of Fornells is famous for its gourmet *caldereta de llagosta* – lobster stew – on the menu at a cluster of attractive seafood restaurants.

13 Palma Cathedral Page **65** • Dominating the waterfront, the monumental bulk of Palma's magnificent cathedral offers one of Spain's finest examples of the Gothic style.

14 Talatí de Dalt Page **221** • In an attractive rural setting close to Maó, this extensive site is the most satisfying of Menorca's many prehistoric remains.

15 Artà Page **183** • The sun-bleached roofs of tiny Artà clamber up the steepest of hills to a castle-like shrine, below which lies the remarkably intact prehistoric village of Ses Paisses.

16 **Maó** Page **211** • Menorca's modest capital retains a pleasantly small-town feel, with an ancient centre, long-established cafés and old-fashioned shops.

17 **Sóller** Page **108** • Tucked away in an exquisite mountain setting high above the coast, the appealing town of Sóller boasts handsome stone mansions and a picture-perfect main square.

18 **Monestir de Lluc** Page **146** • This rambling monastery holds the Balearics' most venerated icon, La Moreneta, and also has an excellent museum and makes a great base for mountain hikes.

19 **Hiking in the Serra de Tramuntana** Pages **128 & 150** • Rolling along the west coast, this rugged mountain range holds scores of exhilarating hiking trails.

20 **Cala Turqueta** Page **262** • One of the finest of Menorca's enticing clutch of unspoilt cove beaches, with a band of fine white sand set between wooded lime-stone cliffs and crystal-clear waters.

Contents

Using this Rough Guide

We've tried to make this Rough Guide a good read and easy to use. The book is divided into five main sections, and you should be able to find whatever you want in one of them.

Colour section

The front colour section offers a quick tour of Mallorca and Menorca. The **introduction** aims to give you a feel for the place, with suggestions on where to go and information about the weather. Next, our author rounds up his favourite aspects of Mallorca and Menorca in the **things not to miss** section – whether it's great food, amazing sights or a special beach. Right after this comes a full **contents** list.

Basics

The Basics section covers all the **pre-departure** nitty-gritty to help you plan your trip. This is where to find out which airlines fly to Mallorca and Menorca, what paperwork you'll need, what to do about money and insurance, Internet access, food, security, public transport, car rental – in fact just about every piece of **general practical information** you might need.

Guide

This is the heart of the book, divided into user-friendly chapters each of which covers a specific region. Every chapter starts with a list of **highlights** and an **introduction** to help you to decide where to go. Likewise, introductions to the various towns and regions within each chapter should

help you plan your itinerary. We start most town accounts with information on accommodation, followed by a tour of the sights, and finally reviews of places to eat and drink, and details of nightlife. Longer accounts also have a directory of practical listings. Each chapter concludes with **public transport** details for that region.

Contexts

Read Contexts to get a deeper understanding of what makes Mallorca and Menorca tick. We include a brief **history**, an article about Balearic **flora and fauna** and a detailed further reading section that reviews dozens of **books** relating to the islands.

Language

The Language section gives useful guidance for speaking Spanish and Catalan and pulls together all the vocabulary you might need on your trip, including a comprehensive **menu reader**, plus a **glossary** of words and terms peculiar to the region.

Index + small print

As well as a **full index**, this section covers publishing information, credits and acknowledgements, and also has our contact details in case you want to send in updates and corrections to the book – or suggestions as to how we might improve it.

Map and chapter list

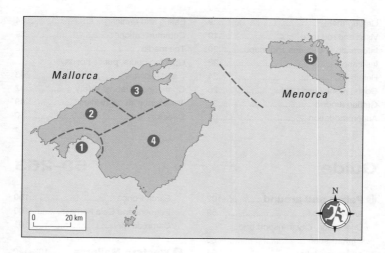

Contents

Contexts   265–307

Language   309–323

small print and **Index**   **341–352**

CONTENTS

Basics

Basics

Getting there

For travellers from the UK and Ireland, the easiest and least expensive way to reach Mallorca and Menorca is to fly. Literally hundreds of charter flights shuttle back and forth between Britain and Ireland and the islands during the summer season and, although they are heavily booked by package-tour operators, there are almost always spare seats for the independent traveller, often at bargain-basement prices. There are also scheduled flights from London and a string of regional UK airports direct to Mallorca, though for Menorca you usually have to change, most conveniently at Barcelona. It's also possible to reach Mallorca and Menorca by driving from the UK to Spain's east coast, from where there are ferries and catamarans over to the islands, but this takes two or three days. Visitors from North America and Australasia will need to fly to London, Madrid or Barcelona – or another European hub – before catching an onward flight to the islands.

Fares to Europe from North America, Australia and New Zealand vary according to the time of year. They're most expensive around Easter and from June to September; fares drop during the "shoulder" seasons – October and the first half of May – and are cheapest during the low season from November to March (excluding Christmas and New Year, when prices are hiked up and seats are at a premium). Flying at weekends ordinarily adds £35/$50 to the round-trip fare. If you're flying to the islands from the UK or Ireland, the same general strictures apply except on the London to Palma route, where competition is so intense that prices can be slashed at any time of the year.

Special deals aside, you can often cut costs by going through a **specialist flight agent** – either a consolidator, who buys up blocks of tickets from the airlines and sells them at a discount, or a **discount agent**, who in addition to dealing with discounted flights may also offer special student and youth fares and a range of other travel-related services such as travel insurance, car rentals, tours and the like. Some agents specialize in charter flights, but note that departure dates are fixed and withdrawal penalties high. In some cases, you may actually find it cheaper to pick up a bargain **package deal** from one of the tour operators listed on p.12, p.14 and p.15 and then find your own accommodation when you get to the islands.

Booking flights online

Many airlines and discount travel websites offer the opportunity of **booking tickets online**, thereby cutting out the costs of agents and middlemen. Good deals are legion.

Online booking agents and general travel sites

Ⓦ **www.cheapflights.com** Flight deals, travel agents, plus links to other travel sites. Bookings from the UK and Ireland only. From the US, Ⓦ www.cheapflight.com; from Canada, Ⓦ www.cheapflights.ca; from Australia, Ⓦ www.cheapflights.com.au.

Ⓦ **www.cheaptickets.com** Discount flight specialists. Bookings from the US only.

Ⓦ **www.etn.nl/discount.htm** A hub of consolidator and discount agent web links, maintained by the non-profit European Travel Network.

Ⓦ **www.expedia.com** Discount airfares, all-airline search engine and daily deals. Bookings from the US only. From the UK, Ⓦ www.expedia.co.uk; from Canada, Ⓦ www.expedia.ca.

Ⓦ **www.flyaow.com** Online air travel info and reservations site.

Ⓦ **www.gaytravel.com** Gay online travel agent, offering accommodation, cruises, tours and more.

@ **www.hotwire.com** Last-minute savings of up to forty percent on regular published fares. Travellers must be at least 18 and there are no refunds, transfers or changes allowed. Log-in required. Bookings from the US only.

@ **www.lastminute.com** Good last-minute holiday package and flight-only deals. Bookings from the UK only. From Australia, @ www.lastminute.com.au.

@ **www.priceline.com** Name-your-own-price website that has deals at around forty percent off standard fares. You cannot specify flight times (although you do specify dates) and the tickets are non-refundable, non-transferable and non-changeable. Bookings from the US only. From the UK, @ www.priceline.co.uk.

@ **www.skyauction.com** Bookings from the US only. Auctions tickets and travel packages using a "second bid" scheme. The best strategy is to bid the maximum you're willing to pay, since if you win you'll pay just enough to beat the runner-up regardless of your maximum bid.

@ **www. travelocity.com** Destination guides, web fares and best deals for car hire, accommodation and lodging as well as flights. Provides access to SABRE, the most comprehensive central reservations system in the US.

@ **www.travelshop.com.au** Australian website offering discounted flights, packages, insurance, and online bookings.

Flights from the UK and Ireland

From the UK, Mallorca and Menorca are readily reached from London and a number of regional airports. There are charter flights to both islands and frequent scheduled flights to Mallorca; scheduled flights to Menorca often require a change of plane, with the quickest connections usually being via Barcelona. Nonstop **flying times** from London to either island are a little over two hours (or 2hr 45min from Manchester).

Fierce competition keeps fares cheap on **scheduled flights** on the London to Palma route, though from regional airports the price picture is much more variable. The least expensive tickets are usually hedged with restrictions, commonly requiring the booking to be made seven days in advance and obliging you to spend one Saturday night abroad. The cheapest flights are with the budget airline Easyjet, whose fares can fall to around £50 for a return from London

Gatwick or Stansted to Palma. A standard, fully-flexible return with British Midland from London Heathrow to Palma costs anywhere between £100 and £400 depending on availability and the time of year. Another option is Iberia's **open-jaw tickets**, whereby you fly to one Balearic island and return from another: London Heathrow–Palma and Menorca–London Heathrow costs as little as £110 in low season, twice that in high season. Fares on **charter flights** vary enormously, but can sometimes represent a significant saving compared to scheduled flights. However, you're unlikely to be able to change the dates and times of travel once you've bought your ticket. It's worth checking out charter fares either online (see booking agents Online, pp.9–10) or with the flight agents listed on p.11.

From Ireland, charter flights are the cheapest and most obvious way to reach Mallorca and Menorca, though there's also a limited range of scheduled flights, mainly with Aer Lingus, British Airways and Iberia, and mostly via Barcelona. Summer charter flights direct to the islands are easy to pick up from either Dublin or Belfast. **Prices** are highest during August – reckon on around £200 return from Belfast, €400 from Dublin – but drop a little in the months either side. Alternatively, taking a budget flight to London and then switching to a London–Palma flight might save you a few pounds. Low-cost carriers flying into London from Ireland include Ryanair, Virgin Express and EasyJet.

Airlines

Aer Lingus Republic of Ireland ☎0818/365 000, @ www.aerlingus.ie. Dublin to Palma and Barcelona.

Air2000 UK ☎0870/240 1402, @ www.air2000.com. Charter flight specialist with departures to Palma from London Gatwick, Stansted and Luton, Birmingham, Bristol, East Midlands, Exeter, Glasgow, Manchester and Newcastle.

Air Europa UK ☎0870/240 1501, @ www.aireuropa.com. London Gatwick to Madrid and (May–Sept only) to Palma.

bmibaby UK ☎0870/264 2229, Republic of Ireland ☎01/236 6130, @ www.bmibaby.com. British Midland's budget airline, with flights from Cardiff, East Midlands and Manchester to Palma, and from East Midlands and Manchester to Barcelona.

Britannia Airways UK ☎01582/424155, ⓦwww.britanniaairways.com. Charter flights from twenty UK airports to Mallorca and Menorca (sometimes via mainland Spain).

British Airways UK ☎0870/850 9850, Republic of Ireland ☎0141/222 2345, ⓦwww.britishairways.com. Flights to Palma from Manchester (via Madrid) and Dublin and Glasgow (via London Gatwick); to Barcelona from London Heathrow and London Gatwick; and to Menorca from London Gatwick.

British Midland UK ☎0870/607 0555, Republic of Ireland ☎01/407 3036, ⓦwww.flybmi.com. London Heathrow to Madrid and Palma.

EasyJet UK ☎0870/600 0000, ⓦwww.easyjet.com. Budget scheduled flights to Palma from Bristol, Liverpool, London Gatwick, Luton and Stansted; to Barcelona from Bristol, East Midlands, Liverpool, London Gatwick, Luton, Newcastle and Stansted; to Madrid from Liverpool, London Gatwick and Luton; and from Belfast to London Gatwick, Luton and Stansted.

Iberia UK ☎0845/601 2854, Republic of Ireland ☎01/677 9846, ⓦwww.iberiaairlines.co.uk. London Heathrow, Manchester and Dublin to Barcelona, and onward connections to Mallorca and Menorca.

Monarch UK ☎0870/040 5040, ⓦwww.monarch-airlines.com. Luton to Menorca and Manchester to Palma.

Ryanair UK ☎0870/156 9569, Republic of Ireland ☎01/609 7800, ⓦwww.ryanair.com. Dublin to London Gatwick, Manchester and Stansted; Cork, Derry, Kerry, Knock and Shannon to Stansted.

Flight agents

CIE Tours International Republic of Ireland ☎01/703 1888, ⓦwww.cietours.ie. General flight and tour agent.

Co-op Travel Care UK ☎0870/112 0099, ⓦwww.travelcareonline.com. Flights and holidays specialist.

Destination Group UK ☎020/7400 7045, ⓦwww.destination-group.com. Good discount airfares.

Flightbookers UK ☎0870/010 7000, ⓦwww.ebookers.com. Low fares on an extensive selection of scheduled flights.

McCarthy's Travel Republic of Ireland ☎021/427 0127, ⓦwww.mccarthystravel.ie. General flight agent.

Neenan Travel Republic of Ireland ☎01/607 9900, ⓦwww.neenantrav.ie. Specialists in European city breaks.

North South Travel UK ☎ 01245/608291, ⓦwww.northsouthtravel.co.uk. Friendly, competitive travel agency offering discounted airfares – profits are used to support projects in the developing world, especially the promotion of sustainable tourism.

Premier Travel Northern Ireland ☎028/7126 3333, ⓦwww.premiertravel.uk.com. Discount flight specialists.

Rosetta Travel Northern Ireland ☎028/9064 4996, ⓦwww.rosettatravel.com. Flight and holiday agent.

STA Travel UK ☎0870/1600 599, ⓦwww.statravel.co.uk. Specialists in low-cost travel for students and under-26s, though other customers welcome.

Top Deck UK ☎020/7244 8000, ⓦwww.topdecktravel.co.uk. Long-established discount flight agent.

Trailfinders UK ☎020/7628 7628, ⓦwww.trailfinders.co.uk, Republic of Ireland ☎01/677 7888, ⓦwww.trailfinders.ie. One of the best-informed and most efficient agents for independent travellers.

usit NOW Republic of Ireland ☎01/602 1600, Northern Ireland ☎028/9032 7111, ⓦwww.usitnow.ie. Student and youth specialists.

Package tours

Few places on earth provide the **package tourist** with as many choices as Mallorca and Menorca, but unfortunately for the island's reputation it's the ugly high-rise hotels – along with the drunken antics of some of their clientele – that have grabbed most of the media attention. However, there are also plenty of countrified villas and apartments, genteel pensions and ritzy hotels on offer, as well as walking holidays around the islands' lesser-known beauty spots.

High-street travel agents will help you trawl through a wide range of packages, some of which are excellent value. If the price is right, it can be worth booking a package simply for the flight – after all, there's no compulsion to stick around at your hotel for the full period of your holiday and it's handy to have your lodgings sorted out at least for a night or two at each end of your trip. Packages are especially worth considering at the height of the season when island accommodation can be very hard to find independently, and the last-minute deals advertised in travel agents' windows can work out almost cheaper than staying at home.

To give yourself a general idea of **prices**, you could start by looking at the Airtours brochures in any travel agent. Prices per person for seven nights in a self-catering **apartment**, including the return flight, start at around £280 in low season and rise to £500 in July and August. Airtours **hotel** holidays begin at about £380 for a week in a standard high-rise with half-board in May (£480 in August). The price of a **villa** for up to six people, with a private pool, starts at around £400 per person per week (£600 in high season), including flights and self-catering facilities.

Packaged **activity holidays** are another option, with **walking** tours being especially popular. The best hiking is in the Serra de Tramuntana mountains of northwest Mallorca. Headwater is one company specializing in this type of holiday. Their seven-night package (Feb–April & mid-Sept–Nov only), which includes five guided walks, three-star hotel accommodation and flight, costs £839 in February, or £967 in September.

Cruises in the Mediterranean are very popular too, and often incorporate visits to one or more of the Balearics. P&O run half-a-dozen cruises a year from Southampton which call at Palma. Prices depend on the length of the voyage and how plush a cabin you have – the fourteen-night "Magnificent Mediterranean" cruise (late April), for example, calls at Palma, Barcelona, Florence and a string of other Mediterranean ports and costs around £1500 per person in a twin cabin with en suite shower. Cruise specialists Costa operate four-night cruises (April–Nov), which incorporate a flight to Barcelona and then a cruise to Mallorca, Menorca and Genoa, from where you catch a flight home. A shared twin cabin with en-suite shower costs around £750 per person.

Tour operators

Costa Cruises ⊕020/7940 4490, ⊛www.costacruises.com. Short cruises in the Mediterranean from May to November. Brochures from any major high street travel agent.
Freelance Holidays UK ⊕01789/297705 ⊛www.freelance-holidays.co.uk. A wide variety of

Mallorcan self-catering accommodation in beautiful locations, including both the Serra de Tramuntana and the central plain, Es Pla – the least commercialized part of the island.
Go Holidays Republic of Ireland ⊕01/874 4126, ⊛www.goholidays.ie. Package-tour specialists.
Headwater UK ⊕01606/720099, ⊛www.headwater.com. Well-regarded walking tour specialist providing guided hikes in the Serra de Tramuntana mountains. Their standard eight-day guided hike takes place from mid-September to November and from February to April.
Ilkeston Co-op UK ⊕08708/708708, ⊛www.ilkeston-coop.co.uk. A wide range of package holidays, often at extraordinarily cheap prices, plus bargain-basement charter flights to both Mallorca and Menorca, especially from Birmingham and East Midlands airports.
Individual Traveller's Spain UK ⊕08700/780194, ⊛www.indiv-travellers.com. Deluxe selection of farmhouses, villas, cottages and village houses, including several tasty offerings near Pollença and others in the small towns of the central plain, Es Pla, especially Sineu.
Joe Walsh Tours Republic of Ireland ⊕01/676 0991, ⊛www.joewalshtours.ie. General budget fares and travel agent.
Madrid and Beyond In Spain, ⊕00 34/917 580 063, ⊛www.madridandbeyond.com. Reputable Madrid-based British operator with a small but enticing range of hotels in out-of-the-way places in Mallorca and Menorca. Also does tailor-made Balearic itineraries.
Magic of Spain UK ⊕0870/888 0228, ⊛www.magictravelgroup.co.uk. Upmarket hotel and villa holidays, often in out-of-the-way places in both Mallorca and Menorca. Several lovely fincas too. Highly recommended.
Mundi Color UK ⊕020/7828 6021 ⊛www.mundicolor.es. Small but well-chosen selection of classy and atmospheric hotels in popular resorts (Cala Fornells, Illetas) and less familiar spots like Banyalbufar, plus city breaks in Palma's better hotels.
P&O Cruises UK ⊕0845/3555 333, ⊛www.pocruises.com. A good range of western Mediterranean cruises, many of which call at Palma. Departures are from Southampton.
Thomson UK ⊕0870/165 0079, ⊛www.thomson-holidays.com. One of the largest UK package-tour companies. Brochures on all manner of Mallorca and Menorca holidays to suit most budgets are available at any high-street travel agent, including vacations in villas and apartments, family-owned hotels and luxury hotels, as well as city breaks in Palma.

Try Holidays UK ☎0870/754 4545
Ⓦwww.tryholidays.com. All-in and
accommodation-only packages at a wide range of
prices in lesser-known parts of Mallorca, as well as
walking and climbing holidays.
Yoga Holidays Mallorca UK ☎01903/746450,
Ⓦwww.yogamallorca.com. Yoga retreats and
holidays in Mallorca from €580 per week.

By train, bus, car and ferry from the UK

Travelling by **train** from London, it takes at
least sixteen hours to reach **Barcelona**, from
where there are regular ferries to Palma and
Maó (see pp.16–18). The first leg of the journey involves taking a **Eurostar** train from
London Waterloo to Paris Gare du Nord. The
easiest option on the second leg is the
overnight **Talgo** service, which leaves Paris
Gare d'Austerlitz daily for Barcelona's
Estació-Sants. A standard return on the
Talgo from Paris to Barcelona costs £125
per person in a two-person sleeper.

The main **bus route** between Britain and
northeastern Spain connects London with
Barcelona. Bus services from Britain are
operated by **Eurolines**, with departures from
London's Victoria Coach Station three times
a week. The journey time is around 26 hours
– long, but just about bearable if you take
enough to eat, drink and read. There are
stops for around twenty minutes every four
to five hours, and the slog is also broken by
the cross-Channel ferry, the price of which is

Train information
Eurostar ☎0870/160 6600,
Ⓦwww.eurostar.com.
Rail Europe ☎0870/584 8848,
Ⓦwww.raileurope.co.uk

Bus information
Eurolines ☎0870/514 3219,
Ⓦwww.eurolines.co.uk.

Ferry information
Brittany Ferries ☎0870/901
2400, Ⓦwww.brittanyferries
.co.uk. Plymouth to Santander
(March–Nov).

P&O Ferries ☎0870/242 4999,
Ⓦwww.poportsmouth.com.
Portsmouth to Bilbao.

---

included in the cost of a ticket. A standard
return fare costs £52 if booked thirty
days in advance, or double that with no
advance booking.

More arduous is the long **drive** to the east
coast of Spain, where regular car ferries from
Barcelona and Valencia depart for Palma
and Maó; these same ports also offer a
summertime catamaran service (see p.18).
Another option is to catch a **ferry** from
Plymouth to Santander or Portsmouth to
Bilbao, which cuts many hours off the driving time through France.

Flights from the USA and Canada

There are no direct flights from North
America to Mallorca or Menorca. The nearest you'll get are the scheduled and charter
flights from various North American cities to
Madrid and Barcelona. Occasionally – and
especially if you're coming from Canada –
you'll find it cheaper to travel to London and
pick up an inexpensive onward flight from
there (see "Flights from the UK and Ireland"
on p.10).

Iberia fly nonstop to Madrid from New
York, Miami and Chicago, and have the
advantage of connecting flights from Madrid
direct to both Mallorca and Menorca.
Alternatively, several **US airlines** fly direct
from the East Coast to Madrid, while Delta
Airlines operate a non-stop flight to
Barcelona. **Air Europa**'s New York–Madrid
flights are less frequent than other services,
but very competitively priced.

You may also find good deals on routings
via other major European cities with various national airlines – KLM via Amsterdam
and British Airways via London are the obvious choices. Remember, though, that you
may be better off continuing with a locally
bought flight. The widest range of deals is on
the New York–London route, served by
dozens of airlines. Competition is intense,
and bargains common. At the time of writing, the major carriers were offering the following round-trip **fares to Madrid**: from
New York $615/925 (low/high season);
Chicago $720/1100; LA $855/1520; and
Miami $695/990. With special promotional
offers, round-trip fares can drop as low as
$300 from New York and $500 from LA.

Flying time is around seven hours from New York to Madrid.

There are no non-stop flights **from Canada** to Spain. However, you should be able to find a fairly convenient routing using a combination of airlines – most likely via another European capital – from any of Canada's major cities. At the time of writing, round-trip **fares** to Madrid started at around CDN\$1200/\$1695 (low/high season) from Toronto and Montréal, and CDN\$1590/2250 from Vancouver.

North American travellers don't have much choice when it comes to **package tours** to Mallorca and Menorca, though the companies listed in the box below provide a few options.

Airlines

Air France US ☎1-800/237-2747, Canada ☎1-800/667-2747, ⓦwww.airfrance.com. From New York, Chicago, Atlanta, Miami, San Francisco, Los Angeles, Washington DC, Toronto and Montréal to Madrid, Barcelona, Málaga and Sevilla, all via Paris.
American Airlines ☎1-800/433-7300, ⓦwww.aa.com. Daily nonstop flights from Miami and Chicago to Madrid.
British Airways ☎1-800/247-9297, ⓦwww.british-airways.com. From 21 cities in the US plus Montréal, Toronto and Vancouver to Madrid and Barcelona, both via London.
Continental Airlines Domestic ☎1-800/523-3273, international ☎1-800/231-0856, ⓦwww.continental.com. Daily nonstop flights from Newark to Madrid.
Delta Airlines Domestic ☎1-800/221-1212, international ☎1-800/241-4141, ⓦwww.delta.com. Daily nonstop flights from New York and Atlanta to Madrid and Barcelona, with connections from most other major North American cities.
Iberia ☎1-800/772-4642, ⓦwww.iberia.com. New York, Miami and Chicago nonstop to Madrid, with frequent connections to Mallorca and Menorca.
Northwest/KLM ☎1-800/447-4747, ⓦwww.nwa.com. From major US and Canadian cities to Madrid and Barcelona via Amsterdam.
United Airlines Domestic ☎1-800/241-6522, international ☎1-800/538-2929, ⓦwww.ual.com. Daily nonstop flights from Philadelphia to Madrid.

Discount travel agents

Air Brokers International ☎1-800/883-3273 or 415/397-1383, ⓦwww.airbrokers.com. Consolidator.
Council Travel ☎1-800/2COUNCIL, ⓦwww.counciltravel.com. Specialist in student/budget travel. Flights from the US only.
Educational Travel Center ☎1-800/747-5551 or 608/256-5551, ⓦwww.edtrav.com. Student and youth discount agent.
New Frontiers ☎1-800/677-0720 or 310/670-7318, ⓦwww.newfrontiers.com. French discount-travel firm based in Los Angeles.
SkyLink US ☎1-800/AIR-ONLY or 212/573-8980, Canada ☎1-800/SKY-LINK, ⓦwww.skylinkus.com. Consolidator.
STA Travel US ☎1-800/781-4040, Canada 1-888/427-5639, ⓦwww.sta-travel.com. Specialists in worldwide independent travel.
Student Flights ☎1-800/255-8000 or 480/951-1177, ⓦwww.isecard.com. Student and youth fares.
Travel Cuts Canada ☎1-800/667-2887, US ☎1-866/246-9762, ⓦwww.travelcuts.com. Canadian student-travel organization.
Worldtek Travel ☎1-800/243-1723, ⓦwww.worldtek.com. Discount travel agency.

Package-tour operators

EC Tours ☎1-800/388-0877, ⓦwww.ectours.com. Pilgrimages, historic city tours, wine and gourmet tours to every corner of Spain. Can arrange customized packages to Mallorca and Menorca.
Escapade Tours ☎1-800/356-2405, ⓦwww.isram.com. Spanish city breaks and multi-city packages. Can arrange customized tours in Mallorca and Menorca.
Far & Wide ☎1-866/327-9433, ⓦwww.farandwide.com. Independent, customized and escorted tours. They specialize in Catalunya and Andalucía, but can also arrange trips to the Balearics.
Hidden Trails ☎1-604/323 1141, ⓦwww.hiddentrails.com. A Canadian site which specialises in horse-riding holidays, including a week-long Mallorcan "Monastery and Beach" holiday.

Flights from Australia and New Zealand

There are no direct flights to Spain from Australia or New Zealand. You'll need to change planes once or twice to reach Madrid or Barcelona, from where there are regular flights to Mallorca and Menorca. Count on 24 hours via Asia or 30 hours via the USA, not including time spent on stopovers.

The most economical scheduled flights **from Australia** are via Asia. The cheapest flight is with Japan Airlines to Madrid, with an overnight stop in either Tokyo or Osaka included in the fare (A$1800/2900 low/high season). There are slightly more expensive (A$2000–3000) flights to Madrid and Barcelona with Thai Airways, Air France and Lauda Air via Bangkok, Paris and Vienna respectively; there's also a Qantas flight to Madrid via Bangkok. The quickest but most expensive option (A$2200–3200) is Singapore Airlines' flight to Madrid, which involves only a short refuelling stop or quick change of planes in Singapore.

Travelling **from New Zealand**, Thai Airways has flights from Auckland to both Madrid and Barcelona (via Sydney and Bangkok), while Japan Airlines (JAL) has flights to Madrid via Tokyo or Osaka for around NZ$2500/3100 (low/high season). In addition, Qantas (via Sydney and Bangkok) and Singapore Airlines (via Singapore), both fly to Madrid, but are more expensive at NZ$2700/3300 (low/high season).

Organized tours are initially more expensive but can be an economic proposition in the long term; see the list of operators below.

Airlines

Air France Australia ℡ 02/9244 2100, New Zealand ℡ 09/308 3352, Ⓦ www.airfrance.fr. Daily flights to Madrid and Barcelona from major Australian gateway cities, via Paris and either Singapore or Bangkok.
Garuda Indonesia Australia ℡ 02/9334 9970, New Zealand ℡ 09/366 1862, Ⓦ www .garuda-indonesia.com. Several flights weekly from major cities in Australia and New Zealand to London and Amsterdam via Denpasar or Jakarta.
Japan Airlines Australia ℡ 02/9272 1111, New Zealand ℡ 09/379 9906, Ⓦ www.japanair.com. Daily flights to Madrid from Brisbane and Sydney, (and several flights a week from Cairns and Auckland) via Tokyo or Osaka.
Lauda Air Australia ℡ 1800/642 438 or 02/9251 6155, New Zealand ℡ 09/522 5948, Ⓦ www.aua.com. Four flights weekly to Barcelona from Sydney via Munich or Vienna.

Qantas Australia ℡ 13 13 13, Ⓦ www.qantas.com.au; New Zealand ℡ 0800/808 767, Ⓦ www.qantas.co.nz. Daily flights to Madrid from major cities in Australia and New Zealand with a transfer in either Singapore or Bangkok and London.
Singapore Airlines Australia ℡ 13 10 11, New Zealand ℡ 0800/808 909, Ⓦ www.singaporeair.com. Daily flights to Madrid via Singapore (and sometimes also Zurich) from Brisbane, Sydney, Melbourne, Perth and Auckland.
Thai Airways Australia ℡ 1300/651 960, New Zealand ℡ 09/377 0268, Ⓦ www.thaiair.com. Several flights weekly to Madrid and Barcelona from Sydney, Melbourne, Brisbane and Auckland via Bangkok and either Rome or Frankfurt.

Flight and travel agents

All the agents listed below offer competitive discounts on air fares as well as a good selection of package holidays, plus tours and car rental.
Flight Centre Australia ℡ 13 31 33 or 02/9235 3522, Ⓦ www.flightcentre.com.au; New Zealand ℡ 0800/243 544 or 09/358 4310, Ⓦ www.flightcentre.co.nz.
Holiday Shoppe New Zealand ℡ 0800/808 480, Ⓦ www.holidayshoppe.co.nz.
New Zealand Destinations Unlimited New Zealand ℡ 09/414 1685, Ⓦ www.holiday.co.nz.
Northern Gateway Australia ℡ 1800/174 800, Ⓦ www.northerngateway.com.au.
STA Travel Australia ℡ 1300/733 035, Ⓦ www.statravel.com.au; New Zealand ℡ 0508/782 872, Ⓦ www.statravel.co.nz.
Student Uni Travel Australia ℡ 02/9232 8444, Ⓦ www.sut.com.au; New Zealand ℡ 09/379 4224, Ⓦ www.sut.co.nz.
Trailfinders Australia ℡ 02/9247 7666, Ⓦ www.trailfinders.com.au.

Package-tour operators

Adventure World Australia ℡ 02/8913 0755, Ⓦ www.adventureworld.com.au, New Zealand ℡ 09/524 5118, Ⓦ www.adventureworld.co.nz. Agents for a vast array of international adventure travel companies (including Headwater see p.12) offering small-group tours.
Ibertours Australia ℡ 03/9867 8833 or 1-800/500 016, Ⓦ www.ibertours.com.au. Package tours to Mallorca and Menorca, with accommodation in top-range resort and country hotels.
IB Tours International Australia ℡ 02/9560 6722, Ⓦ www.ib-tours.com.au. Offers villas in

Spain (and elsewhere), car rental and city stays. Customized Balearic tours on request.

From the rest of Spain

Menorca and more especially Mallorca are easily reached by plane and ferry from mainland Spain and Ibiza. Obviously, the main advantage of **flying** is speed: Barcelona to Palma, for example, takes just forty minutes, compared to the ferry trip of eight hours. By plane, there's also the advantage of a wider range of jumping-off points: regular scheduled flights operated by Iberia link many of Spain's major cities with Mallorca and several with Menorca too. By **ferry and catamaran**, you're confined to three departure ports for Mallorca – Barcelona, Valencia, Ibiza Town – and two for Maó on Menorca – Valencia and Barcelona.

Ticket **prices** also favour aircraft travel: it is less expensive by ferry, but not by all that much, and certainly not enough to justify the extra time and trouble – unless, that is, you're in or near one of the departure ports anyway. The only situation in which the boat is a necessity is if you're taking your own vehicle over to the islands.

For details of **ferries and flights between Mallorca and Menorca**, see p.30.

By air from the mainland

Almost all **scheduled flights** to Mallorca and Menorca from the Spanish mainland are operated by **Iberia** (🌐www.iberia.com), who have sales offices in every major Spanish city. Seat availability isn't usually a problem and fares are very reasonable: a standard, one-way flight from Barcelona to Palma, for instance, can cost as little as €52, double that for a return. There are also a variety of excursion fares available at discounted prices – see the airline website or ask locally for further details. In Spain, Iberia has a nationwide domestic flight reservation and information line on ☎902 400 500 (English spoken).

It's sometimes possible to get a cheaper ticket on a **charter flight**. These are available in most major Spanish cities, but you may have to plod around local travel agents to find one – travel agents are listed in the Yellow Pages under *viajes agencias*.

By air from Ibiza

Flying to Mallorca **from Ibiza** couldn't be simpler. Iberia operate six or seven **flights** daily between the two islands. The journey takes thirty minutes and costs around €73 one-way (double for a return). There's usually no problem with seat availability, but you need to book ahead during the height of the season and on public holidays. There are, however, no direct flights from Ibiza to Menorca – you're routed via Mallorca at a one-way cost of about €150.

By ferry from mainland Spain

Two companies – Trasmediterranea and Balearia – run **car ferry and catamaran** services between mainland Spain and Mallorca and Menorca. Advance booking is strongly recommended on both car ferry and catamaran services. If you're taking a vehicle or need a cabin, book in advance year-round. **Tickets** can be purchased at the port of embarkation or in advance by phone and via the companies' websites or with Trasmediterranea's UK agent (see box on p.18).

Iberia domestic flight frequencies

From Alicante to: Palma (2 daily; 1hr 10min).
From Barcelona to: Maó (3–6 daily; 35min); Palma (10 daily; 40min).
From Bilbao to: Palma (3 daily via Barcelona; 3hr).
From Ibiza Town to: Palma (6–7 daily; 30min).
From Madrid to: Maó (1–3 daily; 1hr 10min); Palma (6–9 daily; 1hr 15min).
From Sevilla to: Palma (2–3 daily via Madrid; 3hr).
From Valencia to: Palma (4 daily; 1hr).

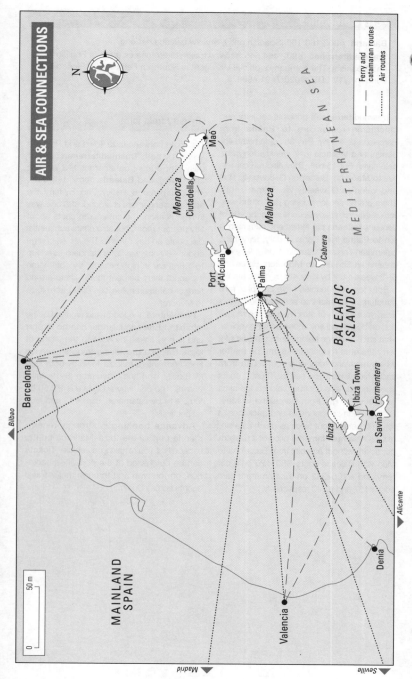

AIR & SEA CONNECTIONS

N

MAINLAND
SPAIN

◄ Bilbao

Barcelona

◄ Alicante

Denia

Valencia

◄ Madrid

◄ Seville

Menorca
Ciutadella
Maó

Port
d'Alcúdia
Mallorca

Palma

Cabrera

BALEARIC
ISLANDS

Ibiza
Ibiza Town
La Savina   Formentera

M E D I T E R R A N E A N   S E A

Ferry and
catamaran routes

Air routes

0   50 m

Ferry companies

Balearia ☎902 160 180 (Spanish only), ⓦwww.balearia.net/eng.
Trasmediterranea ☎902 454 645, ⓦwww.trasmediterranea.es (both in English and Spanish). The company's official UK agent is Southern Ferries, 179 Piccadilly, London W1V 9DB ☎020/7491 4968.

Trasmediterranea's principal car ferry and catamaran routes are **to Palma** from Barcelona (2–4 daily; ferry 8hr, catamaran 4hr 30min) and Valencia (6–7 weekly; ferry 9hr, catamaran 6hr 15min). They also run car ferries **to Maó** from Barcelona (3–8 weekly; 9hr) and Valencia (1 weekly via Palma; 14hr). There are no services during part of the winter, usually from early December to the end of January. **Balearia** car ferries and catamarans run **to Palma** from Dénia (1 daily; ferry 10hr, catamaran 7hr) and Valencia (1 daily; ferry 8hr, catamaran 5hr) and **to Maó** from Barcelona (2–3 weekly; 8hr by ferry, 4hr by catamaran).

Both ferry companies have complex **fare** structures that take into account the time of year, your length of stay, your accommodation on board and any accompanying vehicle. That said, all things being equal, the cost of a ferry ticket is roughly the same no matter which mainland ferry port you depart from and which island you sail to. Thus, it costs about the same to get from Valencia to Palma as it does to get from Barcelona to Maó. Setting aside special deals and packages, a return ticket is about twice as much as a single. As a **sample fare**, the price of a passenger ticket (without a cabin) from Barcelona to Maó with Balearia costs €80–120 on a car ferry and €105–242 on a catamaran; cars cost €137 and €240 respectively.

By ferry from Ibiza

The route between Ibiza Town and Palma is served by both **Trasmediterranea** (ferry: 1 daily; 4hr 30min; catamaran: 1–3 weekly; 2hr 15min), and **Balearia** (ferry: 1–2 daily; 4hr; catamaran: 6 weekly; 2hr). By ferry, the adult passenger fare is around €25 one-way in high season; the catamaran costs about fifty percent more, but also offers substantial discounts on day returns. The ferries charge about €60 one-way for a standard-sized (up to 1.8m) car in high season; by catamaran it's about thirty percent more. There are no ferry or catamaran services direct from Ibiza to Menorca.

Formentera, the fourth and smallest of the inhabited Balearic Islands, has no airport and is only linked by boat to the island of Ibiza. Balearia provides a frequent service from Formentera to Ibiza Town by both ferry (5–8 daily; 1hr) and catamaran (8–12 daily; 25min). The one-way adult fare is €9.50 by ferry, €14 by catamaran, cars €42 and €85 respectively.

Advance booking is strongly recommended on all the Ibiza–Mallorca boats, especially if you're taking a vehicle. **Tickets** can be purchased at the port of embarkation, on the web and through major travel agents across Spain.

Visas and red tape

Citizens of the UK, Ireland and other EU countries – as well as nationals of Australia, New Zealand, Canada and the US – only need a valid passport to enter Spain for up to ninety days. Your passport must be valid for the entire period of the visit.

To stay longer than ninety days, EU nationals can apply for a **permiso de residencia** (residence permit) at the local Aliens Office (*oficina de extranjero*). You'll either have to produce proof that you have sufficient funds to be able to support yourself without working (reckon on €35 per day); a contract of employment (*contrato de trabajo*); or something to prove you are self-employed, which involves registering at the tax office. Citizens of other nationalities will either need to get a **special visa** from a Spanish consulate before departure (see below for addresses) or apply at the local Aliens Office for a ninety-day **visa extension**, showing proof of sufficient funds. Any tourist office will provide the address of the nearest Aliens Office.

Spanish embassies and consulates

Australia 15 Arkana St, Yarralumla, Canberra, ACT 2600 ☏02/6273 3555; 4th floor, 540 Elizabeth St, Melbourne, VIC 3000 ☏03/9347 1966; Floor 24, St Martin's Tower, 31 Market St, Sydney, NSW 2000 ☏02/9261 2433.
Canada 350 Sparks St, #802, Ottawa, Ontario K1R 7SB ☏1-613/237-2193, ⓦwww.docuweb.ca/spainincanada; 1 Westmount Square #1456, Ave Wood, Montréal, Québec H3Z 2P9 ☏514/935-5235; 1200 Bay Street, #400, Toronto, Ontario M5P 2A5 ☏1-416/967-4949.
Ireland 17a Merlyn Park, Ballsbridge, Dublin 4 ☏01/269 1640.
New Zealand No representation.
UK 20 Draycott Place, London SW3 2RZ ☏020/7589 8989; Suite 1a, Brook House, 70 Spring Gardens, Manchester M2 2BQ ☏0161/236 1213; 63 North Castle St, Edinburgh EH2 3LJ ☏0131/220 1843.
USA 2375 Pennsylvania Ave NW, Washington DC

20037 ☏1-202/452-0100, ⓦwww.spainemb.org; 180 N Michigan Ave #1500, Chicago, IL 60601 ☏1-312/782-4588; 5055 Wilshire Blvd #960, Los Angeles, CA 90036 ☏1-323/938-0158; 2655 Lejeune Rd #203, Coral Gables, Miami, FL 33134 ☏305/446-5511; 2102 World Trade Center, 2 Canal St, New Orleans, LA 70130 ☏504/525-4951; 150 E 58th St, New York, NY 10155 ☏1-212/355-4090, ⓦwww.spainconsul-ny.org.

Duty-free allowances

Every adult **EU citizen** has a **traveller's allowance**, whereby items bought in one EU country and brought back directly to another do not attract import/export taxes, so long as they are deemed as being for personal use. The maximum levels per adult are: 800 cigarettes (or 1kg of tobacco), 10 litres of strong spirit or 20 litres of fortified wine, 90 litres of table wine and 110 litres of beer. If you keep within these limits and within the EU, you don't need to make a declaration to customs.

On arrival in Spain, **non-EU residents** have a duty-free import allowance of 200 cigarettes (or 250g of tobacco), one litre of spirits or two litres of fortified wine, and two litres of table wine. Returning home, the limits are generally the same, but check with your carrier if you're uncertain. There are also restrictions as to the value of goods you can take home without paying tax – again, check with your carrier – and remember that the importing of fresh food, plants or animals into Britain, Ireland, the USA, Canada, Australia or New Zealand is severely restricted.

Information, websites and maps

The Spanish National Tourist Office (SNTO) has several overseas branches (see p.21) where you can pick up a wide range of information before you leave home, including free maps, pamphlets and special-interest leaflets on both the islands. They also have a particularly useful booklet listing all the Balearic Islands' hotels, *hostals* and campsites – this can be difficult to obtain on the islands themselves. Another obvious source of information is the Internet. Although Mallorca and Menorca aren't very well represented on the Web, there's a modest selection of general websites, including three operated by the SNTO.

On the islands themselves, information is fairly easy to get hold of, with all the larger towns and resorts equipped with **tourist information offices**. The **maps** printed in this guide – possibly supplemented by the free road and town maps issued by the tourist offices – should be sufficient for most purposes, although if you're planning to explore the islands' byways by bike or car, you'll need a more detailed road map, and prospective hikers will need specialist hiking maps.

Websites

As yet, the **Internet** hasn't really taken off in Mallorca and Menorca. Many sites emanating from the islands are rudimentary and infrequently updated. Furthermore, the majority are only available in Castilian (Spanish) or Catalan, though you can get help in deciphering these from any Internet translation service – for Spanish, try Ⓦ www.babelfish.altavista.com/translate.dy. See also the list of SNTO websites on p.21.

Ⓦ **www.a-palma.es/eng** Useful site, providing detailed street maps, public transport information and "where to go" and "what's on" guides. Primarily in Spanish, but with English sections too, though some of the translations are incomplete.

Ⓦ **www.baleares.com** A multi-lingual tourist guide to all the Balearics with separate sections devoted to a whole raft of special features from art through to cycling and car rental. The site's poorly laid out, but the information it contains is good – once you find it.

Ⓦ **www.baleares.com/tourist.guide/cycling** Details of eight different cycle routes on Mallorca, from 70km to 320km. Routes are designed to avoid

busy roads and to provide sections on the flat as well as steep climbs. In several languages, including English.

Ⓦ **www.caib.es/kfcont.htm** The official site of the Balearic provincial government, and a well-presented source of general information. The tourist information section is presented in several languages, including English, and gives links to sites offering information on accommodation, eating and drinking, sports, and so on.

Ⓦ **www.conselldemallorca.net** One of the best-presented Mallorcan sites, though in Catalan only. Contains all sorts of information and news, and has a useful events page, Novetats, although the translation produced by Babelfish (see above) is rather garbled.

Ⓦ **www.inm.es/wwb** Daily weather forecasts for the whole of Spain – in Spanish.

Ⓦ **www.malhigh.com** Expat heaven, this site hosts private ads from German and English expatriates. Useful and amusing in equal measure.

Ⓦ **www.menorca-info.de** A German guide to the island, partly translated into Spanish and English. It's particularly useful for its comprehensive links to everything from car rental and camping through to boats and apartments, accommodation and eateries.

Ⓦ **www.menorcavirtual.com** This well-organized portal will link you to many Menorcan businesses and official websites. The emphasis is on car rental, accommodation and water sports. Most listings are in English.

Tourist offices

In **Mallorca**, the main provincial and municipal **tourist offices** in Palma (see p.59 and p.61) will provide free maps of the town and the island, and leaflets detailing all sorts of island-wide practicalities – from bus and train timetables to lists of car rental firms, ferry schedules and boat excursion organizers. Outside of Palma, many of the larger towns and resorts have seasonal tourist offices (addresses are detailed in the guide). These vary enormously in quality, and while they are generally extremely useful for local information, they cannot be relied on to know anything about what goes on outside their patch. In **Menorca**, there are efficient year-round tourist offices in the two main towns, Maó and Ciutadella, but nowhere else.

Opening hours vary considerably. The larger tourist offices are all open at least from Monday to Friday from 8 or 9am to 2pm or 3pm. The smaller concerns operate from April or May to September or October, often on weekday mornings only. We've given details of opening times throughout the guide, though in remoter spots you can't always rely on the officially posted hours.

Spanish National Tourist Offices overseas

The SNTO's main website is ⓦwww.spain.info.

Canada 2 Bloor St West, Suite #3402, Toronto, Ontario M4W 3E2 ⓣ416/961-3131, ⓦwww.tourspain.toronto.on.ca.

UK 22–23 Manchester Square, London W1U 3PX; general enquiries ⓣ020/7486 8077; brochure request premium line ⓣ0906/364 0630; ⓦwww.tourspain.co.uk.

USA 666 Fifth Ave, 35th Floor, New York, NY 10103 ⓣ1-212/265-8822; 845 N Michigan Ave, Chicago, IL 60611 ⓣ1-312/642-1992; 8383 Wilshire Blvd, Suite #960, Beverly Hills, Los Angeles, CA 90211 ⓣ1-323/658-7188; 1221 Brickell Ave, Miami, FL 33131 ⓣ305/358-1992; ⓦwww.okspain.org.

Maps

Detailed **road maps of Mallorca** are widely available from island newsagents, petrol stations, souvenir shops and bookshops. There are several different types on offer, but the ones recommended below shouldn't cost more than €5. If you do buy supplementary maps, it's important to remember that all **road, town and street signs** are in the local language, **Catalan**; Castilian (Spanish) maps are either obsolete or impossibly confusing to use. To ensure you're buying a Catalan

map, unfold it and check out the spelling of Port de Pollença on Mallorca's north coast; if it reads "Puerto de Pollença", you've got a Castilian map. Just to confuse matters, however, some maps switch between the two languages for no apparent reason.

The best Catalan map of the island is published by the Ministerio de Obras Públicas (Ministry of Public Works). This accurately portrays the island's most important highways and principal byways, and provides topographical details too. It's not, however, as easy to get hold of as most of its rivals – to buy it you'll need to consult a specialist map shop either before you go (see p.22) or in Mallorca. More readily available Catalan alternatives include the easy-to-follow *Collins Mallorca Holiday Map* (1:175,000), which usefully indicates distances between settlements, marks salient geographical features and provides a street plan and index of central Palma. In Mallorca, the largely Catalan *Mallorca and Palma* map (1:175,000) is a widely available and inexpensive local government publication equipped with a large-scale, indexed plan of Palma and brief descriptions of the city's tourist attractions. Its only drawbacks are the absence of topographical features and some waywardness when it comes to depicting the island's byroads.

As for **Menorca**, the most detailed and up-to-date map (1:75,000) is produced by Distrimapas Telstar; it's produced in several languages, so be sure to get the Catalan edition. The language of the map should be clearly displayed, but if it isn't, check a couple of Catalan spellings – Maó (Mahón in Castilian) and Port de Maó (Puerto de Mahón in Castilian). The map shows all the island's major and most of the minor roads, though sometimes it doesn't effectively indicate which country lanes are easily driveable and which aren't. It's sold at leading bookshops and many larger newsagents on the island, but isn't readily available outside of Menorca, though you might try the specialist map shops detailed on p.22.

Serious **hikers** are poorly provided for. There are no really reliable maps with walking trails marked for either Mallorca or Menorca. The IGN (Instituto Geográfico Nacional) issues **topographical maps** of the Balearics at 1:25,000 and 1:50,000, based on an aerial survey of 1979. These are the best on the market, although many minor roads and footpaths simply don't appear, and even crags and cliffs aren't always shown. They are available from bookshops in Palma (see p.92), Sóller (see p.108), Maó (see p.221) and Ciutadella (see p.260), but supplies are unreliable, so it's best to purchase them before you go from a specialist map shop overseas (see below).

The cartographic void has been partly filled by **Discovery Walking Guides** (ⓦwww .walking.demon.co.uk), whose publications include the very competent *Mallorca North & Mountains Tour & Trail Map* (1:40,000), *Mallorca North Walking Guide* (1:40,000) and an island-wide *Menorca Tour & Trail Map* (1:40,000). Most better UK bookshops, and some on Mallorca, sell these maps, or you can order them worldwide from Amazon (ⓦwww.amazon.co.uk).

Map outlets

In the UK and Ireland

Easons Bookshop 40 O'Connell St, Dublin 1 ☎01/858 3881, ⓦwww.eason.ie.
Hodges Figgis Bookshop 56–58 Dawson St, Dublin 2 ☎01/677 4754.
Newcastle Map Centre 55 Grey St, Newcastle-upon-Tyne NE1 6EF ☎0191/261 5622.
Stanfords 12–14 Long Acre WC2E 9LP ☎020/7836 1321, ⓦwww.stanfords.co.uk.

The Travel Bookshop 13–15 Blenheim Crescent, London W11 2EE ☎020/7229 5260, ⓦwww.thetravelbookshop.co.uk.

In the US and Canada

Elliot Bay Book Company 101 S Main St, Seattle, WA 98104 ☎1-800/962-5311, ⓦwww.elliotbaybook.com.
Globe Corner Bookstore 28 Church St, Cambridge, MA 02138 ☎1-800/358-6013, ⓦwww.globercorner.com.
Map Link 30 S La Patera Lane, Unit 5, Santa Barbara, CA 93117 ☎1-800/962-1394, ⓦwww.maplink.com.
Rand McNally US ☎1-800/333-0136, ⓦwww.randmcnally.com. Around thirty stores across the US; dial ext 2111 or check the website for the nearest location.
The Travel Bug Bookstore 2667 W Broadway, Vancouver V6K 2G2 ☎604/737-1122, ⓦwww.swifty.com/tbug.
World of Maps 1235 Wellington St, Ottawa, Ontario K1Y 3A3 ☎1-800/214-8524, ⓦwww.worldofmaps.com.

In Australia and New Zealand

Mapland 372 Little Bourke St, Melbourne, Victoria 3000 ☎03/9670 4383, ⓦwww.mapland.com.au.
The Map Shop 6–10 Peel St, Adelaide, SA 5000 ☎08/8231 2033, ⓦwww.mapshop.net.au.
MapWorld 173 Gloucester St, Christchurch ☎0800/627967, ⓦwww.mapworld.co.nz.
Perth Map Centre 900 Hay St, Perth, WA 6000 ☎08/9322 5733, ⓦwww.perthmap.com.au.
Specialty Maps 46 Albert St, Auckland 1001 ☎09/307 2217, ⓦwww.specialtymaps.co.nz.

Insurance

Prior to travelling, you'd do well to take out an insurance policy to cover against theft, loss and illness or injury. Before paying for a new policy, however, it's worth checking whether you already have some degree of cover: EU health care privileges apply in both Mallorca and Menorca (see p.24), some all-risks home insurance policies may cover your possessions when overseas, and many private medical schemes include cover when abroad. In Canada, provincial health plans usually provide partial cover for medical mishaps overseas, while holders of official student/teacher/youth cards in Canada and the US are entitled to (albeit meagre) accident coverage and hospital in-patient benefits. Students will often find that their student health coverage extends during the vacations and for one term beyond the date of last enrolment.

After exhausting the possibilities above, you might want to contact a specialist travel insurance company. A typical travel insurance policy usually provides cover for loss of baggage, tickets and – up to a certain limit – cash or cheques, as well as cancellation or curtailment of your journey. Most of them exclude so-called **dangerous sports** – climbing, horse-riding, windsurfing and so forth – unless an extra premium is paid. Many policies can be chopped and changed to exclude coverage you don't need – for example, sickness and accident benefits can often be excluded or included at will. If you do take medical coverage, ascertain whether benefits will be paid as treatment proceeds or only after your return home, and whether there is a 24-hour medical emergency number. When securing baggage cover, make sure that the per-article limit will cover your most valuable possession. If you need to make a claim, keep **receipts** for medicines and medical treatment. In the event you have anything stolen, you must obtain a **crime report** statement or number.

Rough Guides travel insurance

Rough Guides offers a low-cost travel insurance policy, especially customized for our readers. There are five main Rough Guides insurance plans: **No Frills**, for the bare minimum for secure travel; **Essential**, which provides decent all-round cover; **Premier**, for comprehensive cover with a wide range of benefits; **Extended Stay**, for cover lasting four months to a year; and **Annual Multi-Trip**, a cost-effective way of getting Premier cover if you travel more than once a year. Premier, Annual Multi-Trip and Extended Stay policies can be supplemented by a "Hazardous Pursuits Extension" if you plan to indulge in sports considered dangerous, such as scuba-diving or trekking. For a policy quote, call the Rough Guide Insurance Line toll-free in the UK ☎0800/015 09 06 or ☎+44 1392 314 665 from elsewhere. Alternatively, get an online quote at ⌨www.roughguides.com/insurance.

Health

Under reciprocal health arrangements involving the countries of the European Union (EU) – which of course includes Spain – all nationals of EU countries are entitled to free or discounted medical treatment within the respective public health care systems of any member country. In Mallorca and Menorca, however, most doctors are not practitioners within the Spanish health care system, the Instituto Nacional de la Salud, and are more accustomed to – or only deal with – private insurance work. Consequently, EU nationals are well-advised to take out their own travel insurance to avoid having to hunt around for a doctor who will treat them for free. A private insurance policy will also cover the cost of items not within the EU's scheme, such as dental treatment and repatriation on medical grounds, though most don't cover prescription charges – their "excesses" are usually greater than the cost of the medicines. Non-EU nationals should always take out their own medical insurance to travel in Spain. Also note that the more worthwhile insurance policies promise to sort matters out before you pay (rather than after) in the case of major expense; if you do, however, have to pay upfront, get and keep the receipts. For more on insurance, see p.23. No inoculations are currently required for Mallorca or Menorca.

If you're an EU national determined to keep within the public system, you should **complete form E111** before you travel, as it provides proof of your entitlement to treatment under EU arrangements. The form is available from most post offices in the UK and from health boards in the Republic of Ireland. If you don't have an E111 form with you on your travels, you will have to pay upfront for any medical treatment you need.

Minor ailments

For the vast majority of travellers, the only blights to a holiday in the Balearics are likely to be an upset stomach or a ferocious hangover. To avoid the former, wash fruit and avoid *tapas* dishes that look like they were cooked last week. Many islanders also refrain from consuming mayonnaise during the summer. If you do fall ill, **minor complaints** can often be remedied at a **pharmacy** (*farmàcia*) – there are plenty of these, and they're listed in the Yellow Pages. Pharmacists are highly trained, willing to give advice (often in English), and able to dispense many drugs which would only be available on prescription in many other countries. Most keep usual shop hours (Mon–Fri

9am–1pm & 4–7pm, Sat 9am–1pm), but in Palma and Maó some open late and at weekends, and a rota system means at least one is open 24 hours a day. In theory at least, the rota is displayed in the window of every pharmacy, or you can check at reception in one of the better hotels. Outside the towns, you'll find a *farmàcia* in most of the larger villages, though there's not much chance of late-night opening or of an English-speaking pharmacist unless you're staying in a resort area.

Condoms no longer need to be smuggled into Spain as they did during the Franco years. They're available from most *farmàcias* and from all sorts of outlets in the resorts, such as bars and vending machines. It's a good job: a recent survey of 18- to 30-year-old visitors found that the average time between arrival and first sexual contact was 3hr 42min.

Seeking medical treatment

In more serious cases, your local pharmacy, tourist office or hotel should be able to provide the telephone number and address of an **English-speaking doctor** or **dentist**.

If you're seeking treatment under EU health agreements, double-check that the doctor is working within (and seeing you as) a patient of the public health care system. In **medical emergencies**, telephone the general emergency number ☎112 and an ambulance will be dispatched. If you're reliant on free treatment within the EU health scheme, try to remember to make this clear both to the ambulance staff and, if you're whisked off to hospital, to the medic you subsequently encounter. You should hand over a photocopy of your E111 on arrival at hospital, or else you may be mistaken for a private insurance job and billed accordingly.

Costs, money and banks

In terms of food, wine and transport, Mallorca and Menorca remain budget destinations for northern Europeans, North Americans, Australians and New Zealanders. However, Balearic hotel prices have increased considerably over the last few years, so independent travellers on any kind of budget will have to plan their accommodation carefully and, in summer, when vacant rooms are scarce, reserve well in advance. Another serious expense may be partying: nightclubs can relieve you of a wallet load of euros in a wink.

ATMs are the easiest way to get cash, and are common in Palma, Maó and Ciutadella, as well as all the larger resorts. Currency-exchange facilities are also widely available.

Costs

On average, if you're prepared to buy your own picnic lunch, stay in inexpensive *hostals* and hotels, and stick to the cheaper bars and restaurants, you could get by on around £20–25/US$30–35 per person per day, assuming you're sharing a room. If you intend to stay in three-star hotels and eat at quality restaurants, you'll need more like £50/$75 a day per person, with the main variable being the cost of your room – and bear in mind that room prices rise steeply as the season progresses. On £80/$120 a day and upwards, you'll be limited only by your energy reserves, unless you're planning to stay in a five-star hotel, in which case this figure won't even cover your bed.

Eating out is excellent value, and even in a top-notch restaurant in Palma a superb meal will only set you back around £20–25/US$30–37 – though, of course, you may pay well over the odds for food and drink in the tourist resorts. As always, if you're travelling alone you'll spend much more than you would in a group of two or more – sharing rooms saves a lot of money.

One other cost is **IVA**, a seven percent sales tax levied on most goods and services. Check in advance to see if IVA is included in the price of your bigger purchases; otherwise, especially in more expensive hotels and restaurants, you may be in for a bit of a shock.

Currency and the exchange rate

The Spanish currency is the **euro** (€). Each euro is made up of 100 cents. **Notes** come in denominations of 5, 10, 50 and 500 euros, **coins** as 1, 2, 5, 10, 20 and 50 cents, and 1 and 2 euros. Euro notes and coins feature a common EU design on one face, but different country-specific designs on the other. The **exchange rate** for the euro at time of writing was 0.70 to the British pound, 0.78 to the Irish punt, 1.15 to the US dollar, 1.51 to the Canadian dollar, 1.61 to the Australian dollar and 1.84 to the NZ dollar.

ATMs

ATMs are commonplace in both Mallorca and Menorca, especially in the cities and resorts, and are undoubtedly the quickest and easiest way of getting money. Most ATMs give instructions in a variety of languages, and accept a host of **debit cards**, including all those carrying the Cirrus coding. If in doubt, check with your bank to find out whether the card you wish to use will be accepted – and if you need a new (international) PIN. You'll rarely be charged a transaction fee. **Credit cards** can be used in ATMs too, but in this case transactions are treated as loans, with interest accruing daily from the date of withdrawal. All major credit cards, including American Express, Visa and Mastercard, are widely accepted in the Balearics.

Travellers' cheques

The main advantage of buying **travellers' cheques** is that they are a safe way of carrying funds. All well-known brands of travellers' cheque in all major currencies are widely accepted in Mallorca and Menorca, with Euro and US dollar travellers' cheques being the most common. The usual fee for their purchase is one or two percent of face value, though this fee is often waived if you buy the cheques through a bank where you have an account. You'll find it useful to purchase a selection of denominations. When you **cash your cheques**, almost all banks make a percentage charge per transaction on top of a basic minimum charge.

In the event that your cheques are **lost or stolen**, the issuing company will expect you to report it immediately. Make sure you keep the purchase agreement, a record of cheque serial numbers, and the details of the company's emergency contact numbers or the addresses of their local offices, safe and separate from the cheques themselves. Most companies claim to replace lost or stolen cheques within 24 hours.

Banks and exchange

All but the tiniest of settlements in Mallorca and Menorca have a **bank** or **savings bank**, the vast majority of which will change foreign currency and travellers' cheques. Many will also give cash advances on credit cards. **Banking hours** are usually Monday to Friday from 9am to 2pm, with many banks opening on Saturday mornings from 9am to 1pm except in the summer. For changing currency, a small transaction fee is the norm – they make their profits from the rate of exchange. Indeed, if the commission is waived, double-check the exchange rate to ensure it's not unreasonable.

Outside banking hours, most major hotels, many *hostals* and specialist exchange kiosks will change money, but at less generous rates and with varying commissions.

Wiring money

Having **money wired** from home using one of the major money-wiring companies (see below) is expensive and should only be considered as a last resort. It can be slightly cheaper to have your own bank send the money through. For that, you need to nominate a receiving bank on the islands; any local branch will do, but those in the cities and resorts will probably be more familiar with the process. Naturally you need to confirm the co-operation of the local bank before you set the wheels in motion back home. The sending bank's fees are geared to the amount being transferred and the urgency of the service you require – the fastest transfers, taking two or three days, start at around £25/$40 for the first £300–400/$450–600.

Money-wiring companies

Thomas Cook (ⓦ www.thomascook.com) Canada ☎ 1-888/823-4732, Great Britain ☎ 01733/318 922, Northern Ireland ☎ 028/9055 0030, Republic of Ireland ☎ 01/677 1721, US ☎ 1-800/287-7362
Travelers Express MoneyGram (ⓦ www.moneygram.com) Australia ☎ 1800/230 100, Canada ☎ 1-800/933-3278, New Zealand ☎ 0800/262 263, Republic of Ireland ☎ 1850/205 800, UK ☎ 0800/018 0104, US ☎ 1-800/955-7777.
Western Union (ⓦ www.westernunion.com) Australia ☎ 1800/501 500, Canada and US ☎ 1-800/325-6000, New Zealand ☎ 0800/270 000, Republic of Ireland ☎ 1800/395 395, UK ☎ 0800/833 833.

Getting around

On both Mallorca and Menorca you're spoiled for choice when it comes to transport. There's a reliable bus network between all the major settlements, a multitude of taxis, a plethora of car rental firms (which keeps prices down to a minimum, especially off-season), plenty of bicycles and mopeds to rent, as well as a couple of minor train lines on Mallorca. Distances are small and consequently the costs of travel low, whether in terms of petrol or the price of a ticket. On Mallorca, it's only 110km from Andratx in the west to Cala Rajada in the east, and from Palma on the south coast to Alcúdia on the north shore is a mere 60km. Menorca has only one major road, which traverses the island from Ciutadella in the west to Maó in the east, a distance of just 45km.

Hopping from one island to the other is easy and economical too, as there are regular and inexpensive **inter-island flights and ferries** – though it's advisable to book ahead in July and August.

Buses

Both Menorca and Mallorca have an extensive network of **bus services** linking the main towns – Palma, Maó and Ciutadella – with most of the villages and resorts of the coast and interior. These main routes are supplemented by more intermittent local services between smaller towns and between neighbouring resorts. Ticket **prices** are reasonable: the one-way fare from Palma to Colònia de Sant Jordi, for instance, is about €4.50, from Palma to Cala Rajada €6, and from Maó to Ciutadella €4. Only Palma is large enough to have its own public transit system, with a multiplicity of bus services linking the city centre with the suburbs and surrounding beach resorts – see p.60 and p.95. That said, all the larger resorts have some form of local transport, either by bus or electric mini-train.

On all island bus services, **destinations** are marked on the front of the bus. Passengers enter the bus at the front and buy tickets from the driver; alternatively, tickets can be bought in advance at a bus station. **Bus stops** are mostly indicated with the word *parada*. A confusing variety of bus companies operate the various routes on Mallorca; all buses on Menorca are run by

Transportes Menorca. Timetables are readily available from most tourist offices.

On the whole buses are reliable and comfortable enough, the only significant problem being that many country towns and villages do not have a bus station or even a clearly marked *parada*, which can be very confusing, as in some places buses leave from the most obscure parts of town. Remember also that bus services are drastically reduced on **Sundays** and **holidays**, and it's best not even to consider travelling out into the sticks on these days. The Catalan words to look out for on timetables are *diari* (daily), *feiners* (workdays, including Saturday), *diumenge* (Sunday) and *festius* (holidays).

Trains

Mallorca has its own, narrow-gauge **train network**. One line travels through the mountains from Palma to Sóller (28km). The second shuttles across the flatlands of the interior from Palma to Inca, just beyond which it forks, with one branch nudging south to Sineu and Manacor, the other pushing on to Sa Pobla. Work is underway to extend the line from Sa Pobla to Alcúdia. Each line has its own station in Palma, which sit alongside each other on Plaça Espanya. The trip to Sóller (see p.108) takes you through some of Mallorca's most magnificent scenery. The standard return fare from Palma to Sóller is €5, €5.70 to Sa Pobla and €7.40 to Manacor.

Taxis

The excellence of the islands' bus services means it's rarely necessary to take a **taxi**, though they are a fast and easy way of reaching your resort from the airport and, perhaps more importantly, of getting back to your hotel after a day's hiking. In the latter case, you should fix a collection point before you set out – there's no point wandering round a tiny village hoping a taxi will show up. Throughout the Balearics, the taxis of each town and resort area have their own livery: Palma taxis, for example, are black with a cream-coloured roof and bonnet (hood). Local journeys are all metered, though there are supplementary charges for each piece of luggage and for travel at night and on Sundays. For longer journeys there are official prices, which are displayed at the island's airport and at some taxi stands and tourist offices. Naturally, you're well advised to check the price with the driver *before* you get going. Fares are reasonable, but not inexpensive: the journey from the airport to downtown Palma, a distance of around 11km, will cost you in the region of €15, while the fare from Palma airport to Port d'Andratx (37km) is about €35.

Driving and vehicle rental

Getting around on public transport is easy enough, but you'll obviously have a great deal more freedom if you have **your own vehicle** – predictably, most of the more secluded (and attractive) beaches are only accessible under your own steam. Major roads are generally good, though back roads are very variable – unpaved minor roads are particularly lethal after rain. Traffic is generally well-behaved (even if Spain does have one of the highest incidences of traffic accidents in Europe), but noisy, especially in Palma, where the horn is used as a recreational tool as well as an instrument of warning. **Fuel** (*gasolina*) comes in four grades. Different companies use different brand names, but generally *Super Plus* is 98-octane fuel, selling at about €0.80 per litre; *Super* is 96-octane, selling at about €0.75 per litre, and almost always without lead (*sense plom*); while *Mezcla*, or *Normal*, is low-grade 90-octane, available for

about €0.68 per litre. Diesel (*gasoleo* or *gasoil*) costs about €0.63 per litre. Both Menorca and Mallorca are well supplied with petrol stations; a few are open 24 hours a day, seven days a week, though most close around 9pm or 10pm and on public holidays.

Most foreign **driving licences** are honoured in Spain – including all EU, US and Canadian ones – but an **International Driver's Licence** (available at minimal cost from your home motoring organization) is an easy way to set your mind at rest. If you're bringing your own car, you must have adequate insurance, a green card (available from your insurers or motoring organization), and a **bail bond**, a document to be shown to the police if you're involved in anything but the most trivial of accidents. Without a bail bond, the police will almost certainly imprison you and impound your vehicle pending an accident investigation. Extra insurance coverage for unforeseen legal costs is also well worth having, as is an appropriate **breakdown** policy from a motoring organization. In the UK, for example, the RAC and AA charge about £110 for a year's Europe-wide breakdown cover, with all the appropriate documentation, including green card and bail bond. Note, however, that rates vary depending on the age of the vehicle and increase if you're towing anything.

Speed **limits** are posted throughout the Balearics: the maximum on urban roads is 60kph, on other roads 90kph, on motorways 120kph. Speed traps are fairly frequent on the main highways. If you're stopped for any violation, the Spanish police can (and usually will) levy a stiff on-the-spot fine of up to €100 before letting you go on your way, their draconian instincts reinforced by the fact that few tourists are likely to appear in court to argue the case. Most **driving rules** and regulations are pretty standard: seat belts are compulsory, "Stop" signs mean exactly that, and drink-driving will land you in big trouble. A single, unbroken white line in the middle of the road means no overtaking, even if the rule is frequently ignored; note also that drivers often sound their horns when overtaking. You yield to traffic coming from the right at all junctions, whether or not there's a give way sign; and be prepared for road signs that give very little, if any, warning of the turning you might require. On major trunk roads, turnings that take vehicles across oncoming traffic are being phased out and replaced by semi-circular minor exits that lead round to traffic lights on the near side of the major road.

Finally, drivers do not have to stop (and usually don't) at **zebra crossings**, which merely indicate a suitable pedestrian crossing place: if you come to an abrupt stop at a crossing, as you might do in Britain, the pedestrians will be amazed and someone may well crash into your rear end.

Car rental

There are scores of companies offering **car rental** (still rendered in Castilian as *coches de alquiler*), with offices thronging the islands' resorts, larger towns and airports. Most of the major international players have outlets, and there are also dozens of small companies. A selection of companies is given in the Palma, Maó and Ciutadella "Listings", and comprehensive lists are available from the islands' tourist offices. To rent a car, you'll have to be 21 or over (and have been driving for at least a year), and you'll probably need a credit card – though some places will accept a hefty deposit in cash and some smaller companies simply ignore all the normal regulations. However, no car rental firm will allow you to transport their vehicles from one Balearic island to another. If you're planning to spend much time driving on rougher tracks, you'll probably be better off with a moped, or even a four-wheel drive vehicle (about thirty percent more expensive than the average car and available from larger rental agencies).

Rental charges vary enormously: out-of-season costs for a standard car can fall to as little as €15 per day with unlimited mileage; in July and August, by comparison, the same basic vehicle could set you back €40 a day (though weekly prices are slightly better value, and special rates operate at the weekend). The big companies all offer competitive rates, but you can often get a better deal through someone in contact with local vehicle rental firms, such as Holiday Autos. If you choose to deal directly with smaller local companies, proceed with care. In particular,

check the policy for the excess applied to claims, and ensure that it includes a bail bond (see opposite), collision damage waiver or CDW (applicable if an accident is your fault) and, in general, adequate levels of financial cover. **Fly-drive** deals are well worth investigating. In Britain, for example, Iberia offers good car rental deals as long as you book your flight with them.

Car rental agencies

Britain

Avis ☎ 0870/606 0100, ⊛ www.avis.co.uk.
Budget ☎ 0800/181 181,
⊛ www.budget.co.uk.
Europcar ☎ 0845/722 2525,
⊛ www.europcar.co.uk.
National ☎ 0870/536 5365,
⊛ www.nationalcar.co.uk.
Hertz ☎ 0870/844 8844, ⊛ www.hertz.co.uk.
Holiday Autos ☎ 0870/400 0099,
⊛ www.holidayautos.co.uk.
Suncars ☎ 0870/500 5566, ⊛ www.suncars.com.

Ireland

Avis Northern Ireland ☎ 028/9024 0404, Republic of Ireland ☎ 01/605 7500, ⊛ www.avis.ie.
Budget Republic of Ireland ☎ 0903/277 11,
⊛ www.budget.ie.
Europcar Northern Ireland ☎ 028/9442 3444, Republic of Ireland ☎ 01/614 2888,
⊛ www.europcar.ie.
Hertz Republic of Ireland ☎ 01/676 7476,
⊛ www.hertz.ie.
Holiday Autos Republic of Ireland ☎ 01/872 9366, ⊛ www.holidayautos.ie.
SIXT Republic of Ireland ☎ 1850/206 088,
⊛ www.irishcarrentals.ie.
Thrifty Republic of Ireland ☎ 1800/515 800,
⊛ www.thrifty.ie.

Australia

Avis ☎ 13 63 33 or 02/9353 9000,
⊛ www.avis.com.au
Budget ☎ 1300/362 848, ⊛ www.budget.com.au
Dollar ☎ 02/9223 1444, ⊛ www.dollarcar.com.au.
Europcar ☎ 1300/131 390,
⊛ www.deltaeuropcar.com.au.
Hertz ☎ 13 30 39 or 03/9698 2555,
⊛ www.hertz.com.au.
Holiday Autos ☎ 1300/554 432,
⊛ www.holidayautos.com.au.
National ☎ 13 10 45, ⊛ www.nationalcar.com.au.

New Zealand

Avis ☎ 09/526 2847 or 0800/655 111,
Ⓦ www.avis.co.nz.
Budget ☎ 09/976 2222, Ⓦ www.budget.co.nz.
Hertz ☎ 0800/654 321, Ⓦ www.hertz.co.nz.
Holiday Autos ☎ 0800/144 040,
Ⓦ www.holidayautos.co.nz.
National ☎ 0800/800 115,
Ⓦ www.nationalcar.co.nz.
Thrifty ☎ 09/309 0111, Ⓦ www.thrifty.co.nz.

US

Alamo US ☎ 1-800/522-9696,
Ⓦ www.alamo.com.
Avis US ☎ 1-800/331-1084, Canada ☎ 1-800/272-5871, Ⓦ www.avis.com.
Budget US ☎ 1-800/527-0700,
Ⓦ www.budgetrentacar.com.
Dollar US ☎ 1-800/800-4000, Ⓦ www.dollar.com.
Europcar US and Canada ☎ 1-877/940 6900,
Ⓦ www.europcar.com.
Hertz US ☎ 1-800/654-3001, Canada ☎ 1-800/263-0600, Ⓦ www.hertz.com.
Holiday Autos US ☎ 1-800/422-7737,
Ⓦ www.holidayautos.com.
National ☎ 1-800/227-7368,
Ⓦ www.nationalcar.com.
Thrifty ☎ 1-800/367-2277, Ⓦ www.thrifty.com.

Moped rental

Mopeds (scooters) are a popular means of transport, especially for visiting remoter spots, and are widely available. Prices start at about €15 per day, including insurance and crash helmets, which must be worn. Be warned, however, that the insurance often excludes theft – always check with the company first. You will generally be asked to show some kind of driving licence (particularly for mopeds over 50cc) and to leave a deposit on your credit card, though most places will accept cash as an alternative. We've listed names and addresses of rental companies throughout the guide where appropriate; tourist offices can provide comprehensive lists of suppliers.

Cycling

Cycling can be an inexpensive and flexible way of getting around both Menorca and (far hillier) Mallorca, and on the way you'll see a great deal of the countryside that would otherwise pass you by. In general terms, you have to be pretty fit to tackle the steep hills of the northern part of Mallorca, but the island's central plain, Es Pla, and most of Menorca are fairly easy going and, with the exception of the main arterial roads, there is little traffic. The Spanish are keen cycling fans, which means that you'll be well received and find reasonable facilities, while cars will normally hoot before they pass – though this can be alarming at first. Mallorca is more prepared for cyclists than its neighbour, and the main tourist office in Palma (see p.61) produces a free specialist leaflet, the *Guía del Ciclista* (in Spanish only), which details suggested itineraries and indicates distances and levels of difficulty. On the Internet, the **Mallorca Cycling Tourist Guide** (Ⓦ www.baleares.com/tourist .guide /cycling) outlines eight different cycle routes, from 70km to 320km, in several languages including English.

Renting a bike costs anywhere between about €5 and €8 a day for an ordinary bike (€27 to €40 per week), or about thirty percent more for a mountain bike. Renting is straightforward: there are dozens of suppliers (there's usually one at every resort) and tourist offices can provide a list or advise you of the nearest outlet; we've also listed a few in the guide.

Getting **your own bike** to the islands should present few problems. Most airlines are happy to take them as ordinary baggage provided they come within your weight allowance (though it's sensible to check first; crowded charter flights may be less obliging). You'll have to deflate the tyres to avoid explosions in the unpressurized hold and turn the handlebars sideways. **Ferries** from the mainland (and between the Balearic islands) transport bikes for free or at minimal cost. Note, however, that you can't take bikes on the train to Sóller. Bike **parts** can often be found at auto repair shops or garages – look for Michelin signs – and there are bike shops in the larger towns.

Flights, ferries and catamarans between Mallorca and Menorca

Iberia (see p.16) have a monopoly on **inter-island flights**, flying six to eight times daily from Menorca to Mallorca and vice versa. The journey takes thirty minutes and costs around €73 one-way (double for a return ticket). There's rarely a problem with seat availability, though it's best to book ahead at the height of the season and on public holidays.

Trasmediterranea (see p.18) operate a **Maó to Palma car ferry** service once or twice weekly. The sailing time is six hours and the one-way adult fare starts at €26, with a standard-size car costing €70, twenty percent more in high season. Reservations are not required for foot passengers, but are strongly advised for vehicles. Alternatively,

Balearia (see p.18) operate two inter-island fast-ferry catamaran services during the summer, one from **Port d'Alcúdia to Maó** and the other from **Port d'Alcúdia to Ciutadella**. One-way passenger fares on both start at €50, cars from €100). Alternatively, Iscomar (☏ 902 119 128, ⊛ www.iscomar.com) operate a car ferry service from **Port d'Alcúdia to Ciutadella** once or twice daily; the one-way passenger fare costs €31; vehicles up to 4.5m in length cost €51. Remember that car rental firms on the Balearics do not allow their vehicles off their home island.

Accommodation

Package-tour operators have a stranglehold on thousands of hotel rooms, villas and apartments in both Mallorca and Menorca, but nonetheless reasonably priced rooms are still available to the independent traveller, though options can be limited at the height of the season. Off-season you should be able to get a simple, medium-sized double room with shower and sink for around €55, whereas in August the same room, if available, can set you back as much as €80 – though this still compares reasonably well with much of Europe. You can, however, comfortably spend €100 and upwards in hotels with three or more stars – some of them being very firmly in the super-luxury class.

Vacant rooms are at their scarcest from late June to early September, when **advance reservations** are strongly recommended. Most hoteliers speak at least a modicum of English, so visitors who don't speak Catalan or Spanish can usually book over the phone, but a confirmation letter or email is always a good idea. In Mallorca the easiest place to get a room is Palma, with Sóller and Port de Sóller lagging not far behind, while the island's five monasteries that offer accommodation (see p.33) are also a good bet for vacancies, even in high summer. In Menorca, accommodation is much thinner on the ground, with only Maó, Ciutadella and maybe Fornells likely to have high-season vacancies.

It's often worth **bargaining** over room prices, especially outside peak season and at fancier hotels, since the posted tariff doesn't necessarily mean much. Many hotels have rooms at different prices, and tend to offer the more expensive ones first. Most places also have rooms with three or four beds at not a great deal more than the price of a double-room, which represents a real saving for small groups. On the other hand, people travelling alone invariably end up paying over the odds. We've detailed where to find places to stay in most of the destinations listed in the guide, from the most basic of rooms to luxury hotels, and given a price range for each (see box on p.32). We've also indicated where an establishment closes over the winter – a common occurrence in Menorca, though more unusual in Mallorca.

Accommodation price codes

All the **accommodation** detailed in this guide has been graded according to the nine price categories listed below. These represent how much you can expect to pay in each establishment for the **least expensive double room in high season** excluding special deals and discounts; for a single room, expect to pay around two-thirds the price of a double. Our categories are simply a guide to prices and do not give an indication of the facilities you might expect; as such they differ from the star-system applied by the tourist authorities. Note that in the more upmarket *hostals* and *pensions*, and in anything calling itself a hotel, you'll pay a **tax** (IVA) of seven percent on top of the room price.

❶ Under €40
❷ €40–50
❸ €50–65
❹ €65–80
❺ €80–100
❻ €100–150
❼ €150–200
❽ €200–250
❾ Over €250

Fondas, casas de huéspedes, pensions, hostals and hotels

The one thing all travellers to the Balearics need to grasp is the diversity of types of places to stay – though in practice the various categories often overlap. The least expensive places are **fondas**, **casas de huéspedes** and **pensions** (*pensiones* in Castilian), further categorized with either one or two stars. Establishments in these categories are few and far between in the Balearics, and the distinctions between them blurred, but in general you'll find food served at *fondas* and *pensions* (some rent rooms on a meals-inclusive basis only), while *casas de huéspedes* – literally "guest houses" – are often used as long-term lodgings. Confusingly, the name of many *pensions* does not follow their designation: lots of *pensions* call themselves *hostals* and vice versa. As a result, the name isn't always a reliable guide to the establishment's price, though the sign outside usually is (see box below).

Slightly more expensive are **hostals** (*hostales* in Castilian) and **hostal-residencias**, categorized from one to three stars. A one-star *hostal* generally costs about the same as a *pensió*. Many *hostals* offer good, functional rooms, often with a private shower. The *residencia* designation means that no meals other than breakfast are served.

Moving up the scale, **hotels** are also graded, with from one to five stars. One-star hotels cost no more than three-star *hostals* (sometimes less), but three-star hotels cost a lot more, and at four or five stars you're in the luxury class with prices to match. There are also a handful of *hotel-residencias*, where the only meal provided is breakfast.

It's safe to assume that bedrooms in a hotel will be adequately clean and furnished, but in the lower categories you're well advised to ask to see the room before you part with any money. Standards vary greatly between places in the same category (even between rooms in the same *hostal*) and it does no harm to check that there's hot water if there's supposed to be, or that you're not being stuck at the back in an airless box. Note that bathrooms in many *pensions* and *hostals* (some hotels too) will have only showers, not bath tubs.

Accommodation signs

The various categories of accommodation in Spain are identifiable by **square blue signs** inscribed in white with the following letters:

F	CH	P	H^s	HR^s	H
fonda	casa de huéspedes	pensió	hostal	hostal-residencia	hotel

By law, each establishment must display its room rates, and there should be a card on the room door showing the prices for the various seasons. If you think you're being overcharged, take up your **complaint** first with the management; you can usually produce an immediate resolution by asking for one of the *hojas de reclamaciones* (complaints forms) that all places are obliged by law to keep. The threat of filling in a form is usually in itself enough to make the proprietor back down.

Monasteries

In recent times **Mallorca's monasteries** have become severely underpopulated and five of them now let out empty cells to visitors of both sexes. All occupy delightful settings in the hills or on hilltops, and most are dotted across the centre of the island. The five are: the Santuari de Sant Salvador near Felanitx (see p.196); the Ermita de Nostra Senyora de Bonany near Petra (see p.182); the Ermita de Nostra Senyora del Puig outside Pollença (see p.152); the Monastir de Nostra Senyora de Lluc (see p.150); and the Santuari de Nostra Senyora de Cura, on Puig Randa near Algaida (see p.179). There's an increasing demand for this simple, cheap form of accommodation so, although it's possible just to turn up and ask for a room, you'd be well advised to either phone ahead or, if your Spanish isn't good enough, get the local tourist office to make a reservation on your behalf. For a double room, you can expect to pay around €12 at most of these monasteries, though it's rather more at Lluc (€60), the most visited and commercialized of the six. Reasonably priced food is usually available, but check arrangements when you book.

Hostels

There are no **youth hostels** (*albergues juveniles*) on Menorca and only two on Mallorca – one near Palma (see p.96), the other outside Alcúdia (see p.167). The former is open all year, the latter from April to September. Both tend to be block-booked by school groups, so unless you reserve well in advance you shouldn't rely on either as a

viable source of inexpensive accommodation. At both, the price of a bed is about €12.50 (€15.60 if you're over 26) and you'll need a sheet sleeping bag. Both hostels are affiliated to Hostelling International (HI) and they expect you to have a HI membership card, available either from your home hostelling organization or buyable on the spot at minimal cost. Specific details of each hostel are given in the guide.

Fincas

Many of **Mallorca's** old stone **fincas** (farmhouses) have been snaffled up for use as second homes, and some are now leased by their owners to package-tour operators for the whole or part of the season – Individual Traveller's Spain (see p.12) has one of the best selections. Out of the tour operators' main season, these fincas often stand idle. At any time of the year, though preferably well in advance of your holiday, it's worth approaching the **Associació Agroturisme Balear**, Avgda Gabriel Alomar i Villalonga 8a–2a, 07006 Palma (☎971 721 508, ⓦ www.agroturismo-balear.com), which issues a booklet detailing most of the finest fincas and takes bookings. Although some fincas are modest affairs and still a part of working farms, the majority are comparatively luxurious and many are situated in remote and beautiful spots. They are not, however, cheap: prices range from €40 to €80 per person per night, and a minimum length of stay of anything between two nights and two weeks is often stipulated.

Camping

Menorca possesses two official campsites: the well-appointed **Son Bou** (see p.242), a Class 1C establishment just outside the south-coast resort of Son Bou, and the plainer **S'Atalaia** (see p.249), a Class 3C campground, near the resort of Cala Santa Galdana. The Son Bou can accommodate about four hundred campers, the S'Atalaia just one hundred – and both take tents, trailer caravans and motor caravans. Although neither has a seashore location, they're both very popular, and in the summer it's best to make a reservation well ahead of time. Prices and specific details of each site are given in the relevant chapters. There are currently no official campsites on **Mallorca**.

Camping rough is legal, but not encouraged, and has various restrictions attached. Spanish regulations state that you're not allowed to camp "in urban areas, areas prohibited for military or touristic reasons, or within 1km of an official campsite". What this means in effect is that you can't camp on resort beaches (though there is some latitude if you're discreet), but you can camp out almost anywhere in the countryside, providing you act sensitively and use some common sense. Whenever possible, ask locally first and/or get permission from the landowner.

Eating and drinking

Traditional Balearic food, which has much in common with Catalan food, is far from delicate, but its hearty soups and stews, seafood dishes and spiced meats can be delicious. In common with other areas of Spain, this regional cuisine has, after many years of neglect, experienced something of a renaissance, and nowadays restaurants offering *Cuina Mallorquína* (and to a lesser extent *Cuina Menorquína*) are comparatively commonplace and should not be missed. Neither should a visit to one of the islands' many pastry shops (*pastisserias*), where you'll find the sweetest of confections and the Balearics' gastronomic pride and joy: *ensaimadas* (spiralled flaky pastries).

On both islands, the distinction between **cafés** (or *cafeterias*) and **restaurants** is blurred. Most serve both light snacks and full meals, with the best deals often appearing as the *menú del día* (menu of the day). At either end of the market, however, the differences become more pronounced: in the more expensive restaurants, there is usually a *menú del día*, but the emphasis is on à la carte; by contrast, the least expensive cafés serve up only simple snacks, and in their turn are often indistinguishable from **bars**, also known as *cellers* or *tavernas*. Before the tourist boom, these snacks always consisted of traditional dishes prepared as either *tapas* (small snacks) or *racions* (larger ones). Today, it's often chips, pizzas and sandwiches, though there's still a lively *tapas* scene in Palma, allowing you to move from place to place sampling a wide range of local specialities.

Opening hours vary considerably. As a general rule cafés and *tapas* bars open from around 9am until at least early in the evening, and many remain open till late at night. Restaurants open from around noon until sometime between 2pm and 4pm, before reopening in the evening from around 6/7pm until 10/11pm. Those restaurants with their eye on the tourist trade often stay open all day and can be relied upon on Sundays, when many local spots close.

For a glossary of **Catalan and Castilian food and drink terms**, see pp.316–321.

Breakfast, snacks and sandwiches

For **breakfast** you're best off in a bar or café. Some *hostals* and most hotels will serve a basic "continental" breakfast, but it's generally less expensive and more enjoyable to go out. A traditional Balearic breakfast (or lunch) dish is *pa amb tomàquet* (*pan con tomate* in Castilian) – a massive slice of bread rubbed with tomato, olive oil and garlic, which you can also have topped with ham – washed down with a flagon of wine.

Pa amb oli (bread rubbed with olive oil) arrives in similar style, but dispenses with the tomato. If that sounds like gastric madness, other breakfast standbys include *torradas* (*tostadas*; toasted rolls) with oil or butter and jam, and *xocolata amb xurros* (*chocolate con churros*) – long, fried tubular doughnuts that you dip into thick drinking chocolate. Most places also serve *ou ferrat* (*huevo frito*; fried egg) and cold *truita* (*tortilla*; omelette), both of which make an excellent breakfast.

Coffee and **pastries** (*pastas*), particularly croissants and doughnuts, are available at some bars and cafés; for a wider selection of cakes, head for a *pastisseria* (pastry shop) or *forn* (bakery). These often sell a wide array of appetizing baked goods besides the obvious bread, croissants and *ensaimadas*. For coffee see p.39.

Some bars specialize in **sandwiches** (*bocadillos*), both hot and cold – they're usually outsize affairs in French bread which will do for breakfast or lunch. In a bar with *tapas* (see below), you can have most of what's on offer put in a sandwich, and you can often get them prepared – or buy the materials to do so – at grocery shops as well. **Menorcan cheese** (*formatge*), usually known as *queso Mahón*, is popular through Spain – the best is hard and has a rind.

A list of the Catalan and Castilian words for common *bocadillo* fillings is given on p.317.

Tapas and racions

Tapas are small snacks, three or four chunks of fish, meat or vegetables, cooked in a sauce or served with a dollop of salad, which traditionally used to be provided free with a drink. These days you have to pay for anything more than a few olives, but a single helping rarely costs more than €3 unless you're somewhere very flashy. **Racions** (*raciones* in Castilian) are bigger portions of the same, served with bread and usually enough in themselves to make a light meal; they cost around €3–5. (Make it clear when ordering whether you want a *ració* or just a *tapa*.) The more people you're with, of course, the better: half-a-dozen or so different dishes can make a varied and quite filling meal for three or four people.

One of the advantages of eating *tapas* in bars is that you are able to experiment. Most places have food laid out on the counter, so you can see what's available and order by pointing without necessarily knowing the names; others have blackboards.

A list of the Catalan and Castilian words for common types of *tapas* and *racions* is given on p.318.

Cafeterias and restaurants

Meals are usually eaten in a **cafeteria** or **restaurant**, though the distinction between the two, particularly at the cheaper end of the market, is often very blurred. In similar fashion, cafeterias blend seamlessly into café-bars and bars, almost all of which serve at least some food. That said, the average price of an average meal in an average establishment does slide down the scale from restaurant to cafeteria to café-bar to bar. At a *cafeteria*, something like egg and steak, chicken and chips, or *calamars* and salad will generally cost in the region of €4–6, excluding drink, whereas the price of a main course at a good-quality restaurant averages about €12. Restaurants run from simple affairs with formica tables and checked tablecloths to expense-account palaces. Many have a daily set menu – the **menú del día** – in addition to an à la carte menu, though some of the more basic places only serve a *menú del día*. This consists of three or four courses, including bread, wine and service, and usually costs €6–10, quite a bit more in glitzy restaurants and at seaside resorts.

In all but the most rock-bottom establishments it's customary to leave a small **tip**; ten to fifteen percent is generally regarded as sufficient. Service is normally included in a *menú del día*. The other thing to take account of is **IVA**, a sales tax of seven percent, which is either included in the prices (in which case it should say so on the menu) or added to your bill at the end.

Restaurants, *cafeterias* and bars on both islands, especially in the resort areas, are mostly reliant on the tourist industry. Consequently, many ignore the strong flavours of traditional Balearic and Spanish food for the blandness of pizzas, hamburgers and pastas, or else dish up a hotch-potch of sanitized local favourites such as omelettes, paella and grilled meats. However, there are still plenty of places where the food is more distinctive and flavoursome. Fresh **fish and seafood** can be excellent, though it's almost always expensive: much of it is imported, despite the local fishing industries around the Balearics and on the Catalan coast. Nevertheless, you're able to get hake, cod (often salted) and squid at very reasonable prices, while fish stews and rice-based *paellas* are often truly memorable, as is the lobster stew – *caldereta de llagosta* – that turns up in many restaurants in Menorca. **Meat** can be outstanding too, usually either grilled and served with a few fried potatoes or salad, or – like ham – cured or dried and served as a starter or in sandwiches. Veal is common, served in great stews, while poultry is often mixed with seafood (chicken and prawns) or fruit (chicken/duck with prunes/pears).

Vegetables rarely amount to more than a few chips or boiled potatoes with the main dish, though there are some splendid vegetable concoctions to watch out for, such as *tumbet*, a pepper, potato, pumpkin and aubergine (eggplant) stew with tomato purée. It's more usual to start your meal with a **salad**, either a standard green or mixed affair, or one of the islands' own salad mixtures, which come garnished with various vegetables, meats and cheeses. **Dessert** in the cheaper places is nearly always fresh **fruit** or *flam*, the local version of *crème caramel*; look out also for *crema catalana*, with a caramelized sugar coating (the Catalan version of *crème brûlée*), and *músic*, dried fruit-and-nut cake.

A list of common Balearic dishes and specialities is given on p.319.

Vegetarian and vegan options

Palma has a couple of **vegetarian** restaurants (see pp.88–89) and most of the resorts are accustomed to having vegetarian guests, but elsewhere the choice isn't so great and is essentially confined to large salads, fried eggs and chips or omelettes. If

you eat fish, however, there's a magnificent range of seafood and *menús del día* nearly always feature a fish dish. Even out in the country, you'll often find trout on the menu.

If you're a **vegan**, you'll no doubt come prepared to cook your own food at least some of the time. That said, some restaurant salads and vegetable dishes are vegan – like *espinacs a la Catalana* (spinach, pine nuts and raisins) and *escalivada* (aubergine/egg-plant and peppers) – but they're few and far between. Fruit and nuts are widely available, and most pizza restaurants will serve you a vegetarian pizza without cheese: ask for *vegetal sense formatge* (in Castilian, *vegetal sin queso*).

For vegetarian and vegan **shopping**, use the markets – where you can buy ready-cooked lentils and beans, and pasta – or look out for shops marked *Aliments regim* (*dietética* in Castilian), which sell wholefoods, soya milk and desserts, and so on.

Where to drink

You'll do most of your everyday **drinking** – from morning coffee to nightcap – in a **bar** or **café** (between which there's little difference). Very often, you'll eat in here too, or at least snack on some *tapas*. Bars situated in old wine cellars are sometimes called *cellers* or *tavernas*; a *bodega* traditionally specializes in wine. In Palma you also have the choice of drinking in rather more salubrious surroundings in the so-called *bars modernos* – designer bars, for want of a better description. Some of these are extraordinarily chic and stylish, sights in their own right, but their drinks are invariably expensive. Locals hang out here for hours whilst managing to imbibe very little.

If you're a **vegetarian**, try in Catalan *"Sóc vegetarià/ana – es pot menjar alguna cosa sense carn?"* (I'm a vegetarian – is there anything without meat?). In Castilian, that's *"Soy vegetariano/a – hay algo sin carne?"* Alternatively, you may be better understood if you simply resort to the Catalan *"No puc menjar carn"* (I can't eat meat).

Bar **opening hours** are difficult to pin down, but you should have little trouble in getting a drink somewhere in Palma until 2am or even 3am. Elsewhere you're OK until at least 11pm, sometimes midnight. The islands' nightclubs tend to close by 2am or 3am. Some bars close on Sundays, and don't expect much to be happening in the resorts out of season.

A glossary of common Catalan and Castilian drinking terms is given on p.320.

Wine

Wine (*vi* in Catalan, *vino* in Castilian) is the invariable accompaniment to every meal and is, as a rule, inexpensive. In bars, cafés and budget restaurants, it may be whatever comes out of the barrel – either red (*negre/tinto*), white (*blanc/blanco*) or rosé (*rosada/rosado*) – or the house bottled special (ask for *vi/vino de la casa*). In a bar, a small glass of wine will generally cost anything from €0.50 to €0.80; in a restaurant, prices start at around €1.80, and even in the poshest of places you'll be able to get a bottle of house wine for under €15. If you're having the *menú del día*, house wine will be included in the price – you'll get a third- to a half-litre per person.

On both islands, all the more expensive restaurants, supermarkets, and some of the cheaper cafés and restaurants carry a good selection of Spanish wines. The thing to check for is the appellation **Denominació d'Origen (DO)**, which indicates the wine has been passed as being of sufficiently high quality by the industry's watchdog, the Instítuto Nacional de Denominaciónes d'Origen (INDO). Over forty regions of Spain currently carry DO status, including the north central region that produces Spain's most famous and widely distributed red wine, Rioja, which is hard to match for reliability and finesse. The wines are generally made of the *tempranillo* and *garnacha* grapes and are classified according to their age. At one end of the scale, *joven* indicates a young, inexpensive, straightforward wine which has spent no time in wood. Wines labelled *con crianza* (with breeding) or *reserva* have received respectively moderate and generous ageing in oak casks and in the bottle. At the top of the scale, in both price and quality, are the *gran reserva* wines, which are only produced in the best years and which have to spend at least two years in the cask followed by three in the bottle before being offered for sale. The names to look for in red Rioja include **Martínez-Bujanda**, **Tondonia** and **Monte Real**.

The region of **Navarra** also produces excellent wine using similar techniques and grape varieties at a fraction of the price of Rioja. The labels to watch for here are **Chivite** and **Señorío de Sarría**. Around Barcelona, the region of **Penedès** is noted for the wines of **Torres** and **Masía Bach**, whilst the reds of the **Ribera del Duero** region, 120km north of Madrid, include **Protos**, **Viña Pedrosa** and **Pesquera**, all three of which offer the smooth integration of fruit and oak that is the hallmark of good Spanish wine.

Spain's **white wines** have not enjoyed the same reputation as the reds. Traditionally, they tended to be highly alcoholic and overoaked. Spain's best white, the **Rioja Blanca** made by **Marqués de Murrieta**, descends from this tradition, but offers a smooth-tasting marriage of oak and lemony fruit. The demands of the export market have led to new approaches to white wine-making, and the result has been clean, fruity and dry wines that tend to be competent rather than memorable. The best of this style has to be **Marqués de Riscal Blanco** from Rueda, just south of Valladolid.

Spain's excellent reputation for **sparkling wine** has been built on the performance of two producers, Freixenet and Codorniú, which hail from a small area west of Barcelona. Local grape varieties are used and the best examples, known as **cava**, are made by the same doublefermentation process as is used in champagne production.

Sherry, brandy, gin and beer

Fortified wines and spirits in the Balearics are the same as those found throughout Spain. The classic Andalucian wine, **sherry** – *vino de Jerez* – is served chilled or at room temperature, a perfect drink to wash down *tapas*. The main distinctions are between

Mallorcan wine

Wine production has flourished in the Balearics since classical times. In the nineteenth century, sweet "Malvasia" – wine similar to Madeira – was exported in great quantity, until the vineyards were devastated by **phylloxera**, whose root-eating activities changed the course of Spanish wine history in the late nineteenth century. The small yellow phylloxera aphid, about 1mm long, was indigenous to eastern North America. It first appeared in Spain in 1878, carried either in soil or on agricultural tools and footwear, and in the space of twenty years it destroyed Spain's existing vine stock and made thousands bankrupt. Indeed, vine cultivation never re-established itself on Ibiza or Menorca, and, with the best will in the world, Mallorcan wines, produced from newly imported vines, were long regarded as being of only average quality.

During the early 1990s, however, a concerted effort was made to raise the standards of Mallorcan wine-making, driven on one side by the tourist industry and on the other by the realization among local producers that the way forward lay in exporting wine that matched international standards. This meant new methods and new equipment. Mallorca's leading wine is **Binissalem**, from around the eponymous village northeast of Palma. Following vigorous local campaigning, it was justifiably awarded its Denominació d'Origen credentials in 1991.

Red Binissalem is a robust and aromatic wine made predominantly of the local *mantonegro* grape. It is not unlike Rioja, but it has a distinctly local character, suggesting cocoa and strawberries. The best producer of the wine is **Franja Roja**, who make the **José Ferrer** brand – well worth looking out for, with prices starting at around €3 per bottle, or €10 for the superior varieties. Red Binissalem is widely available throughout Mallorca. **White and rosé Binissalem** struggle to reach the same standard as the red. However, the **Binissalem Blanco** made by **Herederos de Ribas** is a lively and fruity white that goes well with fish. Also around the island are various country wineries making inexpensive and unpretentious wine predominantly for local consumption, such as the **Muscat Miguel Oliver** or the **Celler Son Calo**. The best places to sample these local, coarser wines is in the *cellers* and bars of the country towns of the interior – we've recommended several in the guide.

If you're visiting in late September, you can catch Binissalem's **Festival of the Grape Harvest** (Festa d'es Verema), which takes place during the week leading up to the last Sunday of the month. Saturday is the best day, with a procession of decorated floats and a good deal of free wine. On a more sedate level, Palma's **Food Week** (Setmana de Cuina Mallorquína) takes place in the middle of May all over the centre of town, with stalls featuring the cuisine and wine of the island.

The best selection of wines in Mallorca is at Palma's **El Centro del Vino y del Cava**, c/Bartomeu Rossello-Porcel 19 (☎971 452 990).

---

fino or *jerez seco* (dry sherry), *amontillado* (medium), and *oloroso* or *jerez dulce* (sweet); these are the terms you should use to order. In mid-afternoon – or even at breakfast – many islanders take a *copa* of **liqueur** with their coffee. The best – certainly to put *in* your coffee – is **coñac**, excellent Spanish brandy, mostly from the south and often deceptively smooth. If you want a brandy from Mallorca, try the mellow but hard-hitting Suau, or look for Torres, from Catalunya. Other good brands include Magno, Veterano and Soberano. Most other spirits are ordered by brand name, too, since there are generally cheaper Spanish equivalents for standard imports. Larios **gin** from Málaga, for instance, is about half the price of Gordons, but around two-thirds the strength and a good deal rougher. The Menorcans, who learnt the art of gin-making from the British, still produce their own versions, in particular the waspish Xoriguer. Always specify *nacional* to avoid getting an expensive foreign brand.

Almost any **mixed drink** seems to be collectively known as a *cuba Libre* or *cubata*, though strictly speaking this should refer only to rum and Coke. For mixers, ask for orange juice (*suc de taronja* in Catalan), lemon (*llimona*) or tonic (*tònica*).

Pilsner-type beer, **cervesa** (more usually seen in Castilian as *cerveza*), is generally pretty good, though more expensive than wine. The two main brands you'll see everywhere are San Miguel and Estrella. In Palma, keep an eye out for draught *cerveza negra* – black fizzy beer with a bitter taste. Beer generally comes in 300ml bottles or, for a little bit less, on tap: a small glass of draught beer is a *cana*, a larger glass a *cana gran*. Equally refreshing, though often deceptively strong, is **sangría**, a wine-and-fruit punch which you'll come across at *festas* and in tourist resorts.

Soft drinks

Soft drinks are much the same as anywhere in the world, but one local favourite to try is *orxata* (*horchata* in Castilian) – a cold milky drink made from tiger nuts. Also, be sure to try a *granissat*, or iced fruit-squash; popular flavours are *granissat de llimona* or *granissat de café*. You can get these drinks from **orxaterias** and from **gelaterias** (ice cream parlours; *heladerías* in Castilian).

Although you can drink the **water** almost everywhere, bottled water – *aigua mineral* – is ubiquitous, either sparkling (*amb gas*) or still (*sense gas*).

Coffee and tea

Coffee – served in cafés, bars and restaurants – is invariably espresso, slightly bitter and, unless you specify otherwise, served black (*café sol*). A slightly weaker large black coffee is called a *café americano*. If you want it white ask for *café cortado* (small cup with a drop of milk) or *café amb llet* (*café con leche* in Castilian) made with hot milk. For a large cup ask for a *gran*. Black coffee is also frequently mixed with brandy, cognac or whisky, all such concoctions termed *carajillo*; a liqueur mixed with white coffee is a *trifásico*. **Decaffeinated** coffee (*descafeinat*) is increasingly available, though in fairly undistinguished sachet form.

Tea (*te*) comes without milk unless you ask for it, and is often weak and insipid. If you do ask for milk, chances are it'll be hot and UHT, so your tea isn't going to taste much like the real thing. Better are the **infusions** that you can get in most bars, such as mint (*menta*), camomile (*camamilla*) and lime (*tiller*).

Communications

The Spanish postal system is competent and comprehensive, if not especially speedy, with post boxes liberally distributed across the islands. The telephone network is comparable – and public telephone booths are commonplace, though you may have to hunt around a bit in the smaller villages. Internet cafés are few and far between, but there are a handful in Maó and Palma.

Mail

There are **post offices** (*correus*) in every town and most of the larger villages, the majority handily located on or near the main square. Opening hours are usually Monday to Friday 9am to 2pm, though the main post office in Palma is open through the afternoon and on Saturday mornings too. All post offices close on public holidays.

Outbound post is slow but reasonably reliable, with letters or cards taking a week or ten days to reach Britain and Ireland, up to two weeks to North America, and about three weeks to Australasia. You can buy **stamps** (*segells*) at tobacconists (look for the brown and yellow *tabac* or *tabacos* sign) and at scores of souvenir shops as well as at post offices. **Post boxes** are yellow; where you have a choice of slots, pick the flap marked *províncies I estranger* or *altres destinos*. Postal rates are inexpensive, with postcards and small letters attracting two tariffs: one to anywhere in Europe; the other worldwide.

Inbound post is fairly reliable. You can send letters to any post office by addressing them "Poste Restante", followed by the surname of the addressee (preferably underlined and in capitals), and then the name of the town followed by Mallorca/Menorca, Spain. To collect, take along your passport or identity card. If you're expecting post and your first enquiry produces nothing, ask the clerk to check under all of your names: letters are often filed under first or middle names.

Telephones

You can make domestic and international **telephone calls** with equal ease from Spanish public (and private) phones. Most hotel rooms also have phones, but note that there is almost always an exorbitant sur-charge for their use. Within Spain, the **ringing tone** is long, whereas **engaged** (busy) is shorter and rapid. On pickup, the standard Spanish response to a call is to the point: *digáme* (speak to me).

International and domestic **rates** are slightly cheaper after 10pm and before 8am, and after 2pm on Saturday and all day Sunday. Making a **collect** or **reverse-charge call** (*cobro revertido*) can be a bit of a hassle, especially if your Spanish – the language in which the phone company conducts its business – is poor. It's best to call the international operator for advice on ☏1008 for Europe, ☏1005 for rest of the world.

Public telephones are of the usual European kind, where you deposit the money before you make your call, though the vast majority also accept credit cards and **phonecards**, which are available in several denominations, from €5 upwards, from most newsagents and tobacconists. Most public phones display instructions in several languages including English along with a list of Spanish area codes and some international country codes. For international calls on a coin-phone, you're best off shovelling in at least €3 to ensure a connection – and make sure you have a good stock of coins on hand if you're intending to have a conversation of any length.

Useful codes and telephone numbers

Phoning abroad from the Balearics:
Dial the international access code ☏00 followed by:
To the UK: ☏44, then the area code (minus the 0) then the number.
To Ireland: ☏353, then the area code (minus the 0) then the number.
To the US or Canada: ☏1, then the area code, then the number.
To Australia: ☏61, then the area code (minus the 0), then the number.
To New Zealand: ☏64, then the area code (minus the 0), then the number.

Phoning the Balearics from abroad:
Dial your international access code, followed by ☏34 for Spain and then the nine-digit local number. Note that all Balearic phone numbers begin with ☏971, but this is an integral part of the number, not an area code.

Useful telephone numbers:
Directory enquiries ☏1003
European operator ☏1008
International operator (outside Europe) ☏1005

Telephone charge cards and credit-card calls

One of the most convenient ways of phoning home from abroad is via a **telephone charge card** issued by your phone company back home. Using a PIN number, these cards allow you to make calls from most public, private and hotel phones; these are then charged to your home account. Since most major charge cards are free to obtain, it's worth getting one at least for emergencies; bear in mind, however, that rates aren't necessarily cheaper than calling from a Balearic public phone – it's just more convenient not having to carry sufficient change around.

In the UK and Ireland, British Telecom (☎0800/345 144, ⊛www.chargecard.bt.com) issue free BT Charge Cards to all BT customers; these can be used in Spain, along with a host of other countries. **In the US**, AT&T, MCI, Sprint, Canada Direct and other North American long-distance companies all provide charge card services to their customers. Call your company's customer service line for details of the toll-free access code in the Balearics. In **Australia and New Zealand**, charge cards include the Telstra Telecard (☎1800/038 000) and Optus Calling Card (☎1300/300 937) in Australia, and Telecom NZ's Calling Card (☎04/801 9000).

Mobile phones

On both islands, **mobile phone** access is routine in all the larger towns and villages and in most of the countryside. If you want to use your mobile phone bought at home here, you'll need to check cellular access and call charges with your phone provider before you set out. Note in particular that you are very likely to be charged extra for incoming calls when abroad, assuming that is that most people calling you will be calling from your home country and paying the usual domestic rate. The same sometimes applies to **text messages**, though in most cases these can now be received with the greatest of ease – no fiddly codes and so forth – and at ordinary rates. In Spain, the mobile network works on GSM 900/1800 – which means that mobiles bought in **North America** need to be **triband** to gain cellular access.

Email

One of the best ways to keep in touch while travelling is to sign up for a **free Internet email address** that can be accessed from anywhere in the world; two of the biggest providers are Yahoo! (⊛www.yahoo.com) and Hotmail (⊛www.hotmail.com). Once you've set up an account, you can use these sites to pick up and send mail from any computer with access to the Internet.

Internet cafés are few and far between in Mallorca and Menorca, but an increasing number of hotels provide Internet access for their guests free or at a minimal charge. We've given addresses of Internet cafés in the guide where appropriate.

The media

English-language newspapers and magazines are widely available in Mallorca and Menorca, and most hotel (if not *hostal*) rooms have satellite TV.

Newspapers and magazines

British and other European newspapers, as well as *USA Today* and the *International Herald Tribune*, are all widely available in the resort areas and larger towns of Mallorca and Menorca. These are supplemented by a ragbag of locally produced English papers and journals, the most informative of them being the *Majorca Daily Bulletin*.

Of the **Spanish newspapers**, the best two are *El País* – liberal, and the only one with much serious analysis or foreign news – and its rival, *El Mundo*, a left-of-centre broadsheet. Other national papers include *ABC*, solidly elitist with a hard moral line against abortion and divorce, and the equally conservative *La Vanguardia*. Printed in Catalan, *Avui* is the chief nationalist paper, but its main competitor, the Catalan *El Diari de Barcelona,* is more liberal. On the Balearics, there are several rather modest local papers, of which *Ultima Hora* and *Diario de Mallorca* are the most substantial.

Amongst a plethora of glossy **magazines**, Spain's most interesting offering is *Ajo Blanco*, a monthly from Barcelona with an eclectic mix of politics, culture and style. The more arty and indulgent *El Europeo*, a massive quarterly publication from Madrid, can also be worth a browse. And, of course, Spain is the home of *Hola* – the original of *Hello*.

Television and radio

Spaniards love their **television**, and consequently you'll catch more of it than you might expect sitting in bars and cafés. On the whole it's hardly riveting stuff, the bulk being a mildly entertaining mixture of kitsch game shows and foreign-language films and TV series dubbed into Spanish. Soaps are a particular speciality, either South American *culebrones* ("serpents" – they go on and on), which take up most of the daytime programming, or well-travelled British or Australian exports, like *EastEnders* (*Gent del Barri*) and *Neighbours* (*Veins*). Sports fans are well catered for, with regular live coverage of football (soccer) and basketball matches; in the football season, you can watch one or two live matches a week in many bars. The number of TV stations is increasing all the time, but the two main national channels are TVE1 and TVE2, and you'll probably also spot the Catalan TVE3 and Canal 33.

The *Majorca Daily Bulletin* and other local English-language newspapers detail the **BBC World Service radio**'s frequencies and broadcasting schedules; alternatively, consult ⓦwww.bbc.co.uk/worldservice. For **Radio Canada** go to ⓦwww.rcinet.ca; for **Voice of America**, ⓦwww.voa.gov.

Opening hours, public holidays and festivals

Despite the blandishments of the tourist industry, many islanders remain committed to their afternoon siesta, which breaks up their working day between a morning and early evening shift. They also relish their public holidays and their festivals – and indeed it's hard to beat the experience of arriving in a town to discover the streets decked out with flags and streamers, a band playing in the square and the entire population out celebrating the local *festa* (in Castilian, *fiesta*).

Opening hours

Although there's been some movement towards a northern European **working day** in Menorca and Mallorca – especially in Palma and the major tourist resorts – most shops and offices still close for a siesta of at least two hours in the hottest part of the afternoon. There's a lot of variability, but basic working hours are generally Monday to Friday 9am to 1pm & 4pm to 7pm, Sat 9am–1pm; notable exceptions are the extended hours operated by the largest department stores, some important tourist attractions and most tourist and souvenir shops.

Almost without exception, **museums** take a siesta, closing between 1pm and 3pm, while many close on Mondays and some on Saturdays and Sundays too. Don't be surprised if the official opening times of less-visited museums are disregarded. The less significant **churches** are often kept locked, opening (if at all) only for services in the early morning and/or the evening. In these cases, either time your visit to coincide with the Mass, or find someone with a key. This is not as difficult as it sounds, since a sacristan or custodian almost always lives nearby, and someone will know where to direct you. You're often expected to give a small donation.

Public holidays

Public holidays – as well as scores of local festivals (see pp.44–46) – may well disrupt your travel plans at some stage. There are ten Spanish national holidays annually, supplemented by five holidays fixed by the regions. The island's resorts are generally oblivious to public holidays, but elsewhere almost all businesses and shops close, and it can prove difficult to find a room. Similarly, vacant seats on planes and buses (which are in any case reduced to a skeleton service) are at a premium.

Festivals

Everywhere in Mallorca and Menorca takes at least one day off a year to devote to a **festival**. Usually it's the local saint's day, but there are celebrations, too, of harvests, deliverance from the Moors, of safe return from the sea – any excuse will do. Each festival is different, with a particular local emphasis, but there is always music, dancing, traditional costume and an immense spirit of enjoyment. The main event of most *festas* is a **parade**, either behind a revered holy image or a more celebratory affair with fancy costumes and **gigantones**, giant carnival figures that rumble down the streets to the delight, or terror, of children.

Although these *festas* take place throughout the year – and it's often the obscure and unexpected event which proves to be most fun – **Holy Week** (*Setmana Santa*) stands out, its passing celebrated in many places with magnificent processions.

The list below gives the highlights of the festival year. For information about less prominent festivals, try local tourist offices. Remember that although outsiders are nearly always welcome at a *festa*, you will have difficulty finding a room, and should try to book your accommodation well in advance.

43

Public holidays

January 1 New Year's Day (Año Nuevo)
January 6 Epiphany (Reyes Magos)
March 19 St Joseph's Day (Sant Josep)
Good Friday Divendres Sant (Viernes Santo in Castilian).
May 1 Labour Day (Día del Trabajo)
Early or mid-June Corpus Christi
June 24 St John's Day (Sant Joan), King Juan Carlos's name-day.
June 29 St Peter and St Paul Day (Sant Pere i Sant Pau)
July 25 St James's Day (Santiago)
August 15 Assumption of the Virgin (Asunción)
October 12 Discovery of America Day (Día de la Hispanidad)
November 1 All Saints (Todos los Santos)
December 6 Constitution Day (Día de la Constitución)
December 8 Immaculate Conception (Inmaculada Concepción)
December 25 Christmas Day (Nadal; Navidad in Castilian)

January

16: Revetla de Sant Antoni Abat (Eve of St Antony's Day) is celebrated by the lighting of bonfires (*foguerons*) in Palma and several of Mallorca's villages, especially Sa Pobla and Muro. In these two villages, the inhabitants move from fire to fire, dancing round in fancy dress and eating *espinagades*, traditional eel and vegetable patties. Also takes place in Sant Lluís on Menorca.

17: Beneides de Sant Antoni (Blessing of St Antony). St Antony's feast day is marked by processions in many of Mallorca's country towns, notably Sa Pobla and Artà, with farmyard animals herded through the streets to receive the saint's blessing and protection against disease.

17: Processó d'els Tres Tocs (Procession of the Three Knocks). Held in Ciutadella, Menorca, this procession commemorates the victory of Alfonso III over the Muslims here on January 17, 1287. There's a mass in the cathedral first and then three horsemen lead the way to the old city walls, where the eldest of the trio knocks three times with his flagstaff at the exact spot the Catalans first breached the walls.

19: Revetla de Sant Sebastià Palma has more bonfires, singing and dancing for St Sebastian.

20: Festa de Sant Sebastià This feast day is celebrated in Pollença with a procession led by a holy banner (*estenard*) picturing the saint. It's accompanied by *cavallets* (literally "merry-go-rounds"), two young dancers each wearing a cardboard horse and imitating the animal's walk. You'll see *cavallets*, which are of medieval origin, at many of the island's festivals.

February

Carnaval Towns and villages throughout the islands live it up during the week before Lent with marches and fancy dress parades. The biggest and liveliest is in Palma, where the shindig is known as *Sa Rua* (the Cavalcade).

March/April

Setmana Santa (Holy Week) is as widely observed in the Balearics as it is everywhere else in Spain. On **Maundy Thursday** in Palma, a much venerated icon of the crucified Christ, *La Sang*, is taken from the eponymous church on the Plaça del Hospital (off La Rambla) and paraded through the city streets. There are also solemn **Good Friday** (*Divendres Sant*) processions in many towns and villages, with the more important taking place in Palma and Sineu.

Most holy of all, however, is the Good Friday *Davallament* (The Lowering), the culmination of Holy Week in Pollença. Here, in total silence and by torchlight, the inhabitants lower a figure of Christ down from the hilltop Oratori to the church of Nostra Senyora dels Àngels. During Holy Week there are also many *romerias* (pilgrimages) to the island's holy places, with one of the most popular being the climb up to the Ermita Santa Magdalena, near Inca.

The Monestir de Lluc, which possesses Mallorca's most venerated shrine, is another religious focus during this time, with the penitential trudging round its Camí dels Misteris del Rosari (The Way of the Mysteries of the Rosary). In Menorca's Ciutadella, there's also the *Matança dels bruixots* (the Slaughter of the Wizards), in which puppets representing well-known personalities are hung in the streets.

May

8: Festa de la Verge del Toro (The Festival of the Virgin of the Bull). The day of the patron saint of Menorca begins with a special mass at the hilltop shrine of Monte Toro and continues with a shindig down in the little town of Es Mercadal.

Mid-May: Festa de Nostra Senyora de la Victòria in Port de Sóller features mock battles between Christians and infidels in commemoration of the thrashing of a band of Arab pirates in 1561. Lots of booze and firing of antique rifles into the air.

June

Early to mid-June: Corpus Christi At noon in the main square of Pollença an ancient and curious dance of uncertain provenance takes place – the *Ball de les Àguiles* (Dance of the Eagles) – followed by a religious procession.

23–25: Festa de Sant Joan This midsummer festival has been celebrated in Ciutadella since the fourteenth century. There are jousting competitions, folk music, dancing and processions following a special mass held in the cathedral on the 24th. Another highlight is on the Sunday before the 24th, when the *S'Homo d'es Bé* (the Man of the Lamb) leads a party of horsemen through the town. Clad in animal skins and carrying a lamb in honour

of St John, he invites everyone to the forthcoming knees-up.

July

15–16: Día de Virgen de Carmen The day of the patron saint of seafarers and fishermen is celebrated in many coastal settlements – principally Palma, Maó, Port de Sóller, Colònia de Sant Pere, Porto Colom and Cala Rajada – with parades and the blessing of boats.

Third Sunday: Festa de Sant Martí in Es Mercadal Celebrates the feast day of St Martin with a popular religious procession followed by dancing and all sorts of fun and games.

Last Sunday: Festa de Sant Jaume This festival in Alcúdia and Menorca's Es Castell celebrates the feast day of St James with a popular religious procession followed by folk dances, fireworks and the like.

August

2: Mare de Déu dels Àngels Moors and Christians battle it out again, this time in Pollença.

Second weekend: Festa de Sant Llorenç High jinks on horseback through the streets of Alaior.

20: Cavallet (see p.44) dances in Felanitx.

Last week: Festa de Sant Bartomeu Three days of festivities in Ferreries.

September

7–9: Festa de la Mare de Déu de Gràcia This three-day festival in Maó, celebrates the Virgin of Grace, the city's patron saint, and begins with a pilgrimage to the chapel of the Virgin. Thereafter, there are processions and parades along with horseback games in which the horses are trained to rear up on their hind legs.

Second week: Nativitat de Nostra Senyora (Nativity of the Virgin) In Alaró, honouring the Virgin with a pilgrimage to a hilltop shrine near the Castell d'Alaró.

October

Third Sunday *Festa d'es Butifarra* (Sausage Festival). Of recent origins, this festival follows on from tractor and automobile contests held in the village of Sant Joan. It features folk dancing and traditional music as well as the eating of specially prepared vegetable pies (*coca amb trampó*) and sausages (*berenada de butifarra*).

December

Christmas (*Nadal*) is especially picturesque in Palma and Ciutadella, where there are Nativity plays in the days leading up to the 25th.

The bullfight

In recent years the popularity of the **bullfight** (*los toros*) has declined across Spain, though it was never as big a deal in Catalunya and the Balearics as elsewhere. Mallorca has two main rings – one in Palma, the other in Muro – which still attract large crowds. The spectators turn up to see the *matadores* dispatch the bulls cleanly and with "artistic merit", which they greet with thunderous applause and the waving of handkerchiefs. A prolonged and messy kill will get the audience whistling in derision. Some Spaniards do, of course, object to the whole spectacle, but opposition is not widespread and if Spaniards tell you that bullfighting is controversial, they are more likely to be referring to new refinements to the "sport", especially the widespread but illegal shaving down of bulls' horns. The horns are as sensitive as fingernails a few millimetres in, and paring them down deters the animals from charging and affects their balance, thereby reducing the danger to the *matador*.

Whether you attend a bullfight is obviously down to you. If you spend any time in Mallorca and Menorca during the season (there are eight or nine bullfights between March and October), you may well encounter *los toros* on a bar TV, and that will probably make up your mind. Many neutrals are particularly offended by the use of horses: padded up for protection, the horses are repeatedly charged by the bulls, which clearly terrifies them – though they can't make their feelings heard as their vocal chords have been cut.

If you want to know more about the **opposition to bullfighting**, contact Spain's Anti-Bullfight Campaign, *ABC International*, c/Bailén 164, local 2 interior, 08037 Barcelona (🕸 www.adda.org/abc.html).

The corrida

Highly stylized, each bullfighting programme, or ***corrida***, begins with a procession to the accompaniment of a *paso doble* by the band. Leading the procession are two *algauziles* or "constables", on horseback and in traditional costume, followed by the three *matadores*, who will each fight two bulls, and their personal teams, each comprising two mounted assistants – *picadores* – and three *banderilleros*. At the back are the mule teams who will drag off the dead bulls. The picadores stab pikes into the beast's withers to soften it up and the process is continued by the *banderilleros*, who stick beribboned and sharpened sticks into the bull in preparation for the *matador*, who kills the animal off.

Tickets and seating

Tickets for *corridas* cost €15 and up – much more for the prime seats and prestigious fights. The cheapest seats are *gradas*, the highest rows at the back, from where you can see everything that happens without too much of the detail; the front rows are known as the *barreras*. Seats are also divided into *sol* (sun), *sombra* (shade) and *sol y sombra* (shaded after a while), though these distinctions have become less relevant as more and more bullfights start later in the day, at 6pm or 7pm, rather than the traditional 5pm. The *sombra* seats are more expensive, not so much for the spectators' personal comfort as for the fact that most of the action takes place in the shade. On the way in, you can rent **cushions**: two hours sitting on concrete is not much fun. Beer and soft drinks are sold inside.

Football

To foreigners, the bullfight is easily the most celebrated of Spain's spectacles. In terms of popular support in modern Spain, however, it ranks far below **fútbol** (football/soccer). For many years, the country's two dominant teams have been Real Madrid and FC

Barcelona, and these have shared the League title and Cup honours with repetitive regularity. Both teams are in Division 1 – *la Primera Liga* – of Spain's four-division League (Divisions 1, 2A, 2B and 3), the same division as the Palma-based Real Club Deportivo Mallorca, or **Real Mallorca**, as they're generally known (☎971 221 221, ⓦwww.rcdmallorca.es). Real Mallorca are easily the Balearics' best team, winning the Spanish Cup in 1998, finishing third in the Primera Liga in 1999 and progressing the same year to the final of the European Cup Winners' Cup – which they lost after a late goal 2-1 to Italian club Lazio. They're still riding high, and boast a hefty complement of world-class players. They play in the Son Moix stadium, just to the north of Palma city centre beyond the Via Cintura on Camí dels Reis, and a visit to a match is good fun, with a noisy, enthusiastic and usually good-humoured crowd. The season runs from early September to April with a short Christmas break; most matches are on Sunday afternoons, and tickets, which are available at the turnstiles, cost €20–60.

Crime and personal safety

Many northern European expatriates love Mallorca and Menorca for their lack of crime – with good reason. In the islands' villages and small towns petty crime is unusual, and serious offences, from burglary to assault and beyond, extremely rare. Of the three larger towns, only Palma presents any problems, mostly low-key stuff such as the occasional fight and minor theft; commonsense precautions are normally enough to keep you out of any trouble.

However, you should be aware that noisy and aggressive males commonly colonize some of the late-night bars at the seedier resorts – S'Arenal and Magaluf have the worst reputations, but it's more a question of which bar you're in, rather than the resort you're staying at.

If for some reason you do have dealings with the Spanish police, remember that, although they are polite enough in the normal course of events, they can be extremely unpleasant if you get on the wrong side of them. At all times, keep your cool and remember, especially if you are British, just how unpleasant some of your compatriots can be when they are tanked up.

The police

General Franco created a **police force** of labyrinthine complexity and since his death political parties of all persuasions have dodged the fundamental reorganization that is really needed. The reason is simple: no one wants to take them on.

There are three main types of police in Spain: the Guardia Civil, the Policía Nacional and the Policía Municipal, all of them armed. Dressed in green uniforms, the **Guardia Civil** police the highways and the country-side, but they are generally regarded as being officious and best avoided. Even now, many Spaniards are deeply suspicious of them, remembering their enthusiastic support of Franco and the unsuccessful coup led by one of their colonels, Tejero, when he held the Spanish parliament hostage in February 1981. They have, however, had their sails trimmed in recent years – improbably, they've even assumed some environmental responsibilities – and the loathed tri-corn hat has been abandoned except for ceremonial occasions. In fairness, the Guardia Civil has attempted to improve its image, launching what (almost) amounts to a charm offensive; recent tourists' reports of their attitude have been favourable.

A second police force, the brown-uniformed **Policía Nacional**, have made a better fist of the transition to democracy despite their disagreeable origins as Franco's brutal security police, the Policía Armada; they were even instrumental in Tejero's failure. They are mainly seen in Palma, armed with submachine guns and guarding key installations or personnel. They are also used to control crowds and demonstrations and – despite their democratic credentials – are not known for their sensitivity. Consequently, if you do need the police, and above all if you're reporting a serious crime, you're usually better off seeking out the more sympathetic **Policía Municipal**, who wear blue uniforms. The problem is that this force only operates in the towns, and so in the countryside you'll usually have no choice but to throw yourself on the tender mercies of the Guardia Civil, who are inclined to resent the suggestion that any crime exists on their turf. Indeed, you may end up feeling as if you're the one who stands accused. Many police officers **speak English**, especially in the towns and resort areas, but you can't bank on it.

Petty crime

Almost all the problems tourists encounter in the Balearics are to do with **petty crime** – pickpocketing and bag-snatching – rather than more serious physical confrontations. If you're **robbed**, you need to go to the police to report it, not least because your insurance company will require a police report or number. Don't expect a great deal of concern if your loss is relatively small, and be prepared to spend ages completing forms and formalities. In the unlikely event that you're **mugged** or otherwise threatened, *never* resist, and try to reduce your contact with the robber to a minimum. Either just hand over what's wanted, or throw money in one direction and take off in the other.

Emergency phone number

For medical, fire and police emergencies, call ☏ 112

Afterwards, go straight to the police, who will be more sympathetic and helpful on these occasions – tourism is, after all, the islands' economic lifeblood.

It's as well to be on your guard and know where your possessions are at all times. Sensible **precautions** include: carrying bags slung across your neck and not over your shoulder; not carrying anything in pockets that are easy to dip into; making photocopies of your passport, airline ticket and driving licence; leaving passports and tickets in the hotel safe; and noting down travellers' cheque and credit card numbers. When you're **looking for a hotel room**, never leave your bags unattended. If you have a **car**, don't leave anything in view when you park. Vehicles are rarely stolen, but luggage and valuables left in cars do make a tempting target. At **night** in Palma, avoid unlit streets, don't go out brimming with valuables, and try not to appear hopelessly lost.

Thieves often work in pairs and, although theft is far from rife, you should be aware of certain **ploys**, such as the "helpful" person pointing out "birdshit" (shaving cream or something similar) on your jacket, while someone else relieves you of your money; the card or note you're invited to read on the street to distract your attention; the move by someone in a café for your drink with one hand (the other hand is in your bag as you react to save your drink); and if you're studying postcards or papers at stalls, watch out for people standing unusually close.

Minor offences

Should you be **arrested** on any charge, you have the right to contact your nearest consulate; several countries are represented in Palma (see p.93 for the addresses). Unfortunately, many consulates are notoriously reluctant to get involved, though most are required to assist you to some degree if you have had your passport stolen or lost all your money. If you've been detained for a drugs offence, don't expect any sympathy or help.

You ought also to be aware of a couple of **offences** that you might commit unwittingly. In theory, you're supposed to carry some kind of **identification** at all times, and the police can stop you in the streets and demand it. In practice they're rarely bothered if you're clearly a foreigner. **Nude bathing** or **unauthorized camping** (see p.34) are activities more likely to bring you into contact with officialdom, though a warning to cover up or move on is more likely than any real confrontation. Topless tanning is commonplace at all the resorts, but in country areas, where attitudes are more traditional, you should take care not to upset local sensibilities.

Sexual harassment

There are few parts of Mallorca and Menorca where foreign women, travelling alone, are likely to feel threatened, intimidated, or attract unwanted attention. The tendency of Spaniards to move around in mixed crowds, filling central bars, clubs and streets late into the night, also helps to make you feel less exposed. If you are in any doubt as to your safety, flag down a taxi (there are plenty of them) and escape.

The major tourist **resorts** have their own artificial holiday culture, which has much to do with sex. The men (of all nationalities) who hang around in nightclubs and bars here pose a no greater or lesser threat than similar operators at home, though the language barrier makes it harder to know who to trust. Amongst Spaniards, *"déjame en paz"* (leave me alone) is a fairly standard rebuff.

The **remoter parts** of the islands' interior can pose problems for women too. In some areas you can walk for hours without seeing a soul or coming across an inhabited farm or house. It's rare that this poses a threat – help and hospitality are much more the norm – but you are certainly more vulnerable and local men here are still less accustomed to women being on their own.

Travellers with disabilities

Despite their popularity as holiday destinations, Mallorca and Menorca pay scant regard to their disabled visitors, with facilities lagging way behind those of most other EU countries. That said, things are slowly improving. Hotels with wheelchair access and other appropriate facilities are increasingly common and attitudes are beginning to change. By law, all new public buildings in Spain are required to be fully accessible.

Flying to the islands should, however, pose few problems with all the scheduled airlines concerned – including the main carrier, Iberia – more than willing to assist travellers with disabilities. If you're driving from the UK, the Brittany Ferries crossing from Plymouth to Santander offers good facilities, as do most of the cross-Channel ferries. On Mallorca and Menorca themselves, **transport** is the principal problem, as buses are not equipped for wheelchairs, and none of the islands' car rental firms has vehicles with adaptations – though at least the taxi drivers are usually helpful. Note also that the more remote roads along the coast and out in the countryside have very rough surfaces. Toilet facilities for people with disabilities are rare too.

Contacts for travellers with disabilities

In the UK and Ireland

Access Travel UK ☎ 01942/888 844, ⓦ www.access-travel.co.uk. Small tour operator that can arrange flights, transfers and accommodation in Spain and the Balearics, personally checking out all the places they recommend.

Holiday Care UK ☎0845/124 9971, minicom ☎0845/124 9976, ⊛www.holidaycare.org.uk. Provides free lists of accessible accommodation abroad and information on financial help for holidays available.

Irish Wheelchair Association Republic of Ireland ☎01/818 6400, ⊛www.iwa.ie. Provide useful information about travelling abroad with a wheelchair.

RADAR (Royal Association for Disability and Rehabilitation) UK ☎020/7250 3222, minicom ☎020/7250 4119, ⊛www.radar.org.uk. A good source of advice on holidays and travel in the UK and Europe.

Tripscope UK ☎0845/7585 641, ⊛www.tripscope.org.uk. This registered charity provides a national telephone information service offering free advice on UK and international transport for those with a mobility problem.

In the US and Canada

Access-Able ⊛www.access-able.com. Online resource for travellers with disabilities.

Directions Unlimited US ☎1-800/533-5343 or 914/241-1700. Travel agency specializing in bookings for people with disabilities.

Mobility International USA US ☎541/343-1284, ⊛www.miusa.org. Information and referral services, access guides, tours and exchange programmes. Annual membership $35 (includes quarterly newsletter).

Society for the Advancement of Travelers with Handicaps (SATH) US ⊛www.sath.org. Non-profit educational organization that has actively represented travellers with disabilities since 1976.

Wheels Up! ☎1-888/38-WHEELS, ⊛www.wheelsup.com. Provides discounted airfare, tour and cruise prices for disabled travellers, also publishes a free monthly newsletter and has a comprehensive website.

In Australia and New Zealand

ACROD (Australian Council for Rehabilitation of the Disabled) Australia ☎02/6282 4333, TTY ☎02/6282 4333, ⊛www.acrod.org.au. Provides lists of travel agencies and tour operators for people with disabilities.

Disabled Persons Assembly New Zealand ☎04/801 9100 (also TTY), ⊛www.dpa.org.nz. Resource centre with lists of travel agencies and tour operators for people with disabilities.

Directory

Addresses These are usually abbreviated to a standard format – "c/Bellver 7" translates as Bellver Street (*carrer*) no. 7. *Plaça* means square. "Plaça Rosari 5, 2è" means the second floor at no. 5. "Passeig d'es Born 15, 1–C" means suite C, first floor, at no. 15. "s/n" (*sense número*) indicates a building without a street number. In Franco's day, most avenues and boulevards were named after Fascist heroes and, although the vast majority were rechristened years ago, there's still some confusion in remoter spots. Another source of bafflement can be house numbers: some houses carry more than one number (the by-product of half-hearted reorganizations), and on many streets the sequence is impossible to fathom.

Children Most *hostals*, pensions and hotels welcome children and many offer rooms with three or four beds. Restaurants and cafés almost always encourage families too. Many package holidays have child-minding facilities as part of the deal. For babies, food seems to work out quite well (some places will prepare food specially) though you might want to bring powdered milk – babies, like most Spaniards, are pretty contemptuous of the UHT stuff generally available. Disposable nappies and other basic supplies are widely available in the resort areas and the larger towns.

Electricity The current is 220 volts AC, with standard European-style two-pin plugs. Brits will need an adaptor to connect their appliances, North Americans both an adaptor and a 220-to-110 transformer.

Laundries Although there's the occasional self-service laundrette (usually rendered in Castilian as *lavandería automática*), mostly you'll have to leave your clothes for a full and somewhat expensive laundry service. A dry-cleaner is a *tintorería* (same in Castilian).

Time Spain is one hour ahead of Greenwich Mean Time, six hours ahead of US Eastern Standard Time, nine hours ahead of US Pacific Standard Time, nine hours behind Australian Eastern Standard Time and eleven hours behind New Zealand – except for periods during the changeovers made in the respective countries to and from daylight saving. In Spain, the clocks go forward an hour on the last Sunday of March and back an hour on the last Sunday of October.

Toilets Public toilets are rare but averagely clean, though they almost never have any paper; it's best to carry your own. They're commonly referred to as *los servicios* or *el lavabo*. The usual signs are, for "Ladies", *Dones* or the Castilian *Damas* and, for "Gentlemen", *Homes* or the Castilian *Caballeros*. You may also see the potentially confusing *Señoras* (Women) and *Señores* (Men).

Guide

Guide

Palma and around

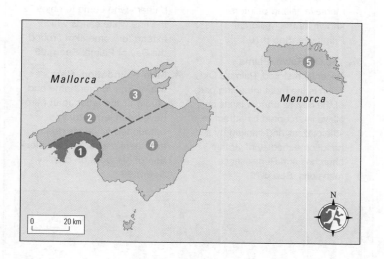

CHAPTER 1 # Highlights

✱ **Palma Cathedral** The city's outstanding attraction, and one of Spain's finest Gothic cathedrals, whose honey-coloured walls and buttresses dominate the waterfront from the crest of a hill. See p.65

✱ **Mallorcan Primitives** The Museu de la Catedral is home to a fascinating selection of works by the distinctive school of medieval island painters known as the Mallorcan Primitives. See p.70

✱ **The Old Town, Palma** Recently restored, Palma's Old Town is the most intriguing part of the city, its narrow lanes and alleys intercepted by attractive little piazzas and flanked by a handsome medley of Gothic churches and Renaissance mansions. See p.73

✱ **Eating in Palma** Palma has the island's widest and liveliest selection of cafés, restaurants and tapas bars, ranging from informal local dives to Michelin-starred palaces offering the latest in international culinary chic. See p.86

✱ **Platja de Palma, S'Arenal** Perhaps the most self–conscious beach in Mallorca, awash with preening sunbathers who come to enjoy the fine white sands which extend for some 4km around the Bay of Palma. See p.95

✱ **Miró Foundation, Cala Major** The former home and studio of the artist Joan Miró have been left virtually untouched since his death, and there's also a wide selection of his work on display. See p.96

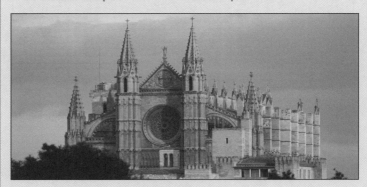

△ Palma cathedral

Palma and around

P**ALMA** is an ambitious city. In 1983 it became the capital of one of Spain's newly established autonomous regions, the Balearic Islands, and since then it has shed the dusty provincialism of yesteryear, developing into a go-ahead and cosmopolitan commercial hub of over 300,000 people. The new self-confidence is plain to see in the city centre, a vibrant and urbane place of careful coiffures and well-cut suits, which is akin to the big cities of the Spanish mainland and a world away from the heaving tourist enclaves of the surrounding bay. There's still a long way to go – much of suburban Palma remains obdurately dull and somewhat dilapidated – but the centre now presents a splendid ensemble of lively shopping areas and refurbished old buildings, mazy lanes, fountains, gardens and sculpture, all enclosed by what remains of the old city walls and their replacement boulevards.

This geography encourages downtown Palma to look into itself and away from the sea, even though its harbour – now quarantined by the main highway – has always been the city's economic lifeline. The Romans were the first to recognize the site's strategic value, establishing a military post here known as Palmaria, but real development came with the Moors, who made their **Medina Mayurka** a major seaport protected by no fewer than three concentric walls. Jaume I of Aragón captured the Moorish stronghold in 1229 and promptly started work on the **cathedral**, whose mellow sandstone still towers above the waterfront, presenting from its seaward side – in the sheer beauty of its massive proportions – one of Spain's most stunning sights.

As a major port of call between Europe and North Africa, Palma boomed under both Moorish and medieval Christian control, but its wealth and prominence came to a sudden end with the Spanish exploitation of the New World: from the early sixteenth century, Madrid looked west across the Atlantic and Palma slipped into Mediterranean obscurity. One result of its abrupt decline has been the preservation of much of the **old town**, with its beguiling tangle of narrow, labyrinthine streets and high-storeyed houses. The pick of Palma's other historic attractions are the fourteenth-century **Castell de Bellver** and the heavyweight Baroque **Basílica de Sant Francesc**.

Yet for most visitors, Palma's main appeal is its sheer vitality: at night scores of excellent **restaurants** offer the best of Spanish, Catalan and Mallorcan cuisine, while the city's **cafés** buzz with purposeful chatter. Palma also boasts **accommodation** to match most budgets, making it a splendid base from which to explore the island. In this respect, the city is far preferable, at least for independent travellers, to the string of resorts along the **Badia de Palma** (Bay of Palma), where nearly all the accommodation is block-booked by tour operators. If you are tempted by a cheap package, it's as well to bear in mind that the more agreeable of the resorts lie to the west of the city, where a hilly

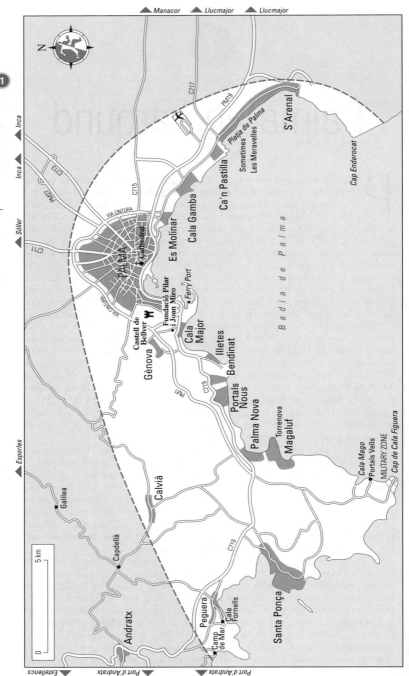

N

Manacor   Llucmajor   Llucmajor

Inca

Inca

Söller

Esporles

Estellencs   Port d'Andratx   Port d'Andratx   Estellencs

C717

PM19

S'Arenal

Platja de Palma

Sometimes

Les Meravelles

Ca'n Pastilla

Cap Enderocat

Cala Gamba

C715

PM20

C713

Es Molinar

Badia de Palma

VIA CINTURA

PALMA

Catedral

Ferry Port

Fundació Pilar
i Joan Miró

VIA CINTURA

Castell de
Bellver

Cala Major

C711

Gènova

Illetes

Bendinat

PM1

C719

Portals
Nous

Palma Nova

Torrenova

Magaluf

Cala Mago

Portals Vells

MILITARY ZONE

Cap de Cala Figuera

Calvià

Galilea

Capdellà

5 km

0

Andratx

Peguera

Cala
Fornells

Camp
de Mar

Santa Ponça

coastline of rocky cliffs and tiny coves is punctuated by small, sandy beaches. Development is ubiquitous, but **Cala Major** is of interest as the home of an excellent museum and the former studio of Joan Miró; well-to-do **Illetes** has several excellent hotels and a couple of lovely cove beaches; and pint-sized **Cala Fornells** has a fine seashore setting and several good hotels, and is within easy reach of the spacious sandy shorelines of family-oriented **Santa Ponça** and **Peguera**. Places to avoid include lager-swilling **Magaluf** and all the resorts to the east of Palma, where the pancake-flat shoreline is burdened by a seamless band of skyscrapers stretching from **Ca'n Pastilla** to **S'Arenal** – behind what is, admittedly, one of the island's longest and most impressive beaches, the **Platja de Palma**.

Arrival

Mallorca's gleaming international **airport** is 11km east of Palma, immediately behind the resort of Ca'n Pastilla. It has one enormous terminal, which handles both scheduled and charter flights, with separate floors for arrivals (downstairs) and departures (upstairs). Both floors have airport **information desks** – a good job, as the airport can be very confusing. On the arrivals floor, a flotilla of **car rental** outlets jostle for position by the luggage carousels. Beyond, through the glass doors, is the main **arrivals hall**, which has 24-hour **ATMs** and **currency exchange** facilities, plus a **provincial tourist office** (Mon–Sat 9am–10pm, Sun 9am–2pm) with public transport timetables, taxi rates, maps, and lists of hotels and *hostals*. They will not, however, help arrange **accommodation** and neither will most of the package-tour travel agents. An exception is the extremely helpful Prima Travel (T971 789 322, Wwww .prima-travel.com), who have a good selection of hotels, apartments and villas in all price ranges, plus English-speaking staff. Alternatively, try the adjacent Jet1 (T971 789 341) or Prestige (T971 789 809) counters: both can help you find last-minute lodgings anywhere on the island in any price range. If you're collecting someone from the airport by car, there's a free five-minute stop zone, plus an enormous if slightly confusing **car park**. When you arrive, grab a ticket from the machine at the car park entrance; before leaving, take the ticket to one of the pay machines.

The airport is linked to the city and the Bay of Palma resorts by a busy highway (*autopista*) which shadows the shoreline from S'Arenal in the east to Palma Nova and Magaluf in the west. The least expensive way to reach Palma from the airport is by **bus #1** (daily every 15min from 5.40am to 2.30am; €1.80), which leaves from the main entrance of the terminal building, just behind the taxi rank. It reaches the city's inner ring road near the foot of Avinguda Gabriel Alomar i Villalonga, at the c/Joan Maragall junction, then heads on to Plaça Espanya, on the north side of the centre, before continuing west to the Passeig Mallorca and then south to the top of Avinguda Jaume III. There are frequent stops along the way. A **taxi** from the airport to the city centre will set you back about €15; taxi rates are controlled and a list of island-wide fares is available from – or displayed in the window of – the provincial tourist office in the arrivals hall.

By ferry

The Palma **ferry terminal** is about 4km west of the city centre. Trasmediterranea ferries arrive at Terminal 2; Balearia ferries at Terminal 3, about 150m away. **Bus #1** (5.40am–2.30am; €1.80) leaves every fifteen minutes from outside Terminal 2 to the Plaça Espanya. There are also **taxi** ranks outside both terminal buildings; the fare to the city centre is about €10.

Orientation, city transport and information

Almost everything of interest in Palma is located in the city centre, a roughly circular affair whose southern perimeter is largely defined by the cathedral and the remains of the old city walls, which in turn abut the coastal motorway and the harbour. The city centre's landward limits are determined by a zigzag of wide boulevards built beside or in place of the old town walls – **Avinguda de la Argentina** and **Avinguda Gabriel Alomar i Villalonga** connect with the coastal motorway, thereby completing the circle. The **Via Cintura**, the ring road around the suburbs, loops off from the coastal motorway to create a much larger, outer circle.

The city centre itself is crossed by four interconnected avenues: **Passeig d'es Born**, **Avinguda Jaume III**, **c/Unió** (which becomes **c/Riera** at its eastern end) and **Passeig de la Rambla**. Your best bet is to use these four thoroughfares to guide yourself round the centre – Palma's jigsaw-like side streets and squares can be very confusing. Central Palma is about 2km in diameter, roughly thirty minutes' walk from one side to the other. If you're in a hurry, **taxi** fares are reasonable. There are ranks outside all the major hotels; alternatively, phone Taxi Palma (☎971 401 414), Taxi Telefono (☎971 744 050), Fono Taxi (☎971 728 081) or Radio Taxi (☎971 755 440).

City transport

To reach the city's outskirts, take the **bus**. City buses are operated by **EMT** (Empresa Municipal de Transports) and almost all their services pass through **Plaça Espanya**, linking the centre with the suburbs and the nearer tourist resorts. In the city centre, each EMT bus stop sports a large route map with timetable details. **Tickets** are available from the driver and cost €1 per journey within the city limits. You can buy a **carnet** of ten at a small discount from the main office in Plaça Espanya. EMT have an information kiosk on Plaça Espanya and an enquiry line in Spanish and Catalan on ☎971 214 444.

The new **Citysightseeing** double-deck tourist bus runs along two routes around the major sights and along the coast. Tickets (€13; available on board

Moving on from Palma

Island-wide buses are operated by several companies. All services depart from the brand-new **bus station** off Plaça Espanya, 200m north of the Inca train station along c/Marquès de la Fontsanta. For timetable information, ask either at the bus station or at the Plaça Espanya tourist information office (see p.61). Timetable information for all island-wide services is also available in Spanish and Catalan on ☎971 177 777.

The city's two tiny **train stations** adjoin the northeast side of Plaça Espanya, each with its own line: one to Sóller; the other to the towns of the central plain, Es Pla, including Binissalem, Inca, Sineu, Manacor and Sa Pobla.

Parking in Palma

Trying to find a **car parking space** in downtown Palma can be a nightmare – you're well advised to leave your vehicle on the city's outskirts, especially for visits of more than an hour or two. If you're staying downtown, choose a hotel which either has its own car park or has an arrangement with a local one (some hotels offer discounts or will reimburse part of the cost). Parking in the city centre requires an **ORA ticket** during busy periods (Mon–Fri 9.30am–1.30pm & 5–8pm, Sat 9.30am–1.30pm). At other times – when the centre is slightly less congested – parking is free. Tickets are readily available from ORA parking meters but, although the cost is minimal (around €1 per hour), the longest-lasting ticket only provides ninety minutes' parking – and fines are immediate and steep. Note also that if the time allowed overlaps into a free period, your ORA ticket is still valid when restricted time begins again.

the bus) are valid for 24 hours, and also get you an audioguide giving a quick overview of the city's sights and history; services depart from in front of the cathedral. A more sedate way of seeing Palma is to take a traditional **horse-and-carriage ride** – they hang around next to the cathedral; count on around €40 for half an hour.

Information

The city's **provincial tourist office** is just off Passeig d'es Born at Plaça de la Reina 2 (Mon–Fri 9am–8pm, Sat 9am–2.30; ☎971 712 216). The main **municipal office** is at c/Sant Domingo 11, in the subway at the end of c/Conquistador (Mon–Fri 9am–8pm, Sat 9am–1.30pm; ☎971 724 090). Both provide city- and island-wide information, dispensing free maps, accommodation lists, bus schedules, ferry timetables, lists of car rental firms, boat trip details and all sorts of special-interest leaflets, including the useful *Artesanía*, which lists specialist suppliers of everything from pottery and pearls to books and handicrafts. A second municipal tourist office (Mon–Fri 9am–8pm, Sat 9am–1pm; ☎971 754 329), located a few metres from the Inca train station on the northeast edge of Plaça Espanya, offers a similar service.

Accommodation

There are dozens of *hostals* and hotels dotted around Palma, although demand can still outstrip supply. Accommodation tends to be in greatest demand during June, early July and September, when you really need to book ahead. From the middle of July to late August, most visitors stay away from the city, either in the relative cool of the mountains or closer to more pristine beaches. Note that in periods of high demand, some places insist on a minimum stay of two or three nights. At other times of the year, things are much easier. If you want help with reservations, contact Prima Travel (☎971 789 322, ⓦwww.prima-travel.com), who specialize in last-minute accommodation and have an office at the airport.

The bulk of Palma's **budget accommodation** is in the city centre – fortunately enough, this is by far the most engaging part of the city; the immediate suburbs are quite unprepossessing. There's a cluster of places along the narrow, cobbled side-streets off the Passeig d'es Born and – rather less appetizingly – around the Plaça Espanya. There's a number of more modern

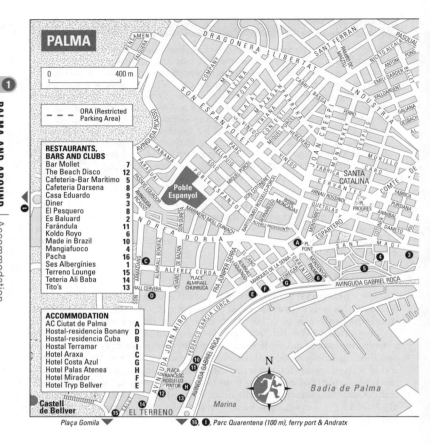

PALMA

| 0 | 400 m |

- - - ORA (Restricted Parking Area)

RESTAURANTS, BARS AND CLUBS

Bar Mollet	7
The Beach Disco	12
Cafeteria-Bar Marítimo	5
Cafeteria Darsena	8
Casa Eduardo	9
Diner	8
El Pesquero	3
Es Baluard	2
Farándula	11
Koldo Royo	6
Made in Brazil	10
Mangiafuoco	4
Pacha	16
Ses Albergínies	1
Terreno Lounge	15
Teteria Ali Baba	14
Tito's	13

ACCOMMODATION

AC Ciutat de Palma	A
Hostal-residencia Bonany	D
Hostal-residencia Cuba	B
Hostal Terramar	I
Hotel Araxa	C
Hotel Costa Azul	G
Hotel Palas Atenea	H
Hotel Mirador	F
Hotel Tryp Bellver	E

Poble Espanyol

SANTA CATALINA

Badia de Palma

Castell de Bellver

EL TERRENO

Plaça Gomila ▼   ▼ ⑯, ❶, Parc Quarentena (100 m), ferry port & Andratx

mid-range hotels on the Passeig Mallorca, a particularly attractive portion of the inner ring road, where two sections of old city wall run down the middle of the boulevard on either side of an ancient watercourse. There's another cluster of modern high-rises, including some quite plush options, to the west of the centre, overlooking the waterfront along Avinguda Gabriel Roca (also known to locals as the Passeig Marítim). The city's **deluxe hotels** are scattered around the old centre; the best occupy beautifully converted old Mallorcan mansions.

Inexpensive

Hostal Apuntadores c/Apuntadors 8 ☎971 713 491, ✉apuntadores@jet.es. Appealingly laid-back *hostal* in an old house on bustling c/Apuntadors. The recently renovated rooms are simple but more than adequate; all have washbasins, and some have showers. Breakfast is also available (€3–5). Closes for a few months in winter. ❶

Hostal-residencia Bonany c/Almirall Cervera 5

☎971 737 924. Newly done-up and very good-value one-star *hostal* on a quiet residential street about 2km west of the city centre, close to Castell de Bellver. All rooms have attached bath, and there's also a small pool. Take bus #6 from Plaça de la Reina and get off at c/Marquès de la Sènia, just before the start of Avgda Joan Miró. Closed Nov–March. ❶

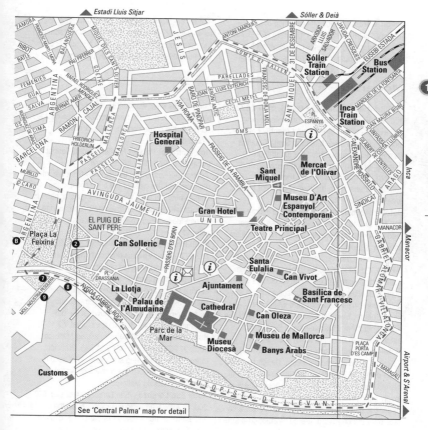

Hostal Brondo c/Ca'n Brondo 1 ☏ & ℻ 971 719 043. In a central but quiet street, this stylish little place has newly refurbished rooms with antiques and charming Rococo plasterwork. Ask for one of the rooms with a wrought-iron balcony. Shared bath ②, en suite ③

Hostal-residencia Cuba c/Sant Magí 1 ☏ 971 738 159, ℻ 971 403 131. Twenty attractive, well-appointed rooms (all en suite) in a beautifully restored *Modernista* stone house of 1904, with a pretty little tower and balustrade and a rooftop sun terrace. Overlooks the harbour and the bottom of busy Avgda Argentina. Two rooms have air-conditioning at no extra cost. ①

Hostal-residencia Pons c/Ví 8 ☏ 971 722 658. Simple rooms (shared bath only) in a lovely old house set around a courtyard and full of house-plants, family portraits and bric-a-brac. ①

Hostal-residencia Regina c/Sant Miquel 77 ☏ 971 713 703, Ⓦ www.hostalregina.com. Ten spartan en-suite rooms above some shops in a plain, two-storey modern building to the north of the old town. There's a roof terrace, but no breakfast. ③

Hostal Ritzi c/Apuntadors 6 ☏ & ℻ 971 714 610. Spartan rooms in an ancient but well-maintained five-storey house on one of central Palma's liveli-est streets. Five rooms have their own showers and two have full bathrooms; the rest have wash-basins. Shared bath ①, en suite ②

Hostal-residencia Terminus Plaça España 5 ☏ 971 750 014, Ⓔ terminus@mail.cinet.es. Attractive two-star establishment by the train station, with a quirkily old-fashioned foyer and fairly large and frugal but still comfortable rooms. The large attached bar is an added attraction, with a Spanish-colonial feel. Shared bath ①, en suite ②

Hostal Terramar Plaça Mediterraneo 8, El Terreno, 1.5km west of the city centre ☎971 739 931 ⓦwww.palma-hostales.com. Newly refurbished, with simple, modern rooms, and convenient for the busy nightlife in the El Terreno district, as well as for the Castell de Bellver, which some of the rooms overlook. No breakfast, but guests can use the kitchen. Shared bath ❶, en suite ❷

Moderate

AC Ciutat de Palma Plaça Pont 3, ☎971 222 300, ⓦwww.ac-hotels.com. Gleamingly new and extremely comfortable and friendly hotel, located close to the interesting Santa Catalina quarter and convenient for the nightlife in Palma's western districts. Rooms are plush, modern and comfortable, and there's free coffee and snacks in the lounge. A great buffet breakfast costs €12. ❻

Hotel-residencia Almudaina Avgda Jaume III 9 ☎971 727 340, ⓔalmudaina@bitel.es. Dapper modern rooms overlooking one of Palma's busiest shopping streets. ❺

Hotel Araxa c/Alférez Cerdá 22 ☎971 731 640, fax 971 731 643. Attractive three-storey modern hotel with pleasant gardens and an outdoor swimming pool. Most rooms have balconies. It's in a quiet residential area about 2km west of the centre, not far from the Castell de Bellver: take bus #6 and get off at c/Marquès de la Sènia, just before the start of Avgda Joan Miró. ❻

Hotel-residencia Born c/Sant Jaume 3 ☎971 712 942, ⓦwww.hotelborn.com. Delightful hotel in an excellent downtown location, set in a refurbished mansion with big wooden doors and a lovely courtyard where you can have breakfast under the palm trees. The rooms, most of which face onto the courtyard, are comfortable if a little plain, and all have a/c, though not all have private bathrooms. It's a popular spot, so book early in high season. Breakfast included. ❸, en suite ❹

Hotel Cannes c/Cardenal Pou 8 ☎ & ⓕ971 726 943. Recently renovated in brisk modern style, this pleasant, fifty-room two-star hotel is located in a residential neighbourhood near Plaça Espanya, close to the principal shopping areas. Breakfast included. ❹

Hotel Costa Azul Passeig Marítim (Avgda Gabriel Roca) 7 ☎971 731 940, ⓦwww.fehm.es/pmi/costa. Recently remodelled, this standard high-rise has balconied rooms overlooking the bay and a heated indoor swimming pool. Breakfast included. ❺

Hotel Dalt Murada c/Almudaina 6 ☎971 425 300, ⓦwww.daltmurada.com. This magnificent sixteenth-century mansion has kept much of its original architecturel and decoration, but without compromising on comforts and conveniences.

Many rooms have wonderful rooftop views of the old city, and some also have terraces. Breakfast is served in the garden on fine days. Breakfast included. ❻

Hotel Mirador Passeig Marítim (Avgda Gabriel Roca) 10 ☎971 732 046, ⓦwww.hotelmirador.es. Down by the waterfront ten minutes' walk to the west of the city centre, this unassuming, recently remodelled four-star hotel is popular with Spanish business folk. Considering its bayside location, room rates are quite reasonable. ❻

Hotel Palau Sa Font c/Apuntadors 38 ☎971 712 277, ⓦwww.palausafont.com. New hotel decorated in earthy Italian colours, with fascinating sculptures and other works of art – at once stylish and homely, and also very friendly. There's a small pool on the roof terrace, and many rooms enjoy inspiring views of the old city, marina and bay. Breakfast included. ❻

Hotel-residencia Palladium Passeig Mallorca 40 ☎971 713 945, fax 971 714 665. Proficient three-star hotel offering spick-and-span accommodation in a modern tower overlooking the handsome Passeig Mallorca. ❺

Hotel San Lorenzo c/San Lorenzo 14 ☎971 728 200, ⓦwww.fehm.es/pmi/sanlorenzo. In the ancient fishermen's quarter of Sant Pere, this aristocratic mansion has been impeccably transformed into a four-star hotel. The antique details have been lovingly preserved, while modern facilities, such as the swimming pool in the garden, have been tastefully added. Many rooms have fantastic views of the cathedral's facade; some have private terraces. ❻

Hotel Saratoga Passeig Mallorca 6 ☎971 727 240, ⓦwww.hotelsaratoga.es. Bright, modern, centrally located hotel in a smart seven-storey block complete with a rooftop café and swimming pool. Rooms are neat and trim, with marble floors and balconies either overlooking the boulevard or an interior courtyard. Breakfast included. ❻

Hotel Sol Jaime III Passeig Mallorca 14 ☎971 725 943, ⓕ971 725 946. Agreeable three-star with smart modern rooms, most with balconies. Front rooms overlook the Passeig Mallorca, and chic shopping is just around the corner. Décor consists of art prints and marble touches. ❺

Expensive

Hotel Convent de la Missió c/de la Missió 7A, ☎971 227 347, ⓦ www.conventdelamissio.com. Owned by two architects, this stunning new hotel is decorated in ultra-minimalist style, with big white spaces punctuated with strategically placed works of art. The elegant *Refectori* restaurant (evenings only) is an additional bonus. ❼

Hotel-residencia Palacio Ca Sa Galesa c/Miramar 8 ☎971 715 400, ⓦ www.palacio-casagalesa.com. Charmingly renovated seventeenth-century mansion set amongst the narrow alleys of the oldest part of town, with just twelve luxurious and tastefully furnished rooms and suites. There's also an indoor heated swimming pool (set in a renovated ancient Roman bath) and fine views of the city from the roof terrace. Opened in the 1980s, this was one of the first deluxe hotels to occupy an old island mansion and its success set something of a trend. ❾

Hotel Palas Atenea Passeig Marítim (Avgda Gabriel Roca) 29 ☎971 281 400, ⓦ www.solmelia.com. A vast, classy 1960s-style foyer leads to attractively furnished, comfortable rooms with balconies overlooking the bay. There's also an inviting bar. ❽

Hotel Portixol c/Sirena 27, 2km east of the city centre in the suburb of Portixol ☎971 271 800, ⓦ www.portixol.com. One of the more tempting hotels in the Palma area, this splendid modern establishment and its first-rate *nouvelle* Mediterranean restaurant have brought new life to this downmarket seashore suburb. There's a large pool, stirring views of the cathedral, plus lots of facilities including free Internet access, video and CD libraries, bicycles and more. Buffet breakfast included. ❼

Hotel Tryp Bellver Passeig Marítim (Avgda Gabriel Roca) 11 ☎971 735 142, ⓦ www.solmelia.com. Well-maintained high-rise chain hotel with smart, spacious rooms decorated in standard modern style, but with some original 1960s fittings. Most rooms have balconies, either overlooking the harbour or (less appealingly) the city. Located a fifteen-minute walk west of the city centre and a popular spot for Spanish conventions and wedding parties. ❼

The City

There's not much argument as to where to start a tour of Palma – it's got to be the **cathedral**, which dominates the waterfront from the crest of a hill. Central Palma's other landmark is the **Palau de l'Almudaina** next door, an important royal residence from Moorish times and now the repository of a mildly engaging assortment of municipal baubles, though successive modifications have robbed the building of much of its character. Spreading northeast behind the cathedral are the narrow lanes and ageing mansions of the most intriguing part of the **old town**. A stroll here is a pleasure in itself, and tucked away among the side streets are two good diversions: the **Museu de Mallorca**, the island's most extensive museum, and the Baroque **Basílica de Sant Francesc**.

North of the old town lies the heart of the early twentieth-century city, where the high-sided tenements are graced by a sequence of flamboyant buildings in the *Modernista* style (the Spanish, and especially Catalan, form of Art Nouveau), particularly on and around **Plaça Weyler**.

West of the city centre, you should consider a visit to the **Castell de Bellver**, an impressive hilltop castle, and perhaps also to the much less interesting **Poble Espanyol**, which comprises detailed, scaled-down reproductions of characteristic buildings from every region of Spain.

The cathedral

Legend has it that when the invasion force of Jaume I of Aragón and Catalunya stood off Mallorca in 1229, a fierce gale threatened to sink the fleet. The desperate king promised to build a church dedicated to the Virgin Mary if the

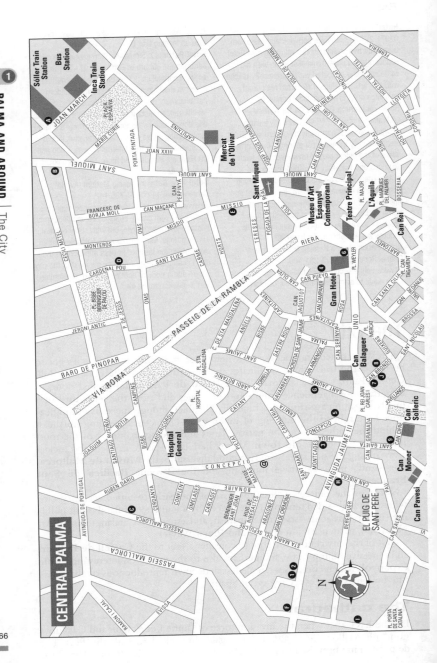

CENTRAL PALMA

Söller Train Station
Bus Station
Inca Train Station

JOAN MARCH

PLAÇA ESPANYA

A

MARIE CURIE

PORTA PINTADA

JOAN XXIII

SANT MIQUEL

B

FRANCESC DE BORJA MOLL

CAN MAÇANET

CAN PERPINYA

SANT MIQUEL

Mercat de l'Olivar

CAPUTXINS

MOLINERS

VILANOVA

CAN GATER

HOSTAL DE L'ESTEL

VOLTA DE LA MERCÈ

SINDICAT

FERRERIA

LLOTGETA

Sant Miquel

Museu d'Art Espanyol Contemporani

Teatre Principal

L'Aguila

PL. MARQUÈS DEL PALMER

PL. MAJOR

BOSSERIA

Can Rei

MISSIO

TERESES

POLS

POSADA DE LA REIAL

RIERA

PL. WEYLER

BARTOMEU

PL. SANTA EULALIA

CAN TAGAMENT

SANT NICOLAU

Gran Hotel

CECILI METEL

MONTEROS

CARDENAL POU

PL. BISBE BERENGUER DE PALOU

OMS

JERONI ANTIC

P. DE JESÚS

SANT ELIES

HORTS

CARME

MISSIO

CAN OLIVA

CAN PUEYO

CAN CAMPANER

ROSA

UNIO

PL. MERCAT

BROSSA

GUIXERS

JOVELLANOS

Can Balaguer

CAN BRONDO

Can Solleric

VIA ROMA

BARO DE PINOPAR

PL. STA. MAGDALENA

JARDI BOTANIC

CAN SERINYA

SANT JAUME

CAN ARMENGOL

PL. REI JOAN CARLES I

Can Chire

PASSEIG DE LA RAMBLA

CAPUTXINS

ANGELS

BISBE

SASTRE ROIG

PALMA

C. DE STA. MAGDALENA

SACRISTIA DE SANT JAUME

CATANY

EMATIA

CAN CAVALLERIA

C. TORNILA

PL. HOSPITAL

Hospital General

MISERICORDIA

BISBE

BONAIRE

C. CATALINA TOMAS

CONCEPCIO

CONCEPCIO

Can Moner

Can Pavesi

EL PUIG DE SANT PERE

BERENGUER

CAN RIBERA

AVINGUDA JAUME III

SANT GAIETA

CAN GRANADA

AIGUA

MONTCADES

METGE MATAS

SANT MARTI

JOAQUIM

SANTIAGO RUSINOL

BOTIA

RUBEN DARIO

CERDANYA

CONVENT

OMELADES

CARLADES

BERENGUER SANT JOAN

PUIG DE RIBESALTES

ARAGONES

JOAN DE CREMONA

STA MARIA DEL SEPULCRE

CAK SALES

PL. PORTA DE SANTA CATALINA

AVINGUDA DE PORTUGAL

PASSEIG MALLORCA

PASSEIG MALLORCA

EIVISSA

RAMON CAJAL

N

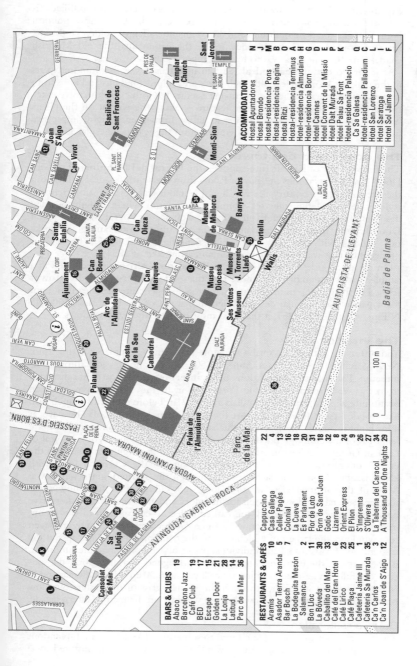

ACCOMMODATION

Hostal Apuntadores	N
Hostal Brondo	J
Hostal-residencia Pons	M
Hostal-residencia Regina	O
Hostal Ritzi	A
Hotel-residencia Terminus	H
Hotel-residencia Almudaina	G
Hotel-residencia Born	D
Hotel Cannes	E
Hotel Convent de la Missió	P
Hotel Dalt Murada	K
Hotel Palau Sa Font	C
Hotel-residencia Palacio	L
Ca Sa Galesa	I
Hotel-residencia Palladium	F
Hotel San Lorenzo	
Hotel Saratoga	
Hotel Sol Jaime III	

BARS & CLUBS

Abaco	19
Barcelona Jazz	19
Café Club	17
BED	15
Escape	21
Golden Door	28
La Lonja	14
Latitud	36
Parc de la Mar	

RESTAURANTS & CAFÉS

Aramis	10
Asador Tierra Aranda	5
Bar Bosch	7
La Bodeguita Mesón Salamanca	2
Bon Lloc	11
La Bóveda	30
Caballito del Mar	33
Café del Gran Hotel	6
Café Lírico	23
Café Plaça	25
Cafetería Jaime III	1
Cafetería Sa Murada	35
Ca'n Carlos	3
Ca'n Joan de S'Aigo	12
Cappuccino	22
Casa Gallega	4
Celler Pagès	13
Colonial	16
La Cueva	18
Es Parlament	20
Flor de Loto	31
Forn de Sant Joan	18
Gòtic	32
Lizarran	8
Orient Express	24
El Pilon	9
S'Imprempta	26
S'Olivera	27
La Taberna del Caracol	34
A Thousand and One Nights	29

expedition against the Moors was successful. It was, and Jaume fulfilled his promise, starting construction work the next year. The king had a political point to make too – he built his cathedral, a gigantic affair of golden sandstone, bang on top of the Great Mosque inside the Almudaina, the old Moorish citadel. The Reconquista was to be no temporary matter.

As it turned out, the **cathedral** (Sa Seu in Catalan) was five hundred years in the making. Nonetheless, although there are architectural bits and bobs from several different eras, the church remains essentially Gothic, with massive exterior buttresses – its most distinctive feature – taking the weight off the pillars within. The whole structure derives its effect from sheer height, impressive from any angle, but startling when viewed from the waterside esplanade.

The doors and bell tower

The finest of the cathedral's three doors is the **Portal del Mirador** ("Lookout Door"), which overlooks the Bay of Palma from the south facade. Dating from the late fourteenth century, the weathered Mirador features a host of Flemish-style ecclesiastical figurines set around a tympanum where heavily bearded disciples sit at a Last Supper. In contrast, the west-facing **Portal Major** ("Great Door"), across from the Almudaina, is a neo-Gothic disaster, an ugly reworking – along with the sixty-metre-high flanking turrets – of a far simpler predecessor that was badly damaged in an earthquake of 1851.

On the north side is a third door, the **Portal de l'Almoina**, decorated in a simple Gothic design of 1498. Above rises the solid squareness of the **bell tower** (closed to the public), an incongruous, fortress-like structure that clearly did not form part of the original design. When the largest of the bells, the 5700-kilo N'Eloi, was tolled in 1857, it shattered most of the cathedral's windows.

The interior

You **enter** the cathedral (April–Oct Mon–Fri 10am–6.15pm, Sat 10am–2pm; Nov–March Mon–Sat 10am–3pm; €3.50) on the north side through its museum. The majestic proportions of its **interior** are seen to best advantage from the western end, from the Portal Major. In the central **nave**, fourteen beautifully aligned, pencil-thin pillars rise to 21m before their ribs branch out, like fronded palm trees, to support the single-span, vaulted roof. The nave, at 44m high, is one of the tallest Gothic structures in Europe, and its 121-metre length is of matching grandeur. This open, hangar-like construction, typical of Catalan Gothic architecture, was designed to make the high altar visible to the entire congregation and to express the mystery of the Christian faith, with kaleidoscopic floods of light filtered in through the **stained-glass windows**. Most of the original glass was lost long ago, but recent refurbishment has returned several windows to their former glory and, now that many others have been un-bricked and cleaned, the cathedral has re-emerged from the gloom imposed by Renaissance, Baroque and neo-Gothic architects. There are seven rose windows, the largest of which crowns the triumphal arch of the apse at the east end and boasts over 1200 individual pieces of glass; providing the sun is out, it's best seen in the morning. The cathedral's designers also incorporated a specific, carefully orchestrated artifice: twice a year, at 6.30am on Candlemas and St Martin's Day, the sun shines through the stained glass of the eastern window onto the wall immediately below the rose window on the main, western facade.

Gaudí's restoration

The first attempt to return the church to something like its original splendour was made at the beginning of the twentieth century when an inspired local bishop commissioned the *Modernista* Catalan architect **Antoni Gaudí** to direct a full-blown restoration. At the time, Gaudí was renowned for his fancifully embellished metalwork, and his functionalist extrapolation of Gothic design was still evolving. This experimentation led ultimately to his most famous and extravagant opus, the church of the Sagrada Familia in Barcelona, but here in Palma his work was relatively restrained – though still deeply controversial. Indeed, certain Catholic dignitaries took the aesthetic hump over the revamp and when, in 1926, a Barcelona tram flattened Gaudí they must have thought their prayers had been answered.

Gaudí worked on Palma's cathedral intermittently between 1904 and 1914, during which time he removed the High Baroque altar and shifted the ornate choir stalls from the centre of the cathedral, placing them flat against the walls of the presbytery. The new high altar, a medieval alabaster table of plain design, was then located beneath a phantasmagorical **baldachin**, a giant canopy, enhanced by hanging lanterns, which was supposed to symbolize the Crown of Thorns. It's not a great success, though to be fair Gaudí never had time to complete it – he wanted it to be made of wrought iron, but what you see today is in fact a trial piece fashioned from cork, cardboard and brocade.

Other examples of Gaudí's distinctive workmanship are dotted around the cathedral. The **railings** in front of the high altar are twisted into shapes inspired by Mallorcan window grilles, while the wall on either side of the **Bishop's Throne**, at the east end of the church, sports ceramic inlays with brightly painted floral designs. Yet Gaudí's main concern was to revive the Gothic tradition by giving light to the cathedral. To this end he introduced **electric lighting**, bathing the apse in bright artificial light and placing lamps and candelabra throughout the church. This was all very innovative: at the time, no choir had ever before been removed in Spain and electric lighting was a real novelty. The artistic success of the whole project, though, was undeniable, and it was immediately popular with the congregation. Like the rest of his work, however, it did not bring Gaudí much international acclaim: it was only in the 1960s that his techniques were championed and copied across western Europe, and that his crucial role in the development of modernism was finally acknowledged.

The chapels

The aisles on either side of the central nave are flanked by a long sequence of **chapels**, dull affairs for the most part, dominated by dusty Baroque altars of gargantuan proportions and little artistic merit. The exception, and the cathedral's one outstanding example of the Baroque, is the **Capella de Corpus Christi**, at the head of the aisle to the left of the high altar. Begun in the sixteenth century, the chapel's tiered and columned altarpiece features three religious scenes, cramped and intense sculptural tableaux showing – from top to bottom – the temptations of St Anthony, the presentation of Jesus in the temple, and the Last Supper. Just across from the chapel is a massive stone pulpit that was moved here by Gaudí, a makeshift location for this excellent illustration of the Plateresque style. Dated to 1531, the pulpit's intricate floral patterns and bustling Biblical scenes cover a clumsy structure, the upper portion of which is carried by telamons, male counterparts of the more usual caryatids.

Though you can't now reach the **Capella de la Trinidad** (Trinity Chapel) – it's at the east end of the church directly behind the high altar – this tiny chapel is also of interest. Completed in 1329, it accommodates the remains of Jaume II and Jaume III, two notable medieval kings of Mallorca (for more on whom, see pp.272–274). Initially, the bodies were stored in a tomb that operated rather like a filing cabinet, allowing the corpses to be venerated by the devout. They were viewed in 1809 by the first British traveller to write an account of a visit to Mallorca, the unflappable Sir John Carr, who calmly observed that, "considering the monarchs had been dead for five hundred years . . . they were in a state of extraordinary preservation". This gruesome practice was finally discontinued during the nineteenth century, and alabaster sarcophagi now enclose the royal bones.

The Museu de la Catedral

The ground floor of the bell tower and two adjoining chapterhouses have been turned into the **Museu de la Catedral** (same times and ticket as the cathedral) in order to accommodate an eclectic mixture of ecclesiastical treasures. The first room's most valuable exhibit, in the glass case in the middle, is a gilded silver monstrance of extraordinary delicacy, its fairy-tale decoration dating from the late sixteenth century. On display around the walls are assorted chalices and reliquaries and a real curiosity, the portable altar of Jaume I, a wood and silver chessboard with each square containing a bag of relics.

The second room is mainly devoted to the Gothic works of the **Mallorcan Primitives**, a school of painters which flourished on the island in the fourteenth and fifteenth centuries, producing strikingly naive devotional works of bold colours and cartoon-like detail. The work of two of the school's leading fourteenth-century practitioners is displayed here, the so-called **Master of the Privileges**, whose love of minute detail and warm colours reveals an Italian influence, and the **Master of Montesión**, who looked to his Catalan contemporaries for his sense of movement and tight draughtsmanship. Later, the work of the Mallorcan Primitives shaded into the new realism of the Flemish style, which was to dominate Mallorcan painting throughout the sixteenth century. **Joan Desí**'s (unlabelled) *Panel of La Almoina* (c. 1500) illustrates the transition – it's the large panel showing St Francis, complete with stigmata, at the side of Christ. In terms of content, look out for the tribulations of **St Eulalia**, whose martyrdom fascinated and excited scores of medieval Mallorcan artists. A Catalan girl-saint, Eulalia defied the Roman Emperor Diocletian by sticking to her Christian faith despite all sorts of ferocious tortures, which are depicted in ecstatic detail here in a large (though unlabelled) panel painting by the Master of the Privileges. She was eventually burnt at the stake; at the moment of her death, white doves flew from her mouth.

The third and final room, the **Baroque chapterhouse**, is entered through a playful Churrigueresque doorway, above which a delicate Madonna is overwhelmed by lively cherubic angels. Inside, pride of place goes to the High Baroque altar, a gaudy, gilded affair surmounted by the Sacred Heart, a gory representation of the heart of Jesus that was very much in vogue during the eighteenth century. Some imagination went into the designation of the reliquaries displayed round the room: there's a piece of the flogging post, three thorns from Christ's crown and even a piece of the gall and vinegared sponge that was offered to the crucified Jesus. Of more appeal are a pair of finely carved, Baroque crucifixes, each Christ a study in perfect muscularity swathed in the flowing folds of a loincloth.

Five of central Palma's museums – the Museu de la Catedral, the Museu Diocesà, Museu de Mallorca, Can Marquès, and Casa Museu J. Torrents Lladó – are covered by a **combined ticket** costing just €10.

The Museu Diocesà

There are several more Mallorcan Primitive paintings in the **Museu Diocesà** (in Castilian, Museo Diocesano; Mon–Fri 10am–1pm & 4–7pm; €2). The museum – which was temporarily closed for refurbishment at the time of writing – is housed in the Bishop's Palace on c/Mirador immediately behind the cathedral; keep going straight past the Portal del Mirador. The palace is a mostly seventeenth-century structure built around an expansive courtyard presided over by a statue of the Sacred Heart. The museum has just two rooms. The first is a tiny antechamber in which is displayed a **panel painting** by the Master of Bishop Galiana, whose crisp draughtsmanship was very much in the Catalan tradition. This particular painting is an intriguing work, a didactic cartoon-strip illustrating the life of St Paul, who is shown with his Bible open and sword in hand, a militant view of the church that must have accorded well with the preoccupations of the powerful bishops of Mallorca. Look out also for the way the artist portrays the conversion on the road to Damascus, with Saul-Paul struck by a laser-like beam of light.

Beyond, in the main room, there are all sorts of bits and pieces, including a selection of **majolica tiles**, the heavy-duty jasper **sarcophagus** built to house the remains of Jaume II in the nineteenth century, and some spectacularly unsuccessful religious sculptures. In addition, two cabinets are packed with shiny, metallic-glaze **pottery** of Moorish and Mudéjar design, rare survivors dating from the fourteenth to the eighteenth century. Two **paintings** stand out here too, the earlier being a panel painting of the *Passion of Christ* by an unknown artist dubbed the Master of the Passion of Mallorca. Dated to the end of the thirteenth century, the painting follows a standard format, with a series of small vignettes outlining the story of Christ, but the detail is warm and gentle: the Palm Sunday donkey leans forward, pushing his nose towards a child; one of the disciples reaches out across the Last Supper table for the fish; and two of Jesus' disciples slip their sandals off in eager anticipation during the washing of the feet. By contrast, Alonso de Sedano's sixteenth-century *Crucifixion* is a sophisticated work of strong, deep colours within a triangulated structure. Above is the blood-spattered, pale-white body of Christ, while down below – divided by the Cross – are two groups, one of hooded mourners, the other a trio of nonchalant Roman soldiers in contemporary Spanish dress.

The Palau de l'Almudaina

Opposite the cathedral entrance stands the **Palau de l'Almudaina**, originally the palace of the Moorish *walis* (governors), and later of the Mallorcan kings (April–Sept Mon–Fri 10am–6.30pm, Sat 10am–2pm; Oct–March Mon–Fri 10am–2pm & 4–6pm, Sat 10am–2pm; €3; free on Wed to EU citizens showing their passport). The present structure, built around a central courtyard, owes much of its appearance to Jaume II (1276–1311), who spent the last twelve years of his life in residence here. Jaume converted the old fortress into a lavish palace that incorporated both Gothic and Moorish features, an uneasy mixture of styles conceived by the Mallorcan Pedro Selva, the king's favourite architect. The two most prominent "Moorish" attributes are the fragile-looking outside walls, with their square turrets and dainty crenellations, and the delicate arcades of the main loggia, which can be seen from the waterside esplanade below.

Once Mallorca was incorporated within the Aragonese kingdom, the Palau de l'Almudaina became surplus to requirements, though it did achieve local notoriety when the eccentric Aragonese king Juan I (1387–1395) installed an alchemist in the royal apartments, hoping he would replenish the treasury by turning base metal into gold. Today the palace serves a variety of official functions, housing the island's legislature, its military – whose camera-shy guards stand outside one of the entrances – and a series of state apartments kept in readiness for visiting dignitaries and the king, which is presumably why those exhibits that are labelled carry Castilian inscriptions. When the king or some other bigwig is in residence, parts of the palace are usually cordoned off.

The interior

An audioguide, issued free at the ticket desk, gives plenty of background information about the *palau's* exhibits in several languages, including English. The tour begins with a series of medieval corridors and rooms that are almost entirely devoid of ornamentation, but things pick up in the **Salón de Consejos** (Hall of Councils; Room 5), where the walls sport a group of admirable Flemish tapestries, fifteenth- and sixteenth-century imports devoted to classical themes. Amongst them is a Roman Triumph, a blood-curdling war scene, and, best of the lot, the suicide of Cleopatra, showing a particularly wan-looking queen with the guilty asp slithering discreetly away. Moving on, the **Comedor de Oficiales** (Officers' Mess; Room 6) possesses a handful of Flemish genre paintings, fine still-life studies including one by the seventeenth-century Antwerp-based artist Frans Snyders – there's no label, but it's the painting with the man, the woman, the cat and several carcasses. Snyders was a contemporary of Rubens and odd-jobbed for him, painting in the flowers and fruit on many of his canvases.

Beyond, there are charming views across the city from the outside **terraza** (terrace; Room 9), which holds a small formal garden, and then it's inside again for the **Sala de Guardia** (Hall of Guards; Room 10), where there are several dire eighteenth-century Spanish tapestries. Crude and inexact, these are in striking contrast to the Flemish tapestries exhibited elsewhere, but by then Spain had lost control of the Netherlands and the Spanish court could no longer acquire pieces from its traditional supplier. In 1725, the Spanish king founded a tapestry factory in Madrid, but its products – as demonstrated here – were poor, and there must have been some aesthetic gnashing of teeth when the Spanish court took delivery. Pressing on, the **Baños Árabes** (Arab Baths; Room 11) are a rare survivor from Moorish times, comprising three stone-vaulted chambers, one each for cold, tepid and hot baths. Enough remains to see how this sophisticated set-up worked and why the Christian kings who supplanted the Moors adopted them lock, stock and barrel.

After the Arab Baths, you move into the central courtyard, from where the **Escalera Real** (Royal Staircase; Room 13), installed by Philip II, leads up to the **state apartments** that fill out the palace's upper level. These apartments are really rather sterile, but there are several splendidly ornate Mudéjar wooden ceilings and a series of fine Brussels tapestries, notably a magnificent seventeenth-century *Siege of Carthage* covering the back wall of the **Salón Gótico** (Gothic Hall; Room 20).

The last room here is the **Despacho de Su Majestad el Rey** (Office of the King; Room 21) after which you emerge back in the courtyard for the final part of the tour, the **Capilla de Santa Ana** (Chapel of St Anne; Room 22). Still used for army officers' masses and weddings, the chapel is an attractive, largely fourteenth-century Gothic structure, though the delicate marble carving above the entrance is Romanesque in style, a deliberate use of what was then an archaic tradition. The three figures above the door are, in the middle, the Virgin Mary, with saints Anne and Joachim to either side. The interior, with its vaulted and embossed ceiling, is decidedly intimate, almost cosy, a suitable home for the Chapel of St Praxedis, which, with its medieval effigy and reliquary, is devoted to a much venerated local saint.

The city walls and the Parc de la Mar

A flight of steps leads down from between the cathedral and the Palau de l'Almudaina to a handsomely restored section of the **Renaissance city walls**, whose mighty zigzag of bastions, bridges, gates and dry moats once encased the whole city. These replaced the city's **medieval walls**, portions of which also survive – look back up from the foot of the steps and a large chunk is clearly visible beneath and to either side of the cathedral. Constructed of sandstone blocks and adobe, the earlier fortifications depended for their efficacy on their height, with a gallery running along the top from which the defenders could fire at the enemy. By the middle of the fifteenth century, however, the development of more effective artillery had shifted the military balance in favour of offence, with cannons now able to breach medieval city walls with comparative ease. The military architects of the day soon evolved a new design in which walls were built much lower and thicker to absorb cannon shot, while four-faced bastions – equipped with artillery platforms – projected from the line of the walls, providing the defenders with a variety of firing lines. The whole was protected by a water-filled **moat** with deep, sheer sides. The costs of re-fortifying the major cities of western Europe were astronomical, but every country joined in the rush. In Palma, the Habsburgs ordered work to start on the new (Renaissance) design in the 1560s, though the chain of bastions was only completed in 1801.

From the foot of the steps below the cathedral, a wide and pleasant **walkway** travels along the top of the walls, providing fine views of the cathedral and an insight into the tremendous strength of the fortifications. Heading west, the walkway leads to the **tiered gardens** of a small Moorish-style park, which tumble down to the foot of Avinguda d'Antoni Maura, an extension of the tree-lined Passeig d'es Born (see p.79). In the opposite direction – east from the steps below the cathedral – the walkway passes above the planted palm trees, concrete terraces and ornamental lagoon of the **Parc de la Mar**, an imaginative and popular redevelopment of the disused land that once lay between the walls and the coastal motorway. Indeed, it has proved so popular that the municipality are considering shoving the road underground so that they can extend the park to the seashore.

Wall and walkway zigzag along the south side of old Palma before fizzling out at Plaça Llorenç Villalonga. After a couple of minutes, you'll pass above the double **Portella** gateway, the outer portal of which carries the Bourbon coat of arms above its arch; you can come off the walkway here, going down either of two wide stone ramps to reach the foot of c/Portella.

The old town

The medina-like maze of streets at the back of the cathedral constitutes the heart of the **old town**, which extends north to Plaça Cort and east to Avinguda Gabriel Alomar i Villalonga. Long a neglected corner of the city, the district is now slowly being refurbished, an ambitious and massively expensive project that's gradually restoring its antique charms. The area's general appearance is its main appeal, rather than any specific sights, and you can spend hours wandering down narrow lanes and alleys, loitering in the squares, gawping at Renaissance mansions and peering at imposing Baroque and Gothic churches. As targets for your wanderings, aim for the district's two finest churches – the

Església de Santa Eulalia and the Basílica de Sant Francesc – plus the city's most extensive museum, the Museu de Mallorca.

The Banys Àrabs and Museo Torrents Lladó

Leaving the city wall walkway at the Portella gate, you'll find yourself in the old town at the foot of c/Portella. North of the gate, take the first turning right for the **Banys Àrabs** (Arab Baths), at c/Can Serra 7 (daily: April–Nov 9.30am–8pm; Dec–March 9.30am–7pm; €1.50). One of the few genuine reminders of the Moorish presence, this tenth-century brick *hammam* (bath house) consists of a small horseshoe-arched and domed chamber which was once heated through the floor. The arches rest on stone pillars, an irregular bunch thought to have been looted from the remains of the island's Roman buildings.

The baths are reasonably well preserved, but if you've been to the baths in Girona or Granada, or even the Baños Árabes in the Palau de l'Almudaina (see p.71), these are anticlimactic. The lush garden outside, with tables where you can picnic, is perhaps nicer.

Close by the Banys Àrabs on c/Portella, the **Casa Museo J. Torrents Lladó** (Tues–Fri 10am–6pm, Sat 10am–2pm; €3; ⓦwww.torrentsllado.com) is home to over a hundred rather forgettable paintings by the twentieth-century Mallorcan artist J. Torrents Lladó (1946–1993), although the picturesque house itself, which was also designed by the artist, is beautifully furnished and decorated.

The Museu de Mallorca

A few metres further north along c/Portella is the **Museu de Mallorca** (Tues–Sat 10am–7pm, Sun 10am–2pm; €2.40). The museum occupies **Can Aiamans**, a rambling Renaissance mansion whose high-ceilinged rooms make a delightful setting for an enjoyable medley of Mallorcan artefacts, the earliest dating from prehistoric times, fleshed out by a superb assortment of Gothic paintings and some exquisite examples of *Modernista* fittings and furnishings. The labelling of the exhibits is very patchy, however.

The collection begins on the **ground floor**, behind and to the right of the entrance, with half a dozen rooms filled with all sorts of bits and pieces retrieved from old buildings and archeological digs. Highlights include Roman votive statuettes, a selection of exquisite Arab and Moorish jewellery, inscribed Arab funerary tablets, and some beautiful, highly decorated wooden panelling that is representative of Mudéjar artistry. Retracing your steps, cross the courtyard and pop into the room at the foot of the stairway, home to a few old documents and one of the most atrocious paintings imaginable, *The Sacking of the City of Troy* by Miquel Bestard (c. 1590–1633), its figures dreadfully executed and the red of the flames thoroughly unconvincing. Fortunately, relief is close to hand, just up the stairs in the first of a couple of rooms devoted to the **Mallorcan Primitive** painters (for more on whom, see p.70). On display in this first room are works by the Masters of Bishop Galiana, Montesión and Castellitx and, best of the lot, a panel painting entitled *Santa Quiteria*, whose lifelike, precisely executed figures – right down to the king's wispy beard – are typical of the gifted Master of the Privileges. In the same room there's also a curious thirteenth-century work of unknown authorship dedicated to St Bernard, with the saint on his knees devotedly drinking the milk of the Virgin Mary.

Beyond a room of religious statues and carved capitals, the second room of Gothic paintings is distinguished by a sequence of works by **Francesc Comes** (1379–1415), whose skill in catching subtle skin textures matches his Flemish contemporaries and represents a softening of the early Mallorcan Primitives' crudeness. In his striking *St George*, the saint – girl-like, with typically full lips – impales a lime-green dragon with more horns than could possibly be useful. One of the last talented exponents of the Mallorcan Gothic, the **Master of the Predellas** – probably a certain Joan Rosató – is represented by his Bosch-like *Life of Santa Margalida*, each crowd of onlookers a sea of ugly, deformed faces and merciless eyes. The work outlines the life of Margaret of Antioch, one of the most venerated saints in medieval Christendom. During the reign of the Roman Emperor Diocletian (284–305 AD) she refused to marry a pagan prefect and was consequently executed after being tortured with extravagant gusto. As if this weren't enough, she also had to resist more metaphysical trials: Satan, disguised as a dragon, swallowed her, but couldn't digest her holiness, so his stomach opened up and out she popped unharmed. This particular tribulation made Margaret the patron saint of pregnant women.

The ensuing rooms display the stodgy art of the Counter-Reformation, though Palma's own Miquel Bestard makes a second, much more successful appearance in his whopping *Feeding of the Five Thousand*. Miraculously, Jesus feeds the hungry crowd from a meagre supply of loaves and fishes, but the subtext is much more revealing: Bestard's crowds are well-behaved and respectful of authority – just what the Catholic hierarchy had in mind.

The museum's **top floor** holds a mildly engaging assortment of nineteenth- and early twentieth-century paintings by foreign artists once resident in Mallorca. There's also a neat sample of works by Mallorca's own **Juli Ramis** (1909–1990), whose striking style is illustrated by his oil-on-fabric *Tres Cavalls* (Three Horses) and the radiant blues of *Tardor en blau* (Blue Autumn). A native of Sóller, Ramis left the island when he was nineteen to spend the next sixty years abroad, travelling widely and becoming acquainted with some of the leading artistic lights of his day, notably Picasso. Ramis mixed his styles, but was essentially an Expressionist with Surrealistic leanings. He returned to Mallorca in the last years of his life and died in Palma.

Also on this floor is a room of *Modernista* fittings and furnishings, mostly retrieved from shops and houses that have since been demolished. Of particular interest are the charming wall tiles manufactured at the island's **La Roqueta** works. The pottery was in production for just twenty years (1897–1918), but this coincided with the vogue for the *Modernista* pieces in which La Roqueta excelled. For once, the labelling is quite good.

North to Santa Eulalia

Continuing on up the hill from the Museu de Mallorca, c/Portella leads to c/Morey where, at no. 9, you'll find **Can Oleza** (no public access), a sixteenth-century mansion with a cool and shaded courtyard embellished by a handsome balustrade and a set of Ionic columns. Nearby **Can Marquès**, at c/Zanglada 2A (Mon–Fri 10am–3pm; €6; ⓦwww.casasconhistoria.net), is one of the few city mansions to be open to the public, but although the rooms are kitted out with original nineteenth-century furnishings and artwork, there's nothing of great historic or aesthetic interest.

At the top of c/Zanglada, turn onto c/Almudaina for a peek at the chunky remains of the old east gate, the **Arc de L'Almudaina** – a remnant of the Moorish fortifications topped with medieval barbicans – and to see **Can Bordils**, at no. 9, one of the city's oldest private mansions (it's now a municipal office building).

Overshadowing the square at the top of c/Morey is the **Església de Santa Eulalia** (Mon–Fri 7am–12.30pm & 5.45–8.30pm, Sat 7am–1pm &

4.30–8.45pm, Sun 8am–1pm & 6.30–8.30pm), which was built on the site of a mosque in the mid-thirteenth century. It took just 25 years to complete and consequently possesses an architectural homogeneity that's unusual for ecclesiastical Palma, though there was some later medieval tinkering, and nineteenth-century renovators added the belfry and remodelled the main (south) facade. The church is typically Gothic in construction, with a yawning nave originally designed – as in the cathedral – to give the entire congregation a view of the high altar. The bricked-up windows of today keep out most of the light and spoil the effect, but suggestions that they be cleared have always been ignored. Framing the nave, the aisles accommodate twelve **chapels**, one of which (the first on the right) sports a delightful Gothic panel painting in finely observed Flemish style. In kitsch contrast, the other chapels are standard-issue Baroque, though they pale into insignificance when compared with the hourglass-shaped **high altarpiece**, a flashy Baroque extravagance of colossal proportions. This holy ground witnessed one of the more disgraceful episodes of Mallorcan history. During Easter week, 1435, a rumour went round that Jewish townsfolk had enacted a blasphemous mock-up of the Crucifixion. There was no proof, but the Jews were promptly robbed of their possessions and condemned to be burnt at the stake unless they adopted Christianity. The ensuing mass baptism was held here at Santa Eulalia.

Just west of the Plaça Santa Eulalia lies the fetching Plaça Cort (see p.79), whilst around the back of the church, at c/Can Savella 4, is **Can Vivot**, an especially opulent early eighteenth-century mansion, whose spacious main courtyard, with its fetching columns and arches, is distinguished by an elegant staircase. Look out, too, for the wonderful curvilinear iron gate to the right of the courtyard – and the shadow it casts when the light is streaming in. Built on top of a Moorish palace, the interior of the mansion is decorated in fine Neoclassical style, especially the sumptuous library, which is filled with scientific instruments of the age, though it's only occasionally open to the public.

Mansions in Palma

Most of medieval Palma was destroyed by fire, so the patrician **mansions** that characterize the old town today generally date from the reconstruction programme of the late seventeenth and early eighteenth centuries. Consequently they were built in the fashionable Renaissance style, with columns and capitals, loggias and arcades tucked away behind outside walls of plain stone three or four storeys high, and are surprisingly uniform in layout. Entry to almost all of these mansions was through a great arched **gateway** that gave onto a rectangular courtyard around which the house was built. Originally, the **courtyard** would have been cheered by exotic trees and flowering shrubs, and equipped with a fancy stone and ironwork well-head, where visitors could water their horses. From the courtyard, a stone **exterior staircase** led up to the main public rooms – with the servants' quarters below and the family's private apartments up above.

Very few of these mansions are open to the public, and all you'll see for the most part is the view from the gateway – the municipality has actually started to pay people to leave their big wooden gates open. Several have, however, passed into the public domain, the Can Aiamans, now the home of the Museu de Mallorca, being the prime example. Others worth making a detour to see are Can Bordils (p.75), Can Oleza (p.75), Can Vivot (above) and Can Solleric (p.79). Only the last of these is open to the public, along with the rather less impressive Can Marquès (see p.75).

The Basílica de Sant Francesc

A short walk east of the Plaça Santa Eulalia along c/Convent de Sant Francesc is the **Basílica de Sant Francesc** (daily 9.30am–12.30pm & 3.30–6pm; closed Sun afternoon; €0.60), a domineering pile that occupies the site of the old Moorish soap factory. Built for the Franciscans towards the end of the thirteenth century, the original church was a vast Gothic edifice which benefited from royal patronage after Jaume II's son, also named Jaume, became a member of the order in 1300. Subsequent Gothic remodellings replaced the initial wooden ceiling with a single-span, vaulted stone roof of imposing dimensions and added stately chapels to the nave and apse. The Basílica became the most fashionable church in medieval Palma and its friars received handsome kickbacks for entombing the local nobility within its precincts. Increasingly eager to enrich themselves, the priests came to compete for possession of the corpses, while the various aristocratic clans vied with each other in the magnificence of their sarcophagi. These tensions exploded when a certain Jaume Armadams had a jug of water emptied over his head on All Saints' Day, 1490. The congregation went berserk and over three hundred noblemen fought it out in the nave before the priests finally restored order. The scandal caused the Basílica to be closed for several decades.

In the seventeenth century the church was badly damaged by lightning, prompting a thoroughgoing reconstruction which accounts for most of its present-day appearance. The main **facade**, which dates from this period, displays a stunning severity of style, with its great rectangular sheet of dressed sandstone stretching up to an arcaded and balustraded balcony. The facade is pierced by a gigantic rose window of Plateresque intricacy and embellished by a **Baroque doorway**, the tympanum of which features a triumphant Virgin Mary engulfed by a wriggling mass of sculptured decoration. Above the Madonna is the figure of St George, and to either side and below are assorted saints – look out for the scholar and missionary Ramon Llull, shown reading a book. The strange statue in front of the doorway of a Franciscan monk and a young Native American celebrates the missionary work of **Junípero Serra** (see p.181), a Mallorcan priest despatched to California in 1768, who subsequently founded the cities of San Diego, Los Angeles and San Francisco.

The church is entered through its outstanding trapezoidal Gothic **cloister**, featuring tiered arcades carved in different styles. The church's **interior** is disappointingly gloomy – too dark, in fact, to pick out any but the most obvious of its features. However, you can push a switch to light the monumental **high altar** – it's on the right-hand side near the door to the sacristy. The altar is a gaudy Baroque affair featuring balustrades, lattice-work and clichéd figurines beneath a painted wooden statue of *St George and the Dragon*. Less overblown are the rolling scrolls and trumpeter-angel of the eighteenth-century **pulpit** on the wall of the nave, and the ornate Gothic-Baroque frontispiece of the nearby organ. The first chapel on the left of the ambulatory shelters the **tomb of Ramon Llull**, whose bones were brought back to Palma after his martyrdom in Algeria in 1315. Considering the sanctity of the man's remains, it's an odd and insignificant-looking affair, with Llull's alabaster effigy set in the wall to the right of the chapel altarpiece at a disconcertingly precarious angle.

The Templar chapel

Follow c/Ramon Llull east from the basilica and you'll soon spy the large and distinctive fortified **gateway** at the end of the street. Dating from the thirteenth century, the gateway once marked the entrance to the castle-like compound of the **Knights Templar**, a military order founded to support

Ramon Llull

The life of **Ramon Llull** (1235–1315) – a figure beloved of Catholic propagandists – was an exercise in redemption following carnal excess. As a young man, Llull was an ebullient rake in the retinue of the future Jaume II. His sexual adventures were not impeded in the least by his marriage, but they ground to a dramatic halt when a certain Ambrosia de Castillo, his latest amatory target, whom he had pursued into the church of Santa Eulalia on horseback, revealed to him her diseased breasts. A deeply shocked Llull devoted the rest of his life to the Catholic faith, becoming a fearless missionary and dedicated scholar of theology, philosophy and alchemy. Exemplifying the cosmopolitan outlook of thirteenth-century Mallorca, Llull learnt to read, write and speak several languages including Arabic, and travelled to France, much of Spain and North Africa. He also founded a monastery and missionary school on **Puig Randa** (see pp.178–179), 35km east of Palma, where he spent ten years in seclusion, writing no fewer than 250 books and treatises. It was Llull's scholarship that attracted the attention of his old friend Jaume II, who summoned him to court in 1282. With royal patronage, Llull then established a monastic school of Oriental languages near Valldemossa, where he trained his future missionary companions. Llull was killed on his third evangelical excursion to Algeria in 1315, his martyrdom ensuring his subsequent beatification.

the Crusades. The knights established bases right across the Mediterranean and this was one of the more important – though they were soon to be dispossessed. The order was rich and secretive, its independence resented by the papacy and just about every secular ruler in Europe. In 1312, following trumped-up charges of heresy, sorcery and bestiality, the pope disbanded the order and their Palma compound passed into the hands of the Hospitallers of St John, a rival knightly order. The Knights Hospitallers struggled on until 1802, when the Spanish king disbanded them and confiscated their property.

An alley leads through the gateway to the only other surviving part of the military compound, the **Templar chapel** (in theory open Mon–Fri 9.30am–1pm & 3.30–7pm, Sat 9.30am–1pm), whose Gothic and Romanesque features were extensively remodelled in the 1880s. Inside, the gloomy nave is divided into three bays with ribbed vaulting and a wooden ceiling over the atrium. The Romanesque side-chapels in the entrance area are perhaps the church's most diverting feature, all slender columns, rounded arches and intense foliate and geometric decoration.

Plaça Sant Jeroni and around

From the gateway, head south along c/Temple for a couple of minutes to reach **Plaça Sant Jeroni**, a pretty little piazza set around a diminutive water fountain. The severe stone walls of a former convent, now a college, dominate one side of the square, while the **Església de Sant Jeroni** fills out another. The church facade is mostly a plain stone wall, but it does sport two elaborate doorways, the one to the left a swirl of carved foliage and some cheeky cherubim. The tympanum portrays the well-known story of Saint Jerome in the desert, during which the saint endures all sorts of tribulations and temptations, but still sticks true to the faith; above, two heraldic lions stand rampant. The **interior** is a seventeenth-century affair with heavy stone vaulting and a whopping organ, though unfortunately it's rarely open to the public. The highlights here are various paintings, amongst them several works by the Mallorcan Primitives including Pere Terrencs' lively *Sant Jeroni*.

From the square, c/Seminari and then c/Monti-Sion run west past the **Església de Monti-Sion** (most likely to be open Mon–Fri 7–8.30am), whose thundering facade is a hectic heap of angels and saints, coats of arms and wriggling foliage. Below the figure of the Virgin, look out for a strangely inconclusive representation of the Devil – half-sheep, half-dragon. Beyond the church, c/Monti-Sion leads to a crossroads: turn right along c/Pare Nadal to reach the Basílica de Sant Francesc (see p.77); alternatively, keep dead ahead and the twisting side streets will deliver you onto c/Cadena, a short distance from Plaça Cort.

Plaça Cort

With its elegant nineteenth-century facades, bustling **Plaça Cort** was named after the various legal bodies – both secular and religious – which were once concentrated here. Along with much of the rest of Spain, Mallorca possessed a truly byzantine legal system until the whole caboodle was swept away and rationalized during the Napoleonic occupation. On one side, the square is dominated by the **Ajuntament** (Town Hall), a debonair example of the late Renaissance style. Pop in for a look at the grand and self-assured foyer, which mostly dates from the nineteenth century, and the six folkloric *gigantones* (giant carnival figures) stored here – four in a corner, the other two tucked against the staircase.

From Plaça Cort, it's a pleasant five-minute stroll to the Passeig d'es Born via c/Sant Domingo and c/Conquistador, which weaves downhill lined by attractive nineteenth-century town houses with wrought-iron grilles and stone balconies. Alternatively, a short walk from Plaça Cort along c/Palau Reial brings you to the cathedral.

Passeig d'es Born and around

Distinguished by the stone sphinxes at its top and bottom, the **Passeig d'es Born** has been the city's principal promenade since the early fifteenth century, when the stream that ran here was diverted following a disastrous flash flood. Nowadays, this leafy avenue is too traffic-congested to be endearing, but it's still at the heart of the city, and close to some of Palma's most fashionable bars and restaurants.

At no. 27, overlooking the *passeig*, is the fine Italianate loggia of **Can Solleric** (Tues–Sat 10.30am–1.45pm & 5.30–9pm, Sun 10am–1.45pm; free), a lavish mansion of heavy wooden doors, marble columns and vaulted ceilings built for a family of cattle and olive oil merchants in 1763. Recently restored, the house now displays temporary exhibitions of modern art.

From **Plaça de la Reina**, the tiny, leafy square at the foot of the Passeig d'es Born, a wide and elegant flight of steps, the **Costa de la Seu**, leads up beneath the spiky walls of the Palau de l'Almudaina to the cathedral. At the foot of the steps is another noteworthy mansion, the **Palau March**, a heavyweight affair whose arcaded galleries, chunky columns and large stone blocks were erected in the 1930s in the general style of the city's earlier Renaissance mansions. It was built for the Mallorcan magnate and art collector **Joan March** (1880–1962), who became the wealthiest man in Franco's Spain by skilfully reinvesting the profits he made from his control of the government monopoly in tobacco – though his enemies always insisted that it was smuggling that really made him rich. The palace's magnificent interior, including the Italianate courtyard, have been transformed into an art **museum** (April–Oct Mon–Fri 10am–6.30pm, Sat 10am–2pm; Nov–Mar Mon–Fri 10am–6pm, Sat

△ *Modernista* architecture, Palma

10am–2pm; €4.50 Ⓦwww.fundbmarch.es). The collection is a bit of a hotch-potch of mainly twentieth-century works, including many by Spanish artists, plus some Romanesque and Gothic carvings. Highlights include sculptures by Rodin and Henry Moore, eighteenth-century Neapolitan Nativity figures, and some works by the celebrated Spanish painter Josep Maria Sert, whose frescoes adorn the UN Palace in Geneva. (Further exhibits from the art collection of the March family are displayed at the recently reopened and expanded Banca March – see p.83).

South of Plaça de la Reina, **Avinguda d'Antoni Maura** runs down to the wide breakwater that marks the start of Palma harbour. The avenue takes its name from **Antoni Maura** (1853–1925), a Mallorquin who served as prime minister of Spain four times between 1903 and 1921. An outstanding orator and extraordinarily forceful personality, Maura was a conservative who opposed universal suffrage as "the politics of the mob", preferring a limited franchise and a constitution which gave power to the middle classes, as long as they marched to the tune of the church and the crown. To give the man some credit, his conservatism with regard to universal suffrage – which was in place from 1887 – was prompted by Spain's particular circumstances. In a backward, largely agrarian society, most Spaniards were largely indifferent to national issues and power was concentrated in the hands of district bosses, or *caciques*, who would bring out the vote for any candidate provided they were guaranteed control of political patronage. Some bosses ruled by intimidation, others by bribery, but the end result was a dense mixture of charity and jobbery, dubbed *caciquismo*, which made national government well-nigh impossible. Maura struggled against this chicanery, and his assertive nationalism was quite enough for Franco to have this avenue named after him.

El Puig de Sant Pere

The ancient neighbourhood of **El Puig de Sant Pere** (St Peter's Mount) covers the area west of the Passeig d'es Born and north to Avinguda Jaume III. Here, the narrow lanes and alleys shelter another sprinkling of patrician mansions, though most of the old houses were divided up into apartments years ago to cater for the district's sailors, dockers and fishermen. Again, it's the general flavour of the area that appeals rather than specific sights, but it's still worth seeking out two late Renaissance facades on c/Sant Feliu, which runs off Passeig d'es Born. At no. 8 is **Can Moner**, whose ornate doorway sports telamons, cherubs and cornucopia, whilst no. 10, **Can Pavesi**, offers a mythical beast with its tongue stuck right out.

There's a gruesome story behind the name of a lane off nearby c/Estanc. **Mà del Moro**, "The Hand of the Moor", harks back to Ahmed, an eighteenth-century slave who murdered his master in a house on this alley. Ahmed was executed for the crime, and his hand chopped off and stuck above the door-way of the house where the murder was committed.

From Passeig d'es Born to Passeig de la Rambla

At the top of Passeig d'es Born, the sturdy shops and office blocks of **Avinguda Jaume III**, dating from the 1940s, march west towards the Passeig Mallorca. It's here you'll find some of the island's chicest clothes shops, as well as downtown's biggest department store, **El Corte Inglés**. There's something very engaging about the avenue – a jostle of beshorted tourists and besuited Spaniards – and the web of ancient alleys immediately to the north is another attractive corner of the city, all high stone walls and dignified old mansions focused on c/Concepció.

Eastwards from the top of the Passeig d'es Born runs **c/Unió**, a new if rather unimaginative appellation – it means "unity" – for a street Franco had previously named after General Mola, one of the prime movers of the Nationalist rebellion of 1936. Mola was killed in a plane accident during the Civil War, possibly to Franco's relief. Hitler, for one, thought that Mola was the more competent, remarking that his death meant that "Franco came to the top like Pontius Pilate in the Creed." **Can Balaguer**, the Renaissance mansion at c/Unió 3, has imposing doors and a grand cobbled courtyard. It is now used to display the work of local artists under the auspices of the city's art society, the Círculo de Bellas Artes; some of the work is very good, but there are no bargains.

A few metres further east along c/Unió is tiny **Plaça Mercat**, the site of two identical *Modernista* buildings commissioned by a wealthy baker, Josep Casasayas, in 1908. Each is a masterpiece of flowing, organic lines tempered by graceful balconies and decorated with fern-leaf and butterfly motifs. Just down the street, on **Plaça Weyler**, stands a further *Modernista* extravagance, the magnificent **Gran Hotel** of 1903. Recently scrubbed and polished, the facade boasts playful arches, balconies, columns and bay windows enlivened with intricate floral trimmings and brilliant polychrome ceramics inspired by Hispano-Arabic designs. The interior houses a café-bar, a good art bookshop and the spacious **art gallery** (Tues–Sat 10am–9pm, Sun 10am–2pm; free) of the Fundació La Caixa, which organizes an excellent and wide-ranging programme of exhibitions. The permanent collection is confined to a large sample of work by the Catalan impressionist-expressionist **Hermen Anglada-Camarasa**, who is best known for the evocative Mallorcan land- and seascapes he produced during his sojourn on the island from 1914 to 1936, though the works on display here are mainly compellingly original – and enormous – paintings of women.

There's another excellent example of *Modernismo* across the street from the Gran Hotel in the floral motifs and gaily painted wooden doorway of the **Forn des Teatre** (theatre bakery) at Plaça Weyler 9. A few metres away looms the Neoclassical frontage of the **Teatre Principal** – the city's main auditorium for classical music, ballet and opera – whose tympanum sports a fanciful relief dedicated to the nine Muses of Greek mythology.

At the theatre, the main street – now c/Riera – does a quick about-face to join the **Passeig de la Rambla**, whose plane trees shelter Palma's main flower market. The two statues at the foot of the boulevard, representing Roman emperors, were placed here in 1937 in honour of Mussolini's Italy – one set of Fascists tipping their municipal hats to another.

Plaça Major and around

On both sides of the Teatre Principal, steep flights of steps lead up to **Plaça Major**, a large pedestrianized square built on the site of the former headquarters of the **Inquisition** (see box opposite). The square, a rather plain affair with a symmetrical portico running around its perimeter, once housed the fish and vegetable market, but nowadays it's popular for its pavement cafés. On the south side of Plaça Major lies the much smaller **Plaça Marquès del Palmer**, a cramped setting for two fascinating *Modernista* edifices. The more dramatic is **Can Rei**, a five-storey apartment building splattered with polychrome ceramics and floral decoration, its centrepiece a gargoyle-like face set between a pair of winged dragons. The facade of the adjacent **L'Àguila** building is of similar ilk, though there's greater emphasis on window space, reflecting its original function as a department store.

To the south, the shopping area between Plaça Marquès del Palmer and Plaça Cort retains an agreeably old-fashioned air, with three- and four-storey buildings flanking its main streets – principally pedestrianized **c/Jaume II** – and embellished with an abundance of fancy iron-grilled balconies.

The Museu d'Art Espanyol Contemporani and around

Running north from Plaça Major, **c/Sant Miquel** is another popular and pleasant shopping street. Here, at no. 11, the **Banca March** occupies a fine Renaissance mansion whose *Modernista* flourishes date from a tasteful refurbishment of 1917. The building has two entrances, one to the bank, the other to the upper-floor **Museu d'Art Espanyol Contemporani** (Mon–Fri 10am–6.30pm, Sat 10am–1.30; €3), which features changing selections from

The Spanish Inquisition

In 1478, mindful of his need for their military support, the pope granted Spain's Isabella I and Fernando V the right to establish their own **Inquisition**. It was much appreciated. The dual monarchs had realised that the Catholic faith was the most powerful force binding a fragmented Spain together, and were sure the Inquisition would both consolidate the church's position and buttress their own. Installed in Castile in 1480 and in Aragón and Catalunya – including the Balearics – seven years later, the Inquisition began its work with the **Jews**. During the Middle Ages, the Jews had played a leading role in Spain's cultural and economic life and were generally treated with tolerance. This began to change in the late fourteenth century, when many Spaniards became increasingly resentful of the Jews' commercial clout and their role as rent collectors for the big landowners. In 1391, anti-Semitic riots broke out across much of Spain – including Mallorca – and many Jews, in fear for their lives, hastily submitted to baptism. These new Christians were subsequently called **conversos**. In the event, though, baptism merely staved off disaster. The riots continued – like the disturbance in Palma in 1435 (see p.76) – and matters came to a head after the capture of Spain's last Moorish kingdom, Granada, in 1492. Flush with military success but short of cash, Fernando and Isabella **expelled** from Spain all those Jews who had not turned Christian – about 120,000 – and confiscated their property, leaving the remaining *conversos* isolated and vulnerable.

Following the Reformation, the Inquisition turned its gaze onto the **Protestants**, though in truth there were very few of them – only two thousand were indicted in Spain in the whole of the sixteenth century. Nevertheless, despite the limited nature of the Protestant threat, the Inquisition was profoundly influential. Most Spaniards regarded it as a bastion against heresy and, acting in this spirit, the Inquisitors kept all progressive thought at bay. Thus, whereas much of Europe was convulsed by disputation, Spain sank into ritual and dogma with the threat of the Inquisition in the background: in Palma few potential heretics could ignore the louring presence of its headquarters, plonked on a hill overlooking the city (now occupied by Plaça Major). Furthermore, by its very processes the Inquisition created an atmosphere of fear and mistrust. The Inquisitors acted on charges of heresy brought to them by the public, but these accusations were often frivolous or motivated by personal enmity. Worse still, even the most orthodox Catholic could not be sure of acquittal. The Inquisitor's examinations were often so theologically complex and long-winded that the danger of self-condemnation was ever-present – under torture, many would confess to anything and everything.

Opposed by reforming clerics in the eighteenth century and increasingly ignored by the state, the Inquisition gradually lost influence. It was finally **abolished** during the Napoleonic occupation of Spain in 1808. Fifteen years later, in 1823, the headquarters of the Inquisition in Palma was demolished.

the contemporary art collection of the March family (see p.79). Dozens of works by twentieth-century Spanish artists are displayed, the intention being to survey the Spanish contribution to modern art (the theme is further developed by temporary exhibitions). The earliest piece, Picasso's *Tête de Femme* (1907), is of particular interest, being one of the first of the artist's works to be influenced by the primitive forms that were to propel him, over the following decade, from the re-creation of natural appearances into abstract art. Miró and Dalí are also represented, and there's one still life by the Spanish Cubist Juan Gris, as well as a number of pieces by the leading contemporary Catalan artist Antoni Tàpies. The bulk of the collection is remorselessly modern, however, and though there are some touches of humour, most of it is hard to warm to, especially the allegedly "vigorous" abstractions of both the El Paso (Millares, Saura, Feito, Canogar) and the Parpalló (Sempere, Alfaro) groupings of the late 1950s.

It's worth continuing a few metres up along c/Sant Miquel from the museum to the **Església Sant Miquel** (Mon–Sat 8am–1.30pm & 5–7.30pm, Sun 10am–1.30pm & 5.30–7.30pm). The sturdy exterior of this church, the result of all sorts of architectural meddlings, hides a gloomy barrel-vaulted nave and rib-vaulted side chapels. The poorly lit high altarpiece, a Baroque classic with a central image celebrating St Michael, is a good example of the intricate work of Francesc Herrara, a much-travelled Spanish painter of religious and genre subjects known for his purposeful compositions and tangy realism.

West along the harbourfront

The various marinas, shipyards, fish docks and ferry and cargo terminals that make up Palma's **harbourfront** extend west for several kilometres from the bottom of Avinguda d'Antoni Maura to the edge of Cala Major (see p.96). The harbour is at its prettiest at this eastern end, where a cycling and walking path skirts the seashore, with boats to one side and bars, restaurants, apartment blocks and the smart hotels of the **Avinguda Gabriel Roca** – often dubbed the Passeig Marítim – on the other.

Sa Llotja

The first harbourfront landmark is the fifteenth-century **Sa Llotja**, the city's former stock exchange (Tues–Sat 11am–2pm & 5–9pm, Sun 11am–2pm; free). This carefully composed late-Gothic structure is one of the masterpieces of Mallorcan **Guillermo Sagrera**, one of the most original European architects of his day, and is distinguished by its four octagonal turrets, slender, spiralling columns and tall windows. The building now hosts frequent, and occasionally excellent, exhibitions (some of which you'll have to pay to get into). It also boasts a series of fierce-looking gargoyles and a muscular angel – appropriately the Guardian Angel of Commerce – above the front door. Next door, the distinguished **Consolat de Mar** was built in the 1660s to accommodate the Habsburg officials who supervised maritime affairs in this part of the empire. Today, as the home of the president of the Balearic Islands, it's closed to the public, but the outside is worth a second look for its pair of crusty old cannons and elegant Renaissance gallery. The forlorn-looking gate between the two buildings – the **Porta Vella del Moll** – originally stood at the end of Avinguda d'Antoni Maura, where it was the main entrance into the city from the sea, but was moved here when portions of the town wall were demolished in the 1870s.

To the Jardins La Quarentena

At the foot of **Avinguda Argentina** – opposite the jetties where the fishing boats come in – is a pleasant terraced **park**, whose trees, lawns, flower beds and fountains step north to Plaça La Feixina. The park abuts both the walled water-course which once served as the **city moat** and the sheer **bastion** that anchored the southwest corner of the Renaissance city wall, the only blot being the whopping **column** erected by Franco in honour – as they say – of those Balearic sailors who were loyal to the Fascist cause. The looming bastion is now being converted into the **Es Baluard** art museum, the island's largest, which will house works by Picasso, Miró, Picabia, Magritte, Nicolas de Stäel and Barceló, along with temporary exhibits.

Continuing west from the foot of Avinguda Argentina, it's a further fifteen or twenty minutes' walk along the palm-lined esplanade to the next worthwhile objective, the delightful **Jardins La Quarentena**, a leafy little park whose cool and shaded terraces, with their aromatic trees and shrubs, clamber up the hillside from the harbourfront.

The Poble Espanyol

A couple of kilometres west of the old town, and reachable by EMT bus #5 from Plaça Espanya – the nearest stop is on Avinguda Andrea Doria – is the **Poble Espanyol** (Spanish Village; daily: April–Nov 9am–8pm; Dec–March 9am–6pm; €6). This kitsch, purpose-built tourist attraction was constructed between 1965 and 1967, its Francoist intentions apparent in its celebration of everything Spanish. Walled like a medieval city, the village contains accurate, scaled-down reproductions of about twenty old and important buildings, such as Barcelona's Palau de la Generalitat, Seville's Torre del Oro, a segment of Granada's Alhambra, El Greco's house in Toledo, and the Ermita de San Antonio in Madrid. These are dotted round the village's streets and squares, where you'll also find craft workshops, souvenir shops, restaurants and bars. It's all a bit daft – and school parties swamp the place – but it's an easy way of introducing yourself to Spanish architecture.

The Castell de Bellver

Boasting superb views of Palma and its harbour from a wooded hilltop some 3km west of the city centre, and 1km southwest of the Poble Espanyol, is the **Castell de Bellver** (April–Sept Mon–Sat 8am–8pm, Sun 10am–7pm; Oct–March Mon–Sat 8am–7pm, Sun 10am–5pm; €3; free on Sun, when the castle museum is closed). To get there, take **bus** #6 from Plaça de la Reina to Plaça Gomila, which leaves a steep one-kilometre walk up the hill. If you're driving, turn off Avinguda Joan Miró (one-way west) onto the circuitous c/Camilo José Cela.

This handsome, strikingly well-preserved fortress was built for Jaume II at the beginning of the fourteenth century. Of canny circular design, the castle's immensely thick walls and steep ditches encircle a central **keep** that incorporates three imposing towers. In addition, an overhead, single-span **stone arch** connects the keep to a massive, freestanding tower, built as a final refuge. To enhance defence, the walls curve and bend and the interconnecting footbridges are set at oblique angles to each other. It's all very impressive – and looks well-nigh impregnable – but the castle was also intended to serve as a royal retreat from the summer heat, and so the austere outside walls hide a commodious, genteel-looking **circular courtyard**, surrounded by two tiers of inward-facing arcades that once belonged to the residential suites. The whole construction is ingenious, incorporating many skilful touches: the flat roof, for example, was designed to channel every drop of rainwater into a huge underground cistern.

Improvements in artillery, however, soon rendered the fortress obsolete, and it didn't last long as a royal residence either. As early as the 1350s the keep was in use as a prison, a function it performed until 1915. More recently, the castle interior has been turned into a **museum** tracking through the history of the city. The Roman statuary is the real highlight, a miscellany of busts and effigies of Roman dignitaries plus a rare and perfectly preserved column of highly decorated *cippolino* marble and, most extraordinary of all, a rare alabaster sleeping Hermaphrodite, apparently troubled by a confusing dream, half-in and half-out of her toga. Other exhibits include carved seals, marble inscriptions, lamps, first-century pots, burnt-orange Samian pottery and a funeral stele. The Roman finds were collected by **Cardinal Antonio Despuig** (1745–1817), a local antiquarian and ecclesiastical bigwig, who bequeathed his collection to the city (the terraced gardens of his old country home, Raixa, south of Sóller, are also open to the public – see p.115). The only problem is that there's absolutely no labelling, so unless you're a classical expert it's impossible to know quite what you're looking at.

After you've explored the castle, you can wander through the pine-scented woods that surround it. There's a network of **footpaths**, but no signs.

Eating and drinking

Eating well in Palma can be less pricey than anywhere else in Mallorca. Inexpensive **cafés** and **tapas bars** are liberally distributed around the city centre, with a particular concentration in the side streets off the Passeig d'es Born and Avinguda d'Antoni Maura. Many downtown cafés are up and running by 9am, but with most visitors taking breakfast at their hotel there's not much demand for early-morning eating places. For light lunches and snacks (*tapas*), however, you're spoiled for choice. You can chomp away in chic modernist surroundings, or join the crowds in simple formica and wallpaper diners where the food more than compensates for the decor – and then there's everything in between.

There's not much distinction between *tapas* bars and **restaurants**, as many of the former serve full meals as well as snacks – and, of course, put a couple of *tapas* together and you've got a full meal anyway. Indeed, the differences often have more to do with appearance than food: if you've got a tablecloth, for instance, you're almost certainly in a restaurant. **Opening times** vary enormously, but many places close one day a week – usually Sunday or Monday, but sometimes only out of season – and the majority take a siesta from about 3pm or 4pm to 7pm or, in the case of smarter joints, 8pm.

Many of Palma's restaurants and *tapas* bars are geared up for the tourist trade, especially those along the harbourfront and amongst the side streets off Avinguda d'Antoni Maura, and multilingual menus (in English, German, Catalan and Castilian) are commonplace. It's foolish to be snooty about them, however, as some serve delicious food. If you venture a little further into the city centre, you'll discover more exclusively local haunts, some offering the finest of Catalan and Spanish cuisine. A smattering of restaurants specialize in ethnic foods, and there are a couple of vegetarian café-restaurants too.

At all but the most expensive of places, €25 will cover the cost of a starter and main course, as well as a bottle of wine – though prices are jacked up during the summer. In addition, almost all the city's establishments offer excellent-value *menús del día* at lunchtime.

Cafés and tapas bars

Bar Bosch Plaça Rei Joan Carles I. One of the most popular and inexpensive *tapas* bars in town, the traditional haunt of the city's intellectuals and usually humming with conversation. At peak times you'll need to be assertive to get served.

Bar Mollet c/Contramuelle Mollet 2 ☎971 719 871. Located just across from the fish market, and with the freshest fish in town. The fine *menú del día* (Mon–Fri; €8.75) includes wine, water and dessert. Lunchtimes only; closed Sun.

La Bodeguita Mesón Salamanca c/Sant Jaume 3. In a glossily refurbished, warren-like town house off Avgda Jaume III, this establishment has a ground-floor wine bar offering tasty *tapas* from €6 and up; it's much better than the stuffy restaurant next door.

Bon Lloc c/Sant Feliu 7. One of the few vegetarian café-restaurants on the island, with good food at low prices (the set menu goes for under €20) and an informal, homely atmosphere. Open Tues–Sat 1–4pm.

La Bóveda c/Boteria 3, off Plaça Llotja. Classy, fashionable bar, one of several on this short alley, with long, wide windows and wine stacked high along the back wall – come early or be prepared to queue to get in. There's also a separate tapas restaurant here, one of the city's best, a popular place with big, good-value portions of very authentic fare (it's entered on the seafront side at Passeig de Sagrera 3) – a great place for lunch or dinner.

Café del Gran Hotel Plaça Weyler 3. A good lunch spot, with tables inside or out on a pleasant square. The *menú del día* is excellent value at €13.90.

Café Lirico Avgda d'Antoni Maura 6. Most of Palma's downtown cafés have been modernized, but not this one – its large mirrors, imitation marble and weatherbeaten clientele are reminiscent of Spanish cafés of yesteryear. Not much in the way of food.

Café Plaça Plaça Santa Eulalia s/n ☎971 726 915. Great spot on this busy square, facing the severe facade of Santa Eulalia. The wide range of snacks and drinks includes tasty crab croquettes, delicious pastries (try the scrumptious *dulce de leche* with coconut) and cappuccinos heaped with whipped cream.

Cafeteria-Bar Marítimo c/Jardines de Santo Domingo de la Calzada s/n, Passeig Marítim ☎971 738 192. Tranquil and appealing garden setting, right under the walls and overlooked by old windmills – an ideal spot to take a break halfway between the city centre and the port. Good *menú del día* for €8.90.

Cafeteria Darsena Darsena de Sant Matgi 1896, Passeig Marítim ☎971 180 504. In an attractive setting right on the marina, just opposite the Royal Nautical Club, with good fresh fish, seafood tapas and full meals, including salads.

Cafeteria Jaime III Avgda Jaume III 20. Popular with office workers and shoppers, this brisk modern café serves up a good line in snacks – try their *pa amb oli* with smoked ham.

Cafeteria Sa Murada Between the two sets of city walls at the foot of c/Portella. Tasty snacks and light meals, with the emphasis on traditional Mallorcan fare. If you've been walking the old town, this is a good spot to soak up the sun from the relative quiet of a pedestrianized mini-plaza.

Ca'n Joan de S'Aigo c/Can Sanç 10. A long-established coffee house with wonderful, freshly baked *ensaimadas* (spiral pastry buns) and fruit-flavoured mousses to die for. Charming decor too, from the kitsch water fountain to the traditional Mallorcan green-tinted chandeliers. It's on a tiny alley near Plaça Santa Eulalia – take c/Sant Crist and its continuation c/Canisseria then turn right. Closed Tues.

Cappuccino c/Conquistador, Palau March. Beautiful terrace café in a great setting on the patio of the Palau March, with an interesting selection of salads and sandwiches. There's another branch at c/Sant Miquel 53.

Colonial c/Palau Reial 3. This spick-and-span old café, a couple of doors down from the Ajuntament (Town Hall), prepares its brews from all sorts of coffee beans and offers a variety of infusion teas, a few *tapas* and good pastries.

La Cueva c/Apuntadors 5. Small and busy *tapas* bar, one of several on this street, with a rack of liquors behind the bar and hocks of meat hanging up in front. Reasonable prices and tasty food, including grilled prawns and other seafood.

Diner c/Sant Magi 23, Santa Catalina ☎971 736 222. A little slice of Americana, serving hamburgers, milkshakes, hash browns, pancakes, BLTs and Dixie fried chicken – all homemade and using only the best ingredients. Open seven days a week, 24 hours a day. Phone for take-away.

Gotic Plaça Llotja 2. One of several cafés and restaurants on this popular and appealing square. Dishes focus on Spanish and international cookery; alternatively, just have a drink and enjoy the atmosphere.

Lizarran c/Ca'n Brondo 6. Delightful and popular little place dishing up Basque-style tapas – things like smoked salmon with chopped onions, and artichoke hearts with pepper and bacon, all served on a small slice of French bread.

Orient Express c/Llotja de Mar 6, beside Sa Llotja. Idiosyncratic café-restaurant with an interior like the inside of a railway carriage. Salads are the speciality; you'll have to wait for a seat at lunchtime.

El Pesquero (also known as *Café Port Pesquer*) Avgda Gabriel Roca s/n. Bright and breezy café on the harbourfront a few minutes' walk west of Avgda d'Antoni Maura, overlooking the jetty where the fishing boats come in. The open-air terrace bar is a good spot to soak up the evening sun, and there's an excellent *menú del día* (Mon–Fri; €12.50).

El Pilon c/Can Cifre 4. Vibrant, cramped and crowded *tapas* bar on a side-street off the north

end of Passeig d'es Born serving all manner of Spanish and Mallorcan dishes at very reasonable prices. Bags of atmosphere. Closed Sunday.

S'Impremta c/Morey 2. Amiable neighbourhood café-restaurant with medieval-looking wood-beam ceilings and traditional shuttered windows. The French chef turns out a delicious melon soup, grilled salmon with vegetables and some tempting desserts, and there's also a delicious range of *tapas* plus a great-value *menú del día* for only €8. Open lunchtimes only.

La Taberna del Caracol c/Sant Alonso 2 ☎971 714 908. Great *tapas* and fabulous desserts in a Gothic setting. Closed Sat evening and Sun.

Teteria Ali Baba Avgda Joan Miró 48. Equipped with the traditional low tables and cushions, this Moroccan-style tea-room serves strong mint tea, snacks like hummus and babaganoush, and you can even try a flavoured water pipe (€6.90).

Restaurants

Inexpensive and moderate

Ca'n Carlos c/Aigua 5 ☎971 713 869. Charming, family-run restaurant featuring exquisite Mallorcan cuisine that takes in dishes such as cuttlefish and snails. The menu isn't extensive, but everything is beautifully and imaginatively prepared and there's a daily special as well as a fish of the day. Main courses average around €13. Reservations recommended. Open for lunch and from 8pm; closed Sun.

Casa Eduardo Moll Industria Pesquera 4 ☎971 721 182. Spick-and-span restaurant located upstairs in one of the plain modern buildings beside the fish dock. There's an enjoyable view of the harbour, but the real treat is the fresh fish – a wonderful range, all simply prepared – grilled is best. It's about five minutes' walk west along the harbourfront from Avgda d'Antoni Maura; the fish dock is just before Avgda Argentina. Closed Sun and Mon.

Casa Gallega c/Can Pueyo 6 ☎971 714 377. Long-established place offering quality Galician cuisine, particularly seafood, though the cooking might be a bit heavy for some tastes. There's a downstairs *tapas* bar and a more formal restaurant upstairs. It's just north of Plaça Weyler, down the side street beside the Gran Hotel.

Celler Pagès Off c/Apuntadors at c/Felip Bauza 2 ☎971 726 036. Tiny, inexpensive restaurant with an easy-going family atmosphere serving tradi-

tional Mallorcan food – try the stuffed marrows with homemade mayonnaise on the side, while the roast leg of duck with dried plums and grilled vegetables is delicious. Reserve at weekends. Closed Sun.

Es Baluard Plaça Porta Santa Catalina 9 ☎971 719 609. Located on a handsome square right next to the old fort (*baluard*), with good Mallorcan-style cooking. Reservations recommended.

Es Parlament c/Conquistador 11 ☎971 726 026. All gilt-wood mirrors and chandeliers, this old and polished restaurant specializes in paella. The tasty and reasonably priced *menú del día* is recommended, too. A favourite hangout of local politicians and lawyers. Reserve for dinner. Closed Sun.

Flor de Loto c/Vallseca 7 ☎971 717 778. Specializing in vegetarian and fish dishes, including risottos and curries (€9–13), this delightful new place has a relaxing atmosphere enhanced by discreet world music and the occasional live guitarist. Try the cold yoghurt soup with tiny grilled shrimps (€5.20). Closed Mon.

Forn de Sant Joan c/Sant Joan 4 ☎971 728 422. Set in an old bakery, this smart and extremely popular family-run Catalan restaurant does a range of fine fish dishes (€15–20) and *tapas* (from €6) – try the red peppers stuffed with shellfish, followed by the lemon and cinnamon mousse.

Specialist food and drink shops

Amongst the city's specialist **food shops**, Colmado Santo Domingo, c/Sant Domingo 1, is a tiny, old-fashioned store packed with hanging sausages and local fruit and veg; Colmado Colom, just down the street, is similar; both are in the city centre in the subway adjoining c/Conquistador. In the appealing Santa Catalina quarter, immediately to the west of Avinguda Argentina, La Favorita, c/Pou 33, is a wonderful gourmet boutique carrying every imaginable local delicacy, while Colmado Manresa, just around the corner at c/Fábrica 19, has an equally tempting selection. Palma has lots of good **cake and pastry** shops (*pastelerías*), including Forn des Teatre, Plaça Weyler 9, and the excellent Forn Fondo, c/Unió 15. Many Palma shops and most supermarkets stock a reasonable range of Spanish **wines**, and some also carry Balearic vintages. A central outlet is Vins, Plaça Cort 7, while a couple of kilometres west of the centre off Avgda Andrea Doria is the even better El Centro del Vino y del Cava, c/Bartomeu Rosselló-Porcel 19. The biggest **department store** in the city centre, El Corte Inglés, Avgda Jaume III 15, has a substantial food and drink section in its basement. For details of Palma's **markets**, see p.93.

Mangiafuoco Plaça Vapor 4, Santa Catalina ☎971 451 072. Tuscan-owned restaurant-cum-wine bar offering top-notch Italian food and specializing in dishes featuring truffles, which are flown in weekly from Tuscany. Try the *pappardelle al tartuffo* and prepare to be wowed, especially when it's washed down with one of the superb wines. Best to reserve.
S'Olivera c/Morey 5 ☎971 729 581. Appealing restaurant, with antique bric-a-bric and paintings dotted round the walls. Food includes a first-rate range of *tapas* (around €4 per portion), plus quality Spanish cuisine and a good-value lunchtime *menú del día* (€7.50). Closed Sat evening and all day Sun.
A Thousand and One Nights c/Vallseca 12 ☎971 723 020. Persian cuisine (somewhere between Indian and Middle Eastern) in a charming setting replete with oriental artefacts and prepared with a wide array of spices whose fragrance fills the restaurant. Main courses €13–17. Open evenings only.

Expensive

Aramís c/Montenegro 1 ☎971 725 232. Set in an old stone mansion on a sidestreet off Passeig d'es Born, though the décor inside is smart and minimalist. The menu is imaginative and international – ravioli and pumpkin, wild mushrooms en croute – and there's an unbeatable *menú del día* (€12.50) plus wonderful house red. Reservations always recommended. Closed Sun and Mon.
Asador Tierra Aranda c/Concepció 4, off Avgda Jaume III ☎971 714 256. A high-class and fairly formal carnivore's paradise in an old

mansion: meats either grilled over open fires or roasted in wood-fired ovens, with suckling pig and lamb a speciality. You can also eat in the very pleasant garden. Closed Sun and Mon. It closes for part of the summer, so best to phone ahead to check opening hours.
Caballito del Mar Across the plaza from Sa Llotja at Passeig Sagrera 5 ☎971 721 074. Trim little restaurant with an extensive range of fish to choose – the *daurada amb sal al forn* (sea bream baked in salt) is excellent. A full meal costs about €40. Reservations recommended.
Koldo Royo Passeig Marítim (Avgda Gabriel Roca) 3 ☎971 732 435. Very expensive (count on €70 and up for a meal), but well worth it to experience the outstanding modern Mediterranean creations of the Michelin-starred Basque chef – strawberry gazpacho, chestnut risotto with wild mushrooms, white asparagus with black truffles, and so on. Closed Sun. Reservations a must.
Ses Albergínies c/Rector Vives 2, where it crosses Na Burguesa in Gènova ☎971 404 779. Top-notch gourmet cuisine, and worth a special trip for its elegant nouvelle Mediterranean cuisine, perhaps combined with a visit to the Fundació Miró (see p.96). Bus #4 provides frequent access to Gènova from Palma. Phone for reservations.
Terreno Lounge c/Bellver 8, El Terreny district ☎971 454 787. Luxurious, hacienda-style place with patio, pool, cool hangings and tropical plants – a romantic place for a candlelit dinner. Food is Mallorcan, with international touches. Count on around €40 a head. Reservations recommended.

Nightlife and entertainment

Most of the cafés and *tapas* bars listed above are quite happy just to ply you with drink until midnight or beyond, making the distinction between them and the **bars** we've listed below somewhat artificial. Nonetheless, there is a cluster of lively **late-night bars** – mostly with music as the backdrop rather than the main event – amongst the narrow and ancient side streets backing onto **Plaça Llotja**. Alternatively, a number of more modish bars can be found strung out along **Avinguda Gabriel Roca** in the vicinity of the Jardins La Quarentena, an area of ritzy hotels and apartment blocks which hums at night with fashionable locals, dressed to the nines, hopping from bar to bar.

Clubs (*discotecas*) are not Palma's forte, but there are a few decent ones on Avinguda Gabriel Roca. They're rarely worth investigating until around 1am and entry charges will rush you anything up to €20, depending on the night and what's happening (although entry is sometimes free). The doorstaff often operate an informal dress code of one sort or another – if you want to get in, avoid beach gear and (heaven forbid) white trainers.

Traditionally, Palma has had little to offer in terms of **performing arts**, but matters are on the mend. The grand nineteenth-century Teatre Principal, Plaça Weyler 16 (℡971 725 548), has been resuscitated and now features classical music and opera, whilst the revamped Teatre Municipal, Passeig Mallorca 9B (℡971 739 148), has a more varied programme of contemporary drama, classic films, dance and ballet. Major international pop acts frequently use the Plaça del Toro as a venue, and in summer there's almost always something going on at the Parc de la Mar. Other venues for music and dance in the warm months include the Castell de Bellver, the Fundació Miró and the Auditorium (Passeig Marítim 18, ℡971 734 735). Ask a tourist office for a complete listing of upcoming events.

Late-night bars

Abaco Just off c/Apuntadors at c/Sant Joan 1 ℡971 715 974. Set in a charming Renaissance mansion, this is easily Palma's most unusual bar, with an interior straight out of a Busby Berkeley musical: fruits cascading down its stairway, caged birds hidden amid patio foliage, elegant music and a daily flower bill you could live on for a month. Drinks, as you might imagine, are extremely expensive (cocktails cost as much as €15) but you're never hurried into buying one. It is, however, too sedate to be much fun if you're on the razzle.

Barcelona Jazz Café Club c/Apuntadors 9. Groovy little spot on one of the busiest streets in town, with jazz, blues and Latin sounds.

BED c/Jaume Ferrer 14. Wine bar and chill-out lounge which is popular with twenty- and thirty-something foreign tourists and residents from about 10pm till 1am before they head off to other nightspots.

Escape Plaça Draçana 13. Friendly little place, and always lively, set just off a square that gets busier and prettier every year.

Farándula Passeig Marítim, across from the Club de Mar, ℡971 400 665. This new bar specializes in salsa, sometimes hosting live bands and promising lots of "Latin Chemistry" – things start reacting well after midnight.

Golden Door c/Apuntadors 3. Classic, dimly lit, old-fashioned cocktail lounge.

Gotic Plaça Llotja 4. Tiny bar with a candlelit patio and pavement tables which nudge out across the square, adding a touch of romance.

Latitud c/Felip Bauza 8, off c/Apuntadors. Tiny, upbeat bar, playing jazz, blues and sometimes classical music.

La Lonja c/Llotja de Mar 2. A popular, well-established haunt, with revolving doors and pleasantly old-fashioned decor; the background music caters for (almost) all tastes. There's *tapas* too, and you can sit out in the square right in front of Sa Llotja.

Made in Brazil Avgda Gabriel Roca 27, close to the Jardins La Quarentena. Great Brazilian sounds and cocktails (including the inevitable *caipirinhas*) in a pocket-sized club-cum-bar with alarming tropical decor.

Parc de la Mar Across the lagoon in front of the cathedral. This bar stays busy until at least midnight and stages frequent musical performances and movies.

Clubs

In addition to the places listed below, the **Santa Barbara** area, just south of *Pacha* (see below), is currently known for its chill-out and house music clubs, such as *113* and *Garito*, though the names and exact musical styles change from season to season.

Pacha Avgda Gabriel Roca 42 ☎971 455 908. Loud, popular and raucous housey disco with a dance floor and a couple of bars inside and another bar outside in the garden. A ten-minute walk west of the Jardins La Quarentena, and 800m east of the ferry terminal. There's generally a gay night, "Pacha Loca", at least once a week, usually Sunday. Entrance (usually) €15.

Tito's Plaça Gomila 3 ☎971 730 017. With its stainless steel and glass exterior, this long-established nightspot looks a bit like something from a sci-fi film. Outdoor lifts carry you up from Avgda Gabriel Roca (the back entrance) to the dance floor, which pulls in huge crowds from many countries – or you can go in through the front entrance on Plaça Gomila. The music (anything from house to mainstream pop) lacks conviction, but it's certainly loud. The Avgda Gabriel Roca entrance is just on the city centre side of the Jardins La Quarentena. Admission €18.

Gay and lesbian Palma

The suburb of **El Terreny**, also west of the centre, below the Castell de Bellver, is the focus of the city's **gay** life, with two rainbow-flagged hotels, a gay-owned-and-operated restaurant and a decent selection of gay and lesbian bars. Ben Amics ("Good Friends") operates an info line (☎971 777 500; 7pm–9pm); alternatively, stop by the centre, which is on the first floor at c/Impremta 1, or call them on ☎971 715 670.

Hotel and restaurant

La Casita Avgda Joan Miró 68 ☎971 737 557. Delightful gay-owned and -managed little restaurant appealingly decorated in soft tones and offering an interesting menu of Mediterranean and French dishes.

Rosamar Hotel & Bar Avgda Joan Miró 74 ☎971 732 723. A friendly gathering place for an international array of men and a few women, this basic hotel also features an appealing terrace bar that fills up in warm weather. Ask for a room with a balcony that overlooks the terrace – or just come by for a drink. ❸

Bars and clubs

Café Lorca c/Federico Garcia Lorca 21. Located at the downtown end of the main gay strip, this café gets busy around 10pm and buzzes until about 1am, when everyone troops off to their favourite discos.

Isidoro c/D'Alvaro Debazan 2. Just off Avgda Joan Miró, this arty bar is the main lesbian venue in town, adorned with interesting paintings and patronized by a mainly local crowd.

Marcus Avgda Joan Miró 54. Recently done up with moody décor and a new dark room.

Pacha Avgda Gabriel Roca 42 ☎971 455 908. This popular disco (see above) hosts a gay night, "Pacha Loca", at least once a week, usually Sunday. Entrance (usually) €15.

Papillon Avgda Joan Miró 73. This downstairs venue is usually packed from about 11pm on thanks to its pleasantly cruisy atmosphere and the fact that it's free, with no pressure to buy a drink.

Shopping

Palma has an interesting range of specialist shops. For **souvenirs**, head to La Concha, c/Jaume II 19, which stocks brightly coloured Spanish fans, olive-wood trinkets, garish Spanish plates, model cherubs, mini-gigantones (carnival figures) and *siurells*. The latter are white clay whistles flecked with red and green paint and shaped to depict a figure, an animal or a scene (a man sitting on a donkey, for instance) – cheap and cheerful gifts which have been given as tokens of friendship in Mallorca for hundreds of years. **Glass-making** is a traditional island craft (see p.177). Vidrias Gordiola, c/Victoria 2, near the Ajuntament, has a fine range of clear and tinted glassware, from bowls, vases and lanterns through to some wonderfully intricate chandeliers. The old-fashioned La Casa del Olivo, on c/Pescateria Vella, a tiny alley off c/Jaume II, is an Aladdin's cave of **olive-wood carvings**, with everything from spoons, bread boards and salad bowls to more eccentric-looking items. **Artificial pearls** are made at Manacor (see p.183) by Majorica, who have dozens of official agents in Palma, as well as their own outlet at Avgda Jaume III 11. Mallorca is renowned for its unique style of fine, handmade **embroidery**. Check it out at lovely Casa Bonet at Plaça Federic Chopin 2, near Plaça Cort. For pottery and other handmade wares from around the island (including olive wood products, clay whistles, glassware and wrought-iron items), head for Fet a Mà, c/Sant Miquel 52. For **antique books** and a few authentic **vintage posters** at great prices, visit musty El Bazar del Libro, c/Sant Crist 4, just to the side of Santa Eulalia church. Finally, **art** of all types abounds; just one of the many tiny galleries you'll see is ArteFacto, c/Sant Pere 8, featuring whimsical works by neighbourhood artists. The ritziest **clothes** stores are concentrated on and around Avgda Jaume III; Loewe, at no. 1, is one of the most chic shops in Spain.

For **books and maps**, El Corte Inglés, Avgda Jaume III 15, sells a small and rather eccentric assortment of English-language books from Ken Follett to Anne Frank, and also has a modest selection of Mallorca guidebooks and maps. Librería Fondevila, near the Teatre Principal at Costa de Sa Pols 18, has a fairly good selection of general maps of Mallorca, plus a reasonably comprehensive selection of IGN hiking maps. Palma's one specialist map shop, the Casa del Mapa, c/Sant Domingo 11, has a good selection of IGN hiking maps as well as various maps of the island and Palma.

Listings

Airlines Air Europa ☎ 902 401 501; British Airways ☎ 971 787 737; Bmibaby ☎ 971 453 112; EasyJet ☎ 902 299 992; Iberia ☎ 902 400 500; Spanair-SAS ☎ 902 131 415.

Airport information ☎ 971 789 000.

Banks and exchange There are plenty of banks on and around the Passeig d'es Born and Avgda Jaume III. Banco de Crédito Balear has branches at Avgda Jaume III 27 and Plaça Espanya 1; Banca March at Plaça Rei Joan Carles I 5 and c/Sant Miquel 30; Banco Santander at c/Jaume II 18 and c/Bonaire 4. The two biggest savings banks, which also handle currency exchange, have branches all over the city. La Caixa has a handy downtown branch at Passeig d'es Born 23; for Sa Nostra go to Avgda Jaume III 18. ATMs are commonplace.

Beaches The closest beach to the city centre is the narrow strip of sand next to the *autopista* just beyond Avgda Gabriel Alomar i Villalonga. Swimming is not, however, recommended here as the water is too polluted. Instead most locals make the half-hour trip on bus #15 east to the Platja de Palma (see p.94).

Bike shops Bimont, Plaça Progrés 19 (☎ 971 731 866), runs a bicycle repair service, but bicycle rental is not possible anywhere in the city.

Bullfights Palma's bullfighting ring, Plaça de Toros (☎ 971 755 245), is a few blocks northeast of the

Plaça Espanya along c/Reina Maria Cristina. You can get tickets and details from travel agents and hotel receptions.

Buses Details of all major Mallorcan bus services are available from all the city's tourist offices (see p.61). For information on EMT city buses, call ☎971 214 444 (press 1 after the pre-recorded message in Catalan, and you'll get an operator who might speak a bit of English) or visit the kiosk on Plaça Espanya. Information on buses island-wide is available on ☎971 177 777 (in Spanish and Catalan).

Car rental Mallorca's airport heaves with car rental companies, as does Palma – there's a concentration of both large and small companies along Avgda Gabriel Roca. Amongst the big companies, there are branches of Atesa-National at Avgda Gabriel Roca 25 ☎971 456 762 (at the airport ☎971 789 896); Avis, Avgda Gabriel Roca 16 ☎971 730 720 (airport ☎971 789 187); Betacar-Europcar, Avgda Gabriel Roca 20 ☎971 455 200 (airport ☎971 789 135); and Hertz, Avgda Gabriel Roca 13 ☎971 734 737 (airport ☎971 789 670). The tourist office can supply a complete list.

Cinema Teatro Cine Rialto, c/Sant Feliu 3, presents mainstream Spanish films plus international blockbusters, usually dubbed.

Consulates Ireland, c/Sant Miquel 68A ☎971 719 244; UK, Plaça Major 3 ☎971 712 445; US, Avgda Jaume III 26 ☎971 725 051.

Doctors and dentists In the resort areas and in Palma most hotel receptions will be able to find an English-speaking doctor or dentist. For complete lists look under *metges* (Castilian *médicos*) or *clíniques dentals* (*clínicas dentales*) in the Yellow Pages.

Email and Internet *La Red* cybercafé, c/Concepció 5, just off Avgda Jaume III (Mon–Fri 11am–1am, Sat & Sun 4pm–midnight; €3-4 per hour) has fifteen PCs plus fax machines, scanners and snacks and drinks. The more central *Cyber Central*, c/Soledad 4, in the heart of the old city (daily 9am–10pm; €2.50 per hour), is also proficient.

Emergencies ☎112.

Ferries and catamarans Palma's tourist offices have ferry and catamaran schedules and tariffs. Tickets can be purchased either at travel agents or direct from the two ferry companies concerned.

These are Trasmediterranea (☎902 454 645, ⓦ www.trasmediterranea.es) and Balearia (☎902 160 180, ⓦ www.balearia.net/eng). They both have offices down at the ferry port, about 3.5km west of the city centre along Avgda Gabriel Roca. Trasmediterranea are at Terminal 2, Balearia at Terminal 3, a couple of minutes' walk away. For ferries from mainland Spain and Ibiza, see p.16. Trasmediterranea operate the only car ferry service from Palma to Menorca (Maó).

Hospital Policlinica Miramar ☎971 767 500 and Clinica Juaneda ☎971 222 222.

Laundry There's a downtown self-service laundry, Lavandería Self Press, at c/Anníbal 14, off Avgda Argentina.

Libraries There's a quaint municipal library inside the Ajuntament (Town Hall) on Plaça Cort (Mon–Fri 8.30am–8.30pm, Sat 9am–1pm).

Markets Palma's big Rastrillo (flea market) is held every Saturday morning (8am–2pm) on Avgda Gabriel Alomar i Villalonga, between Plaça Porta d'es Camp and c/Manacor. There's a fresh fruit and vegetable market on Plaça Navegació, just west of Avgda Argentina (Mon–Sat 7am–2pm); and a daily flower market on Passeig de la Rambla.

Moped rental Mopeds and scooters can be rented from RTR Rental, Avgda Joan Miró 340 (☎971 702 775).

Pharmacies Central pharmacies include Farmacia Castañer, Plaça Rei Joan Carles I 3; Farmacia Llobera, Plaça Santa Eulalia 1; and Farmacia A Nadal, Plaça Cort 1. A full list of pharmacies is in the Yellow Pages under *farmàcies* (Castilian *farmacias*).

Post office The central *correu* is at c/Constitució 5 (Mon–Fri 8.30am–8.30pm, Sat 9.30am–2pm).

Trains The tourist office has train timetables or you can phone direct: Palma to Manacor and Sa Pobla on ☎971 177 777; Palma to Sóller on ☎971 752 051.

Travel agencies There are dozens of travel agencies in Palma, listed in full in the Yellow Pages under *agències de viatges* (Castilian, *agencias de viajes*). Two helpful downtown choices are Viajes Iberia, Passeig d'es Born 14 ☎971 726 743, and Mallorca Tours, Sant Miquel 50 ☎971 722 606. There's also a good travel agent at El Corte Inglés (see p.81).

Around Palma

Strewn around the sheltered waters of the **Badia de Palma** are the package tourist resorts that have made Mallorca synonymous with the cheap and tacky. In recent years the Balearic government have done their best to improve matters – greening resorts, restricting high-rise construction and redirecting traffic away from the coast – but their inherited problems remain. In the 1960s and 1970s, the bay experienced a building boom of almost unimaginable proportions as miles of pristine shoreline sprouted concrete and glass hotel towers, overwhelming the area's farms and fishing villages. There were few planning controls, if any, and the legacy is the mammoth sprawl of development that now extends, almost without interruption, from **S'Arenal** in the east to **Magaluf** in the west – with Palma roughly in the middle. To make matters worse, it is also debatable as to whether the recent move away from high-rise construction is well-conceived. The new villa complexes that are now the fashion gobble up the land at an alarming rate and multiply traffic. Furthermore, although the new villas are rarely more than three storeys high and built in a sort of pan-Mediterranean style – some with Neoclassical features, others more reminiscent of Spanish design – they end up looking terribly, remorselessly suburban. As a consequence, although the thirty-kilometre-long stretch of coast between S'Arenal and Magaluf is divided into a score or more resorts, it's often impossible to pick out where one ends and the next begins. That said, most of the resorts have evolved their own identities, either in terms of the nationalities they attract, the income group they appeal to, or the age range they cater for.

East of Palma lies **S'Arenal**, mainly geared up for young German tourists, with dozens of pounding bars and all-night clubs. S'Arenal also fringes one of Mallorca's best **beaches**, the **Platja de Palma**, which stretches from S'Arenal round to **Ca'n Pastilla**, but although the beach is superb, the flat shoreline behind it accommodates an unprepossessing, seemingly endless strip of restaurants, bars and souvenir shops.

West of Palma, the coast bubbles up into the low, rocky hills and sharp coves that prefigure the mountains further west. The sandy beaches here are far smaller – and some are actually artificial – but the terrain makes the tourist development seem less oppressive. **Cala Major**, the first stop, was once the playground of the jetset. It's hit grittier times, but some of the grand old buildings have survived and the **Fundació Pilar i Joan Miró**, which exhibits a fine selection of Miró's work in what was once his home and studio, makes a fascinating detour. The neighbouring resort of **Illetes** is a good deal more polished, boasting comfortable hotels and attractive cove beaches, while, moving west again, **Portals Nous** has an affluent and exclusive air born of its swanky marina. Next comes British-dominated **Palma Nova**, a major package holiday destination popular with all ages, and the adjacent **Magaluf**, where modern high-rise hotels, thumping nightlife and a substantial sandy beach cater to a youthful and very British crowd. South of Magaluf, the charming cove beach of **Portals Vells** is a real surprise, sheltered by an undeveloped, pine-studded peninsula. West of Magaluf, the coastal highway leaves the Badia de Palma for unpretentious **Santa Ponça** before pushing on to **Peguera**, a large, sprawling resort with attractive sandy beaches and a relaxed family atmosphere. Next door – and much more endearing – is tiny **Cala Fornells**, where pretty villas thread along the coastal hills and a pair of first-rate hotels overlook a wooded cove (and concrete-slab beaches). From here, it's another short hop to the good-looking bay which encloses the burgeoning resort of **Camp de Mar**.

Practicalities

Although these resorts boast hundreds of **hotels**, *hostals* and apartment buildings, nearly all are block-booked by the package tourist industry from May or

June through to September or October, with frugal pickings for the independent traveller. We've selected some of the more interesting and enjoyable package hotels, as well as picking out several relatively inexpensive places where there's a reasonable chance of finding a vacancy independently in high season. Two smallish resorts on this coast where the tourist development is not too oppressive are Illetes and Cala Fornells; the former has its own sandy beaches, though they are small, while the latter is within easy reach of the fine beaches of Peguera. Swimming is particularly good at both. Out of season, many places simply close down, but at those which remain open, it's well worth haggling over the price.

We haven't highlighted resort **nightlife** at all, since the liveliest discos and clubs are, as a general rule, concentrated in the tackier spots. This coast also has hundreds of **restaurants** and cafés, but the choice is not as diverse as you might expect, and for the most part standards are not very high: the vast majority of places serve either low-price pizzas and pastas or a sort of pan-European tourist menu.

Transport

Public **transport** along the coast is fast and efficient, with most services starting from Palma's Plaça Espanya. **EMT** bus #15 travels the old coastal road east through Ca'n Pastilla to S'Arenal; bus #21 heads west as far as Palma Nova; and bus #3 runs through Cala Major to Illetes. In addition, the **TransaBús** bus company operates the "Playasol" routes, with frequent buses from Plaça Espanya, Plaça Rei Joan Carles I and other Palma city centre points west to Magaluf, Santa Ponça, Peguera and Camp de Mar. For frequencies and journey times, see p.102.

Driving is straightforward: the *autopista* shoots along the coast from S'Arenal right round to Palma Nova and then slices across a narrow peninsula to reach Santa Ponça and Peguera. Alternatively, you can take the much slower old coastal road (numbered the C719 west of Palma), which meanders through most of the resorts.

East of Palma

The *autopista* rushes **east** out of Palma with tourist resorts on one side and the **airport** on the other. The flatlands backing onto the coast were once prime agricultural land whose pastoral days are recalled by the ruined windmills – built to pump water out of the marshy topsoil – that lie scattered over the landscape. The alternative route, along the old coastal road, is a bit more interesting and a lot slower; take the turning off the *autopista* just beyond the city walls (signposted to Ca'n Pastilla) which tracks through the gritty suburb of Es Molinar en route to **CALA GAMBA**, an unassuming little place with a pleasant horseshoe-shaped harbour. Close by, **CA'N PASTILLA** is the first substantial tourist resort on this part of the coast, its fifty-odd hotels and apartment buildings set in a rough rectangle of land pushed tight against the seashore. The place is short on charm and certainly too close to the airport for sonic comfort, but it does herald the start of the fine Platja de Palma beach.

Sometimes, Les Meravelles and S'Arenal

The **Platja de Palma**, the four-kilometre stretch of sandy beach that defines the three coterminous (and indistinguishable) resorts of **SOMETIMES**, **LES MERAVELLES** and **S'ARENAL**, is crowded with serious sun-seekers, a sweating throng of bronzed and oiled bodies slowly roasting in the heat. The beach is also a busy pick-up place, the spot for a touch of verbal foreplay before the night-time bingeing begins. It is, as they say, fine if you like that sort of thing – though older visitors look rather marooned. A wide and pleasant walkway lined with palm trees runs behind the beach and this, in turn, is edged by a long sequence of bars, restaurants and souvenir shops. A toy-town tourist "train" shuttles up and down the walkway, but there's so little to distinguish one part of the beach from another that it's easy to become disoriented. To maintain your bearings, keep an eye out for the series of smart, stainless-steel beach bars, each numbered and labelled, in Castilian, "*balneario*", strung along the shore: Balneario no. 15 is by the Ca'n Pastilla marina, while no. 1 is near S'Arenal harbour.

Singling out any part of this massive complex is a pretty pointless exercise, but the area around S'Arenal harbour does at least have a concentration of **facilities**. There's car rental, currency exchange, boat trips and nightclubs, and you can eat well at the lively terrace bar of the harbourside *Club Nàutico*, where the paella is delicious. S'Arenal also boasts **Aquacity** (May–Oct daily 10am–5pm; closed Sat in Oct; €16), a huge leisure complex of swimming pools, water flumes and kiddies' playgrounds. It's between the *autopista* and the eastern edge of the resort, about 15km east of Palma.

Accommodation

All three resorts extend a few blocks inland and encompass dozens of **places to stay**. The cheapest accommodation is provided by the **youth hostel**, the *Playa de Palma*, at c/Costa Brava 13 in Sometimes (☏971 260 892; €12.50–15.60 per person), which has four-bed dorms with en-suite bathrooms). It's a 25-minute journey on EMT bus #15 from Palma's Plaça Reina or Plaça Espanya; ask to be put off at the giant *Hotel Iberostar Royal Cristina Aparthotel* on the main road. The hostel is a couple of hundred metres further along the road on the left, a couple of minutes' walk from Balneario no. 9. It's fairly clean but has only 65 beds, so advance reservations are strongly recommended. It should be open all year, but sometimes closes for a month or two in the winter.

At the other end of the market, the four-star **hotel** *Iberostar Royal Cristina Aparthotel*, on Arenas de Bilbao (☏971 492 211, ⊛www.iberostar.com; ❻), offers luxury rooms and apartments, although it doesn't overlook the beach. Another mid-range option is the three-star *Royal Cupido*, a bright, modern 200-room hotel which backs onto the beach a couple of minutes' walk west of the *Royal Cristina* at c/Marbella 32 (☏971 264 300, ℉971 265 510; ❼).

West from Palma to Cala Major

Crowded **CALA MAJOR** snakes along a hilly stretch of coastline a kilometre or two **west** of Palma's ferry port. Overlooking the main street (which comprises a section of the C719 coast road), occasional *Modernista* mansions and the luxurious *Nixe Hotel* are reminders of halcyon days when the resort was a byword for elegance. The king of Spain still runs a palace here – the Palacio de Marivent, on the main street close to the *autopista* at the east end of the resort.

The Fundació Pilar i Joan Miró

Opposite the Palacio de Marivent, a turning signposted to Gènova leads up the hill for 500m to the **Fundació Pilar i Joan Miró** (Tues–Sat 10am–7pm, Sun 10am–3pm; mid-Sept to mid-May Tues–Sat closes 6pm; €4), where the painter

Joan Miró lived and worked for much of the 1950s, 1960s and 1970s. The Fundació is at c/Joan de Saridakis 29; EMT bus #4 passes every twenty minutes on its way between Palma's Plaça Espanya and Gènova.

Initially – from 1920 – the young Miró was involved with the Surrealists in Paris and contributed to all their major exhibitions: his wild squiggles, supercharged with bright colours, prompted André Breton, the leading theorist of the movement, to describe Miró as "the most Surrealist of us all". In the 1930s he adopted a simpler style, abandoning the decorative complexity of his earlier work for a more minimalist use of symbols, though the highly coloured forms remained. Miró returned to Barcelona, the city of his birth, in 1940, where he continued to work in the Surrealist tradition, though as an avowed opponent of Franco his position was uneasy. In 1957 he moved to Mallorca, its relative isolation offering a degree of safety. His wife and mother were both Mallorcan, which must have influenced his decision, as did the chance to work in his own purpose-built studio with its view of the coast. Even from the relative isolation of Franco's Spain he remained an influential figure, prepared to experiment with all kinds of media, right up until his death in Cala Major in 1983.

The expansive hillside premises of the Fundació include Miró's old **studio**, an unassuming affair with views over the bay that has been left pretty much as it was at the time of his death. It's worth a quick gander for a flavour of how the man worked – tackling a dozen or so canvases at the same time – but unfortunately you're only allowed to peer through the windows. Opposite are the angular lines of the bright-white art gallery, the **Edificio Estrella**, which displays a rotating and representative sample of the prolific artist's work. Miró was nothing if not productive, and the Fundació holds 134 paintings, 300 engravings and 105 drawings, as well as sculptures, gouaches and preliminary sketches – more than six thousand works in all. There are no guarantees as to what will be on display, but you're likely to see a decent selection of his paintings, the familiar dream-like squiggles and half-recognizable shapes that are intended to conjure up the unconscious, with free play often given to erotic associations. The gallery also stores a comprehensive collection of Miró documents and occasionally hosts exhibitions.

Illetes

Well-heeled **ILLETES** (sometimes written Illetas), just along the coast from Cala Major and 7km west of Palma, comprises a ribbon of restaurants, hotels and apartment buildings which bestride the steep hills that rise high above the rocky shoreline. There's precious little space left, but at least the generally low-rise buildings are of manageable proportions. A string of tiny cove beaches punctuates the coast, the most attractive being the pine-shaded **Platja Cala Comtesa**, at the southern end of the resort, alongside a military zone.

The long main street, Passeig d'Illetes, runs past several good **hotels**. The most enjoyable is the *Bon Sol*, about halfway along (☎971 402 111, ⊛www.ila-chateau.com/bon_sol; ❽), which tumbles down the cliffs to the seashore and its own artificial beach. A family-run concern, the hotel has all the conveniences you could want and the better rooms have fine views out over the bay. Its clientele is staid and steady, befitting the antique-crammed interior. Another good choice is the *Gran Hotel Albatros*, located near the north end of Passeig d'Illetes (☎971 402 211, ⊛www.barcelo.com; half board only, ❻); rooms here have balconies and air conditioning and there's a swimming pool and private beach. There are similar facilities at the luxurious, five-star *Hotel Melià de Mar* (☎971 402 511, ⊛www.melia-hotels-mallorca.com; breakfast included, ❾), which overlooks the seashore close to the *Bon Sol*, while equally spacious lodging is to be found a couple of minutes' walk south along the coast at the attractive *Hotel-residencia Illetas* (☎971 402 411, ℱ971 401 808; ❻, breakfast included). Most visitors eat in their hotels, but there's a smattering of smart **cafés** on the main drag, including *Es Parral* towards the south end of the resort (☎971 701 127), which serves Mallorcan cuisine.

Bendinat and Portals Nous

The C719 avoids Illetes but cuts through the peripheries of **BENDINAT**, a couple of kilometres further along the coast. On the south side of the road, the resort's leafy streets meander down to the seashore, lined by the villas of the well-to-do. It's a pretty spot, and tucked away on a quiet, rocky cove is the charming *Hotel Bendinat*, c/Rossegada (☎971 675 725, ⓦwww .hotelbendinat.es; ❾), dating from the 1950s and built in the traditional *hacienda* style, with a beautiful arcaded terrace overlooking the sea. You can stay either in the main building, where most of the bedrooms have balconies, or in one of the trim, whitewashed bungalows that dot the gardens.

On its west side, Bendinat merges with the larger **PORTALS NOUS**, another ritzy settlement where polished mansions fill out the green and hilly terrain abutting the coast. There's a tiny beach too, set beneath the cliffs and reached via a flight of steps at the foot of c/Passatge del Mar. In contrast to the studied elegance of the side streets, the resort's main drag (also the C719) is disappointingly drab, though it does lead to the glitzy **marina**, one of Mallorca's most exclusive, where the boats look more like ocean liners than pleasure yachts – it's a favoured hang-out for the king and his cronies. Close by, **Marineland** is one of the tackiest but most popular attractions on the island, with shark tanks and a tropical fish aquarium, as well as exploitative dolphin, sealion and parrot shows (daily: April–Sept 9.30am–6pm; Jan–March & Oct to mid-Nov 9.30am–5pm; €14). Kids love the place; adults mostly suffer in silence.

Portals Nous has few **hotels** – much of the shoreline is occupied by private villas and apartments – and the best local accommodation is outside the resort in the direction of Andratx at the luxurious *Hotel Punta Negra Resort*, Ctra Andratx, km 12, Costa d'en Blanes (☎971 680 762, ⓦwww .hotelpuntanegra.com; ❻, including breakfast), set on two rugged, unspoilt coves with crystal clear water. The best **restaurant** is *Flanigan* (☎971 676 117; from €30 per head), which has nautical decor and international fusion cuisine with the emphasis on seafood. Seating is either in plush rooms inside or on the marina-facing terrace. Other choices include the very superior *Tristan's*, boasting two Michelin stars (count on around €100 per person) and the much more affordable *Ritzi's* (☎971 684 104), with excellent Italian cuisine, and *Dahini* (open evenings only; ☎971 676 025), which does good Japanese fare.

Palma Nova and Calvià

Old Mallorca hands claim that **PALMA NOVA**, 4km west of Portals Nous, was once a beauty spot, and certainly its wide and shallow bay, with good beaches among a string of bumpy headlands, still has its moments. But for the most part, the bay has been engulfed by a broad, congested sweep of hotels and tourist facilities. With the development comes a vigorous **nightlife** and a plethora of accommodation options on or near the seashore – though, as elsewhere, most are block-booked by tour operators throughout the season.

Amongst the resort's many **hotels**, recommendable places include the *Hotel Playa Comodoro*, Passeig Cala Blanca 9 (☎971 682 061, ⓦwww.bqhoteles.com; ❻, including breakfast), a standard-issue high-rise with balconied double rooms looking out over the bay; and the slightly more luxurious *Hotel Delfín Playa* (☎971 680 100, ⓔdelfin.hotels@atlas-iap.es; ❻, including breakfast), which faces the beach at the centre of the resort from behind Passeig de la Mar. A third option is the giant *Hotel Sol Mirlos*, a five-minute walk from the beach on c/Pinzones (☎971 681 900, ⓦwww.iespana.es/calvianet; ❻, including breakfast).

Some 6km north of Palma Nova, tucked away in the hills behind the coast, is the tiny town of **CALVIÀ**, the region's administrative centre – hence the oversized town hall, paid for by the profits of the tourist industry. The parish church of **Sant Joan Baptista** (daily 10am–1pm), dating from 1245, dominates the town, though the building's Gothic subtleties mostly disappeared during a nineteenth-century refurbishment that left a crude bas-relief carving of the Garden of Gethsemane above the main door. There are pleasant views across the surrounding countryside from the church, and the adjacent square is home to a modern mural showing a rather neat depiction of the island's history. Opposite the square, *Bar Bauza* serves *bocadillos*, coffee and pastries, either inside or in the picturesque courtyard, while just down the hill the excellent *Méson Ca'n Torrat* (☎971 670 682; dinner only in summer, closed Tues) specializes in roast legs of lamb and suckling pig. EMT **bus** #20 runs from Palma through Palma Nova to Calvià nine or ten times daily.

From Calvià, it's a short drive west to **Capdellà** and the **Serra de Tramuntana**, covered in Chapter 2.

Magaluf and around

Torrenova, on the chunky headland at the far end of Palma Nova, is a cramped and untidy development that slides into **MAGALUF**, whose high-rise towers march across the next bay down the coast. For years a bargain-basement package holiday destination, Magaluf finally lost patience with its youthful British visitors in 1996. The local authorities won a court order allowing them to demolish twenty downmarket hotels in an attempt to end – or at least control – the annual binge of "violence, drunkenness and open-air sex" that, they argued, characterized the resort. The high-rise hotels were duly dynamited and an extensive clean-up programme subsequently freshened up the resort's appearance. However, short of demolishing the whole lot, there's not too much anyone can do with the deadening concrete of the modern town centre – and the demolished blocks will anyway be replaced, albeit by more upmarket hotels. These draconian measures have brought some improvement, but the resort's British visitors remain steadfastly determined to create, or at least patronize, a bizarre caricature of their homeland: it's all here, from beans-on-toast with Marmite to pubs like *Tom Brown's Chicken & Steak Inn*.

Stuck on the western edge of Magaluf, **Aquapark** (daily: June–Sept 10am–5pm; May & Oct 1pm–5pm; €15) is a giant-sized water park with swimming pools, water chutes and flumes which rivals S'Arenal's Aquacity – like Aquacity, it's immensely popular, drawing kids in their hundreds. Across the road is a second theme park, **Western Park: Crazy Wet West** (or simply "Wild West Park"; 9.30am–7pm; €14). The main event here is a replica Wild West town – one of the most incongruous sights in Spain – as well as a water-park, with all the Wild West clichés.

In the unlikely event that you want to find a room in Magaluf, you can get a free map giving the location of all the resort's hotels at the seasonal **tourist office**, on the square one block back from the beach at Avinguda Pere Vaquer Ramis 1 (June–Aug Mon–Fri 9am–1pm & 3–5pm; ☎971 131 126).

South to Portals Vells

Things pick up beyond Magaluf: the eastern reaches of the pine-clad peninsula that extends south of the resort have been barely touched by the developers. In consequence, however, there aren't any **buses** beyond Magaluf, so you'll have to drive, walk or cycle.

The clearly signposted road south to Portals Vells begins on the west side of Magaluf, where the *autopista* merges into the C719. After about 1.5km, the road cuts past the Aquapark theme park and then keeps straight at a fork where the road to Santa Ponça curves off to the right. South of the fork, the road narrows into a country lane, passing a golf course before heading off into the woods. After about 4km, a steep turning on the left leads down 1km to **Cala Mago** (still signposted in Castilian as Playa El Mago), where a rocky little headland with a shattered guard house has lovely beaches to either side. Park and walk down to whichever cove takes your fancy: the **nudist beach** on the right with its smart café-restaurant, or the delightful pine-shaded strand on the left with its beach bar, tiny port and sprinkling of villas. Both provide sunbeds and showers.

Continuing a further 600m past the Cala Mago turning, a second side road cuts for a kilometre down to the cove beach of **PORTALS VELLS**. Despite a bar-restaurant and a handful of villas, it remains a pleasant, pine-scented spot of glistening sand, rocky cliffs and clear blue water, especially appealing early in the morning before it gets crowded. Clearly visible from the beach are the **caves** of the headland on the south side of the cove. A footpath leads to the most interesting, an old cave church where the holy-water stoup and altar have been cut out of the solid rock – the work of shipwrecked Genoese seamen, according to local legend.

Beyond the Portals Vells turning, the road continues south for 1.5km as far as a broken-down barbed-wire fence at the start of a disused military zone. You can't drive any further and you're not supposed to walk beyond the fence either, but some people do, braving the no-entry signs to scramble through the pine woods and out along the headland for about 1.5km to reach the solitary **Cap de Cala Figuera** lighthouse.

Santa Ponça and around

West of Magaluf, the C719 trims the outskirts of **SANTA PONÇA**, one of the less endearing of the resorts that punctuate this stretch of coast. Mostly a product of the 1980s, this sprawling conurbation has abandoned the concrete high-rises of yesteryear for a pseudo-vernacular architecture that's littered the hills with scores of tedious villas. That said, the setting is magnificent, with rolling green hills flanking a broad bay, whose spacious white sandy beaches offer safe bathing, and there's good-value family-oriented accommodation at the comfortable and inviting *Hotel Playas del Rey*, Via Jaime I 76 (℡971 691 213, ℻971 699 642; Ⓦwww.playasdelray.com; ❺, breakfast included), located just a few steps from the beach. There's good **food** just across the street at *Sa Terrassa*, Avgda Rey Jaime I 97, (℡971 692 964), which has fresh, homemade Mexican dishes, a big menu of local dishes, plus great terrace views over the whole bay. If you want to go **diving**, Zoea Mallorca, at the Club Náutico Santa Ponsa, Via de la Cruz s/n (℡971 691 444, Ⓦwww.zoeamallorca.com) organizes dives and courses for all levels.

Peguera and Cala Fornells

Sprawling **PEGUERA**, about 6km north of Santa Ponça, is strung out along a lengthy, partly pedestrianized main street – the Avinguda de Peguera – immediately behind several generous sandy beaches. There's nothing remarkable about the place, but it does have an easy-going air and is a favourite with families and older visitors. The C719 loops right round Peguera and the easiest approach, if you're just after the beach, is from the west. Head into the resort along the main street and park anywhere you can before you reach the pedestrianized part of the Avinguda de Peguera, where the town's baffling one-way system sends you weaving through the resort's side streets – best avoided, if you can.

The two signed turnings that lead to the neighbouring (and much prettier) resort of **CALA FORNELLS** are also reached along the main street on the west side of Peguera. The first turning is on the edge of Peguera, the second is at the Casa Pepe supermarket. Take the second turning and the road climbs up to a string of chic, *pueblo*-style houses that perch on the sea cliffs and trail round to the tiny centre of the resort, where a wooded cove is set around a minuscule beach and concreted sunbathing slabs. Although Cala Fornells tends to be over-crowded during the daytime, at night the tranquillity returns, and it makes a good base for a holiday. You can also stroll out into the surrounding woods along a wide, dirt track which runs up behind the hotels, cutting across the pine-scented hills towards the stony cove beach of **Caló d'es Monjo**, 1.5km to the west.

Cala Fornells has two fetching **hotels**, both behind the beach at the end of the access roads: the sprucely modern, four-star *Coronado* (☎971 686 800, ⓦwww.hotelcoronado.com; ❻; closed Nov & Dec), where all 140 bedrooms have sea views and balconies; and the more sympathetic, green-shuttered and white-painted *Cala Fornells* (☎971 686 950, ⓦwww.calafornells.com; ❻, including breakfast). If your wallet won't stretch to either of these, Peguera has plenty of bargain-basement *hostals* (❷–❸) in the characterless side streets sloping up from the seafront. Peguera's seasonal **tourist office** at the east end of the resort, Avinguda de Peguera 76 (Mon–Sat 9am–1pm & 3–5pm; ☎971 687 083), issues comprehensive accommodation lists as well as local maps giving the location of all the resort's hotels.

Peguera has dozens of bright, inexpensive **cafés** and **restaurants**, from pizza joints through to seafood places. The best spot in town is *La Gran Tortuga* (☎971 686 023; closed Mon), which overlooks the seashore on the road from the Casa Pepe supermarket to Cala Fornells. It serves superb seafood, has a terrace bar and even boasts its own swimming pool. A three-course evening meal will set you back about €35, but you can enjoy its excellent lunches for much less.

Camp de Mar

Tucked away among the hills 3km west of Peguera, **CAMP DE MAR** has an expansive beach and fine bathing, though the scene is marred by the presence of two thumping great **hotels** dropped right on the seashore – the *Hotel Playa*, a British favourite, and the smarter, four-star *Club Camp de Mar*, which caters mainly to Germans. Both are modern high-rises equipped with spacious, balconied bedrooms, and both can be booked only through packaging agents – which gives you a clear idea of what this resort is like. It's also in the middle of a massive expansion, with brand-new villa complexes now trailing back from the beach in an all-too-familiar semi-suburban sprawl. All the same, the beach is an amiable spot to soak up the sun, and it's hard to resist the eccentric café stuck out in the bay and approached via a rickety walkway on stilts; or try the *Bar La Siesta*, overlooking the beach, for romantic sunsets and wonderful paellas.

A minor road twists west from Camp de Mar over wooded hills to **Port d'Andratx** (see p.137).

Travel details

Local buses

EMT buses from Palma to: the airport (#1; every 15min; 25min); Cala Major (#3; every 10min; 15min); Gènova (#4; every 20min; 30min); Illetes (#3; every 10min; 20min); Palma Nova (#20; every 30min; 30min); Portals Nous (#20; every 30min; 25min); S'Arenal (#15; every 10min; 30min).

TransaBús from Palma (Plaça Porta des Camp and Plaça Reina) to: Andratx (hourly; 45min); Camp de Mar (hourly; 40min); Magaluf (May–Oct 22 daily; Nov–April 11 daily; 25min); Palma Nova (May–Oct 22 daily; Nov–April 11 daily; 20min); Peguera (May–Oct hourly; Nov–April Mon–Fri 12 daily, Sat & Sun 6 daily; 35min); Port d'Andratx (hourly; 45min).

Island-wide buses

Palma to: Alcúdia (May–Oct Mon–Sat hourly, 5 on Sun; Nov–April Mon–Sat 5 daily, 3 on Sun; 1hr); Andratx (hourly; 45min); Artà (Mon–Sat 4 daily, 1 on Sun; 1hr 25min); Banyalbufar (Mon–Sat 4 daily, 1 on Sun; 35min); Bunyola (Mon–Sat 8 daily; 5 on Sun; 1hr); Cala d'Or (May–Oct Mon–Sat 8 daily, 2 on Sun; Nov–April 2–4 daily; 1hr 10min); Cala Figuera (May–Oct Mon–Sat 1 daily; 1hr 20min); Cala Millor (Mon–Sat 8 daily, 2 on Sun; 1hr 15min); Cala Rajada (Mon–Sat 4 daily, 2 on Sun; 1hr 30min); Ca'n Picafort (Mon–Sat hourly, 4 on Sun; 1hr); Colònia de Sant Jordi (May–Oct Mon–Fri 8 daily, Sat & Sun 2–5 daily; Nov–April Mon–Sat 4 daily, 2 on Sun; 1hr); Coves del Drac (May–Oct Mon–Sat 4 daily, 2 on Sun; Nov–April 1 daily; 1hr); Covetes, for Es Trenc beach (May–Oct 1 daily; 1hr); Deià (Mon–Fri 5 daily, 2 on Sat & Sun; 45min); Esporles (Mon–Fri 7 daily, Sat & Sun 2–4 daily; 20min); Estellencs (Mon–Sat 4 daily, 1 on Sun; 45min); Felanitx (Mon–Fri 9 daily, Sat & Sun 5–6 daily; 50min); Formentor (May–Oct Mon–Sat 1 daily; 1hr 15min); Inca (Mon–Sat hourly, Sat & Sun 3–5 daily; 30min); La Granja (Mon–Sat 4 daily, 1 on Sun; 25min); Lluc (Mon–Fri 4 daily, Sat & Sun 2–3 daily; 1hr); Manacor (Mon–Sat 8 daily, 2 on Sun; 45min); Montuïri (Mon–Fri 5 daily, Sat & Sun 2–4 daily; 40min); Petra (Mon–Fri 5 daily, Sat & Sun 2–4 daily; 45min); Pollença (Mon–Sat 8 daily, 2 on Sun; 1hr); Port d'Alcúdia (May–Oct Mon–Sat hourly, 5 on Sun; Nov–April 3–5 daily; 1hr 5min); Port d'Andratx (hourly; 45min); Port de Pollença (Mon–Sat 8 daily, 2 on Sun; 1hr 10min); Port de Sóller (via the tunnel: Mon–Fri 5 daily, 2 on Sat; 35min; via Valldemossa: 5 daily; 55min); Porto Colom (Mon–Fri 3–6 daily; 1hr 10min); Porto Cristo (Mon–Sat 8 daily, 3 on Sun; 1hr 10min); Santanyí (May–Oct Mon–Sat 8 daily, 2 on Sun; Nov–April 2–4 daily; 1hr 10min); Sóller (via the tunnel: Mon–Fri hourly, Sat & Sun 3–6 daily; 30min; via Valldemossa: Mon–Fri 5 daily, Sat & Sun 2 daily; 50min); Valldemossa (Mon–Fri 5 daily, Sat & Sun 2 daily; 30min).

Peguera to: Andratx (Mon–Fri 1 daily; 10min); Estellencs (Mon–Fri 1 daily; 1hr); Port d'Andratx (hourly; 10min); Sant Elm (Mon–Sat 6 daily, 5 on Sun; 20min); Valldemossa (Mon–Fri 1 daily; 1hr 10min).

Trains

Palma to: Alaró (hourly; 25min); Binissalem (hourly; 30min); Inca (hourly; 40min); Sineu (hourly; 45min); Manacor (hourly; 1hr); Muro (hourly; 50min); Petra (hourly; 50min); Sa Pobla (hourly; 55min); Sóller (5–6 daily; 1hr 15min).

Western Mallorca

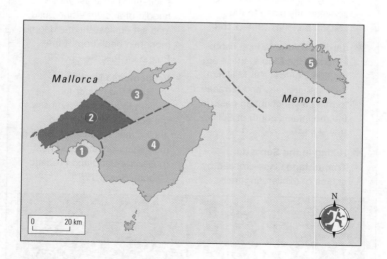

CHAPTER 2 # Highlights

* **Palma–Sóller train** Ride the antique train over the mountains from Palma to Sóller for a wonderful introduction to the island's varied and dramatic topography. See p.108

* **Sóller** The enjoyable town of Sóller boasts handsome stone mansions, a dinky main square and an exquisite setting tucked away amongst craggy mountains – but still conveniently close to the coastal beaches. See p.108

* **Jardins d'Alfabia** First established by the Moors, these are the finest gardens in Mallorca, their lush trellises and terraces forming an enchanting oasis in the mountains south of Sóller. See p.114

* **Hiking in the Serra de Tramuntana** Criss-crossed by scores of exhilarating trails, the rugged mountains of the Serra de Tramuntana offer the Balearics' finest hiking. See p.105

* **Scotts Hotel, Binissalem** Delightful hotel occupying a sympathetically restored old almond grower's mansion in the appealing inland town of Binissalem. See p.118

* **Deià** One of Mallorca's most enchanting villages, with a huddle of ancient stone buildings set against the handsome mountain backdrop of the Puig d'es Teix. See p.120

* **Valldemossa** Nestling amongst the hills at the ancient town of Valldemossa, the echoing cloisters and ancient cells of this fascinating monastery once played host to George Sand and Frédéric Chopin. See p.125

△ Valldemossa

Western Mallorca

Mallorca is at its scenic best in the gnarled ridge of the **Serra de Tramuntana**, the imposing mountain range which stretches the length of the island's northwestern shore, its rearing peaks and plunging seacliffs intermittently punctuated by valleys of olive and citrus groves. Midway along and cramped by the mountains is **Sóller**, an antiquated merchants' town that serves as a charming introduction to the region, especially when reached on the scenic narrow-gauge train line from Palma. From Sóller, it's a short hop down to the coast to **Port de Sóller**, a popular resort on a deep and expansive bay. (This geographical arrangement – the town located a few kilometres inland from its eponymous port – is repeated across Mallorca, a reminder of more troubled days when marauding corsairs obliged the islanders to live away from the coast.) The mountain valleys in the vicinity of Sóller shelter the bucolic stone-built villages of **Fornalutx**, **Orient** and **Alaró**, close to **Binissalem**, one of the most diverting little towns of the central plain, Es Pla. Also within easy reach of Sóller are two appealing gardens: the oasis-like **Jardins d'Alfàbia** and the Italianate terraces of **Raixa**.

Southwest of Sóller, the principal coastal road, the **C710**, threads up through the mountains to reach the beguiling village of **Deià**, tucked at the base of formidable cliffs and famous as the former home of Robert Graves. Beyond lies the magnificent Carthusian monastery of **Valldemossa**, whose echoing cloisters briefly accommodated George Sand and Frédéric Chopin during the 1830s, and the gracious *hacienda* of **La Granja**, another compelling stop. Continuing southwest, the C710 wriggles high above the shoreline, slipping through a sequence of mountain hamlets, of which **Banyalbufar** and **Estellencs** are the most picturesque, their tightly terraced fields tumbling down the coastal cliffs. A few kilometres further and you leave the coast behind, drifting inland out of the mountains and into the foothills that precede the market town of **Andratx**. Beyond, on Mallorca's western tip, lie the safe waters of **Port d'Andratx**, a medium-sized resort draped around a handsome inlet, its villas announcing the start of the intense tourist development that eats up the coast eastwards to Palma.

The Serra de Tramuntana provides the best walking on Mallorca, with scores of **hiking trails** latticing the mountains. Generally speaking, paths are well marked, though apt to be clogged with thornbushes. There are trails to suit all aptitudes and all levels of enthusiasm, from the easiest of strolls to the most gruelling of long-distance treks. Details of several walks are given in the text, and two hikes, beginning in Valldemossa and Deià, are described in depth. Spring and autumn are the best times to embark on the longer trails; in mid-summer the heat can be enervating and water is scarce. Bear in mind also that the mountains are prone to mists, though they usually lift at some point in the day.

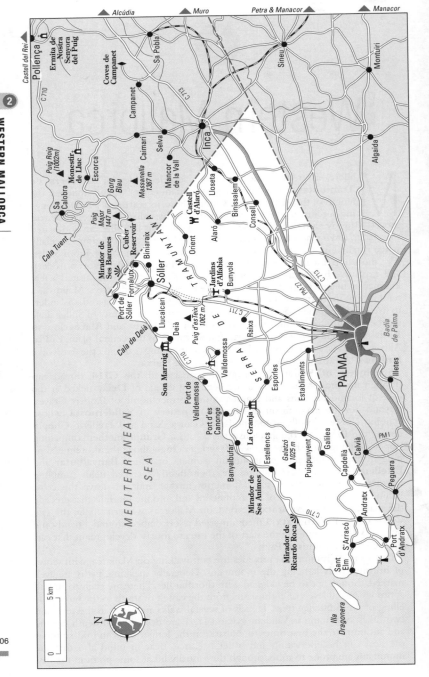

For obvious safety reasons, lone mountain walking is not recommended: the dangers are very real at any time of year, and fatalities are not unheard of, often caused by – or related to – heat stroke or dehydration. If you're looking for **beaches**, most of the region's coastal villages have a tiny, shingly strip – but nothing more. The longest strip of sand is at Port de Sóller, but this is no great shakes. Deià's modest strand has a wild and wonderful setting, as does its equivalent at Estellencs.

Port d'Andratx, Sóller and Port de Sóller have the widest range of **accommodation**, but all the villages in the region have at least a couple of places to stay. That said, from June to early September (or sometimes beyond), vacancies are extremely thin on the ground and advance reservations are strongly advised. To compensate, distances are small – from Andratx to Sóller via the C710 is only about 75km – the roads are good and the **bus** network is adequate for most destinations. **Taxis** can work out a reasonable deal too, if you're travelling in a group: the fare for the forty-kilometre trip from Palma to Sóller, for instance, is about €40.

Sóller and around

At the end of the train line from Palma lies **Sóller**, one of the most laid-back and enjoyable towns on Mallorca, and an ideal and fairly inexpensive base for exploring the surrounding mountains. Most visitors, though, stick religiously to the coast, taking the rumbling tram down to the popular and amenable seaside resort of **Port de Sóller**. There are much nicer bathing spots not far away – especially Cala Deià – but the port does offer good restaurants and a cluster of budget hotels. However, the best of the region lies just inland. To the northeast, Sóller's mellow mansions fade seamlessly into the orchards and farmland that precede the charming hamlets of **Biniaraix** and **Fornalutx**, both within easy walking distance of town. Further afield, on the landward side of the Serra de Tramuntana, spread the verdant gardens of the **Jardins d'Alfàbia** and the hamlet of **Orient**, on the road to the remote ruins of the **Castell d'Alaró**. Beyond the castle are the attractive little towns of **Alaró** and **Binissalem**, the centre of Mallorca's wine industry.

Getting around

The quickest route from Palma to Sóller is along the **C711** road, which tunnels straight through the mountains. The twenty-kilometre journey takes about thirty minutes; it costs €3.80 per car to use the three-kilometre **tunnel**. You can avoid the tunnel by driving along a serpentine road over the mountains, though this adds about 6km to the trip.

There's a fast and frequent direct **bus** service from Palma to Sóller and Port de Sóller via the tunnel; other buses are routed via Valldemossa and Deià. More intermittent services run along the main coastal road, the C710, from Andratx to Valldemossa and on to Sóller and Port de Sóller.

Trains from Palma to Sóller (see box on p.108) link with ramshackle old **trams** that clunk down to the coast at Port de Sóller, 5km away. The trams, some of which date back to 1912, depart every half-hour or hour daily from 7am to 9pm; the fifteen-minute journey costs €1 one-way. A second (recently extended) train line runs from Palma through Binissalem and Lloseta and on to Manacor and Sa Pobla.

The train from Palma to Sóller

The 28-kilometre **train** journey from Palma to Sóller is a delight, dipping and cutting through the mountains and fertile valleys of the Serra de Tramuntana. The line was completed in 1911 on the profits of the orange and lemon trade: the railway was built to transport the fruit to Palma, at a time when it took a full day to make the trip by road. The rolling stock is tremendously atmospheric too, with narrow carriages – the gauge is only 914mm – which look like they've come out of an Agatha Christie novel.

After clearing the scratchy suburbs of Palma, the train runs across pancake-flat farmland with the impenetrable-looking peaks of the Serra de Tramuntana dead ahead. After clunking through the outskirts of Bunyola, the train threads upwards to spend five minutes tunnelling through the mountains, where the noisy engine and dimly lit carriages give the feel of a rollercoaster ride. Beyond, out in the bright mountain air, are the steep valleys and craggy thousand-metre peaks at the heart of the Serra de Tramuntana, and everywhere there are almond groves, vivid with blossom in January and February.

There are six departures daily from Palma station throughout the year; the whole ride takes just under an hour and a quarter. An ordinary one-way ticket costs €2.47; a return costs double. There are also two "Panoramic" trains (10.50am and 12.15pm), though the only difference is that these make a brief photo-stop in the mountains at the Mirador Pujol d'En Banja; a one-way ticket on these trains costs €6 single (€8.47 return).

Sóller

Rather than any specific sight, it's the general flavour of **SÓLLER** that appeals, with the town's narrow, sloping lanes cramped by eighteenth- and nineteenth-century stone houses adorned with fancy grilles and big wooden doors – the former dwellings of the region's rich fruit merchants. A couple of low-key attractions fill out a wander around town, while the picturesque villages of **Biniaraix** and **Fornalutx** are within walking distance.

Arrival and information

Buses from Lluc and Pollença drop passengers beside the Campsa petrol station on the main Sóller–Palma road to the west of the town centre. From here, it's a five-minute stroll into the centre: walk south from the petrol station and take the first left down Costa d'en Llorenç, at the end of which turn right onto c/Capità Angelets and keep going east. Buses from Palma, Valldemossa and Deià arrive beside Plaça Amèrica, from where it's about five minutes' walk south to Plaça Constitució.

The **tourist office** (Mon–Fri 9.30am–2pm & 3–5pm, Sat & Sun 10am–1pm; ☏971 630 200, ⓦwww.sollernet.com) is housed in an old train carriage in the centre of Plaça d'Espanya, where the tram from Port de Sóller terminates. The office can provide lists of local accommodation, maps of the town and environs, and a synopsis in English of local hikes, quaintly entitled "Walking between the Mountains and the Sea". Many of the most popular hikes are now well signposted, but for the more arcane ones you'll need an IGN **hiking map**; the newspaper shop in Plaça Constitució sometimes has a limited supply, but don't rely on it in high season. You could also try the well-stocked Libreria Calabruix at c/Sa Lluna 7, facing the main square.

Leaving Sóller, buses heading both east and west along the coast are often full. To make sure of a seat, you'll need to go down to Port de Sóller, where these services originate.

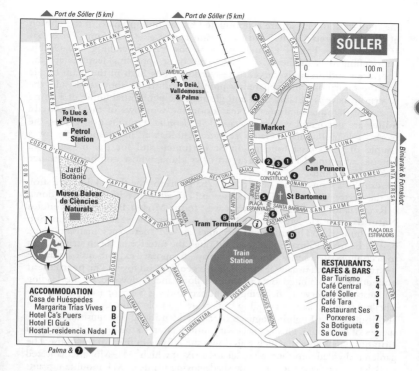

Port de Sóller (5 km)   Port de Sóller (5 km)

SÓLLER

0   100 m

To Deià, Valldemossa & Palma

To Lluc & Pollença

Petrol Station

Jardí Botànic

Museu Balear de Ciències Naturals

Market

Can Prunera

PLAÇA CONSTITUCIÓ

St Bartomeu

Tram Terminus

Biniaraix & Fornalutx

Train Station

Palma & 7

RESTAURANTS, CAFÉS & BARS
Bar Turismo   5
Café Central   4
Café Soller   3
Café Tara   1
Restaurant Ses
 Porxeres   7
Sa Botigueta   6
Sa Cova   2

ACCOMMODATION
Casa de Huéspedes
 Margarita Trías Vives   D
Hotel Ca's Puers   B
Hotel El Guía   C
Hostal-residencia Nadal   A

Accommodation

Although Sóller's **accommodation** options are very limited, there's actually as much chance of finding a vacant room here during the high season as there is down at the port.

Hotel Agroturismo Ca's Xorc About 5km from Sóller on the Ctra Sóller–Deià, Km56.1 ☎971 638 280, ⊛www.casxorc.com. Spectacular mountain retreat perched high up in the mountains, overlooking the entire valley and face to face with the island's highest peak. The whole place exudes luxury, set in a converted rural mansion surrounded by gardens, with Moroccan furnishings, peacocks and lots of attentive staff. ❼
Casa de Huéspedes Margarita Trías Vives c/Reial 3 ☎971 634 214. Pleasant rooms in an attractive old terraced house close to the train station. Stay at the back (away from the road) if you're a light sleeper. Closed Nov–March. ❷
Hotel Ca's Puers c/Isabel II 39 ☎971 638 004, ⊛www.caspuers.com. Plush hotel occupying a

handsome old stone house about 300m from the main square. Has just six, immaculately decorated rooms, and is also home to a Michelin-starred restaurant. Closed Nov, early Dec & Jan. ❼
Hotel El Guía c/Castanyer 2 ☎971 630 227, ℻971 632 634. Easily the best place in town: a lovely, old-fashioned one-star hotel set back behind a pretty little courtyard. Bygones litter the foyer, which leads to pleasantly furnished and attractive rooms. To get there, walk down the steps from the train station platform and turn right. Closed Nov–March. ❹
Hostal-residencia Nadal c/Romaguera 27 ☎ & ℻971 631 180. Simple, central two-star with 26 rooms with and without showers set in a neatly decorated and well-kept house about five minutes' walk north of Plaça Constitució. ❷

The Town

All streets lead to the main square, **Plaça Constitució**, an informal, pint-sized affair of crowded cafés and grouchy mopeds just down the hill from

109

the train station. The square is dominated by the hulking mass of the church of **St Bartomeu** (Mon–Thurs 10.30am–1pm & 2.45–5.15pm, Fri & Sat 10.30am–1pm). This is a crude but somehow rather fetching neo-Gothic remodelling of a medieval original – the most appealing features are the enormous and precisely carved rose window stuck high in the main façade and the enormous and apparently pointless balustrade above it. Inside, the cavernous nave is suitably dark and gloomy, the penitential home of a string of gaudy Baroque altarpieces. Next door, the windows of the **Banco de Sóller** are decorated with extravagant *Modernista* wrought iron grilles, the work of Joan Rubiò, a Gaudí acolyte. Rubiò was also responsible for a couple of *Modernista* touches on St Bartomeu and for the mosaics and frescoes adorning **Can Prunera**, on c/Sa Lluna, whose colourful entrance you can peep into.

From Plaça Constitució, head down c/Sa Lluna for the three-kilometre stroll to the pretty village of Biniaraix (see p.111); alternatively, turn right down c/Rectoria for the five-minute walk west to the **Museu Balear de Ciències Naturals** (Balearic Museum of Natural Sciences; Tues–Sat 10am–6pm, Sun 10am–2pm; €3). This museum occupies an old merchant's mansion stuck beside the main Palma–Sóller road, although the interior has been stripped out to accommodate a series of modest displays. Temporary exhibitions occupy the top two floors and usually feature Balearic geology and fossils. The **permanent collection** is exhibited on the ground floor and is devoted to the leading botanists of yesteryear, including Archduke Ludwig Salvator (see p.124). The labelling is in Catalan, but English leaflets are available at the ticket desk, which also issues a free English-language brochure identifying and illustrating many species of local flora. This is a necessary introduction to the neat and trim **Jardí Botànic** (same hours), which rolls down the hillside in front of the house. The garden is divided into thirteen small areas, six of which (M1–M6) are dedicated to Balearic species – these include shade-loving plants in M4, mountain plants in M5, and dune and sea-cliff species in M2.

Eating and drinking

Sóller's **café-bars** provide an abundance of low-cost snacks and light meals during the day and early evening. The **restaurant** scene is more limited, but there are still a couple of decent places, and one top-class option.

Bar Turismo Avgda d'es Born 8. By the tram lines just up from Plaça Constitució, this convivial little bar is an amenable spot to nurse a drink.

Bens d'Avall 4km from Sóller on the road to Deià ☎971 632 381. Top-notch Mallorcan, Spanish and Mediterranean cuisine in an elegantly rustic setting amidst dramatic mountain scenery. Expect to pay at least €50 a head. Closed Nov to mid-March.

Café Central Plaça Constitució s/n. Dominating one side of the square, this modern establishment with handsome shutters and wrought iron touches does just about everything and does it well, from breakfasts to cheap full meals, with specialities including pizza, spaghetti, bocadillos and loads of exotic fruit juices and pastries.

Café Soller Plaça Constitució 13. One of several cheerful cafés on the main square, this place

serves up fresh *ensaimadas* plus tasty *tapas* (€4) and *racions* (€6). A good bet for breakfast.

Café Tara c/Sa Lluna 5. A straightforward café just off Plaça Constitució serving shoppers with delicious pastries during the day, and concentrating in the evening on pizzas (averaging €5). Usually closes around 6 or 7pm.

Restaurant El Guia c/Castanyer 2 ☎971 630 227. In the hotel of the same name, this is a real treat. A little formal for some tastes, perhaps, but the prices are very reasonable, with a delicious *menú del día* for around €18. Closed Mon; plus limited opening hours Nov–March.

Restaurant Ses Porxeres Carretera Sóller s/n ☎971 613 762. Something of an island institution, this rustic restaurant is well known for its game, prepared in the traditional Catalan manner, along with other Catalan-style dishes – reckon on about

€12 for a main course. You'll need to reserve, and note that on Sundays it can get booked up weeks in advance. It's located 4km from the centre of Sóller, just beyond the south end of the C711 Sóller tunnel beside the Jardins d'Alfàbia.

Sa Botigueta Avgda Jeroni Estades 9 (there's another entrance at c/Es Born 5). Large, old-fash-ioned and atmospheric café, with good cheap tapas, hot chocolate and freshly squeezed orange juice.

Sa Cova Plaça Constitució 7 ☎971 633 222. Elegant and inviting restaurant offering appetizing versions of traditional Mallorcan dishes (from around €9), including fish.

East of Sóller: Biniaraix and Fornalutx

Following c/Sa Lluna east from Sóller's main square, it takes about half-an-hour to stroll to the village of **BINIARAIX**, passing orchards and farmland criss-crossed with ancient irrigation channels and dry-stone walls. The village, nestled in the foothills of the Serra de Tramuntana, is tiny – just a cluster of handsome old stone houses surrounding a dilapidated church and the smallest of central squares – but it is extraordinarily pretty. It is also the starting point for one of Mallorca's busiest **hiking** routes, commonly called the **Cornadors Circuit**. This comprises a thirteen-kilometre trail which takes about six hours to negotiate, weaving a circuitous course through the mountains to finish up back in Sóller (although a local landowner has been restricting access to hikers beyond the Barranc de Biniaraix, so check with the Sóller tourist office in advance if you want to hike the whole circuit). To get to the trailhead, walk uphill from the square along c/Sant Josep. After about 200m you'll reach a spring and cattle trough, where a sign offers a choice of hiking routes: left for the Camí del Marroig, right for the more interesting **Camí d'es Barranc**, the first, and most diverting, part of the Cornadors Circuit.

The Camí d'es Barranc follows an old cobbled track – originally built for pilgrims on their way to Lluc – which ascends the **Barranc de Biniaraix**, a beautiful gorge of terraced citrus groves set in the shadow of the mountains. After about ninety minute's walking you'll reach the head of the ravine and a large barn sporting painted signs on its walls. Beyond this point the going gets appreciably tougher and the route more difficult to work out, so you'll need to have a hiking map with you. Otherwise, you'll have to return the way you came.

Fornalutx

FORNALUTX, a couple of kilometres east of Biniaraix along a narrow, sign-posted country lane, is often touted as the most attractive village on Mallorca, and it certainly has a superb location. Orange and lemon groves scent the valley as it tapers up towards the settlement, whose honey-coloured stone houses huddle against a mountainous backdrop. Matching its setting, the quaint centre of Fornalutx fans out from the minuscule main square, its narrow cobbled streets stepped to facilitate mule traffic, though nowadays you're more likely to be hit by a Mercedes than obstructed by a mule: foreigners love the place and own about half of the village's three hundred houses. This sizeable expatriate community sustains one excellent **restaurant**, the *Bella Vista* (☎971 631 590), just down from the main square on the road back towards Sóller. Enjoying fabulous views over the valley, it offers seafood and traditional Mallorcan cuisine, with full meals costing around €25. It's fine just to have a drink here too. There are also a couple of small cafés on the main square.

As for **accommodation**, the smartest place in town is the *C'an Verdera*, at c/des Toros 1, just off the main road through town (☎971 638 203, Ⓦwww.canverdera.com; ❼). It's coolly and tastefully furnished in a mix of the medieval and the modern, and has a garden patio, pool and great views. A cheaper option is the charming one-star *Fornalutx Petit Hotel*, c/Alba 22 (T 971 631 997; 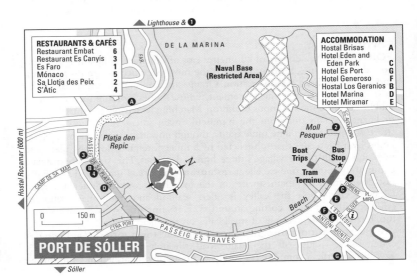), which occupies an attractively furnished and spotlessly clean old stone house with a terraced garden overlooking the orchards behind. Reservations are essential here and at the neighbouring – and very similar – *Ca'n Reus*, c/Alba 26 (T & F 971 631 174;), though the chic-rustic decor at the latter is a tad more self-conscious. To get to c/Alba, walk down the main street from the square (as for the *Bella Vista*) and take the first left just beyond the conspicuous railings – a minute's stroll.

A taxi from Fornalutx to Sóller costs €10. If you can't see one hanging around, call T 971 630 571.

Port de Sóller

PORT DE SÓLLER is one of the most popular spots on the west coast, and its handsome, horseshoe-shaped bay, ringed by forested hills, must be one of the most photographed places on the island after the package resorts around Palma. The high jinks of the Badia de Palma, however, are a world away from this low-key, family-oriented resort, grafted onto an old fishing port and naval base. Attractions here include a pleasant strip of **beach** with generally clean and clear water, plus an excellent selection of restaurants. It's also worth making the enjoyable hour-long hike west to the **lighthouse** (*far*) which guards the cliffs of Cap Gros above the entrance to its inlet. From here, the views out over the wild and rocky coast and back across the harbour are truly magnificent, especially at sunset. There's a tarmac road all the way: from the tram terminus, walk round the southern side of the bay past Platja d'en Repic and keep going, following the signs.

Arrival and information

Trams from Sóller shadow the main road and clank to a stop beside the jetties, bang in the centre of town. From here, it's a couple of minutes' walk east to the **tourist office**, located beside the church on c/Canonge Oliver 10

The Festa de Nostra Senyora de la Victòria

If you're around Port de Sóller in the second week of May, be sure to catch the **Festa de Nostra Senyora de la Victòria**, which commemorates the events of May 1561 when a large force of Arab pirates came to a sticky end after sacking Sóller. The Mallorcans had been taken by surprise, but they ambushed and massacred the Arabs as they returned to their ships and took grisly revenge by planting the raiders' heads on stakes. The story – bar decapitations – is played out in chaotic, alcoholic fashion every year at the festival. The re-enactment begins with the arrival of the pirates by boat, and continues with fancy-dress Christians and Arabs battling it out through the streets of the port, to the sound of blanks being fired in the air from antique rifles. The tourist office can give you a rough idea of the schedule of events, plus details of the dances and parties that follow.

(Mon–Fri 9am–12.50pm & 2.40–4.50pm; Sat 10am–12.50pm; ☎971 633 042, ⓦwww.sollernet.com). They carry a reasonable range of local information, including restaurant and accommodation lists, maps and boat-trip details.

Bike rental is available from Vivas, back towards Platja d'en Repic at Passeig Es Través 14–15 (☎971 630 088). In summer, **boats** leave the dock by the tram terminus for day excursions along the coast – northeast to Cala Tuent (May, June & Sept Mon–Fri 1 daily; €10), Sa Calobra (May, June & Sept 3 daily; €10) and Formentor (June, July & Sept on Sat at 10.30am; Aug on Sun at 10.30am; €18) and southwest to Sa Foradada via Cala Deià (May, June, Sept & Oct on Wed at 10am & 3pm; July & Aug at 3.15pm; €10). Cala Tuent (see p.146) is the most diverting of the destinations, though each trip is a good way of seeing a chunk of coast, and Cala Deià (see p.120) is well worth a day out.

Accommodation

Most of the town's hotels and *hostals* overlook the bay and although **rooms** are hard to find in high season, there are usually lots of vacancies at other times of the year. There are no hotel tower blocks here, but rather a ring of three- to four-storey blocks dating back to the 1960s. The pick of these overlook the **Platja d'en Repic**, a narrow wedge of sand about 1.5km round the bay from the tram terminus.

Hostal Brisas Camí del Far 11–14 ☎971 631 352, ☏971 632 146. On the far side of the bay, this simple but friendly place makes a perfect retreat and is close to the town's best nightlife. ❷
Hotel Eden and Eden Park Passeig Es Través 26 ☎971 631 600, ⓦwww.hoteleden.com. Mainstream, family-oriented hotel in two adjacent blocks, with large pools and comfortable facilities. ❺
Hotel Es Port c/Antoni Montis 43 ☎971 631 650, ⓦwww.hotelesport.com. This three-star hotel at the back of the port, a few minutes' walk from the waterfront, boasts lovely gardens, a swimming pool and a charming reception area set inside a renovated manor house. The guest rooms are, however, far less endearing, occupying a sprawling modern extension. ❹
Hotel Generoso c/Marina 4 ☎971 631 450, ⓦwww.hotelgeneroso.com. Routine modern block

near the tram terminus with a hundred rather plain and simple rooms. ❺
Hostal Los Geranios Passeig de Sa Platja 15 ☎971 631 440, ⓦwww.hotel-losgeranios.ch. Straightforward two-star seafront hotel overlooking the Platja d'en Repic, with a hundred rooms on four floors. ❻
Hotel Marina Passeig de Sa Platja 3 ☎971 631 461, ⓦwww.hotelmarinasoller.com. Pleasant two-star hotel overlooking the Platja d'en Repic. The rooms are kitted out in brisk, modern style and most have bayside balconies. Closed mid-Nov to Jan. ❺
Hotel Miramar c/Marina 12 ☎971 631 350, ⓦwww.hotelmiramarsoller.com. A standard-issue modern block overlooking the bay from near the tram terminus, with just thirty functional rooms. ❹

Eating and drinking

Port de Sóller heaves with **cafés** and **restaurants**, but standards are very variable: some serve up mediocre food with the package tourist in mind, others are more authentically *Mallorquín* – or at least Spanish. The majority are dotted along the bayshore, though the cluster of mainly tourist-oriented joints on c/Santa Caterina d'Alexandria is best avoided.

Restaurant Embat c/Església 8 ☎971 634 971. This French-run restaurant offers a quiet, low-key hideaway up a sidestreet. The – mainly fish – dishes (from €8) are prepared and served with care and style, and the *menú del día* (lunch only; €10.50) is a real bargain, and offers lots of choice.
Restaurant Es Canyís Passeig de Sa Platja d'en Repic 32 ☎971 631 406. Bright and cheerful bistro-style restaurant offering a good range of Spanish dishes from its bayshore premises behind the Platja d'en Repic. The snails are a house special. Main courses average €9–12.
Es Faro Cap Gros ☎971 633 752. Set in a wonderful location, high up on the cliffs at the entrance to the harbour – the views from the outside terrace are nothing short of spectacular. During the day, the *Es Faro* offers coffees, light

meals and an excellent *menú del día*; at night it's à la carte – and the seafood is delicious. Mains from €20. Reservations recommended.
Mónaco Plaça Sa Torre 7 ☎971 631 025. The only place in town where you can put your feet in the sand while you dine, with great seafood at moderate prices.
Sa Llotja des Peix Muelle Pesquero s/n ☎971 632 954. The town's leading fish and seafood restaurant, if a bit touristy, located right above the fish market and using fresh catch plucked straight out of the boats. Mains from around €10.
S'Àtic On the top floor of the *Hotel Los Geranios*, Passeig de Sa Platja 15 ☎971 638 113. Elegantly understated establishment, with views of the bay and outstanding nouvelle Mediterranean cuisine. Mains from €20. Expensive but worth it.

Nightlife

Pubs and **clubs** are plentiful on the busy northern side of the port – check out the friendly *Bar Claridge*, Passeig Es Través 48; the jumping *Asgard Pub*, Passeig Es Través 15; or the large and teen-packed *Discoteca Altamar*, on the corner of Passeig Es Través and c/Antonio Montis. However, the best place in town is the *Café Prop del Mar*, located on the opposite shore at Camí del Far 2, which has indoor and beachside seating and a sophisticated range of world music and jazz on the sound-system.

The Jardins d'Alfàbia and Raixa

Heading south from Sóller, the main road to Palma tunnels through the Serra de Tramuntana. An alternative, scenic (though longer) road hairpins up and over the mountains, threading its way past the **Coll de Sóller**, a rocky pass with a car park and lookout point offering splendid views out over the coast. Whichever route you choose, be sure to stop by the **Jardins d'Alfàbia** (Mon–Fri 9.30am–6.30pm, Sat 9.30am–1pm; Sept–May Mon–Fri 9.30am–5.30pm; €5). These lush and beautiful terraced gardens surround a genteel *hacienda* close to the southern entrance to the tunnel. Shortly after the Reconquista, Jaume I granted the estate of Alfàbia to a prominent Moor by the name of Benhabet. Seeing which way the historical wind was blowing, Benhabet, as governor of Pollença, had given his support to Jaume, provisioning the Catalan army during the invasion. There was no way Jaume I could leave his Moorish ally in charge of Pollença (and anyway it was already pledged to a Catalan noble), but he was able to reward him with this generous portion of land. Benhabet planned his new estate in the Moorish manner, channelling water from the surrounding mountains to irrigate the fields and fashion oasis-like gardens. Generations of island gentry added to the estate without marring Benhabet's original design, thus creating the homogenous ensemble that survives today.

From the roadside, you follow a stately avenue of plane trees towards the house. Before you reach it, you're directed up a flight of stone steps and into the **gardens**, where a footpath leads past ivy-covered stone walls, gurgling watercourses and brightly coloured flowers cascading over narrow terraces. Trellises of jasmine and wisteria create patterns of light and shade, while palm and fruit trees jostle upwards, allowing only the occasional glimpse of the surrounding citrus groves. At the end of the path, the gardens' highlight is a verdant jungle of palm trees, bamboo and bullrushes tangling a tiny pool. It's an enchanting spot, especially on a hot summer's day, and an outdoor **bar** sells big glasses of freshly squeezed orange juice, a snip at €1.50. A few paces away is the **house**, a rather mundane, veranda'd *hacienda* whose handful of rooms house an eccentric mix of antiques and curios. Pride of place goes to a superb fourteenth-century **oak chair** adorned with delightful bas-relief scenes depicting the story of Tristan and Isolde. The uncrowned Jaume IV ordered the chair, though he never had a chance to sit on it: after the Battle of Llucmajor in 1349, in which the Aragonese killed his father, Jaume III, he was captured and spent the rest of his days in exile.

At the front of the house, the cobbled **courtyard** is shaded by a giant plane tree and surrounded by good-looking, rustic outbuildings. Beyond lies the **gatehouse**, an imposing structure sheltering a fine coffered ceiling of Mudéjar design, with an inscription praising Allah.

If you fancy something **to eat**, the outstanding *Restaurant Ses Porxeres* (see p.115) is right beside the gardens.

Raixa

Pushing on south along the C711 from the Jardins d'Alfàbia, it's about 5km to the short gravel lane that leads west to **Raixa**, the one-time country estate of the eighteenth-century antiquarian Cardinal Antonio Despuig (whose collection of classical sculpture can be seen in Palma – see p.86). The cardinal carved a sequence of terraced **gardens** (Wed–Sun 11am–7pm; €5) out of the hill beside his country home and then proceeded to decorate them with Neoclassical statues, water fountains and even bits of old masonry recovered from medieval buildings in Palma – all in the fashionable Italian style of his day. Despuig saw himself as a leading light of the Enlightenment, but underneath the cultured cassock was a medieval piety: he died in Italy and on his deathbed he left instructions for his heart to be cut out and buried close to the body of Mallorca's favourite saint, Catalina Thomàs (see p.125). Today, the manor house is out of bounds, and the gardens are in need of repair, but it's still a lovely secluded spot, and you can climb up through the gardens to reach the belvedere, which offers extensive views out across the surrounding countryside.

The small purple road sign to Raixa is easy to miss: travelling south from Sóller, if you reach the traffic island at the junction of the C711 and the PM114/PM203, you've gone too far. Double back and the Raixa turning is about 500m to the north.

Orient and around

In between Alfàbia and Raixa, a country road (the PM201 and then the PM210) forks east off the C711, looping past the plane trees and sun-bleached walls of the unassuming market town of **BUNYOLA** before snaking across the forested foothills of the Serra de Tramuntana. It's a beautiful drive (the tarmac's in good condition too, though some of the bends are nerve-jangling), and after about 13km you'll come to **ORIENT**. This remote hamlet of ancient houses is scattered along the eastern side of the lovely Vall d'Orient, with hills rising all around olive and almond groves. There are even a couple of places **to stay** in the village: the simple, tiny *Hotel Muntanya*, c/Bordoy 6 (☎971 615 373, ⓦwww.daltmuntanya.com; ❺); and the beautiful, recently renovated *Agroturismo Finca Son Palou*, Plaça de l'Església s/n (☎971 148 282 ⓦwww.sonpalou.com; ❻). However, these are as nothing compared to the romantic *Hotel L'Hermitage* (☎971 180 303, ⓦwww.hermitage-hotel.com; closed mid-Nov to Jan; ❾), a luxuriously renovated medieval manor house roughly 1km east of Orient on the PM210. The hotel gardens are lovely, the scenery gorgeous, and the **restaurant**, with its mammoth antique olive press, excellent, even if the decor is a little twee. Advance reservations are pretty much essential and, if you're paying this sort of money, try to get one of the four rooms in the old manor house, rather than one of the sixteen in the modern annexe.

The Castell d'Alaró

Beyond the *Hotel L'Hermitage*, the PM210 sticks to the ridge overlooking the narrow valley of the Torrent d'en Paragon for around 3km, before veering south to slip between a pair of molar-like hills whose bare rocky flanks tower above the surrounding forest and scrub. The more westerly of the two sports the sparse ruins of the **Castell d'Alaró**, originally a Moorish stronghold but rebuilt by Jaume I. Visible for miles around, the castle looks impregnable on its lofty perch, and it certainly impeded the Aragonese invasion of 1285: when an Aragonese messenger suggested terms for surrender, the garrison's two commanders responded by calling the Aragonese king Alfonso III "fish-face", punning on his name in Catalan (*anfos* means "perch"). When the castle finally fell, Alfonso had the two roasted alive. Goodness knows what he'd have done if they'd called him something really rude.

Access to the castle is from the south: coming from Orient, watch for the signposted right turn just beyond the Kilometre 18 stone marker. The first 3km of this narrow side road are well-surfaced, but the last 1.3km is gravel and dirt, with a tight series of hairpins negotiating a very steep hillside – especially hazardous after rain. The road emerges at a car park and an old ramshackle farmstead, whose barn now holds the *Es Verger* **restaurant** (opening hours vary; best to check on ☎971 510 711). It's tempting to linger here: the views down over the plain are sumptuous and the food delicious, particularly the house speciality, oven-baked lamb. From the restaurant, you can also spy the ruins of the castle above, about an hour's walk away along a clearly marked track. The trail leads to the castle's stone gateway, beyond which lies an expansive wooded plateau accommodating the fragmentary ruins of the fortress, plus the tiny pilgrims' church of **Mare de Déu del Refugi**. There's a simple restaurant and bar up here too, serving traditional Mallorcan food: the *pa amb oli* is a snip at under €4.

Alaró

Back on the PM210, it's about 1.5km south from the castle turn-off to the town of **ALARÓ**, a sleepy little place of old stone houses fanning out from an attractive main square, **Plaça Vila**. A long and elegant arcaded gallery flanks one side of the square, and a second is shadowed by the **church**, a fortress-like, medieval affair whose honey-coloured sandstone is embellished with Baroque details. The square also has a couple of first-rate **restaurants**, where local families gather at weekends. There's not much to divide the two, but *Traffic*, at no. 8 (℡971 879 117; closed Tues), is perhaps the better, with Mallorcan specialities — notably casseroles — served up in a pleasantly renovated old mansion with a wood-beamed ceiling or in the spacious garden out the back. Less specifically *Mallorquín* is the *Restaurant Gaia*, just off the main square at c/Petit 11 (April–Oct Mon–Sat 7.30–11.30pm; ℡971 518 119), which features an inventive international menu with, for instance, quiche and artichokes (in season) in a cheese sauce for €11.

Should you want to **stay**, there is a *hostal* here, the two-star *Ca'n Tiu*, whose eleven modest rooms are located above the *Restaurant Gaia* at c/Petit 11 (℡ & ℻971 510 974; ❸). The street is quite busy, so ask for a room at the back.

Binissalem and Lloseta

Just south of Alaró, you leave the foothills of the Serra de Tramuntana behind for the central plain of Mallorca, **Es Pla**. The northern peripheries of the plain hold **BINISSALEM**, an appealing country town that has long been the centre of the island's wine industry (for more on which, see p.38). Binissalem looks dull and ugly from the main C713 Palma–Alcúdia road, but the tatty, semi-industrial sprawl that straddles the main road camouflages an antique town centre, whose narrow streets contain a proud ensemble of old stone mansions dating from the seventeenth and eighteenth centuries. The Romans settled here, and so did the Moors — Binissalem could be derived from the Arabic "Bani Salaam", meaning Sons of Peace — but the town's commercial heyday began in the sixteenth century, boosted by its vineyards and stone quarries.

The old town zeroes in on its main square, the **Plaça Església**, a pretty, stone-flagged piazza lined with benches where old-timers shoot the breeze in the shade of the plane trees. The north side of the square is dominated by the **Església Nostra Senyora de Robines**, the clumpy, medieval nave of which is attached to a soaring neo-Gothic bell tower added in 1908. Inside, the single-vaulted nave is dark and gloomy, its most distinctive features being its glitzy Baroque altarpiece and the grooved stonework that graces the ceilings of the transepts and the apse. This grooved stonework pops up all over town, representing the cockle-shell emblem of **St James the Greater**, one of the apostles. James witnessed the Transfiguration and the capture of Jesus in the Garden of Gethsemane and was the first of the apostles to be martyred, at the hands of Herod in 44 AD. Despite his early demise, however, Spanish legend insists that he visited Spain and preached here; tradition also claims that James's body was brought from Jerusalem to Spain and buried at Santiago de Compostela in the far northwest of Spain. Although these tales verge on the ridiculous, they made St James one of Spain's most venerated saints and transformed Santiago de Compostela into one of the greatest pilgrimage centres of medieval Europe. An especially good time to visit Binissalem is in the third week of July, during the week-long **festivities** that precede the saint's feast day on July 25.

Strolling southwest from the Plaça Església, along c/Concepció, it's a short distance to the **Ajuntament** (Town Hall), and a few minutes more to **Can Sabater**, c/Bonaire 25, one of the town's most distinguished patrician mansions. This was once the home of the writer Llorenç Villalonga (1897–1980), whose most successful novel was *The Dolls' Room*, an ambiguous portrait of Mallorca's nineteenth-century landed gentry in moral decline. In his honour, the house has been turned into the **Casa Museu Llorenç Villalonga** (Mon–Sat 10am–2pm; also Tues & Thurs 4–8pm; free), with detailed Catalan explanations of his life and times as well as his library and study. The house is typical of its type, with elegant stone arches and high-ceilinged rooms redolent of oligarchic comfort. It also has its own chapel: the island's richer families usually had their own live-in priests.

Double back along c/Bonaire and take a right turn along c/Sant Vicenç de Paul, just before you reach the Ajuntament, to reach **c/Pere Estruch**, a cobbled street flanked by the town's most complete sequence of old stone houses, adorned by a medley of wooden shutters and wrought-iron balconies.

Practicalities

Buses pull in beside the C713 road at the foot of c/Bonaire, a five- to ten-minute walk from the Plaça Església. Binissalem is also on the **train** line from Palma to Manacor and Sa Pobla, and regular trains from both directions stop at the station on the northern edge of the town centre. From the train station, it's a five- to ten- minute walk straight down c/S'Estació and right at the end along c/Porteta, to Passeig d'es Born beside the church on Plaça Església. Binissalem has no tourist office as such, but there are free town **maps** and brochures in the foyer of the Ajuntament, close to the church on c/Concepció – just help yourself.

Binissalem boasts one of Mallorca's finest **hotels**, *Scotts*, right in the centre of town at Plaça Església 12 (℡971 870 100, Ⓦwww.scottshotel.com; ❼). The house was originally owned by an almond grower, and has been immaculately restored, its sweeping stone arches and high ceilings enclosing three suites decorated in elegant, broadly nineteenth-century style. At the back, the old stone outbuildings surround a leafy courtyard and contain more recent rooms, each decorated in crisp modern style. Breakfast is served on a sunny terrace at the back of the hotel, and there's a swimming pool. The American owner, George Scott, is familiar with every nook and cranny of the island; his first novel, *The Bloody Bokhara* (see p.306), was published in 2000.

Scotts offers light suppers three evenings a week (advance reservations required) and there's also a cosy, polished **restaurant** in the town centre – *El Suizo*, c/Pou Bo 20 (℡971 870 076), where they present an imaginative international menu featuring local ingredients. It's about five minutes' walk from Plaça Església: walk south down c/Bonaire, turn right along c/Reg, left down c/Llorenç Moya and it's on the right at the fork. On Plaça Església itself is the inexpensive locals' hangout, *Café Plaça*, where they serve up tasty *tapas* in spartan surroundings.

If you can't be in Binissalem for the July festivities around the day of St James (see p.117), try to aim for the delightful **Festa d'es Vermar** (Festival of the Grape Harvest) in the third week of September, when the cordoned-off streets are lined with trestle tables weighed down with all sorts of local wines and foods, proudly presented by their makers.

Lloseta

The old shoemaking town of **LLOSETA**, about 4km east of Binissalem, is draped over a steep little hill, its pleasant central square, the **Plaça Espanya**, decorated by a medieval church surmounted by the most petite of bell towers. Otherwise, Lloseta is really rather humdrum, although it is home to the **Palau Aiamans**, the grand eighteenth-century, L-shaped mansion of the local bigwig, located next to the church on the main square. The house has recently been converted into a luxury **hotel**, the *Ca's Comte* (℡971 873 077, Ⓦwww.cascomte.com; ❻), whose modernist interior – all stone arches, glass tables and marble floors – contains just eight splendid rooms, though the out-of-the-way location means that they're quite reasonably priced.

Plaça Espanya is a ten-minute walk north up c/Mestre Antoni Vidal from ⸱ Lloseta **train station**. There's a good **restaurant** nearby in the shape of the family-run *Ca'n Carrossa*, c/Guillem Santandreu 38 (☎971 514 023; closed Sun), which has outstanding Mallorcan cooking at reasonable prices. It's about 200m west of Plaça Espanya's southern edge.

Deià to Port d'Andratx

The western reaches of the Serra de Tramuntana rise out of the flatlands around Palma, with the range's forested foothills and sheltered valleys soon giving way to the craggy, wooded mountains that crimp most of the **southwest coast**. Several fast roads link Palma with the coast – the prettiest runs to Valldemossa – and a delightful network of country roads patterns the foothills, but the key sights and the best scenery are most readily reached along the main coastal road, the **C710**.

From Sóller, the C710 skirts the broad and wooded slopes of the Puig d'es Teix to reach **Deià**, an ancient mountain village which perches precariously high above the seashore, clinging to the fame brought by associations with the writer Robert Graves. The next 20km of coastline boasts three of Mallorca's star attractions, allied to some of its finest coastal scenery: **Son Marroig**, the well-appointed mansion of the Mallorca-loving archduke, Ludwig Salvator; the hilltop monastery of **Valldemossa**, complete with its echoing cloisters and choice examples of modern art; and the old grandee's mansion and estate of **La Granja**. This captivating trio is hard to beat, although the tiered hamlets that decorate the coast further down the road are also instantly beguiling. Of these, both **Banyalbufar** and **Estellencs** occupy fine sites and are well worth at least a fleeting visit. Alternatively, you can travel inland from La Granja, climbing the slopes of the leafy foothills and rambling through secluded valleys of almond, olive and carob trees to reach the charming village of **Galilea**. Both the Galilea route and the C710 coast road emerge from the Serra de Tramuntana at **Andratx**, a crossroads town with easy access to the tiny port of **Sant Elm** and the more commercialized harbour-cum-resort of **Port d'Andratx** in the far southwest.

Beach lovers have meagre pickings in this part of the island. There's a good sandy beach with safe swimming at Sant Elm, but further up the coast, shingle strips will have to suffice. The most impressive of these is **Cala Deià**, set in the shadow of the mountains at the end of a narrow ravine. **Accommodation** can be hard to find, too. Each of the destinations mentioned above, with the exception of Galilea, has at least a couple of places to stay, but you're strongly advised to book well ahead for any stays between June and September or even October. Deià, Banyalbufar and Port d'Andratx have a cluster of hotels and *hostals*, and so represent the best bets for a last-minute vacancy, with Sant Elm the fourth favourite.

Getting around

A **bus** service runs regularly from Palma to Valldemossa, Son Marroig and Deià, continuing on to Sóller and Port de Sóller. There are also fast and frequent buses from Palma to Andratx and Port d'Andratx. Along the C710 coast road between Andratx and Valldemossa, however, you're limited to a five-times-a-week bus service from Peguera. For frequencies and journey times, see p.139.

between destinations are short, so **taxis** can work out a reasonable if you're in a group: the fare for the twenty-kilometre trip from Port o Valldemossa, for example, is about €24, or €28 from Palma to Deià.

Deià, 10km west of Sóller, is beautiful. The mighty Puig d'es Teix (1062m) meets the coast here, and, although the mountain's lower slopes are now gentrified by the villas of the well-to-do, it retains a formidable, almost mysterious presence, especially in the shadows of a moonlit night. Deià's main street, c/Arxiduc Lluís Salvador, doubles as the coastal highway, skirting the base of the Teix and showing off most of the village's hotels and restaurants. **Buses** between Palma, Valldemossa and Port de Sóller scoot through Deià five times daily in each direction (Nov–March reduced service on Sat & Sun). The town hall, just up from the bus stop, houses a **tourist office** (Mon–Fri 10am–2pm, Sat 10am–noon; ☎971 639 077). The village's hotels and *hostals* will gladly provide local advice on walks and weather and can fix you up with a **taxi**; alternatively, call Sóller's Autotaxis on ☎971 630 571.

At times, Deià's main street is too congested to be much fun, but the tiny heart of the village, tumbling over a high and narrow ridge on the seaward side of the road, still retains a surprising tranquillity. Labyrinthine alleys of old peasant houses curl up to a pretty country **church**, in the precincts of which is buried **Robert Graves**, the village's most famous resident – his headstone marked simply "Robert Graves: Poeta, E.P.D" (*En Paz Descanse*, "Rest In Peace"). From the graveyard, there are memorable views out over the coast and of the Teix, with banks of carefully terraced fields tumbling down from the mountain towards the sea. The church itself is a modest little affair, decked out with Baroque altar pieces.

Graves put the village on the international map, and nowadays Deià is the haunt of long-term expatriates, mostly ex-hippies and artists presumably living on ample trust funds, judging from the kind of monthly rents that are charged here. These inhabitants congregate at **Cala Deià**, the nearest thing the village has to a beach – some 200m of shingle at the back of a handsome rocky cove of jagged cliffs, boulders and white-crested surf. It's a great place for a swim, the water is clean, deep and cool, and there's a ramshackle beach bar. Most of the time, the cove is quiet and peaceful, but parties of day-trippers do sometimes stir things up. It takes about twenty minutes to walk from the village to the *cala*, a delightful stroll down a wooded ravine margin – directions are given in the first part of the "Coastal Walk" route to Port de Sóller described on p.122. To drive there, head north along the main road out of Deià and watch for the sign about 600m beyond the *Restaurant El Olivo*.

Accommodation

Deià boasts two of the most luxurious **hotels** on the island as well as a handful of delightful, less expensive places. There's a reasonable chance of finding a room on spec at any time of the year, but you're really much better off making a reservation at least a day or two in advance.

Fonda Villa Verde c/Ramón Llull 19 ☎971 639 037, ℱ971 639 485. This lovely little pension perches on the side of a hill in the antique centre of the village, between the main road and the church. The rooms are immaculate and there's a charming shaded terrace overlooking Puig d'es Teix. Closed Dec–Feb. ❸

Hostal Miramar c/Ca'n Oliver s/n ☎ & ℱ971 639 084. A pleasant one-star *hostal* above – and signposted from – the C710 about halfway through the village, with just nine frugal rooms both with and without private shower. Closed Nov–March. ❹
Hotel Costa d'Or 2km east along the C710 coast road at the hamlet of Llucalcari ☎971 639 025,

Robert Graves in Deià

The English poet, novelist and classical scholar **Robert Graves** (1895–1985) spent two periods living in Deià, the first in the 1930s, and the second from the end of World War II until his death. During his first stay he shared a house at the edge of the village with **Laura Riding**, an American poet and dabbler in the mystical. Riding had arrived in England in 1926 and, after she became Graves's secretary and collaborator, the two of them began an affair – unknown to either of their spouses. Their tumultuous relationship created such a furore that they decided to leave England, settling in Mallorca on the advice of Gertrude Stein in 1930. The fuss was not simply a matter of morality – many of their friends were indifferent to adultery – but more to do with the self-styled "**Holy Circle**" they had founded, a cabalistic and intensely self-preoccupied literary-mystic group. The last straw came when Riding, in her attempt to control the group, jumped out of a window, saying "Goodbye, chaps", and the besotted Graves leapt after her. No wonder his mate T.E. Lawrence ("of Arabia") wrote of "madhouse minds" and of Graves "drowning in a quagmire".

The two both recovered, but the dottiness continued once they'd moved to Deià, with Graves acting as doting servant to Riding, whom he reinvented as a sort of all-knowing matriarch and muse. Simultaneously, Graves thumped away at his prose: he had already produced *Goodbye to All That* (1929), his bleak and painful memoirs of army service in the World War I trenches, but now came his other best-remembered books, **I, Claudius** (1934) and its sequel **Claudius the God** (1935), historical novels detailing the life and times of the Roman emperor. Nonetheless, to Graves these "potboilers", as he styled them, were secondary to his poetry – usually carefully crafted love poems of melancholic tenderness in praise of Riding – which were well received by critics of the time.

At the onset of the Spanish Civil War, Graves and Riding left Mallorca, not out of sympathy for the Republicans – Graves was far too reactionary for that – but to keep contact with friends and family. During their exile Graves was ditched by Riding, and he subsequently took up with a mutual friend, **Beryl Hodge**. After Graves had returned to Deià in 1946, he worked on *The White Goddess*, a controversial study of prehistoric and classical myth that argued the existence of an all-pervasive, primordial religion based on the worship of a poet-goddess. Hodge joined him in the midst of his labours (the book was published in 1948), and in 1950 they were married in Palma. They were not, however, to live happily ever after. Graves had a predilection for young women, claiming he needed female muses for poetic inspiration, and although his wife outwardly accepted this waywardness, she did so without much enthusiasm. Meanwhile, although Graves's novels became increasingly well-known and profitable, his poetry, with its preoccupation with romantic love, fell out of fashion, and his last anthology, *Poems 1965–1968*, was widely criticized by the literary establishment.

Nevertheless, Graves's international reputation as a writer attracted a steady stream of visitors to Deià from the ranks of the literati, with the occasional film-star dropping by to add to the self-regarding stew. By the middle of the 1970s, however, just as an acclaimed BBC TV production of *I, Claudius* was bringing his books to a wider public in his native country, Graves had begun to lose his mind, and ended his days in sad senility.

Ⓕ971 639 347. This splendid one-star hotel occupies a wonderful setting, overlooking an undeveloped slice of coast and surrounded by pine groves and olive terraces. There's a shaded terrace bar and a splendid outdoor swimming pool. The rooms vary, although all are spotlessly clean: there are some doubles in two buildings at

the back of the complex, while the more expensive rooms look directly over the sea. Closed Nov–March. ❹

Hotel Es Moli Carretera Deià s/n ☏971 639 000, Ⓕ971 639 333. One of Mallorca's best hotels, offering four-star luxury in a grand, lavishly refurbished old mansion overlooking the C710 at the west end of the village, surrounded by lovely gardens and equipped with a swimming pool. The ninety air-conditioned bedrooms are kitted out in dapper, modern style; most have balconies with sea views. Closed Nov to mid-April. ❼

Hotel d'es Puig c/Es Puig 4 ☎971 639 409, Ⓔpuig@futurnet.es. A smart and tastefully furnished hotel with eight bedrooms in an elegantly converted, four-storey old stone house located in the centre of the village, between the C710 and the church. Closed mid-Nov to Feb. ❻

Hotel-residencia La Residencia c/Arxiduc Lluís Salvador s/n ☎971 639 011, Ⓔlaresidencia @atlas-iap.es. Deià's second luxury hotel is also sited in a gracious old mansion – on the main drag at the east end of the village, opposite the old centre – but its furnishings and fittings are more self-conscious than the rival *Es Moli*. The hotel's clean, modern lines are superimposed on rooms with an antique appearance boasting big wooden bedsteads, timbered ceilings and the like. ❾

Eating and drinking

As for eating and drinking in Deià, you're spoiled for choice. Dotted along the main street c/Arxiduc Lluís Salvador are several smart and polished **restaurants** plus a number of more modest **café-bars**, ideal for nursing a drink and, especially in the off-season, checking out the expat scene.

A coastal walk from Deià to Port de Sóller

12km; 4hr–4hr 30min
This delightful **walk** starts in Deià village and ends in Port de Sóller. There's a fairly regular bus service between the two places, which makes the round trip relatively straightforward, but be sure to confirm bus times before you set out. The coast north of Deià is dotted with pine trees and abandoned olive terraces, and slopes steeply down to the sea from the high massif of Sa Galera. On such steep terrain, run-off water plays havoc with terrace walls and paths, so although this walk is mainly easy, care is needed where erosion has occurred. All the way the **views** are superlative, beginning with the panorama of the blue-green waters of Cala Deià. The views from the bus on your return journey are equally outstanding: notice especially the picturesque hamlet of **Llucalcari**, which cannot be seen from the coastal path below. The walking route, which sometimes drops almost to sea-level and at other times rises to avoid difficult ground, is partially waymarked with red paint and cairns, although a certain amount of route-finding is required. There are stiles at all the boundary fences the path crosses.

The route
From the **bus stop** in Deià, walk in the Palma direction to a sharp right bend in the main road. Turn right down the shallow steps and continue downhill, past the Archeological Museum-cum-Historical Research Centre. After a few minutes take a right fork, where the road is marked with a "no through way" sign. Where the lane ends, follow the signposted footpath which continues in the same direction. About 150m further, the footpath is marked by a green painted wooden arrow. After about five minutes, turn right (north) by a white "Cala" sign painted on a stone. Some 200m further on, the path joins a surfaced road, veering slightly to the left before reaching, after about 500m, tiny **Cala Deià**, with its cluster of small boats and a beach bar serving meals in summer.

The **coastal path** begins up a flight of steps some 50m before the road ends. There is another flight of steps closer to the beach, but this just leads to a public toilet (the key for which is kept at the beach bar). After ascending the steps of the coastal path, ignore a left branch after about five minutes, but only a couple of minutes later follow the line of red painted stones left where the stepped path swings right. The path immediately turns right along a terrace, crosses a low wall and then turns sharp left downhill beside the wall. One minute later it turns right

Bar-restaurant Deià c/Arxiduc Lluís Salvador s/n. Light meals and snacks with a pan-European slant. Occupies an attractive setting at the west end of the village, with an outdoor terrace overlooking a steep ravine.

Café La Fábrica c/Arxiduc Lluís Salvador s/n. An unpretentious café-bar at the west end of the village, offering reasonably priced *tapas, bocadillos* and the traditional *pa amb oli* (bread rubbed with olive oil). Limited opening hours in winter.

Restaurant Es Racó d'es Teix c/Vinya Vella 6 ☎ 971 639 501. Delightful little Michelin-starred restaurant in an old stone house with an exquisite shaded terrace, located a steep 30m or so above the main road, about halfway into the village – watch for the sign. The Mediterranean fusion cuisine is memorable, as are the prices (up to €100 for a meal). Closed Tues.

Restaurant Jaime c/Arxiduc Lluís Salvador s/n ☎ 971 639 029. First-rate restaurant, on the main drag about halfway into the village, specializing in traditional Mallorcan cuisine, with dishes from around €10.

Restaurant El Olivo c/Arxiduc Lluís Salvador s/n ☎ 971 639 011. If your wallet is stuffed, try this chi-chi restaurant located in a former mill that's now part of *Hotel La Residencia*. Gourmets recommend the place – and the broadly Mediterranean menu is widely regarded as top-notch.

Restaurant Sa Dorada c/Arxiduc Lluís Salvador 24 ☎ 971 639 481. One of the best places in town for fish, with main courses from around €12.50. It's located about halfway into the village on the main road.

again and leads to an attractive headland among pine trees, overlooking the sea and the white rocks of Cala Deià.

Continue straight on along the path to the north, passing a **mirador** (viewpoint) with a private path descending to it from an unseen house above. Below the *mirador*, steps descend to a rocky inlet. Go halfway down these, then turn off right and ascend the earth path waymarked with red paint spots. Later, after crossing two stiles, there are notices saying **"No picnic"** next to a large circular table with surrounding seats – a useful landmark. Here the path forks left downhill, leading to another stile and, a few minutes later, passes below a stone enclosure and then past the left edge of a wall where the ground rises steeply inland. After the wall follow the direction of the red paint marks leading uphill to a headland with a few almond trees growing in bare red earth.

Round the corner beyond the headland there's an eroded gully, its edge protected with a wire fence. The path becomes less clear hereabouts. Go inland past a **white house**. Ascend to a terrace, which contours round the hillside to a two- or three-metre gap in the gully fence. At this point the stream which created the gully has been culverted. At the end of this terrace follow the lower path to reach the next stile and another terrace, quite low down near the sea. Next, go uphill by a **fallen tree**, cross a headland among boulders and heather, and then go fairly steeply upwards through terraces of olive trees. This part of the route is well marked and leads in about fifteen minutes to a path which contours left above a steep cliff to reach another stile.

The path then descends into and out of a stream bed and goes over a stile into a lane. Turn left, and when the lane ends find the continuation of the footpath on the right. Five minutes later this reaches a **concrete road** near some houses. Follow it uphill and, after a few minutes of steep walking, cross another stream bed (usually dry) by means of the metal pegs in the enclosing dry-stone walls – an awkward manoeuvre which requires two free hands. Turn right along the wide road by the well known *Bens d'Avall* **restaurant** (see p.110), and follow the road uphill for 1.5km to reach the Muleta road junction. Turn left, then right, heading along a track towards a **large farmhouse with a square tower**.

The most direct route to **Port de Sóller** is to turn right and go through the gate towards the house with tower, following a path to the right between the buildings. Continue through a gate to the mule track, which leads down to the *Rocamar* hotel. Below the *Rocamar*, turn left for the Platja d'en Repic, Port de Sóller's largest beach, or right for the trams on the main road to Sóller.

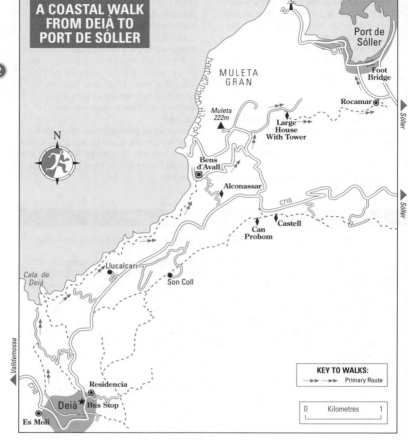

A COASTAL WALK
FROM DEIÀ TO
PORT DE SÓLLER

MULETA
GRAN

Port de
Sóller

Foot
Bridge

Rocamar ◉

Muleta
222m ▲

Large
House
With Tower

Sóller ▶

Bens
d'Avall ◼

Alconassar

C710

Sóller ▶

Can
Prohom

Castell

Llucalcari ▼

*Cala de
Deià*

Son Coll

◀ Valldemossa

Residencia

C710

Deià ★ Bus Stop

Es Moli ◉

KEY TO WALKS:
➤➤ ➤➤ Primary Route

0   Kilometres   1

Son Marroig

South from Deià, the C710 snakes through the mountains for 3km to reach
Son Marroig, an imposing L-shaped mansion perched high above the
seashore (and just below the road). The house dates from late medieval times,
but was refashioned in the nineteenth century to become the favourite residence of the Habsburg archduke **Ludwig Salvator** (1847–1915). Dynastically
insignificant but extremely rich, the Austrian noble was a man in search of a
hobby – and he found it in Mallorca. He first visited the island at the age of
19, fell head-over-heels in love with the place, and returned to buy this chunk
of the west coast. Once in residence, Ludwig immersed himself in all things
Mallorquín, learning the dialect and chronicling the island's topography, arche-
ology, history and folklore in astounding detail. He churned out no fewer than
seven volumes on the Balearics and, perhaps more importantly, played a leading role as a proto-environmentalist, conserving the coastline of his estates and,

amongst many projects, paying for a team of geologists to chart the Coves del Drac (see p.194).

The Son Marroig estate (Mon–Sat 9.30am–2pm & 3–5pm; €4) comprises the house, its gardens and the headland below. The **house** boasts a handful of period rooms, whose antique furnishings and fittings are enlivened by an eclectic sample of Hispano-Arabic pottery. On display too are some of the archduke's manuscripts and pen drawings, as well as several interesting photographs of him. It won't be long, however, before you're out in the **garden**, whose terraces are graced by a Neoclassical belvedere of Tuscan Carrara marble. The views along the jagged, forested coast are gorgeous.

Down below the garden is a slender promontory, known as **Sa Foradada**, "the rock pierced by a hole", where the archduke used to park his yacht. The hole in question is a strange circular affair, sited high up in the rock face at the end of the promontory. It takes about forty minutes to **walk** the 3km down to the tip of land, a largely straightforward excursion to a delightfully secluded and scenic spot. A sign on the gate at the beginning of the path (up the hill and to the left of the house) insists you need to get permission at Son Marroig before setting out – but this is just to make sure you pay the admission fee to the house and estate. There should be few problems with direction-finding on the walk: about 100m beyond the gate, keep right at the fork in the track, and as you approach the end of the promontory, think carefully before deciding to attempt the precarious climb beyond the old jetties. On your return, you can slake your thirst at the **café-bar** *Son Marroig* overlooking the coast from beside the car park near the house.

Valldemossa and around

South of Son Marroig, the C710 stays high above the coast, twisting through what was once the archducal estate en route to the intriguing ancient hill-town of **VALLDEMOSSA**. Approaching from Deià, the town at first appears disappointing, as the C710 cuts through the drab western outskirts. The approach from the south, however, is delightful. Here, with the mountains closing in, the road squeezes through a narrow, wooded defile before entering a lovely valley, whose tiered and terraced fields ascend to the town, a sloping jumble of rusticated houses and monastic buildings backclothed by the mountains.

The origins of Valldemossa date to the early fourteenth century, when the asthmatic **King Sancho** built a royal palace here in the hills where the air was easier to breathe. Later, in 1399, the palace was gifted to Carthusian monks from Tarragona, who converted and extended the original buildings into a **monastery**, now Mallorca's most visited building after Palma cathedral. Besides the monastery, there's not much to Valldemossa. The narrow cobbled lanes of the oldest part of town tumble prettily down the hillside beneath the monastery, but it only takes a few minutes to explore them and there are only two specific sights: the imposing bulk of the church of **Sant Bartomeu** and – round the back along a narrow alley, c/Rectoria 5 – the humble birthplace of **Santa Catalina Thomàs**, a sixteenth-century nun revered for her piety. The interior of the house has been turned into a simple little shrine, with a statue of the diminutive saint holding a small bird.

Valldemossa is a stop for the regular **buses** between Palma, Deià and Sóller and, on five days a week, for the once-daily bus from Peguera, Andratx and Estellencs. Orientation is easy: a modern bypass skirts the centre of Valldemossa to the north; there are several car parks along this road, as well as a bus stop at the west end of town, from where it's a couple of minutes'

VALLDEMOSSA

▲ Palma

Hike to Puig d'es Teix ◄

◄ Deià & the C710

N

0   100 m

School

JOAN MIR DE LA CONCEPTION

JOAN FUSTER

AMETLERS

SON GUAL

LLUIS VIVES

MAS

AVINGUDA PALMA

FILOSES

PARE FRANCESC FRAU

REI SANXO

PLAÇA
PÚBLICA

BUGER

DONANTS DE SANG

CAMÍ DE SA COMA

PARE CASTANYEDA

RECTORIA

Santa Thomas
Shrine

PLAÇA SANTA
CATALINA
TOMAS

Sant
Bartomeu

SA DRAGONERA

ROSA

ROSA

UETAM

Ca'n Mario ◉

PLAÇA RAMON
LLULL

PLAÇA
CARTOIXA

Valldemossa ◉

CANONGE

P

Costa Nord

ⓘ

P

VENERABLE SOR AINA

ES COS

ANGDA A.L. SALVADOR

Ca'n Pedro

Bus Stop

VIA BLANQUERNA

URUGUAI

Jardines Joan
Carlos I

Valldemossa
Monastery

Palace of
King Sancho

walk to the monastery. The new **tourist office** is right next to the main car park (Mon–Sat 10am–1pm & 2.30–7pm, Sun 10am–5pm; ☎971 612 106).

The monastery

Most of the present complex of Valldemossa's **Real Cartuja de Jesús de Nazaret** (Royal Carthusian Monastery of Jesus of Nazareth; Mon–Sat 9.30am–6pm, Sun 10am–1pm; Nov–Feb Mon–Sat closes 4.30pm; €8) is of seventeenth- and eighteenth-century construction, having been remodelled on several occasions. It owes its present notoriety almost entirely to the novelist and republican polemicist **George Sand** (1804–76), who, with her companion, the composer **Frédéric Chopin**, lived here for four months in 1838–39. They arrived just three years after the last monks had been evicted during the liberal-inspired suppression of the monasteries, and so were able to rent a commodious set of vacant cells. Their stay is commemorated in Sand's *A Winter in Majorca*, a sharp-tongued and sharp-eyed epistle that is available hereabouts in just about every European language (an extract is given on p.296). Reading the book today, what comes through strongly is Sand's frustration with the ossified social structures on the island, though her diatribes against reaction sometimes merge into a mean-spirited contempt for her Spanish neighbours. Ungraciously, Sand explains that her nickname for Mallorca, "Monkey Island", was coined for its "crafty, thieving and yet innocent" inhabitants, who, she asserts, are "heartless, selfish and impertinent". Quite what the islanders made of Sand is unknown, but her trouser-wearing, cigar-smoking image – along with her "living in sin" – could hardly have made the woman popular in rural Mallorca.

There's an obvious, though limited curiosity in looking around Sand and Chopin's old quarters, but the monastery boasts far more interesting diversions, and it's easy to follow the multilingual signs around. A visit begins in the gloomy, aisle-less **church**, a square and heavy construction with a kitsch high altar and barrel vaulting that's distinguished by its late Baroque ceiling paintings and fanciful bishop's throne, though the lines of the nave are spoiled by the clumsy wooden stalls of the choir. Beyond the church lie the shadowy **cloisters**, where the first port of call is the **pharmacy**, which survived the expulsion of the monks to serve the town's medicinal needs well into the twentieth century. Its shelves are crammed with a host of beautifully decorated majolica jars, antique glass receptacles and painted wood boxes, each carefully inscribed with the name of a potion or drug.

The nearby **prior's cell** is, despite its name, a comfortable suite of bright, sizeable rooms, enhanced by access to a private garden with splendid views down the valley. The cell, and the adjoining library, dining and audience rooms, are graced by a wide assortment of religious *objets d'art*. These include handsome majolica and tin-glazed tiles and, displayed in the library, two fine but unattributed medieval triptychs: the *Adoration of the Magi*, a charmingly naive painting in the Flemish style, and an intricate three-panel marble sculpture celebrating the marriage of Pedro II of Aragón. This degree of luxury – the other cells are of similar proportions – was clearly not what the ascetic St Bruno had in mind when he founded the Carthusian order in the eleventh century. Nevertheless, it's hard to blame the monks at Valldemossa for lightening what must have been a very heavy burden of privations. Bruno's rigorous regime, inspired by his years as a hermit, had his monks in almost continuous isolation, gathering together only for certain church services and to eat in the refectory on Sundays. At other times, lay brothers fed the monks through hatches along the cloister corridors, though this was hardly an onerous task:

three days a week the monks had only bread and water, and they never ate meat. The diet and the mountain air, however, seemed to suit them: the longevity of the Valldemossa monks was proverbial.

Along the corridor, **Cell no. 2** exhibits miscellaneous curios relating to Chopin and Sand, from portraits and a lock of hair to musical scores and letters (it was in this cell that the composer wrote his "Raindrop" Prelude). There's more of the same next door in **Cell no. 4**, plus Chopin's favourite

From Valldemossa to Puig d'es Teix by the Archduke's Path

12.5km; 674m of ascent; 4hr 30min–5hr

The terrain between Valldemossa and Deià is mountainous and wild, abounding in steep cliffs and rocky summits; the lower slopes are wooded but the tops are almost devoid of vegetation, with numerous dramatic viewpoints, many of them overlooking the sea. The land is rough but, as elsewhere in Mallorca, the mountains are crisscrossed by footpaths first made by charcoal burners, olive growers and hunters. These paths can be stony, but this area was also subject to the attentions of the nineteenth-century Austrian archduke **Ludwig Salvator** (see p.124), who had some wonderful paths constructed so that he could ride around on horseback admiring the scenery. Today, walkers can still benefit from the archduke's efforts because his estate was acquired in 1967 by ICONA, Mallorca's organization for nature conservation. This circular walk – which can be lengthened or shortened to suit – is a classic, showing the area at its best.

The route

From Valldemossa's bypass near the monastery, proceed along c/Venerable Sor Aina past the small car park and take the first right – c/Joan Miró – up to the school. Climb the steps at the left-hand side of the school, then turn right and almost immediately left. Go to the end of the street, turn right, ascend slightly, then turn left up a wide path that leads into the woods, entered by a stile over a gate. The stony path twists up quite steeply to reach an opening in the wall at the edge of the wooded plain, the **Pla d'es Pouet**; a shortcut near the top is waymarked, but it makes little difference which way you go. From the wall, go straight on across the level ground to reach an old **well** (now polluted) in a large clearing with a rotten fallen tree. This well is a vital reference point in a confusing area, and it is essential that you take your bearings carefully here. An **extension** of the walk, via the Mirador de Ses Puntes, begins here (see below).

For the main walk, take the path bearing slightly right (northeast at first, and then north), which leads easily up to the **Coll de S'Estret de Son Gallard**. On the col is a barrier of brushwood set up by hunters who still practise the traditional *caza a coll* method, which you can observe: birds are lured into flying along artificial tunnels created by cutting passages through the trees, then captured in nets.

From the nearby V-shaped stone seats, the path continues uphill to the right. To the south of the main path lies the **Cova de Ermita Guillem**, an interesting hermit's cave, containing icons and candles; this offers excellent shelter if you're unlucky with the weather – look for a branch path on the right, which leads to the enclosure in front of the cave. To rejoin the uphill main path, retrace your steps for about 100m and then branch sharply off to the right. The most spectacular part of the walk begins here: it's a wide and easy walkway on the edge of cliffs with a breathtaking view.

As you approach the summit of Caragolí, a path branches off left towards the cliffs, offering the possibility of an adventurous **descent to Deià** by a thrilling, but precarious, cliff path. If you're tempted to try this, find the start by making for the largest of the holm oaks on the horizon, growing out of a pothole. A path from this holm oak descends into the woods below, where you should look out for a large *sitja* (charcoal-worker's

piano which, after three months of unbelievable complications, arrived just three weeks before the couple left for Paris. Considering the hype, these incidental mementos are something of an anticlimax. Nor do things improve much in the ground-floor galleries of the adjacent **Museu Municipal**, which feature local landscape painters and take a stab at tracing the diligent endeavours of Archduke Ludwig Salvator (see p.124). But don't give up: the upstairs section of the museum, entitled the Museu Municipal Art Contemporani, has a small

shelter), with two stone shelters and a stone bread oven; turn right here, join another track and turn left. Reaching a gate, double-back along terraces to a *caseta* (fieldhouse), from where a path leads down to *Es Moli* hotel in Deià.

From the main path, you can spy Port de Sóller down on the coast and the mountains Major, Teix and Galatzó rising high above the seashore. Then the path climbs southeast to 944m before descending gently over a sloping, arid plain, the **Pla d'es Aritges** (*aritge* is smilax, a plant with vicious backward-curving thorns). A path junction at an isolated group of pine trees offers a shortcut back to Valldemossa **via Fontanelles**. To continue on the main route, take the left fork northeast, which brings you over a 935-metre top and, shortly after, to a viewpoint overlooking Deià. After this the path swings southeast and begins to descend to the Teix path junction.

A metre-high cairn marks the Teix path junction. Here, branch left (northeast) on a path that scrambles up a little gully and then proceed over a wall positioned at right angles to the edge of a cliff. Stone steps take you to the top of the wall and an iron ladder down the far side. From here, it's an easy walk to the **Pla de Sa Serp**, a plain where there is a spring, the **Font de Sa Serp**. A well-used path leads up to the col between the two tops and on to the main west summit of **Puig d'es Teix** (1062m), where the views are especially good to the northeast, looking over the Sóller valley to Mitx Dia, the western summit of Puig Major, with the tops of Cornadors, L'Ofre and the Alfàbia ridge forming a stunning skyline.

Return to the Teix path junction by the same route (avoid the difficult-to-follow route southwest from Teix towards Sa Bussa) and turn left to follow the main track down the **Cairats valley**. First you'll come to an old "snowhouse" (a deep hole used for storing ice in winter), then a mountain hut and below that a spring and picnic site, the **Font d'es Poll** (Well of the Poplar). The wide track beyond is rather stony but you'll have no trouble finding the route. On the way down the valley you'll see reconstructions of a *sitja*, a charcoal-worker's shelter. Keep on the main track down the Cairats valley, going over a wall via stone steps to the left of a locked gate. Ignore two branches to the left and then join a road which leads past a number of large new houses down to an old house with a square tower, **Son Gual**, from where there's a splendid view over the old part of Valldemossa.

Extension of the walk to Mirador de Ses Puntes and Veià
1.5km; 116m of ascent; 45min

From the well in the clearing on the Pla d'es Pouet, take the path which leads northwest at first, before zigzagging uphill and swinging west. Fork left shortly after passing an old bread oven to reach the **Mirador de Ses Puntes**. From this superb viewpoint, return to the fork and take the left branch, which rises through the trees to the top of **Pouet** (858m) and, after a little dip, **Veià** (871m). For much of the way the path is the wide bridleway built by the archduke and from it you can look down on Sa Foradada, a rocky headland near his old house, Son Marroig. From the ruined shelter on Veià the path descends to the Coll de S'Estret de Son Gallard, where you rejoin the main path a little up from the well.

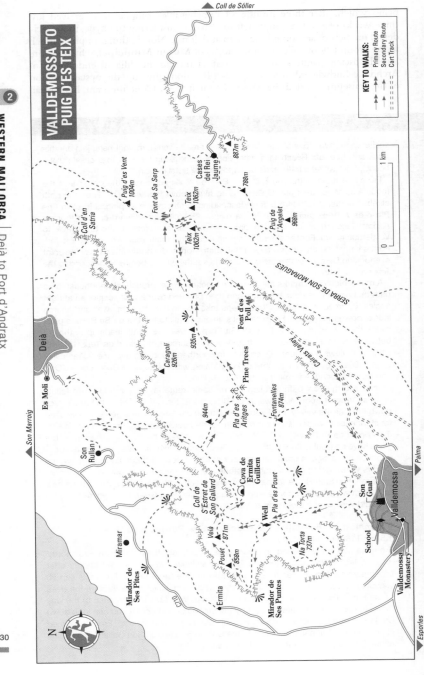

VALLDEMOSSA TO
PUIG D'ES TEIX

▲ Coll de Sóller

Puig d'es Vent
1004m

Font de Sa Serp

Teix
1062m

Teix
1062m

Cases
del Rei
Jaume

887m

788m

Puig de
L'Angelet
968m

Col d'en
Satria

935m

SERRA DE SON MORAGUES

Caragolí
926m

Font d'es
Poll

944m

Pla d'es
Aritges

Pine Trees

Fontanelles
874m

Carates Valley

Es Molí

Deià

Son Marroig ▶

Son
Rullan

Cova de
Ermita
Guillem

Coll de
S'Estret de
Son Gallard

Pla d'es Pouet

Well

Son
Gual

Valldemossa

Palma ▶

Miramar

Veiá
871m

Pouet
858m

Na Torta
737m

School

Valldemossa
Monastery

Mirador
de Ses Pites

Ermita

Mirador de
Ses Puntes

◀ Esporles

N

KEY TO WALKS:
Primary Route
Secondary Route
Cart Track

0   1 km

2

130

but outstanding collection of **modern art**, including work by Miró, Picasso, Francis Bacon and sketches by Henry Moore. There's also a substantial sample of the work of the Spanish modernist Juli Ramís (1909–1990), from geometric abstractions through to forceful, expressionistic paintings like *The Blue Lady* (*Dama Blava*).

Back beside the prior's cell, be sure to take the doorway which leads outside the cloisters to the **Palace of King Sancho**. It's not the original medieval palace – that disappeared long ago – but this fortified mansion is the oldest part of the complex and its imposing walls, mostly dating from the sixteenth century, accommodate a string of handsome period rooms cluttered with faded paintings and other curios. There's also an eccentric wooden drawbridge linking two rooms above the original entrance situated on the far side of the building, away from the cloisters. The "palace" was used as a political prison for much of its history, its most celebrated internee being the liberal reformer Gaspar de Jovellanos, a victim of the royal favourite Manuel de Godoy, who had him locked up here from 1801 to 1802. Nowadays, the palace has regular displays of folk dancing, and there are hourly free **concerts** of Chopin's piano music.

Practicalities

There are a couple of **accommodation** options in Valldemossa. *Ca'n Mario*, c/Uetam 8 (☏971 612 122, ☏971 616 029; ❷), is a very attractive little *hostal* with an elegant, antique-cluttered foyer and comfortably old-fashioned rooms. It's situated just a minute's walk from the monastery – from the pedestrianized area between the cloisters and the palace, go down the slope and take the first turning on the right – and is a popular spot, so reservations are pretty much essential. The only other option in town is the brand new *Valldemossa*, ctra Vieja de Valldemossa s/n (☏971 612 626, ⓦwww.valldemossahotelrural.com; ❾), a luxury property with pretensions to practically regal grandeur. It has a gorgeous restaurant and one of the most beautiful views on the island. Outside town, off the C710 just over 2km to the west, is the solitary *Hotel Residencia Vistamar* (☏971 612 300, ☏971 612 583; ❼), an opulently converted eighteenth-century *finca* whose gardens and swimming pool abut a deep green gully that plunges down towards the sea; rooms are decorated in traditional style, with dark wood and bright fabrics.

The centre of Valldemossa is packed with **restaurants and cafés**. Many are geared up for day-trippers and offer dire fast food at inflated prices, but there's a handful of recommendable places amongst the dross. Probably the best choice is the pocket-sized, family-run restaurant on the upper floor of the *Hostal Ca'n Mario*, c/Uetam 8 (☏971 612 122), where they serve traditional Mallorcan food at affordable prices. A reserve option is the inexpensive *Ca'n Pedro*, Avgda Arxiduc Lluís Salvador s/n (☏971 612 170; closed Sun eve), a large and traditional café-restaurant serving from an extensive menu; the food isn't exactly memorable and the place can heave with tourists, but it's just about good enough. Alternatively, about 2km outside of town on the Deià road, *Ca'n Costa* (☏971 616 134; closed Tues) is a popular restaurant occupying an ancient *finca*; the decor is over the top – old farm equipment and other rustic baubles – but the shaded terrace is lovely, and the Mallorcan cuisine is excellent and affordable, with main courses from around €9. The area's top restaurant, however, is the excellent *Costa Nord*, Avgda Palma 6, bang in the town centre across from the car park (☏971 612 425, ⓦwww.costanord.com), with great views and Mediterranean cuisine; full meals cost around €30. The restaurant is attached to an **information centre** (free entrance), the brainchild of

American actor Michael Douglas, who owns an estate nearby. Here you can see a documentary (featuring Douglas himself) on the history of the Serra de Tramuntana, along with exhibits on Archduke Luis Salvador and local wildlife.

Port de Valldemossa

The closest spot to Valldemossa for a swim is **PORT DE VALLDEMOSSA**, a hamlet set in the shadow of the mountains at the mouth of a narrow, craggy cove. There's no public transport, but the drive down to the hamlet, once Valldemossa's gateway to the outside world, is stimulating: head west out of Valldemossa along the C710 and, after about 1.5km, turn right at the sign and follow the twisty side road for 6km through the mountains. Port de Valldemossa's beach is small and shingly, and tends to get battered by the surf, but the scenery is stunning and the village sports a handful of **restaurants**. Pick of the bunch is the busy *Es Port* (℡971 616 194), which has a well-deserved reputation for its superb seafood, with main courses from around €12.

La Granja and around

Nestling in a tranquil wooded and terraced valley some 10km southwest from Valldemossa is the *hacienda* of **La Granja** (daily: April–Oct 10am–7pm; Nov–March 10am–6pm; €8; Ⓦ www.la-granja.net). To get there, follow the C710 for about 8.5km from Valldemossa and take the signposted left turn; the once-daily Palma–Estellencs **bus** stops by the entrance. The house and its grounds make for a popular package-tourist trip, but, despite the many visitors, the estate maintains a languorous air of old patrician comfort. There's hardly anything new or modern on view, but somehow this doesn't seem contrived. La Granja was occupied until very recently by the Fortuny family, who took possession in the mid-fifteenth century; after about the 1920s, it seems that modernization simply never crossed their minds.

From the entrance in front of the main forecourt, signs direct you up round the back of the house, past an incidental collection of well-weathered farming tackle and on into the tiny formal **gardens**. Next door, a small patio leads to the main **house**, a ramshackle sequence of apartments strewn with domestic clutter – everything from children's games and mannequins, through old costumes, musical instruments and a cabinet of fans, to a fully equipped antique kitchen. There's also a delightful little theatre, where plays were once performed for the household in a manner common amongst Europe's nineteenth-century rural landowners. Likewise, the dining room, with its faded paintings and heavy drapes, has a real touch of country elegance, as does the graceful first-floor loggia. Look out also for the finely crafted, green-tinted Mallorcan chandeliers and the beautiful majolica tile-panels that embellish several walls.

Tagged onto the house, a series of **workrooms** recall the days when La Granja was a profitable and almost entirely self-sufficient concern. A wine press, almond and olive-oil mills prepared the estate's produce for export, whilst plumbers, carpenters, cobblers, weavers and sail makers all kept pace with domestic requirements from their specialized workshops. The Fortunys were one of Mallorca's more enlightened landowning families, and employees were well fed by the kitchen staff, who made cheeses, bread and preserves by hand. The main kitchen is in one of the **cellars**, where you'll also find a grain store and a "torture chamber", an entirely inappropriate recent addition which holds a harrowing variety of instruments once regularly used by the Inquisition. Moving on, you'll soon reach the family **chapel**, a diminutive affair with kitsch silver-winged angels, and then the expansive **forecourt**, shaded by plane trees and surrounded by antiquated workshops where costumed artisans practise traditional crafts such as wood-turning and candle-making. This part of the visit is a bit bogus, but good fun all the same – and the home-made pastries and doughnuts (*bunyols*) are lip-smacking. Your visit may also coincide with a mildly diverting display of Mallorcan **folk dancing** (summer Wed & Fri 3.30–5pm).

Esporles

It's a couple of kilometres along the Palma road southeast from La Granja to **ESPORLES**, an amiable, leafy little town whose elongated main street follows the line of an ancient stone watercourse. This is Mallorca away from the tourist zone, and although there's no special reason to stop, it's an attractive place to overnight. The town has several places **to stay**, the best being the one-star *Hostal Esporles* (☎971 610 202; ❺), a handsomely renovated, family-run *hostal* in an appealing old stone house just off the main drag by the church at Plaça Espanya 8; breakfast is served on an outside terrace overlooking the mountains. They also have an excellent restaurant serving *Mallorquín* cuisine – the best place **to eat** in town.

Galilea and around

Heading southwest from La Granja, a narrow and difficult country road heads up a V-shaped valley before snaking through the foothills of the Serra de Tramuntana. After 10km you come to **PUIGPUNYENT**, a workaday farmers' village marginally enhanced by a seventeenth-century church with a squat bell tower. The main attraction here is the *Gran Hotel Son Net* (☎971 147 000, ⓦwww.sonnet.es; ❾), set in a deliciously pink Renaissance palace which sits atop the imposing hill in the town centre. One of the finest of Mallorca's growing number of super-luxury resorts, this sumptuous establishment has inspiring views, excellent international cuisine (with Mediterranean leanings) and attentive service. It's only a fifteen-minute drive from Palma, but enjoys a wonderfully tranquil setting.

Continuing southwest, the road threads for another 4km along a benign valley of citrus groves and olive trees on its way to **GALILEA**, an engaging scattering of whitewashed farmsteads built in sight of a stolid hilltop church. There's a rusty old café-bar beside the church, but the best place to soak up the bucolic atmosphere is at the *Restaurant-Bar Galilea* (☎971 614 329; closed Wed), below the church and beside the through road. The views from the terrace are gorgeous and the Mallorcan **food** is both delicious and cheap, with filling snacks from just €4.

Southwest of Galilea, the road wriggles its way through to the unremarkable settlement of **CAPDELLÀ**, before squeezing through the mountains – the most beautiful, and nerve-jangling, part of the drive – for a further 9km to enter Andratx from the east.

Banyalbufar and around

Back on the C710, just beyond the turning for La Granja, a narrow side road forks down to the coast at **PORT D'ES CANONGE**. The five-kilometre journey down through thickly forested hills is splendid, but the settlement itself is disappointing, a scrawny, modern *urbanització* flanking a shingle beach.

You'd do far better to stay on the main coast road for a further 6km, enjoying spectacular views on the way to the attractive village of **BANYALBUFAR**,

△ Fishing nets, Port de Sóller

whose terraced fields cling gingerly to the coastal cliffs. The land here has been cultivated since Moorish times, with a spring above the village providing a water supply that's still channelled down the hillside along slender watercourses into open storage cisterns (which are the unlikely-looking home for a few carp). The village itself is bisected by its main street, the C710, which is flanked by whitewashed houses and narrow cobbled lanes. The cute main square perches above the C710, overlooked by a chunky parish church dating from the fifteenth century.

Banyalbufar is a fine place to unwind and there's a rough and rocky **beach** fifteen minutes' walk away down the hill – ask locally for directions since the lanes that lead there are difficult to find. The village has several appealing places **to stay**. The nicest is the *Hotel Mar y Vent*, on the main street towards the east end of the village (℡971 618 000, ⓦwww.hotelmarivent.com; ❺; closed Dec–Jan), which has an enticing exterior and elegantly appointed rooms with Mallorcan antiques and modern comforts – most also have balconies with views of the sea, and there's a rooftop swimming pool. However, there's probably more chance of a vacancy at the *Hostal Baronia*, at the west end of the main drag (℡971 618 146, ⓕ971 148 738; ❸; closed Nov–March), a modern building with an outside pool and forty plain but perfectly adequate balconied bedrooms. Less appealing is the *Hotel Sa Coma* (℡971 618 034; ❹; closed Nov–Jan), a modern concrete lump with tidy rooms facing the sea down below the main street.

Banyalbufar has a fair selection of **cafés** and **restaurants** strung along the main drag. The *Café Bellavista* (closed Sun) serves salads, omelettes and light meals and has a seaview terrace, as does the best restaurant hereabouts, the *Son Tomas*, towards the west end of the village (℡971 618 149; closed Tues), which has great steaks and a delicious fish of the day (around €17), as well as an excellent *menú del día* (€14).

Estellencs

About 1km southwest of Banyalbufar stands perhaps the most impressive of the lookout points that dot the coastal road, the **Mirador de Ses Ànimes**, a sixteenth-century watchtower built as a sentinel against pirate attack and now providing stunning views along the coast. **ESTELLENCS**, 6km further on, is similar to Banyalbufar, with steep coastal cliffs and tight terraced fields, though if anything it's even prettier. There's almost no sign of tourist development in the village, whose narrow, winding alleys are adorned with old stone houses and a trim, largely eighteenth-century parish **church** – peep inside for a look at the exquisite pinewood reredos. A steep, but driveable, two-kilometre lane leads down from the village, past olive and orange orchards, to **Cala Estellencs**, a rocky, surf-buffeted cove that shelters a shingly beach and a summertime bar.

Estellencs has several **hotels**. The pick is the exquisite little *Hotel Nord*, smack in the middle of the village at Plaça Triquet 4 (℡971 149 006, ⓦwww.hotelruralnord.com; ❺). This occupies a beautiful and newly refurbished medieval building, with antiques, old paintings and beautiful rugs and textiles. Another delightful – and slightly cheaper – option is the *Sa Plana Petit Hotel*, c/Eusebi Pascual s/n (℡971 618 666, ⓦwww.saplana.com; ❹), a rustic, family-run converted farmhouse with plenty of atmosphere set on its own hill at the southern edge of town. There's also the routinely modern, two-star *Maristel*, which offers great views down over the coast (℡971 618 529, ⓕ971 618 511; ❹; closed Nov–Dec). Amongst the village's handful of **cafés**, the *Vall-Hermós* has good range of snacks and stunning views from its terrace, while the

Maristel's café-restaurant does a good *menú del día* for only €9. The best **restaurant** is the *Montimar* (☎971 618 576), in a graceful old mansion across from the church, which serves splendid traditional meals, including rabbit dishes for about €10. Its principal rival is the adjacent *Son Llarg* (☎971 618 564), also set in a fine old house and specializing in traditional Mallorcan cuisine.

Andratx and around

Heading southwest from Estellencs, the C710 threads along the littoral for 6km before slipping through a tunnel and – immediately beyond – passing the stone stairway up to the **Mirador de Ricardo Roca**. At 400m above the sea, this lookout point offers some fine coastal views, and you can wet your whistle at the *Es Grau* **restaurant** next door (☎971 618 527), which does acceptable local food (around €15 for a full meal).

Beyond the mirador, the C710 makes a few final flourishes before turning inland and worming its way up and over forested foothills to **ANDRATX**, a small and unassuming town 19km southwest of Estellencs and just 23km west of Palma. The main event here is the Wednesday morning **market**, a tourist favourite, but otherwise there's not much to detain you, though the old houses and cobbled streets of the upper town form a harmonious ochre ensemble. The upper town culminates in the fortress-like walls of the thirteenth-century church of **Santa Maria**, built high and strong to deter raiding pirates, its balustraded precincts offering panoramic views down to the coast.

Sant Elm

From Andratx, a handsome country road heads west through the coastal hills to the low-key resort of Sant Elm (sometimes signposted in Castilian as San Telmo). After 3km you'll stumble across the hillside hamlet of S'Arracó, the prelude to a pretty, orchard-covered landscape, which buckles up into wooded hills and dipping valleys as it nears the seashore.

SANT ELM is little more than one main street draped along the shore, with a sandy beach at one end and a harbour at the other. There are plans to expand the resort, but at present it's a quiet spot where there's a reasonable chance of a **room** in high season, either at the conspicuous *Hotel Aquamarín*, c/Cala Conis 4 (☎971 239 105, ℗971 239 125; ❸; closed Nov–April), a spectacularly unsuccessful concrete edifice built in the style of an old watchtower and equipped with spartan rooms; or, preferably, at the *Hostal Dragonera*, Avgda Rey Jaume I 5 (☎971 239 086, ℗971 239 013; ❸), a simple modern building with clean and neat rooms, the best of which have balconies with sea views.

For such a small place, there's a surprisingly wide choice of **cafés** and **restaurants** dotted along the main street. The seafront *Bar-Restaurant Flexas* serves delicious and cheap snacks and meals, while the set meal at the *Hostal Dragonera* costs a very reasonable €12. The harbourside *Restaurant Na Caragola* (☎971 109 299) has a charming terrace and sea views, as well as a wide-ranging menu – from pizzas to paella with main courses anywhere between €7.50 and €22. A local favourite is the *Vista Mar*, c/Jaume I 46 (☎971 239 044), which has great views across the picturesque harbour and does an excellent fish soup (€8.15) and other fish dishes (from around €11), including *zarzuela*.

There's a regular **bus** service to Sant Elm from Andratx and Peguera during the summer (May–Oct), and a reasonable service the rest of the year. Buses pull in beside the *Hotel Aquamarín* at the south end of the main drag. There are also **boats** between Sant Elm and Port d'Andratx (March–Sept daily at 4pm; €6; reservations on ☎639 617 545).

Illa Dragonera

From Sant Elm's minuscule harbour, **boats** take a few minutes to shuttle across to the austere offshore islet of **Illa Dragonera**. This uninhabited chunk of rock, some 4km long and 700m wide, lies at an oblique angle to the coast, with an imposing ridge of seacliffs dominating its northwestern shore. Behind the ridge, a rough track travels the length of the island, linking a pair of craggy capes and their lighthouses. Most people visit for the scenic solitude, but the island is also good for **birdlife**: ospreys, shags, gulls and other seabirds are plentiful, and you may also see several species of raptor.

There are two ways of getting to the island. A passenger **ferry** rattles across from Sant Elm, dropping passengers about halfway up the east shore at a tiny cove-harbour (July–Sept Tues–Thurs, Sat & Sun 5 daily; €8; Oct–May Mon–Sat 4 daily; €6). You should make arrangements for your return trip, which is included in the fare, on the outward journey. Alternatively, there's a two-hour **cruise** (July–Sept Mon & Fri 2 daily; €11), which allows half an hour on Dragonera and spends the rest of the time nosing along the local coastline. Reservations are a good idea, though not essential. For sailing times of both boats, ask at the harbour or call ☎639 617 545 or ☎696 423 933.

Port d'Andratx

The picturesque port and fishing harbour of **PORT D'ANDRATX**, 6km southwest of Andratx, has been transformed by a rash of low-rise shopping complexes and Spanish-style villas. However, it's not at all a classic case of overdevelopment: the heart of the **old town**, which slopes up from the south side of the bay, preserves a cramped network of ancient lanes, and there's no denying the prettiness of the setting, with the port standing at the head of a long and slender inlet flanked by wooded hills. Sunsets show the place to best advantage, casting long shadows up the bay, and it's then that the old town's gaggle of harbourside restaurants crowd with holidaymakers and expatriates, a well-

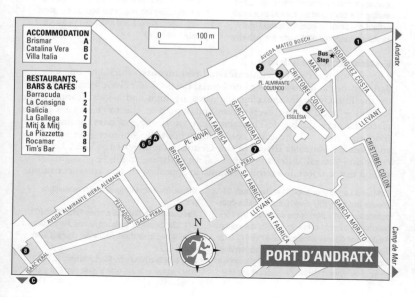

ACCOMMODATION	
Brismar	A
Catalina Vera	B
Villa Italia	C

RESTAURANTS, BARS & CAFÉS	
Barracuda	1
La Consigna	2
Galicia	4
La Gallega	7
Mitj & Mitj	6
La Piazzetta	3
Rocamar	8
Tim's Bar	5

PORT D'ANDRATX

heeled crew, occasionally irritated by raucous teenagers, who come here for the nightlife. Port d'Andratx may be rather sedate, but it's still an enjoyable place to spend a night or two, especially as it possesses several outstanding seafood restaurants and is easy to reach. The one thing it doesn't have, however, is a sandy beach – the nearest one is east over the hills at Camp de Mar (see p.101).

Arrival and information

There are regular **buses** from Andratx, Camp de Mar and Palma; these pull in at the back of the bay, a brief walk from both the old town (on the left as you face the sea) and the big, modern marina (on the right). From March to October there are once-daily **boats** from Sant Elm (€6) and Peguera (€13); for timetable details call ☎639 617 545 or ☎696 423 933. There's a **taxi** rank about halfway along the old town harbourfront, or you can call Radio Taxi Andratx on ☎971 136 398; the fare to Camp de Mar is about €5, to Sant Elm about €10.

Accommodation

Even in the height of the season, there's a good chance of finding a vacant **room** in Port d'Andratx, but you're much safer making a reservation ahead. The options are, however, limited to an inexpensive *hostal* and two hotels, one a bargain, the other full-blown luxury. All are located on or near the old town's harbourfront.

Hotel Brismar c/Almirante Riera Alemany 6 ☎971 671 600, ⓕ971 671 183. A pleasant, old-fashioned two-star place with fifty spotless, en suite rooms, the pick of which have port-facing balconies (though avoid these if you're a light sleeper – there's a bar next door). Closed Dec–Feb. ❹

Hostal-residencia Catalina Vera c/Isaac Peral 63 ☎971 671 918. This appealing establishment occupies a neatly shuttered and whitewashed building in a quiet location, flanked by a small orchard one block up from the harbourfront. Rooms are frugal but neat; some are with show-

ers, some without. Closed Dec–March. ❸

Hotel Villa Italia Cami Sant Carles s/n ☎971 674 011, ⓦwww.hotelvillaitalia.com. An opulent, 1920s twin-towered Italianate mansion set behind a steeply terraced garden with luxuries such as a rooftop swimming pool, as well as gorgeous views out over the bay. It's located a five-minute stroll west of the old part of town along Camí Sant Carles, an extension of c/Isaac Peral. Don't miss the *menú del día*, one of the best on the island, with superb service and knock-out views – and it's only €16.50. ❽

Eating and drinking

The old town is packed with **cafés** and **restaurants**, which line up along the harbourfront and crowd the more central portions of c/Isaac Peral, one block up the hill. Generally speaking, standards are high and a local feature is the seafood – good almost everywhere and superb at the town's two Galician places. Eating is the big deal here, but there are a couple of **bars** too, lively little spots that hum till the early hours throughout the summer. The very large and popular *Barracuda* **disco**, in the Centro Commercial Las Velas, Local 11, comprises several different venues offering theme nights, gay nights (Fri), several dance floors and a mix of music to appeal to all ages and inclinations.

Cafeteria La Consigna Avgda Mateo Bosch 26. Popular and enjoyably modern coffee house-cum-patisserie about a third of the way along the harbourfront with great cakes, croissants and coffees.
Restaurant Galicia c/Isaac Peral 37 ☎971 672 705. Highly recommended Galician place serving mouthwatering seafood without the pretensions of some of its rivals down on the harbourfront. Has

simple, traditional decor and very reasonable prices.
Restaurant La Gallega c/Isaac Peral 52 ☎971 671 338. Excellent, bistro-style Galician restaurant specializing in seafood, with main courses from about €12.
Mitj & Mitj c/Almirante Riera Alemany 8. The flashiest bar in town, with a wide range of sounds,

from house through to jazz, and imaginative decor including art installations on the outside balcony.
Restaurante La Piazzetta Plaça Almirante Oquendo 2 ℡971 672 700. Large, popular restaurant and pizzeria on a pleasant pedestrianized square just up from – and about one-third of the way along – the harbourfront, serving tasty pizzas and pastas from €5.50 as well as reasonably priced seafood dishes.

Restaurant Rocamar c/Almirante Riera Alemany 29 ℡971 671 261. A well-established restaurant at the west end of the harbourfront, away from the crowds and offering delicious seafood; also has a lovely waterside terrace. About €40 per person for a full meal.
Tim's Bar c/Almirante Riera Alemany 10. More subdued than the *Mitj & Mitj* next door, this cosy little bar caters to an older crowd.

Travel details

Buses

Andratx to: Camp de Mar (every 1–2hr; 10min); Palma (hourly; 45min); Peguera (every 1–2hr; 10min); Port d'Andratx (every 1–2hr; 10min); Sant Elm (May–Oct 5–6 daily; Nov–April 1 daily; 10min); Valldemossa (Mon–Fri 1 daily; 1hr).
Bunyola to: Palma (3–5 daily; 30min)
Deià to: Palma (Mon–Fri 5 daily, Sat & Sun 2–3 daily; 45min); Port de Sóller (5 daily, Mon–Fri 5 daily, Sat & Sun 2 daily; 25min); Sóller (Mon–Fri 5 daily, Sat & Sun 2 daily; 20min); Valldemossa (Mon–Fri 5 daily, Sat & Sun 2 daily; 15min); Peguera (Mon–Fri 4 daily; 50min).
Esporles to: Palma (Mon–Fri 7 daily; Sat 4 daily, Sun 2 daily; 20min).
Estellencs to: Palma (Mon–Fri daily; Sat & Sun 1 daily; 45min).
Port d'Andratx to: Andratx (every 1–2hr; 10min); Camp de Mar (every 1–2hr; 20min); Palma (hourly; 45min); Peguera (every 1–2hr; 10min).
Port de Sóller to: Alcúdia (May–Oct Mon–Sat 2 daily; 2hr); Ca'n Picafort (May–Oct Mon–Sat 2 daily; 2hr 30min); Deià (Mon–Fri 6 daily, Sat & Sun 2–3 daily; 25min); Lluc (May–Oct Mon–Sat 2 daily; 1hr 15min); Palma (via the tunnel: Mon–Fri 14 daily, Sat & Sun 2–3 daily; 35min; via Valldemossa: Mon–Fri 5 daily, Sat & Sun 2–3 daily; 55min); Sóller (7 daily; 5min); Pollença (May–Oct Mon–Sat 2 daily; 1hr 45min); Port d'Alcúdia

(May–Oct Mon–Sat 2 daily; 2hr 5min); Port de Pollença (May–Oct Mon–Sat 2 daily; 1hr 50min); Valldemossa (Mon–Fri 6 daily, Sat & Sun 2–3 daily; 35min).
Sant Elm to: Andratx (May–Oct 4–6 daily; Nov–April 1 daily; 10min); Peguera (May–Oct 4–6 daily; Nov–April 1 daily; 20min).
Sóller to: Deià (Mon–Fri 6 daily, Sat & Sun 2–3 daily; 20min); Palma (via the tunnel: Mon–Fri 14 daily, Sat & Sun 2–3 daily; 30min; via Valldemossa: Mon–Fri 5 daily, Sat & Sun 2–3 daily; 50min); Port de Sóller (7 daily; 5min); Valldemossa (Mon–Fri 5 daily, Sat & Sun 2 daily; 30min).
Valldemossa to: Andratx (Mon–Sat 1 daily; 1hr); Banyalbufar (Mon–Fri 1 daily; 30min); Deià (Mon–Fri 6 daily, Sat & Sun 2–3 daily; 15min); Estellencs (Mon–Sat 1 daily; 45min); Palma (Mon–Fri 14 daily, Sat 4 daily, Sun 9 daily; 20–30min depending on route); Peguera (Mon–Sat 1 daily; 1hr 10min); Port de Sóller (Mon–Fri 6 daily, Sat & Sun 2–3 daily; 35min); Sóller (Mon–Fri 6 daily, Sat & Sun 2 daily; 30min).

Trains

Binissalem to: Inca (hourly; 10min); Lloseta (hourly; 5min); Palma (hourly; 30min).
Lloseta to: Binissalem (hourly; 5min); Inca (hourly; 5min); Palma (hourly; 35min).
Sóller to: Palma (7–8 daily; 1hr 15min).

Northern Mallorca

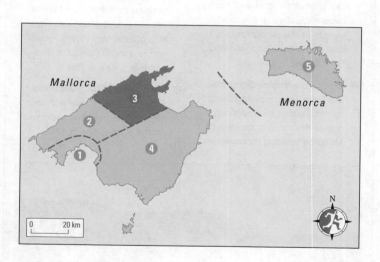

CHAPTER 3 **Highlights**

* **Lluc** Home to the Balearics' most venerated icon, La Moreneta, this rambling monastery also has an excellent museum and makes a great base for mountain hikes. See p.146

* **The Davallement, Pollença** Held in the beguiling little town of Pollença, the torchlit lowering of the Cross – the Davallement – is one of the most evocative of the many events in the Balearics celebrating Holy Week (Setmana Santa). See p.154

* **Ermita de Nostra Senyora del Puig** This rambling assortment of old stone buildings is one of the most appealing of Mallorca's hilltop monasteries, perched on a hilltop high above Pollença. See p.154

* **Hotel Formentor** Opened in 1930, this distinguished hotel once played host to Charlie Chaplin and F. Scott Fitzgerald and still offers a sandy beach, delightful sea views and immaculate gardens. See p.160

* **Cap de Formentor** This tapered promontory of bleak sea-cliffs and scrub-covered hills offers magnificent views and is a fruitful area for bird-watching. See p.160

* **Parc Natural de S'Albufera** Small pocket of rare wetland offering the best birdwatching on the island. See p.170

△ Parc Natural de S'Albufera

Northern Mallorca

The magnificent **Serra de Tramuntana** mountains reach a precipitous climax in the rearing peaks of northern Mallorca, beginning just to the northeast of Sóller. This is the wildest part of the island, long the haunt of brigands and monks, and even today the ruggedness of the terrain forces the main coastal road, the C710, to duck and weave inland, offering only the most occasional glimpse of the sea. A rare exception is the extraordinary side road that snakes down to both overcrowded **Sa Calobra** and the attractive beach at **Cala Tuent**, but it's the well-appointed monastery of **Lluc** that remains the big draw here – for religious islanders, who venerate an effigy of the Virgin known as La Moreneta, and tourists alike. Pushing on along the coast, the C710 emerges from the mountains to reach **Pollença**, a tangle of stone houses clustered around a fine, cypress-lined Way of the Cross. Pollença is one of Mallorca's most appealing towns and it's also within easy reach of both the comely coastal resort of **Cala Sant Vicenç** and the wild and rocky **Península de Formentor**, the bony, northernmost spur of the Serra de Tramuntana. The peninsula shelters the northern shore of the Badia de Pollença, which is home to the laid-back and low-key resort of **Port de Pollença**, whilst the next bay down holds the more upbeat and flashy **Port d'Alcúdia**. Close by, the old walled town of **Alcúdia** has a clutch of modest historical sights and pocket-sized **Muro** has a splendid main square. The **Parc Natural de S'Albufera** takes the prize as the best birdwatching wetland in Mallorca.

The Serra de Tramuntana is fine **hiking country**. Suggestions for several comparatively easy walks are given in the text, and we have also described in detail one outstanding day-long hike starting at Lluc and another, shorter hike from Port de Pollença. Northern Mallorca also boasts fine **beaches**, from the long golden strands that stretch round the bays of Pollença and Alcúdia to the more discreet charms of the cove beaches at Cala Sant Vicenç.

As regards **accommodation**, the resorts of northern Mallorca – primarily Port de Pollença, Port d'Alcúdia and Cala Sant Vicenç – muster a veritable phalanx of hotels and *hostals*, but this is predominantly package territory, and from June to early September (and sometimes beyond) independent travellers are well advised to make advance reservations. In the shoulder season and in winter things are much easier and cheaper, though many places do close down. More promisingly, the number of inland *hostals* and hotels is on the increase – Pollença, Alcúdia, Sineu and Petra all now have places to stay – and there's not quite the seasonal crush here that there is on the coast. Finally, you could also stay at one of the region's two **monasteries** – at Lluc and just outside Pollença: the rooms are frugal but inexpensive, and there's usually space at any time of the year.

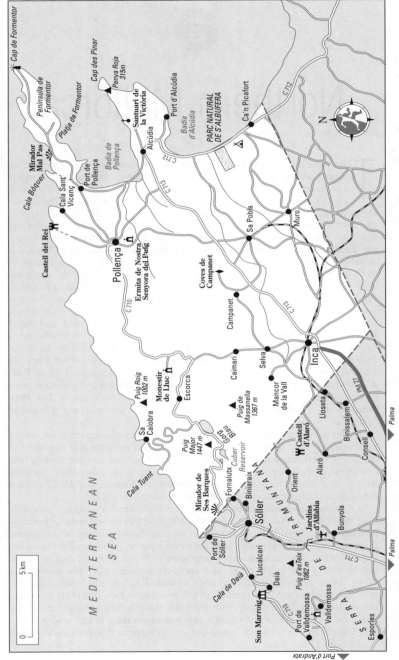

Artà

Cap de Formentor

Peninsula de Formentor

Platja de Formentor

Mirador Mal Pas

Cala Boquer

Cala Sant Vicenç

Port de Pollença

Badia de Pollença

Castell del Rei

Penya Roja 315m

Santuari de la Victòria

Cap des Pinar

Port d'Alcúdia

Alcúdia

Badia d'Alcúdia

Ca n Picafort

C-712

PARC NATURAL DE S'ALBUFERA

N

Pollença

Ermita de Nostra Senyora del Puig

C-710

C-713

Sa Pobla

Muro

Coves de Campanet

Campanet

Selva

Caimari

Mancor de la Vall

Inca

C-713

Palma

PM-27

Lloseta

Binissalem

Consell

Puig Roig 1002 m

Monestir de Lluc

Escorca

Puig de Massanella 1367 m

Sa Calobra

Puig Major 1447 m

Cúber Reservoir

Gorg Blau

Mirador de Ses Barques

Fornalutx

Biniaraix

Castell d'Alaró

Alaró

Orient

Bunyola

Cala Tuent

MEDITERRANEAN SEA

Port de Sóller

Sóller

Jardins d'Alfàbia

C-711

Palma

SERRA DE TRAMUNTANA

Llucalcari

Deià

Cala de Deià

Puig d'es Teix 1062 m

Son Marroig

Port de Valldemossa

Valldemossa

C-710

Esporles

Port d'Andratx

5 km

0

Getting around by public transport is easy enough – even the smaller places have a reasonable **bus** service – though service is a mite patchy on Sundays and in the winter.

The northern coast and Pollença

Beyond Sóller, the **C710** slips through the highest and harshest section of the Serra de Tramuntana. For the most part, the mountains drop straight into the sea – precipitous and largely unapproachable cliffs with barely a cove in sight. The accessible exceptions are the comely beach at **Cala Tuent** and the horribly commercial hamlet of **Sa Calobra** next door. The best place to break your journey, however, is inland at the monastery and pilgrimage centre of **Lluc**, which offers a diverting museum, excellent hiking trails in the mountains and a reliable supply of inexpensive rooms.

There's more low-priced monastic accommodation at the hilltop Ermita de Nostra Senyora del Puig, just outside **Pollença**, a beguiling old town of grandee mansions sitting at the foot of a beautiful calvary. Nearby, at the end of the C710, is **Port de Pollença**, a medium-sized but low-key resort with a long sandy beach draped around the Badia de Pollença. The resort is a popular summertime retreat for the inhabitants of Palma and abounds in places to stay; it's also within easy striking distance of the dramatic seacliffs of the **Península de Formentor** at the northernmost tip of the island.

Several **buses** serve the area, including year-round services between Palma and Lluc, Pollença and Port de Pollença and (May–Oct) a once-daily bus on weekdays from Palma to Formentor. However, perhaps the most useful bus runs along the C710 from Port de Sóller, stopping at Sóller, Lluc, Pollença, Port de Pollença, Alcúdia and Port d'Alcúdia. This operates from May to October twice daily on weekdays, though it's so popular that would-be passengers often can't get on. You'll have a better chance of grabbing a seat if you get on board at Port de Sóller rather than waiting at the second stop, Sóller. For the frequencies and journey times of all buses, see p.172.

Cala Tuent, Sa Calobra and Escorca

Heading northeast from Sóller, the C710 zigzags up into the mountains. After about 5km, it passes the steep turning down to Fornalutx (see p.111) before offering a last lingering look over the coast from the **Mirador de Ses Barques** vantage point. Thereafter, the road snakes inland and tunnels through the western flanks of **Puig Major** (1447m), the island's highest mountain. Beyond the tunnel is the **Gorg Blau** (Blue Gorge), a bare and bleak ravine that was a well-known beauty spot until a hydroelectric scheme filled it with a trio of puddle-like reservoirs. The second of the three is the **Embalse de Cúber** (Cúber Reservoir), an unappetizing expanse of water redeemed by its abundant birdlife, notably several different types of raptor. For a better look, follow the easy footpath which circumnavigates the reservoir; it takes a couple of hours to complete. To the immediate north rear the craggy flanks of Puig Major, but the dramatic trail which twists up to the summit from the military base beside the main road remains off-limits because of its radar station. This makes **Puig de Massanella** (1367m), which looms over the gorge to the east, the highest mountain that can be climbed on Mallorca – the climb up it from Lluc is described on p.150.

Cala Tuent

At the far end of the Gorg Blau the road tunnels into the mountains, to emerge just short of a left turn leading to Cala Tuent and Sa Calobra. This turn-off makes for an exhilarating, ear-popping detour to the seashore, the well-surfaced road hairpinning its way down the mountain slopes so severely that at one point it actually turns 270 degrees to run under itself.

About 10km down this road, there's a fork: head left over the hills for the four-kilometre journey to the **Ermita de Sant Llorenç**, a tiny medieval church perched high above the coast, and **CALA TUENT**, where a smattering of villas cling to the northern slopes of Puig Major as it tumbles down to the seashore. Ancient orchards temper the harshness of the mountain, and the gravel and sand beach is one of the quietest on the north coast. It's a lovely spot to while away a few hours and – if you can wrangle a parking spot (space is extremely limited) – and provided you stay close to the shore, the swimming is safe. There's nowhere to stay, though there is an excellent **restaurant** up on a ridge on the far side of the cove, the *Es Vergeret* (☎971 517 105), which offers a wide range of fish and meat dishes from €12, best devoured at the terrace bar in sight of the sea.

Sa Calobra

Heading right at the fork, it's just 2km more to **SA CALOBRA**, a modern resort occupying a pint-sized cove in the shadow of the mountains. The setting itself is gorgeous, but the place is an over-visited disaster, and you'll have to pay €4 just to park. Almost every island operator deposits a busload of tourists here every day in summer and the crush is quite unbearable – as is the overpriced and overcooked food at the local cafés. The reason why so many people come here is to visit the impressive box canyon at the mouth of the **Torrent de Pareis** (River of the Twins). It takes about ten minutes to follow the partly tunnelled walkway round the coast from the resort to the mouth of the canyon. Here, with sheer cliffs rising on every side, the milky-green river trickles down to the narrow bank of shingle that bars its final approach to the sea – though the scene is transformed after heavy rainfall, when the river crashes down into the canyon and out into the sea.

Escorca

Back on the C710, about 4km northeast of the Cala Tuent and Sa Calobra turnoff and 26km northeast of Sóller, is **ESCORCA**, a poorly defined scattering of houses that is the starting point for the **descent of the Torrent de Pareis**, a famous though very testing and potentially dangerous hike-cum-climb which requires rock-climbing skills, wetsuits and ropes. The river drops from here to Sa Calobra through a formidable, seven-kilometre-long limestone gorge, which takes about six hours to negotiate. The descent is not practicable in winter, spring, or after rainfall, when the river may be waist-high and the rocks dangerously slippery. The descent starts on the main road opposite the conspicuous *Restaurant Escorca*, but the old sign has been taken down and a new one has yet to arrive.

The Monestir de Lluc

Tucked away in a remote valley about 35km northeast of Sóller, the austere, high-sided dormitories and orange-flecked roof tiles of the **Monestir de Nostra Senyora de Lluc** (Monastery of Our Lady of Lluc) stand out against the greens and greys of the surrounding mountains. It's a magnificent setting for what has been Mallorca's most important place of pilgrimage since the middle of the thirteenth century. The religious significance of the place, however, goes back much further: the valley's prehistoric animistic inhabitants deified the local holm-oak woods, and the **Romans** picked up on the theme, naming the place from *lucus*, the Latin for "sacred forest". After the Reconquista, however, the **monks** who settled here were keen both to coin a purely Christian etymology and to enhance their reputation. They invented the story of a shepherd boy named Lluc (Luke) stumbling across a tiny, brightly painted **statue** of the Virgin in the woods. Frightened by his discovery, the lad collared the nearest monk, and when the pair returned heavenly music filled their ears, bright lights dazzled their eyes, and celestial voices declared the statue to be an authentically heaven-sent image.

Buses to Lluc, which is situated 700m off the C710, stop in the car park right outside the monastery. In addition to the bus which runs from Port de Sóller and Sóller to Pollença (May–Oct only), there are also services to Lluc two to four times a day from Palma via Inca.

The monastery church and museum

The monastic complex (daily: April–Sept 10am–11pm; Oct–March 10am–8pm; free) is an imposing and formal-looking affair mostly dating from the eighteenth and early nineteenth centuries. At the centre of the complex is the main shrine and architectural highlight, the **Basílica de la Mare de Déu de Lluc**, graced by an elegant Baroque facade. To reach it, pass through the monastery's stately double-doored entrance and keep straight on to the second – and final – courtyard, where there's a dreary statue of Bishop Campins, who overhauled Lluc in the early part of the last century. Dark and gaudily decorated, the church is dominated by heavy jasper columns, the stolidness of which is partly relieved by a dome over the crossing. On either side of the nave, stone steps extend the aisles round the back of the Baroque high altar to a small chapel. This is the holy of holies, built to display the statue of the Virgin, which has been commonly known as **La Moreneta** ("the Little Dark-Skinned One") ever since the original paintwork peeled off in the fifteenth century to reveal brown stone underneath. Just 61cm high, the Virgin looks innocuous, her face tweaked by a hint of a smile and haloed by a much more modern jewel-encrusted gold crown. In her left arm she cradles a bumptious baby Jesus, who holds the "Book of Life" open to reveal the letters alpha and omega. Every day, during the 11am mass and again at around 7pm, the **Escolania de Lluc**, a boys' choir founded in the early sixteenth century with the stipulation that it must be "composed of natives of Mallorca, of pure blood, sound in grammar and song", performs in the basilica. They're nicknamed *Ses Blavets*, "The Blues", for the colour of their cassocks.

Just inside and to the right of the basilica's main entrance a small door leads through to the monastery's information desk and a stairway that climbs up to the enjoyable **Museu de Lluc** (daily: 10am–1.30pm & 2.30–5.15pm; €2). After a modest section devoted to archeological finds from the Talayotic and Roman periods come cabinets of intricate old vestments, exquisite gold and silver sacred vessels, medieval religious paintings and an intriguing assortment of votive offerings – folkloric bits and bobs brought here to honour La Moreneta. The museum also boasts an extensive collection of **majolica** (see box on p.148), glazed earthenware mostly shaped into two-handled drug jars and show dishes or plates, of which some two or three hundred are on display. The designs vary in sophistication from broad and bold dashes of colour to carefully painted naturalistic designs, but the colours remain fairly constant, restricted by the available technology to iron red, copper green, cobalt blue, manganese purple and antimony yellow. There are also some rare examples of Islamic **lustreware** and a recently opened section showing a captivating selection of Mallorcan, Spanish and Italian **paintings**. Island artists represented include nineteenth- and twentieth-century canvases by Rusinyol, Cerdà, and Ribas, plus the Goya-esque works of Mayol, and romantic landscapes of Palma by Sureda. There are also some anonymous seventeenth-century Italian Baroque still-lifes featuring flowers, fruit and parrots. The last, disappointing section of the museum displays the paintings and drawings of the early twentieth-century artist **José Coll Bardolet** – the video about his life and ideas is more interesting than his work itself.

The Camí dels Misteris del Rosari

Back outside the monastery's double-doored entrance, walk a few metres to the west and you'll soon spot the large, rough-hewn column at the start of the **Camí dels Misteris del Rosari** (Way of the Mysteries of the Rosary), a broad pilgrims' footpath that winds its way up the rocky hillside directly behind the monastery. Dating from 1913, the solemn granite stations marking the way are of two types: simple stone pediments and, more intriguingly, rough trilobate columns of Gaudí-like design, each surmounted by a chunky crown and cross. The prettiest part of the walk is round the back of the hill where the path slips through the cool, green woods with rock overhangs on one side and views out over the bowl-shaped Albarca valley on the other. It takes about ten minutes to reach the top of the hill, where a wrought-iron *Modernista* cross stands protected by ugly barbed-wire. Afterwards it's possible to stroll or drive down into the Albarca valley by following the country road that begins to the left of the monastery's main entrance. The valley is shadowed by **Puig Roig** (1002m), but there's nowhere in particular to aim for and the road fizzles out long before you reach the coast. For a longer **hike** into the mountains, see p.150.

On the other side of the main complex lie the monastery's extensive **botanical gardens** (same hours as monastery; free); they're through the broad arch to your right as you face the main building. The gardens are laid out with local plants as well as exotics, with small ponds and waterfalls, little footbridges and a stone shed that serves as a tiny museum for antique tools, ancient household crockery and the like.

Majolica

The fifteenth century witnessed a vigorous trade in decorative pottery sent from Spain to Italy via Mallorca. The Italians coined the term **"majolica"** to describe this imported Spanish pottery after the medieval name for the island through which it was traded, but thereafter the name came to be applied to all tin-glazed pottery. The process of making majolica began with the mixing and cleaning of clay, after which it was fired and retrieved at the "biscuit" (earthenware) stage. The biscuit was then cooled and dipped in a liquid glaze containing tin and water. The water in the glaze was absorbed, leaving a dry surface ready for decoration. After painting, the pottery was returned to the kiln for a final firing, which fused the glaze and fixed the painting. Additional glazings and firings added extra lustre. Initially, majolica was dominated by greens and purples, but technological advances added blue, yellow and ochre in the fifteenth century. Majolica of one sort or another was produced in Mallorca up until the early twentieth century.

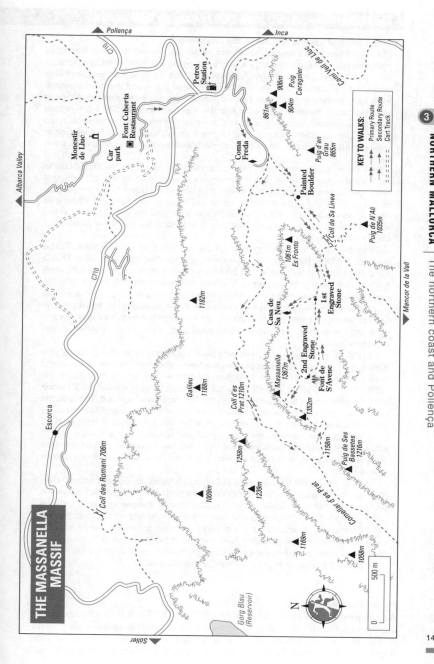

THE MASSANELLA MASSIF

KEY TO WALKS:
Primary Route
Secondary Route
Cart Track

▲ Pollença

▲ Inca

Petrol Station

Font Cuberta Restaurant

Monestir de Lluc

Car park

◄ Albarca Valley

Camí Vell de Lluc

906m

Puig Caragoler

861m

904m

Coma Freda

Puig d'en Grau 865m

Painted Boulder

Coll de Sa Linea

Puig de N'Ali 1035m

1182m

Es Fronto 1061m

Casa de Sa Neu

1st Engraved Stone

▶ Mancor de la Vall

Galileu 1188m

2nd Engraved Stone

Massanella 1367m

Font de S'Avenc

Coll d'es Prat 1210m

1352m

Escorca

Coll des Romani 706m

1258m

1009m

1239m

·1158m

Puig de Ses Bassetes 1216m

Comellar d'es Prat

1169m

1058m

N

◄ Sóller

Gorg Blau (Reservoir)

0   500 m

The Massanella massif: from Lluc to Puig de Massanella

14km; 887m of ascent; 5hr 30min–6hr round-trip.

The large **Massanella massif** has eleven peaks over 1000m and is defended by many crags and steep rocky slopes. Since the construction of a military establishment put Puig Major out of bounds, Massanella has become the best-loved summit of the island. There are several well-defined paths and the classic **ascent from Lluc monastery**, with magnificent views, uses the best of these. Although quite strenuous, the route is not difficult and is deservedly popular. The top is all bare rock, although some small plants grow where moisture lingers in the crevices. Keep an eye open for black vultures, and for the friendly Alpine accentors who often appear on the summit or down by **Font de S'Avenc**, the spring on the southern flank.

From the front of the monastery, walk up through the car park to the **Font Cuberta restaurant** – you can fill up your water bottle at the ancient font through the gated entrance just across from the restaurant. Turn left behind it and follow the road up to join the C710 at a junction on the Coll de Sa Batalla (ignore the sign for Font d'es Prat, which points right). Turn towards Inca and go past the petrol station, where walkers arriving by car may park. The ascent of Massanella from here takes about two and a quarter hours.

Cross the bridge and turn right through the iron gates onto a wide track. Follow the track for 250m past a spring and water trough. Ignoring the Camí Vell de Lluc, a restored footpath to Caimari which continues straight on, swing sharp right uphill following the red painted waymarks. Continue on the wide track through a gate into the area of the Coma Freda farm, whose owner charges €3 at this gate. Pause when you come to a wide opening into a field to look at the impressive **Es Fronto**, a high spur of Massanella with precipitous cliffs. At this point the track to the farm turns right and the path to the Puig de Massanella goes straight on, outside the wall enclosing the field.

This path is well used and marked with paint signs and cairns. Rising through the woods, it joins a wide track by a **painted boulder** (remember this point, as it's useful during the descent). The wide track actually reaches the bottom of a dip at this point, which helps identify it on the way back. Turn left to reach the **Coll de Sa Linea** at 822m, where there is a clearing among the trees and two engraved stones on the right. The main track begins to descend here towards the village of Mancor de la Vall. A possible diversion for strong walkers is to make the ascent of **Puig de N'Ali** by a winding route marked with some cairns and red paint signs; it's not easy to follow, especially at first because of the trees. The top is unusual, with an immense boulder supported in three places to form a sheltered cave with a southern outlook over the plain.

For Puig de Massanella, turn right at Coll de Sa Linea up a clearly defined path rising in big swings at first, then twisting and turning to reach a junction where the two paths to the top diverge. At the junction, there's a **stone** engraved with the words "Puig y Font" ("Mountain and Spring") on the right-hand side and "Font y Puig" on the left, showing the order of arrival at these points. For the ascent, the route to the right is recommended, following an old track which was formerly used to carry ice down on mules. Later on, above the treeline, you'll see the old dry-stone walls of the **Casa de Sa Neu** on the right, where ice was stored.

Practicalities

Accommodation at the monastery (☎971 871 525, ✉info@lluc.net; ❶) is highly organized, with simple, self-contained apartment-cells and apartments. In summer, phone ahead if you want to be sure of space; at other times simply book at the monastery's information office on arrival. There's

Beyond here the path almost levels out, meandering through boulders and clumps of carritx grass in a shallow valley. The southerly path coming up from Font de S'Avenc (described below as part of the descent) passes a second engraved stone, and joins the northerly path about 100m or 200m northeast of this second stone.

Beyond here, head towards the dip between the highest peak of **Massanella** (1367m) and the secondary peak to the southwest (1352m), then veer right to the main peak, which is where you're most likely to see a black vulture. Be careful how you go as there's a pothole some 20m deep close to the summit. On a good day the view from the top encompasses almost the entire island, from the Formentor headland in the northeast to the Bay of Palma. To the north, vertical cliffs plunge 150m to the **Coll d'es Prat** (1210m), above which lies the northern section of the Massanella massif. Puig Major is readily identified by the radar domes on the summit and the splendid cliffs below.

The descent
To descend, retrace your steps to where the southerly path joins the route up. This southerly path offers an awkward but exhilarating descent over sharp cornered limestone boulders lying at all angles, with deep crevices in between. To go down it, turn right to the second engraved stone, on the edge of a sloping shelf below the summit. An obvious rocky staircase leads down to a spring, the **Font de S'Avenc**, by which is a red earth platform, conspicuous in the grey rocky landscape. Steps lead down to an upper cave where a table and benches have been cut out of the rock, and a further set of steps leads down to a lower chamber with two basins of water (you'll need a torch to see inside the lower cave). The flies that infest this cavern make it an unlikely picnic spot, but it offers shelter from lightning and rain.

The path from the spring contours to the east at first, splitting briefly into two; take either branch. The route is marked, but pay careful attention to where you're going as there are many goat paths and natural ledges to lead walkers astray. Follow the marked path back into the trees and on to reach the first engraved stone, which signals the junction with the old mule track used on the ascent. Now it's a question of retracing your steps, turning left at the Coll de Sa Linea and right at the painted boulder, before passing through Coma Freda farm again.

Alternative ascent via Coll d'es Prat
With descent as above, 16km; 1022m of ascent; 6hr–6hr 30min round-trip.
An alternative and longer ascent can be made by following the old track from Coma Freda up the valley on the north side of Massanella to the high Coll d'es Prat (1210m), then descending the Comellar d'es Prat valley for about 1km, from where a path climbs up to the 1158-metre col between Puig de Ses Bassetes (1216m) and Massanella by a short easy scramble. From this col, the direct ascent of the southwest ridge to a secondary peak of Massanella (1352m) is for rock-climbers only, but a walkable path makes its way up a rising traverse, heading east at first, then following the cairns which show the way up the steep and rocky ground. These cairns are difficult to see in the grey rocky wilderness and a descent by this route is not recommended.

an 11pm curfew, except for the apartments, which have their own separate entrance.

For **food**, there's a small general store and several adequate cafés and restaurants, but the star turn is the monks' former refectory, *Sa Fonda* (☎971 517 022; closed Mon evening, Tues and July), a beautifully restored old hall complete with wooden beams, wide stone arches and red marble Ionic pillars. The food is traditional Spanish, with main courses from around €9; the meat dishes are much better than the fish. An interesting alternative is *Restaurant Es Guix* (T971 517 092, lunch only), a curious and solitary little place hidden away in a lushly wooded ravine about 3km from the monastery. The restaurant has a traditional rustic look and good meat dishes – goat is a speciality. To get there, take the Inca turning off the C710 near the monastery and look out for the sign. Reservations are a must in high season.

Pollença and around

Founded in the thirteenth century, the tranquil little town of **POLLENÇA** nestles among a trio of hillocks 20km northeast of Lluc, where the Serra de Tramuntana fades into coastal flatland. Following standard Mallorcan practice, the town was established a few kilometres from the seashore to militate against sudden pirate attack, with its harbour, **Port de Pollença** (see p.157), left as an unprotected outpost. For once the stratagem worked. Unlike most of Mallorca's old towns, Pollença successfully repelled a string of piratical onslaughts, the last and most threatening of which was in 1550, when the notorious Turkish corsair Dragut came within a hair's breadth of victory. In the festival of **Mare de Déu dels Àngels** on August 2, the townspeople celebrate their escape with enthusiastic street battles, the day's events named after the warning shouted by the hero of the resistance, a certain Joan Más: "Mare de Déu dels Àngels, assistiu-mos!" ("Our Lady of Angels, help us!").

Arrival and information

Buses to Pollença (the most frequent services are from Palma, Port de Pollença and Lluc) stop immediately to the south of Plaça Major, at the foot of c/Antoni Maura. The town's **tourist office** (Mon–Sat 9am–1pm & 5–8pm, Sun 9am–1pm; T971 535 077) is just across the street at c/Sant Domingo 2, in front of the church of Nostra Senyora del Roser. Pollença's tiny centre is best explored on foot, but outlying attractions such as the resort of Cala Sant Vicenç (see p.156) can be affordably reached by **taxi**. There's a taxi rank in the centre at the corner of Avinguda Pollentia and c/Reina Maria Cristina, or call Radio Taxi Pollença on T971 866 396. If you're **driving**, you can avoid the baffling one-way streets of the old town by entering Pollença from the south, turning off the main Inca–Port de Pollença road along Avinguda Pollentia.

Accommodation

Desbrull c/Marquès Desbrull 7 T971 535 055, Wwww.desbrull.com. Small hotel with black marble touches and elegant – if rather spartan – rooms. **5**

Ermita de Nostra Senyora del Puig 2km south of town (see p.154) T971 184 132. Ten of the original monks' cells here have been renovated to provide simple rooms sleeping between two and four guests for just €6 per person per night. There's also space for thirty on the floor of another room, but in this case you have to bring your own sleeping bag and you don't save any money – the price is the same. Be warned that it can get cold and windy at night, even in the summer. All guests have access to shared showers and there's a refectory, but the food is only average. Most guests turn up on spec: to be sure of a room, book ahead. **1**

Hotel Juma Plaça Major 9 (T971 535 002, Wwww.hoteljuma.com. First-rate hotel occupying a smart and tastefully converted old merchant's stone house in the heart of the old town. The guest rooms are tidily furnished in brisk modern style with air-conditioning. Rooms overlooking the square cost €7 extra. Closed Nov–Feb. **6**

Posada de Lluc c/Roser Vell 11 T971 535 2200, Wwww.posadalluc.com. Set in a charmingly converted medieval town house; rooms come with a/c, satellite TV, minibar, and there's also a pleasant garden and a small swimming pool. **6**

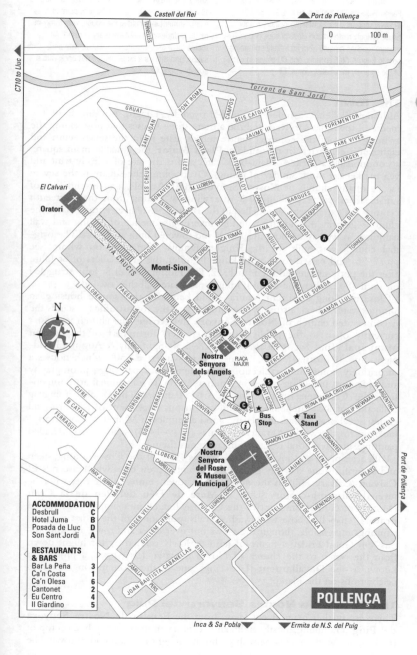

Castell del Rei ▲   ▲ Port de Pollença

◄ C710 to Lluc

0   100 m

Torrent de Sant Jordi

El Calvari

Oratori ✝

TERNELLES
GRUAT
SANT JOAN
LES CREUS
Q311
PONT ROMA
CAMPOS
REIS CATOLICS
JAUME III
FOREMENTOR
PARE VIVES
BINIRELLS
GENTERIA
SION
VERGER
MAR
BARTOMEUALOI
B.CANAVIS
DR. FABREGUES
BARQUES
ADAN DIEM
RULL

HORTA
BONAVISTA
SALUT
ESTRELLA
PADRIMADA
BOU
PT. CERDA
LEO
ROCA TOMAS
M. LLOBERA
PADRO
MENA
AGUILA
ROCA
ST. SEBASTIA
STA. BARBARA
PAU
METGE SUREDA
TORRES

VIA CRUCIS
PORQUER
LLOBERA
PAGESES
FERRA
GAMBOVERIA
MARTELL
GARRIGA
LLUNA
GRAL BOSCH
JESUS
BALANZA
HORTA
JOAN MAS
Monti-Sion ✝
MONTESION
MIRO
COSTA
ANGELS
LLOBERA
SANT SEBASTIA
RAMON LLULL
②
①
CIFRE
B CATALA
FERRAGUT
ALACANTI
CORONEL
JOAN GUIRAUD
GONZALO FERRAGUT
L'OMBRA
FERRA VEN
❸
❹
Nostra Senyora dels Àngels ✝
PLAÇA MAJOR
COLON
SOL
MERCAT
MUNAR
PIO XI
JONQUET
RAMON MARIA CRISTINA
VIA ARGENTINA
B
CONVENT
SANT JOSEP
M. DESBRULL
⑤
❻
A. MAURA
SANT ISIDRE
ALCUDIA
PHILIP NEWMAN
CECILIO METELO
Port de Pollença ▶
N
CGE. LLOBERA
CABRELLES
MALLORCA
C
ℹ
★ **Bus Stop**
★ **Taxi Stand**
REINA MARIA CRISTINA
CERVANTES
FRAY J SERRA
MARE ALBERTA
D
Nostra Senyora del Roser & Museu Municipal ✝
RAMON I CAJAL
AVGDA POLLENTIA
JAUME I
DONES DE L' SALA
MENENDEZ
PELAYO
ROSER VELL
GUILLEM CIFRE
PUIG DE MARIA
BISBE DESBACH
SANT DOMINGO
CECILIO METELO
CAMILA
JOAN BAUTISTA CABANELLAS
SINIA
REIS

ACCOMMODATION
Desbrull   C
Hotel Juma   B
Posada de Lluc   D
Son Sant Jordi   A

RESTAURANTS & BARS
Bar La Peña   3
Ca'n Costa   1
Ca'n Olesa   6
Cantonet   2
Eu Centro   4
Il Giardino   5

POLLENÇA

Inca & Sa Pobla ▼   ▼ Ermita de N.S. del Puig

153

Son Brull A few kilometres west of town on the Crta Palma-Pollença PM 220 Km 49.8 ☎971 535 353, ⓦ www.sonbrull.com. Eighteenth-century manor house lovingly restored and cleverly equipped with modern touches ranging from an infinity swimming pool to Bang & Olufsen video and CD player in each of the serenely minimalist rooms. ❾

Son Sant Jordi c/Sant Jordi 29 ☎971 530 389, ⓦ www.sonsantjordi.com. Lavishly appointed establishment in an old stone house, with a mix of rustic antiques and contemporary comfort. All rooms have a/c, satellite TV, minibar, safe and sauna, and there's a large garden out back with a sizeable pool. ❻

The Town

Although Pollença avoided being destroyed by Dragut, not much of the medieval town has survived, and the austere stone houses that now cramp the twisting lanes of the compact centre mostly date from the seventeenth and eighteenth centuries. In the middle, **Plaça Major**, the amiable main square, accommodates a cluster of laid-back cafés and is the site of a lively fruit and veg market on most Sunday mornings. Overlooking the square is the severe facade of the church of **Nostra Senyora dels Àngels**, a sheer cliff-face of sun-bleached stone pierced by a rose window. Dating from the thirteenth century but extensively remodelled in the Baroque style five centuries later, the church's gloomy interior has a mildly diverting sequence of ceiling and wall paintings, as well as a whopping, tiered and towered high altarpiece. The original church was built for the Knights Templar (for more on whom, see pp.77–78) and passed to another knightly order, the Hospitallers of St John, after the pope suppressed them in 1312. The Hospitallers of St John struggled on until 1802, when the Spanish king appropriated all they owned.

Close by, along c/Antoni Maura – and behind a tiny square housing an antique water wheel, a stumpy watchtower and the tourist office – stands the deconsecrated church of **Nostra Senyora del Roser**. The church itself isn't currently open to the public, but the cloisters form part of the **Museu Municipal** (Tues–Sat 10.30am–1.30pm & 5.30–8pm, July & Aug until midnight, Sun 10.30am–1.30pm, 11am–1pm in winter; €1.50), which houses a surprisingly compelling collection of contemporary paintings, photography and video art, including pieces by winners of the town's annual art competition, the Certamen Internacional d'Arts Plàstiques. There's also a ragbag collection of local archeological finds, a curious assortment of folkloric and ecclesiastical bric-a-brac, and several good examples of Mallorcan Gothic art – look out for the work of Francesc Comes (1379–1415), whose finely detailed paintings give temporal reality to his religious themes.

Pollença's pride and joy is its **Via Crucis** (Way of the Cross), a long, steep and beautiful stone stairway, graced by ancient cypress trees which ascends **El Calvari** (Calvary Hill) to the north of the town centre. At the top, a much-revered thirteenth-century statue of **Mare de Déu del Peu de la Creu** (Mother of God at the Foot of the Cross) is lodged in a simple, courtyarded **oratori** (chapel), whose whitewashed walls sport some of the worst religious paintings imaginable, though the views out over coast and town are sumptuous. On Good Friday, a figure of Jesus is slowly carried by torchlight down from the *oratori* to the church of Nostra Senyora dels Àngels, a procession known as the **Davallament** (Lowering), one of the most moving religious celebrations on the island.

The Ermita de Nostra Senyora del Puig

There are further magnificent views from the **Ermita de Nostra Senyora del Puig**, a rambling, mostly eighteenth-century monastery perched on top of the Puig de Maria, a 320-metre-high hump facing the south end of town. The monastic complex, with its fortified walls, courtyard, chapel, refectory and cells, has had a chequered history, alternately abandoned and restored by both monks and nuns. The Benedictines now own the place, but the monks are gone and today a custodian supplements the order's income by renting out cells to tourists (see p.152). There's nothing specific to see, but the setting is extraordinarily serene and beautiful, with the mellow honey-coloured walls of the monastery surrounded by ancient carob and olive trees, a million miles from the tourist resorts visible far below.

It takes around an hour to walk to the monastery from the centre of town. Take the signposted turning off the main Pollença–Inca road just south of town and head up this steep lane until it fizzles out after 1.5km, to be replaced by a cobbled footpath which winds up to the monastery's entrance. It's possible to drive to the top of the lane, but unless you've got nerves of steel, you're better off parking elsewhere. Note that there have been reports of cars left at the foot of the lane overnight being vandalized; although this is unusual, you might prefer to park in town instead.

Eating and drinking

Pollença does very well for **restaurants**, supported by the villa owners who gather here every evening from the surrounding countryside. The **bar** scene is less convincing, but there are several reasonably lively spots in the vicinity of Plaça Major, with one or two occupying the converted basements of old mansions. All these bars serve food of some description, mostly inexpensive *tapas*.

Bar La Peña c/Temple 2. This traditional neighbourhood café-bar has long been one of the best places in town for an inexpensive meal, with a wide range of delicious *variados* (mixed plates; €3.5–7.25).

Café-Bar Juma Plaça Major 9. Good range of tasty *tapas* sold in the brisk, modern bar of the *Hotel Juma*. Rapid-fire service and reasonable prices – a standard portion of *tapas* costs about €3.60. The outside terrace overlooking the main square is especially enticing.

Ca'n Costa c/Costa i Llobera 11 ☏971 531 276. Beautiful place tucked away in an old mansion on a picturesque side street, featuring expensive international gourmet cuisine with a Mediterranean slant; the *menú del día* (€18.50) is a treat. Mon-Sat evenings only, Sun lunch only.

Ca'n Olesa Plaça Major 12 ☏971 532 908. Good

central location and low prices, but stick to the *cocina mallorquina* dishes and grilled fish and meat rather than the bland pastas and pizzas. Open Mon-Sat evenings only, Sunday all day.

Cantonet c/Monti-Sion 20 ☏971 530 429. This fashionable restaurant just north of Plaça Major offers top-notch international cuisine from a limited menu (mains €10–20). In the summer, you can eat out on the terrace of the large church next door. Evenings only, closed Tues.

Eu Centro c/Temple 3. This very central restaurant is one of the town's mainstays and popular with locals and tourists alike for its solid Mallorcan fare. Main courses €6.50–11. Closed Wed.

Il Giardino Plaça Major 11 ☏971 534 302. One of the best restaurants in town, this smart bistro-style place offers a superb range of Italian dishes from about €14, all prepared with great flair.

North of Pollença: the Castell del Rei

Some 7km north of Pollença lie the battered ruins of the medieval **Castell del Rei** (Castle of the King), attached to an isolated and inhospitable crag which rears high above the sea. This remote fastness was founded by the Moors and strengthened by Jaume I to guard the northerly approaches to Pollença against pirate attack. In this regard, however, it was something of a failure: the pirates simply ignored it, preferring to land at nearby Cala Sant Vicenç instead. More successfully, it held out for months against the Aragonese invasion of 1285 and was the last fortress to surrender to Pedro of Aragón, the supplanter of the Mallorcan king Jaume III, in 1343. Subsequently, the castle was used as a watchtower, finally being abandoned in 1715.

It takes about two hours to **walk** to the castle from Pollença, an undemanding hike along a country lane and then a forest footpath leading through the pretty Ternelles valley. On the northern edge of Pollença, a turning signposted to **Ternelles** leads off the C710, twisting north past attractively renovated old *fincas* and olive and citrus groves (note that the Ternelles sign is small, faded and easy to miss; the turning is about 800m to the west of the junction of the C710 and the roads to Port de Pollença and Inca). After 1.6km on the Ternelles road, you'll reach a guarded gate set in the narrow defile at the entrance to the Ternelles valley (if you're driving, you have to park here). An easy-to-follow, rough and dusty track leads to another set of gates, beyond which the path starts to rise, climbing through oak woods to a stretch of mixed woodland dominated by pines. Further on, the trees thin out and the castle ruins can be spied in the distance. About 100m after the start of a fenced-off area on the right-hand side, fork left off the main track – which continues down to the shingly beach at **Cala Castell** – for the climb up to the castle. You can't actually go inside the ruins, but it's worth climbing up for the view. Be aware that this walk is across private land; check with the Pollença tourist office (see p.152) before you set out.

Northeast of Pollença: Cala Sant Vicenç

One of Mallorca's more agreeable resorts, **CALA SANT VICENÇ**, 6km northeast of Pollença, boasts an attractive, solitary setting, its medley of well-heeled villas and modern hotels gambolling over and around a wooded ravine just behind a pair of pint-sized sandy **beaches**. The fly in the aesthetic ointment is the overpowering *Hotel Don Pedro*, insensitively located on the minuscule headland separating the beaches, but the resort is still a delightful spot for a swim – the water is crystal clear and the beach is sheltered from the wind. In addition, you can **hike** out onto the wild and wind-licked seashore that extends to either side of the resort. One tempting option is the moderately strenuous hoof north up the adjoining headland to the top of **Puig de l'Àguila** (206m), from where there are grand views over the surrounding coast and back over the resort. This six-kilometre hike takes around three hours; the first part uses a rough stone road, the second follows a well-defined path which

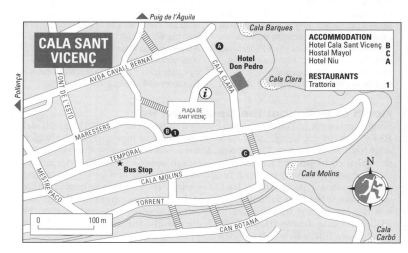

leads to the base of Puig de l'Àguila – but you'll still need a proper IGN map to find your way.

Buses from Lluc and Pollença stop in town on Avinguda Temporal, from where it's a short walk northeast to the **tourist office** on Plaça Sant Vicenç (June–Sept Mon–Fri 9am–2pm, Sat 9.30am–12.30pm; ☎971 533 264). This is package territory, so vacant **rooms** are extremely thin on the ground in summer. Your best bets are the *Hotel Niu*, a comfortably old-fashioned low-rise next to the beach (☎971 530 100, ⓦwww.hotelniu.com; ❻), or the more secluded two-star *Hostal Mayol* (☎971 530 440; ❷) at Cala Molins, a homely and friendly place with its own pool; it's down the steep hill from the main part of the resort. Cala Sant Vicenç's smartest hotel is the four-star *Cala Sant Vicenç*, located in the centre of the resort away from the beach off Avinguda Temporal at Maressers 2 (☎971 530 250, ⓦwww.hotelcala.com; ❼; closed Dec–Jan); it's a tasteful spot with all mod cons.

The resort has a good supply of **cafés** and **restaurants**, beginning with the *Trattoria*, operated by – and adjacent to – the *Hotel Cala Sant Vicenç*. Arguably the best restaurant is the *Cavall Bernat* (☎971 530 250), also in the *Hotel Cala Sant Vicenç*, which offers an impressive gourmet menu that includes traditional Mallorcan dishes.

Port de Pollença

Things are much busier over at **PORT DE POLLENÇA**, but it's still all pleasantly low-key. With the mountains as a shimmering backcloth, this family-oriented resort arches through the flatlands behind the Badia de Pollença, a deeply indented bay whose sheltered waters are ideal for swimming. The **beach** is the focus of attention, a narrow, elongated sliver of sand that's easily long enough to accommodate the crowds, though as a general rule you'll have more space the further south (towards Alcúdia) you go. A rash of apartment buildings and hotels blights the edge of town, and the noisy main road to Alcúdia cuts through the centre, but there are no high-rises to speak of and the resort is dotted with attractive whitewashed and stone-trimmed villas. All together it's quite delightful, especially to the north of the marina, where a portion of the old beachside road – along **Passeig Anglada Camarasa** – has been pedestrianized.

Arrival, information and accommodation

Buses to Port de Pollença from, amongst many places, Pollença, Palma, Alcúdia, Port d'Alcúdia and Port de Sóller stop by the marina right in the town centre. A couple of minutes' walk away is the **tourist office**, just up behind the seafront at c/Monjes s/n (June–Sept Mon–Fri 8am–3pm & 5–7pm, Sat 9am–2pm; Oct–May Mon–Fri 8am–3pm, Sat 9am–1pm; ☎971 865 467), which has loads of local information and accommodation lists.

Port de Pollença has around a dozen **hotels** and not quite as many **hostals**. Needless to say, most of the rooms are block-booked by tour operators, but there's a fairly good chance of finding a vacancy in the places listed below, especially in the shoulder season.

Hostal Bahía Passeig Voramar 31 ☎971 866 562, ⓔmafigueiras@vianwe.com. In a lovely location a few minutes' walk north of the marina along the seashore, this pleasant, unassuming one-star *hostal* offers thirty rooms in one of the port's older villas. Closed Nov–March. ❹

Hotel Capri Passeig Anglada Camarasa 69 ☎971 866 601, ⓦwww.hoposa.es. Standard-issue modern hotel just north of the marina with thirty pleasant rooms. Overlooks the beach where it's flanked by the pedestrianized walkway – the prettiest part of town. Closed Nov–April. ❹

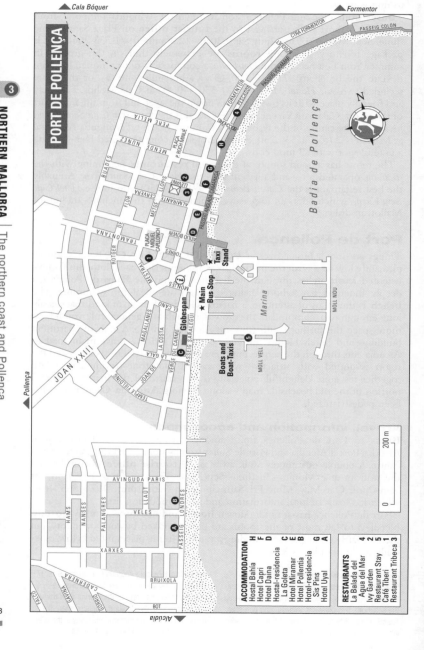

PORT DE POLLENÇA

▲ Cala Bóquer   ▲ Formentor

▲ Pollença

▲ Alcúdia

Badia de Pollença

N

Marina

MÒLL NOU

MÒLL VELL

★ Taxi Stand

★ Main Bus Stop

Boats and Boat-Taxis

Globespan

PASSEIG COLÓN

CTRA FORMENTOR

PASSEIG SARALEGUI

JOAN XXIII

AVINGUDA PARIS

PASSEIG LONDRES

0   200 m

Hotel Daina c/Atilio Boveri 2 ℡971 866 250, ⓦwww.hoposa.es. Straightforward block-like hotel with three stars and sixty rooms. The public areas are decorated in brisk modern style and the rooms are somewhat bleak – and come equipped with some ponderous neo-baronial furniture – but everything is in order. Closed Dec–April. ❺

Hostal-residencia La Goleta Passeig Saralegui 118 ℡971 865 902, ⓔhrlagoleta@hotmail.com. No fuss, two-star *hostal* with sixteen rooms in an attractive five-storey building on the traffic-heavy seafront south of the marina. The front rooms have balconies, but suffer from the noise below. Closed Dec–Feb. ❷

Hotel Miramar Passeig Anglada Camarasa 39 ℡971 866 400, ⓔh.miramar@fehm.es. Attractive three-star hotel in an elegant building – all iron grilles and stone lintels. Every room has its own balcony, but try to get a room at the front with a sea view, or you might be plonked at the back looking out over Carretera Formentor. Closed Nov–March. ❻

Hotel Pollentia Passeig Londres s/n ℡971 865 200, ⓦwww.hoposa.es. Cheerful and friendly place, right across from the beach and just steps away from the town centre. ❻

Hotel-residencia Sis Pins Passeig Anglada Camarasa 77 ℡971 867 050, ⓕ971 534 013. Medium-sized three-star hotel occupying a handsome whitewashed and balconied villa on the waterfront. Closed Nov–March. ❻

Hotel Uyal Passeig Londres s/n ℡971 865 500, ⓦwww.hoposa.es. Pleasant three-star in a white, Spanish-style building on the busy beachfront road. Has its own pool. ❻

The town and around

The flatlands edging the Badia de Pollença and stretching inland as far as Pollença and along the bay to Alcúdia make for easy, scenic cycling. **Mountain bikes** can be rented from March, c/Joan XXIII 89 (Mon–Sat 9am–1pm & 3–8pm, Sun 9am–12.30pm; ℡971 864 784), as can **mopeds** and **motorcycles**. Mountain bikes cost in the region of €8 per day or €40 per week. Ordinary bicycles work out at about half the price. **Car rental** companies include La Parra, c/Joan XXIII 20 (℡971 866 721), and Avis, along the street at no. 80 (℡971 865 394).

The walking holiday specialists **Globespan** (℡971 867 050, ⓦwww .globespan.com) have an office on the waterfront at the *Hotel-Residencia Sis Pins* (see above), where you can sign up for one of their day-long **guided walks**. These are graded according to difficulty and cost €10–25, including transport (but you'll need to take your own food and water); book a minimum of 24 hours beforehand. **Water taxis** shuttle between the marina and the Platja de Formentor, one of Mallorca's most attractive beaches (April–Oct 5–7 daily; 30min; €7.30 each way) and **boat trips** cruise the bay (June to mid-Oct Mon–Sat 1 daily; 2hr 30min; €16), working their way along to Cap de Formentor (Mon, Tues, Wed & Fri 1 daily; 1hr each way; €17 return) or going around to Cala Sant Vicenç and back (Thurs & Sat 1 daily; 1hr 30min one way; €21 return). There's also a delightful six-kilometre **hike** across the neck of the Península de Formentor to Cala Bóquer (see box on p.162).

Eating and drinking

Port de Pollença heaves with **restaurants**. Many offer run-of-the-mill tourist fodder and there's a plethora of pizza places, but others serve the freshest of seafood and skilfully blend Catalan and Castilian cuisines. As a general rule, competition keeps **prices** down to readily affordable levels, with around €9–15 covering a main course at all but the ritziest establishments.

La Balada del Agua del Mar Passeig Voramar 5 ℡971 864 276. Set in a lovely garden alongside the pedestrianized promenade, with international dishes including a wide range of omelettes, curries, and salads. Mains €11–17.

Ivy Garden c/Llevant 14 ℡971 866 271. This outstanding restaurant, arguably the best in town, features an inventive modern menu at reasonable prices. Dishes change, but include things like fillet of salmon with pesto and lemon dressing (€12) and duck with ginger sauce (€14).

Restaurant Stay on the Moll Vell jetty ☎971 864 013. This long-established restaurant, with its crisp modern decor and attentive service, is renowned for the quality of its seafood – though the main courses tend towards the minimal. Prices are a bit above average, but well worth it for the romantic setting out on the pier. It's a very popular spot, so reservations are pretty much essential.

Café Tiberi c/Migjorn 6 ☎971 866 195. Busy, arty place with tapas and specialities including fresh pasta, homemade desserts, and a tasting menu.

Restaurant Tribeca Carretera Formentor 43 ☎971 866 423. Small and intimate bistro-style restaurant with an imaginative modern menu – anything from crêpes to lamb couscous. Smart but competitively priced, with dishes averaging about €15. Centrally located at the junction with c/Llevant. Evenings only; closed Sat.

The Península de Formentor

Heading northeast out of Port de Pollença, the road clears the military zone at the far end of the resort before weaving up into the hills at the start of the twenty-kilometre-long **Península de Formentor**, the final spur of the Serra de Tramuntana. At first, the road (which suffers a surfeit of tourists from mid-morning to mid-afternoon) travels inland, out of sight of the true grandeur of the scenery, but after about 4km the **Mirador de Mal Pas** rectifies matters with a string of lookout points perched on the edge of plunging, north-facing seacliffs. There are further stunning views, in this case over the south shore, from the **Talaia d'Albercutx** watchtower view-point, up the rough side road that climbs the ridge opposite the Mirador de Mal Pas.

The Platja de Formentor

It's a couple of kilometres along the main road from the Mirador de Mal Pas to a roadside car park (€4), from where a ten-minute walk through the woods leads to the **Platja de Formentor**, a pine-clad beach of golden sand in a pretty cove. It's a beautiful spot, with views over to the mountains on the far side of the bay, though it can get a little crowded. From May to October, you can get here from Palma and Port de Pollença on a once-daily **bus** serv-ice (daily except Sun), and there's also a twice-daily bus year-round from Alcúdia and Port d'Alcúdia (daily except Sun). The best way to arrive, however, is by **water taxi** from Pollença (April–Oct 5–7 daily; 30min; €7.30 each way).

At the far end of the beach, and with its own access road from near the car park, stands the **Hotel Formentor** (☎971 899 100, ⓦwww.hotelformentor .net; ❾). Opened in 1930, this grand old hotel – in its heyday the island's best – lies low against the forested hillside, its *hacienda*-style architecture enhanced by Neoclassical and Art Deco features and exquisite terraced gardens. The place was once the haunt of the rich and fashionable – Charlie Chaplin and F. Scott Fitzgerald both stayed here – and although its socialite days are long gone, the hotel preserves an air of understated elegance. It has every facility, and dinner is served on an outside terrace perfumed by the flowers of the gardens; break-fast is taken on the splendid upper-floor loggia with spectacular views over the bay. The rooms are not quite as grand as you might expect, but are still charm-ing. Stay here if you can afford it; there's a good chance of a vacant room, even in high season.

The Cap de Formentor

Beyond the turn-off for the hotel, the main peninsula road runs along a wooded ridge before tunnelling through Mont Fumat to emerge on the rocky mass of the **Cap de Formentor**, a tapered promontory of bleak sea-cliffs and scrub-covered hills which offers magnificent views and good **birdwatching**. The silver-domed lighthouse stuck on the cape's windswept tip is out of bounds, but you can wander round its rocky environs, where the sparse vegetation offers a perfect habitat for lizards and small birds, especially the deep-blue feathered rock thrush and the white-rumped rock dove. From near the lighthouse you can also see the steep, eastward-facing sea-cliffs which shelter colonies of nesting Eleonora's falcons from April to October, whilst circling overhead there are often ravens, martins and swifts. During the spring and summer migrations, thousands of seabirds fly over the cape, Manx and Cory's shearwaters in particular.

If you fancy a snack before heading back from the cape, there's a **coffee bar** next to the lighthouse.

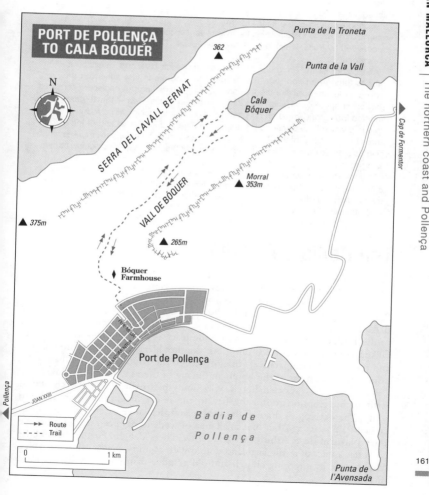

A valley walk from Port de Pollença to Cala Bóquer

6km; 101m of ascent; 1hr 30min.

The walk through the sheltered **Vall de Bóquer** is an attractive, easy stroll over gently undulating ground across the neck of the Península de Formentor. Return is by the same route, about 3km each way. The walk is suitable for most ages and abilities – though the last leg down to the beach can be overgrown and difficult for young children – and is also favoured by ornithologists for the variety of resident and migrant bird life.

Start by walking along the seafront north of Port de Pollença's marina and turn left up **Avinguda Bocchoris**. Proceed across the Formentor road and keep straight along a wide footpath fringed with pine trees and tamarisk. Beyond the end of the footpath is an untidy area whose tarmac marks the layout of a proposed housing development. Ahead, at a sign saying "Predio Bóquer Propriedad Privada Camin Particular," take the wide path north with the ridge of Serra del Cavall Bernat straight ahead. After 150m the path swings to the northeast past olive trees. On the right is a striking example of the lentisk or mastic tree, a dark evergreen with a resinous smell that grows to three metres. Its flowers vary in colour from red to brown and are succeeded by fruits, which are first red then black. The other trees with long pods are carobs.

About 75m further on, the path veers left at the car park and, after about 250m, passes through an iron gate. The **Bóquer farmhouse** is just ahead on the right, while on the left, opposite the farmhouse, is an interesting but neglected **terraced garden** shaped like a ship with its prow facing out to sea – the terraces were watered from stone irrigation channels fed from holding tanks, all now dry. There's a splendid view of the Badia de Pollença from here and, at the far end of the garden, some fine examples of the *Agave americana*, a succulent whose flower spikes reach heights of three metres. On the farmhouse side of the path there's an equally impressive two-metre-high opuntia cactus.

Beyond the farmhouse, the path turns round to the right, heading north through a small iron gate, then ascends steadily for about 500m, passing between large rocks. Niches in the rocks are occupied by clumps of dwarf fan palms, and you'll probably see the blue rock thrushes that inhabit the area. Here and further along

The Badia d'Alcúdia

Moving south from Port de Pollença, it's just 10km round the bay to the compact old town of **Alcúdia**, whose main claims to fame are its imitation medieval walls and the rubbly remains of the old Roman settlement of Pollentia. Within easy striking distance lies the mega-resort of **Port d'Alcúdia**, where glistening sky-rises sweep around the glorious sandy beach of the **Badia d'Alcúdia**. In summer the place is probably best avoided – it's far too crowded to be much fun – but the shoulder seasons are more relaxing and the beach is comparatively uncrowded. In the wintertime you'll barely see a soul, but then most of the hotels and many of the restaurants are closed.

Port d'Alcúdia's assorted hotels, villas and apartment blocks stretch almost without interruption round the bay to the resort of **Ca'n Picafort**, 10km south. The developers drained the swampland that once extended behind this coastal strip years ago, but one small area of wetland has been protected as the **Parc Natural de S'Albufera**, a real birdwatchers' delight. Further behind the coast lies a tract of fertile farmland dotted with country towns, amongst which **Muro**, with its imposing church and old grandee mansions, is easily the most diverting.

the walk, you may also spot wheatears, black-eared wheatears, black redstarts, rock sparrows and wryneck, as well as buzzards, peregrines, kestrels, booted eagles, the occasional osprey, Eleonora's falcons in spring and summer, stone chats and goldfinches. Various warblers pass through this area on migration too, but the big ornithological sight here is the **black vulture**, with a wingspan of around two metres, which glides the air currents of the north coast. There's a fairly good chance of spotting one from the Vall de Bóquer, and if you're really lucky you'll get a close view, its large, black body contrasting with a brownish head, beak and ruff.

Beyond the boulders the path descends, becoming less rocky, then passes through a gap in a dry-stone wall before ascending gently for about 150m – a scattering of pine trees 50m to the left offers a shady spot for a picnic. This area has been heavily grazed by the valley's semi-wild goats, leaving the vegetation sparse and scrubby. The most noticeable plant is *Asphodelus microcarpus*, which grows up to two metres high, bearing tall spikes of white flowers with a reddish brown vein on each petal. Not even the goats like it. Other common shrubs are the *Hypericum balearicum*, a St John's wort whose yellow flowers are at their best in spring and early summer, and the narrow-leaved cistus and spurges, whose hemispherical bushes bear bright yellow glands.

At the top of the next incline the path passes through another wall. About 50m off to the right of the junction of wall and path, more or less due south, is a 1.5m-high **tunnel**, inside which is a spring. Be careful, however, if you venture in, as it's popular with goats, who like the water and shade. They'll sometimes panic and charge out if they see you coming.

To descend to the sea take the path which bears to the left and then runs down alongside a dried-up watercourse amidst the cries of sea birds and the whispering of the tall carritx grass. Patches of aromatic blue-flowered rosemary line the path. The **beach** at the end of the walk at Cala Bóquer is disappointing, being predominantly shingle, and it can also be dirty, although the water is clean and is good for a swim.

To return to Port de Pollença, retrace your steps along the same route.

Accommodation is concentrated in Port d'Alcúdia, but in the summertime it's nearly all reserved for package tourists and getting a last-minute room can be problematic – your best bet is in Alcúdia town, where there are a couple of *hostals*. Transport connections, particularly from May to October, are very good. Frequent **buses** link Port de Pollença, Pollença, Alcúdia, Port d'Alcúdia and Ca'n Picafort. There are also regular services to Alcúdia and its port from Palma, and reasonable summertime connections from Port de Sóller and Sóller as well. **Trains** connect Palma with Muro and Sa Pobla.

Alcúdia and around

To pull in the day-trippers, pint-sized **ALCÚDIA** wears its history on its sleeve. The crenellated wall that encircles much of the town centre is a modern restoration of the original medieval defences, and although the sixteenth- to eighteenth-century houses behind them are genuine enough, the whole place is overly spick and span. In fact, little can be seen today which reflects the town's true historical importance. Situated on a neck of land separating two large, sheltered bays, the site's strategic value was first recognized by the Phoenicians, who settled here in around 700 BC and used the place as a staging-post for sea trade between northwest Africa and Spain. A few Phoenician

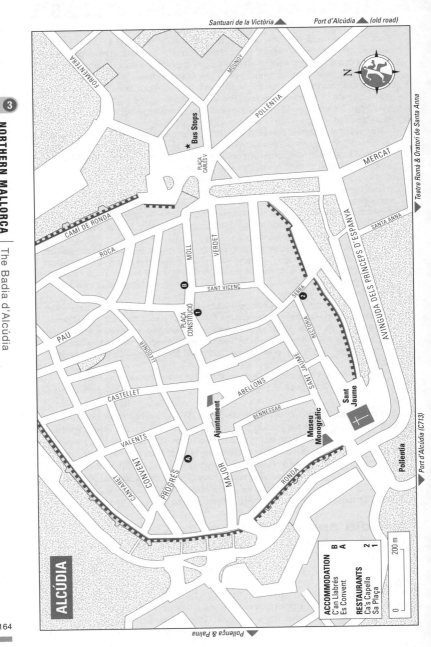

Santuari de la Victòria ▲   Port d'Alcúdia ▲ (old road)

Teatre Romà & Oratori de Santa Anna ▶

Port d'Alcúdia (C713) ▶

▲ Pollença & Palma

N

ALCÚDIA

FORMENTERA

MOLINOT

POLLENTIA

MERCAT

★ Bus Stops

PLAÇA
CARLES V

CAMI DE RONDA

ROCA

MOLL

VERDET

SANTA ANNA

AVINGUDA DELS PRÍNCEPS D'ESPANYA

PAU

LLEDONER

B

①

SANT VICENÇ

PLAÇA
CONSTITUCIÓ

SERRA

②

RECTORIA

CASTELLET

ABELLONS

SANT JAUME

**Sant
Jaume**

VALENTS

CONVENT

PROGRÉS

A

Ajuntament

BENNESSAR

**Museu
Monogràfic**

CANYARET

MAJOR

RONDA

Pollentia

ACCOMMODATION
C'an Llabrés   B
Es Convent   A

RESTAURANTS
Ca's Capella   2
Sa Plaça   1

0   200 m

trinkets have been unearthed here – most notably examples of their delicate, coloured glass jewellery – but their town disappeared when the Romans built their island capital, **Pollentia**, on top of the earlier settlement. In 426, Pollentia was destroyed by the Vandals and lay neglected until the Moors built a fortress in about 800, naming it Al Kudia (On the Hill). After the Reconquista, Alcúdia prospered as a major trading centre for the western Mediterranean, a role it performed well into the nineteenth century, when the town slipped into a long and gentle decline – until tourism refloated its economy.

The Town

It only takes an hour or so to walk around the antique lanes of Alcúdia's compact centre and explore the town wall and its fortified gates. This pleasant stroll can be extended by a visit to a series of minor sights which combine to make an enjoyable whole, although none of them is compelling in itself.

Beginning at the old town's eastern entrance, on Plaça Carles V, walk through the gateway and keep to the main drag – here c/Moll – and you'll soon reach the slender Plaça Constitució, lined with pavement cafés. Just beyond, on c/Major, is Alcúdia's best-looking building, the **Ajuntament** (Town Hall), a handsome, largely seventeenth-century structure with an elegant stone balcony and overhanging eaves. From c/Major, take any of the several sidestreets that lead to the southwest corner of the old town, where you'll find perhaps the most diverting of Alcúdia's sights, the **Museu Monogràfic**, c/Sant Jaume 2 (April–Sept Tues–Fri 10am–1.30pm & 5–7pm, Sat & Sun 10.30am–1pm; Oct–March Tues–Fri 10am–1.30pm & 3.30–5.30pm, Sat & Sun 10.30am–1pm; €2, which also includes admission to the ruins of the Roman town of Pollentia – see below). The museum consists of just one large room, but it's stuffed with a satisfying assortment of archeological bits and bobs, primarily Roman artefacts from Pollentia, including amulets, miniature devotional objects, tiny oil lamps and some elegant statues.

Across the street, dominating this portion of the old town, is the heavyweight and heavily reworked Gothic church of **Sant Jaume**, which holds a modest religious museum (Tues–Fri 10am–1pm, Sun 10am–noon; €1). Close by, on the other side of the ring road just beyond the church, lie the broken pillars and mashed-up walls that comprise the meagre remains of Roman **Pollentia** (same times and ticket as the Museu Monogràfic; €2). Nearly all the stone from the site has been looted by the townsfolk over the centuries so, disappointingly, it's no longer possible to discern the layout of the former capital.

By contrast, the open-air remains of the **Teatre Romà** (Roman Theatre; open access; free) are much more substantial. Dating from the first century BC, this is the smallest of the twenty Roman theatres to have survived in Spain. Nonetheless, despite its modest proportions, the builders were able to stick to the standard type of layout with eight tiers of seats carved out of the rocky hillside, divided by two gangways. Inevitably, the stage area, which was constructed of earth and timber, has disappeared. It's a lovely spot, set amidst fruit and olive trees, a ten-minute stroll to the south of the old town. The short, signed footpath to the Roman theatre begins on c/Santa Anna, a pretty country lane lined by old stone walls that runs south from the ring road a couple of hundred metres east of the remains of Pollentia.

About 500m north from the path to the Roman theatre, another short, clearly signposted footpath heads off c/Santa Anna, this one leading to the **Oratori de Santa Anna**, a diminutive medieval chapel overlooking the C713.

△ Serra de Tramuntana

Practicalities

Buses halt beside the town walls on Plaça Carles V. There are two places **to stay**, beginning with the no-frills *Hostal Ca'n Llabrés* (☎971 545 000; ❷), which has a handful of **rooms** above a café-bar right in the middle of town on Plaça Constitució. Far nicer is *Es Convent*, c/Progrés 6 (☎971 548 716, ⓦwww.esconvent.com; ❻), an exquisitely restored medieval building which also boasts a very fine restaurant serving gourmet local cuisine. There are several other good places **to eat**. The smart *Restaurant Sa Plaça* (☎971 546 278), also on Plaça Constitució, has traditional Mallorcan cuisine, with main courses averaging around €11. A less expensive choice is the cosy café-bar of *Ca's Capella*, just east of the church of Sant Jaume, in an old stone building at the far end of c/Rectoria. It's nothing special, but the pizzas and salads are fine, and it's a little off the beaten track – which is useful, since Alcúdia heaves with day-trippers in the summer.

The Santuari de la Victòria

East of Alcúdia a steep and rocky promontory pokes a wild finger out into the ocean, its northern shore traversed by a narrow road which begins at the easternmost intersection on Alcúdia's ring road. This promontory road slices past the suburban villas of Bonaire before emerging into more scenic terrain, offering fine views of the Badia de Pollença as it bumps over the steep, pine-clad ridges that fringe the coast. After 4.3km, the road slips past the barracks-like, 120-bed *Albergue de la Victòria* **youth hostel** (☎971 545 395, ⓦwww.reaj.com; ❶; closed Oct–Feb). This place has dorm beds only – school parties predominate, and vacant beds are a rarity. There's precious little point in turning up here on the off-chance, and even reservations need to be made well in advance. There's no public transport.

About 1km further along the headland, a turning on the right climbs 500m up the wooded hillside to the **Santuari de la Victòria**, a fortress-like church built in the seventeenth century to hold and protect a crude but much-venerated statue of the Virgin. It was a necessary precaution: this part of the coast was especially prone to attack and, even with these defences, pirates still stole the statue twice, though on both occasions the islanders eventually got it back. The adjacent **restaurant**, the *Mirador de la Victòria* (reservations required; ☎971 547 173; closed Mon), occupies a magnificent location with sweeping sea views, which can be enjoyed from an expansive terrace. The food is first-rate too; guinea fowl and chicken are two specialities.

The Santuari is also the starting point for **hikes** further along the promontory, whose severe peaks are dotted with ruined defensive installations, including a watchtower and an old gun emplacement. The obvious draw is the 315-metre **Penya Roja** mountain, from whose summit there are more great views. The outward part of the hike, leading up through woods and beneath steep cliffs, is quite strenuous; return is by the same route. Allow thirty to forty-five minutes each way. It begins on the wide and clearly signposted dirt road that climbs up behind the Santuari, but the later sections are on trails that require an IGN (or similar) hiking map.

Port d'Alcúdia

PORT D'ALCÚDIA, 2km south of Alcúdia, is easily the biggest and busiest of the resorts in the north of the island: a seemingly interminable string of high-rise hotels and apartment buildings serviced by myriad restaurants and

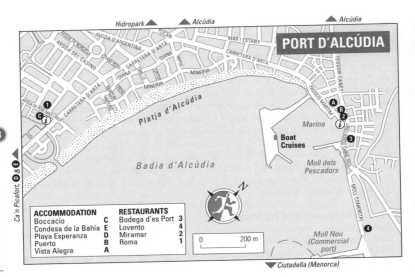

café-bars. Despite the superficial resemblance, however, Port d'Alcúdia is a world away from the seamy resorts on the Badia de Palma. The tower blocks are relatively well distributed, the streets are neat and tidy and there's a prosperous and easygoing air, with families particularly well catered for. Predictably, the daytime focus is the **beach**, a superb arc of pine-studded golden sand which stretches south for 10km from the two purpose-built jetties of Port d'Alcúdia's combined marina, cruise boat and fishing harbour. About 500m east of the marina along the headland lies the **commercial port**, Mallorca's largest container terminal after Palma.

Arrival and information

Port d'Alcúdia acts as northern Mallorca's summertime transport hub, with **bus** services to and from Palma, Port de Sóller, Artà, Cala Millor and Cala Rajada, as well as neighbouring towns and resorts. There's no bus station; instead, most local and long-distance bus services travel the length of the **Carretera d'Artà**, the main drag, dropping off passengers at clearly signed stops along the way. The main **tourist office** (Easter–Oct Mon–Sat 9am–7pm; ☎971 892 615) is at Carretera d'Artà 68, about 2km south round the bay from the marina, while there's a second, more conveniently located tourist booth on the Passeig Marítim (Easter–Oct Mon–Sat 9am–2pm & 4–7pm; ☎971 547 257). Both have all sorts of information, including useful free maps marked with all the resort's hotels and apartments.

Accommodation

In season, vacant **rooms** are few and far between, but there's a vague chance of finding something amongst the low-priced *hostals* clustered behind the marina in the oldest and tattiest part of the resort. The least expensive rooms here – basic, no-frills affairs – are provided by the mundanely modern *Puerto*, c/Teodor Canet 29 (☎ & ☎971 545 447; ◑; closed Nov–March), and the even cheaper *Vista Alegre*, Passeig Marítim 22 (☎971 547 347; ◐), which also has the advantage of being on the seafront and open year-round.

In winter most of the hotels and *hostals* close down, but in the shoulder seasons it's sometimes possible to get a good deal at one of the plusher **hotels**. Places to try include the whopping 300-room, three-star *Boccacio*, near the tourist office at Avgda Pere Mas i Reus 3 (℡971 891 375, ℱ971 891 987; ❻; closed Nov–Jan), and the comparable, though more luxurious, five-star *Playa Esperanza*, about 4km south of the marina along the seashore (℡971 890 568, ℱ971 890 938; ❻; closed mid-Nov to Jan). Both have the full range of facilities, including swimming pools and sports facilities, but the *Esperanza* has the advantage of a beachside location, as does the *Hotel Condesa de la Bahía* (℡971 890 120, ℱ971 890 049; ❺), a huge L-shaped complex about 3km south of the marina, open year-round with every facility from bike rental to a children's playground.

The town and around

Port d'Alcúdia lies at the beginning of an intensively developed tourist zone which takes advantage of the great swath of pine-studded sandy beach stretching around the Badia d'Alcúdia. Some lessons have been learnt from earlier developments – there are more recreational facilities and at least some of the coast has been left unscathed – but first impressions are primarily of concrete and glass. The beach and the sky-rises end on the outskirts of **CA'N PICAFORT**, once an important fishing port; its harbour–marina still preserves vestiges of its earlier function but today the town is an uninteresting suburban sprawl.

A tourist "**train**" (on wheels, with clearly marked roadside stops) runs up and down the length of the resort every hour from June to September, transporting sunbaked bodies from one part of the beach to another. Not that there's very much to distinguish anywhere from anywhere else – the palm-thatched *balnearios* (beach bars) are a great help in actually remembering where you are. A walkway runs along the back of the beach, which is usually more crowded to the north. Just as crowded, and located a kilometre or so inland along Avinguda del Tucan, is the much-vaunted **Hidropark**, a gigantic pool complex with all sorts of flumes and chutes (May–Oct daily 10am–6pm; €14).

There's a superabundance of **car, moped and bike rental** companies strung out along the Carretera d'Artà. Mountain bikes work out at about €8 per day; cars are €25. Summer **boat trips**, leaving from the marina, explore the rocky, mountainous coastline to the northeast of Port d'Alcúdia: the shorter excursion travels as far as the tip of the headland, the Cap des Pinar, without venturing into the Badia de Pollença (April–Oct 3 daily; 3hr; €12); the longer version continues round this headland, across the bay to the Platja de Formentor and around to Cala Sant Vicenç (July & Aug Sat & Sun; 4hr; €20).

Ferries to Menorca

Balearia (℡902 160 180, ⓦwww.balearia.net/eng) operate a fast-ferry **catamaran** service during the summer from Port d'Alcúdia to Maó and Ciutadella on Menorca. In both cases, the one-way passenger fares start at €50 (cars from €100). In addition, Iscomar (℡902 119 128, ⓦwww.iscomar.com) operate **car ferries** from Port d'Alcúdia to Ciutadella once or twice daily; the one-way passenger fare costs €31, vehicles up to 4.5m in length €51. Remember that local car rental firms do not allow their vehicles to leave Mallorca.

Eating and drinking

There are dozens of **cafés** and **restaurants** in Port d'Alcúdia, and although many of them are identikit pizzerias and tourist-style places serving mediocre versions of Spanish food, there are a number of distinctive exceptions.

Bodega d'es Port c/Gabriel Roca 1. Set on the waterfront, between the marina and the commercial port and decked out in an appealing version of traditional bodega style with wide windows, wooden chairs and a stone façade. It's a great place for a drink, accompanied by a first-rate selection of *tapas*.
Restaurant Lovento c/Gabriel Roca 33 ☎971 545 048. Just away from the main tourist zone, along the waterfront near the commercial port, this smooth and polished spot offers superb seafood at affordable prices – try the monkfish.

Restaurant Miramar c/Vicealmirante Moreno 4 ☎971 545 293. Well-established seafront restaurant serving a fine range of seafood. A full meal will set you back about €45.
Pizzeria Roma Restaurant Avgda Pere Mas i Reus s/n. This is one of the more authentically Italian of Port d'Alcúdia's many pizzerias, with a wide-ranging menu offering pizzas and pastas through to crêpes (which are particularly good) and steaks. It's located just off Carretera d'Artà, across and just up the street from the main tourist office.

The Parc Natural de S'Albufera

Given all the high-rise development along the Badia d'Alcúdia, the pristine wetland of the 2000-acre **Parc Natural de S'Albufera** (daily: April–Sept 9am–7pm; Oct–March 9am–5pm; free), on the west side of Ca'n Picafort, makes a wonderful change. Swampland once extended round much of the bay, but large-scale reclamation began in the nineteenth century, when a British company dug a network of channels and installed a steam engine to pump the water out. These endeavours were prompted by a desire to eradicate malaria – then the scourge of the local population – as much as by the need for more farmland. Further drainage schemes accompanied the frantic tourist boom of the 1960s, and only in the last decade has the Balearic government recognized the ecological importance of the wetland and organized a park to protect what little remains.

The **park entrance** is clearly signposted on the C712, about 6km southeast of Port d'Alcúdia's marina. From the entrance, a country lane leads just over 1km inland to the reception centre, **Sa Roca** (daily 9am–1pm & 2–7pm; Oct–March closes 5.30pm; free; ☎971 892 250), where you can pick up a free map, a permit and a list of birds you might see. There's a small wildlife display here too, and an adjacent building houses a second flora and fauna identity parade. Note that you can't drive down the country lane; the best bet is to **cycle** here or take a **bus** to the entrance and walk. (Buses from Port d'Alcúdia to Ca'n Picafort and points southeast stop close to the entrance.) If you do bring a vehicle you'll have to find a parking space near the entrance, either in the sidestreets or at the conspicuous *Hotel Parc Naturel*, where there's a dedicated parking area for S'Albufera visitors. The hotel is located a few metres east of – and opposite – the park entrance.

Footpaths and cycle trails head out from Sa Roca into the reedy, watery tract beyond, where ten well-appointed hides allow excellent **birdwatching** – the best on the island. Over 200 different types of birds have been spotted, including resident wetland-loving birds from the crake, warbler and tern families; autumn and/or springtime migrants such as grebes, herons, cranes, plovers and godwits; and wintering egrets and sandpipers. Such rich pickings attract birds of prey in their scores, especially kestrels and harriers. The open ground edging the reed beds supports many different **wild flowers**, the most striking of which are the orchids that bloom during April and May.

Muro and around

From the C712 on the west side of Ca'n Picafort, a gentle country road heads west across a pancake-flat, windmill-studded hinterland to reach the hilltop town of **MURO**, a sleepy little place dotted with big old town houses built by wealthy landowners. There's a big bash here on January 16 at the **Revetla de Sant Antoni Abat** (Eve of St Antony's Day), when locals gather round bonfires to drink and dance, tucking into specialities like sausages and eel pies (*espinagades*), made with eels from the nearby marshes of S'Albufera. Quite what St Antony – an Egyptian hermit and ascetic who spent most of his long life in the desert – would have made of these high jinks it's hard to say. There again, he certainly wouldn't have been overwhelmed by temptation if he had stuck around Muro for the rest of the year.

The Town

Long-distance **buses** from Palma and local services from Ca'n Picafort and Port d'Alcúdia pull in close to Muro's handsome main square, Plaça Constitució, an attractive open area flanked by old stone houses. The square is shadowed by the domineering church of **St Joan Baptista**, a real hotchpotch of architectural styles, its monumental Gothic lines uneasily modified by the sweeping sixteenth-century arcades above the aisles. A slender arch connects the church to the adjacent **belfry**, an imposing seven-storey construction partly designed as a watchtower; it's sometimes possible to go to the top, where the views out over the coast are superb. The church's cavernous interior holds a mighty vaulted roof and an immense altarpiece, a flashy extravaganza of columns, parapets and tiers in a folksy rendition of the Baroque.

From the main square, it's a couple of minutes' walk east to the **Museu Etnològic**, c/Major 15 (April–Oct Tues–Sat 10am–2pm & 5–8pm, Sun 10am–1pm; Oct–March Tues–Sat 10am–1pm & 4–6pm, Sun 10am–1pm; €1.80). This is one of the least visited museums on the island, and the custodians seem positively amazed when a visitor shows up. It occupies a rambling old mansion and showcases a motley assortment of local bygones, from old agricultural implements, pottery and apothecary jars through to Mallorcan bagpipes and traditional costumes. Amongst the agricultural equipment there's a broken-down example of a mule- or donkey-driven water wheel, a *noria*. Introduced by the Moors, these were common features of the Mallorcan landscape for hundreds of years, though there are few of them left today. Among the pottery, look out for the *siurells*, miniature white-, green- and red-painted figurines created in a naive style. Now debased as a mass-produced tourist trinket, they were originally made as whistles – hence the spout with the hole – shaped in the form of animals, humans and mythological or imaginary figures.

That's just about it for Muro, though on a hot summer's day you'll be glad of a drink at one of the **cafés** around the main square. Best of the bunch is *Los Arcos*, a neat modern little place with a good range of inexpensive *tapas*; it's located at the back of a mini-square, just off Plaça Constitució and across from the church.

Sa Pobla

From Muro, it's just 4km northwest to the dusty little agricultural town of **SA POBLA**, whose straightforward grid-iron of old streets is at its prettiest in the main square, the Plaça Constitució, which is also the site of a busy Sunday morning **market**. Also of interest is **Can Planes**, c/Antoni Maura 6 (Tues–Sat 10am–2pm & 4–8pm, Sun 10am–2pm; €3; Ⓦwww.museu.org), a late nineteenth-century *Modernista* mansion which has been turned into a cultural centre incorporating a contemporary art gallery and toy museum. The mansion is poorly signed and can be hard to find – it's located at the north end of c/Antoni Maura (which runs north–south across the west side of the town centre), close to its intersection with Carretera Inca, the main road to Inca. The gallery's permanent collection features the work of Mallorcan artists and foreign artists resident on the island since the 1970s and there's an ambitious programme of temporary exhibitions too. Upstairs, the toy museum boasts an assortment of nineteenth- and early to mid-twentieth-century toys and games – some four thousand exhibits in all, from miniature rocking horses and carousels to baffling board games.

Travel details

Buses

Alcúdia to: Ca'n Picafort (May–Oct every 15min; Nov–April 11 daily; 30min); Lluc (May–Oct Mon–Sat 2 daily; 1hr 10min); Palma (May–Oct Mon–Sat hourly, Sun 5 daily; Nov–April 3–5 daily; 1hr 5min); Platja de Formentor (May–Oct Mon–Sat 2 daily; 35min); Pollença (May–Oct every 15min; Nov–April 11 daily; 30min); Port d'Alcúdia (May–Oct every 15min; Nov–April 11 daily; 15min); Port de Pollença (May–Oct every 15min; Nov–April 11 daily; 20min); Port de Sóller (May–Oct Mon–Sat 2 daily; 2hr).

Cala Sant Vicenç to: Pollença (4–5 daily; 15min); Port de Pollença (4–5 daily; 20min).

Ca'n Picafort to: Alcúdia (May–Oct every 15min; Nov–April 11 daily; 30min); Lluc (May–Oct Mon–Sat 2 daily; 1hr 45min); Muro (2–3 daily; 10min); Palma (2–5 daily; 1hr); Pollença (May–Oct every 15min; Nov–April 11 daily; 30min); Platja de Formentor (May–Oct Mon–Sat 2 daily; 50min); Port d'Alcúdia (May–Oct every 15min; Nov–April 11 daily; 20min); Port de Pollença (May–Oct every 15min; Nov–April 11 daily; 1hr); Port de Sóller (May–Oct Mon–Sat 2 daily; 2hr 30min); Porto Cristo (May–Oct Mon–Sat 3 daily; 50min).

Lluc to: Alcúdia (May–Oct Mon–Sat 2 daily; 1hr 10min); Ca'n Picafort (May–Oct Mon–Sat 2 daily; 1hr 45min); Palma (1–2 daily; 1hr); Pollença (May–Oct Mon–Sat 2 daily; 50min); Port d'Alcúdia (May–Oct Mon–Sat 2 daily; 1hr 15min); Port de Pollença (May–Oct Mon–Sat 2 daily; 55min); Port de Sóller (May–Oct Mon–Sat 2 daily; 1hr 15min).

Muro to: Ca'n Picafort (2–3 daily; 10min); Palma (2–8 daily; 50min); Port d'Alcúdia (2–3 daily; 20min); Sa Pobla (2–8 daily; 10min).

Platja de Formentor to: Alcúdia (May–Oct Mon–Sat 2 daily; 35min); Palma (May–Oct Mon–Sat 1 daily; 1hr 15min); Port d'Alcúdia (May–Oct Mon–Sat 2 daily; 25min); Port de Pollença (May–Oct Mon–Sat 1 daily; 20min).

Pollença to: Alcúdia (May–Oct every 15min; Nov–April 11 daily; 30min); Cala Sant Vicenç (4–5 daily; 15min); Ca'n Picafort (May–Oct every 15min; Nov–April 11 daily; 30min); Lluc (May–Oct Mon–Sat 2 daily; 50min); Palma (3–5 daily; 1hr); Port d'Alcúdia (May–Oct every 15min; Nov–April 11 daily; 25min); Port de Pollença (6–16 daily; 10min); Port de Sóller (May–Oct Mon–Sat 2 daily; 1hr 45min).

Port d'Alcúdia to: Alcúdia (May–Oct every 15min; Nov–April 11 daily; 15min); Cala Rajada (May–Oct Mon–Sat 2 daily; 40min); Ca'n Picafort (May–Oct every 15min; Nov–April 11 daily; 20min); Lluc (May–Oct Mon–Sat 2 daily; 1hr 15min); Palma (May–Oct Mon–Sat hourly, 5 on Sun; Nov–April 3–5 daily; 1hr 10min); Platja de Formentor (May–Oct Mon–Sat 2 daily; 25min); Pollença (May–Oct every 15min, Nov–April 11 daily; 25min); Port de Pollença (May–Oct every 15min; Nov–April 11 daily; 20min); Port de Sóller (May–Oct Mon–Sat 2 daily; 2hr).

Port de Pollença to: Alcúdia (May–Oct every 15min; Nov–April 11 daily; 20min); Ca'n Picafort (May–Oct every 15min; Nov–April 11 daily; 1hr); Palma (3–5 daily; 1hr 10min); Platja de Formentor (May–Oct 2 daily; 20min); Pollença (6–16 daily; 10min); Port d'Alcúdia (May–Oct every 15min; Nov–April 11 daily; 20min); Port de Sóller (May–Oct Mon–Sat 2 daily; 1hr 55min); Sóller (May–Oct Mon–Sat 2 daily; 2hr).

Trains

Muro to: Palma (hourly; 50min); Sa Pobla (hourly; 5min).

Sa Pobla to: Muro (hourly; 5min); Palma (hourly; 55min).

Southern Mallorca

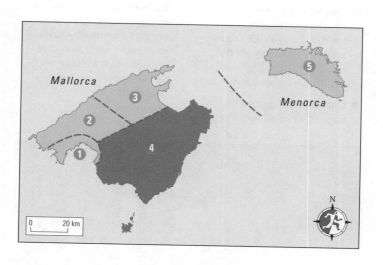

CHAPTER 4

Highlights

※ **Gordiola Glassworks**
Mallorca has long been famous for its glassware, and this factory outlet is the place to buy it. See p.177

※ **Sineu** The most attractive of the ancient agricultural towns of central Mallorca, home to the island's finest parish church and a bustling market. See p.180

※ **Artà** Ancient hill town of sun-bleached roofs clustered beneath a castellated chapel-shrine, while nearby lies the remarkably intact prehistoric village of Ses Paisses. See p.183

※ **Cala Rajada** Perched on the edge of a bumpy headland, this busy resort is within easy striking distance of several excellent, pine-clad sandy beaches. See p.186

※ **Coves del Drac** Perhaps the finest of eastern Mallorca's numerous cave systems, with fantastically shaped stalactites and stalagmites and one of the world's largest subterranean lakes. See p.194

※ **Cabrera** The fiercely hostile terrain of this offshore islet makes for an unusual day's excursion – and lots of rare Lilfords wall lizards will help you with your sandwiches. See p.204

△ Castell de Santueri

Southern Mallorca

Most of **southern Mallorca** comprises the island's central plain, **Es Pla**, a fertile tract bounded to the west by the mountainous Serra de Tramuntana and to the east by the hilly range that shadows the coast, the Serres de Llevant. For many visitors the region is no more than a monotonous interlude between airport and resort, but although it now seems like a sleepy backwater, until the twentieth century Es Pla largely defined Mallorca: the majority of the island's inhabitants lived here; it produced enough food to meet almost every domestic requirement; and Palma's gentry were reliant on Es Pla estates for their income. Mallorca's medieval kings constructed hilltop fortresses along the Serres de Llevant to defend the plain from marauding pirates, leaving the eastern shoreline's smattering of insignificant fishing villages and tiny ports unprotected. This situation persisted until the 1960s, when the tourist boom stood everything on its head and the developers simply bypassed Es Pla to focus on the picturesque coves of the east coast.

The towns of Es Pla have largely chosen to ignore the tourist industry and, although things are beginning to change, few put themselves out to attract visitors: accommodation is scarce, restaurants are thin on the ground and tourist offices are even rarer. Nevertheless, it's here that you can get the full flavour of an older, agricultural Mallorca, whose softly hued landscapes are patterned with olive orchards, chunky farmhouses and country towns of low, whitewashed houses huddled beneath outsized churches. Admittedly, there's precious little to distinguish one settlement from another, but there are exceptions, most notably **Sineu**, which has a particularly imposing parish church, and **Petra**, with its clutch of sights celebrating the life and times of the eighteenth-century Franciscan monk and explorer Junipero Serra. Other sights worth making a beeline for are the impressive monastery perched on the summit of **Puig Randa** and, in the Serres de Llevant, the hilltop shrine at **Artà** and the delightful medieval castle at **Capdepera**. All these destinations are readily accessible from the C715, which runs the 70km from Palma to Artà.

The ancient fishing villages of the **east coast** have mostly been swallowed up within mega-resorts, whose endless high rises and villa complexes blotch the land for miles. There are, however, a couple of enjoyable seaside towns which have avoided the worst excesses of concrete and glass: **Cala Rajada**, a lively holiday spot bordered by fine beaches and a beautiful pine-shrouded coastline, and **Cala Figuera**, which surrounds a lovely, steep-sided cove. The former fishing villages of **Porto Colom** and **Porto Petro** have also managed to retain much of their original charm, as has the ramshackle old port of **Porto Cristo**. Different again is tiny **Cala Mondragó**, where a slice of coast has been belatedly protected by the creation of a park. The east coast also boasts the cave

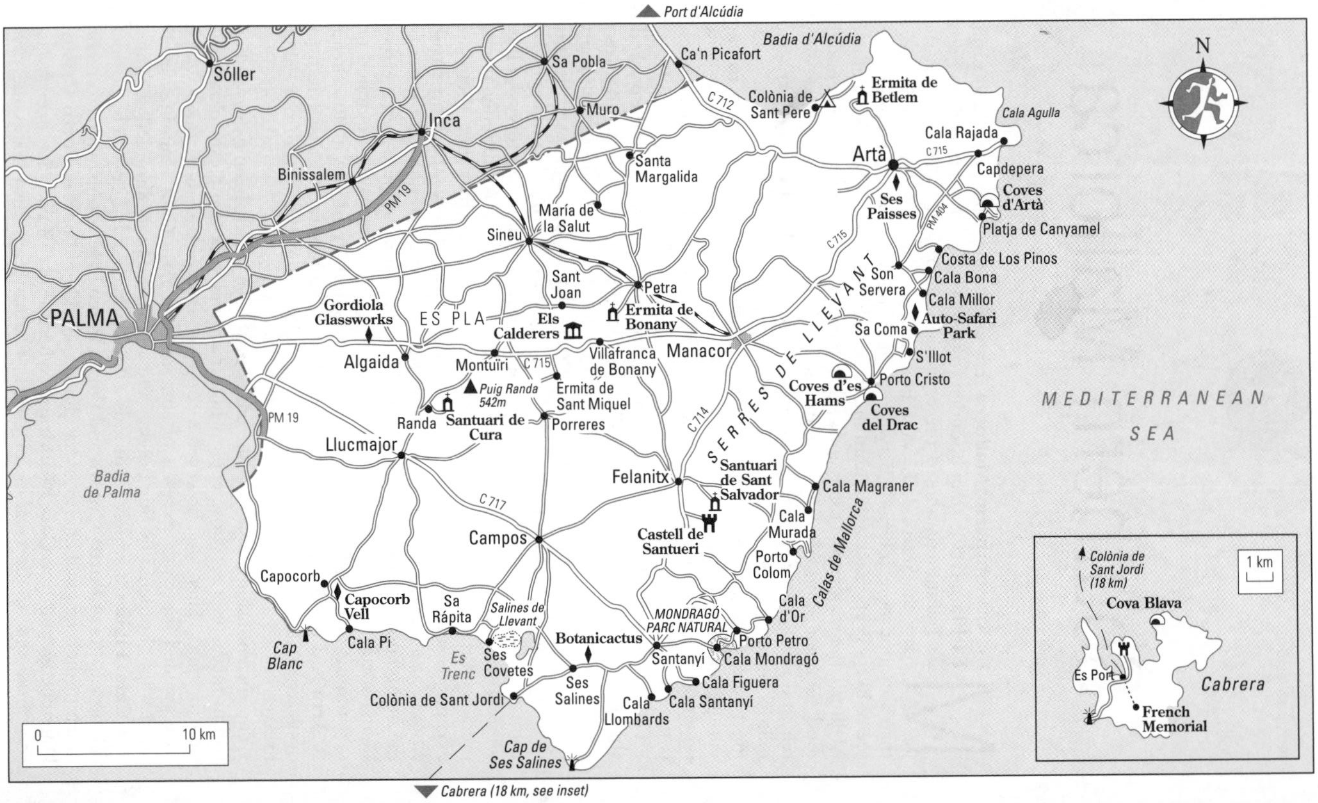
Port d'Alcúdia
Badia d'Alcúdia
Ca'n Picafort
Sóller
Sa Pobla
Muro
Inca
Colònia de Sant Pere
Ermita de Betlem
Cala Agulla
Cala Rajada
C 715
Artà
Capdepera
Coves d'Artà
Ses Paisses
PM 404
Platja de Canyamel
Binissalem
PM 19
Santa Margalida
María de la Salut
Sineu
C 712
C 715
Costa de Los Pinos
Son Servera
Cala Bona
Cala Millor
Auto-Safari Park
Sa Coma
S'Illot
Sant Joan
Petra
Ermita de Bonany
Gordiola Glassworks
ES PLA
Els Calderers
PALMA
Algaida
Montuïri
C 715
Villafranca de Bonany
Manacor
SERRES DE LLEVANT
Coves d'es Hams
Porto Cristo
Coves del Drac
MEDITERRANEAN SEA
Puig Randa 542m
Ermita de Sant Miquel
Randa
Santuari de Cura
Porreres
PM 19
Llucmajor
C 714
Badia de Palma
Felanitx
Santuari de Sant Salvador
Cala Magraner
C 717
Castell de Santueri
Cala Murada
Calas de Mallorca
Campos
Porto Colom
Capocorb
Capocorb Vell
Sa Rápita
Salines de Llevant
MONDRAGÓ PARC NATURAL
Cala d'Or
Cap Blanc
Cala Pi
Es Trenc
Ses Covetes
Botanicactus
Santanyí
Porto Petro
Cala Mondragó
Ses Salines
Cala Figuera
Colònia de Sant Jordi
Cala Llombards
Cala Santanyí
0
10 km
Cap de Ses Salines
Cabrera (18 km, see inset)
N
Colònia de Sant Jordi (18 km)
1 km
Cova Blava
Es Port
Cabrera
French Memorial

systems of **Coves d'Artà** and **Coves del Drac**, justifiably famous for their extravagant stalactites and stalagmites.

On the **south coast**, the scenery changes again, with hills and coves giving way to sparse flatlands, whose only star turn is the port-cum-resort of **Colònia de Sant Jordi,** from where boat trips leave for the scrubby remoteness of the fauna-rich island of **Cabrera**.

Practicalities

Given the difficulty of finding a room in the coastal package resorts and the general dearth of **accommodation** in the interior, advance reservations are a good idea – and pretty much essential in the height of the season. In addition, four of the region's **monasteries** offer simple, inexpensive lodgings, and usually have space at any time of year. These are the Santuari de Nostra Senyora de Cura, on Puig Randa near Algaida (see p.179); the Santuari de Monti-Sion near Porreres (see p.180; dorm accommodation only); the Ermita de Nostra Senyora de Bonany, near Petra (see p.182); and the Santuari de Sant Salvador outside Felanitx (see p.196).

Direct **buses** link Palma with almost every resort and town in the region, but services between the towns of Es Pla are virtually nonexistent, while those along the coast are patchy. Broadly speaking, you can manage to get a bus almost anywhere from Manacor, as well as between Cala Rajada, Artà and Cala Millor in the north, and between Cala d'Or, Cala Figuera and Colònia de Sant Jordi in the south. Elsewhere, you'll be struggling without a car. The new **train** line from Palma to Manacor via Sineu and Petra offers an alternative way of reaching the heart of the area.

East from Palma to Artà

The C715, which whizzes through the agricultural landscape due east from Palma, is lined with roadside tourist attractions. The most successful of these are the **Gordiola Glassworks**, which houses a superb glassware museum, and **Els Calderers**, a big old country house which is now a museum illustrating *hacienda* life in the nineteenth century. The third choice, the pearl-making factory of **Perlas Majorica** at Manacor, lags some way behind. By far the most interesting detours from the highway are to the monastery surmounting **Puig Randa** and to **Sineu**, once the site of a royal palace and now the prettiest town on the plain. Neither should **Artà**, tucked away amongst the Serres de Llevant, be overlooked, not only for its delightful location, but also for its proximity to the fascinating Talayotic settlement of **Ses Paisses** and the laid-back mini-resort of **Colònia de Sant Pere**.

Buses from Palma to Manacor and Artà are fast and frequent and there's also a reasonably regular service to Montuïri, Sineu and Petra. As for **accommodation**, both Artà and Sineu have one excellent hotel each, and there are monastery rooms near Algaida, Montuïri, Porreres and Petra.

The Gordiola Glassworks

Some 19km east of Palma along the C715 is the **Gordiola Glassworks** (April–Oct Mon–Sat 9am–8pm, Sun 9am–1pm; Nov–March Mon–Sat 9am–1.30pm & 3–7pm, Sun 9am–1pm; free), which occupies a conspicuous castle-like building, Ca'n Gordiola, whose crenellated walls and clumsy loggias date from the 1960s. Don't be put off by its appearance, however, or by the herd of tourist coaches parked outside. Inside, you can watch highly skilled glass-blowers in action, practising their precise art in a gloomy hall designed to resemble a medieval church and illuminated by glowing furnaces, while guides explain the techniques involved – the fusion of silica, soda and lime at a temperature of 1100°C. Perhaps inevitably, this is all part of a public relations exercise intended to push you towards the adjacent **gift shops**. Here, amongst a massive assortment of glass and ceramic items, you'll find everything from the most abysmal tourist tat to works of great delicacy, notably green-tinted chandeliers of traditional Mallorcan design costing anything up to €3000 – even a single simple goblet fetches about €30.

The gift shops are one thing, but the **museum**, on the top floor, is quite another. The owners of the glassworks, the Gordiola family, have been in business in Mallorca since the early eighteenth century, when the first of the line, Gordiola Rigal, arrived from the Spanish mainland. Since then, seven successive generations have accumulated an extraordinary collection of glassware, now displayed in fifty-odd cabinets, each devoted to a particular theme or country. Guidebooks (€6) are available from the gift shop.

On display are the earliest Gordiola work, green-coloured jugs of a frothy consistency, where both the shade and the trapped air bubbles were unwanted. Heated by wood and coal, the original hoop-shaped furnaces had windows through which works in progress could be rotated. With such limited technology, it was impossible to maintain a consistently high temperature, so the glass could neither be clarified nor cleared of its last air bubbles. Aware of these deficiencies, the next of the line, Bernardo Gordiola, spent years in Venice cultivating the leading glassmakers of the day, and the results of what he learnt can be seen in the same display case. He developed a style of Mallorcan-made jugs decorated with *laticinos*, glass strips wrapped round the object in the Venetian manner, and, in general, improved the quality of the glass. Amongst later Gordiola work, kitchen- and tableware predominate – bottles, vases, jugs and glasses – in a variety of shades, of which green remains the most distinctive. There's also a tendency to extrapolate functional designs into imaginative, ornamental pieces, ranging from hideous fish-shaped receptacles designed for someone's mantlepiece to the most poetic of vases.

Yet Gordiola glassware is just a fraction of the collection. Other cabinets feature pieces from every corner of the globe, beginning with finds from Classical Greece, the Nile and the Euphrates. There's also an exquisite sample of early Islamic glassware, Spanish and Chinese opalescents, and superb Venetian vases dating from the seventeenth and eighteenth centuries. More modern items include goblets from Germany and Austria, devotional pieces from Poland, traditional Caithness crystal from Scotland, and a striking melange of Norwegian Art Nouveau glasswork. The museum also exhibits decorative items from cultures where glass was unknown – an eclectic ensemble of pre-Columbian pieces worked in clay, quartz and obsidian, along with the zoomorphic and anthropomorphic basalt figures characteristic of the Sahara.

Algaida and around

ALGAIDA, just off the main highway 2km east of the glassworks, is typical of the small agricultural towns that sprinkle Mallorca's central plain – low, white-washed houses fanning out from an old Gothic-Baroque church. There's nothing remarkable about the place, but if you're travelling the C715 you'll need to pass through here to reach **Puig Randa**, the highest of a slim band of hills on the north side of Llucmajor. Beginning around 3km south of Algaida, the road to the 542-metre summit – a well-surfaced but serpentine affair, some 5km long – starts by climbing through the hamlet of **RANDA**, a pretty little place of old stone houses harbouring a comfortable three-star *hotel-residencia, Es Reco de Randa*, at c/Font 21 (☎971 660 997, Ⓦwww.fehm.es/pmi/esreco; ⑥). The hotel, with just fourteen rooms and an outdoor swimming pool on a balustraded terrace with panoramic views, is usually booked up months in advance during the summer, but there's often a vacancy out of season. It also has a delightful terraced restaurant, where the specialities include roast lamb and suckling pig.

Puig Randa

The top of **Puig Randa** is flat enough to accommodate a substantial walled complex, the **Santuari de Nostra Senyora de Cura** (Hermitage of Our Lady of Cura – Cura is the name of the upper part of Puig Randa). Entry is through a seventeenth-century portal, but most of the buildings beyond are plain and modern, the work of the present incumbents, Franciscan monks who arrived in 1913 after the site had lain abandoned for decades. The scholar and missionary **Ramon Llull** (see pp.77, 78) founded the original hermitage in the thirteenth century, and it was here that he prepared his acolytes for their missions to Asia and Africa. Succeeding generations of Franciscans turned the site into a centre of religious learning, and the scholastic tradition was maintained by a grammar school, which finally fizzled out in 1826. The Llull connection makes the monastery an important place of pilgrimage, especially for the **Bendición de los Frutos** (Blessing of the Crops), held on the fourth Sunday after Easter.

Nothing remains of Llull's foundation. The oldest surviving building is the quaintly gabled **chapel**, parts of which date from the 1660s. Situated to the right of the entrance, the chapel is homely and familiar, its narrow, truncated nave spanned by a barrel-vaulted roof. Next door, in the old school, there's a modest **museum** (donation requested) with a collection of ecclesiastical bric-a-brac and a few interesting old photos taken by the Franciscans before they rebuilt the place. It only takes a few minutes to look around and you'll soon be moving on to the nearby terrace **café**, which offers average food and superb views out across the island. There are a couple of other belvederes on the hill-top, plus an information office by the main entrance where you can get free maps and fix yourself up with a **room** in the guest quarters – a self-contained, modern block of basic bedrooms (advance bookings on ☎971 120 260; ❶).

There are two other, less significant sanctuaries on the lower slopes of Puig Randa. Heading back down the hill, past the radio masts, it's a couple of kilometres to the easily missable sharp left turn for the **Santuari de Sant Honorat**, which comprises a tiny church and a few conventual buildings of medieval provenance. Back on the main summit road, a further 1.2km down the hill, is the more appealing third and final monastery, the **Santuari de Gràcia**, which is approached through a signposted gateway on the left and along a short asphalt road. Founded in the fifteenth century, the whitewashed walls of this tiny sanctuary are tucked underneath a severe cliff face, which throngs with nesting birds. The simple barrel-vaulted church boasts some handsome majolica tiles, but it's the panoramic view of Es Pla's rolling farm-land that holds the eye.

Montuïri and around

Travelling east of Algaida on the C715, you'll soon reach the giant-sized Munper leather shop and then the **Perlas Orquidea factory**, where artificial pearls are made from glass globules, an industry for which Mallorca is internationally famous. The sales rooms are extensive and you can glimpse aspects of the production process, though the factory tours of the Perlas Majorica plant in Manacor are a tad more illuminating. Better still, leave the C715 and pop into **MONTUÏRI**, a gentle sweep of pastel-shaded stone houses on a low hill immediately north of the main road. In the heart of the town, it's worth taking a peek at the largely Gothic church of **Sant Bartomeu**, an imposing pile plonked next to the small main square; there are several fine Baroque retables inside.

The next place of interest on the C715 east of Montuïri is the fascinating old country house of Els Calderers (see p.182), but the town is also a convenient starting point for the short detour north along country roads to Sineu and Petra. In addition, Montuïri is close to the hilltop **Ermita de Sant Miquel**, (℡971/646314), signposted south off the C715 just east of the town and the location of a café-restaurant with smashing views over Es Pla. There are more panoramic views near Montuïri at another former monastery, the **Santuari de Monti-Sion** (℡971 647 185; closed Aug), which overlooks the country town of **PORRERES**, 12km to the southeast of Montuïri and also signposted south off the C715. In medieval times, Porreres was one of the island's most prosperous towns, its economy built on wine, apricots and almonds, but today it's of no particular interest. On the southwest edge of Porreres, a narrow country road snakes up to the Santuari, threading through almond orchards and a light dusting of pine trees. From the car park, a wide flight of steps leads to the deep arches of the main entrance, beyond which the central courtyard is flanked by an arcaded gallery and shadowed by a chapel, a cheerless affair dating from 1513. Until fairly recently, there was a school here, and the old refectory now houses a simple bar-restaurant. If you want to **stay**, there are bunk beds (€5 per night without linen) in one large room sleeping 22 people.

Sineu

SINEU, 12km north of Montuïri, is undoubtedly the most interesting of the ancient agricultural towns of Es Pla. Glued to a hill at the geographical centre of the island, the town had obvious strategic advantages for the independent kings of fourteenth-century Mallorca. Jaume II built a royal palace here; his asthmatic successor Sancho came to take the upland air; and the last of the dynasty, Jaume III, slept in Sineu the night before he was defeated and killed at the battle of Llucmajor by Pedro of Aragón. The new Aragonese monarchs had no need of the Sineu palace, which disappeared long ago, but former pretensions survive in the massive stone facade of **Nostra Senyora de los Angeles**, the grandest parish church on the island. Built in the thirteenth century, the church was extensively remodelled three hundred years later, but the majestic simplicity of the original Gothic design is still plain to see – though it's in a poor state of repair. At the side, a single-span arch connects with the colossal free-standing bell tower, and at the front, at the top of the steps, a big, modern and aggressive statue of a winged lion – the emblem of the town's patron, St Mark – stands guard, courtesy of Franco's cronies.

Beside the church is the unassuming main square, Sa Plaça, where you'll find the first of two excellent, traditional Mallorcan **bar-restaurants**, the *Celler Ca'n Font* (℡971 520 313), which serves hearty, inexpensive snacks from €5. The cavernous interior doubles as a wine vault, hence the enormous wooden barrels. A couple of minutes' walk away, the *Celler Es Grops*, c/Major 18 (℡971

520 187), has similar decor but a more welcoming atmosphere, and the food, if anything, is even better; count on around €20 for a full meal. Both places are at their busiest on Wednesdays, when the town fizzes with one of Mallorca's biggest fresh produce and livestock **markets**.

Sineu also has a nicely turned out **hotel**, the *Leon de Sineu*, c/Bous 129 (☎971 520 211, ⊛www.hotel-leon-sineu.com; ❻), set in a beautifully refurbished, 500-year-old mansion five minutes' stroll from Sa Plaça: walk down the hill from the square, turn first right and keep going. The hotel's wood-beamed foyer is spacious and elegant, and each of the bedrooms is tastefully furnished in an uncluttered antique style. At the back, the well-tended garden has an outdoor swimming pool and a breakfast terrace; it's all quite delightful. Around 6km southeast from Sineu is *Sa Rota d'en Palerm*, ctra Lloret de Vistalegre–Montuïri, Km 8 (☎971 726 934, ⊛www.sa-rota.com; ❻), a charming and peaceful rural retreat, set in a beautifully restored eighteenth-century country house. To reach the hotel from Sineu, take the road towards Lloret. About 500m before you reach that village, take the left turn towards Montuïri. After about 800m there's a sign to the hotel on the left. Continue for 2.5km to reach the hotel.

Petra and around

Nothing very exciting happens in **PETRA**, 11km east of Sineu, but it was the birthplace of **Junipero Serra**, the eighteenth-century Franciscan friar who played an important role in the settlement of Spanish North America. Serra's missionary endeavours began in 1749 when he landed at Veracruz on the Gulf of Mexico. Despite a particularly unpleasant voyage, he and his band of monks promptly walked 500km to Mexico City, thereby completing the first of many mind-boggling treks. For eighteen years Serra thrashed around the remoter parts of Mexico until, entirely by chance, political machinations back in Europe saved him from obscurity. In 1768, Carlos III claimed the west coast of the North American continent for Spain and, to substantiate his claim, dispatched a small expeditionary force of soldiers and monks north. Serra happened to be in the right place at the right time, and was assigned to lead the priests. Even by Serra's standards, the walk from Mexico City to California was pretty daunting, but almost all the force survived to reach the Pacific Ocean somewhere near the present US–Mexico border in early 1769. Over the next decade, Serra and his small party of priests set about converting the Native Americans of coastal California to the Catholic faith, and established a string of nine missions along the Pacific coast, including San Diego, Los Angeles and San Francisco. Pope John Paul II beatified Serra in 1988.

Petra makes a reasonable hand of its connection with Serra. In the upper part of town, on c/Major, is the chunky church of **Sant Bernat**, beside which – down a narrow side street – lies a modest sequence of majolica panels honouring Serra's life and missionary work. This simple tribute is backed up by a self-effacing **museum** in a pleasant old house at the end of this same side street (Mon–Fri 9am–8pm; donation requested), with several rooms devoted to Serra's cult: the honours paid to him, the books written about him, and the paintings of him. Another room focuses on Serra's work in California, with photos and models of his foundations. Three doors up the street, at no. 6, is the humble whitewashed stone and brick **house** where he was born (same hours). The museum and house are sometimes locked, but there are instructions posted outside explaining how to collect the key from the custodian.

Other than that, the only reason to hang around is to visit the elegantly old-fashioned *Sa Plaça* **restaurant**, Plaça Ramon Llull 4 (☎971 561 646), where you can eat either in the antique-filled interior, or outside facing the main square.

Ermita de Nostra Senyora de Bonany

Some 5km southwest of Petra is the hilltop **Ermita de Nostra Senyora de Bonany**, which offers extensive views over Es Pla. To get there, take the Felanitx road out of Petra and look out for the sign on the edge of the village. The monastery is at the end of a bumpy, four-kilometre country lane, and takes its name from events in 1609 when desperate locals gathered here at the chapel to pray for rain. Shortly afterwards, the drought broke and the ensuing harvest was a good one – hence *bon any* ("good year"). The prettiest feature of the complex is the **chapel**, which is approached along an avenue of cypress and palm trees and comes complete with a rose window, twin towers and a little cupola. The monastery's conspicuous stone cross was erected in honour of Junipero Serra, who left here bound for the Americas in 1749. It also has five simple double **rooms** (☎971 561 101; ❶). There's hot water (in one bathroom) and cooking facilities, but you'll have to bring your own food and bedding.

Els Calderers

Tucked away at the end of a country lane 2km north of – and clearly sign-posted from – the C715 between Montuïri and Villafranca de Bonany is **Els Calderers** (daily: April–Sept 10am–6pm; Oct–March 10am–5pm; €7). Dating mostly from the eighteenth century, this charming country house bears witness to the wealth and influence once enjoyed by the island's landed gentry – in this case the Veri family. The house was the focus of a large estate which produced a mixed bag of agricultural produce: the main cash crop was origi-nally grapes, though this changed in the 1870s when phylloxera, a greenfly-like aphid, destroyed Mallorca's (and most of Europe's) vineyards. The Veris switched to cereals, and at the beginning of the twentieth century were at the forefront of efforts to modernize Mallorcan agriculture, much to the conster-nation of some of their more stick-in-the-mud neighbours, and to the horror of a workforce used to more traditional methods.

Flanked by a pair of crumpled-looking lions, the entrance to the **house** leads to a sequence of handsome rooms surrounding a cool courtyard with a well. All are kitted out with antique furniture, *objets d'art* and family portraits, and each has a clearly defined function, from the dainty music room to the hunt-ing room, with assorted stuffed animal heads, and the master's office, with big armchairs and a much-polished desk. You can also see the family's tiny chapel (like every landed family on the island, the Veris had a live-in priest), and there's more religious material upstairs in the assorted prints that line the walls. They're neither original nor of good quality, but they give the flavour of the mawkish piety that characterized the island's landed class in the late nineteenth century. Attached to, but separate from, the family house are the living quarters of the *amo* (farm manager), the barn and the farmworkers' kitchen and eating area. To complete your visit, take a stroll round the animal pens, though don't expect to see much farmyard activity in the heat of the day. The animals are breeds traditionally used on Mallorcan farms, though they're here to illustrate the past rather than to be of any practical use.

It takes an hour or so to wander round the house and the adjacent animal pens, more if you stop at the simple little **café**, where they serve traditional

Mallorcan snacks – the *pa amb oli* (bread rubbed with olive oil) with ham and cheese is delicious.

Manacor

MANACOR declares its business long before you arrive, with vast roadside hoardings promoting its furniture, wrought-iron and artificial pearl factories. On the strength of these, the city has risen to become Mallorca's second urban centre, smaller than Palma, but large enough to have spawned sprawling suburbs on all sides. Fortunately, the historic centre has been attractively restored and this is where you should head for – though first you have to brave the modern attractions that line up beside the C715 on the west side of town, each designed to catch the passing tourist trade. The first, the **Oliv-Art** olive wood shop and museum, is more shop than museum, churning out thousands of household ornaments – oversized ashtrays and the like – stained a sticky-looking brown. Sometimes these verge on the kitsch, but mostly they're just ugly. The life-size plastic dinosaurs outside don't make things any better.

A few doors down is the first of the town's several Perlas Majorica **artificial pearl** shops, though it's better to skip it in favour of the Perlas Majorica factory, signposted as the **Pearl Centre** (Mon–Fri 9–10.30am & 12.30–7pm, Sat & Sun 10am–1pm; free), 300m further east along the main road. The somewhat perfunctory **free factory tour** here offers a general insight into the manufacturing process. The core of the imitation pearl is a glass globule on to which are painted many layers of a glutinous liquid primarily composed of fish scales. The finished items – anywhere between soft yellow and metallic grey – are gently polished and then included within many different types of jewellery. Artificial pearls last longer than, and are virtually indistinguishable from, the real thing, but are consequently expensive – as you'll discover if you visit the showroom and gift shop (9am–7pm) across the street from the factory.

In the centre of town, the **tourist office**, Plaça Ramon Llull s/n (☎971 847 241), has a useful selection of local information, including a map marking the town's architectural high points on and around the main square. The most impressive building is the **Església Nostra Senyora Verge dels Dolors**, the principal church, whose left transept holds an idiosyncratic full-sized polychrome crucified Christ wearing a sort of skirt. While you're here, be sure to try the local speciality – spicy pork sausage made from the Iberian black pig (*sobrasada de cerdo negro*) at the *Palau Café*, Plaça Rector Rubí 8 (☎971 844 492; closed Sun).

A few kilometres to the north of Manacor lies the fabulous *La Reserva Rotana* (☎971 845 685, ⓦwww.reservarotana.com; ❾), an unpretentious yet luxurious resort in a large converted stone hacienda, sporting its own nine-hole golf course, spa, a large pool and acres of private nature reserve. Each of the suites is individually decorated with unusual antiques collected by the owner, and there's also a top-notch restaurant with fresh-flavoured Mediterranean cuisine (count on around €60 a head for a full dinner).

Artà and around

Beyond Manacor the C715 veers northeast to run parallel to the coast, with the flatlands soon left behind for the easy peaks of the **Serres de Llevant**. The top end of this mountain range bunches to fill out Mallorca's eastern corner, providing a dramatic backdrop to **ARTÀ**, an ancient hill town of sun-bleached roofs clustered beneath a castellated chapel-shrine. It's a delightful scene, though at close quarters the town is something of an anticlimax, and the cobweb of cramped and twisted alleys doesn't quite match the setting.

Buses to Artà from several directions, including Palma, Cala Rajada and Ca'n Picafort, stop on the C715 at the edge of the town centre. From the bus stops, it's a couple of hundred metres west to the foot of the short main street, **c/Ciutat**. If you've driven here, finding somewhere **to park** can be a hassle – try along c/Ciutator adjoining Plaça Conqueridor.

The ten-minute trek up to the **Santuari de Sant Salvador**, the panoramic shrine at the top of Artà, is a must. It's almost impossible to get lost – just keep going upwards. Follow c/Ciutat as it slices across the edge of Plaça Conqueridor, and then head straight on up to **Plaça Espanya**, a leafy little piazza that is home to the town hall. Beyond, a short stroll through streets of gently decaying mansions brings you to the gargantuan parish church of Sant Salvador. From this unremarkable pile, steep stone steps and cypress trees lead up the Via Crucis (Way of the Cross) to the *santuari*, which, in its present form, dates from the early nineteenth century, though the hilltop has been a place of pilgrimage for much longer. During the Reconquista, Catalan soldiers demolished the Moorish fort that stood here and replaced it with a shrine accommodating an image of the Virgin Mary which they had brought with them. This edifice was, in its turn, knocked down in 1820 in a superstitious attempt to stop the spread of an epidemic that was decimating the region's population. Built a few years later, the interior of the present chapel is hardly awe-inspiring – the paintings are mediocre and the curious statue of Jesus behind the altar has him smiling as if he has lost his mental marbles – but the views are exquisite, with the picturesque town below and Es Pla stretching away to distant hills.

There are several **café-restaurants** along c/Ciutat, the best being *Café Parisien,* at no. 18 (T 971 835 440), a trendy little place with an outside terrace, modernist decor and tasty *tapas* and salads at reasonable prices. The *Restaurant Ca'n Balaguer* (T 971 835 003), on the other side of the street at no. 19, is a more traditional place where the emphasis is on Mallorcan dishes. Artà has one first-rate **hotel**, the *Casal d'Artà*, which occupies an immaculately restored, three-storey grandee mansion overlooking Plaça Espanya at c/Rafael Blanes 19 (T & F 971 829 163; O).

Ses Paisses

About 1km south of Artà lie the substantial and elegiacally rustic remains of the Talayotic village of **Ses Paisses** (April–Sept daily 9am–1pm & 3–7pm; Oct–March Mon–Fri 9am–1pm & 2.30–5pm, Sat 9am–1pm; €2). To get there, walk to the bottom of c/Ciutat, turn left along the main through-road (the C715) and watch for the signposted and well-surfaced country lane on the right. A clear footpath explores every nook and cranny of the site, and its numbered markers are thoroughly explained in the English-language **guide-book** available at the entrance (€1.80).

Tucked away in a grove of olive, carob and holm-oak trees, the prehistoric village is entered through a monolithic gateway, whose heavyweight jambs and lintel interrupt the Cyclopean walls that still encircle the site. These outer remains date from the second phase of the Talayotic culture (c.1000–800 BC), when the emphasis was on consolidation and defence; in places, the walls still stand at their original size, around 3.5m high and 3m thick. Beside the gate, there's also a modern plinth erected in honour of Miquel Llobera, a local writer who penned romantic verses about the place. Beyond the gateway, the central **talayot** is from the first Talayotic phase (c.1300–1000 BC), its shattered ruins flanked by the foundations of several rooms of later date and uncertain purpose. Experts believe the horseshoe-shaped room was used, at least towards the end of the Talayotic period, for cremations, whilst the three rectangular rooms were probably living quarters. In the rooms, archeologists discovered various items such as iron objects and ceramics imported from elsewhere in the Mediterranean. Some of them were perhaps brought back from the Punic Wars (264–146 BC) by mercenaries – the skills of Balearic stone slingers were highly prized by the Carthaginians, and it's known that several hundred accompanied Hannibal and his elephants over the Alps in 218 BC.

Around Artà: the Ermita de Betlem

Hidden away in the hills 10km northwest of Artà is the **Ermita de Betlem**, a remote and minuscule hermitage founded in 1805. The road to the *ermita* begins immediately to the west of Artà's Plaça Espanya, but the start is poorly signed and tricky to find. The road's rough surface and snaking course also make for a difficult drive, so it's far better to **walk** – reckon on five or six hours for the return trip from Artà to the *ermita* and back. The first portion is an easy stroll up along the wooded valley of the Torrent d'es Cocones, but then – after about 3km – the road squeezes through the narrowest of defiles, with the hills rising steeply on either side. Beyond, the road begins to climb into the foothills of the Serra de Llevant (here classified as the **Massís d'Artà**) until, some 3km after the defile, a signposted left turn signals the start of the strenuous part of the journey. Here, the track wriggles for 4km up the steep hillside before finally reaching the *ermita*.

The buildings, which date from the hermitage's foundation, are unassuming – although, if you've come this far, you'll undoubtedly want to peep into the tiny **church**, where the walls are decorated with crude religious frescoes. The hermitage doesn't offer accommodation or food, just picnic tables, which does seem a bit cruel if you've hiked all the way here, but the views over the Badia d'Alcúdia are magnificent. The adventurous can head down to the bay to the east of Colònia de Sant Pere, but this is a difficult hike and you'll need to be properly equipped.

Colònia de Sant Pere

West of Artà the C712 weaves through the hills on its way to Ca'n Picafort and Port d'Alcúdia. On the way, it passes the turning for **COLÒNIA DE SANT PERE**, a downbeat resort and one-time fishing village nestling beside the Badia d'Alcúdia, with the stern escarpments of the Massís d'Artà for a back-drop. New villa complexes have sprouted along the foreshore, but mercifully the developers have pretty much left the village alone – not that there's much to the place. Founded in 1881, Colònia de Sant Pere is no more than a few blocks across, its plain, low-rise modern buildings set behind a small sandy beach. It's all very low-key and laid-back, and this, along with the setting, is the place's charm.

There's just one convenient **hostal**, the agreeable *Rocamar*, c/Sant Mateu 9 (T & F 971 589 312; ❷), an unassuming whitewashed and blue-shuttered building right in the centre three blocks back from the sea, with a restaurant on the ground floor and eight simple rooms up above. You can **eat** well at the cosy *Acuàrium* restaurant (T 971 589 106), which serves the freshest of fish; it's on c/Sant Mateu, opposite the *Rocamar*. There are several seafront reataurants too, the pick being the *Blau Mari* (T 971 589 407; closed Nov–Feb), which specializes in seafood and paellas.

The east coast

Mallorca's **east coast**, stretching for about 60km from Cala Rajada all the way south to Cala Llombards, is fretted by narrow coves, the remnants of prehistoric river valleys created when the level of the Mediterranean was much lower. All of these inlets have accrued at least some tourist development, ranging from a mild scattering of second homes to intensive chains of tower blocks. An attractive minor road links the resorts, running for the most part a few kilometres inland along the edge of the **Serres de Llevant**, a slim band of grassy hills which rises to over 500m at its two extremities, south outside Felanitx and north around Artà. If you have your own transport, this coastal route enables you to pick and choose destinations with the greatest of ease, dodging the crassest examples of over-development – principally Cala Millor, Calas de Mallorca and Cala d'Or – altogether.

Amongst the larger resorts, boisterous **Cala Rajada** is easily the most enticing, and is also within easy reach of excellent sandy beaches and the lovely medieval fortress of **Capdepera**. South of here, the old port of **Porto Cristo** has a ramshackle charm, as does the fishing village-cum-resort of **Porto Colom**. By contrast, **Porto Petro** and **Cala Figuera** are more upmarket – the latter is now a lively, medium-sized resort which possesses some fine restaurants and a top-notch diving centre. At the southern end of the east coast are the relatively untouched beaches of **Cala Mondragó**, now protected within a park, and **Cala Llombards**. The east coast is also famous for its limestone cave systems, with the most impressive formations found at the **Coves d'Artà** in the north, and the **Coves del Drac** at Porto Cristo.

It would be lovely to work your way down the coast, stopping for a couple of nights here and there, but the problem is **accommodation**. In the height of the season, locating a vacant room in one of the more attractive resorts can be a real tribulation – if you do find somewhere reasonable, you'll probably want to stay put. An alternative is to select a less popular spot, such as Porto Cristo or Porto Colom, where there's far more chance of a bed. Things ease up in the shoulder season, but in winter many hotels and *hostals* close down.

To explore the east coast thoroughly you'll need your own **transport**. All the major resorts have regular bus links with Palma, and in summer there are good connections to Port d'Alcúdia from Porto Cristo and points north, but services up and down the coast are generally inadequate.

Cala Rajada

Awash with cafés, bars and hotels, vibrant **CALA RAJADA** lies on the southerly side of a stubby headland in the northeast corner of Mallorca. The town centre, an unassuming patchwork of low-rise modern buildings, is hardly prepossessing, but it's neat and trim, while around town is a wild and rocky coastline, backed by pine-clad hills and sheltering a series of delightful **beaches**.

Arrival, information and accommodation

Most **buses** stop in the town centre near the intersection of c/Juan Sebastian Elcano and c/Castellet (note that there are no buses on Sundays). From here, it's a couple of minutes' walk southeast to the main square, **Plaça dels Pins**, where you'll find the **tourist office** (Mon–Fri 9.30am–1.30pm & 2.30–5.30pm, Sat 9.30am–1.30pm; March–Oct also Sun 10am–1.30pm; ☎971 563 033). The office can supply an excellent range of local information includ-

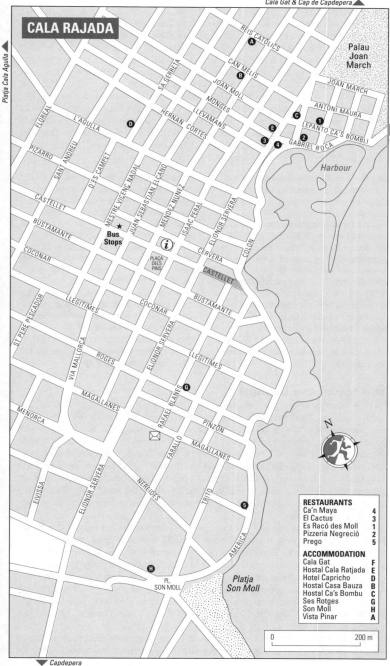

CALA RAJADA

Cala Gat & Cap de Capdepera ▲

Platja Cala Agulla ◀

REIS CATÓLICS

Ⓐ

CAN MELIS

Ⓑ

Palau
Joan
March

JOAN MARCH

SA GENERA

JOAN MOLL

ANTONI MAURA

MONGES

Ⓒ

LEPANTO CA'S BOMBLI

FLOREAL

L'AGULLA

LLEVAMANS

Ⓓ

HERNAN CORTES

Ⓔ

Ⓕ

PIZARRO

SANT ANDREU

DES CAMPET

Ⓓ

③

②

④

GABRIEL ROCA

①

Harbour

CASTELLET

MESTRE VICENÇ NADAL

JUAN SEBASTIAN EL CANO

MENDEZ NUÑEZ

ISAAC PERAL

ELIONOR SERVERA

COLON

BUSTAMANTE

★
Bus
Stops

ⓘ

PLAÇA
DELS
PINS

CERVERA

COCONAR

CASTELLET

ST PERE PESCADOR

LLEGITIMES

COCONAR

BUSTAMANTE

VIA MALLORCA

ROGES

ELIONOR SERVERA

LLEGITIMES

MAGALLANES

RAFAEL BLANES

Ⓖ

MENORCA

PINZON

FARALLO

MAGALLANES

EIVISSA

ELIONOR SERVERA

NEREIDES

TRITO

⑤

AMERICA

Ⓗ

PL.
SON MOLL

Platja
Son Moll

Platja Son Moll

Capdepera ▼

N

RESTAURANTS
Ca'n Maya   4
El Cactus   3
Es Racó des Moll   1
Pizzeria Negreció   2
Prego   5

ACCOMMODATION
Cala Gat   F
Hostal Cala Ratjada E
Hotel Capricho   D
Hostal Casa Bauza   B
Hostal Ca's Bombu   C
Ses Rotges   G
Son Moll   H
Vista Pinar   A

0   200 m

187

ing restaurant lists, bus schedules, details of car and bicycle rental firms, and free town maps marked with all accommodation. They also have a popular, though not very detailed, pamphlet on **hiking tour routes** for €3.

The town centre is easy to explore on foot, but for the outlying beaches you'll probably want a **local bus**. Among several summertime services from the bus stops along c/Castellet, a short distance north of Plaça dels Pins, the most useful are to Cala Agulla, Platja de Canyamel and the Coves d'Artà.

The only real problem with Cala Rajada is finding **accommodation**. The town is a favourite German package resort and in high season you'll be lucky to find a room. The best place to try is among the *hostals* and hotels dotted around the busy commercial streets just up from the harbour. In the shoulder season, it's probably worth trying one of the popular seafront hotels. All the places listed here are closed between November and March.

Cala Gat ℡971 563 166, ⊛www.hotelcalagat .com. Unassuming but particularly good-value choice in a secluded location in the pine woods above Cala Gat. ❷

Hostal Cala Ratjada Corner c/Monges and c/Elionor Servera ℡971 563 202, ℻971 818 025. Good-value *hostal*, close to the port, set in a nicely renovated and characterful white-stucco building with rustic touches. ❶

Hotel Capricho Off c/L'Agulla at c/Sa Gerreta 5 ℡971 563 500, ⊛www.calarajada.info. Modern, air-conditioned three-star establishment with a pool and sports facilities. Good value. ❷

Hostal Casa Bauza c/Méndez Núñez 61 ℡971 563 844, ⊛www.calarajada.info. One-star *hostal* with clean, simply furnished rooms and a pool. ❷

Hostal Ca's Bombu c/Elíonor Servera 86 ℡971 563 203, ⊛www.casbombu.com. Stylish and appealing place with a pool and a wonderful terrace restaurant overlooking the water. Breakfast included. ❶

Ses Rotges c/Rafael Blanes 21 ℡971 563 108, ⊛www.sesrotges.com. Delightful three-star establishment in an elegantly restored antique villa just out of earshot of the main square. ❺

Son Moll c/Tritó 25 ℡971 563 100, ⊛www.calaratjada.com. Workaday seafront option in a modern block overlooking the Platja Son Moll, with light and airy rooms, most with balconies, and magnificent views out to sea. ❹

Vista Pinar c/Reis Catòlics 11 ℡971 563 751, ⊛www.calaratjada.com. Large, adequate two-star with its own swimming pool. ❸

The town and around

Cala Rajada was once a fishing village, but there's little evidence of this today, and the **harbour** is now used by pleasure boats and overlooked by restaurants. From the harbour, walkways extend along the headland's south coast. To the southwest, past the busiest part of town, it takes about ten to fifteen minutes to stroll round to **Platja Son Moll**, a slender arc of sand overlooked by Goliath-like hotels. More rewarding is the ten-minute stroll east from the harbour to **Cala Gat**, a narrow cove beach tucked tight up against the steep, wooded coastline. The beach is far from undiscovered – there's a beach bar and at times it gets decidedly crowded – but it's an attractive spot all the same.

Up above the footpath to Cala Gat you can glimpse the gardens of the **Palau Joan March**, a lavish mansion built in 1916 for the eponymous tobacco merchant, who was to become the richest man in Franco's Spain. Most of the sculptures which until recently decorated these gardens are now on display in Palma (see p.79), and the mansion is now closed to the public. Beyond the gardens, continuing east along c/Elíonor Servera, the road twists steeply up through the pine woods to reach, after about 1km, the bony headlands and lighthouse of the **Cap de Capdepera**, Mallorca's most easterly point. The views out along the coast are a treat.

On the northern side of Cala Rajada, c/L'Agulla crosses the promontory to hit the north coast at **Platja Cala Agulla**. The approach road, some 2km of

Boats leave Cala Rajada's harbour for regular summer excursions down the east coast and back. Destinations include Porto Cristo (Feb–Oct Mon–Sat 1 daily; €10); Platja de Canyamel (April–Oct 3 daily; €8); and the Coves d'Artà (April–Oct 3 daily; €8).

tourist tackiness, is of little appeal, but the beach, a vast curve of bright golden sand, is big enough to accommodate hundreds of bronzing pectorals with plenty of space to spare. The further you walk – and there are signed and shaded footpaths through the pine woods to assist you – the more isolation you'll get.

Eating

The *Hotel Ses Rotges* (see p.188) boasts the best **restaurant** in town, but it's pricey and there are scores of less expensive rivals serving everything from sauerkraut and sausages through to traditional Spanish cuisine. There are several good spots down at the harbour. There's tasty *tapas* at the *Es Racó des Moll*, a fashionable little café-restaurant just a few metres back from the harbour, while the waterfront *Pizzeria Negrecio* is a popular and cheerful cafeteria with low-price pizzas, sandwiches, steaks and spaghetti. The expensive *El Cactus* Spanish restaurant, just up from the harbour at c/Elíonor Servera 83 (☏971 564 609; dinner only), is central and has a view of the port, and you'll find superb seafood at the *Ca'n Maya*, close by at c/Elíonor Servera 80 (☏971 564 035). Strolling southwest along c/America en route to Platja Son Moll, *Prego* is a nice, scenic place for sandwiches, salads and desserts.

Capdepera

Spied across the valley from the west or south, the crenellated walls dominating **CAPDEPERA**, a tiny village 8km east of Artà and 3km west of Cala Rajada, look too pristine to be true. Yet the triangular fortifications are genuine enough, built in the fourteenth century by the Mallorcan king Sancho to protect the coast from pirates. The village, snuggled below the walls, contains a pleasant medley of old houses, its slender main square, Plaça de L'Orient, acting as a prelude to the steep steps up to the **Castell de Capdepera** (daily: April–Oct 10am–8pm; Nov–March 10am–5pm; €1.20). The steps are the most pleasant way to reach the castle, but you can also follow the signs and drive up narrow c/Major. Flowering cactuses give the fortress a special allure in late May and June, but it's a beguiling place at any time, with over 400m of walls equipped with a parapet walkway and sheltering neat terraced gardens. At the top of the fortress, **Nostra Senyora de la Esperança** (Our Lady of Good Hope) is the quaintest of Gothic churches: its aisle-less, vaulted frame is furnished with outside steps leading up, behind the bell gable, to a flat roof, from where the views are superb.

Run-of-the-mill **cafés** line up on Plaça de L'Orient – the best is *Pizzeria L'Orient*, with tasty *tapas* from €3–5. Capdepera also has several excellent **restaurants**. The pick is *La Fragua*, c/Es Pla d'en Coset 3 (☏971 565 050; dinner only, closed Tues), an intimate, romantic spot where they serve delicious Thai meals. It's located just off Plaça de L'Orient, on the way up towards the castle steps. There's nowhere to **stay** in Capdepera, but it's easy enough to visit by bus from Artà, Cala Rajada, Cala Millor or even Palma.

△ Windmill, central Mallorca

The Coves d'Artà

The succession of coves, caves and beaches notching the seashore between Cala Rajada and Cala Millor begins promisingly with the memorable **Coves d'Artà** (often signposted in Castilian as "Cuevas de Artà"), reached along the first turning off the main coastal road (the PM404) south of Capdepera. This is the pick of the numerous cave systems of eastern Mallorca, its sequence of cavernous chambers, studded with stalagmites and stalactites, extending 450m into the rock face. Artificial lighting exaggerates the bizarre shapes of the caverns and their accretions, especially in the **Hall of Flags**, where stalactites up to 50m long hang in the shape of partly unfurled flags. Exiting the caves, you're greeted with a stunning view, courtesy of a majestic stairway straight out of a horror movie which leads up to the yawning hole, beckoning like the mouth of hell high in the cliffs above the bay.

The caves have had a chequered history. During the Reconquista, a thousand Moorish refugees from Artà were literally smoked out of the caves to be slaughtered by Catalan soldiers waiting outside. In the nineteenth century, touring the caves for their scientific interest became fashionable amongst the rich and famous – Jules Verne was particularly impressed – and visits now feature prominently on many a package-tour itinerary.

From May to October, **buses** run two or three times a day (but not on Sundays) from Artà and Cala Rajada, or you could elect for a **boat cruise** here from Cala Rajada (April–Oct 3 daily; €8). **Tours** of the caves run every half-hour (daily: July–Sept 10am–7pm; Oct–June 10am–5pm; €8) and the guides give a complete geological description in tedious detail and in several languages including English as you wander the illuminated abyss. Allow about an hour for the visit – more if there's a queue, as there sometimes is.

Platja de Canyamel

PLATJA DE CANYAMEL (not to be confused with the tedious Costa de Canyamel *urbanització* immediately to the south) is a cove resort with smart modern villas draped around a pine-backed sandy beach in sight of a pair of rocky headlands. It's situated about 1km south of the Coves d'Artà, though there's no connecting road: you have to return to the main coastal road, the PM404 running a few kilometres inland, to make the journey. From May to October, local **buses** run from Cala Rajada (Mon–Sat 3–4 daily) and Artà (Mon–Sat 2 daily) via the Coves d'Artà, stopping in Platja de Canyamel outside the *Laguna* hotel (see below).

The *platja* makes an agreeable spot for a few hours sunbathing, and there are a couple of good **restaurants** here too. In the centre, a short walk up from the beach, is the *Isabel*, where the seafood is fresh and well prepared, or you can sample traditional Mallorcan cuisine at the excellent *Porxada de Sa Torre* (☎971 841 310; closed Mon & Nov–April), which occupies a tastefully converted old watchtower about 3km west of the beach along the access road.

There are several **hotels** in Platja de Canyamel, but they're usually block-booked by German tour operators and the only vague chance of a room is at the *Laguna* (☎971 841 150, ⓦwww.calarajada.info; ❷; closed Nov–April), an attractive whitewashed hotel plonked right on the beach.

Cala Millor and around

Continuing south along the main coast road, you'll soon pass the turning for the well-heeled villas of **COSTA DE LOS PINOS**, the most northerly and prosperous portion of a gigantic resort conurbation centred on **CALA BONA** and **CALA MILLOR**. This is development gone quite mad, a swathe of apartment buildings, sky-rise hotels and villa-villages overwhelming the contours of the coast as far as the eye can see. The only redeeming feature – and the reason for all this frantic construction in the first place – is the **beach**, a magnificent two-kilometre stretch of sand fringed by what remains of the old pine woods. You can get plenty of information, including free maps, from the principal **tourist office** at Parc de la Mar 2, just behind the beach at the south end of Cala Millor (Mon–Fri 9am–1pm & 3–7pm, Sat 9am–1pm; ☎971 585 864).

To avoid this visual assault, stay on the main coastal road, which runs just inland from the resort, threading through the unappealing town of **SON SERVERA** before passing the **Auto–Safari Park** (daily: April–Sept 9am–7pm; Oct–March 9am–5pm; €10), 4km north of Porto Cristo, where a motley assortment of African animals roams open countryside. Beyond, there are yet more acres of concrete and glass at **SA COMA** and **S'ILLOT**, though the main road, still set back from the coast, cuts a rustic route through vineyards and almond groves before reaching the multicoloured billboards which announce the cave systems of Porto Cristo.

Porto Cristo

Although **PORTO CRISTO** prospered in the early days of the tourist boom, sprouting a string of hotels and *hostals*, it's fared badly since mega-resorts such as Cala Millor and Cala d'Or were constructed nearby. Don't be deceived by the jam of tourist buses clogging the town's streets on their way to the nearby **Coves del Drac** – few of their occupants will actually be staying here. Consequently, this is one of the very few places on the east coast where you're likely to find a room in July and August, and it's not too bad a spot to spend a night either. The **beach** is fine enough for sunbathing (though the swimming isn't great); it's tucked inside the harbour, a narrow V-shaped channel entered between a pair of rocky promontories that is one of the most sheltered ports on Mallorca's east coast.

Porto Cristo's origins are uncertain, but it was definitely in existence by the thirteenth century, when it served as the fishing harbour and seaport of the inland town of Manacor. Nothing remains of the medieval settlement, however, and today the centre, which climbs the hill behind the harbour, consists of high-sided terraced buildings mostly dating from the late nineteenth and early twentieth centuries.

In August 1936, Porto Cristo was the site of a **Republican landing** to try to capture the island from the Falangists. The campaign was a fiasco: the Republicans disembarked over seven thousand men and quickly established a long and deep bridgehead, but their commanders, completely surprised by their initial success, quite literally didn't know what to do next. The Nationalists did: they counterattacked and, supported by the Italian air force, soon had the Republicans dashing back to the coast. Barcelona radio put on a brave face, announcing, "The heroic Catalan columns have returned from Mallorca after a magnificent action. Not a single man suffered from the effects of the embarkation."

Arrival, information and accommodation

The main coastal road passes along Porto Cristo's seafront, and a sizeable number of long-distance **buses**, principally from Palma and Port d'Alcúdia, terminate in the centre beside the harbour and the beach. The **tourist office**

PORTO CRISTO

Son Servera

Beach

Marina

Buses

Acuàrium

Bus Stop

Coves del Drac

N

ACCOMMODATION	
Estrella	B
Felip	A
Sol i Vida	C

RESTAURANTS	
Flamingo	2
Sa Carrotja	1
Sassecador	3
Siroco	4

0   100 m

is on the seafront directly behind the beach at c/Bordils 53A (Mon–Fri 8am–3pm; ☎971 815 103); they can provide useful maps of the town and neighbouring resorts. Beyond the beach, the harbour accommodates a large marina and then meets the oily-green Es Rivet river, which forms the town centre's southern perimeter.

For **accommodation**, Porto Cristo has half-a-dozen hotels and *hostals*. They're an undistinguished lot, but there's a good chance of a vacancy here even in July and August. The three-star *Hotel Felip*, c/Bordils 61 (☎971 820 750, ⓦwww.thbhotels.com; ⑥; closed Nov–Jan) has a great location, in a big old balconied building overlooking the beach. The interior has been revamped in modern style and the rooms are neat and trim – ask for a harbour view. Other less well-appointed options include the spick-and-span one-star *Hotel Estrella*, c/Curricà 16 (☎971 820 833, ⑤971 820 892; ❷; closed Nov–April), which occupies a plain postwar three-storey building between the town centre and the caves. To get there, follow the main road south over the river and it's the third turning on the right. Alternatively, the *Sol i Vida* is a small, tidy

Boat cruises from Porto Cristo

Boat trips from Porto Cristo head to Cala Rajada (up to five daily; €18 return) and various other destinations including Sa Coma (5 daily; €16), Cala Bona (2 daily; €20) and Calas de Mallorca (4 daily; €20). There are also one- and two-hour cruises up and down the coast in glass-bottomed boats (€10–12).

two-star hotel in a pleasant wooded location on a residential street a few metres from the Coves del Drac caves, Avgda Joan Servera Camps 11 (☎ & ☏971 821 074; ②).

The town and around

Across the river, about fifteen minutes' walk south of the centre along the coastal road, lies Porto Cristo's pride and joy, the **Coves del Drac** (often signposted in Castilian as "Cuevas del Drach"). Locals had known of the "Dragon's Caves" for hundreds of years, but it was the Austrian archduke Ludwig Salvator (see p.124) who recruited French geologists to explore and map them in 1896. The French discovered four huge chambers that penetrated the coast's limestone cliffs for a distance of around 2km. In the last cavern they found one of the largest subterranean lakes in the world, some 177m long, 40m wide and 30m deep. The eccentric shapes of the myriad **stalactites and stalagmites** adorning each chamber immediately invited comparison with more familiar objects. As the leader of the French team, Edouard Martel, wrote, "On all sides, everywhere, in front and behind, as far as the eye can see, marble cascades, organ pipes, lace draperies, pendants of multi-faceted gems hang suspended from the walls and roof."

Since the French exploration, the caves have been thoroughly commercialized. The present complex accommodates a giant car park, ticket office and restaurant, behind which lurk the gardens that lead to the flight of steps down to the caves. You may come to know each step well, as you can wait in line for ages, especially at the weekend. **Guided tours** of the caves run every hour (daily: April–Oct 10am–5pm; Nov–March 10.30am–3.30pm; €7.50).

Inside, the innumerable concretions of calcium carbonate, formed by the dissolution of the soft limestone by rainwater, are shrewdly illuminated. Shunting you through the hour-long, multilingual tour, the guides invite you to gawp and gush at formations such as "the Buddha", "the Pagoda" and "the Snowy Mountain", and magnificent icicle-like stalactites, some of which are snowy white, others picking up hints of orange and red from the rocks they hang off. The *tour de force* is the larger of the two **subterranean lakes**, whose translucent waters flicker with reflected colours, the mysterious atmosphere further enhanced by a small group of musicians drifting by in boats (performances usually begin on the hour). At the end of the tour, some visitors leave on foot, but you can also take a brief boat ride (included in the admission price) across part of the lake. From the cave complex, it's a short walk across the car park to the well-stocked **Acuàrium** (daily: April–Oct 10.30am–6pm; Nov–March 11am–3pm; €5). Mediterranean creatures lurk on the upper floor, while displays of international ocean life can be found on the ground floor, where the glass tanks magnify such exotic horrors as electric eels, piranhas and stinging fish.

There's another cave system situated 2km west of Porto Cristo on the road to Manacor – though you'd hardly want to visit both. The **Coves d'es Hams** (or "Cuevas del Hams" in Castilian) follow the same format as their rival, with a sequence of somewhat smaller caverns lit to emphasize the beauty of the stalagmites and stalactites. Guided tours run about every half-hour (daily: April–Oct 10am–6pm; Nov–March 10.30am–5pm; €9). As at the Coves del Drac, musicians play from boats on an underground lake (every 20min until 4.30pm).

Eating

Although most of Porto Cristo's restaurants and cafés are geared up for the passing tourist trade, there are a few decent **places to eat**. Two good inexpensive places are *Sa Carrotja*, a low-key family-run restaurant at the first intersection north from the beach along c/Bordils at Avgda Joan Amer 45 (℡971 821 503); and the rather more polished *Siroco* (℡971 822 444), whose cosy terrace abuts the harbour a few metres south from the beach on c/Veri. *Sassecador*, c/Mar 11 (℡971 820 826) is a perhaps even classier choice, with several beautifully decorated antique dining rooms; a traditional Mallorcan meal here will cost about €25. In the other direction, heading away from the port, is the gorgeous *Flamingo*, c/Bordils s/n (℡971 822 259), offering panoramic views of the town and port. The homemade paellas are great, or try the steamed mussels (€9), pizzas (from €6) or the mixed fish grill (€20).

South to Porto Colom

The modern resorts disfiguring the pint-sized coves to the south of Porto Cristo reach their nadir at the **CALAS DE MALLORCA**, the collective name for a band of tourist settlements extending from Cala Magraner to Cala Murada. This part of the shoreline didn't have much charm in the first place – the coves are mostly scrawny and shadeless – and it's even less compelling now. Inland, however, the main coast road gives few hints of these scenic disasters as it wends its pastoral way past honey-coloured dry-stone walls and a smattering of ancient farmhouses in the lee of the Serres de Llevant.

Porto Colom

PORTO COLOM straggles round a long and irregular bay some 20km south of Porto Cristo. Originally a fishing village supplying the needs of the neighbouring town of Felanitx, the port boomed throughout most of the nineteenth century from the export trade in wine to France. The good times, however, came to an abrupt end when phylloxera wiped out the island's vines in the 1870s. The villagers returned to **fishing**, which still makes up a significant part of the local economy: the boats they use, as well as some old boat sheds, litter the kilometre-long **quay** on the southwest side of the bay. The quayside, along with the modest settlement immediately behind it, constitutes the heart of the present village and although there's little to grab your attention, it's still an amiable, downbeat spot. The oldest part of the village is about 300m from the west end of the quay, round the back of the harbour, and comprises a small parcel of pastel-shaded houses by the water, and some rather elegant townhouses shadowing a little square above. Elsewhere, the headlands overlooking the entrance to the bay house a lighthouse and an unappetizing mix of villas and hotels, while over the hill behind the village (about 1km to the south) is **Cala Marçal**, a crowded, shadeless wedge of sand overlooked by the concrete flanks of the eponymous hotel.

Buses, principally from Palma, arrive at the quayside. There's a smattering of inexpensive and largely mundane **accommodation**, including the *Hostal-residencia César*, c/Llaud s/n (℡971 825 302; ❶; closed Nov–March), and the equally undistinguished *Hostal Bahía Azul*, Ronda Creuer Baleares 88 (☎971 825 280, ℱ971 824 452; ❷), both situated amongst the scrubland at the far (east) end of the quay. For something rather more comfortable, especially in the shoulder season, try the three-star *Hotel Cala Marsal* (☎971 825 225, ℱ971 825 250; ❸; closed Nov–March) in Cala Marçal, a package-tour favourite with sea-facing rooms. *El Vistamar*, Hos Pinzón, behind the main port (☎971 825 101, ⓦwww.olahotels.com; ❻) is a great-value resort with loads of amenities, including a couple of tennis courts and no less than four pools.

Porto Colom does rather better with its **restaurants**, the pick of which are dotted along the quayside. The cream of the crop at the west end of the quay is the *Celler Sa Sínia* (☎971 575 323; closed Mon), which has reasonably priced and very tasty fish dishes. At the other end of the quay the best option is *El Cinco* (☎971 826 020), on Plaça Sant Jaume, which has an inventive international menu ranging from vegetable curry (€14) to fresh scampi with Thai glass noodle salad (€10.90). Ask for a table on the candlelit terrace upstairs if you come for dinner. Nearby at 59 Ronda Creuer Baleares, the smart *Ses Portadores* (☎971 825 271) is a good alternative; it's a bit pricier, but the fish is just as fresh and there's a wider selection.

Felanitx and around

Thirteen kilometres inland from Porto Colom lies **FELANITX**, the main town hereabouts. It's an industrious place, producing wine, ceramics and pearls, and although hardly beautiful, it does have more than a modicum of charm, its tangle of narrow streets lined by handsome old houses mostly dating from the eighteenth and nineteenth centuries. The finest building is the church of **Sant Miquel**, whose honey-gold, Baroque facade adds a touch of elegance to the largely modern main square, the **Plaça Constitució**. A plaque on the church recalls the worst disaster to hit the town since the days of pirate attack, when a wall collapsed killing over four hundred people on their way from church. There are no other sights as such, but strolling the old streets and alleys is an agreeable way to pass the odd hour; the best time to visit is on Sunday morning, when the main square is given over to a lively fresh produce and craft **market**. In particular, look out for the capers (Catalan *tapèras*; Castilian *alcaparras*), produced locally and sold by size; the smallest are the most flavourful, either as *nonpareilles* (up to 7mm) or *surfines* (7–8mm).

Buses, which run to and from Palma and Porto Colom, stop by the main square. There is no tourist office, and neither is there anywhere **to stay** except the nearby Santuari de Sant Salvador.

The Santuari de Sant Salvador

Within easy striking distance of Felanitx is one of the more scenic portions of the Serres de Llevant. The best approach is to head east along the road to Porto Colom for about 2km then take the signposted, four-kilometre tarmac byroad that wriggles up the mountain to the **Santuari de Sant Salvador**, recognizable from miles around by its conspicuous stone cross and enormous statue of Christ. Long an important place of pilgrimage, the monastery occupies a splendid position near the summit of the highest mountain in these parts, the 510-metre Puig de Sant Salvador, with sumptuous views out over the east coast. The sanctuary was founded in the mid-fourteenth century, but the original buildings were razed by raiding pirates and most of today's complex is Baroque. The heavy gatehouse is its most conspicuous feature while, inside the compound, the eighteenth-century church shelters a much-venerated image of the Virgin Mary.

This was the last of Mallorca's monasteries to lose its monks – the last ones moved out in the early 1990s. It now has fourteen spartan **guest rooms** (reservations on ☎971 827 282) sleeping between two and nine people. Ten of the rooms have shared bathrooms and cost €8 per person; four are en suite and cost €10 per person. There's hot water and a **café-restaurant** (it's best to call ahead to confirm opening hours), and bedding is provided. If you've got a car, you could make the sanctuary an unusual base for exploring the locality. It's certainly a very quiet place to stay.

The Castell de Santueri

The custodians at the Santuari de Sant Salvador should be able to point you towards the footpath to the **Castell de Santueri**, about 4km away across the hills to the south. The route is fairly easy to follow and the going isn't difficult, although it's still advisable to have a walking map and stout shoes. The path meanders through a pretty landscape of dry stone walls, flowering shrubs and copses of almond and carob trees, bringing you to the castle after about an hour and a half. Glued to a rocky hilltop, the battered ramparts date from the fourteenth century, though it was the Moors who built the first stronghold here. Getting inside the ruins is pot luck: sometimes you can (in which case a small entry fee is levied at the main gate), and sometimes you can't. If you don't fancy the walk, you can drive to the castle along a five-kilometre country lane, signed off the Santanyí road about 2km south of Felanitx.

Cala d'Or and around

South along the coast from Porto Colom, the pretty little fishing villages that once studded the quiet coves as far as Porto Petro have been blasted by development. The interconnected resorts that now stand in their place are largely indistinguishable, a homogeneous strip of whitewashed, low-rise villas, hotels, restaurants and bars, all designed in a sort of *pueblo* style. Confusingly, this long string of resorts is now usually lumped together under the title **CALA D'OR**, though this name in fact refers to one particular cove, which is also one of the smallest. The "Cala d'Or" we refer to in this account is the original cove and not the whole development.

To be fair, the pseudo-Andalucian style of the new resorts blends well with the ritzy *haciendas* left by a previous generation of sun-seekers. The latter are largely concentrated on the humpy little headland which separates Cala d'Or from its northerly neighbour, **CALA GRAN**. These two fetching little coves, tucked between the cliffs and edged by narrow golden beaches, are the highlights of the area. The beaches are jam-packed throughout the season, but the swimming is perfect and the wooded coastline here is far preferable to the more concentrated development all around. Of equal appeal is the genteel and leafy headland on the south side of Cala d'Or, though this is a brief and flattering preamble to the massive marina and endless villas of **CALA LLONGA**.

Practicalities

Buses stop on Cala d'Or's crowded and charmless main drag, Avinguda Fernando Tarrago, two minutes' walk from the beach. Under various designations, this same street links the main cove resorts, from Cala Esmeralda in the north to Cala Llonga in the south –about a twenty-minute walk from one end to the other. From around May to September, a tourist "train" on wheels, the **mini tren** (hourly; €3), links Cala d'Or, Porto Petro and Cala Mondragó, stopping along the main street and beside all the beaches.

The **tourist office** (Mon–Fri 8.30am–2pm; May–Sept also Sat 8.30am–2pm; ☎971 657 463) is situated a few metres up from the Cala Llonga waterside at c/Perico Pomar 10. They can provide free maps marked with all the local hotels and *hostals*, though finding a place **to stay** is well-nigh impossible in the summer – a better bet is to try the *Nereida* at Porto Petro (see below). The most luxurious option – where you'll almost certainly need an advance reservation – is the four-star *Hotel Cala d'Or*, right above Cala d'Or's beach on Avinguda Bèlgica (☎971 657 249; ❻; closed Nov–March). The hotel has seventy balconied bedrooms, each furnished in an attractive modern style with fine sea views, while the equally appealing public areas include a bar, restaurant and an outside swimming pool. Cala Gran also has a good upmarket hotel, the *Cala Gran* (☎971 657 100; ❻; closed Nov–March), a bigger and brisker affair at the back of the beach. The modern bedrooms here have balconies and sea views, and there's every convenience, including a swimming pool.

There are lots of **cafés and restaurants** around Cala d'Or and Cala Llonga, especially along Avinguda Fernando Tarrago. One that's worth hunting down is the popular *Ca'n Trompé*, close to the *Hotel Cala d'Or* at Avgda Bèlgica 12 (☎971 657 341; closed Dec–Feb), which serves delicious, though pricey, meals, with the emphasis on Mallorcan mainstays – the suckling pig is a real treat.

Porto Petro

PORTO PETRO rambles round a twin-pronged cove a couple of kilometres south of Cala Llonga, its minuscule village centre perched on the headland above the marina, with a cluster of whitewashed houses recalling the days before the tourists. Although it's now all but swallowed up by the Cala d'Or conurbation, Porto Petro still somehow manages to hang onto its original character. Because there's no beach here, development has been fairly restrained, and although the old fishing harbour has been turned into a marina and villas dot the gentle wooded hillsides edging the coast, it remains a quiet and tranquil spot – the only real activity is the promenade round the crystal-watered cove.

There's a reasonable chance of getting a **room** here at the two-star *Hostal Nereida* (☎971 657 223, ☏971 659 235; ❸; closed Nov–March), a comfortable and neat little place with its own pool and rooftop sun terraces. The village has all the amenities to make for a good base: there's car and bike rental, and regular *mini tren* connections up and down the coast to all the resorts between Cala d'Or and Cala Mondragó. In addition, from May to October there are once-weekly **boat cruises** from Porto Petro to Cabrera island (see p.204), currently on Tuesdays, departing at 9.30am and returning by 5pm. The cost is €27 per person, and you should book ahead on ☎971 657 012.

There are also a couple of fine, moderately priced harbourside **restaurants**: the *Ca'n Martina* (☎971 657 517), at the head of the marina, boasts a paella to die for and a lovely outside terrace, whilst the nearby *Restaurant Porto Petro* (☎971 657 704) serves wonderful seafood from upper-floor premises overlooking the bay – try the sardines.

The Mondragó Parc Natural and Cala Mondragó

A few kilometres south of Porto Petro, the **Mondragó Parc Natural** protects a small slice of the east coast whose diverse terrain covers almost two thousand acres of wetland, farmland, beach, pine and scrub. The park is still fairly undeveloped, and the road signs are a bit confusing, but there are two **car parks** to aim for, both signposted from the C717 between Porto Petro and Santanyí. The better target is the **Fonts de N'Alis** car park, 100m from the tiny resort of Cala Mondragó (see below); the other car park, **S'Amarador**, is on the low-lying headland to the east of the cove. The very scenic park is latticed with footpaths and country lanes, and you can pick up a (rather poor) map from the Fonts de N'Alis **visitor centre** (℡971 181 022), at the Fonts de N'Alis car park. This shows the park's three hiking trails: all are easy loops, two of forty minutes, one of twenty. Until the visitor centre sorts itself out with proper hiking maps, the only reliable reference is the billboard map displayed outside.

CALA MONDRAGÓ, about 4km south of Porto Petro, is one of Mallorca's prettiest resorts. There was some development here before the creation of the park in 1990, but it's all very low key and barely disturbs the cove's beauty, with low, pine-clad cliffs framing a pair of sandy beaches beside crystal-clear waters. Predictably, the cove's "unspoilt" reputation and safe bathing acts as a magnet for sun-lovers from miles around, but you can escape the crowds by **staying** the night (if there's space) at either of two beachside *hostals*. Choose between the *Hostal Playa Mondragó*, a straightforward, modern concrete block with forty plain but adequate rooms (℡ & ℻971 657 752; ❷; closed Nov–March), or the rather more enticing *Hostal Condemar*, about 300m from the beach, where most of the rooms have balconies (℡ & ℻971 657 756; ❷; closed Nov–April).

There are no **buses** to Cala Mondragó, but it is the terminus of the summertime *mini tren* which runs along the coast to and from Porto Petro and Cala d'Or (May–Sept hourly; €3).

Santanyí and around

The crossroads town of **SANTANYÍ**, 18km southwest of Porto Colom, was once an important medieval stronghold guarding the island's southeastern approaches. Corsairs ransacked the place on several occasions, but one of the old town gates, **Sa Porta**, has survived along with the occasional chunk of masonry from the old city walls. However, it's Santanyí's narrow alleys, squeezed between high-sided stone houses, that are the town's main appeal. Several pavement **cafés** edge the main square: the place to hang out is *Sa Cova*, Plaça Major 30 (℡971 163 146), a lively art gallery and café-bar with live music and salads, sandwiches and snacks.

Cala Figuera and Cala Santanyí

Travelling southeast from Santanyí, a 5km-long byroad cuts a pretty, rustic route through to **CALA FIGUERA**, whose antique harbour sits beside a fjord-like inlet below the steepest of coastal cliffs. Local fishermen still land their catches and mend their nets here, but nowadays it's to the accompaniment of scores of photo-snapping tourists. Up above, the pine-covered shoreline heaves with villas, hotels and *hostals*, although the absence of high-rise buildings means the development is never overbearing.

Cala Figuera is extremely popular, and there are precious few vacant **rooms** at its dozen or so establishments, even in shoulder season. If you do decide to chance your arm the obvious place to start is on the steep pedestrianized ramp – c/Verge del Carmen – which leads up from the harbour. In this prime location, at no. 50, is the unassuming *Hostal Cala*, with twenty rooms stashed above a restaurant (℡971 645 018; ❸; closed Nov–March). Close by at no. 58, the year-round *Hostal Marina* has just six simple bedrooms, also over a restaurant

(℡ & ℱ971 645 035; ❶). Up the hill in the centre of the resort is another good choice, the two-star family-run *Hostal Ventura*, c/Pintor Bennareggi 17 (℡971 645 102; ❶; closed Nov–March), which has a swimming pool and forty plain but perfectly adequate rooms. The nicest place is probably the *Hotel Villa Sirena*, c/Virgen del Carmen 37 (℡971 645 303, ℱ971 645 106, ⓦwww .hotelvillasirena.com; ❸), located at the end of the promontory at the end of the cove, which has its own swimming platforms above the water.

Of Cala Figuera's many **restaurants**, the most distinguished are the seafood places lining c/Verge del Carmen. It's difficult to select – and hard to go wrong – but *Mistral* (℡610 453 972), *Ca'n Jordi* (℡971 645 035) and *Es Port* (℡971 165 140) are all excellent, with good views, and not too pricey. There are also several lively music **bars** and **discos** dotted along the main street. In terms of amenities, the resort has car and bike rental outlets, and, down by the harbour, a **diving school** (℡971 645 015) which rents out a wide range of gear to experienced divers, and arranges novice courses – three days of tuition go for around €300.

What you won't get is a beach. The nearest is 4km west at **CALA SANTANYÍ**, a busy little resort with a medium-sized (and frequently crowded) beach at the end of a steep-sided, heavily wooded gulch. To get there, head back towards Santanyí for about 2km and follow the signs.

Cala Llombards

The next bay west from Cala Santanyí is little-developed **CALA LLOMBARDS**, a good-looking, pine-forested cove of gleaming sand, turquoise sea and sheer cliffs. There's a scrawny villa-village behind, not visible from the beach, a seasonal beach-bar and a dirt car park, but otherwise it's comparatively pristine – though litter louts do tend to spoil the place. Only rarely will you have the beach to yourself, but it's seldom crowded and makes a relaxing spot to while away a few hours.

There are no **buses** to Cala Llombards, and even driving here can be a baffling experience on the narrow country roads that cover this part of the island. Your best bet is to take the road southwest from Santanyí towards Colònia de Sant Jordi and watch for the signed turning before you get to the roadside hamlet of **Es Llombards**; thereafter, Cala Lombards is 5km away – keep your eyes peeled for further signs. There's an alternative turnoff in Es Llombards itself.

The south coast

Mallorca's **south coast** – stretching from the island's most southerly point, Cap de Ses Salines round to the rim of the Bay of Palma – has hardly been developed at all, but the reasons for this lack of interest are pretty obvious when you come here. Most of the shoreline is unenticingly spartan, a long and low rocky shelf with barely a decent beach in sight. The flat, sparsely populated hinterland behind offers little shade or variety, villages are few and far between, and in places the land has an eerie sense of desolation – especially at the wind-buffeted **Cap de Ses Salines** – though some visitors find this barrenness strangely fascinating.

A smattering of modern resorts gamely make the most of these disheartening surroundings. The best is undoubtedly **Colònia de Sant Jordi**, a curious amalgamation of plush tourist settlement and old seaport, which thoroughly deserves an overnight visit, not least because it offers boat trips to the remote islet of **Cabrera** and is near the wildlife-rich saltflats that back onto the region's longest beach, **Es Trenc**. Of the other resorts, **Cala Pi**, where a deep ravine frames a sandy beach, is the best-looking and although it doesn't offer much it is close to the substantial remains of prehistoric **Capocorb Vell**. East of Cala Pi things get much worse with the grim and untidy resorts of Valgornera, S'Estanyol and Sa Rapita, no more than clumps of mundane second homes decorating the treeless shoreline.

Planning an itinerary is straightforward. The best advice is to use the **C717** road, which runs from Santanyí northwest to Ca'n Pastilla on the Bay of Palma, as your baseline, branching off as you wish. As ever, **accommodation** is at a premium. Throughout the season, your best chance by a long chalk is in Colònia de Sant Jordi, but from November to March nearly everything is closed and you'll almost certainly have to visit on a day trip. **Bus** services are adequate if you're heading somewhere specific from Palma, but are dreadful when you attempt to move between the resorts themselves.

Cap de Ses Salines and Botanicactus

Heading southwest from Santanyí, a fast and easy country road drifts through a landscape of old dry stone walls, broken-down windmills, ochre-flecked farmhouses and straggling fields on its way towards Colònia de Sant Jordi. After about 4km, you pass through tiny **Es Llombards** and shortly afterwards reach the turning that leads the 10km down through coastal pine woods to the lighthouse on **Cap de Ses Salines**, a bleak, brush-covered headland which is Mallorca's most southerly point. The lighthouse itself is closed to the public, but there are fine views out to sea. Thekla larks and stone curlews are often to be seen on the cape, whilst gulls, terns and shearwaters glide about offshore, benefiting from the winds which, when they're up, can make the place intolerable.

Back on the road to Colònia de Sant Jordi, billboards welcome you to **Botanicactus** (daily: April–Sept 9am–7pm; Oct–March 9am–5pm; €6.20), a huge botanical garden mostly devoted to indigenous and imported species of cactus. A surprise here is the artificial lake, which encourages the growth of wetland plants – a welcome splash in arid surroundings – but otherwise the place has all the atmosphere of a garden centre and is definitely missable.

Colònia de Sant Jordi and around

About 13km west of Santanyí is **COLÒNIA DE SANT JORDI**, whose wide streets pattern a substantial and irregularly shaped headland. **Buses**, principally from Palma, stop at several central locations, including the bus-stop at the north end of the old harbour, but the town is confusing, at least at first. During the season, a toytown **mini-train** shuttles around town every hour or two, and there's a central **taxi** stand (℡908 142 187) at the c/Gabriel Roca and c/Pescadors intersection.

The main approach road is the **Avinguda Marquès del Palmer**, at the end of which – roughly in the middle of the headland – lies the principal square, the unremarkable **Plaça Constitució**. From here, c/Sa Solta and then Avinguda Primavera lead west. At the end of the avenue, the sprawling *Hotel Marquès del Palmer* sits tight against the **Platja d'Estanys**, whose gleaming sands curve round a dune-edged cove. South of Avinguda Primavera is the surprisingly pleasant main tourist zone, whose domineering lines of flashy hotels are broken by low-rise villas and landscaped side streets. To the north are the **Salines de S'Avall**, the saltpans which once provided the town with its principal source of income.

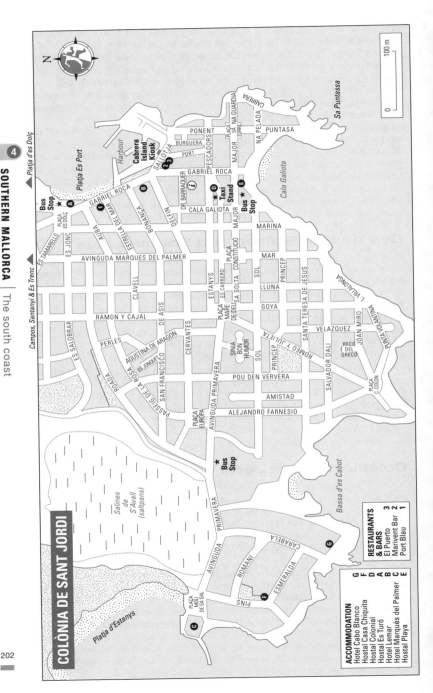

COLÒNIA DE SANT JORDI

Platja d'es Dolç ▲

Campos, Santanyi & Es Trenc ▲

Platja Es Port ▲

100 m

0

N

Harbour

Cabrera Island Kiosk

Sa Puntassa

PONENT

CABRERA

SA NA GUARDIA

PLAÇA SA NA GUARDIA

LLOBE

NA PELADA

PUNTASA

BURGUERA

PORT

SALIOTA

2 3

GABRIEL ROCA

PESCADORS

MAJOR

Platja Es Port

Bus Stop

★ A

GABRIEL ROCA

1

B

DR BARRAQUER

i

DELFIN

D

Taxi Stand

E

Bus Stop ★

Cala Galiota

PLAÇA ES DOLÇ

ES TAMARELLS

ALBA

ES JONC

ESTRELLA DEL MAR

BONANÇA

CALA GALIOTA

MAJOR

MARINA

Sa Puntassa

ES SALOBRAR

AVINGUDA MARQUES DEL PALMER

CLAVELL

DE ASIS

ESTANYS

PLAÇA ES CARRERO

SA SOLTA

PLAÇA CONSTITUCIÓ

MAR

SOL

PRINCEP

L VILALONGA

RAMON Y CAJAL

PLAÇA MARE DE DÉU

LLUNA

SANTA TERESA DE JESUS

JOAN MIRO

PERLES

AGUSTINA DE ARAGON

CERVANTES

SINIA BON HUMOR

GOYA

VELAZQUEZ

PUNTA VOLANTINA

ROAJA

PASSEIG DE LA ROSA

ES JONQUET

SAN FRANCISCO

SOL

PRINCEP

ROMEO Y JULIETA

SALVADOR DALI

RECO DEL GRECO

AVINGUDA PRIMAVERA

POU DEN VERVERA

PLAÇA C. COLON

PLAÇA EUROPA

AMISTAD

ALEJANDRO FARNESIO

Salines de S'Avall (saltpans)

Bus Stop ★

Bassa d'es Cabot

AVINGUDA PRIMAVERA

CARABELA

G

ROMANI

ESMERALDA

PINS

F

PLAÇA MOLI DE SA SAL

G

Platja d'Estanys

ACCOMMODATION
- G Hotel Cabo Blanco
- F Hostal Casa Chiquita
- D Hostal Colonial
- A Hostal Es Turó
- B Hotel Lemar
- C Hotel Marqués del Palmer
- E Hostal Playa

RESTAURANTS & BARS
- 3 El Puerto
- 2 Marivent Bar
- 1 Port Blau

East from Plaça Constitució along c/Major, and then left (north) down c/Gabriel Roca, is the old **harbour**, the most diverting part of town. Framed by an attractive, early twentieth-century ensemble of balconied houses, the port makes the most of a handsome, horseshoe-shaped bay. There's nothing special to look at, but it's a relaxing spot with a handful of restaurants, fishing smacks, a marina and a pocket-sized beach, the **Platja Es Port**. From here, it's a five-minute walk along the footpath north round the bay onto the slender, low-lying headland that accommodates the much more extensive sands of the **Platja d'es Dolç**.

The **tourist office** is on the upper floor of the town hall at c/Doctor Barraquer 5 (Mon–Fri 9am–1pm & 5–7.30pm, Sat 9am–1pm; ☎ 971 656 073). Staff issue free town maps and have information about local **bike rental** shops (cycling in the flatlands around the resort is a popular and enjoyable pastime), as well as details of local accommodation.

Accommodation

In the budget range of **accommodation**, there's a handful of hotels and *hostals* beside and behind the harbour – and these are your best chance if you're looking for a last-minute room in season. In addition, there is a selection of glossy modern hotels in the resort zone at the west end of Avinguda Primavera, all glistening towers of air-conditioned, balconied bedrooms offering panoramas of the sea.

Hotel Cabo Blanco c/Carabela 2 ☎ 971 655 075, ⓦ www.fehm.es/pmi/caboblanco. One of the town's better package-tour hotels, this polished three-star hotel has pools and attractive gardens, plus a great seashore location. Closed Nov–March. Half board only, ❺

Hostal Casa Chiquita c/Esmeralda 14 ☎ 971 655 121, ⓦ www.casachiquita.es. This smart and well-tended *hostal* occupies a rambling, *pueblo*-style modern villa in the tourist zone at the west end of Avinguda Primavera. It has a good-looking garden, with lots of exotic cactuses, and 18 smartly decorated en-suite guest rooms. Closed mid-Nov to Feb. Half board only, ❻

Hostal Colonial c/Gabriel Roca 9 ☎ 971 656 182, ⓦ www.hostal-colonial.com. The cheapest place in town, with eight spartan rooms in a basic one-star *hostal*. Closed Nov–Feb. ❷

Hostal Es Turó c/Ingeniero Roca 38 ☎ 971 655 057. Unassuming, recently done-up one-star *hostal* in a solid three-storey building plonked right on Es Port beach. There's a rooftop swimming pool and eighteen guest rooms – those at the back look out over the beach. Closed Nov–April. ❸

Hotel Lemar c/Bonança 1 ☎ 971 655 178, ⓕ 971 655 162, ⓦ www.hotel-lemar.com. Old balconied building right in the centre of things, with ninety two-star rooms overlooking the harbour. Ask for one at the front. Closed Nov to mid-April. ❸

Hotel Marquès del Palmer Avgda Primavera s/n ☎ 971 655 100, ⓦ www.universalhotels.org. Right on the beach at the west end of Avinguda Primavera, this isn't quite as new and glitzy as some of its neighbours, but is still a good-quality and comfortable three-star hotel. Closed Nov–April. ❹

Hostal Playa c/Major 25 ☎ & ⓕ 971 655 256. About five minutes' walk from the harbour, this cosy and well-cared-for little *hostal* has folksy bygones in its public areas and eight spotless en-suite rooms. Breakfast is served on a pretty patio terrace with views along the seashore. ❸

Eating

There's a cluster of first-rate **restaurants** beside the harbour, a pleasant low-key ensemble of places that attracts tourists for evening relaxation. Things get busy from around 8pm.

El Puerto Sa Llotja s/n. This popular harbourfront spot divides into two: a café-bar offering bargain-basement pizzas and spaghetti, and a restaurant specializing in seafood (around €10 for a main course).

Marivent Bar Sa Llotja s/n. The best place in town for *tapas* – from around €4 – and a drink.

Port Blau c/Gabriel Roca 67 ☎ 971 656 555. Hogs the port's best location and lives up to its setting with some of the town's top food, including big, beautifully presented portions of the freshest fish, plus big salads and great bread. *Menú del día* €10.25. Closed Tues & Jan & Feb.

Around Colònia de Sant Jordi: Es Trenc

One of Colònia de Sant Jordi's attractions is its proximity to **Es Trenc**, a 4km strip of sandy beach that extends as far as the eye can see. It's neither unknown, nor unspoilt, but the crowds are easily absorbed except at the highest point of high season, and development is virtually non-existent. To drive there, head north from Colònia de Sant Jordi and, about 1km out of town, turn left towards Campos; after 2.8km, take the signed left turn and follow the country lanes leading across the salt flats to the large car park (€4) at the east end of the beach – a total distance of around 7km. This end of the beach is far more appealing than the other, at **Ses Covetes**, which is splotched by improvised shacks and drinks stalls.

The saltpans backing onto the beach – the **Salines de Llevant** – and the surrounding farmland and scrubland support a wide variety of **birdlife**. Residents such as marsh harriers, kestrels, spotted crakes, fan-tailed warblers and hoopoes make a visit enjoyable at any time of year, but the best time to come is in the spring when hundreds of migrants arrive from Africa. Commonly seen in the springtime are avocets, little ringed plovers, little egrets, common sandpipers, little stints, black-tailed godwits, collared pratincoles and black terns. Several **footpaths** lead from Es Trenc beach into the saltpans, but it's not a good area to explore on foot: the scenery is boring, it's smelly and for much of the year insects are a menace. It's much better to drive or cycle round using the maze-like network of narrow country lanes that traverse the saltpans, stopping anywhere that looks promising.

Cabrera island

Cabrera ("Goat Island") is a bumpy, scrub-covered chunk lying 18km offshore from Colònia de Sant Jordi. Bare, almost entirely uninhabited and no more than 7km wide and 5km long, it is nonetheless easily the largest of a cluster of tiny islets. The only significant hint of Cabrera's eventful past is the protective **castle** above its supremely sheltered harbour. Pliny claimed the island to have been the birthplace of Hannibal; medieval pirates hunkered down on it to plan future raids; and during the Napoleonic Wars, the Spanish stuck nine thousand French prisoners of war out here and forgot about them – two-thirds died from hunger and disease during their three-year captivity. More recently, the island was taken over by Franco's armed forces, and now they've departed the island has been designated a national park.

A tiny kiosk beside Colònia de Sant Jordi harbour (April–Sept daily 8am–1pm & 5–9pm) has information on, and takes reservations for, **boat trips** to the island (April–Oct daily; 8hr; €28–34 depending on demand; ☎971 649 034, ⓦwww.excursionsacabrera.com). There's nowhere to eat on Cabrera, so you'll either have to take your own food or shell out €6 for the buffet provided by the boat company (drinks are extra). There are also once-weekly summer cruises to Cabrera from Porto Petro – see p.198.

The day-trip starts with a sixty-minute voyage to the island followed by a speedy circumnavigation, weather permitting. On the final stretch, the boat nudges round a hostile-looking headland to enter the harbour, **Es Port** – a narrow finger of calm water edged by hills and equipped with a tiny jetty. From here, it's a stiff hoof up the path to the ruins of the fourteenth-century **castle** perched high above on Cabrera's west coast. The views from the fortress back to Mallorca are magnificent, and all sorts of **birds** can be seen gliding round the sea-cliffs, including Manx and Cory's shearwaters and the rare Audouin's gulls, as well as peregrine falcons and shags. It is, however, the blueunderbellied **Lilfords wall lizard** that really steals the show: after you've completed the walk to the castle and back (which takes about twenty minutes each way), take time to have a drink down by the jetty, where you can tempt the Lilfords lizards out from the scrub with pieces of fruit. Note that parts of Cabrera are unsafe to explore, as there's still a real danger from **unexploded armaments** left here by the military – check with the park staff before you wander off into the interior.

You can also visit **Cabrera Museum** (free), with displays tracing the history of the island illustrated by a ragbag of archeological finds recovered from the island and its surrounding waters. The museum is housed in an attractively converted old wine cellar about ten minutes' walk from the jetty. The cellar was actually never used for its original purpose, since its construction coincided with the phylloxera louse epidemic that destroyed the island's vineyards in the 1870s. One further sight is the sombre **memorial** to the dead French prisoners of war, a short distance west of the museum.

On the return journey, the boat bobs across the bay to visit the **Cova Blava** (Blue Grotto), and heads right into the cave through the fifty-metre-wide entrance and on into the yawning chamber beyond. The grotto reaches a height of 160m and is suffused by bluish light, from which it gets its name; you can swim in it too.

Campos, Llucmajor and around

The unassuming town of **CAMPOS**, 13km northwest of Santanyí and 12km north of Colònia de Sant Jordi, hardly fires the imagination, though the fine facade of the immaculately restored Renaissance town hall and the chunky sixteenth-century church opposite both merit a look. Much more importantly, Campos boasts what many consider to be the best **patisserie** on the island – *Pastisserie Pomar*, in the main square at Plaça 20 (☎971 650 606).

LLUCMAJOR, the next settlement to the west, has little to detain you, despite its medieval origins as a market town and its long association with the island's shoemakers. It was here, just outside the old city walls, that Jaume III, the last of the independent kings of Mallorca, was defeated and killed by Pedro IV of Aragon.

Llucmajor is at the head of the byroad which leads south to Cap Blanc and Cala Pi. About 13km along this road lies **Capocorb Vell** (often signposted in Castilian as "Capicorp Vey"; Mon–Wed & Fri–Sun 10am–5pm; €2), whose extensive remains date from around 1000 BC. Surrounded by arid scrubland and enclosed within a modern dry-stone wall, this prehistoric village incorporates the battered ruins of five *talayots* and 28 dwellings. A footpath weaves round the haphazard remains, but most of what you see is not very inspiring and gives little idea of how the village was arranged. The most impressive features are the Cyclopean walls, which reach a height of four metres in places. To make more sense of what you see, pick up the free English leaflet at the entrance.

A short distance further south, just beyond the village of Capocorb, there's a choice of routes: straight on for **Cap Blanc**, a desultory cape with a lighthouse, or left for the four-kilometre trip to **CALA PI**. Spreading over a bleak headland, this resort is the remote setting for the glitzy *Club Cala Pi*, a self-contained resort complex that's a favourite with French tourists. The cove conceals a lovely **beach**, a tiny finger of sand wedged between high, pine-studded cliffs and fringed by ramshackle fishing huts. There's nowhere to **stay**, but you can refuel at the *Miguel* **restaurant**, which has tasty grilled fish, or snack at the **bar** next door.

Travel details

Buses

Artà to: Cala Rajada (Mon–Sat 6–8 daily, 1–2 on Sun; 10min); Ca'n Picafort (May–Oct Mon–Sat 2 daily; 45min); Coves d'Artà (May–Oct Mon–Sat 2–4 daily; 10min); Palma (Mon–Sat 4 daily, 2 on Sun; 1hr 25min); Platja de Canyamel (May–Oct Mon–Sat 2 daily; 15min); Port d'Alcúdia (May–Oct Mon–Sat 3 daily; 30min).

Cala d'Or to: Cala Rajada (May–Oct 5 daily; 20min); Coves del Drac (May–Oct Mon–Sat 6 daily; 20min); Palma (May–Oct Mon–Fri 5 daily, Sat & Sun 2–3 daily; Nov–April 2–4 daily; 1hr 10min); Santanyí (May–Oct Mon–Fri 6 daily, Sat & Sun 2–3 daily; Nov–April 2–4 daily; 1hr 10min).

Cala Figuera to: Cala Santanyí (May–Oct Mon–Sat 1 daily; 5min); Palma (May–Oct Mon–Sat 1 daily; 1hr 20min); Santanyí (Mon–Sat 2 daily; 15min).

Cala Millor to: Cala Rajada (May–Oct Mon–Sat 12 daily, 2 on Sun; Nov–April Mon–Sat 2 daily; 25min); Coves del Drac (May–Oct Mon–Sat 6 daily, 1 on Sun; 25min); Palma (Mon–Sat 7–8 daily, 2 on Sun; 1hr 15min); Port d'Alcúdia (May–Oct Mon–Sat 3 daily; 1hr).

Cala Pi to: Palma (May–Oct Mon–Sat 1–2 daily; 45min).

Cala Rajada to: Artà (Mon–Sat 6–8 daily, 1–2 on Sun; 10min); Cala Agulla (May–Oct Mon–Sat 4 daily; 5min); Cala de Sa Font (May–Oct Mon–Sat 4 daily; 10min); Cala Millor (May–Oct Mon–Sat 12 daily, 2 on Sun; Nov–April Mon–Sat 2 daily; 25min); Cala d'Or (May–Oct 5 daily; 20min); Ca'n Picafort (May–Oct Mon–Sat 4 daily; 35min); Capdepera (Mon–Sat 6–8 daily, 1–2 on Sun; 5min); Coves d'Artà (Mon–Sat 2–4 daily; 25min); Palma (Mon–Sat 4 daily, 2 on Sun; 1hr 30min); Platja de Canyamel (May–Oct Mon–Sat 4 daily; 20min); Port d'Alcúdia (May–Oct Mon–Sat 2 daily; 45min).

Capdepera to: Cala Rajada (Mon–Sat 6–8 daily, 1–2 on Sun; 5min); Palma (Mon–Sat 4 daily, 1–2 on Sun; 1hr 30min).

Colònia de Sant Jordi to: Palma (May–Oct Mon–Sat 5–7 daily, 2 on Sun; Nov–April Mon–Sat 4 daily, 2 on Sun; 1hr); Santanyí (2–4 daily; 25min).

Coves d'Artà to: Artà (May–Oct Mon–Sat 2–4 daily; 10min); Cala d'Or (May–Oct Mon–Sat 6 daily; 20min); Cala Rajada (May–Oct Mon–Sat 2–4 daily; 25min).

Coves del Drac to: Cala Rajada (May–Oct Mon–Sat 6 daily, 1 on Sun; 25min); Palma (May–Oct Mon–Sat 3 daily, 1 on Sun; Nov–April 1 daily; 1hr).

Felanitx to: Palma (Mon–Fri 9, Sat & Sun 5–6 daily; 50min); Porto Colom (1–3 daily; 15min).

Manacor to: Palma (Mon–Sat hourly, 5 on Sun; 45min); Porto Cristo (8–12 daily; 25min).

Montuïri to: Petra (Mon–Sat 4 daily, 2 on Sun; 10min); Palma (Mon–Sat 4–5 daily, 2 on Sun; 40min).

Palma to: Algaida (Mon–Fri 9, Sat & Sun 5–6; 20min); Artà (Mon–Sat 4 daily, 2 on Sun; 1hr 25min); Cala d'Or (May–Oct Mon–Fri 5 daily, Sat & Sun 2–3 daily; Nov–April 2–4 daily; 1hr 10min); Cala Figuera (May–Oct Mon–Sat 1 daily; 1hr 20min); Cala Millor (Mon–Sat 8 daily, 2 on Sun; 1hr 15min); Cala Pi (May–Oct Mon–Sat 1–2 daily; 45min); Cala Rajada (Mon–Sat 4 daily, 2 on Sun; 1hr 30min); Calas de Mallorca (May–Oct Mon–Sat 2 daily; 1hr); Colònia de Sant Jordi (May–Oct Mon–Sat 5–7 daily, 2 on Sun; Nov–April Mon–Sat 4 daily, 2 on Sun; 1hr); Coves del Drac (May–Oct Mon–Sat 3 daily, 1 on Sun; Nov–April 1 daily; 1hr); Covetes (for Es Trenc beach; May–Oct 1 daily; 1hr); Felanitx (Mon–Fri 9, Sat & Sun 5–6 daily; 50min); Manacor (Mon–Sat hourly, 5 on Sun; 45min); Montuïri (Mon–Sat 4–5 daily, 2 on Sun; 40min); Petra (Mon–Sat 4 daily, Sun 2; 45min); Porto Colom (Mon–Fri 6 daily, Sat & Sun 4 daily; 1hr 10min); Porto Cristo (Mon–Sat 8 daily, 2 on Sun; 1hr 10min); Porto Petro (May–Oct 2 daily; 1hr 10min); Santanyí (May–Oct Mon–Fri 5 daily, Sat & Sun 2–3 daily; Nov–April 2–4 daily; 1hr 10min).

Petra to: Montuïri (Mon–Sat 4 daily, 2 on Sun; 10min); Palma (Mon–Sat 4 daily, 2 on Sun; 45min).

Porto Colom to: Palma (Mon–Fri 6 daily, Sat & Sun 4 daily; 1hr).

Porto Cristo to: Ca'n Picafort (May–Oct Mon–Sat 3 daily; 1hr); Palma via Manacor (Mon–Sat 8 daily, 2 on Sun; 1hr 10min); Port d'Alcúdia (May–Oct Mon–Sat 3 daily; 1hr).

Santanyí to: Cala Santanyí (May–Oct Mon–Sat 1 daily; 10min); Palma (May–Oct Mon–Fri 5 daily, Sat & Sun 2–3 daily; Nov–April 2–4 daily; 1hr 10min).

Train

Manacor to: Inca (hourly; 20min); Palma (hourly; 1hr); Petra (hourly; 10min); Sineu (hourly; 15min).

Petra to: Inca (hourly; 10min); Manacor (hourly; 10min); Palma (hourly; 50min); Sineu (hourly; 5min).

Sineu to: Inca (hourly; 5min); Manacor (hourly; 15min); Palma (hourly; 45min); Petra (hourly; 5min).

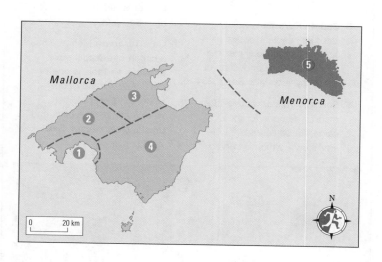

5

Menorca

Mallorca

3

2

1

4

Menorca

5

0   20 km

N

CHAPTER 5

Highlights

✳ **Maó** The labyrinthine lanes and alleys of Menorca's engaging capital ramble along the top of a ridge, high above the town marina and its outstanding assortment of restaurants. See p.211

✳ **Talatí de Dalt** The most satisfying of Menorca's many prehistoric remains, in a charming rustic setting just outside Maó. See p.221

✳ **Cap de Favaritx** Wind-stripped headland where a solitary lighthouse shines out over a lunar-like landscape of tightly layered slate. See p.234

✳ **Fornells** This attractive little resort is famous for its *caldereta de llagosta* – lobster stew – which is served

up at a batch of fine seafood restaurants. See p.235

✳ **Monte Toro** Menorca's highest point, offering wonderful vistas of the whole island on a clear day. See p.243

✳ **Ciutadella** The island's prettiest town, its compact centre an inordinately appealing maze of handsome stone buildings culminating in a pocket–sized Gothic cathedral. See p.251

✳ **Cala Turqueta** Menorca has a clutch of unspoilt cove beaches and this is one of the finest: a band of fine white sand set between wooded limestone cliffs and crystal-clear waters. See p.262

△ Ciutadella

5

Menorca

econd largest of the Balearics, boomerang-shaped **MENORCA** stretches from the enormous natural harbour of **Maó** in the east to the smaller port of **Ciutadella** in the west, a distance of just 45km. Each of these two towns, which together boast around seventy percent of the population, has preserved much of its eighteenth- and early nineteenth-century appearance, though Ciutadella's labyrinthine centre, with its grandee mansions and Gothic cathedral, has the aesthetic edge over Maó's plainer, more mercantile architecture. Running through the rustic interior between the two, the main **C721** highway forms the island's backbone, linking a trio of pocket-sized market towns – **Alaior**, **Es Mercadal** and **Ferreries** – and succouring what little industry Menorca enjoys, a few shoe factories and cheese-making plants. Branching off the highway, a sequence of asphalted side roads lead to the resorts that notch the north and south coasts. Mercifully, however, the tourist development is largely confined to individual coves and bays, and only amongst the sprawling villa-villages of the southeast and on the west coast has it become overpowering. What's more, there are still many remote cove **beaches** with not a speck of concrete in sight, though access to them is usually along rough and dusty lanes. Neither is the development likely to spread: determined to protect their island from the worst excesses of the tourist industry, the Menorcans have clearly demarcated development areas and are meanwhile pushing ahead with a variety of environmental schemes. The most prominent is the creation of a chain of conservation areas that will eventually protect around forty percent of the island, and there are also plans to revamp the old mule track that once circled the entire island and turn it into a footpath.

The C721 also acts as a rough dividing line between Menorca's two distinct geological areas. In the north, sandstone predominates, giving a red tint to the low hills which roll out towards the bare, surf-battered coastline, one of whose many coves and inlets shelters the lovely fishing village and resort of **Fornells**. To the south all is limestone, with low-lying flatlands punctuated by bulging hills and fringed by a cove-studded coastline. Straddling the two zones, **Monte Toro**, Menorca's highest peak and the site of a quaint little convent, offers panoramic views which reveal the topography of the whole island. Clearly visible from here are the wooded ravines that gash the southern zone, becoming deeper and more dramatic as you travel west – especially around **Cala Santa Galdana**, a popular resort set beneath severe, pine-clad seacliffs.

This varied terrain supports a smattering of minuscule villages and solitary farmsteads, present witnesses to an **agriculture** that had become, before much of it was killed off by urbanization, highly advanced. A dry-stone wall (*tanca*)

MENORCA

protected every field – the island boasts no less than 15,000 kms of stone wall – and prevented the Tramuntana, the vicious north wind, from tearing away the topsoil. Even olive trees had their roots individually protected in little stone wells, while compact stone ziggurats sheltered cattle from both the wind and the blazing sun. Nowadays, apart from a few acres of rape and corn, many of the fields are barren, but the walls and ziggurats survive, as do many of the old twisted gates made from olive branches.

The landscape is further cluttered by hundreds of crude stone memorials, mostly dating from the second millennium BC. Yet, despite this widespread physical evidence, little is known of the island's prehistory. The most common monuments are thought to be linked to those of Sardinia and are attributed to the so-called Talayotic culture (see p.222), whose distinctive remains can be seen across the island: three of the finest sites are at **Talatí de Dalt**, just outside Maó, and **Torrellafuda** and the **Naveta d'es Tudons**, near Ciutadella.

In more recent times, the deep-water channel of the port of Maó promoted Menorca to an important position in European affairs. The **British** saw its potential as a **naval base** and captured the island in 1708 during the War of the Spanish Succession – five years later it was ceded to them under the Treaty of Utrecht. Spain regained possession in 1783, but with the threat of Napoleon in the Mediterranean, a new British base was temporarily established under admirals Nelson and Collingwood until Britain finally relinquished all claims to the island in 1802. The British influence on Menorca, especially its architecture, is still manifest: the sash windows so popular in Georgian design are even now sometimes referred to as *winderes*, locals often part with a fond *bye-bye*, and there's a substantial expatriate community. The British also introduced the art of distilling juniper berries, and Menorcan gin (Xoriguer, Beltran or Nelson) is now world-renowned.

Maó

Despite its status as island capital, **MAÓ** (in Castilian, Mahón) has a comfortable, small-town feel – the population is just 24,000 – and wandering around the ancient centre, with its long-established cafés and old-fashioned shops, is a relaxing and enjoyable way to pass a few hours. Nowadays, most visitors approach Maó from its landward side, but this gives the wrong impression. The town has always been a port, thanks to its position on the largest natural harbour in the Mediterranean, and it's only from the water that the logic of the

---

Flights, ferries and catamarans between Mallorca and Menorca

Iberia fly six to eight times daily from Menorca to Mallorca and vice versa. The journey takes thirty minutes and costs around €73 one-way (double for a return ticket). There's rarely a problem with seat availability, though it's best to book ahead at the height of the season. By boat, **Trasmediterranea** (℡902 454 645, Ⓦwww.trasmediterranea.es) operate a Maó to Palma car ferry service once or twice weekly (for more details see p.31), whilst **Balearia** (℡902 160 180, Ⓦwww.balearia.net/eng) run inter-island fast-ferry catamaran services during the summer, from **Port d'Alcúdia to Maó** and **Ciutadella**; more details are given on p.31. Finally, Iscomar (℡902 119 128, Ⓦwww.iscomar.com) operate a car ferry service from **Port d'Alcúdia to Ciutadella** once or twice daily – see p.31. Note that car rental firms in the Balearics do not allow their vehicles off their home island.

place becomes apparent, with its centre crowding a steeply inclined ridge set tight against the south side of the harbour. From this angle, Maó is extraordinarily beautiful, its well-worn houses stacked high up on the crest of the ridge interrupted by fragments of the old city walls and the occasional church. The town centre possesses two highlights, the Churrigueresque chapel in the church of **St Francesc** and the exquisite prehistoric artefacts of the **Museu Menorca** next door, but it's the general flavour of the place that appeals rather than any individual sight. The icing on the cake is the town's striking and unusual hybrid architecture: tall, monumental Spanish mansions stand cheek-by-jowl with classical Georgian sash-windowed town houses, elegant reminders of the British occupation. Outside the centre, you might also consider visiting the enjoyable **Xoriguer gin distillery**, down on the harbour, where you can sample as many of the island's liquors as you like, and two prehistoric sites, **Trepucó** and the more substantial **Talatí de Dalt**.

Port it may be, but there's no seamy side to Maó. Nightlife is limited to a few clubs near the ferry terminal, and the harbourfront's main draw is the string of excellent **restaurants and cafés** which attract tourists in their droves, though few stay the night, preferring the purpose-built resorts close by. As a result, Maó has surprisingly few *hostals* and hotels, which means that you can base yourself here and – if you avoid the waterfront – escape the tourist throngs with the greatest of ease. The lack of places to stay also means that rooms are in exceedingly short supply in July and August, and reserving in advance during this period is strongly recommended.

Arrival and information

Menorca's **airport** (☎971 157 000), just 5km southwest of Maó, is a smart, compact affair with a handful of car-rental outlets, currency-exchange facilities and a **tourist information desk**, which has a good selection of free literature (May–Oct Mon–Fri 8am–9pm, Sat 9am–1.30pm; ☎971 157 115). There are no buses into town; the taxi fare will set you back €8–10.

Ferries from Barcelona and Palma sail right up the Port de Maó to Maó harbour, mooring next to the Trasmediterranea offices, which are located directly beneath the town centre. From the ferry dock, it's a brief walk up the wide stone stairway of Costa de Ses Voltes to Plaça Espanya and the oldest part of town. All local and island-wide **buses** arrive at – and depart from – the stops just to the west of the town's main square, the Plaça S'Esplanada, in what was formerly an army barracks; a new terminal is due to be built here at some point, though no one's too sure when.

Driving through the labyrinthine lanes of central Maó is well-nigh impossible and you're better off **parking** on the periphery. The obvious – and easiest – spot is the underground car park below Plaça S'Esplanada, though this is a good deal more expensive than on-street parking (when you can find a place). On-street parking is metered during shopping hours (Mon–Fri 9am–2pm & 4.30–7.30pm; mid-June to mid-Sept 5.30–8.30pm, plus Sat 9am–2pm) and there's a maximum stay of two hours (€1.35). At other times, it's free – and there's more chance of a space. Note that if the time you've paid for overlaps into a free period, your ticket will be valid for the time you've got left when the next restricted period begins.

There are **tourist information offices** near Plaça S'Esplanada on c/Rovellada de Dalt 24 (June–Aug Mon–Fri 9am–1.30 & 5–7pm, Sat 9am–1.30pm; ☎971 363 790), and down by the port on the landward side of the Edificio de Autoridad Portuaria (Mon–Fri 8am–9pm, Sat 9am–1pm; ☎971

MAÓ

Port de Maó

Naval Base

Illa Pinto

Xoriguer Gin Distillery

Sant Francesc

Museu de Menorca

Ferry Port

Gobierno Militar

Ajuntament

Santa Maria

Fish Market

Claustre del Carme

Església del Carme

Teatre Principal

Bus Stops ★

ACCOMMODATION
Hotel del Almirante	**F**
Hotel Capri	**C**
Hostal La Isla	**B**
Hostal-residència Jume	**A**
Hostal-residència Orsi	**D**
Hotel Port-Mahón	**E**

RESTAURANTS & CAFÉS
Andaira	18
L'Arpó	11
Café Baixamar	9
Café-bar La Farinera	13
Cafetería La Bombilla	15
Gregal	2
Jàgaro	3
J&J	19
Mesón del Puerto	5
La Minerva	14
Mirador Café	16
Il Porto	1
Roma	4
Varadero	10

BARS AND CLUBS
Bar Akelarre	7
Café Mó Blues	21
Discoteca Sí	20
Mambo	12
Nou Bar	17
Salsa Bar	8
Tse-Tse	6

0   100 m

N

Barcelona

Bellavista

Santa Cecília

Santa Nicolau

Santa Sebastià

Santa Rosa

Concepció

Santa Catarina

Santa Teresa

Santa Anna

El Carme

Nord

Anuncivel

Infanta

Noble

Ciutadella

Sa Ravaleta

Portal de Mar

Costa de ses Voltes

Moll de Ponent

Moll de Llevant

Plaça Miranda

Plaça Príncep

Plaça Carme

Plaça Espanya

Plaça Conquesta

Plaça Reial

Plaça Constitució

Plaça Colón

Plaça Bastió

Plaça Esplanada

Plaça S'Esplanada

Isabel II

Sant Jaume

Es Frares

Avgda Dr. Guardia

S'Arraval

Sa Rovellada de Baix

Sa Rovellada de Dalt

Forn

Bonaire

Sant Roque

Alaior

Bastió

Moreres

Sant Jordi

Sant Josep

Es Còs de Gràcia

Cami d'es Castell

Comèdia

Vassallo

Av Josep Maria Quadrado

MENORCA | Maó

5

213

Sant Lluís

Trepucó

Sant Lluís

& Airport

& Airport

355 952). Both can provide a map of the island and free leaflets giving the lowdown on almost everything you can think of, from archeological sites and beaches to bus timetables, car rental, taxis, accommodation and banks. They won't help you find accommodation, however.

Accommodation

Maó has a very limited supply of **accommodation**, though despite this it remains along with Ciutadella the best bet on Menorca for bargain lodgings. There are a few inexpensive **hostals** close to the town centre: none is especially inspiring, but they're reasonable enough and convenient – unlike Maó's two classier **hotels**, which are stuck out on the edge of town. **Prices** vary considerably according to season, with rates in July and August about thirty percent more than in winter; advance reservations are advised from June to October and are pretty much essential in July and August.

Hostals

Hostal La Isla c/Santa Caterina 4 ☎971 366 492. Recently refurbished, this excellent one-star *hostal* is run by a very friendly couple. Rooms are on the small side, but are attractive and comfortable, and all have private bathroom and TV. There's a popular bar and restaurant downstairs. ❷

Hostal Residencia Jume c/Concepció 6 ☎971 363 266, ⓕ971 364 878. Centrally located on a narrow side street, this large, one-star *hostal* occupies a five-storey modern block and has thirty-five frugal rooms. ❷

Hostal Residencia Orsi c/Infanta 19 ☎ & ⓕ971 364 751. In a large old terrace house a couple of minutes' walk from Plaça Reial, this unassuming *hostal* has seventeen rooms, with mostly shared showers, and a rooftop terrace. The owners are English-speakers – one an American, the other a Scot. ❷

Hotels

Hotel del Almirante Carretera de Maó ☎971 362 700, ⓦwww.hoteldelalmirante.com. Once the residence of British admiral Lord Collingwood, this maroon and cream Georgian house has a delight-

ful, antique-crammed interior, though some of the bedrooms are modern affairs overlooking the swimming pool round the back. The package-tour operators Thomson use the place, but there are often vacancies. It's located about 2km east of Maó beside the coastal road to Es Castell. To get there from the town centre, take a taxi or the Es Castell bus and ask to be dropped off. ❺

Hotel Capri c/Sant Esteve 8 ☎971 361 400, ⓔcapri@rtmhotels.com. Large, proficiently modern three-star hotel in the centre of Maó, popular with business travellers. The rooftop spa and pool, and a huge buffet breakfast are pluses. It's a brief walk west of the tourist office along Avgda Quadrado, just after Plaça S'Esplanada. ❹

Hotel Port-Mahón Avgda Fort de l'Eau s/n ☎971 362 600, ⓕ971 351 050. Elegant colonial-style hotel in a superb location overlooking the Maó inlet. There's a swimming pool and a chic patio café, plus each of eighty-odd rooms is decked out in smart, modern style with air conditioning. Room prices vary enormously, with the top whack a hefty €192. Situated a twenty-minute walk east of the town centre via c/Carme or c/Barcelona at the corner of Avinguda Fort de L'Eau and Avinguda Port de Maó. ❺

The Town

With its good-looking mansions and grand churches, the oldest and most diverting part of **Maó** rolls along the clifftop above the harbour for roughly 1km. Behind, immediately to the south, the predominantly nineteenth-century town clambers up the hill, its complicated pattern of tiny squares and short lanes bisected by the principal shopping street and pedestrianized main drag, which goes under various names, with **Costa de Sa Plaça** and **c/Moreres** being the longest individual strips. It takes five to ten minutes to walk from one end of the main street to the other and you emerge at **Plaça S'Esplanada**, the mundane main square.

Plaça Espanya

From just behind the ferry terminal, a graceful stone stairway and a narrow, twisting street – the Costa de Ses Voltes – tangle together as they climb up the hill to emerge in the old town at the compact **Plaça Espanya**. On the north side of the square, a sociable little **fish market** is plonked on top of a sturdy bastion that was originally part of the **Renaissance city wall**. This mighty zigzag of fortifications, bridges and gates once encased the whole city and replaced the city's **medieval walls**, sections of which also survive – look back up from the foot of the stairway and several chunks are clearly visible. Work on the new Renaissance walls started under the Habsburgs in the middle of the sixteenth century, though the chain of bastions took over one hundred years to complete.

Plaça Carme

Immediately to the east of the fish market, **Plaça Carme** is overshadowed by the massive facade of the eighteenth-century **Església del Carme**, a Carmelite church whose barn-like interior is almost entirely devoid of embellishment. The adjoining cloisters, the **Claustre del Carme**, have, after long service as the municipal courts, been refurbished to house the town's fresh meat, fruit and vegetable market, with the market stalls set against sculpted angels and religious carvings. The cloisters were originally taken from the Carmelites in 1837 under the terms of a national edict that confiscated church property, passing vast estates and buildings to the state in what was the largest redistribution of land since the Reconquista. For the liberals, who pushed the edict through, the church was the acme of reaction, and its monks and priests, who usually opposed progressive reform, the representatives of arcane medievalism. Their legislation was, as might be expected, bitterly resented by the church, but it caught the popular mood, a volatile mix of anti-clericalism and self-interest, with many small farmers hoping to buy the confiscated land from the state at knock-down prices. The confiscation was just one aspect of the prolonged struggle between conservatives and progressives that destabilized Spain throughout the nineteenth century, but it had permanent effects: later conservative administrations did return some of the ecclesiastical property, but most of the land was lost to the church for good.

A narrow, dead-end alley on the right-hand side of the Plaça Espanya fish market offers fine views back down over the port and is home to the chic, pastel-painted *Mirador Café* (see p.219).

Plaça Conquesta and the Església de Santa Maria

North of Plaça Espanya lies slender **Plaça Conquesta**, whose full-length but poorly crafted statue of Alfonso III, the Aragonese king who expelled the Menorcan Moors, was donated by Franco in a typically nationalist gesture. At the far end of the square, turn left along the cobbled lane – c/Alfons III – and you'll soon spy the genteel arcades, bull's-eye upper windows and wrought-iron grilles of the seventeenth-century **Ajuntament** (town hall). This was built by the Spanish, but subsequently occupied by the island's first colonial governor, Sir Richard Kane (see box on p.239), who donated its distinctive clock as well as the portraits of King George III and Queen Charlotte, which still hang in the entrance hall.

The Ajuntament is on the northern edge of **Plaça Constitució**, a narrow piazza overshadowed by the **Església de Santa Maria** (7.30am–1pm & 6–8.30pm), a heavy-duty pile founded in 1287 by Alfonso III to celebrate the island's reconquest. Rebuilt in the middle of the eighteenth century and remodelled on several subsequent occasions, the church is an enjoyable architectural hybrid. The Gothic features of the exterior are encased within later Neoclassical additions, while inside the **nave** is all Catalan Gothic, a hangar-like, aisle-less, single-vaulted construction designed to make the high altar visible to the entire congregation – and indeed there's no missing it: its larger-than-life Baroque excesses shoot up to the roof flanked by spiral columns. Unfortunately, the nave is dark and gloomy, as most of the windows are bricked up – in contradiction to the original design in which kaleidoscopic floods of light would have poured in through soaring, stained-glass windows.

In contrast to the clean lines of the nave, the truncated **transepts** and the ceiling above the high altar sport intricate stuccowork, with dozens of cherubs peering out from a swirling, decorative undergrowth. Several side chapels exhibit similar Baroque flourishes, but the church's pride and joy is really its **organ**, a monumental piece of woodwork filling out the elevated gallery above the south entrance. The instrument, with its trumpeting angels, four keyboards and three thousand pipes, was made in Austria in 1810 and lugged across half of Europe at the height of the Napoleonic wars. Britain's Admiral Collingwood helped with the move, probably as a crafty piece of appeasement: defiance of their new Protestant masters had played a large part in the locals' decision to rebuild the church during the British occupation.

Carrer Isabel II

Georgian doors and fanlights, sash and bay windows and fancy ironwork distinguish **Carrer Isabel II** as it runs west from Plaça Constitució. This narrow, elongated street, lined by a string of fine patrician mansions backing onto the cliffs above the harbour, once lay at the heart of the British administration. Halfway along, the present **Gobierno Militar** (military governor's house) is the most distinctive building today, with its elaborate paintwork and shaded, colonial-style arcades.

There's a useful – and extremely pleasant – shortcut down to the harbour from c/Isabel II: head down **Costa d'es General**, an alley at the foot of c/Rector Mort, which tunnels through the old city wall before snaking its way down the cliff to the waterside below.

The Església de St Francesc

At the end of c/Isabel II the Baroque facade of the **Església de St Francesc** (daily 10am–noon & 5–7.30, closed Fri morning) appears as a cliff-face of pale golden stone set above the rounded, Romanesque-style arches of its doorway. The church was a long time in the making, its construction spread over the seventeenth and eighteenth centuries following the razing of the town by Barbarossa in 1535 – a random piece of piracy during the protracted struggle for control of the Mediterranean between the Ottomans and the Habsburgs which lasted until the destruction of the Turkish fleet at the Battle of Lepanto in 1571. Inside, the mighty nave, with its lofty vaulted roof, encloses a crude but flamboyant high altar with panels of biblical scenes designed to edify the (illiterate) congregation. The nave is poorly lit, but it's still possible to pick out the pinkish tint in much of the stone and the unusual spiral decoration of the pillars. In contrast, the **Chapel of the Immaculate Conception**, tucked away off the north side of the nave, is flooded with light – an octagonal wonderland of garlanded vines and roses in the Churrigueresque style. The chapel is attributed to Francesc Herrara, the painter, engraver and architect who trained in Rome and worked in Menorca before moving on to Palma in Mallorca.

The Museu de Menorca

The monastic buildings adjacent to the Església de St Francesc now house the **Museu de Menorca** (Tues–Sat 10am–2pm & 4–8.30pm, Sun 10am–2pm; €2.40), easily the island's biggest and best museum, with multilingual labels to explain most of the exhibits. Entry to the collection is through the cloister, whose sturdy pillars and vaulted aisles illustrate the high point of the Menorcan Baroque.

The first floor holds a wide sampling of prehistoric artefacts, beginning with bits and pieces left by the Neolithic pastoralists who were well established here by about 4000 BC. There's also an extensive range of material from the **Talayotic period**. The early stuff, household objects and the like, is pretty crude, but the displays ably illustrate the increasing sophistication of the Talayotic people, both in their homemade goods and in their use of imported items. In particular, look out for the dainty, rather quizzical-looking bronze bull, probably of Phoenician manufacture, found at the Torralba d'en Salord Talayotic site (see p.241). Other imported items include several enormous amphorae, a few pieces of charming, multicoloured Punic jewellery and a small Egyptian bronze of Imhotep found at Torre d'en Gaumés (see p.242). These reflect the final flourishing of Talayotic culture when Menorca became a major port of call for ships sailing through the Mediterranean, particularly between Italy and Spain.

The collection deteriorates on the **second floor**, where a series of skimpy displays gallop unconvincingly through the Moorish period and continue all the way to 1900. The only items of interest are a small selection of majolica pottery and the whimsical wooden figurines, representing various *Menorquín* folkloric characters, carved by the Monjo i Monjo Brothers in the late nineteenth century.

Plaça Bastió and Plaça S'Esplanada

From the Museu de Menorca it's a brief walk southeast to **Plaça Bastió**, an expansive square that holds Maó's one remaining medieval gateway, the **Portal de Sant Roc**, a sturdy affair of roughly hewn stone comprising two turrets, a connecting arch and a projecting parapet. The gateway is named after Saint Roch, a fourteenth-century hermit who was popular hereabouts as a talisman to ward off the plague: Christian legend asserted that he both recovered from a bout of the plague and cured fellow sufferers, a good recommendation at a time when every city in Europe feared an outbreak.

From Plaça Bastió, it's a few paces along narrow c/Alaior to the steeply sloping main street, here known as **Costa de Sa Plaça** (also signed as c/Hannover), whose old-fashioned shops and tiny piazzas form the town's commercial centre. There are more shops up the hill along **c/Moreres**, which brings you to the flowerbeds and benches of the principal square, **Plaça S'Esplanada**, liveliest at weekends, when it fills up with crowds converging on its ice-cream vendors and kiddies' swings. The square is overlooked from the west by an unpleasant reminder of Fascist days in the form of a monumental Civil War memorial endowed with Francoist insignia. The column is inscribed with the old fable, "Honor todos los que dieron su vida por Espanya" ("Honour to all those who gave their life for Spain"). The former army barracks behind the monument is now where all local and island-wide buses arrive and depart.

The quayside

Below the town stretches the three-kilometre-long **quayside**, in the middle of which lies Maó's ferry terminal. To the west, beyond a few bars and restaurants, are the fishing boats and jetties, followed by an industrial area, which extends round the murky waters at the head of the inlet. To the east, it's a couple of hundred metres to the departure point for **boat tours** of Port de Maó (see box below), beyond which lies the town's elongated marina, where flashy chrome yachts face a string of restaurants, bars and cafés. By day, the half-hour stroll east along the quayside is tame verging on boring; at night, with tourists converging on the restaurants, it's slightly more animated, but not much.

There is, however, one enjoyable daytime attraction a couple of minutes' walk west of the ferry terminal. This is the showroom of the **Xoriguer gin distillery** (June–Aug Mon–Fri 8am–7pm, Sat 9am–1pm; Sept–May Mon–Fri 9am–1pm & 4–7pm; free), where you can help yourself to free samples of gin, various liqueurs and other spirits. Multilingual labels give details of all the different types, and there are some pretty obscure examples, such as *calent*, a sweet, brown liqueur with aniseed, wine, saffron and cinnamon; and *palo*, a liquorice-flavoured spirit supposedly of Phoenician provenance. The lime-green *hierbas*, a favourite local tipple, is a sweet and sticky liqueur, partly made from camomile collected on the headlands of La Mola outside Maó (see p.227). In all its guises, it is, however, gin which remains the main product, and *pomada*, a gin cocktail with lemonade, is now as near as damn it Menorca's national drink. Gin was first brought to the island by British sailors in the late eighteenth century, but a local businessman, a certain Beltran, obtained the recipe in obscure circumstances and started making the stuff himself. Nowadays, Xoriguer is the most popular island brand, mostly sold in modern versions of the earthenware bottles once used by British sailors, known locally as *canecas*.

Boat trips from Maó

Departing from the jetty near the foot of Costa de Ses Voltes, various companies run regular boat trips along the **Port de Maó** inlet, with an hour-long scoot down and around the port costing €8.50 per person. Frequency depends on the season: in summer there are departures every hour or so, whereas in January there are only a handful of sailings every week. You can also rent boats privately for **longer trips** (summer only), including to Fornells or even all the way around the island to Ciutadella, with stops for swimming and snorkelling. Half-day trips to, say, Fornells or Cala Galdana, cost around €60 per adult; a full-day trip to Ciutadella costs €90 per adult. The busiest company is Yellow Cats (☎639 676 351); other outfits include Don Joan (☎689 322 526), Pirata Azul (no phone), Blue Mediterranean (☎609 305 314) and Rutas Marítimas de la Cruz (☎607 214 455).

These boat trips are the only ways to get close to the three islets that dot the Port de Maó – four if you count tiny **Illa Pinto** (just opposite the Yellow Cats jetty), which is used by the military and attached to the north shore by a causeway. The first of the three islands is the **Illa del Rei**, whose dilapidated buildings once accommodated a military hospital and where Alfonso III landed at the start of his successful invasion of Muslim Menorca in 1287. Next comes tiny **Illa Plana**, also known as Illa Quarentena, a pancake-flat islet which has been used variously as a quarantine station, a US naval base and now a Spanish one. Finally, the larger **Illa del Llatzeret** is the site of a former hospital for infectious diseases, surrounded by imposing walls built of stone retrieved from Fort Sant Felip (see p.224) – the Menorcans were convinced that contagion could be carried into town by the wind, so they built the walls to keep the germs inside (internal walls separated patients suffering different diseases for precisely the same reason). The hospital remained in service until 1917, since when – oddly enough – it has been used as a holiday retreat for health workers. Llatzeret was only separated from the mainland in 1900 when a canal was cut on its landward side to provide a more sheltered route to the daunting La Mola fortress (see p.227).

Eating, drinking and nightlife

Maó has a place in culinary history as the eighteenth-century birthplace of **mayonnaise** (*mahonesa*). Various legends, all of them involving the French, claim to identify its inventor: take your pick from the chef of the French commander besieging Maó; a peasant woman dressing a salad for another French general; or a housekeeper disguising rancid meat from the taste buds of a French officer. The French also changed the way the Menorcans bake their bread, while the British started the dairy industry and encouraged the roasting of meat. Traditional Balearic food is, however, not very much in evidence these days, as most of Maó's **restaurants** specialize in Spanish, Catalan or Italian dishes. These tourist-oriented establishments are mainly spread out along the quayside – the Moll de Ponent west of the main stairway, the Moll de Llevant to the east. There's also a smattering of more economical **cafés** and **café-bars**, both down on the quayside and in the town centre, though there are surprisingly few *tapas* bars.

As far as **opening hours** are concerned, almost all the town's cafés and restaurants open daily during high season, though restaurants usually take a siesta between 4pm and 7pm or 8pm, and things can get eerily quiet on Sundays. Out of season, many places shut completely, while others close early.

Nightlife isn't Maó's forte, though there are some fairly lively bars dotted along the harbourfront; there's a cluster just up from the ferry terminal and another towards the east end of the harbour on Moll de Llevant. These open late – some not until midnight – and keep going until well into the small hours, and until dawn at weekends.

Cafés and café-bars

Café Baixamar Moll de Ponent 17. An attractively decorated little café-bar, with old-fashioned mirrors and soft-hued paintwork, serving tasty traditional Menorcan snacks and tapas – island cheese and sausage, for example, costs just €3.

Café-bar La Farinera Moll de Llevant 84. Located near the ferry port, this spruce and modern café-bar offers tasty snacks, and also has a selection of interesting photographs of old Menorca on the walls. Usually open from 6am.

Cafeteria La Bombilla c/Sant Roc 31. This modest little café in the town centre on Plaça Bastió offers a good range of tapas, averaging about €3 per portion.

J&J Plaça S'Esplanada s/n. A retreat for homesick Brits, this English-owned and -run place does fish and chips and other simple meals, and you can take in the square from the terrace seating. Mon, Tues & Sat closes at 4pm; Wed–Fri open evenings as well.

Mirador Café Plaça Espanya s/n. Located just steps from the fish market at the top of the main stairway leading from the harbour to the town centre, this little café-bar offers tasty snacks, and has great views over the harbour from its terrace. Jazz is the favoured background music.

Varadero Moll de Llevant 4. Close to the ferry terminal – and adjacent to the Yellow Cats jetty – this smart, modern place has a restaurant on one side and a café-bar on the other. The café-bar is the place to aim for – a stylish spot to nurse a drink and sample a small range of tapas. Very popular with tourists in the summer.

Restaurants

Andaira c/Forn 61 ☏971 366 817. A very intimate and stylish family-run place featuring Mediterranean fusion cuisine, with main courses costing around €14. It's near Plaça S'Esplanada: leave the square along c/Pi, a short pedestrianized alley on its north side, take the first right and then the first left. Dinner only; closed Mon, and sometimes Sun too.

L'Arpó Moll de Llevant 124 ☏971 369 844. Cosy and intimate restaurant featuring a superb selection of fish dishes from €11. Try the paella.

Gregal Moll de Llevant 306 ☏971 366 606. The decor is uninspired, but the food is outstanding, with mouthwatering seafood dishes prepared in all sorts of delicious (and often traditional) ways. Try the John Dory in leek sauce (€27) or the sea-anemone fritters (€10).

Jàgaro Moll de Llevant 334 ℡ 971 362 390. At the east end of the waterfront, with a smart, traditional interior and a terrace packed with greenery. The ambitious menu is perhaps a little too wide-ranging for its own good, featuring everything from hamburgers to paella. It's best to stick to the fish (mains €12–18).

Mesón del Puerto Moll de Ponent 66 ℡ 971 352 903. Just west of the ferry terminal, this pleasant, old-fashioned bodega-style café-restaurant, with big wooden tables and agricultural bric-a-brac pinned on the walls, has a good, very Spanish, menu – the squid and the cod (both €12) are especially tasty.

La Minerva Moll de Llevant 87 ℡ 971 351 995. One of – if not the – smartest restaurants in town, with glossy furnishings and fittings, a harbourside terrace, and a menu featuring dishes with a Mediterranean slant. The paella is outstanding, and so is the *menú del día*, a relative snip at €14. Save room for the wonderful desserts – the vanilla custard boats in syrup speak for themselves.

Il Porto Moll de Llevant 225 ℡ 971 354 426. An enjoyable place to eat, with a fountain and an arcaded terrace. The cooks perform in full view, turning out tasty fish and meat dishes from a wide-ranging menu that features Italian fare – the pizzas are particularly good. Popular with families. Closed in winter.

Roma Moll de Llevant 295. Popular, fast-service eatery specializing in well-prepared Italian food at bargain prices, with pasta and pizzas from €5.50. The decor is a tad old-fashioned, but that seems to suit the clientele. Closed in winter.

Bars and nightclubs

Bar Akelarre Moll de Ponent 41. Set down on the waterfront near the ferry terminal, this is probably the best – and certainly the most fashionable – bar in town, occupying an attractively renovated ground-floor vault with stone walls and a miniature garden-cum-terrace at the back, right at the foot of the old city walls. Jazz and smooth modern sounds form the backcloth, with occasional live acts.

Café Mô Blues c/Santiago Ramon i Cajal 3. A favourite with local twenty-somethings, this amenable basement bar features jazz through to R&B. It's located a couple of minutes' walk south of Plaça Reial, along c/Infanta then first right up c/Verge de Gràcia and dead ahead at the first intersection. Fri & Sat only, from 10pm.

Discoteca Si c/Verge de Gràcia 16. Low-key, locals' late-night disco-bar south of Plaça Reial.

Usually open from 11.30pm to around 3am.

Mambo Moll de Llevant s/n.One of the best of the various bars which dot the waterfront east of the ferry terminal, this busy little place occupies a pleasantly converted old premises with stone walls and beamed ceiling. Standing room only.

Nou Bar c/Nou 1. The ground-floor café here, with its crummy armchairs and gloomy lighting, is a dog-eared old place much favoured by locals. During festivals, it's the place to be, especially on the balcony upstairs.

Salsa Bar Moll de Ponent 29. Tiny, lively, first-floor bar playing mostly Latin sounds.

Tse-Tse Costa des General 14. Head up the ramped lane across from the ferry terminal to find this nightclub; there are several other tiny places close by, all of which come to life after midnight and rave on till dawn.

Listings

Banks Amongst many, there's Banco de Credito Balear, Plaça S'Esplanada 2; Banca March, c/S'Arravaleta 7; and Banco de Santander, c/Moreres 46 and 69.

Bicycle rental VRB, c/S'Arraval 52 (℡ 971 353 798) rents out ordinary and mountain bikes for around €10 per day.

Car rental There are branches of Avis (℡ 971 361 576) and Atesa (℡ 971 366 213) at the airport; downtown there's Betacar Menorca office at Plaça S'Esplanada 8 (℡ 971 360 620), plus many smaller concerns – the tourist office has a complete list.

Email and internet access Cyber Princip@l, c/Nou 25 (Mon–Sat 9.30–10pm; €3.50 per hour).

Ferries and catamarans Balearia (℡ 902 160 180, ⓦ www.balearia.net/eng) operate an inter-island fast-ferry catamaran service during the summer from Port d'Alcúdia, on Mallorca, to Maó (one-way passenger fares from €50, cars from €100); Trasmediterranea (℡ 902 454 645, ⓦ www.trasmediterranea.es) run car ferries to Maó from Palma once or twice weekly. The sailing time is six hours and the one-way adult fare starts at €26, with a standard-size car costing €70, twenty percent more in high season. Reservations are not required for foot passengers, but are strongly advised for vehicles. Note that local car rental firms do not allow their vehicles to travel from Mallorca to Menorca or vice versa.

Schedules, tariffs and tickets are available direct from the operators, Trasmediterranea and Balearia, down at the ferry terminal.
Maps & books Llibrería Fundació, facing Plaça Colón at Costa de Sa Plaça 14 (Mon–Fri 9.30am–1.30pm & 5–8pm, Sat 9.30am–1.30pm; ☎971 363 543), stocks a fair selection of English-language guidebooks and is strong on birdwatching guides. It also has general maps of Menorca – including the Distrimapas Telstar – plus a reasonable, though far from exhaustive, assortment of IGN walking maps.

Mopeds Moped rental at Motos Gelabert, Avinguda J. A. Clavé 12 (☎971 360 614) or down by the port at Motos Rayda, Moll de Llevant 21 (☎971 354 786).
Pharmacies Amongst several downtown pharmacies, there's one at c/S'Arravaleta 5 and another at c/Moreres 28.
Post office The central *correu* is at c/Bonnaire 15, just east of Plaça Bastió (Mon–Sat 9am–9pm).
Taxis There are taxi ranks on Plaça S'Esplanada and Plaça d'Espanya; alternatively, phone Radio Taxis on ☎971 367 111. Advance booking is recommended.

Around Maó: Trepucó and Talatí de Dalt

There are two notable prehistoric sites close to Maó, both with open access and no entry charge. One of them, **Trepucó**, is on the southern edge of town near the ring road, the other – the more appealing **Talatí de Dalt** – is about 4km to the west of Maó beside the C721. If you've ventured this far, you may as well drop by a third site, **Rafal Rubí**, about 2.5km further west on the C721. All three sites are signed.

Trepucó

It takes about thirty minutes to walk to **Trepucó** from Plaça S'Esplanada. Follow c/Moreres from the eastern corner of the square, take the first right onto c/Cós de Gràcia and then go straight on down c/Verge de Gràcia to the ring road. Here, go over the traffic island and follow the twisting lane dead ahead, past the cemetery. Thereafter the route is not, at present, clearly signed. Look out for the Ermita de Gràcia and go past it. After 200m beyond the Ermita, go straight at the fork, and then – 500m later – veer left at the fork and, after a further 100m, turn right. Surrounded by olive trees and dry-stone walls, the tiny site's focal point is a 4.2-metre-high and 2.75-metre-wide **taula**, one of the largest and best-preserved of these T-shaped megaliths on the island. The *taula* stands inside a circular compound which is edged by the remains of several broadly circular buildings. These were thoroughly excavated by a team of archeologists from Cambridge University in the late 1920s, but even they couldn't work out how the complex was structured. There are two cone-shaped **talayots** close by, the larger one accessible, the other not. The shape of the larger talayot is, however, not entirely authentic, as the French increased its width to mount their guns during the invasion of 1781.

Talatí de Dalt and Rafal Rubí

Another illuminating Talayotic remnant, **Talatí de Dalt**, lies 4km from Maó, just south of the main C721 highway. If you're driving, take the short and signposted country lane on the left; by public transport, take any Alaior bus, but check first that the driver is prepared to let you off. Much larger than Trepucó, the site is partly enclosed by a Cyclopean wall and features an imposing *taula* set within a circular precinct. The *taula* here appears to be propped up by a T-shaped pillar, though it's generally agreed that this is the result of an accidental fall, rather than by prehistoric design. Next to the *taula* are the heaped stones of the main *talayot*, whilst all around lie the meagre remains of prehistoric dwellings. The exact functions of these are

Menorca's Talayotic sites

Menorca's **Talayotic sites** conform to a common pattern, though there are of course differences in the condition in which each has been preserved. The tallest structure on each site is generally the **talayot** (from *atalaya*, Arabic for "watchtower"), a cone-shaped mound between 5m and 10m high, built without mortar or cement. There are dozens of ruined *talayots* on both islands and the detail of their original design varies from site to site: some are solid, others contain one or more chambers. Most are found in settlements, but there are solitary examples too. This diversity has helped generate considerable debate about their original purpose, with scholars suggesting variously that they were built for defence, as dwellings for chieftains, as burial sites or as storehouses. Popular belief has it that they functioned as watchtowers, but it's a theory few experts accept: they have no interior stairway and only a handful are found on the coast. Even so, no one has come up with a more convincing explanation. The mystery of the *talayots* is compounded by their unusualness. The only Mediterranean structures they resemble are the Nuragh towers found on Sardinia. A Sardinian connection would support the view that this phase in the Balearics' development resulted from contact with other cultures, though Sardinia is but one of several options, with Egypt, Crete and Greece also touted as possible influences.

These talayots are often positioned a few metres from a **taula**, a T-shaped structure comprising two huge stones up to 4.5m high. Some sites may contain several *talayots*, but there's only ever one *taula*, and this almost always sits in the middle of a circular enclosure whose perimeter is (or was) marked by a low wall. Archeologists have unearthed objects in these enclosures and the remains of firepits have been found against the perimeter wall, both of which seem to imply a religious function, though this is only conjecture – there's certainly insufficient evidence to justify referring to these enclosures as "shrines", as they've sometimes been called. There's general agreement, however, that the *taula* and its enclosure formed the public part of the settlement, and – as confirmation – on many sites the remains of circular family dwellings surround them. Finally, Menorca also holds a number of **navetas**, stone-slab constructions shaped like inverted loaf tins and dating from between 1400 and 800 BC. Many have false ceilings, and although you can stand up inside, they were clearly not living spaces, but rather communal tombs, or ossuaries. The prime example is the **Naveta d'es Tudons**, outside Ciutadella. Navetas are never found in the same place as the *talayots* and *taulas*.

Archeologists divide the Talayotic period into several different periods, but as far as the non-specialist is concerned, the only significant difference between the various phases is the encircling **wall**, a dry-stone affair often several metres high and made up of large stones. These walls were for defence and probably reflect an increase in piracy across the western Mediterranean: the earlier settlements don't have them; the later ones – from around 1000 BC – do. For more on the Talayotic period, see pp.267–268.

not known, but there's no doubt that the *taula* was the village centrepiece, and probably the focus of religious ceremonies. The rustic setting is charming – olive and carob trees abound and a tribe of hogs roots around the undergrowth.

Back on the C721 and heading west, it's about another 2.5km to **Rafal Rubí**, where two smallish *navetas* (see box above) occupy adjacent fields just north of the main road. Made of large stones and resembling inverted loaf tins, they hardly set the pulse racing, but if you visit on a moonlit night they really are very spooky.

Port de Maó

Port de Maó, as Menorcans term the whole of the extended inlet that links Maó with the Mediterranean, is one of the finest natural harbours in the world. Over 5km long and almost a kilometre wide in places, the channel also boasts the narrowest of deep-sea entrances, strategic blessings that have long made it an object of nautical desire. The high admiral of the Holy Roman Emperor Charles V quipped that "June, July, August and Mahon are the best ports in the Mediterranean", and after Barbarossa's destruction of Maó in 1535, the emperor finally took the hint and had the harbour fortified. Later, the British eyed up the port as both a forward base for Gibraltar and a lookout against the French naval squadron in Toulon. Using the War of the Spanish Succession as an excuse, they occupied Menorca in 1708 and, give or take occasional French and Spanish interventions, stayed in control until 1802. They poured vast resources into the harbour defences and, since their departure, the Spaniards have updated and remodelled the fortifications on several occasions.

Nowadays, both shores – as well as a trio of islets in mid-channel (see p.218) – are covered in the remains of all this military history and are pockmarked by ruined **fortifications**, thick-walled affairs hugging the contours of the coast. The two highlights of Port de Maó's **south shore** are the unusual subterranean fortress of **Fort Marlborough** and **Sant Esteve**, the pretty fishing village where it is located. Of lesser interest is the former garrison town of **Es Castell**, purpose-built by the English in the 1770s. The **north shore** is formed by a hilly promontory which nudges out into the ocean, protecting the channel from the Tramuntana. The promontory's steep terrain has deterred the islanders from settling here, and although development has spawned a pair of ritzy suburbs – Sant Antoni and Cala Llonga – the north shore's key features remain the handsome old colonial villa, **Golden Farm**, and the out-of-bounds fortress of **La Mola**, which sprawls over the headland at its very tip. Also of interest are the two dinky little fishing villages that snuggle around rocky coves just over the hills on the island's northeast shore – **Es Murtar** and **Sa Mesquida**, with its wide sandy beach.

To explore either shore thoroughly you'll need your own transport, though there's a frequent **bus** service from Maó to Es Castell. Alternatively, the walk on p.224 offers a good introduction to the area.

Port de Maó's south shore

Tucked in tight against the shore just 3km from Maó, the grid-iron streets of **ES CASTELL** (formerly known as Villa Carlos) have a militaristic and very English air. Originally called Georgetown, the town is ranged around **Plaça S'Esplanada**, the old parade ground-cum-plaza. The square's Georgian-style town hall, graced by a stumpy, toy-town clock tower, and the elongated facades of its three barracks, bear witness to British influence. Elsewhere, sash windows, doors with glass fanlights, and wrought-iron grilles adorn many of the older houses, though nowadays the centre looks rather bedraggled. As a garrison town, the fortunes of Es Castell have always been tied to those of the military, and, with Franco gone, the army no longer has the same prestige. This is reflected in the town's general demeanour – and especially on the main square, where two of the barracks stand abandoned and neglected.

Nevertheless, Es Castell is still worth a brief wander, beginning in the Plaça S'Esplanada, where one of the barracks houses a modest military **museum**, equipped with a motley collection of old rifles and uniforms (Mon, Thurs & first Sun in the month 11am–1pm; €2.40). From the plaza it's a couple of minutes' walk east down c/Stuart to the harbour, a pleasant spot occupying the thumb-shaped cove of **Cales Fonts**. Stroll north along the waterside and you'll pass a string of **restaurants**, two of the best being the *Rocamar*, at Cala Fonduco 32 (℡971 365 601), and the *Siroco* at no. 39 (℡971 367 965); both serve tasty seafood at reasonable prices. At the north end of the harbour, a sullen **bastion** is all that remains of the town's fortifications; from here c/Bellavista leads south back towards the main square – hang a left at either c/Sant Ignasi or c/Victori.

Buses from Maó stop on c/Gran, just steps away from the main square along c/Victori.

Fort Sant Felip and Sant Esteve

Beyond Es Castell, the main coastal road continues down towards the mouth of Port de Maó before veering right for Sant Lluís (see p.229). Keeping

A coastal walk from Maó to Punta Prima

16km; 100m ascent; 4–5hr

Starting in the centre of **Maó**, this long and varied walk winds around the south-eastern corner of the island, initially following the **Port de Maó**, then detouring inland before rejoining the coast to finish at the resort of **Punta Prima**, from where buses run (May–Oct) back to Maó. The coastal scenery is magnificent throughout, while the walk also gives a good impression of the successive layers of fortification that grew up to protect Maó's seaward approaches. The going is generally easy, except for one brief section of overgrown track, and is almost entirely flat – but be sure to check bus schedules back from Punta Prima before setting out.

Beginning in Maó's **Plaça Espanya**, descend Costa de Ses Voltes and turn right along the waterfront, walking around the headland and the narrow inlet of Cala Figuera to reach, after 1.5km, the **Hostal Rocamar** (currently closed). Just past here, before the road turns into a slipway and disappears under water, a flight of steps (arrowed up to "13D") ascends to the right. Climb these, go through the gap in the wall at the top and you'll find yourself in an area of overgrown scrub, divided into tiny fields by a lattice of stone walls. Follow the clifftop path, from where there are expansive views across the Port de Maó – of the Illa de Rei, and of the elegant pastel-painted Golden Farm mansion (see p.227) behind on the northern shore. Ahead in the distance, stacked up above the mouth of the seaway, are the sombre barracks of La Mola (see p.227).

Continue along the cliffs to reach the pink apartment building at the edge of the old garrison town of **Es Castell** (see p.223). Follow the road in front to a T-junction, head left for 50m, then right down c/San Cristòfol to reach Cala Corb. Cross the cala using the steps, carry on ahead to Es Castell's main square, Placa S'Esplanada, then continue straight on to rejoin the waterfront at **Cales Fonts**, with its string of restaurants. Head right here for 50m, then left onto c/Llevant (opposite the *Cafeteria Can Omi*) and follow this road for 200m, across a T-junction, to reach the top of **Cala Padera**. Continue to the *Sol Naciente* restaurant ahead, then turn left along the road behind it, passing a block of memorably kitsch pueblo-style development. After 50m, opposite a (nameless) *supermercat*, a narrow path heads off along the low clifftops, rounding a line of desirable holiday villas to reach open country.

Continue along, passing a walled enclosure marked "Propriedad de La Armada Español" and containing a Civil War bunker. The path zigzags through the scattered outer remains of the **Fort de Sant Felip**, Port de Maó's main defensive emplacement until Carlos III obligingly had it demolished, allowing the British to retake the island in 1798 without a single casualty. Carry on until you reach the barbed-wire fence of the Sant Felip military zone, still off limits, then follow the path round the fence and, straight, you'll come to a narrow country lane that leads past the turning to Sant Esteve (see below) and then reaches – after a further 300m – a dead end at the zona militar. This restricted military area sprawls over the inlet's final headland, where the Emperor Charles V built an imposing star-shaped fortress in the 1550s, naming it **Fort Sant Felip** after his son, later Philip II. Once Menorca's greatest stronghold, the fort was adapted by the British, who controlled the seaway from here. This irritated the Spanish so much that when Menorca was returned to them in 1782 they promptly destroyed the fort in a fit of pique – a rather misguided move, as it turned out, since the lack of defences allowed the British to recapture the island with the greatest of ease just a few years later. Today, nothing survives except the most fragmentary of ruins, though rumours persist of secret tunnels.

Doubling back from Fort Sant Felip, it's a short hop to **SANT ESTEVE**, an extraordinarily picturesque little village, whose old whitewashed houses are

when it runs out, bear right across a field past two huge cairns to reach the road leading to the fort entrance.

Turn right briefly, then go left down the road with the dead-end sign for 400m to reach a second dead-end sign, where a track heads off right – the solid-looking cobbles underfoot here are reputedly of Roman provenance, part of a road that once stretched back to Maó. Follow this track down to reach the sequestered inlet of **Sant Esteve** (see above), then rejoin the road and head round the cove, passing the subterranean entrance to **Fort Marlborough** (see p.226), built by the British to complement the firepower of Fort de Sant Felip.

When the road ends, head left (literally) through the bushes and scramble up to the top, then continue around the clifftop through further decaying military remains until you hit, more or less simultaneously, the high stone wall of the **Villa Eugenia** *finca* and the **Torre d'en Penyat** ("The Hanging Tower"). Built by the British in 1798 at the beginning of their third and final occupation of the island, the tower has acquired a lurid reputation as a place in which local miscreants were executed – you can go inside to enjoy the fine acoustics and a large collection of Balearic trash. Continue inland behind the tower, where the path swings left, following the walls of Villa Eugenia to reach an old mule trail between high stone walls. This is the **Camí de Cavalls**, once a major agricultural thoroughfare that extended around the entire coast of the island.

Turn left, following the *camí* for 1km, straight over the access road at the entrance to Villa Eugenia, after which the track has unfortunately become extremely over-grown. Push your way through the branches to reach the handsome farmstead of **Binissaida de Damunt**, where the path emerges on a track. Go right, past the farm entrance, then left onto a gravel road and right at the next junction at the Camí de Cavalls sign. Follow this track past the entrance to Son Vidal and onto a T-junction and the gate to **Rafalet Nou** farm. Go left, climbing over the gate (it's usually locked), heading past the farmhouse and straight on through another gate. Continue 150m to a fork, then go right 200m to a T-junction. Turn right again (the left turn has been walled off), following the path over a treacherous cattlegrid and past the drab outlying buildings of **S'Algar** until you reach a metalled road. Head straight across for 500m to reach a second road. Turn left, then right, following the signs down to tiny **Xuroy** beach, where there's a bar in summer.

Walk to the top of the beach, then go left through the gap in the wall and up around the clifftop, heading to the right of the large **Torre d'Alcaufar Vell**, constructed by the Spanish in 1787 and recently restored. The final 2km is along a restored stretch of the Camí de Cavalls, as it follows the magnificently unspoilt coast to **Punta Prima**.

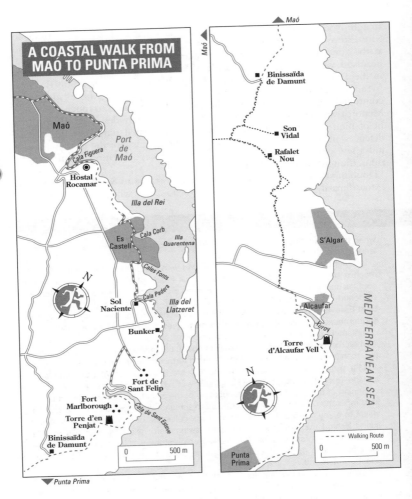

A COASTAL WALK FROM MAÓ TO PUNTA PRIMA

strung out along a slender cove with a turquoise sea lapping against crumbly dark cliffs. On the far side of the cove, near the end of the village, a tunnel burrows into the hillside to enter what was once **Fort Marlborough** (June–Sept Tues–Sat 10am–1pm & 5–8pm, Sun 10am–1pm; Oct–May Tues–Sun 10am–1pm; €3), an intricate, largely subterranean stronghold built to guard the southern approach to Fort Sant Felip by the British between 1710 and 1726. The fort, which was named after one of Britain's most talented generals, Sir John Churchill, the Duke of Marlborough, is a complicated affair, beginning with a long gallery dug into the soft rock with counter-galleries cut at right angles to detect enemy attempts to mine into the fortress. In addition, the main gallery encircles an interior moat – dry now, but once filled with water – and comes complete with gun slits that would have been used to fire on the moat from every angle. In turn, the moat encircles a small fortified hillock, the most protected part of the fortress and once the site of an artillery battery that had this stretch of the coast in its sights. Fort Marlborough was besieged twice – once by the French in 1756 and once by the Spanish in 1781; it was captured on both occasions, but only after a prolonged siege. One of the advantages of this type of fortress was that it could tie up a large enemy force for weeks and yet require a minuscule garrison – the British put just sixty men here. The self-guided tour round the fort takes about forty minutes.

Port de Maó's north shore

From the traffic island at the west end of Maó's harbour, a narrow byroad soon leaves the city behind, twisting up past the ugly, modern power station to thread over grassy hills with old stone walls and whitewashed farmhouses. After 2.5km, the road slips past the turning for Sa Mesquida (see p.228) to reach – after another 700m – **Golden Farm**, a fine old mansion in the British colonial style, perched on the hillside overlooking the Port de Maó. You can't go into the house and the only decent view is as you approach from La Mola (see below) to the east. From this direction, you can see the house's large portico, whose two arcaded galleries dominate the south (Maó) side of the house. The upper gallery – the balcony – is equipped with a delicate balustrade; above, classical deities decorate the tympanum, a trio of languorous figures in vaguely erotic poses. This mansion may have been **Admiral Nelson**'s headquarters, albeit briefly, during the island's third British occupation (1798–1802), and there's all sorts of folkloric tittle-tattle alluding to romantic trysts here between Nelson and his mistress, Emma Hamilton. In fact, Nelson was much too concerned with events in Naples, where the Hamiltons were ensconced and where he was involved in supporting the Neapolitan king, the Bourbon Ferdinand, against the incursions of the French. Indeed, Nelson did his best to avoid visiting Menorca at all – he only came here once or twice for a couple of days apiece – despite it being crucial for Britain's naval control of the Mediterranean. In July 1799, his superior, Lord Keith, mustered his fleet at Port de Maó to resist a possible French attack and ordered Nelson to join him. Nelson refused point blank, writing to the Admiralty "I am fully aware of the act I have committed, but, sensible of my loyal intentions, I am prepared for any fate which may await my disobedience." The Admiralty let it go – a good job considering Trafalgar was just round the corner – and Keith ranted and raved in vain.

East to La Mola

Further on from Golden Farm, the road skirts the well-heeled suburb of **Cala Llonga**, where modern villas tumble down the hillside to the water's edge, and offers fine but fleeting panoramas of the harbour and two of its small islands, **Illa del Rei** and **Illa Quarentena** (see p.218).

Beyond, the road weaves over a stretch of wind-raked heathland to reach its conclusion at the truncated causeway leading to the formidable fortress of **La Mola**, at the end of the promontory, some 6.5km from Maó. Work began on the fortress in the 1830s, its tiers of complementary bastions and gun emplacements designed to resist the most intensive of artillery bombardments. As an attempt to bolster Spain's military position in the Mediterranean, the stronghold failed to impress anyone – Spain's decline was too advanced for that – but it did provide work for hundreds of Menorcans at a time of high unemployment. Much less savoury is La Mola's connection with Franco, who used several of its barracks as a high-security political prison until 1968. The army is no longer in possession of the fortress and today you can walk across the causeway, past the battered old barrier, to explore the fort most days from May to

August, and on Sunday mornings (only) in winter. However, it's a forlorn spot, and with the army gone, no one is quite sure what should be done with it.

To the right of the road as it approaches the causeway is the **Illa del Llatzeret**, a former isolation hospital for infectious diseases (see p.218).

Es Murtar and Sa Mesquida

Returning from La Mola, take the signposted turning just to the west of Golden Farm north over the hills for 1.2km to reach the short side road to **ES MURTAR**, a tiny fishing village whose whitewashed houses are tucked in between the cliffs and a narrow, sandless cove. It's a pretty spot, though there's nothing specific to see or do.

Back on the road, a further 600m or so will take you to **SA MESQUIDA**, whose charming whitewashed houses flank a rough and rocky shoreline spiked by miniature pinnacles and bony islets, three of which guard the tiny harbour. Overlooking the scene is the prominent **Torre de Sa Mesquida** (no access), a watchtower of medieval provenance. The tower's battered stonework culminates in a machicolation (projecting parapet), from the apertures of which defenders could could dump boiling oil and water and whatever else came to hand on the heads of their attackers. There's nowhere to stay in Sa Mesquida, but there is a first-rate **restaurant**, *Cap Roig* (☎971 188 383), which offers tasty seafood and fine views out to sea from the cliffs at the start of the village.

The road pushes on through the village, swinging up and over the hills to reach, after 800m, the **beach**, a wide arc of pale-brown sand overlooked by bare hills. It's not an especially appetizing spot, but it is the nearest beach to Maó.

Southeast Menorca

Beyond Port de Maó, the **southeast corner** of Menorca, bounded by the road between Maó and Cala en Porter, consists of a low-lying limestone plateau fringed by a rocky shoreline with a string of craggy coves. In recent years this stretch of coast has been extensively developed, and today thousands of villas cover what was once empty scrubland. The result is not pretty and, although many prefer this low-rise architecture to the high-rise hotels of the 1960s, it's difficult to be enthusiastic, especially in **Cala en Porter**, the biggest and perhaps the ugliest *urbanització* of the lot. That said, the coast itself can be beautiful, and the resort of **Cala d'Alcaufar**, one of the earliest developments, fringes a particularly picturesque cove. Inland lies an agricultural landscape crisscrossed by country lanes and dotted with tiny villages, plus one town – mildly diverting **Sant Lluís**.

Most of the district is devoted to villa-style **accommodation** and package-tour operators rule the local roost, so there are only lean pickings for the independent traveller. That said, there's a reasonable chance of finding a room here and there amongst the southeast's scattering of hotels and *hostals*, with Cala d'Alcaufar being the best bet.

From May to October, getting around by **bus** is fairly straightforward. There are hourly services from Maó to Sant Lluís and Punta Prima, as well as regular services to Cala en Porter and Cala d'Alcaufar; in winter, there's a good bus service from Maó to Sant Lluís and Cala en Porter, but nothing at all to Punta Prima and Cala d'Alcaufar (see p.229 for full details). Bear in mind, however, that, with the exception of compact Cala d'Alcaufar, all of these resorts spread for miles, and if you've rented a villa you could be facing a very long, hot and confusing trek from the nearest bus stop. You might prefer to ring for a **taxi** from Maó's Radio Taxis on ☎971 367 111.

Sant Lluís

It's just 4km south of Maó along the main road to **SANT LLUÍS**, a trim, one-square, one-church town of brightly whitewashed terraced houses. As at Es Castell, the town's grid plan betrays its colonial origins. A French commander, the Duc de Richelieu, built Sant Lluís to house his Breton sailors in the 1750s, naming the new settlement after the thirteenth-century King Louis IX, who was beatified for his part in the Crusades. The French connection is further recalled by the trio of coats of arms carved on the west front of the **church** – those of the royal household and two French governors.

Buses from Maó stop at the north end of town beside Plaça Nova. There are no *hostals* here, but the *Biniarroca Hotel Rural* (☎971 150 059, ⓦwww.biniarroca.com; ❼; closed Nov–Easter), occupying a lavishly renovated *finca* just east of town on the road to Es Castell at Camí Biniarroca 57, is one of the island's most luxurious hotels, with plush rooms, a swimming pool and a first-rate **restaurant** (reservations required), serving from an international menu. Two other good places **to eat** hereabouts are *La Venta* (☎971 150 995), beside the traffic island at the south end of town, where the speciality is suckling pig, and the *Sa Pedrera* (☎971 150 717), a smart restaurant with a wide-ranging international menu, including Chinese dishes, and an outside terrace located in the nearby hamlet of **Torret**. Torret is just south of Sant Lluís along the main road – but be sure to ring for reservations and directions.

South to Punta Prima

At the south end of Sant Lluís, keep on the main road (the PM702) and you'll soon reach the turning for Punta Prima (see below) and then the fork that leads to either **S'ALGAR**, where rank upon rank of suburban-looking villas sprawl along the coast, or – a far better option – the pretty little resort of **CALA D'ALCAUFAR**. The development here is restrained, with just a smattering of holiday homes and old fishermen's cottages set beside a handsome inlet of flat-topped limestone cliffs and a turquoise sea. You can stroll out across the surrounding headlands, one of which has a Martello tower, or just enjoy the sandy beach. The main footpath down to the beach runs through the *Hostal Xuroy* (☎ & ☎971 151 820; ❺; closed Nov–April), a pleasant two-star establishment with 46 modern rooms – though most of them are booked up months in advance by package-tour companies.

Doubling back from S'Algar, it's only a few kilometres to **PUNTA PRIMA**, a sprawling, standard-issue resort whose villas and supermarkets back onto a wide and windy beach at the island's southeastern tip. Frankly, the place doesn't have much going for it, though at least the view from the beach does'nt take in the offshore **Illa de l'Aire**, an inaccessible and uninhabited chunk of rock equipped with an automatic lighthouse. Unfortunately, swimming in the choppy channel between the island and the shore can be dangerous – watch for the green or red flags. The wind, however, attracts windsurfers, and wind-surfing equipment is available for rent, as are pedalos and sunbeds.

West from Punta Prima to Sant Climent

Travelling Menorca's south coast from Punta Prima to Binidalí, a distance of around 10km, is a depressing experience: poorly signposted roads meander across the coastal scrubland traversing patches of undistinguished tourist development. On the map, it looks as if there are about half a dozen resorts, but on the ground it's impossible to determine where one settlement ends and another begins. The only vague light in the architectural gloom is a purpose-built settlement of second homes at **BINIBECA**, specifically **Binibeca Vell**, where the narrow, whitewashed alleyways, wooden balconies and twisting flights of steps are designed to resemble an old Mediterranean fishing village. At the end of the coastal road is scrawny Binidalí, from where (with relief) you can head inland to **SANT CLIMENT**, a tiny village with a minuscule main square and a dinky little church. The village is also home to the *Restaurant-bar Casino* (T971 153 418), where there's live jazz Tuesday evening, of variable styles and quality. Unfortunately for the inhabitants, the village is also within earshot of the airport and is bisected by the busy Maó–Cala en Porter road.

Cala en Porter

Back on the main road, it's a short haul west to **CALA EN PORTER**, one of the first *calas* (cove beaches) to be developed, and now a sprawling *urbanització* which has engulfed a bumpy plateau with hundreds of villas of such similar appearance and proportions that it soon becomes disorienting. Nor is there any focus to the development, which is limited to the south by plunging seacliffs and in the west by a steep bluff that flanks a deep ravine with marshes at the back and a wide sandy beach at the front. Access to the beach is either by road down into the ravine or by flights of steps running down the bluff.

One redeeming feature – and one of the island's most popular attractions – is the **Cova d'en Xoroi** (June–Sept daily 10am–9pm; €4.90, including snacks and a drink), a large cave stuck spectacularly high in the cliff-face above the ocean. A stairway from the entrance on the clifftop winds down to the cave, offering stirring views along the coast. From June to September, the cave turns into a bar and disco from 11pm nightly until around dawn; entry costs a pricey €20 or so, depending on the night; it's also open during the rest of the year, though opening hours are more restricted.

Fornells and the north coast

Menorca's **north coast** holds some of the island's prettiest scenery, and its craggy coves, islets and headlands have only rarely been rattled by the developers, since the harsh prevailing wind – the Tramuntana – makes life a tad too blustery for sun-seeking packagers. There are developed coves for sure – and four of them contain substantial villa resorts of little immediate appeal – but

---

The one-eared Moor

The Cova d'en Xoroi is the subject of one of the island's best-known folk tales. Legend has it that a shipwrecked Moor named **Xoroi** (literally, "One Ear") hid out here, raiding local farms for food. Bored and lonely, he then kidnapped a local virgin – the so-called "Flower of Alaior" – and imprisoned her in his cave. Eventually, Xoroi's refuge was discovered when locals picked up his tracks back to the cave after a freak snowstorm. Cornered, Xoroi committed suicide by throwing himself into the ocean, while the girl (and her children) were taken back to Alaior, where they lived happily ever after.

these are the exception rather than the rule, and for the most part this stretch of coast remains delightfully unspoilt.

Apart from the good-looking village of **Sa Mesquida**, reached from Port de Mao's northern shore (see p.228), most of the northeast coast is approached via the enjoyable, 25km-long minor road linking Maó and Fornells. This runs alongside cultivated fields protected by great stands of trees, with the low hills that form the backbone of the interior bumping away into the distance. At regular intervals you can turn off towards the seashore. The first turning takes you to **Es Grau**, the starting point for a delightful two- to three-hour hike along the coast or a shorter stroll along the marshy shores of **S'Albufera**, a freshwater lake noted for its birdlife. The next turning lead north to the windy bleakness of the **Cap de Favàritx**, and the two turnings after that head north again for the four big resorts hereabouts – **Port d'Addaia**, **Na Macaret**, **Arenal d'en Castell** and **Son Parc**. Much more rewarding than this quartet, however, is **Fornells**, whose delightful bayside location and measured development makes it one of the most appealing resorts on the island. Fornells is also renowned for its excellent restaurants, and none of its three *hostals* is block-booked by package-tour operators, so you've a reasonable chance of a room even in the height of the season. There's no **beach** at Fornells itself, apart from a pocket-sized blot of sand, but it makes a good base for visiting some of the more remote cove beaches nearby, such as **Cala Pregonda** and **Platja de Binimel-Là**, to name but two.

There's a real shortage of non-package **accommodation** on the north coast – only Fornells is likely to have anything, though of course Maó is within easy striking distance too. Public transport is fairly good: **buses** run from Maó to Fornells five times daily except on Sunday from May to October, and once daily on four days a week from November to April.

Es Grau and the Illa d'en Colom

The first right turn off the Maó–Fornells road threads its way up through wooded hills and clips past pastureland to **ES GRAU**, a neat and trim little village overlooking a horseshoe-shaped bay, where pine trees and sand dunes fringe an unenticing arc of greyish sand. The shallow waters here are, however, ideal for children, and on weekends the handful of **bars** and **restaurants** that dot the main street are crowded with holidaying Mahonese. The most popular place is the *Bar Es Grau*, with a charming shaded terrace, located on the water's edge at the start of the village. Alternatively, you could head a few metres beyond to the *Tamarindos* (☎971 359 420), a café-restaurant noted for its inexpensive seafood.

Easily reached from Es Grau by boat is the **Illa d'en Colom** (Pigeon Island), a rocky, one-kilometre-square islet lying just offshore. It's now uninhabited, but in the eighteenth century, the British quarantined sick sailors here, and the Spanish followed suit until they built the hospital on the Illa del Llatzeret in Maó harbour (see p.218). The exposed east side of the Illa d'en Colom is bleak and bare, its vegetation stunted by the prevailing winds, but the sheltered west side is a bit more luxuriant and has a couple of **beaches**, the most scenic of which is **S'Arenal d'en Moro**. **Boats** to the island leave from the tiny jetty at the far end of Es Grau's main street. There's no sailing schedule as such, but boats leave every half-hour or so daily throughout the summer from 10am – just wait around at the jetty or ask at the *Ca'n Bernat* bar. You can get off the boat at either beach and the return fare will set you back about €5.

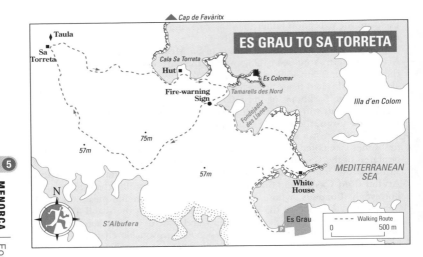

A coastal walk from Es Grau to Sa Torreta

9km; 100m ascent; 2hr–2hr 30min

This **coastal walk** leads from Es Grau along one of the wilder sections of the Menorcan seaboard, before detouring inland around the S'Albufera lagoon to visit the remote Talayotic site of Sa Torreta. The going is easy throughout, along well-marked tracks, with only one modest ascent towards the highest point of the walk at Sa Torreta farm. There's also a small section of backtracking at the end of the walk, though this is no hardship given the splendour of the coastal scenery hereabouts.

Starting at the car park at the entrance to **Es Grau**, walk round the long sandy beach and follow the path on the far side as it climbs up onto the low cliffs. At the top, ignore the well-defined track that heads off left and continue straight on, descending sharply, then follow the path as it bears right until you see a solitary white house ahead.

About 50m before you reach the house, a path branches off up to the left. Follow this to the top of the hill, where you'll see the craggy Illa d'en Colom off the coast directly ahead. The path goes straight on, then swings left, giving increasingly expansive views of the rugged coast to either side, without any sign of human habitation until the **lighthouse** on Cap de Favàritx hoves into view way ahead.

As soon as you see the lighthouse, look for the path that descends to your right. Go down this path, past a curious abandoned rock-dwelling built into the cliffside, then continue left along the coast, following any of the various paths which cross the scrub. The walk here takes you between low, convoluted clumps of mastic and wild olive dotted with spiky pin-cushions of Launaea cervicornis (try not to sit on them). Aim for the **Martello tower** at the tip of the headland of Es Colomar ahead, passing the trash-covered inlet of Fondejador des Llanes to reach the small sandy beach of **Tamarells des Nord**.

Cross the beach to the **fire-warning sign** on the far side (remember this point for later on), then go through the gap in the wall and head left to reach, after 25m, a major track. Turn left and follow this track inland as it climbs into a beautifully

S'Albufera Parc Natural

The scrub-covered dunes behind Es Grau's beach form the northeastern periphery of an expanse of dunes encircling the freshwater lagoon of **S'Albufera**. Only 2km from east to west and a couple of hundred metres wide, the lagoon has just one outlet, the faint stream – La Gola – that trickles out into the bay beside Es Grau. The lake was once fished for bass, grey mullet and eels – a real island delicacy – but fishing and hunting have been banned since the creation of the **Parc Natural S'Albufera d'es Grau** in the 1990s. The park boasts a varied terrain, including dunes (which are glued together by a combination of Aleppo pine, marram grass and beach thistle), and wetland, concentrated at the west end of the lake and containing patches of saltworts and rushes. The lagoon and its surroundings are rich in birdlife, attracting thousands of migrant birds in spring and autumn; for more on Menorca's birds, see pp.291–292.

The access road into the park begins 2km back from Es Grau on the road to Maó. Just 1.5km long, it skims past the plush villas of the Shangril-Là development before terminating at a car park, from where clearly marked paths run (in either direction) along the lake's southern shore. It's easy walking and the scenery is gentle on the eye, with the blue of the lake set against

enclosed and secluded valley. After 750m, the track swings right and you have your first proper view of the **S'Albufera** lagoon ahead, one of Menorca's richest ornithological sites, although you're just too far away from the lake here to see much of its birdlife. (For more on the lagoon, see above.) The path gradually ascends through cow pasture before splitting into three. Take the middle track and climb to another fork at the top, then go right, up along a beautiful stonewalled lane, through a gate and across a field, making for the farmhouse of **Sa Torreta** ahead. Monte Toro (see p.243) begins to fill the view in the distance as you ascend, while to your left there's an overgrown and impassable walled track, typical of many of the island's abandoned mule trails.

You'll soon arrive at a T-junction. Turn left to reach the farm and, at the first farm building, continue straight ahead over the gate, cross the yard, then immediately go right to reach an old circular threshing floor after 25m. Stop here and look behind you to spot Sa Torreta **taula and talayot**. Now you can see it, turn round, retrace your steps for 10m and cross the fields through the gap in the wall on your right to reach the walled enclosure, one of the least-visited prehistoric sites on Menorca, and one of the few on the northern side of the island. The fine four-metre taula and partly collapsed talayot here are proof of the longevity of Menorca's megalithic culture, post-dating the earlier and more famous examples at Trepucó (see p.221) by as much as a thousand years.

You're now at the highest point of the walk, with grand views to the coast below and Illa d'en Colom in the distance. Rejoin the path by the threshing floor and follow it for 1.2km down to the sea at **Cala Sa Torreta**, a remote, sandy beach covered in dried seaweed and seaborne rubbish – not much good for swimming, though the clump of Aleppo pines behind the beach is a good spot for a picnic and some birdwatching. From the beach, take the wide track that climbs up to your right, past a small hut, and continue across the headland back towards Tamarells des Nord. As you rejoin the seafront the path swings right. Walk inland for 100m to a fork, then go left another 100m and you should see the fire-warning sign you passed earlier. Head for this, and then retrace your steps back to Es Grau.

the rolling greens and yellows of the dunes. Birders – both casual and enthusiasts – should aim for **Es Prat**, the large patch of wetland at the west end of the lake, and be sure to pack your binoculars. Nature walks open to interested visitors are organized by park naturalists – ring ☎971 352 502 for details.

Cap de Favàritx

Back on the Maó–Fornells road and heading northwest from the Es Grau turning, it's just over 5.5km to the right turn that weaves its way north to **Cap de Favàritx**. This side road cuts along a slender valley and slips through dumpy little hills to reach, after 6km, an unsigned fork where you veer right for the final leg of the journey. The further you go, the barer the landscape becomes – grass gives way to succulents, but even they can't survive on the wind-stripped headland where the solitary **lighthouse** shines out over a bare lunar-like landscape of tightly layered, crumbly slate. The lighthouse is closed to the public, but the views out over the coast are dramatic and you can pick your way along the sharp adjacent rocks, though if the wind is up this isn't much fun.

In 1756, Cap de Favàritx witnessed one of the British Navy's more embarrassing moments when admiral **John Byng** (1704–57) anchored his fleet off here for no particular reason. The French had besieged the British garrison at Fort San Felipe (see p.224) at the start of the Seven Years' War and Byng had been dispatched to Menorca to relieve them. Instead, he dillied and he dallied, allegedly reading and re-reading the Admiralty's instruction book, and managed to get caught with his nautical trousers down when the French fleet turned up off Cap de Favàritx, too. The resulting battle was an inconclusive affair, but Byng faint-heartedly withdrew to Gibraltar, abandoning the British garrison to its fate. Back in London, the Prime Minister, the Duke of Newcastle, fumed: "He shall be tried immediately; he shall be hanged directly" – and proceeded to carry out his threat. On his return, Byng was court-martialled and shot by firing squad on his own flagship in Portsmouth harbour, an event which famously prompted **Voltaire** to remark in *Candide* that the British needed to shoot an admiral now and again "pour encourager les autres".

Port d'Addaia and Son Parc

"I shall ever think of Adaia, and of the company I enjoyed at that charming little Retirement, with the utmost Complacency and Satisfaction," wrote John Armstrong, an engineer in the British army, in the 1740s. If he could only see it now. The old **PORT D'ADDAIA**, at the mouth of a long, wooded inlet, has mushroomed dreary holiday homes, supermarkets and a marina, and as if that weren't bad enough, the neighbouring headlands now heave with the villas and apartment buildings of two oversized resorts: low-key **NA MACARET** and the more boisterous **ARENAL D'EN CASTELL**, which at least boasts a wide and sandy beach set within a circular, cliff-edged cove.

The next turning along the Maó–Fornells road leads to **SON PARC**, a workaday grid of holiday homes and apartment blocks flanking a golf course and overlooking the water. One of the more upmarket resorts, Son Parc is fringed by thick pine woods and has a wide, pink-tinged sandy beach, backed by nice dunes and equipped with a seasonal restaurant and beach bar. For a tad more isolation, walk the 1km north to **Cala Pudent**, a peaceful sandy strip set beside a narrow inlet. A stony track connecting the two beaches runs just behind the seashore.

Fornells

FORNELLS, a low-rise, classically pretty fishing village at the mouth of a long and chubby bay, has been popular with tourists for years, above all for its **seafood restaurants**, whose speciality, *caldereta de llagosta* (*langosta* in Castilian), is a fabulously tasty – and often wincingly expensive – lobster stew. Nevertheless, there's been comparatively little development, just a slim trail of holiday homes extending north from the old village in a suitably unobtrusive style. Behind the village and across the bay lie rockily austere headlands where winter storms and ocean spray keep vegetation to a minimum. This bleak terrain envelops various ruined **fortifications** – evidence of the harbour's past importance – of which two are easy to reach: an old **watchtower** (Tues–Sat 11am–2pm & 5–8pm, Sun 11am–2pm; €2.40, free on Sun), peering out over the coast on the headland beyond Fornells, and the shattered **Castell de Sant Antoni**, in the village itself. Built to protect the inlet from Arab and Turkish corsairs in the late seventeenth century, these fortifications were refurbished by the British, who constructed another on an island in the middle of the bay and posted a garrison. In a controversial piece of early tourist development, one of the British commanders also exceeded his military brief, turning a local chapel into a tavern and thereby incurring the disapproval of fellow officer John Armstrong: "In the Temple of Bacchus, no bounds are set to their [the soldiers'] Debauches and such a quantity of Wine is daily swallowed down, as would stagger Credulity itself." Quite – but there again, there wasn't much else for the squaddies to do.

Fornells has no **beach** to speak of apart from a tiny patch of sand in front of *Sa Nansa* restaurant, round the corner from the main square. There is, however, a long strip of sand 1.5km back down the access road beside the Ses Salines apartment complex, and other, even more attractive beaches in the area, such as Platja de Binimel·Là and Cala Pregonda (see p.238). The village's sweeping inlet also provides ideal conditions for **scuba diving** and **windsurfing** – you'll see flocks of windsurfers scooting across the calm waters at the southern end of the bay as you approach the town. The Menorca Diving Club (☎971 376 412), on the seafront at the south end of the village, rents out equipment and organizes diving courses, as does Diving Center Fornells (☎971 376 431), just across the street. Advance reservations for courses and equipment are strongly advised. As for windsurfing, Windsurf Fornells (☎971 188 150), situated beside the main access road on the southern edge of the village, offers tuition to both novices and more experienced hands, and teaches **sailing** skills too. Lessons include the use of their wetsuits, boards or boats. General information about all sorts of water-related activities is also available at the Club Náutico de Fornells, in the Ses Salines complex 1.5km south of town (☎971 376 358).

Practicalities

Buses from Maó and Es Mercadal pull in beside the minuscule main square, Plaça S'Algaret (see p.263 for more details). There's no tourist office, but this is hardly a hindrance as almost all of the amenities are within a few metres of the square, beginning with the village's three reasonably priced and comfortable **hostals**. Perhaps surprisingly, there's a fair chance of a vacancy in one or other of them even in the high season – but it's best to book ahead just in case.

Hostal Fornells c/Major 17 ☎971 376 676, ⓔfornells@chi.es. Fornells' smartest *hostal*, this pleasant three-story establishment occupies a well-kept two-storey building half a block up the main pedestrian-only street from the village's central square, Plaça S'Algaret. It has a good swimming pool and attractive gardens, and bills itself as a "health eco-resort", with natural herbal treatments and massage available. **⑤**

Hostal-residencia La Palma Plaça S'Algaret 3 ☎

& ⓕ971 376 634. Bang in the centre of Fornells on the main square, this two-star hostal is a neat little place, with quaintly authentic local decor and simple but cheerfully bright and colourful rooms. There's also a small swimming pool. Closed Nov–April. **④**

S'Algaret Plaça S'Algaret 7 ☎971 376 674, ⓕ971 376 666. Straightforward two-star establishment with some thirty guest rooms, all en suite and decorated in brisk modern style, plus a small swimming pool. April–Oct. **④**

Eating

With the British garrison long gone, nightlife in Fornells is confined to the expensive **restaurants** that edge the waterfront on either side of the main square. Such is their reputation that King Juan Carlos has been known to drop by on his yacht, and many people phone up days in advance with their orders.

Es Cranc c/Escoles 31 ☎971 376 442. A couple of minutes' walk north of Plaça S'Algaret in the heart of the old village, this smooth and polished restaurant offers a wide variety of fish dishes. The signature *caldereta de llagosta* goes for €60, although the mouth-watering fish soup is a mere €5.75. Closed Wed.

Es Pla Passeig Es Pla s/n ☎971 376 655. The royal favourite, this harbourside restaurant, metres from Plaça S'Algaret, with its sedately bourgeois dining room, offers a superb paella (minimum two people) for around €45.70 per head, as well as the traditional lobster stew, weighing in at €59 – that's per person, as well.

Es Port c/Riera 5 ☎971 376 403. On the waterfront, just off Plaça S'Algaret, this relaxed and easygoing restaurant concentrates on a magnificent *caldereta de llagosta* (€54).

Sibaris Plaça S'Algaret 1 ☎971 376 619. Hard-to-beat seafood with a superb, and relatively cheap, *caldereta de llagosta* (€42) and lobster paella (minimum two people; €45 per head).

Sa Nansa c/Viveros s/n ☎971 376 453. Relatively sensible prices, for once, and meals are served on a small terrace facing a tiny beach round the corner from the main square – try the black paella with squid ink (minimum two people; €13.90 per head) or the grilled monkfish (€11.50).

Beyond Fornells

The wild and rocky coastline west of Fornells boasts several cove beaches of outstanding beauty, including **Cala Pregonda** and **Platja de Binimel-Là**. Getting to them, however, can be a problem: the developers have barely touched this portion of the island, so the remoter spots are sometimes poorly signposted and the access roads are of very variable quality. Some are gravel or dirt tracks, particularly slippery after rain; others are asphalted but extremely narrow, and others are a mixture of all three. These byroads branch off from the narrow but metalled country lane which crosses the lovely pastoral hinterland between Fornells and Castell de Santa Àgueda. There's also dramatic coastal scenery at **Cap de Cavalleria**, whose louring seacliffs rise precipitously from the ocean.

Public transport around here is, as you might expect, non-existent and there's nowhere to stay.

Cala Tirant to Cap de Cavalleria

About 3km south of Fornells, the roads from Maó and Es Mercadal meet at a staggered crossroads. From here, a signposted turning leads west down a country lane to pass, after 2km, the clearly marked turning to **Cala Tirant**. This unmade side road offers a rough and dusty two-kilometre drive down to the cove, where a thick arc of ochre-coloured sand lies trapped between bumpy headlands, with grassy dunes and marshland to the rear. It's an attractive spot, but not perfect – there are villa developments on both sides of the cove and the beach is exposed to the Tramuntana wind. There's a beach bar, loungers, pedalos and windsurfing equipment for hire.

West of the Cala Tirant turn-off, the country lane continues through a charming landscape of old stone walls and scattered farmsteads. After about 1km, keep straight on at the intersection and proceed for another 1km or so to the signposted right turning that leads north (along an asphalted byroad) towards Cap de Cavalleria. This is easy driving, and 4km later, halfway to the cape, you stumble across the **Ecomuseu Cap de Cavalleria** (daily: April, May, June & Oct 10am–7pm; July, Aug & Sept 10am–8pm; €7), an odd little museum occupying an old farmstead perched on a hillock with wide views of the cape. The Romans settled on the sheltered side of this headland in 123 AD, and it was here they built the town and port of **Sanisera** on the ruins of an earlier Phoenician settlement, though almost nothing survives from either period. This ancient history convinced the European Union to fund the Ecomuseu, though it's hard not to think it was more of a job-creation scheme – an impression the museum's paltry if gallant collection of Roman and Talayotic bits and pieces does little to dispel. The long cove which the Romans colonized – the **Port de Sanitja** – lies some 700m north of the museum, just west of the road to the cape. Archeologists have explored the site, but the main historical artefact is the Martello Tower – the **Torre de Sanitja** – built at the mouth of the inlet by the British at the end of the eighteenth century.

North of the museum, the road becomes bumpy and narrow as it slices across a sparse plateau that rises abruptly as it reaches the **Cap de Cavalleria**, named after the *cavalleries* – baronial estates – into which Menorca was divided after the Reconquista. This is Menorca's northernmost point, a bleak and wind-buffeted hunk of rock with mighty seacliffs, 90m high, and a lonely lighthouse (no access).

Platja de Binimel-Là and Cala Pregonda

Back on the country lane, it's a further 1.6km west to the signposted turning for **Platja de Binimel-Là**. At first, the dirt access road is wide and fairly easy to negotiate, but, after 1.5km you take a left and the last bit of road deteriorates – 500m of bone-jangling motoring, so most people park short of the beach. It's a rocky beach, but the waters are clear and good for swimming and snorkelling. This is a fairly popular spot, though there are several more secluded and much smaller beaches on the east side of the cove, reached by clambering along the seashore. In the summer, there's sometimes an ad-hoc beach bar, but there are no other facilities.

One significant problem at Binimel-Là is the seaweed and detritus that sometimes get driven onto the beach by a northerly wind. If this has happened and

The Martello Tower

Popular with the British military in the late eighteenth and early nineteenth centuries, the design of the **Martello Tower**, a combined barracks, gun battery and storehouse, was copied from a Corsican tower (at Martello Point) that had proved particularly troublesome to the Royal Navy when they had tried to capture it. These self-contained, semi-self-sufficient defensive fortifications, equipped with thick walls and a protected entrance, proved so successful and easy to build that they were erected in every corner of the empire, only becoming obsolete in the 1870s with advances in artillery technology.

if you've come equipped with reasonably stout shoes and a hiking map, move on to **Cala Pregonda**, a splendid, seastack-studded bay with a wide sandy beach, thirty minutes' walk away to the west. There's no clear path except at the start, but the terrain isn't difficult: climb the whitewashed steps over the wall at the west end of Binimel-Là beach and follow the wide track beyond across the salt flats and round a pebble-strewn cove; then keep straight to clamber over a small headland and you'll see the beach below.

Central Menorca

Central Menorca is the agricultural heart of the island, its rippling hills and rolling plains dotted with scores of whitewashed farmsteads, and although the tourist boom has knocked some of the stuffing out of the island's agriculture – witness the many unkempt fields – it's still surprising, considering Menorca's package popularity, just how traditional things are here. The land still carries the myriad marks of past agrarian endeavours in its dry-stone walls, stone ziggurats (called *barraques*), which were built to shelter cattle from wind and sun, and old twisted gates made from olive branches. In addition, the land is dotted with scores of prehistoric stone memorials – primarily *navetas*, *taulas* and *talayots* – left by its earliest inhabitants, and representing the island's most distinctive historical sights. None of the four little towns of the interior – Alaior, Es Mercadal, Ferreries and Es Migjorn Gran – has been much modernized, and each contains a comely ensemble of old houses dating back to the eighteenth century, sometimes further. All four towns are either on or easily reached from the 45km-long C721 Maó–Ciutadella road which bisects the island.

West from Maó, the **C721** begins by traversing a flattish agricultural district on its way to the hilltop town of **Alaior**, which boasts a pretty little centre of mazy cobbled streets. Alaior also hosts a couple of cheese-making factories where you can sample local brands, and is just 3km from one of the island's most extensive prehistoric sites, **Torralba d'en Salord**. Further west, the C721 slides into the antique village of **Es Mercadal**, overlooked by **Monte Toro**, the island's highest peak, its summit occupied by both a military lookout point and a convent. The road to the mountaintop is excellent and the views superb, revealing the geological make-up of the island: to the north, reddish sandstone hills bump down to a fretted coastline, while to the south the limestone plain is gashed by wooded gorges (*barrancs*). This is an essential detour – unlike the excursion south to the seaside resort of **Son Bou**, a grimly modern affair redeemed only by its long sandy beach.

From Es Mercadal, it's a short journey southwest to **Es Migjorn Gran**, a pleasant if unremarkable little town that's the starting point for an excellent two- to three-hour hike down the **Barranc de Binigaus** (see box on p.244) and is also situated close to another sprawling resort, **Sant Tomàs**. Back on the C721, you'll soon reach **Ferreries**, the fourth of the towns of the interior and the starting point for another recommended hike (see box on p.248). Ferreries is also near to the **Binisues** manor house and the shattered ruins of the hilltop **Castell de Santa Àgueda**, once an important Moorish stronghold. A short excursion south from Ferreries leads to **Cala Santa Galdana**, an attractive resort of manageable proportions that's within easy hiking distance of several superb and isolated cove beaches.

For part of the way at least, there is an alternative to the C721 – the **Camí d'en Kane**, named after Richard Kane, Menorca's first British governor (see box below), who devoted much time and energy to improving the island's communications. His principal achievement was the construction of a highway between Maó and Ciutadella – funded by a tax on alcohol – and although much of Kane's original road has disappeared beneath the C721, a healthy portion has survived, running north of the C721 between Maó and Es Mercadal. A lovely route, this old road follows the agricultural contours of the island, passing ancient *haciendas*, olive groves, pasture and mile after mile of dry-stone wall. To reach it, take the Fornells road out of Maó and, 1.2km after the Es Grau turning, watch for the Camí d'en Kane sign on the left.

There's no public transport along the Camí d'en Kane, but fast and frequent **buses** ply the C721, with supplementary summertime services running from Maó to Sant Tomàs and Son Bou, and from Ferreries to Cala Santa Galdana. Es Migjorn Gran is reachable by bus from both Maó and Ciutadella. **Accommodation**, on the other hand, is difficult to come by for independent travellers. The resorts are dominated by the package-tourist industry, though you can, of course, try pot luck. Of the four inland towns, only Es Mercadal and Es Migjorn Gran have recommendable accommodation options – and even these muster just three places in total.

Alaior and around

Cheese is as good a reason as any to stop at **ALAIOR**, an old market town 12km from Maó, which has long been the nucleus of the island's dairy industry. There are two major companies, La Payesa and COINGA, both of which have factory shops near to – and signposted from – the old main road as it cuts through the southern periphery of town. From the new bypass, which swings round the town to the south, the easiest option is to come off at the eastern-

Richard Kane

Born in Ulster in 1666, **Richard Kane** was the quintessential military man. His long career in the British army included service in Canada and campaigns with the Duke of Marlborough. In 1713, following the Treaty of Utrecht, Kane was appointed Lieutenant-Governor of Menorca. He was transferred in 1720 but returned a decade later for a second stint, staying until 1736, the year of his death.

When Kane arrived in Menorca, he found a dispirited and impoverished population, governed from Ciutadella by a reactionary oligarchy. Kane's initial preoccupation was with the island's **food supply**, which was woefully inadequate. He promptly set about draining swampland near Maó and introduced new and improved strains of seed corn. The governor also had livestock imported from England – hence the Friesian cattle that remain the mainstay of the island's cheese-making industry. Meanwhile, a tax on alcohol provided the cash to develop Menorca's infrastructure, resulting in improved port facilities at Maó and the construction of the first **road** right across the island.

These innovations were not at all to the taste of the Menorcan aristocracy, who, holed up in Ciutadella, were further offended when Kane arranged for the capital to be moved to Maó. They bombarded London with complaints, eventually inducing a formal governmental response in an open letter to the islanders entitled A Vindication of Colonel Kane. Most Menorcans, however, seem to have welcomed Kane's benevolent administration, except in religious matters, where the governor caused offence by holding Protestant services for his troops in Catholic churches. That apart, there's little doubt that, by the time of his death, Kane was a widely respected figure, whose endeavours were ill served by the colonial indifference of some of his successors.

5

MENORCA | Central Menorca

239

△ Christ statue, Monte Toro

most of the three Alaior exits. From this direction, the first – and rather more folksy – shop you reach is owned by **La Payesa**, at c/d'Es Banyer 64 (Mon–Fri 9am–1pm & 4–7pm), while the second is the larger outlet of **COINGA**, c/Es Mercadal 8 (Mon–Fri 9am–1pm & 5–8pm). Both companies sell a similar product, known generically as Queso Mahon, after the port, Maó, from which it was traditionally exported. It's a richly textured, white, semi-fat cheese made from pasteurized cow's milk with a touch of ewe's milk added for extra flavour. The cheese is sold at four different stages of maturity, either *tierno* (young), *semi-curado* (semi-mature), *curado* (mature) or *añejo* (very mature). Both shops have the full range and, although quite expensive, their prices are the most competitive you'll see.

Both cheese shops are in the lower part of Alaior; the medieval centre, a tangle of narrow streets and bright white houses, climbs the steep hillside above. It's a quick two-minute drive or a strenuous one-kilometre walk up c/Bassa Roja to the top, where the imposing parish church of **Santa Eulàlia**, a magnificent edifice of fortress-like proportions built between 1674 and 1690, has recently been restored. The main doorway is a Baroque extravagance, its exuberant scrollwork dripping with fruits and fronds, while the facade above accommodates a rose window and a pair of balustrades. Beyond the church – just up the hill to the northwest along the L-shaped c/Moli de l'Angel – a mini-watchtower is plonked on top of the **Munt de l'Angel**, a hill from where you can look out over the countryside. From the end of c/Moli de l'Angel, it's a few metres north to the old town's main square, **Plaça Nova**, an attractive piazza flanked by pastel-painted civic buildings of considerable age.

Practicalities

Buses to Alaior pull in beside the school to the east of – and about ten minutes' walk from – the old town. There's nowhere to stay. For **food**, the outstanding *Cobblers Restaurant*, set in a beautiful old mansion at c/Sant Macari 6 (☎971 371 400; open for dinner only; closed Dec to mid-March), does excellent meat dishes – try the lamb – served in charming surroundings, either inside under the beamed ceiling or outside in the flower-filled courtyard. The restaurant is just to the east of Santa Eulàlia: take c/Pare Diego Saura, turn right onto c/Verge Sa Muntanyeta and it's straight ahead.

Apart from a bite to eat and a quick gambol round the town, there's not much reason to hang around – unless, that is, you happen to be here in the second weekend of August, when Alaior lets loose for the **Festa de Sant Llorenç**, a drunken celebration and display of horsemanship. As its climax, a procession of horses tears through the packed town square, bucking and rearing, with their riders clinging on for dear life. Although no one seems to get hurt, you might prefer to enjoy the spectacle from the safety of a balcony.

Around Alaior: the Torralba d'en Salord

One of the island's more extensive Talayotic settlements, **Torralba d'en Salord** (Mon–Sat 10am–8pm; €2.40) lies about 3km southeast of Alaior beside the road to Cala en Porter. The site is muddled by the old (and disused) Cala En Porter road, which slices right through the site, and by the modern stone walls built alongside both the old and new roads. Nevertheless, it doesn't take too long to figure things out. From the car park, signs direct you round the Talayotic remains, beginning with the *taula*, one of the best preserved on the island. The rectangular enclosure surrounding it is also in good condition, and has been the subject of much conjecture by archeologists, who discovered that several of the recesses contained large fire pits, which may well have been used for the ritual slaughter of animals. It was, however, the unearthing of a tiny bronze bull (now in the Museu de Menorca in Maó) that really got the experts going. The theory was that the Menorcans (in common with several other prehistoric Mediterranean peoples) venerated the bull, with the *taula* being a stylized representation of a bull's head. The argument continues to this day. Beyond the *taula*, the signed trail circumnavigates the remainder of the site, which contains a confusion of stone remains, none of them especially revealing. The most noteworthy are the battered remains of a *talayot* just across from the *taula* and, about 30m further to the north, an underground chamber roofed with stone slabs.

From Torralba d'en Salord, it's just 3km to the south coast resort of Cala en Porter (see p.230).

Torre d'en Gaumés, Son Bou and Sant Jaume Mediterrani

West of Alaior on the C721, the Son Bou turning leads to the beaches of the south coast and the rambling Talayotic settlement of **Torre d'en Gaumés** (free; open access). The drive to both is easy enough – for the coast keep straight, for the ruins go left at the signposted fork 2.5km south of the C721 and follow the asphalted lane for another 2km. The site possesses no fewer than three *talayots*, the largest of which is next to a broken-down *taula* in the centre of a badly ruined circular enclosure. Together, these remains form what is presumed to have been the public part of the village, and it was here in the enclosure that archeologists unearthed a little bronze figure of the Egyptian god of knowledge, Imhotep (now in the Museu de Menorca in Maó), a discovery which reinforced the theory that these enclosures possessed religious significance. It's impossible to interpret precisely the remains surrounding the outside of the enclosure, as the site was inhabited – and continually modified – well into Roman times. That said, you can pick out the broadly circular outlines of a sequence of private dwellings dating from as early as 1500 BC.

Son Bou and Sant Jaume Mediterrani

At **SON BOU**, 8km south of Alaior, the antiquarian interest is maintained by an extensive **cave complex**, cut into the cliff-face above the final part of the approach road, and the foundations of an early Christian **basilica**, set behind the beach at the east end of the resort. They're hardly popular attractions, however, when compared with the **beach**, a whopping pale-gold strand some 3km long and 40m wide. This is Menorca's longest beach, and behind it has mushroomed a massive tourist complex of skyscraper hotels and villa-villages that spreads west into the twin resort of **SANT JAUME MEDITERRANI**. The sand shelves gently into the sea, but the bathing isn't quite as safe as it appears: ocean currents are hazardous, particularly when the wind picks up, and you should watch for the green and red flags. The beach accommodates several beach bars, and **watersports** equipment is widely available – everything from jet-skis, snorkels and windsurfing boards to sunbeds and pedalos.

The development is at its crassest – and the crowds at their worst – towards the east end of the beach, where the foreshore is dominated by several huge sky-rise hotels, including the *Club Sol Milanos* (☎971 371 200, ⓦwww.solmelia.com; ❼; closed Nov–April) and the *Club Sol Pinguinos* (same details). These two hotels share facilities, including sun terraces, outside pools, bars and restaurants, and have spruce modern balconied bedrooms. A little to the west, a strip of dune-fringed, marshy scrubland runs behind the beach, providing the shoreline with some much needed protection and pushing the villa developments a kilometre or so inland. As a result, the bathing along this stretch of coast is far more secluded. In addition, this is where you'll find one of Menorca's two **campsites**, the Son Bou (☎971 372 727, ⓦwww.campingsonbou.com; closed mid-Oct to March), which is 3.5km inland from Sant Jaume Mediterrani on the road linking it and the Torre-solí Nou *urbanització* (but not Son Bou itself) with the C721. This well-equipped campsite has 430 pitches, as well as its own swimming pool, tennis courts, laundry, supermarket and restaurant. In high season (July & Aug), campers pay €6 each, plus €3.30–10.75 for a site, depending on size; cars (€4) and tax (7 percent) further add to the bill, and there are small supplementary charges for electrical hook-ups and hot water. Shoulder-season rates are around ten percent less.

To get to the Son Bou campsite from the C721 you need to go down the road to Sant Jaume Mediterrani, just west of the Son Bou turning, from where the campsite is signed.

Es Mercadal

Ten kilometres northwest of Alaior along the C721, **ES MERCADAL** squats amongst the hills at the very centre of the island. Another old market town, it's an amiable little place of whitewashed houses and trim allotments whose antique centre straddles a quaint watercourse. Tucked down c/Major, at no.16, is a Ruritanian **Ajuntament** (town hall), while the minuscule main square, a few paces away, has a couple of sleepy cafés. The town also boasts one top-notch **restaurant**, the *Can Aguedet*, just metres from the C721 at c/Lepanto 30 (☎971 375 391; daily 1–4pm & 8–11.30pm). It's popular with tourists and serves up outstanding Menorcan cuisine at reasonable prices; monkfish in leek sauce, for instance, costs €15, and grilled squid is €9. Es Mercadal also has a one-star **hostal–residencia**, the spick-and-span *Jeni* (☎971 375 059, ⓦwww.hotel-jeni.de; ❸), in a modern building at c/Miranda del Toro 81. This has 36 comfortable rooms with attractive modern furnishings and a rooftop swimming pool. To get there, leave the main square – Sa Plaça – along c/Nou and take the first left and then the first right. **Buses** to Es Mercadal from Maó, Ciutadella and Sant Tomàs stop just off the C721 on Avinguda Metge Camps, which leads on to c/Nou; for full details, see p.263.

Monte Toro

Es Mercadal is the starting point for the ascent of **Monte Toro**, a steep 3.2km climb along a serpentine but easily driveable road. At 357m, the summit is the island's highest point and offers wonderful vistas: on a good day you can see almost the whole island; on a bad one, you can still see at least as far as Fornells. From this lofty vantage point, Menorca's geological division becomes apparent: to the north, Devonian rock (mostly reddish sandstone) supports a rolling, sparsely populated landscape edged by a ragged coastline; to the south, limestone predominates in a rippling plain that boasts the island's best farmland and, as it approaches the south coast, its deepest valleys.

It's likely that the name of the hill is derived from the Moorish Al Thor ("high point"), but medieval Christians invented an alternative etymology. In predictable fashion, this involves villagers (or monks) spotting a mysterious light on the mountain and, on closer investigation, being confronted by a bull (*toro*) which, lo and behold, obligingly leads them to a miracle-making statue of the Virgin. Whatever the truth, a statue of the Virgin – the Verge del Toro – was installed in a shrine in the thirteenth century and Monte Toro has been a place of pilgrimage ever since. The ceremonial highlight is May 8, when the **Festa de la Verge del Toro** (Festival of the Virgin of the Bull) begins with a special mass at the Monte Toro church and continues with a knees-up down in Es Mercadal.

The Augustinians plonked a monastery on the summit in the seventeenth century, but panicky islanders soon interrupted their monkish reveries by building a small fortress here against the threat of an Ottoman invasion. Bits of both the monastery and the fort survive, the former incorporated within the present **convent**, the latter in a square stone **tower** that is now part of an army outpost bristling with all sorts of aerials and radar dishes. Overshadowing both is a monumentally ugly **statue** of Christ erected in honour of those Menorcans who died in a grubby colonial war launched by Spain in Morocco in the 1920s.

All the army post and much of the convent is out of bounds. The public area, approached across a handsome courtyard with a dinky little well, includes a couple of gift shops, a delightful terrace café – from where there are more great views – a simple restaurant, where the *menú del día* costs €9.90, and a charming **church**, entered through a shallow porch packed with bright flowers and deep-green shrubs. Inside, the barrel-vaulted nave is a modest, truncated affair

A walk from Es Migjorn Gran to the coast

8km; 110m ascent; 2hr–3hr

Despite its modest dimensions, Menorca packs a surprising degree of scenic diversity into its landscape. One of the island's most unexpected – and best hidden – topographical features is the series of dramatic limestone gorges, or *barrancs*, which score the southern coast, running from the inland hills down to the sea. Starting in the town of **Es Migjorn Gran**, this walk follows one of these, the **Barranc de Binigaus**, down to the coast near Sant Tomàs, passing through an area rich in Talayotic remains and impressive natural limestone formations.

The walk starts on the western edge of **Es Migjorn Gran**, where the main road from Ferreries reaches the first houses at the edge of the town. Approaching from Ferreries, look for the unsigned road off on the right, opposite houses number 26 and 28 and the street sign for Avinguda Binicurdell. Walk down this road, past a school and a fine old enclosure housing the substantial remains of two **talayots**. Beyond here, the road becomes rougher, running picturesquely between limestone walls flanked by handsome Aleppo pines. Some 200m further on you'll pass another *talayot* on your right, followed by an attractive ensemble of white houses and arched, Menorcan-style wooden gates. Continue, passing overgrown enclosures littered with limestone boulders, until you reach the farm of **Binigaus Vell** after 1km (the word *bini*, incidentally, is a Moorish legacy, meaning "sons" in Arabic, and a common component of many place names across the island).

Just past here you'll have your first sight of the sea, with views of Mallorca on a clear day. The path swings right, through an intricate but overgrown system of terraces and enclosures before climbing past a strangely eroded limestone outcrop to reach the brow of the hill. From here, the farmhouse of Binigaus Nou is visible ahead with the dramatic limestone gorge of the **Barranc de Binigaus** behind it, issuing into the sea via a narrow defile – your eventual goal – far ahead and below.

Two more *talayots* become visible to your left on the far side of the gorge, part of a landscape which is hereabouts an incredible jumble of stone, with natural limestone

dating from 1595, its gloominess partly dispelled by a central dome and racks of candles. The most prominent feature is the gaudy, 1940s high altarpiece, whose fancy woodwork swarms with cherubs and frames the much-venerated **Verge del Toro**, depicting the crowned Virgin holding Jesus in her arms with the enterprising bull of folklore fame at her feet. The statue is typical of the so-called black Catalan Madonnas, made either from black-stained wood or dark stone.

Es Migjorn Gran and Sant Tomàs

Southwest from Es Mercadal, the road weaves a rustic route to **ES MIGJORN GRAN**, a sleepy little town that trails along a gentle ridge overlooking intricate terraced fields. Of the several towns founded on the island in the eighteenth century, this is the only one not to have been laid out by foreigners. Consequently, the grid-iron street plan of the likes of Es Castell and Sant Lluís is replaced here by a more organic lay-out, the houses of the old agricultural workers straggling along the elongated main street, **c/Major**, as it curves through town.

Es Migjorn Gran is linked by **bus** to Maó and Ferreries (see p.263 for details) and is the starting point for an excellent hike (see box on p.244). It also has two **places to stay**. The cheaper is the fourteen-room *La Palmera* (☎971 370 023; ❷), a simple *casa de huéspedes* (guesthouse) which occupies an older three-storey house in the middle of town at c/Major 85. The other is the *Fonda S'engolidor*,

formations and prehistoric remains mixed chaotically with more modern agricultural enclosures and terracing. Descend to the farmhouse of **Binigaus Nou**, a curiously baronial-looking – but now largely derelict – structure, and walk round to the left rear-hand side of the house. Here, there's an unusual Talayotic **hypostyle chamber** – a gloomy little semi-subterranean burrow supported by a few rudimentary pillars – and a terrific view of the stacked-up field terracing on the hillside behind.

Beyond here the path descends into the *barranc*. Go down to the bottom, passing more overgrown terracing to either side, until the track swings right and narrows at the bottom to reach a Menorcan gate and a well. Walk through the gate and head on 100m to reach the beach next to a gun emplacement buried in the dunes, surrounded – and virtually covered – by fantastically windswept vegetation. If you're in need of rest and refreshment, head left and walk along the coast for 500m to reach the resort of Sant Tomàs (see p.246).

Return to the gate and well and now, instead of going left along the track, head straight ahead over the filled-in gap in the wall and contour round the hill to the right (there's no track here), keeping to the edge of the fields. After 200m you'll see a gap in the wall ahead. Head for this and pick up the trail on the far side, then follow this path for 500m as it runs along the top of a stone terrace until you reach a walled enclosure. Go right here, along the narrowing gorge, beneath increasingly impressive limestone cliffs, pockmarked with caves, until after a further 500m you reach a small T-junction. Go right 20m to the top of the path, then follow the zigzagging stone terrace up to reach the **Cova dels Coloms** – a huge, damp, natural cave, impressive for its size if nothing else.

Return to the T-junction and go left. A few metres beyond, there's another insignificant-looking split in the path – take care to choose the upper trail, or you'll get stuck in the *barranc*. Follow the path as it climbs briskly out of the gorge, returning you to the original path you came down on between Binigaus Vell and Binigaus Nou, and retrace your steps to Es Migjorn Gran, a walk of about 25 minutes.

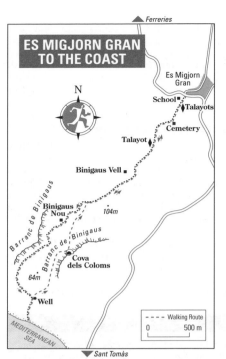

ES MIGJORN GRAN TO THE COAST

Ferreries

Es Migjorn Gran

School
Talayots
Cemetery
Talayot
Binigaus Vell

Barranc de Binigaus

Binigaus Nou

104m

Barranc de Binigaus

Cova dels Coloms

64m

Well

N

MEDITERRANEAN SEA

--- Walking Route
0   500 m

Sant Tomàs

c/Major 3 (℡971 370 193; ❷; closed Dec–April), with four spick-and-span guest rooms in an attractively restored eighteenth-century house towards the south (Ferreries) end of town. Down below is the best **restaurant** in town, the reasonably priced *S'engolidor 58*, c/Major 3 (℡971 370 193), where the emphasis is on traditional Menorcan cuisine. The restaurant also possesses a delightful garden terrace (open summer only), with views over a wooded gorge. A good second choice is *Ca'n Pilar*, a café-restaurant at the north (Es Mercadal) end of town on c/Major.

Sant Tomàs

South of Es Migjorn Gran, the road shuttles along a wooded ravine that leads down to the south coast – and the crass hotel and apartment buildings of **SANT TOMÀS**. The three-kilometre-long sandy **beach**, however, is superb, very similar to that of Son Bou, a couple of headlands away to the east – though all is not quite as it seems. A thunderous storm stripped the existing sand away in 1989, and what you see has been imported. The beach looks very inviting as it slopes gently into the ocean, but there are sometimes dangerous undercurrents – look out for green or red flags. The road reaches the shore halfway along the beach, which is called **Platja Sant Adeodat** to the west and **Platja Sant Tomàs** to the east. The latter is easily the more congested, and it's here you'll find the high-rise hotels, among which the air-conditioned, ultra-modern *Santo Tomàs* is the most lavish (℡971 370 025, ⓦwww.sethotels.com; ❽; closed Nov–March), while the marginally less expensive *Sol Menorca* will do just as well (℡971 370 050, ⓦwww.solmenorca.solmelia.com; ❼; closed Nov–April). Both have pools, restaurants, night-time entertainment and many types of sports facility. Windsurfing boards, jet-skis and pedalos can all be rented on the beach nearby.

Ferreries

Tucked into a hollow beneath a steep hill, 8km from Es Mercadal on the C721 and 7km from Es Migjorn Gran, lies **FERRERIES**, whose narrow, sloping streets are prettily framed by terraced fields. A surprise here is the pagoda-like piece of modern sculpture in the main square, the **Plaça Espanya**, while, just up the hill, the old town centre is marked by the neatly shuttered **Ajuntament**, primly facing the old parish church of **Sant Bartomeu**, a largely eighteenth-century edifice with a belfry of 1884 tacked on to the top. The liveliest time to be here is Saturday morning, when a modest fresh produce **market** is held on Plaça Espanya. Otherwise, there's not much to detain you unless you're after a country hike (see p.248) or keen to visit the Jaime Mascaró **factory shoe and leather shop**, 1km or so east of town along the C721.

One definite plus here is the *Vimpi* **café-bar**, beside the C721 on Plaça Joan Carles, which serves some of the tastiest *tapas* on the island for about €3. You wouldn't choose to stay in Ferreries – it's just too quiet – which is just as well because there's no recommendable accommodation. **Buses** stop in front of the *Vimpi*, which is a couple of minutes' walk from Plaça Espanya, straight up Avinguda Verge del Toro.

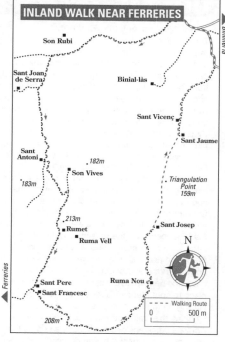

INLAND WALK NEAR FERRERIES

Cala Santa Galdana

South from Ferreries, an excellent eight-kilometre road breezes through a picturesque pastoral landscape down to **CALA SANTA GALDANA**. Once a much-loved beauty spot, the bay has experienced a rash of development since the building of the road and is now cluttered with high-rises. But, despite the concrete, there's no denying the beauty of the setting, the curving sandy **beach** framed by pine-studded, limestone cliffs and intercepted by a rocky promontory adjacent to a narrow river. Early in the morning or out of season is the best time to appreciate the scene – or you can escape the crowds by hiking round the headland beside the *Hotel Audax* at the west end of the bay. It's possible to hire out all sorts of **watersports** equipment here – from pedalos and water scooters to windsurfing boards and snorkelling tackle; and small boats ply regularly to other more secluded beaches (see p.249).

Among the resort's three high-rise **hotels**, you're most likely to find a vacant room at the luxurious, four-star *Audax* (☎971 154 646, ⓦwww.rtmhoteles.com; ➐; closed Nov–March), though if you're prepared to pay this much, make sure you get a sea-facing balcony. The *Cala Galdana*, set just back from the beach (☎971 154 500, ⓦwww.galdana.com; half board only, ➐; closed Nov–March) and the massive, four-star *Sol Elite Gavilanes* (☎971 154 545, ⓦwww.solmelia.es; ➑; closed Nov–March) both have spick-and-span modern rooms, but lack style or special interest. At the other end of the market, the simple S'Atalaia **campsite** is located about 4km back down the road towards Ferreries (☎ & Ⓕ971 374 232; open all year). Pine trees shade much of the site, which has an outdoor swimming pool and a restaurant–bar. It

An inland walk near Ferreries

11km; 220m ascent; 2hr 30min–3hr

This circular inland walk takes you through the miniature hills north of the small town of **Ferreries**, with fine views out over the interior of the island and down to either coast. Although most of the walk uses the access tracks of the many farms you'll pass en route, there are precious few signs of cultivation hereabouts. Indeed, apart from the occasional cow pasture, most of the land is given over to scrub and game enclosures, evidence of the declining state of Menorcan agriculture. If you have your own transport, it's best to start at the farm of **Sant Francesc**, though at a pinch you could do the walk from Ferreries itself, which is regularly connected by bus to both Ciutadella and Maó. Note, though, that this adds around 4km to the total distance, plus a steep climb up to Sant Francesc at the beginning of the route.

To reach the start of the walk, first find the **roundabout** on the eastern edge of Ferreries, by the Meubles allés store, where the Es Migjorn road meets the highway to Maó. Take the unsigned northern exit off this roundabout across the industrial estate (*polígon industrial*), past the Lamborghini showroom (displaying tractors, not sports cars), just beyond which the road becomes a country lane. Follow this lane for 1km to a fork at the Camí de Marcona sign, then go right and continue for a further 1km to the top of a steep hill, where you reach the farms of Sant Pere and Sant Francesc and the beginning of the walk.

Park considerately if you've driven here, then head through the gate to **Sant Francesc** and along the ridgetop track, from where there are marvellous views of both the north and south coasts, the heights of Monte Toro, Fornells, and, looking back, the neat white cluster of houses that comprises Ferreries. This is also a good place to spot Menorca's resident birds of prey, such as the booted eagle or red kite, circling on the thermals overhead or on the plains below.

Follow this track for 1km, passing the first of innumerable *coto privado de caza* ("private game enclosure") signs, then swing left in front of a gate festooned with no-entry signs and past a clump of weirdly wind-shaped wild olive on the brow of the hill. Around 500m further on you pass through another set of gates, marked *propriedad privado* (private property) – act responsibly and it's extremely unlikely that anyone will object to your being there. Continue across an area of scrub full of

---

can only accommodate about a hundred guests, and advance reservations are strongly advised. Charges range from €3.30 to €10.75 for a site depending on size, plus €4 for a vehicle, and €6 per person.

Back in the resort, there's a good-quality seafood **restaurant**, *El Mirador* (℡971 154 503), built into the promontory that pokes out from the beach, though you pay over the odds for the setting. If your budget doesn't stretch that far, other less expensive choices are stuck behind the *Hotel Audax* on c/Mirador. Additional facilities include **car rental** outlets – for instance Hertz (℡971 154 567), metres from the *Hotel Cala Galdana* – and Radio-Taxi Salord Ferrerías (℡971 155 068). There are regular **buses** to Cala Santa Galdana from Ferreries from May to October.

Beaches around Cala Santa Galdana

There are several exquisite **cove beaches** within easy reach of Cala Santa Galdana, the most obvious choice being **Cala Mitjana**, just 1km to the east. The footpath to Cala Mitjana begins beside the *Sol Elite Gavilanes* hotel at the Plaça Na Gran in Cala Santa Galdana. A gate at the back of the hotel's parking lot leads onto an easy-to-follow path through coastal pine woods. At the first fork veer right; after a few minutes you'll reach a clear-

small, elusive birds, following the track straight ahead through Ruma Nou farm and on for another 500m to reach **Sant Josep**.

Head round the left side of the farmhouse, crossing a muddy cow pasture then going carefully around the gate at the far end. Follow the track straight on along the ridgetop for 100m until it veers right through a gap in the wall and then disappears. Ahead you'll see the farms of Sant Jaume and Sant Vicenc – your next goal – though the lack of a clear path makes finding a route down to them slightly difficult. Follow the overgrown ridgetop wall for another 100m to reach a semi-ruined **triangulation point** at the highest point of the ridge. From here, you'll spy the ruined fortifications of the Castell Santa Àgueda (see p.250) on the hilltop to your left, and the rocky finger of the Cap de Cavalleria (see p.237) stretching into the sea ahead. The next 500m is a bit of a scramble: climb over the wall by the triangulation point (there's a stepping stone to help you over), then follow the ridgetop wall down to **Sant Jaume**, climbing over a couple more small walls en route, until you emerge on the broad track in front of the farm.

The remainder of the walk is either on surfaced roads or well-defined paths. Follow the track in front of Sant Jaume farm for 500m to hit a metalled road and turn left, with the strange, fortress-like natural rock formation at the summit of El Pujol hill away to your right. Then continue along the road over a T-junction and past the following turn off to the right as the road swings left until the houses of **Son Rubi** appear on the bluff ahead. Carry on past the entrance to Son Rubi, after which the road reverts to dirt track.

At the fork 300m ahead go left, passing a line of small fig trees on your right followed by the entrance to **Sant Joan de Serra**. The path then swings left again, with Castell Santa Àgueda, now closer to hand, rearing into view once more on your right. Some 250m past the Sant Joan de Serra turn-off, pass through the gates to **San Antoni de Ruma**. Climb up to the farmhouse and make a left turn at the fork just beyond onto a metalled road. Gird your loins here for a final climb back up to the ridgetop, ascending steeply into a narrow wooded valley. Reach the T-junction at the top and turn left for the final kilometre back to your starting point at Sant Francesc.

ing. Cross the clearing diagonally to the left then follow the path as it descends to the **beach**, a broad strip of sand set beneath wooded cliffs at the end of a beguiling bay – though there's sometimes an unpleasant seaweed smell. A favourite sport here is jumping into the crystal-clear water from the surrounding cliffs.

Equally beautiful, but also afflicted with periodic seaweed problems, is **Cala Trebalúger**, a further 2.5km east from Cala Mitjana and best reached by boat from Cala Santa Galdana (summer 1–2 daily). Cala Trebalúger boasts a beautiful arc of sand flanked by steep cliffs and crossed by a stream which emerges from the gorge behind. There are no beach facilities, so you'll need to take your own food and drink.

Walking west from Cala Santa Galdana on the footpath starting opposite the *Hotel Audax* (at the top of the small flight of steps beside the telephone boxes) it takes about forty minutes to reach **Cala Macarella**. Here, severe, partly wooded limestone cliffs surround a band of white sand that shelves gently into the Med. It's a beautiful spot, ideal for swimming – and, unlike the other beaches around Cala Santa Galdana, seaweed is never a problem. There's a touch of development in the form of a summertime beach bar, and sunbeds and pedalos for rent, but it's nothing excessive.

Binisues and Castell Santa Àgueda

Heading west out of Ferreries along the C721, it's about 3km to the (clearly signed) right turn leading to the rural manor house of **Binisues** (May–Oct daily 11am–7pm; €5). The house occupies a grand setting, overlooking the valleys and hills of central Menorca, and its elegant symmetries reflect the self-confidence of the island's nineteenth-century landed gentry. The interior, however, is a yawn. Presumably, the intention is to re-create the mansion's old patrician air, but the accumulated knick-knacks look as if they've been thrown in haphazardly. Even worse, if you persevere beyond the family rooms, you'll find an assortment of old agricultural implements on the second floor and a collection of mounted butterflies above – you're much better off sipping coffee at the restaurant and admiring the view.

Returning to the lane below Binisues, it's about 2km more to the deserted schoolhouse (and parking space) on the right-hand side which marks the start of the hour-long hike up the rocky and lightly wooded mountainside to the **Castell Santa Àgueda**, whose modest remains perch atop the peak of the same name, Menorca's second highest at 268m. The Romans were the first to recognize the hill's strategic value, fortifying the summit in the second century BC, but it was the Moors who developed the stronghold, and it was here that they made their final stand against Alfonso III's invasion in 1287. Fresh from their defeat at Maó, the demoralized Moors didn't put up much of a fight – though they would certainly have been more determined if they had known of their ultimate fate. After the surrender, the Catalans demanded a heavy ransom for every captive. Those who couldn't pay were enslaved and those who weren't fit to work as slaves were shoved onto ships, taken out to sea and thrown overboard. Nowadays, little remains of the Moorish castle bar a few crumbling turrets and walls, but the views are spectacular.

About 3km west of the Binisues turning, the C721 leaves the central hills for the flatlands surrounding Ciutadella. Within easy striking distance of the main road in between Binisues and Ciutadella are a clutch of clearly signed prehistoric sites, principally Torrellafuda and the island's best-preserved naveta, the Naveta d'es Tudons (see p.261), 5km from Ciutadella – just after kilometre post 40.

Ciutadella

Like Maó, **CIUTADELLA** sits high above its harbour, but here navigation is far more difficult, up a narrow channel too slender for all but the smallest of cargo ships. Nonetheless, despite this nautical inconvenience, Ciutadella was the island's capital until fairly recently: the Romans chose it, the Moors adopted it as Medina Minurka, and the Catalans of the *Reconquista* flattened the place and began all over again. In the event, the medieval Catalan town didn't last either: in 1558, Turkish corsairs razed the place and carted off three thousand captives – around eighty percent of the population – to the slave markets of Istanbul. As news spread of the disaster, the Pope organized a European whip-round, and, with the money in the bag, an intrepid Menorcan doctor, one Marcos Martí, ventured east to Istanbul to buy the slaves back. Martí was remarkably successful – but there again, the Turks were raiding for the money, not to fight a religious war – and the returning hostages, together with the survivors of the assault,

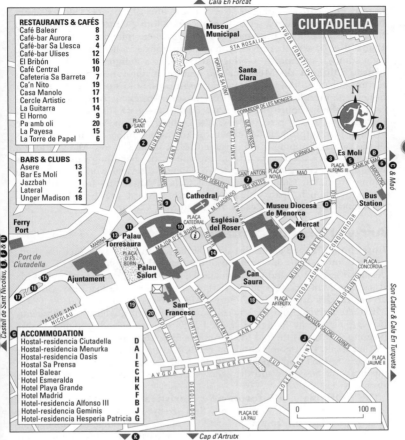

RESTAURANTS & CAFÉS

Café Balear	8
Café-bar Aurora	3
Café-bar Sa Llesca	4
Café-bar Ulises	12
El Bribón	16
Café Central	10
Cafeteria Sa Barreta	7
Ca'n Nito	19
Casa Manolo	17
Cercle Artistic	11
La Guitarra	14
El Horno	9
Pa amb oli	20
La Payesa	15
La Torre de Papel	6

BARS & CLUBS

Asere	13
Bar Es Molí	5
Jazzbah	1
Lateral	2
Unger Madison	18

G ACCOMMODATION

Hostal-residencia Ciutadella	D
Hostal-residencia Menurka	A
Hostal-residencia Oasis	I
Hostal Sa Prensa	E
Hotel Balear	C
Hotel Esmeralda	H
Hotel Playa Grande	K
Hotel Madrid	F
Hotel-residencia Alfonso III	B
Hotel-residencia Geminis	J
Hotel-residencia Hesperia Patricia	G

determinedly rebuilt Ciutadella in grand style. They re-fortified the town's compact centre and then, reassured, set about adorning it with fine stone churches and sweeping mansions.

Throughout the seventeenth century, Menorca's leading landowners hung out in Ciutadella, confident of their position and power. They were, however, in for a shock: for the colonial powers of the eighteenth century, the town's feeble port had no appeal when compared with Maó's magnificent inlet, and the British simply – and abruptly – moved the capital to Maó in 1722. Thereafter, Maó flourished as a trading centre, while Ciutadella stagnated – a long-lasting economic reverie that has, by coincidence, preserved the town's old and beautiful centre as if in aspic.

Despite the fact that Ciutadella had lost its capital status, the bulk of the Menorcan aristocracy decided to remain. The island's foreign rulers pretty much left them to stew in their own juice – an increasingly redundant, landowning class far from the wheels of mercantile power. Consequently, there's very little British or French influence in Ciutadella's **architecture**:

instead, the narrow, cobbled streets boast fine old palaces, hidden away behind high walls, and a set of Baroque and Gothic churches very much in the Spanish tradition. Essentially, it's the whole ensemble, centred on stately **Plaça d'es Born**, that gives Ciutadella its appeal rather than any specific sight, though the mostly Gothic **cathedral** is a delight, as is the eclectic **Museu Diocesà de Menorca**. An ambitious renovation programme has further enhanced the town, restoring most of the old stone facades to their honey-coloured best. Added to this are some excellent **restaurants**, especially on the harbourfront, and a reasonably adequate supply of *hostals* and **hotels**. It's a lovely place to stay, and nothing else on Menorca rivals the evening *passeig* (promenade), when the townsfolk amble the narrow streets of the centre, dropping in on pavement cafés as the sun sets. Allow at least a couple of days, more if you seek out one of the beguiling **cove beaches** within easy striking distance of town. There are several wonderful spots to choose from, but **Cala Turqueta** and **Cala d'Algairens** are probably the pick of the bunch. Spare time also for the prehistoric sites hereabouts, most pertinently the **Naveta d'es Tudons** and **Son Catlar**.

Arrival and information

Buses from Maó and points east arrive at the station on c/Barcelona, just south of the Camí de Maó, an extension of the main island highway, the C721. For details of services to and from Ciutadella, see p.263. **Catamarans** from Cala Rajada on Mallorca dock in the harbour right below the Plaça d'es Born, as do **car ferries** from Mallorca's Port d'Alcúdia — see Listings, p.260.

If you're **driving** in, there's no missing the ring road, which, under various names — principally Avinguda Jaume I El Conqueridor and Avinguda Capità Negrete — encircles the old town. Approaching from the east, turn left when you hit it and keep going until you reach its conclusion beside the Plaça dels Pins. If you can't find a **parking** spot actually on this square, turn left at the top near the bus stops and drive down Passeig Sant Nicolau, where there's always space.

The **Oficina d'Informació Turística** (May–Oct Mon–Fri 9.30am–8.30pm, Sat 9am–1pm, Sun 5–8pm; Nov–April Mon–Fri 10am–7pm, Sat 9am–1pm; ☎971 382 693) has a good range of information on Menorca as a whole and Ciutadella in particular. This includes bus timetables, ferry schedules, lists of *hostals* and hotels, and free maps. They don't, however, help with finding accommodation. The tourist office is directly opposite the Cathedral on Plaça Catedral, bang in the middle of the old town.

Ciutadella's compact centre is easily seen on foot. If you want to explore other parts of the west coast, there's a handy network of **local buses** that leaves from Plaça dels Pins, on the west side of the town centre next to the main square, Plaça d'es Born. **Taxis** leave from Plaça dels Pins and Avinguda Constitució, round the corner from Plaça Alfons III.

Accommodation

There's hardly a plethora of **accommodation** in Ciutadella, but the town does have four quality hotels that aren't booked up by package-tour operators — the *Geminis*, *Hesperia Patricia*, *Playa Grande* and *Sant Ignasi* — and a handful of fairly comfortable and reasonably priced *hostals* dotted in and around the centre. The establishments listed below are open all year, unless otherwise specified.

Inexpensive

Hotel-residencia Alfonso III Camí de Maó 53 ☎971 380 150, ⓔhalfonso@supersonik.com. Located beside the main road from Maó, a couple of minutes' walk from the ring road, this brashly modern hotel has fifty simple one-star rooms – but try to get one at the back away from the noisy road. ❸

Hotel Madrid c/Madrid 60 ☎971 380 328, ⓕ971 482 158. Fourteen quite comfortable rooms in a run-of-the-mill, villa-style building with its own ground-floor café-bar. It's located near the waterfront, a fifteen-minute walk west of the town centre. To get there, follow Passeig Sant Nicolau from the Plaça dels Pins, take the third turning on the left (c/Saragossa) and you'll hit c/Madrid just east of the hostal at the first major intersection. ❸

Hostal-residencia Oasis c/Sant Isidre 33 ☎971 382 197. Just a few metres from Plaça Artrutx, this attractive one-star has nine simple rooms set around a gaudily decorated courtyard-restaurant. ❷

Hostal Sa Prensa c/Madrid s/n ☎971 382 698. Recently refurbished, villa-like, one-star *hostal* with six spartan bedrooms above a café-bar. It's a fifteen-minute walk west of the centre, close to the rocky seashore at the end of c/Madrid. To get there, follow Passeig Sant Nicolau from the Plaça dels Pins, take the fourth turning on the left (c/Joan Ramis i Ramis) and you'll hit c/Madrid just beside the *hostal* at the first major intersection. ❸

Moderate

Hotel Balear Camí de Maó 178 ☎971 482 341, ⓦwww.hotel-balear.com. A modern, three-storey hotel in an unappetizing location, beside the main Maó–Ciutadella road about 500m east from the town centre. The rooms are OK, nothing more, though all are en suite and there's a good chance of a vacancy here when everywhere else is full. ❹

Hostal-residencia Ciutadella c/Sant Eloi 10 ☎ & ⓕ 971 383 462. Unassuming yet comfortable two-star in an old terraced house down a narrow side street off Plaça Alfons III. ❸

Hotel-residencia Geminis c/Josepa Rossinyol 4 ☎971 384 644, ⓕ971 383 683. Distinctively painted in pink and white with blue awnings, this well tended, very comfortable two-star has thirty rooms, each decorated in bright modern style. The rooms at the front have Art Deco-style balconies and overlook a quiet and prosperous suburban street. To get there on foot, walk a few paces down c/Mossèn J. Salord i Farnés from the ring road and watch for the archway on the right; go through the arch and the hotel's on the right. Closed Jan. ❹

Hostal-residencia Menurka c/Domingo Savio 6 ☎971 381 415, ⓦwww.menurka.com. A tidy two-star establishment of 21 rooms, some with balconies, though they overlook a mundane side street. C/Domingo Savio is just east of the town centre, one block up from Camí de Maó. ❹

Expensive

Hotel Esmeralda Passeig Sant Nicolau 171 ☎971 380 250, ⓕ971 380 258. Located at the west end of the street, a fifteen-minute walk from the centre. The sweeping curves of this four-storey hotel are a classic example of 1960s design, with a swimming pool and private gardens out front. Most of the bedrooms have wide and expansive balconies and face out to sea, but the bulk are booked up by package-tour operators. Closed Nov–March. ❻

Hotel-residencia Hesperia Patricia Passeig Sant Nicolau 90 ☎971 385 511, ⓦwww .hoteles-hesperia.es. The smartest hotel in town, popular with business folk and handy for the centre. The extremely comfortable, ultra-modern rooms come with all facilities, the only downer being the lack of a sea view – though the best rooms have rooftop balconies with wide vistas over the town centre. There's also a swimming pool. ❻

Hotel Playa Grande c/Bisbe Juano 2 ☎971 382 445, ⓕ971 381 536. This pleasant hotel with its brisk modern interior is located about ten minutes' walk south of Plaça dels Pins, at the foot of c/Mallorca. At the front, its balconied rooms overlook a narrow cove and a busy road – ask for a room at the back if you're a light sleeper. Closed Jan. ❻

Hotel Sant Ignasi Carretera Cala Morell s/n ☎971 385 575, ⓦwww.santignasi.com. This elegant nineteenth-century manor house has been tastefully converted into an immaculate, excellent-value hotel. Each of the twenty bedrooms is individually decorated in a style that blends with the original building, and there are gardens and an outside pool too. It's in the middle of the countryside, though the surrounding farmland is flat and dull. The hotel is about 4km northeast of the centre of Ciutadella, clearly signposted (down a very narrow 1.5km-long lane) from the road to Cala Morell. ❻

The Town

All of Ciutadella's key attractions are clustered in the compact **town centre**, a rabbit warren of lanes, fringed by fine old mansions and handsome churches. Most of the centre is pedestrianized, but it only takes a few minutes to walk from one side to the other, and keeping your bearings is fairly straightforward – the main square and harbour are on the west side of the centre, the ring road to the east.

Plaça d'es Born

Primarily a nineteenth-century creation, **Plaça d'es Born** is easily the finest main square in the Balearic Islands. In the middle soars an **obelisk** commemorating the futile defence against the Turks in 1558, a brutal episode that was actually something of an accident. The Ottomans had dispatched 15,000 soldiers and 150 warships west to assist their French allies against the Habsburgs. With no particular place to go, the Turks rolled around the Mediterranean for a few weeks and, after deciding Maó wasn't worth the candle, they happened on Ciutadella, where the garrison numbered just forty. For the Menorcans, the results were cataclysmic. The one-sided siege ended with the destruction of the town and the enslavement of its population – there was so much damage that when the new Spanish governor arrived, he was forced to live in a cave. The obelisk's Latin inscription, penned by the mid-nineteenth-century politician and historian Josep Quadrado, reads, "Here we fought until death for our religion and our country in the year 1558." Such grandiose nationalism was typical of Quadrodo, then the region's most prominent politician and leader of the reactionary Catholic Union, which bombarded Madrid with complaints and petitions whenever central government did anything progressive.

On the western side of the Plaça d'es Born stands the **Ajuntament** (town hall), whose early nineteenth-century arches and crenellations mimic Moorish style, purposely recalling the time when the site was occupied by the Wali's *alcázar* (palace). From here, it's a few paces along the north side of the square to the **Teatre d'es Born**, a neat, late nineteenth-century structure built to salvage some municipal pride. The merchants of Maó had just built an opera house and, pricked into cultural action, the oligarchs of Ciutadella promptly followed suit – though they weren't quite as energetic when it came to actually getting people to perform here. After years of neglect the theatre has been restored, and is now used as both a theatre and cinema.

The northeast corner of the Plaça d'es Born is marked by the sweeping lines of the **Palau Torresaura**, built in the nineteenth century, but looking far older, and the grandest of several aristocratic mansions edging the plaza. Embellished by a handsome loggia, its frontage proclaims the family coat of arms above a large wooden door leading into a spacious coutryard. The antique interior, however, is off limits – like most of its neighbours, the house is still owner-occupied. An exception is the adjacent **Palau Salort** (May–Oct Mon–Sat 10am–2pm; €2.50), which is entered round the corner on c/Major d'es Born, the narrow cobbled street that leads to the cathedral. Dating from 1813, this rambling mansion has seen more illustrious days, but it's still of some mild interest for its sequence of high-ceilinged rooms redolent of nineteenth-century aristocratic life.

Tucked away in the southeast corner of the square, the **Església de St Francesc** is a clean-lined, airy structure, whose hybrid architecture reflects the island's ups and downs. The original church was constructed shortly after the *Reconquista* and it was here in 1301 that Jaume II met his nobles to parcel up the island into the feudal estates – the *Cavalleries* (from cavaller, the Catalan for knight) – that cemented his kingdom. In 1558, the Turks fired the church, but it was rebuilt to the original specifications in the 1590s, with further embellishments added later – the Baroque side door in the eighteenth century, the dome in the nineteenth. Like most of Ciutadella's churches, the interior was ransacked by Republicans in the Civil War, but bits and pieces did survive, notably several chintzy carved wood altars and a motley crew of polychromatic saints.

The Cathedral and around

From beside Palau Salort, c/Major d'es Born leads to the **Cathedral** (daily 9am–1pm & 6–9pm), a handsome structure built by Jaume II at the beginning of the fourteenth century on the site of the chief mosque, but remodelled after the Turkish onslaught of 1558. During the rebuilding, the flying buttresses of the original were partly encased within a thick stone wall to guard against future attack, a modification which gives the cathedral its distinctive appearance. The Gothic side door – on the south side of the church – was, however, left intact, its arching columns decorated with strange-looking beasts and the coats of arms of Aragon and Ciutadella, all surmounted by a delicate carving of the Magi honouring the infant Christ. Another survivor was the set of fierce-looking gargoyles that decorates the buttresses at roof level. The principal (west) entrance was added much later, in 1813, its flashy Neoclassical portico contrasting with the rest of the church and the intricate rose window above.

Inside, light filters through the stained glass of the narrow, lofty windows to bathe the high altar in an ethereal glow. There's also a sequence of glitzy Baroque side chapels and a wonderfully kitsch, pointed high-altar canopy or baldachin. The wall behind the high altar carries a medieval panel painting, the Purification of the Virgin, but most of the church's old furnishings and fittings were destroyed in a frenzy of anti-clericalism when the Republicans took control of Menorca during the Civil War. Although the British had made Maó the island's capital in 1722, Ciutadella remained Menorca's ecclesiastical centre and, almost without exception, its resident Catholic hierarchy were rich and reactionary in equal measure. They enthusiastically proclaimed their support for the officers of the Maó garrison when the latter declared for Franco in July 1936, but this turned out to be a major gaffe. The bulk of the garrison stayed loyal to the Republic, and, allied with local left-wing groups, they captured the rebels, shot their leaders and ransacked Ciutadella's main churches as retribution.

Directly opposite the Cathedral's west entrance is the **Palau Olivar** (no access), whose stern, eighteenth-century facade is partly relieved by a pair of miniature balconies fronted by wrought-iron grilles. In 1707, the house witnessed one of the town's crueller episodes, when a reclusive mother and daughter who worked and lived here were accused of witchcraft. Found guilty on palpably potty charges, the older woman was sent to prison for life, and the younger was executed – by any standard, a heavy price to pay for not joining in the town's social life.

From Plaça Catedral, the stone-flagged piazza beside the church, it's a short walk north through to **c/Sa Muradeta**, a wide flight of steps that leads down to the harbour. Here, yachts and fishing smacks bob up and down in front of a series of waterside restaurants (see p.259), with the old town walls forming a scenic background. Alternatively, proceed south along c/Roser and you'll soon pass the tiny **Església del Roser**, whose striking Churrigueresque facade, dating from the seventeenth century, boasts a quartet of pillars festooned with intricate tracery. The church was the subject of bitter controversy when the British governor Richard Kane (see p.239) commandeered it for Church of England services – which was not at all to the liking of the Dominican friars who owned the place.

The Museu Diocesà de Menorca

At the far end of c/Roser, turn left past the palatial, seventeenth-century mansion of **Can Saura**, which is distinguished by its elegant stonework and overhanging eaves, and then left again for c/Seminari and the **Museu Diocesà de Menorca** (Diocesan Museum; Tues–Sat 10.30am–1.30pm, May–Sept also Sun 10.30am–1.30pm; €2). Housed in an old and dignified convent and its church – the Església dels Socors – the museum is a delight. Before you go in, take a look at the elongated perimeter wall, a sober affair cheered by the delicate flutings of a Neoclassical portal that once served as the main entrance to the church. On top of the doorway, a bizarre sculpted cameo is the town's most unusual sight, depicting the Virgin Mary, armed with a cudgel, standing menacingly over a cringing, cat-like dragon-devil. Inside, the conventual buildings surround an immaculately preserved Baroque **cloister**, whose vaulted aisles sport coats of arms and religious motifs. The museum's collection is distributed chronologically among the tiny rooms edging the cloister; the labelling – where it exists – is in Spanish. The first three rooms hold a hotchpotch of Talayotic and early classical archeological finds, notably a superbly crafted, miniature bull and a similarly exquisite little mermaid (*sirena*), almost certainly Greek bronzes dating from the fifth century BC. Room 4 is devoted to the workaday paintings of a local artist, Pere Daura, and Room 5 has scale models of old Menorcan buildings made by one of the priests. Rooms 6–8 occupy parts of the old refectory and display some dreadful religious paintings, as well as all sorts of ecclesiastical tackle. There are elaborate monstrances, communion cups, reliquaries, croziers and such like, but it's the general glitter that impresses, rather than any individual piece. The adjoining **church** is often used for temporary exhibitions featuring local – or at least Catalan – artists.

The market and around

Immediately north of the museum along c/Seminari, turn right down c/Socors to make the quick detour east to the **market** (*mercat*; mornings Mon–Sat), which rambles over two miniature squares, Plaça Francesc Netto and Plaça Llibertat. This is another delightful corner of the old town, where fresh fruit, vegetable, meat and fish stalls mingle with lively and inexpensive cafés selling the freshest of *ensaimadas*. The fish stalls occupy a dinky little structure of 1895; the rest fill out a slender arcaded gallery that was constructed thirty years before as part of a municipal drive to clean up the town's food supply.

Doubling back to c/Seminari along c/Socors, turn right to pass the savings bank which occupies the **Palau Saura**, built in grand style by the British for a Menorcan aristocrat, one Joan Miquel Saura, in return for his help in planning their successful invasion of 1708. Just north along the street is the flamboyant facade of the **Capella del Sant Crist**, a Baroque extravaganza with garlands of fruit and a pair of gargoyle-like faces. Inside, the intimate, candle-lit nave supports an octagonal stone dome and is also home to an unattributed medieval panel painting depicting three saints of local significance. The skeletal crucified Christ above the high altar is supposed to have dripped with sweat in 1661 and remains a popular object of devotion.

From the chapel, it's a few metres north to the narrow, pedestrianized main street that runs through the old town – here c/J. M. Quadrado. Look to the left and you'll spy a perky bronze lamb – the **Estatua des Be** – stuck on a column. The lamb, symbolizing the Lamb of God and carrying a flag bearing the cross of St John the Baptist, is a reminder of Ciutadella's biggest shindig, the Festa de Sant Joan (see p.45).

Santa Clara and the Museu Municipal

Directly opposite the top of c/Seminari, a long, straight street – c/Santa Clara – shoots off north, hemmed in by the walls of old aristocratic palaces. At the top is the convent of **Santa Clara**, a mundanely modern incarnation of a centuries-old foundation. In 1749, this was the site of a scandal that had tongues clacking from Ciutadella to Maó. During the night, three young women hopped over the convent wall and placed themselves under the protection of their British boyfriends. Even worse, as far as the local clergy were concerned, they wanted to turn Protestant and marry their men. In this delicate situation, Governor Blakeney had the room where the women were staying sealed up by a priest every night. But he refused to send them back to the convent and allowed the weddings to go ahead, thereby compounding a religious animosity – Catholic subject against Protestant master – which had begun in the days of Richard Kane.

Beyond Santa Clara, at the end of c/Portal de Sa Font, the **Museu Municipal** (Tues–Sat 10am–2pm; €2) occupies part of the old municipal fortifications, a massive honeysuckle-clad bastion overlooking a slender ravine that once had, until it was redirected, a river running along its base and into the harbour. Inside the museum, a long vaulted chamber is given over to a wide range of archeological artefacts, among which there's a substantial collection of Talayotic remains, featuring finds garnered from all over the island and covering the several phases of Talayotic civilization. The earlier pieces, dating from around 1400 to 700 BC, include many examples of crudely crafted beakers and tumblers. Later work – from around 120 BC – reveals a far greater degree of sophistication, both in terms of kitchenware, with bowls and tumblers particularly common, and bronze weaponry, notably several finely chiselled arrowheads. From this later period comes most of the (imported) jewellery, whose fine detail and miniature size suggests a Carthaginian origin. A leaflet detailing the exhibits in English is available free at reception. Temporary exhibitions take place downstairs.

From the Museu Municipal, it's a five-minute walk back to Plaça d'es Born along c/Sa Muradeta with pleasant views down the ravine to the harbour.

East from c/Seminari to Plaça Alfons III

From the top of c/Seminari, the pedestrianized main street of the old town runs east as c/J. M. Quadrado. The first stretch is crimped by a block of whitewashed, vaulted arches, **Ses Voltes**, distinctly Moorish in inspiration and a suitable

The Rissaga

Almost all of the time, Ciutadella's long and slender harbour is as flat as a mill-pond, but every so often, for reasons that remain obscure, it is subjected to a violent disturbance, the **Rissaga**. This begins with sudden changes to the water level and is followed by a dramatic rush of water into the harbour before normality returns. The last great Rissaga of 1984 submerged the harbourside beneath two metres of water.

setting for a string of busy shops and cafés. Just beyond is **Plaça Nova**, an attractive little square edged by some of the most popular pavement cafés in town. Just off the square along c/Sant Antoni, a narrow archway cuts through what was once the town wall, which explains the name of the alley beyond, "Qui no Passa" ("The one that doesn't go through"). Returning to Plaça Nova, c/Maó leads east to leave the cramped alleys of the old town at **Plaça Alfons III**, a traffic-choked square that was once the site of Ciutadella's east gate. The big old windmill here, the **Moli d'es Comte**, looks as if it should be in the countryside, its forlorn appearance not helped by its partial conversion into a bar.

The Castell de Sant Nicolau

West from Plaça d'es Born, Passeig Sant Nicolau runs along the northern edge of Plaça S'Esplanada and reaches, after about 800m, the headland **Castell de Sant Nicolau** (Mon–Sat 11am–1pm & 6–8pm; free), a dinky little seventeenth-century watchtower equipped with a drawbridge, oil holes and turrets, all stuck on unwelcoming rocks. The interior, however, is disappointingly bare and is, indeed, only usually open in the evening, when people come here to watch the sun set out beyond Mallorca. It also hosts occasional exhibitions.

Beside the castle is a statue honouring **David Glasgow Farragut**, who is shown with telescope in hand and wind in his hair. The son of a Ciutadellan who emigrated to America in 1776, Farragut entered the US navy in 1810, the start of a long naval career distinguished by several audacious attacks on Confederate strongholds in the Civil War. Most famously, Farragut forced the surrender of New Orleans in 1862 and as a result of this and other actions was made an admiral of the US fleet four years later. He visited Menorca in 1867 and was greeted by cheering crowds everywhere he went – in Ciutadella, the throng was so dense that he had to abandon his carriage and walk to his lodgings near the cathedral. At church the next day, his secretary wrote approvingly that "hundreds of eyes were riveted upon the pleasant countenance of the unappalled admiral".

Eating, drinking and nightlife

For an early **breakfast** the best place to go is the market (*mercat*) on Plaça Llibertat, where a couple of simple cafés serve coffee and fresh pastries. Later in the day, around **lunch time**, aim for c/J. M. Quadrado, Plaça Nova and Plaça Alfons III, which together hold a good selection of inexpensive café-bars, offering *tapas* and light meals. In the **evening**, more ambitious and expensive food is available at a string of excellent restaurants down by the harbourside, or at a couple of good establishments tucked away near Plaça d'es Born. Almost all the harbourside places have the advantage of an outside terrace, but note that – unlike those restaurants near the Plaça d'es Born – they usually close down in winter. Most places open daily during the season, though restaurants usually take a siesta between 4pm and 7pm or 8pm.

Ciutadella has several bakeries. One of the best is the *Pastisseria Mol*, c/Roser 2, which sells excellent takeaway pizza slices, filled bread rolls and mouthwatering cakes from Monday to Saturday. It's across the square from the cathedral. *Pastelería Montaner*, at c/Bisbe Torres 11 on the other side of the cathedral, is the oldest pastry shop in town and sells some of the tastiest *ensaimadas* on the island. *Sa Gelateria de Menorca* (open summer only), at Plaça de la Catedral 3, has the island's best Italian-style ice cream.

People don't come to Ciutadella for the **nightlife**, but there's a complement of late-night bars dotted round the old town plus a cluster of touristy places down at the harbourside. If you want to savour the flavour of the old town, head for the pavement cafés of Plaça Nova, where you can nurse a drink and watch the early evening crowds amble by. The youngest and liveliest nightlife can be found around Plaça Sant Joan, in the ravine at the head of the port.

Cafés and café-bars

Café-bar Aurora Plaça Alfons III, 3. Next to the ring road on the eastern edge of the old town. Open all day for both *tapas* (€3–6) and full meals, with the emphasis on Menorcan standards.

Café-bar Sa Llesca Plaça Nova 4. One of several pleasant – and largely indistinguishable – café-bars on this tiny square. The ground-floor terrace café is one of the more popular spots in the old town, and there's a first-floor dining room inside.

Café-bar Ulises Plaça Llibertat. This amenable, low-key café-bar next to the market is a locals' favourite. Their *ensaimadas*, a snip at €1.20 each, are the best in town.

Café Central c/Bisbe 2. Busy little place next to the cathedral's main entrance, serving traditional Menorcan *tapas*, including various sausages and cheeses. Open summer only.

Cafeteria Sa Barreta c/J. M. Quadrado 16. In the vaulted arches – Ses Voltes – bang in the middle of the old town, this unassuming family-run café is great for fresh *pa amb oli* and other traditional Menorcan snacks – sausage and so forth.

Ca'n Nito Plaça d'es Born 12. Specializing in *tapas*, this is one of the liveliest spots in town, and the nice terrace in the square is a popular place for a drink, especially during the Saturday market.

Cercle Artístic Plaça d'es Born 19. Spacious and elegant place, located in the entrance to the Teatre d'es Born and a great spot for people-watching. Good range of local snacks, salads, sandwiches and pastries.

Pa amb oli c/Nou de Julio 4. Just off Plaça d'es Born, kitted out in vaguely rustic style, this excellent café-bar specializes in all things Menorcan, with bowls of peppers and olives liberally distributed on the counter and smoked sausages hanging from the ceiling. The food is filling, delicious and traditional – and inexpensive, too.

La Torre de Papel Camí de Maó 46. The most urbane coffee house in town, all polished wood floors, with a bookshop at the front and a tiny terrace at the back.

Restaurants

Café Balear Passeig de Sant Joan 17 ☏971 380 005. Justifiably popular, this attractively decorated café-restaurant sits at the back of the harbour by the bridge. Its pint-sized terrace is the best place to eat, but there are tables inside too. The food is first-rate – delicious shellfish, pasta and tapas all at reasonable prices.

El Bribón c/Marina 107 ☏971 385 050. Next door to *Casa Manolo*, this superb harbourside restaurant specializes in seafood, often prepared in traditional Menorcan style. Reckon on around €13 for the *menú del día*, €12–16 for a main course.

Casa Manolo c/Marina 117–121 ☏971 380 003. At the end of the long line of restaurants flanking the south side of the harbour, this place does fabulous seafood, with main courses averaging around €15.

La Guitarra c/Nostra Senyora dels Dolors 1 ☏971 381 355. Located a short walk from the cathedral, this is arguably the best restaurant in town, featuring the very best of Menorcan cuisine with main courses – anything from seafood to lamb – averaging a very reasonable €9. The restaurant occupies an old cellar, whose stone walls sport a scattering of agricultural antiques. Closed Sun.

El Horno c/Forn 12 ☏971 380 767. French-style basement restaurant near the northeast corner of Plaça d'es Born, with good and reasonably priced food. Open evenings only.

La Payesa c/Marina 65 ☏971 380 021. Popular tourist restaurant with a wide-ranging menu, featuring everything from pizzas through omelettes to seafood. Very child-friendly.

Bars and clubs

Asere c/Pere Capllonch s/n. Ciutadella's busiest nightspot, offering a mix of Cuban music and tropical cocktails, this late-night tourist bar tunnels into the cliffside beside the harbour – it's at the foot of the steps near the bridge.

Bar Es Molí Camí de Maó 1. Housed in the Moli d'es Comte, the old windmill across the street from Plaça Alfons III, this is a noisy and gritty café-bar, with a (very) young Menorcan crowd. Open till 1am.

Jazzbah Plaça de Sant Joan 3 Live jazz concerts are held here, from time to time, all year round. A chill-out terrace and alternative rock and world music complete the scene. Open from 10pm to 6am.

Lateral Plaça de Sant Joan s/n. The best established of this lively square's various nightspots – there are several other places nearby, though they come and go on a yearly basis.

Tony's Bar Cala Blanca s/n. A music café till the wee hours, but always good for a drink any time,

coffee or one of their popular cocktails. Located out of town to the south. Daily 4pm-4am.

Unger Madison c/Sant Joan 8. Near Plaça Artrutx, this is the chicest bar in town, with angular wooden tables, soft lighting, modern paintings and a first-rate selection of domestic and imported wines. Open Mon–Fri from 6pm till early in the morning, Sat from 8pm; closed Sun.

Listings

Banks Banca March, at Plaça d'es Born 10 and Plaça Alfons III, 5; and Sa Nostra, c/Maó 2, on Plaça Nova.

Bicycle and moped rental Bicicletas Salord, c/Sant Isidre 32, off Plaça Artrutx (℡971 381 576).

Car rental The most centrally located car rental company is Betacar, on the ring road at Avinguda Jaume I El Conqueridor 59 (℡971 382 998).

Email and internet access Café Internet, Plaça dels Pins 37 (€3.75 per hour).

Ferries and catamarans Balearia (℡902 160 180, ⓦwww.balearia.net/eng) operate an inter-island fast-ferry catamaran service during the summer from Port d'Alcúdia, on Mallorca, to Ciutadella (one-way passenger fares from €50, cars from €100); Iscomar (℡902 119 128,

ⓦwww.iscomar.com) operates a car ferry service on the same route once or twice daily, with the one-way passenger fare costing €31, vehicles up to 4.5m in length €51. The journey time is two to two and a half hours. Local car rental firms do not allow their vehicles to travel from Mallorca to Menorca or vice versa.

Maps and books Both Punt i Apart, c/Roser 14, and Libreria Pau, c/Nou de Juliol 23, have a reasonably good selection of travel books, general maps and Menorcan walking maps from the IGN series.

Pharmacies Amongst several downtown options, there's one at Plaça Nova 2.

Post office The main *correu* is handily located at Plaça d'es Born 8 (Mon–Fri 8.30am–2.30pm, Sat 9.30am–1pm).

Around Ciutadella

The diverse attractions of **west Menorca** are within easy striking distance of Ciutadella, beginning with one of the island's finest prehistoric remains, the **Naveta d'es Tudons**, located beside the C721 just east of town. Alternatively, it's southeast across the island's rural interior to the pristine cove **beaches** that notch the southern shore. There are several delightful spots to choose from, including the appealing **Cala des Talaier** and beautiful **Cala Turqueta**. As is common hereabouts, each of these coves is on private land, which means that there's a modest charge to get onto the beach, and the landowner prohibits access during the winter. There's no such restriction to the northeast of Ciutadella at the smart villa-village of **Cala Morell**, though this occupies a singularly bleak and barren cove northeast of town, and there's no sand – only brownish grit.

Entirely different is the intensively developed **west coast**, where long lines of villas carpet the flat and treeless seashore on either side of Ciutadella, from **Cala en Forcat** and **Els Delfins** in the north to the **Cap d'Artrutx**, 14km away to the south. By and large, this is all pretty dreadful, a remorseless suburban sprawl that is ugly and dull in equal measure. Here and there, however, the villas bunch round narrow coves to form reasonably pleasant resorts. The pick of these is **Cala Blanca**, which also possesses a recommendable hotel where there's a reasonable chance of a room in high season.

From May to October, **buses** leave Ciutadella's Plaça dels Pins for the tourist settlements of the west coast hourly and there's a reasonably regular winter service too; see p.263 for more details. There are, however, no buses northeast from town towards Cala Morell or southeast towards Cala Turqueta; buses to Maó pass by the Naveta d'es Tudons regularly, but check the driver is prepared to stop and let you off near the site.

The Naveta d'es Tudons and Torrellafuda

The best-preserved *naveta* on the island, the **Naveta d'es Tudons**, can be found in a field to the east of Ciutadella, approximately 5km along the C721, then five minutes' walk from the roadside car park – but be aware that the sign is easy to miss. Seven metres high and fourteen long, the *naveta* is made of massive stone blocks slotted together using a sophisticated dry-stone technique. The narrow entrance on the west side leads into a small antechamber, which was once sealed off by a stone slab; beyond lies the main chamber where the bones of the dead were stashed away after the flesh had been removed. Folkloric memories of the *navetas*' original purpose survived into modern times – Menorcans were loathe to go near these odd-looking and solitary monuments until well into the nineteenth century.

If your enthusiasm for prehistory has been fired, you should also take in **Torrellafuda**, where a broken *taula* stands in the shadow of olive trees abutting a particularly well-preserved *talayot*. There are Cyclopean walls here too, but it's the setting that appeals as much as the remains, with the site encircled by fertile farmland – a perfect spot for a picnic. To get here, look out for the sign on the C721 about 2.5km east of Naveta d'es Tudons. Turn down the lane, bump the 800m to the car park, from where it's a couple of minutes' walk.

Back on the C721, it's another 600m or so to the signed turning that leads to a third (vaguely) noteworthy Talayotic site, **Torretrencada**, where a wind-scoured *taula* stands surrounded by dry-stone walls and the scant remains of a prehistoric stone circle.

South of Ciutadella

Beginning at the traffic island on c/Alfons V, the cross-country **Camí de Sant Joan de Missa** runs southeast from Ciutadella to the remote coves of the south coast. After about 3km, you reach the clearly marked farmhouse of **Son Vivó**, where the road branches into two, with each (signposted) **fork** leading to several south-coast beaches, the nearest of which are about 8km away from town. Both roads are in (fairly) good condition and the signs are (usually) easy to follow, but the beaches mentioned below are all on private land and access is only permitted in the summer at a cost of about €5 per person. In all cases, the last stretch of the journey is a five- to ten-minute walk down to the beach from a parking lot, though this is hardly a hardship. Incidentally, if you've rented a moped be prepared for a bumpy ride and watch out for the dust and muck churned up by passing cars.

South to Cala des Talaier and Cala Turqueta

Taking the more easterly road from the Son Vivó fork, you arrive after about 1.5km at the **Ermita de St Joan de Missa**, a squat, brightly whitewashed church with a dinky little bell tower. There's a fork here too, but the signs are easy to follow and you keep straight, with the road slicing across the countryside, before swerving round the **Marjal Vella farmhouse**. Shortly afterwards, about 3.7km from the church, the road passes the metal gate that marks the start of the two-kilometre-long, privately owned lane leading to the **Cala des**

Talaier, where a tiny strip of pale sand is backed by pine trees and overlooked by a ruined watchtower.

Back on the road, it's a further 600m or so to the start of the one-kilometre-long private lane that leads down to the little dell behind **Cala Turqueta**, a lovely cove flanked by wooded limestone cliffs. The beach consists of a sheltered horseshoe of white sand sloping gently into the sea, making it ideal for bathing, and because there are no facilities it's most unusual to find a crowd. If you've driven, it costs €5 to park.

Son Catlar and Platges Son Saura

Back at the Son Vivó fork, it's 3km along the more westerly road to **Son Catlar**, the largest prehistoric settlement on Menorca and one which was still expanding when the Romans arrived in force in 123 BC. The most impressive feature of this Talayotic village is its extraordinary stone wall, originally three metres high and made of massive blocks – the square towers were added later. Inside the walls, however, all is confusion. The widely scattered remains are largely incomprehensible and only the *taula* compound and the five battered *talayots* make any sense.

Pushing on south, the asphalt peters out around 1.5km further down the road, just before you reach the ornate gateway that bars the entrance to the **Torre Saura farmhouse**. At the farmhouse, there's a privately owned parking lot on the left and from here a two-kilometre-long trail leads down to a wide horseshoe-shaped cove that shelters two beaches, the **Platges Son Saura**. Sometimes visitors are allowed to drive down the trail, sometimes not, but it's difficult going, especially after rain. The west side of the cove is more exposed and is often sticky with seaweed, so aim for the more sheltered eastern side where a wide arc of white sand is fringed by pines.

South to Cap d'Artrutx

Heading south from Ciutadella along the main coastal road, you're soon amongst the interminable villa complexes that extend almost without interruption as far as **Cap d'Artrutx**, at the southwest tip of the island. This is all rather depressing, but, amidst the aesthetic gloom, the resort of **CALA BLANCA** does at least possess a modicum of charm, its low limestone seacliffs framing a narrow cove and a small sandy beach. The swimming is safe and the beach has all the usual resort facilities, including a bar and water-ski-, lounger- and pedalo-rental. For somewhere to stay, there's little to choose between several sky-rise **hotels**, but the package-dominated *Mediterrani* probably has the edge, with spacious balconied and air-conditioned rooms just seconds away from the beach (℡971 384 203, ℻971 386 162; ❻; closed Nov–April).

Northeast of Ciutadella

Signposted from the C721 on the outskirts of Ciutadella, a well-surfaced country lane carves northeast across a pastoral landscape to the small tourist settlement of **CALA MORELL**, just 8km from Ciutadella. This is one of the island's more refined *urbanitzacions*, its streets – named in Latin after the constellations – hugging a narrow and rocky bay. Besides swimming off the gritty beach, you can visit some of the man-made caves for which Cala Morell is noted, visible beside the road as you approach the village. Dating from the late Bronze and Iron Ages, the caves form one of the largest prehistoric necropolises known in Europe, and are surprisingly sophisticated, with central pillars supporting the roofs, and, in some instances, windows cut into the rock and classical designs carved in relief. No one owns the caves, so there's unlimited access – just scramble up from the road. The sight of one or two is sufficient for most visitors, but if you're after more than a glimpse, bring a torch.

Backtracking along the country lane from Cala Morell, it's about 3km to the signed intersection. A narrow side road forks east from here across farmland to reach – after 2.5km – a guarded gate, where the landowner levies €5 for the one-kilometre onward drive down to **Cala d'Algaiarens**. Backed by attractive dunes and pine forests, the two sandy cove beaches here offer excellent swimming in sheltered waters.

Travel details

Buses

Ciutadella to: Alaior (6–7 daily; 40min); Cala Blanca (11–20 daily; 10min); Cala d'en Focat (13–23 daily; 10min); Cap d'Artuxt (Mon–Sat 5 daily; 15min); Es Mercadal (6–7 daily; 30min); Ferreries (6–7 daily; 20min); Maó (6–7 daily; 1hr) Sant Tomàs (Mon–Sat 2–3 daily; 45min).
Es Mercadal to: Fornells (May–Oct Mon–Sat 1–2 daily; Nov–April 4 weekly; 15min); Maó (6–7 daily; 30min);
Es Migjorn Grand to: Ferreries (3–4 daily; 10min); Maó (4–6 daily; 30min).
Ferreries to: Alaior (6–7 daily; 20min); Cala Santa Galdana (May–Oct 13 daily; 20min); Ciutadella (6–7 daily; 20min); Es Mercadal (6–7 daily; 10min); Es Migjorn Gran (3–4 daily; 10min); Maó (6–7 daily; 40min).
Fornells to: Es Mercadal (May–Oct Mon–Sat 1–2 daily; Nov–April 4 weekly; 15min); Maó (May–Oct Mon–Sat 5 daily; Nov–April 4 weekly; 35min).
Maó to: Alaior (Mon–Sat 12 daily, 6 on Sun; 20min); Arenal d'en Castell (Mon–Sat 5 daily; 25min); Ciutadella (6–7 daily; 1hr); Es Mercadal (6–7 daily; 30min); Es Migjorn Gran (4–6 daily; 30min); Ferreries (6–7 daily; 40min); Fornells (May–Oct Mon–Sat 5 daily; Nov–April 4 weekly; 35min); Punta Prima (8–9 daily; 15min); Sant Tomàs (Mon–Sat 2–3 daily; 45min); Son Bou (Mon–Sat 5 daily; 40min); Son Parc (Mon–Sat 5 daily; 40min).

Contexts

Contexts

History

The earliest inhabitants of the Balearics seem to have reached the islands from the Iberian peninsula, and carbon-dating of remains indicates that human occupation was well established by 4000 BC. The discovery of pottery, flints and animal horns fashioned into tools suggests that these early people were **Neolithic pastoralists**, who supplemented their food supplies by hunting, particularly the *Myotragus balearicus*, a species of mountain goat now extinct. Hundreds of these animals' skulls have been discovered and several are exhibited in the islands' larger museums. The frequency of these finds has encouraged some experts to assert that the *Myotragus* was domesticated, the principal evidence being the remains of what might be crude corrals found on the coast of Mallorca near Valldemossa; this assertion is, however, strongly contested.

Why, or how, these Neolithic peoples moved to the Balearic Islands is unknown. Indeed, the first landfall may have been accidental, made by early seafarers travelling along the shores of the Mediterranean – part of a great wave of migration that is known to have taken place in the Neolithic period. Many of the oldest archeological finds have been discovered in natural **caves**, where it seems likely that these early settlers first sought shelter and protection. Later, cave complexes were dug out of the soft limestone that occurs on both islands, comprising living quarters, usually circular and sometimes with a domed ceiling, as well as longer, straighter funerary chambers. The best example is at the resort of **Cala Morell** (see p.263). These complexes represent the flourishing of what is commonly called the **Balearic Cave Culture**.

The Balearic cave dwellers soon came into regular contact with other cultures; the Mediterranean, with its relatively calm and tide-free waters, has always acted as a conduit of civilization. The discovery of Beaker ware at Deià indicates one of the earliest of these outside influences. The **Beaker People**, whose artefacts have been found right across Western Europe, are named after their practice of burying their dead with pottery beakers. They had knowledge of the use of bronze, an alloy of copper and tin, and they exported their bronze-working skills into the Balearics in around 1400 BC. This technological revolution marked the end of the cave culture and the beginning of the Talayotic period.

The Talayotic period

The megalithic remains of the **Talayotic period**, which extended almost to the Christian era, are strewn all over Mallorca and Menorca – though, surprisingly, there's no evidence of them on Ibiza. The structure that gives its name to the period is the **talayot**, a cone-shaped tower with a circular base, between five and ten metres in height (for more on Talayotic remains, see p.222). Although the original purpose of these talayots remains unknown, it is clear that by 1000 BC a relatively sophisticated, largely pastoral society had developed on both Mallorca and Menorca, with at least some of the islanders occupying the walled settlements that still dot the interior. The three best examples are **Capocorb Vell** (see p.205), south of Llucmajor on Mallorca, where you can still inspect four *talayots* and the remains of up to thirty houses, **Ses Paisses** (see p.184), a settlement of comparable proportions outside Artà, and Menorca's **Son Catlar** (see p.262), not far from Ciutadella. All three were occupied well into the Roman period.

Talayotic culture reached its highest level of development on Menorca, and it's here you'll find the most enigmatic remains of the period. These are the **taulas** ("tables" in Catalan), T-shaped structures standing as high as four metres and consisting of two massive dressed stones. Their purpose is unknown, though many theories have been advanced. One early nineteenth-century writer suggested that they were altars used for human sacrifice, but unfortunately for this lurid theory, the height of most *taulas* makes it very unlikely. Other writers have noted that many *taulas* are surrounded by enclosures and have argued that the "T" formed the centre of a roofed structure, thatched in some way. Another theory is that the "T" was a stylized head of a bull, an animal that was venerated in many parts of the ancient Mediterranean, most notably in Minoan Crete. The idea that these enclosures had a religious purpose was supported by discoveries made during excavations of the *taula* enclosure of **Torralba d'en Salord** (see p.241), where archeologists discovered animal remains and pottery in side recesses of fireplaces, and concluded that these must have been ritual offerings. They also found a bronze sculpture of a bull, suggesting that cattle were, indeed, worshipped. Torralba d'en Salord is one of the many sites where *taulas* and *talayots* stand cheek by jowl. In many places, the remains are too broken down to be of much interest, but two other good spots are **Trepucó** (see p.221) and **Talatí de Dalt** (see p.221), both near Maó. Dating from around 1400 BC, Talatí de Dalt incorporates a *talayot*, a *taula* and several columned chambers or **hypostyles**. Partly dug out of the ground and roofed with massive slabs of stone, these hypostyles must have taken considerable effort to build, and may have been used for important gatherings, possibly of communal leaders.

The other distinctive structure to be found on Menorca is the **naveta**, made of roughly dressed dry-stone blocks and looking like an upturned bread tin. Dating from the beginning of the Talayotic period, the **Naveta d'es Tudons**, near Ciutadella (see p.261), is the finest example, but there are around thirty-five others sprinkled across the island. They were collective tombs, or, more correctly, ossuaries, where, after the flesh had been removed, the bones of the dead were placed along with some personal possessions such as jewellery, pottery and bone buttons.

Phoenicians, Greeks and Carthaginians

Fearful of attack from the sea, the islands' Talayotic peoples built their walled settlements a few kilometres inland. This pattern was, however, modified during the first millennium BC, when the Balearics became a staging post for the **Phoenicians**, maritime traders from the eastern Mediterranean whose long voyages reached as far as Cornwall in southwest England. According to the Roman historian Pliny, the Phoenicians established a large settlement at **Sanisera** on Menorca's north coast (see p.237), and archeologists have also discovered Phoenician artefacts at **Alcúdia** on Mallorca (see p.163). In general, however, very few Phoenician remains have been found on the Balearics – just a handful of bronze items, jewellery and pieces of coloured glass.

The Phoenicians were displaced by **Greeks** from around 800 BC, as several city-states explored the western Mediterranean in search of trade and potential colonies. Like the Phoenicians, the Greeks appear to have used the Balearics primarily as a staging post, for no Greek buildings have survived on either Mallorca or Menorca. The absence of metal apparently made the islands unsuitable for long-term colonization, and the belligerence of the native population may have played a part too: the Greeks coined the islands' name, the "**Balearics**", which they derived from *ballein*, meaning "to throw from a sling". The islanders were adept at this form of warfare, and many early visitors were repelled with showers of polished sling-stones (though some historians dispute this theory, claiming rather that the name comes from the Baleri tribe of Sardinia).

The Greeks were also discouraged from colonization by the growth of the **Carthaginian** empire across the western Mediterranean. The Phoenicians had established Carthage, on the North African coast, under the leadership of the princess Elissa (better known as Dido, the tragic hero of Virgil's *Aeneid*). According to the Greek historian Diodorus Siculus, the Carthaginians began to colonize the Balearics in the early seventh century BC, and the islands were firmly under their control by the beginning of the third century BC, if not earlier. Little is known of the Carthaginian occupation except that they established several new settlements. It is also claimed that the famous Carthaginian general, Hannibal, was born on Cabrera island off Mallorca, though Ibiza and Malta claim this honour too.

In the third century BC, the expansion of the Carthaginian empire across the Mediterranean and up into the Iberian Peninsula triggered two **Punic Wars** with Rome. In both of these wars the Balearics proved extremely valuable, first as stepping stones from the North African coast to the European mainland and second as a source of mercenaries. Balearic slingers were highly valued and accompanied Hannibal and his elephants across the Alps in the Second Punic War, when (for reasons that remain obscure) the islanders refused gold and demanded payment in wine and women instead. After Hannibal's defeat by the Romans at the battle of Zama in 202 BC, Carthaginian power began to wane and they withdrew from Mallorca and Menorca, although they continued to have some influence over Ibiza for at least another seventy years.

Romans, Vandals and Byzantines

As the Carthaginians retreated so the **Romans** advanced, incorporating Ibiza within their empire after the final victory over Carthage in 146 BC. On Mallorca and Menorca, the islanders took advantage of the prolonged military chaos to profit from piracy, until finally, in 123 BC, the Romans, led by the consul Quintus Metellus, restored maritime order by occupying both islands. These victories earned Metellus the title "Balearico" from the Roman senate and two of the islands were given new names, Balearis Major (Mallorca) and Balearis Minor (Menorca).

For the next five hundred years all of the Balearics Islands were part of the **Roman Empire**. Amongst many developments, Roman colonists introduced viticulture, turning the Balearics into a wine-exporting area, and initiated olive-oil production from newly planted groves. As was their custom, the Romans consolidated their control of the islands by building roads and establishing towns. On Mallorca, they founded Pollentia (Alcúdia) in the north and Palmaria on the south coast, near the site of modern Palma, whilst on Menorca they developed Port Magonum (Maó) as an administrative centre, while Sanisera – previously the site of a Phoenician trading post – became an important port. Initially, the Balearics were part of the Roman province of Tarraconensis (Tarragona), but in 404 AD the islands became a province in their own right with the name **Balearica**.

By this time, however, the Roman Empire was in decline, its defences unable to resist the westward-moving tribes of central Asia. One of these tribes, the **Vandals**, swept across the Balearics in around 425 AD, thereby ending Roman rule. So thoroughgoing was the destruction they wrought that very few signs of the Romans have survived – the only significant remains are those of Pollentia at Alcúdia (see p.165).

The Vandals had been Christianized long before they reached the Mediterranean, but they were followers of the **Arian** sect. This interpretation of Christianity, founded by Arius, an Alexandrian priest, insisted that Christ the Son and God the Father were two distinct figures, not elements of the Trinity. To orthodox Christians, this seemed dangerously close to the pagan belief in a multiplicity of gods and, by the end of the fourth century AD, Arianism had been forcibly extirpated within the Roman Empire. However, the sect continued to flourish amongst the Germanic peoples of the Rhine, including the Vandals, who, armed with their "heretical" beliefs, had no religious truck with their new Balearic subjects, persecuting them and destroying their churches. As a consequence, only a handful of Christian remains from this period have survived, primarily the ruins of the basilica at **Son Bou** (see p.242).

In 533 the Vandals were defeated in North Africa by the Byzantine general Count Belisarius (who was the subject of a novel by one of Mallorca's adopted sons, Robert Graves). This brought the Balearics under **Byzantine** rule and, for a time, restored prosperity and stability. However, the islands were too far removed from Constantinople to be of much imperial importance and, when the empire was threatened from the east at the end of the seventh century, they were abandoned in all but name.

The Moors

As the influence of Byzantium receded, so militarized Islam moved in from the south and east to fill the vacuum. In 707–8 the **Moors** of North Africa conducted an extended raid against Mallorca, destroying its entire fleet and carrying away slaves and booty. By 716 the Balearics' position had become even more vulnerable with the completion of the Moorish conquest of Spain. In 798 the Balearics were again sacked by the Moors – who were still more interested in plunder than settlement – and in desperation the islanders appealed for help to **Charlemagne**, the Frankish Holy Roman Emperor. As emperor, Charlemagne was the military leader of Western Christendom (the pope was the spiritual leader), so the appeal signified the final severance of the Balearics' links with Byzantium and the East.

Charlemagne's attempt to protect the islands from the Moors met with some success, but the respite was only temporary. By the middle of the ninth century, the Christian position had deteriorated so badly that the Balearics were compelled to enter a non-aggression pact with the Moors, and, to add to the islanders' woes, the Balearics suffered a full-scale **Viking** raid in 859. Finally, at the beginning of the tenth century, the **Emir of Cordoba** conquered both Menorca and Mallorca. Moorish rule lasted over three hundred years, though internal political divisions among the Muslims meant that the islands experienced several different regimes. In the early eleventh century, the emirate of Córdoba collapsed and control passed to the *wali* (governor) of Denia, on the Spanish mainland. This administration allowed the Christians – who were known as **Mozarabs** – to practise their faith, and the islands prospered from their position at the heart of the trade routes between North Africa and Islamic Spain.

In 1085 the Balearics became an independent emirate with a new dynasty of *walis*, from **Amortadha** in North Africa. They pursued a more aggressive foreign and domestic policy, raiding the towns of the mainland and persecuting their Christian citizens. These actions blighted trade and thereby enraged the emergent city-states of Italy at a time when Christendom was fired by crusading zeal. Anticipating retaliation, the Amortadhas fortified Palma, which was known at this time as Medina Mayurka, and several mountain strongholds. The Christian attack came in 1114 when a grand Italian fleet – led by the ships of Pisa and supported by the pope as a mini-crusade – landed an army of 70,000 Catalan and Italian soldiers on Ibiza. The island was soon captured, but Mallorca, the crusaders' next target, proved a much more difficult proposition. The island's coastal defences proved impregnable, so the Christians assaulted the landward defences instead, the concentric lines of the fortifications forcing them into a long series of bloody engagements. When the city finally fell, the invaders took a bitter revenge, slaughtering most of the surviving Muslim population. However, despite their victory, the Christians had neither the will nor the resources to consolidate their position and, loading their vessels with freed slaves and loot, they returned home.

It took the Moors just two years to re-establish themselves on the islands, this time under the leadership of the **Almoravids**, a North African Berber tribe who had previously controlled southern Spain. The Almoravids proved to be tolerant and progressive rulers, and the Balearics prospered under them: agriculture improved, particularly through the development of irrigation, and trade expanded as commercial agreements were struck with the Italian cities of Genoa and Pisa. The Pisans – Crusaders earlier in the century – defied a papal ban on trade with Muslims to finalize the deal; consciences could, it seems, be flexible even in the "devout" Middle Ages when access to the precious goods of the east (silks, carpets and spices) was the prize.

Jaume I and the Reconquest

In 1203 the Almoravids were supplanted by the **Almohad** dynasty, who forcibly converted the islands' Christian population to Islam and started raiding the mainland. This was an extraordinary miscalculation, as the kingdoms of Aragón and Catalunya had recently been united, thereby strengthening the Christian position in this part of Spain. The unification was a major step in the changing balance of power: with their forces combined, the Christians were able to launch the **Reconquista**, which was eventually to drive the Moors from the entire peninsula. Part of the Christian jigsaw was the Balearics and, in 1228, the Emir of Mallorca imprudently antagonized the young **King Jaume I** of Aragón and Catalunya by seizing a couple of his ships. The king's advisers, with their eyes firmly fixed on the islands' wealth, determined to capitalize on the offence. They organized the first Balearic publicity evening, a feast at which the king was presented with a multitude of island delicacies and Catalan sailors told of the archipelago's prosperity. And so, insulted by the emir and persuaded by his nobility, Jaume I committed himself to a full-scale invasion.

Jaume's expedition of 150 ships, 16,000 men and 1500 horses set sail for Mallorca in September 1229. The king had originally planned to land at Pollença, in the northeast, but adverse weather conditions forced the fleet further south, and it eventually anchored off Sant Elm. The following day, the Catalans defeated the Moorish forces sent to oppose the landing and Jaume promptly pushed east, laying siege to Medina Mayurka. It took three months to breach the walls, but on December 31 the city finally fell and Jaume was hailed as **"El Conqueridor"**.

The cost of launching an invasion on this scale placed an enormous strain on the resources of a medieval monarch. With this in mind, Jaume subcontracted the capture of Ibiza, entering into an agreement in 1231 with the Crown Prince of Portugal, Don Pedro, and the Count of Roussillon. In return for the capture of the island, the count and the prince were to be allowed to divide Ibiza between themselves, provided they acknowledged the suzerainty of Jaume. This project initially faltered, but was revived with the addition of the Archbishop of Tarragona. The three allies captured Ibiza in 1235 and divided the spoils, although Don Pedro waived his rights and his share passed to Jaume.

In the meantime, Jaume had acquired the overlordship of Menorca. Unable to afford another full-scale invasion, the king devised a cunning ruse. In 1232 he returned to Mallorca with just three galleys, which he dispatched to Menorca carrying envoys, while he camped out in the mountains above Capdepera on Mallorca. As night fell and his envoys negotiated with the enemy, Jaume ordered the lighting of as many bonfires as possible to illuminate the sky and give the impression of a vast army. The strategem worked and the next day, mindful of the bloodbath following the invasion of Mallorca, the Menorcan Moors capitulated. According to the king's own account, they informed his envoys that "they gave great thanks to God and to me for the message I had sent them for they knew well they could not long defend themselves against me". The terms of submission were generous: the Moors handed over Ciutadella, their principal settlement, and a number of other strongpoints, but Jaume acknowledged the Muslims as his subjects and appointed one of their leaders as his *rais* (governor).

The retention of Moorish government in Menorca, albeit under the suzerainty of the king, was in marked contrast to events on Mallorca. Here, the land was divided into eight blocs, with four passing to the king and the rest to his most trusted followers, who leased their holdings in the feudal fashion, granting land to tenants in return for military service. In 1230 Jaume consolidated his position by issuing the **Carta de Població** (People's Charter), guaranteeing equality before the law, an extremely progressive precept for the period. Furthermore, Mallorca was exempted from taxation to encourage Catalan immigration, and special rights were given to Jews resident on the island, a measure designed to stimulate trade. Twenty years later, Jaume also initiated a distinctive form of government for Mallorca, with a governing body of six **jurats** (adjudicators) – one from the nobility, two knights, two merchants and one peasant. At the end of each year the *jurats* elected their successors. This form of government remained in place until the sixteenth century.

From a modern perspective, the downside of the Reconquest of Mallorca was the wholesale demolition of almost all Moorish buildings, with mosques systematically replaced by churches (at a later date the same policy was followed on Menorca). The main compensation is the architectural magnificence of **Palma Cathedral** (see p.65), which was consecrated in 1269. Shortly afterwards, Jaume I died at Valencia. In his will he divided his kingdom between his two sons: Pedro received Catalunya, Aragón and Valencia, whilst **Jaume II** was bequeathed Montpellier, Roussillon and the Balearics. Jaume II was crowned in Mallorca on September 12, 1276.

The Balearic Kingdom

Jaume I's division of his kingdom infuriated **Pedro**, as the Balearics stood astride the shipping route between Barcelona and Sicily, where his wife was queen. He forced his brother to become his vassal, but in response Jaume II secretly schemed with the French. Predictably enough, Pedro soon discovered his brother's treachery and promptly set about planning a full-blooded invasion. However, Pedro died before the assault could begin and it was left to his son, **Alfonso III**, to carry out his father's plans. Late in 1285, Alfonso's army captured Palma without too much trouble, which was just as well for its inhabitants: wherever Alfonso met with resistance – as he did later in the campaign at the castle of Alaró – he extracted a brutal revenge. Indeed, even by the standards of thirteenth-century Spain, Alfonso was considered excessively violent and the pope excommunicated him for his atrocities – but not for long.

With Mallorca secured and Jaume deposed, Alfonso turned his attention to Menorca where he suspected the loyalty of the Moorish governor – the *rais* was allegedly in conspiratorial contact with the Moors of North Africa. Alfonso's army landed on Menorca in January 1287 and decisively defeated the Moors just outside Maó. The Moors retreated to the hilltop fortress of Santa Agueda, but their resistance didn't amount to much and the whole island was Alfonso's within a few days. The king's treatment of the vanquished islanders was savage: those Muslims who were unable to buy their freedom were enslaved, and those who couldn't work as slaves – the old, the sick and the very young – were taken to sea and thrown overboard. Alfonso rewarded the nobles who had accompanied him with grants of land and brought in hundreds of Catalan settlers. The capital, Medina Minurka, was renamed **Ciutadella**, and the island's mosques were converted to Christian usage, before being demolished and replaced.

Alfonso's violent career was cut short by his death in 1291 at the age of 25. His successor was his brother, Jaume, also the king of Sicily. A more temperate man, Jaume conducted negotiations through the papacy that eventually led, in 1298, to the restoration of the partition envisaged by Jaume I: he himself presided over Catalunya, Aragón and Valencia, while his exiled uncle, **Jaume II**, ruled as king of Mallorca and Menorca. Restored to the crown, Jaume II devoted a great deal of time to improving the commerce and administration of the Balearics. To stimulate trade, he established a weekly market in Palma, reissued the currency in gold and silver, and founded a string of inland towns, including Manacor, Felanitx, Llucmajor and Binissalem on Mallorca and Alaior and Es Mercadal on Menorca. Jaume II attended to God as well as Mammon, and his reign saw the building of many churches and monasteries. In the same vein, the king also patronized the Mallorcan poet, scholar and Franciscan friar, **Ramon Llull** (see p.77 and p.179), providing him with the finance to establish a monastic school near Valldemossa. Perhaps his most important act, though, was to grant Menorca its own **Carta de Població**, which bestowed the same legal rights as the Mallorcans enjoyed.

On his death in 1311, Jaume was succeeded by his asthmatic son, **Sancho**, who spent most of his time in his palace at Valldemossa, where the mountain air was to his liking. Nonetheless, he did his job well, continuing the successful economic policies of his father and strengthening his fleet to protect his territories from North African pirates. Mallorca and Menorca boomed. Mallorca in particular had long served as the entrepôt between North Africa and Europe, its warehouses crammed with iron, figs, salt, oil and slaves, but in the early fourteenth century its industries flourished too, primarily shipbuilding and textiles. In 1325, the traveller Ramón Muntaner praised Palma as an "honoured city of greater wealth than any with the most businesslike inhabitants . . . of any city in the world." He may have been exaggerating, but not by much, and Palma's merchants were certainly inventive: spotting a gap in the market they went into **crossbow-making** and by 1380 they were exporting them by the boat-load.

Internationally, Sancho worked hard to avoid entanglement in the growing antagonism between Aragón and France, but the islands' future still looked decidedly shaky when he died without issue in 1324. Theoretically, the islands should have passed to Aragón, but the local nobility moved fast to crown Sancho's ten-year-old nephew as **Jaume III**. Hoping to forestall Aragonese hostility, they then had him betrothed to the king of Aragón's five-year-old daughter, though in the long term this marriage did the new king little good. After he came of age, Jaume III's relations with his brother-in-law, Pedro IV of Aragón, quickly deteriorated, and Pedro successfully invaded the Balearics in response to an alleged plot against him. Jaume fled to his mainland possessions and sold Montpellier to the French to raise money for an invasion. He landed on Mallorca in 1349, but was no match for Pedro and was defeated and killed on the outskirts of Llucmajor. His son, the uncrowned **Jaume IV**, was also captured and although he eventually escaped, he was never able to drum up sufficient support to threaten the Aragonese.

Unification with Spain

For a diversity of reasons the **unification** of the Balearics with Aragón – and their subsequent incorporation within Spain – proved a disaster. In particular, the mainland connection meant that the islands' nobility soon gravitated towards the Aragonese court, regarding their local estates as little more than sources of income to sustain their expensive lifestyles. More fundamentally, general economic trends moved firmly against the islands. After the fall of Constantinople to the Turks in 1453, the lucrative overland trade routes from the eastern Mediterranean to the Far East were blocked and, just as bad, it was the Portuguese who discovered the way around the Cape of Good Hope to the Indies. In 1479, **Fernando V of Aragón** married **Isabella I of Castile**, thereby uniting the two largest kingdoms in Spain, but yet again this was bad news for the islanders. The union brought mainland preoccupations and a centralized bureaucracy, which rendered the islands a provincial backwater – even more so when, following Columbus's reaching the Americas in 1492, the focus of European trade moved from the Mediterranean to the Atlantic seaboard almost at a stroke. The last commercial straw was the royal decree that

---

The Jews in Mallorcan history

In 1391, crowds marched on Palma to object to heavy Aragonese taxation and absentee landlords; failing to find satisfaction, they instead vented their spleen on the city's **Jews**, massacring three hundred of them. Mallorca's large Jewish community, concentrated in Palma and Inca, had long played a crucial part in maintaining the island's money supply and supporting trade with North Africa, but they were treated in that strangely contradictory manner which was common across much of medieval Europe, alternately courted and discriminated against. They were, for instance, expected to live in their own ghettos and wear a distinctive type of dress, but were allowed (unlike their Christian neighbours) to divorce and re-marry. Predictably, they were often blamed for things over which they had no control, from famine to plague, and were intermittently subjected to pogroms like this one in 1395 and again in 1435 (see p.76). They were also subject to the attentions of the **Holy Office of the Inquisition**, which set up shop in Palma in 1484 determined to impose orthodoxy on all of the island's citizenry. The Inquisitors bore down on the Jews, most of whom either left or chose the course of least resistance and converted to Christianity, though a small percentage were burnt to death. As late as the 1970s, the descendants of these converts still formed a distinct group of Palma gold- and silversmiths.

forbade Catalunya and the Balearics from trading with the New World. By the start of the sixteenth century, the Balearics were starved of foreign currency, and the islands' merchants had begun to leave, signalling a period of long-term economic decline.

Sixteenth-century decline

Political and economic difficulties destabilized the islands' social structures. As scapegoats, the **Jews** focused some of the swirling antagonisms that perturbed sixteenth-century Mallorca, but there were many other signs of discontent. The aristocracy was divided into warring factions, the country districts were set against the towns, and perhaps most destabilizing of all were high taxes and an unreliable grain supply. In Mallorca, this turbulence coalesced in an **armed uprising** of peasants and artisans in 1521. Organized in a *Germania*, or armed brotherhood, the insurrectionists seized control of Palma, whose nobles beat a hasty retreat to the safety of either Palma's Castell de Bellver or the Alcúdia citadel – those who didn't move fast enough were slaughtered in the streets. The rebels soon captured the Bellver, and polished off the blue-bloods who had sought protection there, but Alcúdia held out until relieved. It was a long wait: only in 1523 did the forces of authority return under the command of **Emperor Charles V**, king of Spain, Habsburg Holy Roman Emperor and the grandson of Fernando and Isabella. Charles negotiated generous terms for the surrender of Palma, but once in possession of the city, promptly broke the agreement and ordered the execution of five hundred of the rebels, who were duly hung, drawn and quartered.

The Balearics witnessed other sixteenth-century horrors with the renewal of large-scale **maritime raids** from North Africa. This upsurge of piratical activity was partly stimulated by the final expulsion of the Moors from Spain in 1492, and partly by the emergence of the Ottoman Turks as a Mediterranean superpower. Muslim raiders ransacked Pollença (1531 and 1550), Alcúdia (1551), Valldemossa (1552), Andratx (1553) and Sóller (1561), whilst the Ottoman admiral Khair ed-Din, better known as **Barbarossa**, ravaged Menorca's Maó after a three-day siege in 1535. Hundreds of Menorcans were enslaved and carted off, prompting Charles V to construct the fort of Sant Felip to guard Maó harbour. Two decades later, the Turks returned and sacked Ciutadella, taking a further three thousand prisoners – about eighty percent of the city's population. Muslim incursions continued until the seventeenth century, but declined in frequency and intensity after a combined Italian and Spanish force destroyed the Turkish fleet at **Lepanto** in 1571.

British and French occupation

The Balearics' woes continued throughout the seventeenth century. Trade remained stagnant and the population declined, a sorry state of affairs that was exacerbated by continued internal tensions. Palma, in particular, was plagued by **vendettas** between its aristocratic families, with the Canavall and Canavant factions regularly involved in street battles and assassinations, whilst the (often absentee) landowners failed to invest in their estates. By the 1630s the population problem had become so critical that Philip IV exempted the islands from the levies that raised men for Spain's armies – though this gain was offset by the loss of 15,000 Mallorcans to the **plague** in 1652.

A new development was the regular appearance of **British** vessels in the Mediterranean, a corollary of Britain's increasing share of the region's seaborne trade and the Royal Navy's commitment to protect its merchantmen from Algerian pirates. The British didn't have much use for Mallorca, and largely ignored it, but they were impressed by Maó's splendid harbour, a secure and sheltered deep-water anchorage where they first put in to take on water in 1621. Forty years later, Charles II of England formalized matters by instructing his ambassador to Spain to "request immediate permission for British ships to use Balearic ports and particularly Port Mahon". The Spanish king granted the request, and the advantages were noted by a poetic British seaman, a certain John Baltharpe:

Good this same is upon Minork
For shipping very useful 'gainst the Turk.
The King of Spain doth to our King it lend,
As in the line above to that same end.

For a time the British were simply content to "borrow" Maó, but their expanding commercial interests prompted a yearning for a more permanent arrangement. It was the dynastic **War of the Spanish Succession** (1701–14), fought over the vacant throne of Spain, which gave them their opportunity. A British force **invaded Menorca** in 1708 and, meeting tepid resistance, captured the island in a fortnight. Apart from the benefits of Maó harbour, Menorca was also an ideal spot from which to blockade the French naval base at Toulon, thereby preventing the union of the French Atlantic and Mediterranean fleets. Indeed, so useful was Menorca to the British that they negotiated its retention at the **Treaty of Utrecht**, which rounded off the war.

Menorca's first British governor, **Sir Richard Kane**, was an energetic and capable man who strengthened Menorca as a military base, and worked hard at improving the administration of the island, its civilian facilities and economy. He built the first **road** across the island from Maó to Ciutadella and introduced improved strains of seed and livestock. During the first forty years of British occupation, the production of wine, vegetables and chickens increased by 500 percent. Relations between the occupying power and the islanders were generally good – though the Catholic clergy no doubt found it difficult to stomach the instruction to "pray for His Britannic Majesty".

The first phase of British domination ended when the **French** captured Menorca in 1756 at the start of the **Seven Years War**. Admiral Byng was dispatched to assist the beleaguered British force, but, after a lacklustre encounter with a French squadron, he withdrew, leaving the British garrison with no option but to surrender. Byng's indifferent performance cost him his life: he was court-martialled and executed for cowardice, prompting Voltaire's famous aphorism that the English shoot their admirals "pour encourager les autres". The new French governor built the township of **Sant Lluís** (see p.229) to house his Breton sailors and, once again, the Menorcans adjusted to the occupying power without too much difficulty. In 1763, Britain regained Menorca in exchange for the Philippines and Cuba, which it had captured from France during the Seven Years War.

The **second period of British occupation** proved far less successful than the first. The governor from 1763 to 1782, General Johnston, was an authoritarian and unpopular figure who undermined the Menorcans' trust in the British. The crunch came in 1781, when, with Britain at war with both Spain and France, the Duc de Crillon landed on the island with 8000 soldiers. In command of a much smaller force, the new British governor, General John Murray, withdrew to the fort of Sant Felip, where he was beseiged for eight months. Succoured by the Menorcans, the Franco–Spanish army finally starved the British into submission; Murray's men were badly stricken with scurvy, and only 1120 survived. With the British vanquished, Menorca temporarily reverted to Spain.

The **third and final period of British rule** ran from 1798 to 1802, when the island was occupied for its value as a naval base in the Napoleonic Wars. Landing at Port d'Addaia, the British took just nine days – and suffered no casualties – in recapturing the island, helped in no small measure by the destruction of fort Sant Felip by the Spaniards in the mid-1780s. It seems that the Spanish high command did not believe they could defend the fortress, so they simply flattened it, thereby denying it to any colonial power – and, of course, making the island vulnerable in the process. The British finally relinquished all claims to Menorca in favour of Spain under the terms of the Treaty of Amiens in 1802.

Meanwhile **Mallorca**, lacking a harbour of any strategic significance, was having a much quieter time, though the islanders did choose the wrong side in the War of the Spanish Succession. Most of Spain favoured the French candidate, Philip of Anjou, but Catalunya and Mallorca preferred the Austrian Habsburg Charles III, who was supported by Britain and the Netherlands. Philip won, and promptly proceeded to strip the island of its title of kingdom and remove many of its historic rights. Otherwise, Mallorca was left pretty much untouched by the European conflicts that rippled around it during the early eighteenth century, but even so it did not prosper. Instead, it turned in on itself, becoming a caste- and priest-ridden backwater preoccupied with its own internal feuds. By the 1740s, however, this reactionary introspection was ruffled by more progressive elements, who, influenced by the **Enlightenment**, brought liberal and rationalist ideas into island society. Conservatives and Liberals came into prolonged conflict over Ramón Llull – the former keen to have him beatified, the latter eager to denigrate his complex mysticism. The traditionalists won, but the bitterness of the dispute combined with its length (1749–77) polarized the middle class and left Mallorcan society unstable. This failure to create a political discourse between rival factions mirrored developments in the rest of Spain, and both here and on the mainland instability was to define the nineteenth century.

One other major change was Madrid's edict pronouncing **Castilian** as the official language of the Balearics in place of the local dialect of Catalan.

The nineteenth century

For both Mallorca and Menorca, the nineteenth century brought difficult times. Neglected and impoverished outposts, they were subject to droughts, famines and epidemics of cholera, bubonic plague and yellow fever. Consequently, the islanders became preoccupied with the art of survival rather than politics, and generally stayed out of the **Carlist** wars between the liberals and the Conservatives which so bitterly divided the Spanish mainland. Many islanders emigrated, some to Algeria after it was acquired by the French in 1830, others to Florida and California. The leading political figure of the period was the historian **Josep Quadrodo**, who led the reactionary Catholic Union, which bombarded Madrid with petitions and greeted every Conservative success with enthusiastic demonstrations.

Matters began to improve towards the end of the nineteenth century, when agriculture, particularly almond cultivation, revived. Modern services, like gas and electricity, began to be installed and a regular steam packet link was established between Mallorca and the mainland. Menorca also developed a thriving export industry in footwear thanks to the entrepreneurial Don Jeronimo Cabrisas, a Menorcan who had made his fortune in Cuba, and later supplied many of the boots worn by the troops in World War I. Around this time too, a **revival of Catalan culture**, led by the middle classes of Barcelona, stirred the Balearic bourgeoisie. In Palma in particular, Catalunyan novelists and poets were lauded, Catalan political groupings were formed, and the town was adorned with a series of magnificent *Modernista* buildings.

Much less positively, Balearic society became bitterly divided between Conservatives and Liberals. This failure to create a political balance between rival factions mirrored developments in the rest of Spain, and both here and on the mainland, instability was to be the harbinger of the military coup that ushered in the right-wing dictatorship of General Primo de Rivera in 1923.

The Spanish Civil War

During the **Spanish Civil War** (1936–39), Mallorca and Menorca supported opposing sides. General Goded made Mallorca an important base for the Fascists, but when General Bosch attempted to do the same on Menorca, his NCOs and men mutinied and, with the support of the civilian population, declared their support for the Republic. In the event – apart from a few bombing raids and an attempted Republican landing at Porto Cristo (see p.192) – the Balearics saw very little actual fighting. Nevertheless, the Menorcans were dangerously exposed towards the end of the war, when they were marooned as the last Republican stronghold. A peaceful conclusion was reached largely through the intervention of the British, who brokered the surrender of the island aboard *HMS Devonshire*. Franco's troops occupied Menorca in April 1939 and the *Devonshire* left with 450 Menorcan refugees.

Modern Mallorca and Menorca

The most significant development in the Balearics since World War II has been the emergence of **mass tourism** as the principal economic activity, though Mallorca's charms had been discovered by the rich and famous long before. Frédéric Chopin and George Sand spent the winter of 1838–39 at Valldemossa (see p.125), and Edward VII and the German Kaiser regularly cruised the Balearics before World War I. The high-water mark of this elitist tourist trade was reached in the 1930s when the Argentinian poet Adan Diehl opened the *Hotel Formentor* (see p.160). Diehl advertised the hotel in lights on the Eiffel Tower and attracted guests such as Edward VIII, the Aga Khan and Winston Churchill. From such small and privileged beginnings, the Balearics' tourist industry mushroomed at an extraordinary rate after World War II. In 1950, Mallorca had just one hundred registered hotels and boarding houses; by 1972 the total had risen to over 1600; similarly, the number of visitors to Menorca rose from 1500 in 1961 to half a million in 1973.

The prodigious pace of development accelerated after the **death of Franco** in 1975, thereby further strengthening the local economy. One twist, however, was the relative price of real estate: traditionally, island landowners with coastal estates had given their younger children the poorer agricultural land near the seashore, but it was this land the developers wanted – and were prepared to pay fortunes for. Inevitably, this disrupted many a household, but the island's economy nevertheless continued to grow at an extraordinary rate. Indeed, the archipelago now has one of the highest per capita incomes in Spain, four times that of Extremadura for instance, and well above the EU average.

The Balearics also benefited from the political restructuring of Spain follow-ing the death of Franco. In 1978, the Spanish parliament, the Cortes, passed a new **constitution** which reorganized the country on a more federal basis and allowed for the establishment of regional Autonomous Communities. In prac-tice, the demarcation of responsibilities between central and regional govern-ments has proved problematic, leading to interminable wrangling, not least because the Socialists, who were in power from 1983 to 1996, waivered in their commitment to decentralization. Nonetheless, the Balearics, constituted as the **Comunidad Autónoma de las Islas Baleares** in 1983, have used their new-found independence to assert the primacy of their native Catalan language – now the main language of education – and to exercise a tighter local control of their economy.

From 1996 to 2000, this trend towards **decentralization** continued under a Conservative government which was only able to secure a majority in the Cortes with the support of several regionally based nationalist parties, includ-ing Basque, Catalan and Balearic groupings. Consequently, these regional groups were in a more powerful position than their numbers would otherwise justify, and were able to keep the momentum of decentralization going despite the innate centralist tendencies of the Madrid Conservatives. In particular, most government expenditure came under the control of the regions, and the Balearic administration used these resources to upgrade a string of holiday resorts and modernize much of the archipelago's infrastructure. In part, this reflected a particular concern with Ibiza and Mallorca's somewhat tacky image and was accompanied by the imposition of stricter building controls, a number of environmental schemes and the spending of millions of pesetas on refur-bishing the older, historical parts of Palma. On Menorca, the money also paid for the creation of a Parc Natural protecting the wetlands of S'Albufera d'es Grau and the adjacent coastline.

In addition, the Conservative-led Balearic administration made moves to curb tourist development, but in this they failed to keep pace with public sentiment – as exemplified by a string of large-scale **demonstrations** during 1998 and 1999. The demonstrations focused on four primary and inter-related concerns: the spiralling cost of real estate, foreign ownership of land (some twenty percent of Mallorca is now in foreign hands), untrammelled develop-ment and loutish behaviour in the cheaper resorts. This failure to keep abreast of popular feeling resulted in the defeat of the Conservatives in the **1999 regional elections** and their replacement by an unwieldy alliance of region-alists, socialists and greens committed to halting further tourist development in its tracks. As one of its spokesmen expressed it: "We need to dignify the tourist sector, not promote it as the cheapest in Europe with the idea that you can come here and do whatever you like." Faced with an annual influx of around eleven million holidaymakers, few islanders disagreed, and the coalition made significant progress, though they came unstuck when the tourist industry hit (comparatively) hard times in 2002 with an eight percent drop in the number of visitors. The main reason for the decline was the economic travails of Germany, but Balearic anxieties focused on the so-called **tourist tax** imposed by the regional government in May 2002. The idea was to impose a modest tax on every visitor over twelve years of age and spend the money – potentially about 30 million euros a year – on environmental improvements. However, the tourist industry created a huge hullabaloo that undermined the Balearic administration, and the Conservatives, who had pledged to rescind the tax, were returned to office in the regional elections of 2003. This was a major set-back for the environmentalist cause at a time when Spain's regionalists were already losing ground to Madrid. In March 2000, **José María Aznar** and his Conservatives won a second general election, but this time with an overall majority in the Cortes. No longer especially mindful of the regionalists, Aznar opposed the proposed tourist tax and was supportive of his fellow Balearic Conservatives in the run up to the 2003 elections. Given the demonstrations of 1998 and 1999, it seems unlikely that the new Balearic administration will be quite as gung-ho in its support of development as some of its conservative predecessors, but only time will tell. They are certainly cagey about being tied too closely with Aznar, as the next Spanish general election is due in 2004.

A chronology of Spanish history

C11th–5th BC	Phoenicians, Greeks and Celts invade Spain and inter-mingle with the native (Iberian) population.
C3rd BC	Carthaginians conquer southeast Spain, incorporating the region within their Mediterranean empire.
C3rd–2nd BC	Carthage and Rome wrestle for control of the Iberian Peninsula in the three Punic Wars. Rome wins all three and their final act is the destruction of Carthage (in present-day Tunisia) in 146 BC.
C2nd BC	Spain becomes part of the Roman Empire, its administrative capital established at Córdoba in 151 BC. The region's mines and granaries bring unprecedented prosperity, and roads, bridges and aqueducts are built to network the peninsula.
C1st AD	Christianity makes rapid progress across Roman Spain.
264–76	Barbarian tribes, the Franks and the Suevi, ravage the peninsula.
414	The Visigoths reach Spain and become the dominant military force, with their capital at Toledo.
711	Islamic Moors (Arabs and Berbers from North Africa) invade and conquer the Visigoths' kingdom in a whirlwind campaign that lasts just seven years. However a Christian victory at the battle of Covadonga (722) halts the Moorish advance and leads to the creation of the kingdom of the Asturias – a Christian toehold on the northwest corner of the Iberian peninsula.
756	Abd ar-Rahman I proclaims the Emirate of Córdoba, confirming Moorish control over almost all of Spain.
778	The Holy Roman Emperor Charlemagne invades Spain from France, but is defeated. In the dash back across the Pyrenees, the Christian rearguard – led by Roland – is hacked to pieces at Roncesvalles, inspiring the epic poem the *Chanson de Roland*. Charlemagne's subsequent endeavours meet with more success and undermine Moorish control of Navarra and Catalunya.
C9th	The Christian kingdoms of Catalunya and Navarra are founded.

C10th–early 11th	The Emirate of Córdoba flourishes, its capital becoming the most prosperous and civilized city in Europe. Abd ar-Rahman III breaks with Baghdad to declare himself caliph of an independent western Islamic empire.
C11th	The caliphate disintegrates into squabbling *taifas*, or petty fiefdoms. A local chieftain, El Cid, leads Christian forces against the Moors of Valencia, but his victories have no lasting effect. Independent Catalunya expands.
1037	Fernando I unites the kingdoms of Castile and León-Asturias.
1162	Alfonso II unites the kingdoms of Aragón and Catalunya.
C13th	The pace of the Christian Reconquest accelerates after the kings of Navarra, Castile and Aragón combine to defeat the Muslims at the crucial battle of Las Navas de Tolosa in 1212. Subsequent Christian victories include the capture of Mallorca (1229), Córdoba (1236), Valencia (1238) and Seville (1248). The reconquered territories are mostly distributed amongst the Christian nobility in great estates, the *latifundia*. Men from the ranks also receive land, forming a lower, larger land-owning class, the *hidalgos*.
1479	Castile and Aragón, the two pre-eminent Christian kingdoms, are united under Isabella I and Fernando V, the so-called Catholic Monarchs (Los Reyes Católicos). Spain subsequently emerges as a single political entity, with the Inquisition acting as a unifying force. The Inquisitors concentrate their attention on the Jews, expelling around 400,000 from Spain for refusing Christian baptism.
1492	The fall of Granada, the last Moorish kingdom. Columbus reaches the Americas.
1494	At the Treaty of Tordesillas, drawn up under the approving eye of the pope, Spain and Portugal divide the New World between them. Portugal gets Brazil and Spain takes the rest of modern-day Latin America.
1516–56	On the death of Fernando, his grandson Carlos I succeeds to the Spanish throne. Three years later Carlos also becomes Holy Roman Emperor – as Charles V – adding Germany, Austria and the Low Countries to his kingdom. Throughout his reign, he wages almost incessant war against his many enemies, principally the French, the Protestants and the

Muslims of North Africa. He funds his campaigns with the gold and silver bullion that is pouring into Spain from the New World, where Spanish adventurers have conquered, colonized and exploited a vast new empire.

1519   Cortés lands in Mexico, seizing its capital two years later.

1532   Pizarro "discovers" Peru, capturing Cuzco the next year.

1539   Hernando de Soto stakes out Florida.

1541   Pedro de Valdivia founds Santiago, Chile.

1555   Charles V finally accepts he is unable to suppress the German Reformation and agrees to a compromise peace with the Protestants at the Treaty of Augsburg.

1556   Charles V abdicates. His son, Felipe II (Philip II), becomes king of Spain and its colonies, Naples, Milan and the Low Countries. His brother, Ferdinand I, becomes Holy Roman Emperor, ruling Germany and Austria. An ardent and autocratic Catholic, Felipe continues the militaristic policy of his father, but concentrates his efforts against the Protestants.

1567   The Protestants of the Low Countries rise against Felipe II, beginning a protracted conflict that will drain Spanish resources and exhaust the Low Countries.

1571   Spain wins control of the Mediterranean after defeating the Turkish fleet at Lepanto.

1581   Spain annexes Portugal.

1588   The English defeat Felipe II's Armada, eliminating Spain as a major sea power.

1598   Felipe II dies. His legacy is an enormous but bankrupt empire: Spain's great wealth, so ruthlessly extracted from its colonies, has been squandered in over seventy years of continuous warfare.

C17th   The decline. Spain's international credibility is undermined by the loss of Portugal (1640) and the Netherlands (1648), emphasizing the country's military degeneration. Domestically, the poverty and suffering of the mass of the population – as compared with the opulence of the royal court – fuels regional discontent and insurrection. Cervantes publishes *Don Quixote* in 1605.

1701–14	Europe's nation states slug it out in the War of the Spanish Succession. The Bourbon (French) claimant – as opposed to that of the Holy Roman Emperor – wins out to become Felipe V. The British pick up Gibraltar and Menorca. As Spain declines, so it moves into the French sphere of influence.
1804	Napoleon crowned Emperor of France. Spain assists him in his war against England.
1805	The British navy, under Nelson, destroys the Franco-Spanish fleet at the Battle of Trafalgar.
1808	Napoleon arrests the Spanish king and replaces him with his brother, Joseph. This starts the War of Independence (otherwise known as the Peninsular War) in which the Spaniards fight the French army of occupation with the help of their new-found allies, the British.
1811 onwards	The South American colonies take advantage of the situation to assert their independence, detaching themselves from Spain one by one.
1815	The end of the Napoleonic Wars.
C19th	Further Spanish decline. The nineteenth century is dominated by the struggle between the forces of monarchist reaction and those of liberal constitutional reform. There are three bitter Carlist wars, named after one of the claimants to the throne. The progressives finally triumph in the 1870s, but the new government's authority is brittle and Spanish society remains deeply divided. Elsewhere, Puerto Rico, the Philippines and Cuba shake off Spanish control with the help of the USA. Spain's American empire is at an end.
1900–31	Liberals and Conservatives fail to reach a secure constitutional consensus, keeping the country on a knife edge. Working-class political movements – of anarchist, Marxist and socialist inclination – grow in strength and stir industrial and political discontent. Spain stays neutral in World War I, but the success of the Russian Bolsheviks terrifies King Alfonso XIII and the bourgeoisie, who support the right-wing military coup engineered by General Primo de Rivera in 1923. Rivera dies in 1930 and the king abdicates in 1931 when anti-monarchist parties win the municipal elections.
1932–36	The new Republican government introduces radical left-of-centre reforms, but separatists (in Catalunya,

Galicia and the Basque country), revolutionaries and rightists undermine its authority. Spain polarizes to the political left and right. Chaos and confusion prevail.

1936–39   The Spanish Civil War. General Francisco Franco leads a right-wing military rebellion against the Republican government. His Nationalists receive substantial support from Hitler and Mussolini. The Republicans get sporadic help from the Soviet Union and attract thousands of volunteers, organized in the International Brigades. The Civil War is vicious and bloody, ending in 1939 with a Fascist victory. Franco becomes head of state and bloody reprisals follow. Pope Pius XII congratulates the dictator on his "Catholic victory".

1939–75   Franco establishes a one-party state, backed up by stringent censorship and a vigorous secret police. By staying neutral during World War II, he survives the fall of Nazi Germany. In 1969, Franco nominates the grandson of Alfonso XIII, Juan Carlos, as his successor, but retains his vice-like grip on the country until his death in 1975.

1976–82   Juan Carlos recognizes the need for political reform and helps steer the country towards a parliamentary system. He reinforces his democratic credentials by opposing the attempted coup of 1981, when Colonel Tejero leads a group of Guardia Civil officers loyal to Franco's memory in the storming of the Cortes (parliament). The coup fails.

1982–96   In 1982, Felipe González's Socialist Workers' Party – the PSOE – is elected to office with the votes of nearly ten million Spaniards. It's an electoral landslide and the PSOE, buoyed up by the optimism of the times, promises change and progress. But González finds it hard to deliver and loses the enthusiasm of the left, his electoral power base. The left feels that González has followed a semi-monetarist policy, putting economic efficiency above social policies and rating the control of inflation as more urgent than the reduction of unemployment. Nevertheless, Spain's economy grows dramatically, the country becomes a respected member of the EU, and the PSOE attempts to deal with Spain's deep-seated separatist tendencies by permitting a large degree of regional autonomy. No effort is made to hunt down Franco's thugs – part of an accommodation between left and right designed to stop Spain from degenerating into a cycle of political revenge.

1996–2000   At the 1996 general election, the Conservative Popular Party led by José Aznar becomes the largest party in the Cortes, but does not get an overall majority. Aznar enlists the support of Catalan and Basque nationalist deputies to form an administration. The price is more powers to the regions. In government, Aznar moves his right-wing party to the political centre, mixing gestures to the unemployed (Spain's unemployment rate is one of the highest in the EU) and substantial investment in the country's infrastructure with privatization (of the national airline, Iberia, for one) and cuts in income tax. His measures are sufficiently well received for Aznar to win a second general election in March 2000 – and this time the Conservatives have an overall majority in the Cortes.

2000–2004

Aznar announces on the day after his election victory that he will seek to govern in conjunction with the regionalists, seeking alliances wherever he can and indicating that he is keen not to threaten the delicate consensus which has developed since the death of Franco. Aznar even acknowledges the role of the rival PSOE in modernizing Spain and pledges himself to keep to the political centre. In 2002, Aznar steers Spain into the single-currency euro zone to general approval. Less encouragingly, Aznar fails to reach a rapprochement with the nationalists (and separatists) of the Basque region, and controversially sends troops to support the American occupation of Iraq in 2003.

Flora and fauna

Despite their reputation as hopelessly over-developed package-holiday destinations, Menorca and more especially Mallorca have much to offer birders and botanists alike. Separated from the Iberian Peninsula some fifty million years ago, the Balearic archipelago has evolved (at least in part) its own distinctive flora and fauna, with further variations between each of the islands. Among the wildlife, it's the raptors inhabiting the mountains of northwest Mallorca – particularly the black vulture – which attract much of the attention, but there are other pleasures too, especially the migratory birds which gather on the islands' saltpans and marshes in April and May and from mid-September to early October. The islands are also justifiably famous for their fabulous range of wild flowers and flowering shrubs.

Some of the islands' most important habitats have, however, been threatened by the developers. This has spawned an influential conservation group, **GOB** (Grup Balear d'Ornitologia i Defensa de la Naturalesa; ⊛www.gobmallorca .com), which has launched several successful campaigns in recent years. It helped save the S'Albufera wetlands from further development, played a leading role in the black vulture re-establishment programme, successfully lobbied to increase the penalties for shooting protected birds, and is now fighting hard to protect and preserve Cabrera island.

The account below of the islands' flora and fauna serves as a general introduction, and includes mention of several important birding sites, cross-referenced to the descriptions given throughout the book. For more specialist information, some recommended **field guides** are listed on p.307.

Habitats

The Balearic Islands are a continuation of the Andalucian mountains of the Iberian Peninsula, from which they are separated by a submarine trench never less than 80km wide and up to 1500m deep. **Mallorca** comprises three distinct geographical areas with two ranges of predominantly limestone hills falling either side of a central plain, **Es Pla**. Mallorca's northwest coast is dominated by the **Serra de Tramuntana**, a slim, ninety-kilometre-long range of wooded hills and rocky peaks, fringed by tiny coves and precipitous seacliffs, that reaches its highest point at Puig Major (1447m). Also edged by steep seacliffs is the **Serres de Llevante**, a range of more modest hills that runs parallel to the island's east shore and rises to 509m at the Santuari de Sant Salvador.

Menorca has less topographical diversity, dividing into two distinct but not dramatically different zones. The **northern half** of the island comprises rolling sandstone uplands punctuated by wide, shallow valleys and occasional peaks, the highest of which is Monte Toro at 357m. To the **south** lie undulating limestone lowlands and deeper valleys. Dramatic seacliffs and scores of rocky coves trim both north and south.

Mallorca and Menorca share a temperate Mediterranean **climate**, with winter frosts a rarity, but there are significant differences between the two. The Serra de Tramuntana protects the rest of Mallorca from the prevailing winds that blow from the north and also catches most of the rain. Menorca, on the other hand, has no mountain barrier to protect it from the cold dry wind (the Tramuntana) which buffets the island from the north, giving much of the island's vegetation a wind-blown look, and obliging farmers to protect their crops with stone walls.

Mallorcan flora

The characteristic terrain of Mallorca up to around 700m is **garrigue**, partly forested open scrubland where the island's native trees – Aleppo pines, wild olives, holm oaks, carobs and dwarf palms – intermingle with imported species like ash, elm and poplar. Between 700m and 950m, *garrigue* is gradually replaced by **maquis**, a scrubland of rosemary, laurel, myrtle and broom interspersed with swaths of bracken. Higher still is a rocky terrain that can only support the sparsest of vegetation, such as an assortment of hardy grasses and low-growth rosemary.

Across much of the island, this indigenous vegetation has been destroyed by cultivation. However, the **Aleppo pine** and the evergreen **holm oak** – which traditionally supplied acorns for pigs, wood for charcoal and bark for tanning – are still common, as is the **carob tree**, which prefers the hottest and driest parts of the island. Arguably the archipelago's most handsome tree, the carob boasts leaves of varying greenness and conspicuous fruits – large pods which start green, but ripen to black-brown. The **dwarf palm**, with its sharp lance-like foliage, is concentrated around Pollença, Alcúdia and Andratx. The **wild olive** is comparatively rare (and may not be indigenous), but the cultivated variety, which boasts silver-grey foliage and can grow up to 10m in height, is endemic and has long been a mainstay of the local economy. There are also **orange** and **lemon** orchards around Sóller and innumerable **almond** trees, whose pink and white blossom adorns much of the island in late January and early February.

Mallorca has a wonderful variety of **flowering shrubs**. There are too many to list here in any detail, but look out for the deep blue flowers of the **rosemary**; the reddish bloom of the **lentisk** (or mastic tree); the bright yellow **broom** which begins blossoming in March; the many types of **tree heather**; and the autumn-flowering **strawberry tree**, found especially around Ca'n Picafort. **Rockroses** are also widely distributed, the most common members of the group being the spring-flowering, grey-leafed cistus, with its velvety leaves and pink flowers, and the narrow-leafed cistus whose bloom is white.

In spring and autumn the fields, verges, woods and cliffs of Mallorca brim with **wild flowers**. There are several hundred species and only in the depths of winter – from November to January – are all of them dormant. Well-known flowers include marigolds, daisies, violets, yellow primroses, gladioli, poppies, hyacinths, several kinds of cyclamen, the resinous St John's wort with its crinkled deep green leaves and, abundant in the pine woods near the sea and in the mountains, many types of orchid. Two common mountain plants are the pampas-like grass **ampelodesmus mauritanica**, giant clumps of which cover the hillsides, and a local variety of the sarsaparilla, **smilax balearica**, which flourishes in limestone crevices where its sharp thorns are something of a hazard for walkers. Other common and prominent plants are the giant-sized **agave** (century plant), an imported amaryllid with huge spear-shaped, leathery leaves of blue-grey coloration, which produces a massive flower spike every ten years (just before it dies). There's also the distinctive **asphodel**, whose tall spikes sport clusters of pink or white flowers from April to June. The asphodel grows on overgrazed or infertile land and its starch-rich tubers were once used by shoemakers to make glue. Another common sight is the **prickly pear**, traditionally grown behind peasants' houses as a windbreak and toilet wall. A versatile plant, the smell of the prickly pear deflects insects (hence its use round toilets) and its fruit is easy to make into pig food or jam.

Finally, many islanders maintain splendid **gardens** and here you'll see species that flourish throughout the Mediterranean, most famously bougainvilleas, oleanders, geraniums and hibiscus.

Mallorcan birds

Mallorca's diverse **birdlife** has attracted ornithologists for decades. The island boasts a whole batch of resident Mediterranean specialists and these are supplemented by migrating flocks of North European birds that descend on the island in their thousands during the spring and autumn.

The limestone **Serra de Tramuntana** mountains crimping the western coast are a haven for birds of prey. The massive black vulture is the real star here. This rare and impressive raptor, with its near three-metre wingspan, breeds in small numbers, but its size and residency means there's a reasonable chance of a sighting. The Puig Roig area (see p.148) is an excellent place to see this vulture, although note that during late spring and summer there are sometimes access restrictions to the bird's active sea-cliff nesting areas. The booted eagle is another mountain highlight, and there's a supporting cast of ospreys, red kites, Eleonora's falcons, kestrels and peregrines.

The **Embalse de Cúber** (Cúber Reservoir; see p.145), just west of Lluc on the C710, provides a natural amphitheatre from where up to ten species of birds of prey can be seen, including ospreys and red-footed falcons hunting over the water itself. The colourful rock thrush breeds in the quarry just west of the reservoir dam and on the nearby crags. The **sea cliffs** of the western coast are the breeding grounds of shearwaters, Mediterranean shag, storm petrels and Audouin's gulls. The most impressive seabird colonies are on the **Illa Dragonera**, off Sant Elm (see p.136), which is home to all these birds as well as over 75 pairs of Eleonora's falcons. If the weather is too rough to get to the island, the seabirds may be viewed from **La Trapa**, a small headland nature reserve of pristine coastal *garrigue* that is owned and operated by GOB. The reserve is about an hour's walk north of Sant Elm, but the going is fairly tough. A similarly good spot for seabirds is **Cap de Formentor** (see p.160), at the other end of the west coast, and birds from here wander the bays of Pollença and Alcúdia.

Characteristic birds of the island's **scrubland** can also be found around the Embalse de Cuber, including a variety of warblers and small songbirds, such as nightingales, larks, pipits and colourful chats. Another area of rich scrubland is the **Vall de Bóquer** (see p.162), near Pollença. Thoughtless development has harmed the olive groves and almond orchards at the base of the valley, but the Bóquer remains a migration hotspot, its pine avenues and denser wooded slopes hosting firecrests and crossbills among more familiar woodland birds like tits and woodpigeons. If you venture to the north end of the valley, you should be rewarded with the colourful delights of Marmora's warbler and the blue rock thrush. In spring, hundreds of bee-eaters can be heard and seen in and around the valley, as these stunning birds move through to breed elsewhere in the Mediterranean.

Wetlands are a magnet for birds in the arid climate of the Mediterranean. Mallorca boasts the most important birdwatching spot in the whole of the Balearics in the marshes of the **Parc Natural de S'Albufera** (see p.170). Here, resident species are augmented by hundreds of migrating birds, who visit to find fresh water after their long journey north or south. Amongst scores of species, the shorter grasses shelter moorhens, coots, crakes and the recently re-introduced purple gallinule, while the reeds hide healthy numbers of several species of herons, bitterns and egrets as well as occasional flamingos. A wide

The list below describes many of the most distinctive **birds** to be found on Mallorca and/or Menorca. We have given the English name, followed in italics by the Latin, a useful cross-reference for those without a British field guide.

Serin (*Serinus serinus*) Menorca: winter visitor. Tiny, green-and-yellow canary-like bird of the finch family, with characteristically buoyant flight. Appears in virtually any habitat.

Fan-tailed warbler (*Cisticola juncidis*) Mallorca and Menorca. Very common breeding resident. Typical small brown bird, but with very distinctive "zit-zit-zit" song, usually uttered in flight. Prefers wetland areas.

Nightingale (*Luscinia megarhynchos*) Mallorca and Menorca. Common breeding summer visitor. Rich-brown-coloured robin-like bird with astonishingly rich, vigorous and varied song. Prefers to sing from small bushes, often deep inside and out of sight.

Wryneck (*Jynx torquilla*) Mallorca: breeding resident; Menorca: spring, autumn and winter visitor. Medium-sized bird with a complex pattern of brown, grey and lilac plumage. A member of the woodpecker family. Favours olive groves.

Hoopoe (*Upupa epops*) Mallorca and Menorca. Common breeding resident. Pigeon-sized pinky-brown bird with black head-crest. It is named after its distinctive "upupu upupu" call. Its wings sport a complex black and white barring, creating a striking sight when in flight. Favours open areas with some trees nearby for nesting.

Black vulture (*Aegypius monachus*) Mallorca: breeding resident only in the northern mountains. Massive, dark, powerful and solitary raptor with a wingspan approaching three metres. The most distinctive of the islands' birds. Probably fewer than fifty remain.

Booted eagle (*Hieraaetus pennatus*) Mallorca and Menorca. Resident breeder. A small and very agile eagle, similar in size to a buzzard. Prefers the mountains, but happily hunts over scrub and grasslands.

Eleonora's falcon (*Falco eleonorae*) Mallorca: fairly common breeding summer visitor; Menorca: spring and autumn migrant. Dark, slim, elegant falcon. Hunts small birds and large insects with fantastic speed and agility. Often seen hunting insects near water.

Rock thrush (*Monticola saxatilis*) Mallorca: breeding summer visitor; Menorca: spring and autumn migrant. Beautifully coloured rock- and quarry-loving thrush. Males have a pale blue head and orangey-red breast and tail. Females are a less distinctive brown and cream.

Blue rock thrush (*Monticola solitarius*) Mallorca and Menorca. Common breeding resident. Blue-coloured thrush, recalling a deep blue starling. Can be found in any rugged, rocky areas at any time of year.

Firecrest (*Regulus ignicapillus*) Mallorca and Menorca. Common breeding resident. The smallest bird on the islands. This tiny pale green bird is named after its vivid orange and yellow crown. Abundant in any woodland.

Crossbill (*Loxia curvirostra*) Mallorca: abundant breeding resident. The vivid red males and the lemon-green females of this bulky finch have an unusual crossed bill and a distinctive parrot-like appearance. The bill is adapted to extract seeds from pine cones.

Marmora's warbler (*Sylvia sarda*) Mallorca: common breeding resident. A small blue-ish grey warbler with a long, often-upright tail and distinctive red eye-ring. Prefers the bushy cover of the coastal lowlands.

Purple gallinule (*Porphyrio porphyrio*) Breeding resident at Mallorca's S'Albufera only. This purple-blue oddity was re-introduced to its marshland habitat at S'Albufera in 1991. It is now well established. Its incredibly long feet and swollen red bill make this hen-like bird very distinctive.

Little egret (*Egretta garzetta*) Mallorca: breeding resident; Menorca: spring and autumn migrant. Long-legged, elegant white wading bird. In summer has beautiful long white plumes trailing from the back of its head. Breeds at S'Albufera only. A wetland specialist, though well adapted to treetop life.

Little bittern (*Ixobrychus minutes*) Spring and autumn visitor to Menorca. Secretive wetland specialist. This is the smallest member of the heron family breeding in Europe, measuring little more than 30cm tall. The male is an attractive pink-cream colour with contrasting black wings and cap. Males advertise themselves with a far-carrying gruff basal note, repeated regularly.

Purple heron (*Ardea purpurea*) Breeding summer visitor to Mallorca. Large, slender heron fond of reed beds. The male plumage has beautiful purple and rich-brown tones. Despite its size it can be rather elusive, hiding deep inside the reeds.

Black-winged stilt (*Himantopus himantopus*) Mallorca: common breeding resident; Menorca: summer visitor. Incredibly long-legged black-and-white wader. Its medium size is somewhat extended by its long, straight, fine, red bill. Can appear anywhere there is mud, but particularly common on saltpans.

Kentish plover (*Charadrius alexandrinus*) Mallorca: common breeding resident; Menorca: spring and autumn visitor. Small, delicate wader of saltpans and marshes. Its pale brown upper body contrasts with its gleaming white head-collar and underparts.

Cetti's warbler (*Cettia cetti*) Mallorca and Menorca. Very common breeding resident. This rather nondescript, chunky, wren-like warbler prefers dense thickets close to water. It possesses an astonishingly loud explosive song: "chet-chet-chet-chetchetchet".

Great reed warbler (*Acrocephalus arundinaceus*) Mallorca and Menorca. Breeding summer visitor. This large, unstreaked, brown warbler can be found in significant numbers where there is reed and marsh vegetation. Its song is a loud and harsh mixture of unusual grating, croaking and creaking noises.

Scops owl (*Otus scops*) Mallorca and Menorca. Common breeding resident. This tiny owl (only 20cm tall) is stubbornly nocturnal. At night, its plaintive "tyoo" note is repeated every few seconds often for long (monotonous) periods. Groves, plantations, small clumps of trees, conifer woodland and even gardens can host this bird.

Greater flamingo (*Phoenicopterus ruber*) Winter/spring visitor in small numbers. The unmistakable silhouette of this leggy wader with roseate wings, bill and legs can be seen on any wetland in spring. In winter, it's confined to the southern reaches of Mallorca – and especially the S'Albufera wetland.

Great white egret (*Egretta alba*) Mallorca and Menorca. Winter visitor. This marshland specialist is really just a large version of the commoner Little Egret – an all-white, tall, elegant heron.

Audouin's gull (*Larus audouinii*) Mallorca and Menorca. Resident breeder. This rare gull favours the rocky coastline of both islands. It's the size and light grey colour of a typical "seagull" but boasts a rather splendid red bill. Unfortunately it takes three years for birds to reach this adult plumage and prior to this they are much less distinctive.

Bee-eater (*Merops apiaster*) Mallorca: common spring visitor, rare summer breeder; Menorca: breeding summer visitor. A brightly coloured, medium-sized bird, with a slim body, long pointed wings and slightly de-curved bill. If the iridescent greens, orange, yellow and blue of this bird aren't distinctive enough, its bubbling "pruuk" call is almost as recognizable. It prefers open, relatively flat, rugged countryside.

Egyptian vulture (*Neophron percnopterus*) Mallorca: rare migrant; Menorca: breeding resident. Medium-sized raptor with small rather pointed protruding head and featherless face. Wings held flat when soaring.

Cattle egret (*Bubulcus ibis*) Mallorca and Menorca. Mainly winter visitor. This small heron-like wader is a regular winter visitor to the larger Balearic marshes. In winter it is white, but is distinguished from the Little Egret by its stubby all-yellow bill and stockier gait.

Night heron (*Nycticorax nycticorax*) Mallorca: small resident population, increasing in summer with migrants; Menorca: spring and autumn migrant. Adults of this stocky, medium-sized heron are an attractive combination of black, grey and white. In contrast younger birds up to three years old are a rather nondescript brown with cream speckling. This water bird is most active at night or dawn and dusk. By day they roost in the tree canopy or large bushes.

Stone curlew (*Burhinus oedicnemus*) Mallorca and Menorca. Resident breeder, more common in summer. Thick-set wader that prefers dry rolling countryside to mud. Has a large, yellow, almost reptilian eye. Largely dull brown with some darker streaking, but with relatively distinctive long yellow legs. When in flight, its strikingly black and white wings become apparent.

Cory's shearwater (*Calonectris diomedia*) Mallorca and Menorca. Common breeder on offshore islands, but seen regularly all along the coast from March to August. Fairly large seabird. Like all the shearwaters, this bird flies close to the sea's surface with stiff outstretched wings. This pattern of flight as well as its size (nearly half a metre long with a wing span of more than a metre) are its most distinctive features as its plumage is rather boring. At sea it appears dark-backed and dirty white below. A close view should reveal some yellow on the bill and a white eye ring. Thousands breed on offshore islands across the Balearics and at sea they will often mix with the smaller pale brown Mediterranean shearwater.

---

variety of small wading birds visit the marsh, including the distinctively long-legged black-winged stilt and the abundant Kentish plover. The open water is popular with ducks and in spring large numbers of terns may be seen. In winter the variety of duck species increases and kingfishers are common. This rich diversity of birdlife attracts birds of prey and this is as good a place as any to see ospreys and marsh harriers. In addition, over one hundred Eleonora's falcons have been seen together over the marsh in spring. Among the smaller birds, the spring dusk and dawn choruses provided by wetland warblers such as Cetti's, moustached and great reed are unforgettable. Neither is the sound of birds restricted to the daytime. At night, listen for the plaintive single note of the scops owl against a backdrop of warblers, crakes and crickets.

The scops owl can be heard in the south of the island too, usually preferring almond groves and olive clumps. Generally speaking, the south is not as rich in birdlife as other parts of the island, the main exception being the **saltpan** habitat of the **Salines de Llevant**, near Colònia de Sant Jordi (see p.204). Here, a wide variety of migrant wading birds, wintering duck and small flocks of wintering flamingos and cranes can be seen. The site also has a breeding flock of over a hundred black-winged stilts in summer and the abundance of prey attracts raptors, most frequently marsh harriers, kestrels and ospreys. The pans also host terns and Audouin's gull; this red-billed gull is a Mediterranean specialist and can be chanced upon at many coastal spots but the southern saltpans are favoured.

The country lanes that lattice Mallorca's **central plain**, Es Pla, also have their own distinctive birdlife. In spring and summer, the calls and songs of small birds like serins, corn buntings and Sardinian warblers and the ubiquitous fan-tailed warbler create a busy backdrop to hot, lazy afternoons. Nightingales seem to be everywhere and their rich song leaves a lasting impression. In the shade of the abundant olive groves, the subtly plumaged wryneck can be found all year, often sharing this ancient landscape with the striking hoopoe.

Other Mallorcan fauna

Mallorca's surviving **mammals** are an uninspiring bunch. The wild boar and red fox were eliminated early in the twentieth century, leaving a motley crew of mountain goats, wild sheep, pine martens, genets, weasels and feral cats, as well as commonplace smaller mammals such as hedgehogs, rabbits, hares and shrews.

As far as **reptiles** go, there are four types of snake – all hard to come by – and two species of gecko (or broad-toed lizard), the lowland-living wall gecko and the mountain-dwelling disc-fingered version. With any luck, you'll spot them as they heat up in the sun, but they move fast since warm gecko is a tasty morsel for many a bird. Off the south coast of Mallorca, the desolate island of Cabrera (see p.204) has a large concentration of the rare, blue-bellied **Lilfords wall lizard**.

Among **amphibians**, Mallorca has a healthy frog population, concentrated in its marshlands but also surviving in its mountain pools (up to around 800m). There are also three types of toad, of which the **Mallorcan midwife toad**, hanging on in the northern corner of the island, is the rarest. With no natural predators, its evolution involved a reduction in fecundity (it produces only a quarter of the number of eggs laid by its mainland relative) and the loss of its poison glands. However, with the introduction of the viperine snake, the resident midwife toads were all but wiped out – only about five hundred pairs remain.

Common **insects** include grasshoppers and cicadas, whose summertime chirping is so evocative of warm Mediterranean nights, as well as over two hundred species of moth and around thirty types of **butterfly**. Some of the more striking butterflies are red admirals, which are seen in winter, and the clouded yellows and painted ladies of spring. One of the more unusual species is the two-tailed pasha, a splendidly marked gold-and-bronze butterfly that flits around the coast in spring and late summer, especially in the vicinity of strawberry trees.

Menorcan flora

Far flatter than its neighbour, Menorca's indigenous vegetation is almost all **garrigue**, though intensive cultivation has reduced the original forest cover to a fraction of its former size – nowadays only about fifteen percent of the island is wooded. Native trees are the holm oak, the dwarf palm, the carob and, commonest of all, the **Aleppo pine**, which has bright green spines, silvery twigs and ruddy-brown cones. Olive trees are endemic and dramatically illustrate the effects of the prevailing Tramuntana, with grove upon grove almost bent double under the weight of the wind.

Menorca's soils nourish a superb range of **flowering shrubs** and **wild flowers**. There is less variety than on Mallorca, but the islands have many species in common. Menorca also boasts a handful of species entirely to itself, the most distinguished of them being the dwarf shrub **daphne rodriquezii**, a purple-flowering evergreen, present on the cliffs of the northeast coast. In addition, the cliffs of much of the coast have a flora uniquely adapted to the combination of limestone yet saline soils. Here, **aromatic inula**, a shrubby perennial with clusters of yellow flowers, grows beside the **common caper**, with its red pods and purple seeds, and the **sea aster**.

Menorcan birds

The varied **birdlife** of Menorca includes birds of prey, wetland specialists, seabirds, waders and characteristic Mediterranean warblers, larks and pipits, but perhaps the most striking feature is the tameness of many of the birds – presumably because there is less **shooting** here than in almost any other part of the Mediterranean.

There are several hot-spots for birds, but wherever you are birds of prey should be evident. Of these, the Egyptian vulture is the most impressive; there are around a hundred of them, the only resident population in Europe. Red kites, booted eagles and ospreys can also be seen year round, and they are joined by marsh and hen harriers in winter. Peregrines, kestrels and, in winter, sparrowhawks complete the more reliable raptors, although in spring and autumn several others – such as the honey buzzard and black kite – may turn up. **Monte Toro** (see p.243), the highest point on Menorca, is as good a vantage point for birds of prey as any.

The island's best birdwatching spot is the marshland, reeds and garigue (partly forested scrubland) fringing the lake of **S'Albufera**, near Es Grau (see p.233), a nature reserve which is itself part of a larger Parc Naturel that extends north to Cap de Favaritx. The lake and its environs are popular with herons and egrets, the most elegant of wetland birds. Over a year, little and cattle egrets, purple, grey, night and squacco herons will all be seen, too. Booted eagles are also common, flying over the area, and the muddy parts of the marsh attract many smaller waders in spring, the leggy black-winged stilt in summer. The lake itself hosts several thousand ducks in winter. The nearby pine woodland, next to the beach at Es Grau, is used by night herons that rest high in the trees by day and then move onto the marsh at dusk. Also at dusk, listen out for the plaintive single note of the scops owl against a backdrop of warblers, crakes, crickets; and, most strikingly, the rich-toned song of the nightingale. The tiny firecrest is common in the woodland, and in the spring this whole area comes alive with hundreds of migrants.

There are smaller marshes elsewhere on the island and those at Cala Tirant in the north and Son Bou in the south are very good. The wetland at **Son Bou** (see p.242) holds the island's largest reedbed and the characteristic species of such a rich habitat are the noisy great reed warblers, moustached warbler and Cetti's warbler. The wetland at **Cala Tirant** (see p.236) can be just as good and the sandy area just inland of the beach is a first-rate place to see the spectacular bee-eater, which breeds in several small colonies on the island. Nearby, the **Cap de Cavalleria** (see p.237), at the northern tip of the island, attracts the curious-looking stone curlew, several larks and pipits; and ospreys can often be seen fishing in the cape's **Port de Sanitja** (see p.237). Another special Balearic bird is the distinctive red-billed Audouin's gull, one of the world's rarest. A good place to see these is just off the coast by the lighthouse at the end of the cape, where Mediterranean shags and shearwaters are also regularly seen. Audouin's gulls can also be seen in and around Maó.

The lush vegetation in the bottom of the Algendar Gorge, just inland of **Cala Santa Galdana** (see p.248), is a magnet for small birds and a perfect setting to hear nightingales and the short explosive song of the Cetti's warbler. Above the gorge, booted eagles, Egyptian vultures and Alpine swifts nest. The ravine also attracts a wonderful array of butterflies.

Finally, although the barren, stony landscape of the northwest coast may seem an unpromising environment, **Punta de S'Escullar** is the site of one of the largest colonies of Cory's shearwaters in the western Mediterranean. Thousands return to their cliffside burrows in the late afternoon in summer. This rugged terrain also hosts the attractive blue rock thrush and migrant chats, wheatears and black redstarts. Pallid swifts and crag martins also breed on the cliffs.

Other Menorcan fauna

Menorca's **mammals** are a low-key bunch, an undistinguished assortment of weasels, feral cats, hedgehogs, rabbits, hares, mice and shrews. The one highlight is the island's **reptiles**. Of the four species of Balearic lizard, Menorca has three. There are two types of wall lizard – Lilfords, a green, black and blue version, and the olive-green and black-striped Italian lizard – as well as the Moroccan rock lizard, with olive skin or reticulated blue-green coloration.

Common **insects** include grasshoppers and cicadas as well as over a hundred species of moth and around thirty types of **butterfly**. Three of the more striking butterflies are red admirals, which are seen in winter, and the clouded yellows and painted ladies, seen in spring.

Writers on Mallorca

M allorca and Menorca have produced few writers of note, but Mallorca has been the subject of many foreign jottings, beginning with the well-heeled travellers who nosed around the island in the nineteenth century. The most distinguished of these was George Sand, the partner of Frédéric Chopin, who wintered here in 1838–39. More recently, Mallorca has been used as a backdrop in the works of several English-language thriller writers and has also produced Tomás Graves, who was born and raised on the island and is fluent in its language and culture.

George Sand

George Sand (1804–76) was the pen name of the French aristocrat Armandine Lucile Aurore Dupin, the Baroness Dudevant. She married the eponymous baron in 1822, and left him nine years later for the literary life of Paris, where she embraced the Republican cause. A prolific author, dramatist and journalist, Sand campaigned against conservatism in its many forms and became a well-known figure in French political circles. She travelled occasionally and one of her excursions, along with her partner, the pianist and composer Frédéric Chopin, was in 1838 to the then backward and remote island of Mallorca (for more on their visit, see p.127). This extract is from Sand's memoir of the time, A Winter in Majorca.

A visit to Valldemossa

It is three leagues from Palma to Valldemosa, but three Majorcan leagues, which can't be covered driving fast in under three hours. The road rises imperceptibly for the first two. During the third it enters the mountains and leads up a well-paved slope (possibly a former work of the Carthusian monks), but very narrow, horribly steep, and more dangerous than the rest of the way.

There one has one's first chance to admire the Alpine part of Majorca. But it is not enough that the mountains rise up on either side of the gorge, and that the torrent leaps from rock to rock; only in the heart of winter do these regions take on the wild, untamed aspect that the Majorcans attribute to them. In the month of December, and in spite of recent rains, the torrent was still a delightful stream which glided along among tufts of grass and clusters of flowers; the mountain was in a smiling mood, and the valley in which Valldemosa nestled opened before us like a garden in spring.

To reach the Cartuja you have to leave the coach, for it is impossible for any vehicle to clamber up the stony track that leads to it. It is a fascinating approach with its sudden twists and bends among magnificent trees, and with wonderful views that are unfolded at every step, and increase in beauty the higher one rises. I have seen nothing more pleasing; nor at the same time more melancholy than these prospects where the green holm oak, the carob tree, the pine, the olive, the poplar and the cypress mix their various hues in dense masses of foliage, veritable abysses of verdure amongst which the torrent pursues its course through thickets of gorgeous richness and inimitable attraction. I will never forget a certain bend in the defile from where, turning round, one can see high up on a mountain one of those pretty Arabic-type cottages, half-hidden among the leaves of the prickly pears, and, projecting its silhouette into the air, a great palm tree leaning over the chasm. When the mud and fog of Paris overwhelm me with depression, I shut my eyes and see again, as in a dream, that mountain full of greenery, those bare rocks, and that solitary palm, alone in a rose-coloured sky.

The Valldemosa cordillera rises up in a series of plateaux, becoming narrower and narrower until they form a kind of funnel, surrounded by high mountains and shut in on the north by the slope of the last plateau, at the entrance to which stands the monastery.

The Carthusian monks, through the work of years, have modified the ruggedness of this romantic spot. At the head of the valley where it reaches the hillside, they have made a vast garden, surrounded by walls that do not block the view, and to which a belt of cypress trees, in pyramidal form and disposed irregularly in pairs, give an appearance appropriate to a stage-set graveyard.

This garden, with palm and almond trees, occupied the whole inclined background of the valley, and rises in a succession of wide terraces on the lower slopes of the mountain. By moonlight, and when its irregularity is masked by the darkness, it could be taken for an amphitheatre carved out for the battles of giants. In the centre and under a group of lovely palms, a stone-built reservoir collects the water from the mountain springs, and distributes it to the lower terraces by means of paved channels, similar to those which irrigate the environs of Barcelona. These works are on too great a scale and too ingenious not to have been the creation of the Moors. They are spread over the whole interior of the island, and the channels that start at the garden of the Carthusian monks, skirt the bed of the torrent and take running water to Palma at all seasons.

The Cartuja, situated at the highest point of this gorge, looks on the north side over an extensive valley which widens out and rises in a gentle slope to the coastal cliffs, whose base is battered and eroded by the sea. One arm of the cordillera points towards Spain, and the others towards the Orient. From this picturesque Carthusian monastery therefore, the sea can be glimpsed or sensed on two sides. Whilst its roar is audible to the north, it can be descried to the south like a fine, brilliant line beyond the descending mountain slopes and the immense plain which is revealed to the eye. It is a surpassing picture, framed in the foreground by dark, pine-covered crags; beyond that by the sharply outlined profiles of mountains set off by superb trees; and in the background by the rounded humps of hills, which the setting sun gilds with the warmest shades, and on whose crests one can still distinguish, from a distance of a league, the microscopic outlines of the trees, as fine as the antennae of butterflies, as black and distinct as a trace of Chinese ink on a backdrop of sparkling gold. ...

In accordance with the Carthusian rule, thirteen monks, including the superior, lived in the Cartuja in Valldemosa. It had escaped the decree which in 1836 ordered the demolition of monasteries occupied by less than a dozen persons conjointly; but, like all the others, they had been dispersed and the convent suppressed, to be considered, as it were, the property of the State. The Majorcan government, not knowing what to do with these immense buildings, had decided to let the cells to persons who would care to occupy them, in the expectation that time and negligence would cause the place to decay and fall down. In spite of the rents being extremely moderate, the villagers in Valldemosa had not chosen to take advantage of the offer, possibly because of their extreme piety and the affection they had felt for the monks, and perhaps also through superstitious fear; this did not prevent them going there to dance on carnival nights, although they did not cease to look very much askance at our irreverent presence among those venerable walls.

Nevertheless, the Cartuja was inhabited during the summer months by middle-class people from Palma who, at that altitude and under the monastery's thick arches, undoubtedly found the air fresher than on the plain or in the city. But with the approach of winter, the cold drove them away, and when we lived in it, the Cartuja had as its only inhabitants, besides myself and my family, the apothecary, the sacristan, and Maria Antonia.

Maria Antonia was a kind of housekeeper who had come from the mainland I believe to get away from squalor and poverty, and she had rented a cell in order to exploit the transient occupants of the Cartuja. Her cell was located next to ours and we made use of it as a kitchen, while she declared herself to be our factotum and help. She had been good-looking and was elegant, clean in appearance and pleasant. She said she came from a good family, had delightful manners, a nice voice, and an ingratiating demeanour. She exercised a very curious sort of hospitality; she would offer her services to the new arrivals and refuse, with an offended air and almost turning pale at the idea, any kind of recompense for her attentions. She did it, she asserted, for the love of God, to be of assistance, and with the sole object of winning the friendship of her neighbours. Her entire furniture consisted of a small folding bed, a foot-warmer, two wicker chairs, a crucifix, and some earthenware crockery, all of which she put at our disposal with great generosity, allowing us to accommodate our new servant, and store our pots and pans, in her dwelling.

But she would immediately take charge of all your belongings, and reserve for herself the best of your finery and food. I have never seen a godly person so fond of her stomach, nor fingers so quick to dip down into a boiling pot without getting burnt, nor a throstle so supple to swallow the coffee and sugar of her dear lodgers, stealthily, whilst she hummed a popular air or a bolero. It would have been interesting and amusing, if one had been completely disinterested in the matter, to see the good Antonia, Catalina the queer witch-like Valldemosa woman who was our maid, and the *niña* (little girl), a small dishevelled monstrosity who acted as our errand girl, quarrelling among themselves over our food. It was the hour of the Angelus and the three never failed to recite it. The two elders, praying in unison, put their hands into every dish, and the small one, as she answered *Amen*, succeeded in palming some chop or candied fruit with unequalled dexterity. It was quite something to watch and worthwhile pretending not to notice; but when the rains cut communication with Palma and our provisions diminished, the "assistance" of Maria Antonia and her party became less pleasing; and my children and I found ourselves in the role of sentinel and relieving each other, in order to keep a watch on our food stores. I remember once hiding under the head-board of my bed a few packets of biscuits which were earmarked for breakfast the next day; and on another occasion, I had to keep a vulture's eye on some plates of fish in our cooking-stove, so as to scare away those birds of prey who would have left us only the bones.

The sacristan was a lusty young fellow who had possibly served at mass with the Carthusian monks since his childhood; he was now the keeper of the keys of the monastery. There was a scandalous story about him. He was once convicted of and confessed to having seduced a *señorita* who had stayed some months in the Cartuja with her parents. He excused himself on the grounds that the State had only entrusted him with the guardianship of the virgins in the pictures. He was not a good type by any standard, but he put on very pretentious airs. Instead of the semi-Arabic attire used by people of his class, he wore European trousers with braces, which certainly dazzled the girls of the district. His sister was the most beautiful Majorcan girl that I've seen. They didn't live in the monastery. They were rich and proud and had a house in the village; but they made a daily round of the Cartuja and were often in Maria Antonia's cell, who invited them to partake of our provender when she had no appetite herself.

The apothecary was a Carthusian who used to shut himself in his cell, put on his former white robe, and recite his office all alone. As soon as anyone knocked on his door to ask him for some marsh-mallow or couch-grass root (the only specific remedies he possessed), he would quickly hide his habit under his bed and appear in black breeches, stockings and a short pea jacket, the same as worn by the male ballet dancers in Molière's interludes. He was a very mistrustful person who never ceased complaining, and who perhaps prayed for the triumph of Don Carlos and the return of the Holy Inquisition, but he meant no harm to anybody. He sold us his herbs at the price of gold, and consoled himself with these small gains, having been released from his vow of poverty. His cell was a fairly long way from ours, being situated at the entrance to the monastery in a hidden corner, whose door was camouflaged by castor-oil bushes and other medicinal plants of pleasing aspect.

Tomás Graves

*Born in 1953, **Tomás Graves**, the son of Robert (see p.121), lives on Mallorca, where he works as a guitarist, printer and author. His knowledge of – and enthusiasm for – the island and its people permeates every page of Bread and Oil, a diverse and intriguing book, first published in Catalan in 1998, that describes many aspects of Mallorcan life via its gastronomy.*

Olive cultivation

The vegetation on Majorca's terraced hillsides hardly changes colour with the seasons. There are several shades of evergreen: the dark holm-oak forest, the vivid pines which sprout on any untended terraces, the grey-green olive groves which flash silver when the strong winds turn up the undersides of their leaves; and among the olives, the occasional broad-leaved carob tree.

Our olive groves have drifted into the realms of what some Majorcan farmers derisively call *hobby farming*. We've reached this point because it's not worth a peasant's while to become a registered olive-grower and pay the corresponding social security if he and his family are only going to gather a few sacks of olives in the best of years. It's hardly worth it even to pick up a few subsidies to repair any of the centuries-old stone terraces that collapse. What really subsidizes the continuing existence of the olive groves is our seasonal tourism. Most Majorcans from the *serra* who work in the hotels and restaurants, sign on the dole in November and have all winter to spend looking after their olive groves and go hunting, as well as doing a little moonlighting on the side. If the harvest were in summer, all the olives would rot on the ground.

Spain's olive groves produce forty per cent of the world's olive oil and represent 146,000 permanent jobs as well as temporary labour to the tune of 46 million day's wages a year. Economically speaking, Majorca's share of the oil business is negligible. Not only does the size of the small-holdings make them unprofitable – property is usually divided up *ad absurdam* between heirs – but the local topography limits the kind of mechanization that you see in parts of Andalucia. There's no way you could get a tractor with a tree-shaking attachment up the Moorish steps of the Barranc de Biniaraix, nor could you manoeuvre a crop-dusting plane between those crags. Throughout the Mediterranean, the olive is a crop which, in spite of mechanization, gives work to entire families and is responsible for preserving the social fabric of the mountainous regions, culturally as well as economically. If the olive groves were to disappear, the rural exodus would be catastrophic because no other crop can be cultivated in the mountainous areas. At least, for the moment, no *legal* crop.

Olive cultivation in the *possessions* or large estates was based first on a slave economy, later on serfdom, and then (until the tourist boom) on the exploitation of the fact that an island's work force can't afford to look for work elsewhere. After a couple of decades of plunging olive oil prices (due to bad press and cheap imported sunflower and soya oil) they began to steadily rise in the 1980s, and today a litre of Majorcan oil fetches double what is paid in Andalucia, due to the demand for local produce. But even so, it doesn't begin to pay for the labour-intensive work of picking olives, maintaining the dry-stone terraces, ploughing and pruning the trees in the high groves which are accessible only by foot or donkey.

Olive picking

"The degree of acidity is set by the olive, there's no part of the process at the oil-press that can affect it," explains professional oil-taster Gaspar, shouting over the noise of the newly-imported Italian machinery at the Sóller Co-op oil-mill. "Olive oil must be one of the few products which has absolutely no additives. You can't mix anything in with it. Every year it's different; some years the acidity is higher, nobody knows exactly why. The weather may have been exactly the same as the year before, the trees are pruned the same way, given the same fertilizer, but the oil is different from one season to the next

"Here on the island, ninety per cent of the olives are picked off the ground. No other fruit is harvested off the floor, it's always better straight from the tree. On the mainland they pull the olives straight off the branches; they're a little greener and the oil they produce has a fruitier smell, a bitterer taste. It's a bit spicy and has a lower acid content; this is the extra virgin oil, the best there is. The green olive – in fact it's neither green nor black but mottled – produces less oil but the quality is better. It's best to beat or comb the tree; you can do it mechanically or with hand-held rakes which don't damage the branches."

It seems that the habit of picking green originated in the northern Mediterranean where the olives had to be harvested before the frost set in. In southern Italy they tend to gather ripe olives from the ground, while in the north they pick them green. Many Majorcan inventors have come up with contraptions to gather olives off the ground, yet whether the principle is suction, a brushing action, or a spiked roller, no mechanical picker seems to be able to distinguish this year's juicy olives from last year's shrivelled ones . . . or from sheep's droppings.

"The Majorcans are used to an oil which can reach four or five degrees of acidity and that's what they're after because it's tasty, but it's the musty taste of an olive that's been on the damp ground too long. We're telling the members of our co-op to put their olives in crates instead of in sacks where the air doesn't get to them, where there are bacteria. That's when the olive gets spoiled, it ferments and the acidity increases."

In medieval times when strong olive oil was set aside for preserving food, recipe books would recommend adding honey to counteract the excess acidity. In this [the twentieth] century, in the postwar years when even the sharpest oil was better than none, a bit of sugar on your *pa amb oli* would stop the oil grating at the back of your throat.

"Here people pick olives the same way they did a hundred years ago. You could say that if Majorcan oil hasn't the quality of the mainland oil it's partly because here the problem is the terrain; it's not easy to get the olives to the press quickly."

Gathering olives off the ground can be, for someone unaccustomed to this work and to the damp winter climate of the *serra*, an ordeal for the knees and kidneys. Every basketful of four kilos of olives renders a scant litre of oil; not much to show for an hour's work poking about between damp shrubs and under thistles. Many of us who still go for gathering from the ground have found we can save a lot of time by using a strimmer to clear the grass under the trees a week or so before the olives change colour. To go olive picking as a family outing or in order to spend the weekend with friends is a profitable way to commune with nature, each according to his humour. You can work in a group chatting away, but it is equally conducive to solitary meditation.

Why don't we follow the rational northern method of knocking the olives down as soon as they begin to turn colour and thus only have to pick once instead of our weekly pass under the same tree? Well, a Majorcan would say that the only way of ensuring the olive is ripe is to wait for it to fall to the ground... but the hidden argument is that beating or combing the trees not only gives you a crick in the neck, it's also harder work than gathering off the ground. Besides, we've always done it this way and, as they say in the southern US, "if it ain't broke, don't fix it".

The *tafona*, or oil press

The first operation of the traditional oil press, after sifting out any leaves and stones, is to crush the olives on the *jaç*, a flat circular bed about a metre high and three across, fashioned out of a single piece of local stone. A contrivance consisting of a wooden funnel connected to a conical millstone rotates on a vertical axle set in the centre of the stone bed, driven by a blinkered donkey or mule which walks round and round the *jaç*. The sorted olives are tipped into the funnel, the *tremuja*, which feeds them, a few at a time, into the path of the rumbling *trull*. As the olives are crushed to a paste, the *trull* pushes the dark sludge outwards into the gutter which runs around the rim of the *jaç*. From here the virgin oil seeps out of the paste and trickles into a vat.

"The olive contains more water than oil. What flows from the *trull* is pure olive juice, the true virgin olive oil, a mixture of oil and water. When I was a little girl I used to go to school in Estellencs," remembers Maria Riera, "and there was a *tafona* in the village where they'd make oil. The *tafoners* would let the schoolmistress know the day before a *trullada*, and we'd all troop in with our slices of bread, and they'd toast them over the coals. Then they'd take the toasted bread with a pair of tongs and dip it in the oil which had just come out, and it was so good... it was delicious just like that, you didn't even have to put salt on."

Antoni Pinya explains that "in the *possessions*, at the end of the working day when the olives had been crushed and were ready for the hot pressing the next morning, a bottle of virgin oil would be collected from the *trull* for the *Senyors* of the estate. After the token bottle had been given to the landowner, all the paste left on the *trull* would be shovelled into a stone vat, the *esportinador*. Then the *madona* – the overseer's wife – would roll up her sleeve, make a fist and stick it into the paste up to her forearm. As she took out her arm it would leave a good sump-hole in the olive paste, into which more virgin oil would seep overnight. The next morning, the *tafoners* would toast their bread and dunk it into the oil that had gathered in the sump. This was the *tafoner's* breakfast, the rien-ne-va-plus, the Number One in the world of bread and oil, known as *pa amb oli de tafona*."

After the 'cold pressing' comes the hot or 'scalded' pressing. In a traditional *tafona* this is done under the weight of an enormous wooden beam, weighing well over a ton: one end of the beam rests on the ground while the other end is raised and then lowered – by means of a vertical wooden screw, turned by arms of the *tafoners* – onto the tall stack of circular esparto mats, *esportins*, spread with olive paste. As the beam is lowered, one *tafoner* 'scalds' the paste by ladling hot water onto the pile; it seeps down through the mats, drawing the oil out of the paste. Some people still refer to hot-pressed oil as *oli de bigues*, 'beam oil'.

Having pressed the paste under a beam until it will yield no more liquid, the process is still not over. The dry paste is scooped out of the *esportins* and thrown back into the *esportinador* where it is beaten with more hot water. The mats are again spread with this rehydrated paste and submitted once more to the heavy pressure treatment, doused with a continuous flow of boiling water to extract that little bit more. The oil obtained by this pressing is known as 'seconds': the quality is lower than the first hot pressing because the continuous heat destroys the vitamin E content as well as part of the flavour and bouquet.

The traditional way of pressing olives produced several qualities of oil, from the virgin pressing for the immediate use of the landowner's family, right down to the 'thick' oil from the second or third pressing, which was used for making soap, lubricating cart axles and for treating woodwork.

Extract from Bread and Oil: Majorcan Culture's Last Stand, © 2000, *Tomás Graves*. Bread and Oil *is published by Prospect Books, Totnes, England.*

Books

Most of the following books are readily available in the UK, US, Australia, New Zealand and Canada, apart from those few titles we mention which are currently out of print (o/p). You might also find it more difficult to track down those few books which are published locally in Mallorca – in these cases we've given the name of the publisher. The UK's *Books on Spain* can supply all manner of rare in- and out-of-print books about the Iberian Peninsula. Their comprehensive, free catalogue includes sections on topics such as travel, the arts, history and culture, plus separate sections (and separate brochures) on the regions, including the Balearics – it's available from PO Box 207, Twickenham TW2 5BQ, UK (☎020/8898 7789, ⓦwww.books-on-spain.com).

Titles marked with the ☆ symbol are especially recommended.

Impressions and travelogues

Tom Crichton *Our Man in Majorca*. The American sailor, adventurer and journalist Tom Crichton was briefly a package-tour representative on Mallorca in the early 1960s. With the encouragement of Robert Graves, he published this account of a comical, disaster-filled fortnight. A book for the sunbed.

Paul Richardson *Not Part of the Package*. Richardson spent a year in the heady 1960s observing and enjoying the razzle-dazzle of Ibiza. His idiosyncratic tales are diverting and revealing in equal measure – and, by implication, throw light on the way mass tourism works in the Balearics as a whole.

☆ **George Sand** *A Winter in Majorca*. Accompanied by her lover, Frédéric Chopin, Sand spent the winter of 1838–39 on Mallorca,

holing up in the monastery of Valldemossa. These are her recollections, often barbed and sharp-tongued – and very critical of the islanders. Readily available in Valldemossa and Mallorca's better bookshops. Read an extract on p.296.

Gordon West *Jogging Round Majorca*. This gentle, humorous account of an extended journey round Mallorca by Gordon and Mary West in the 1920s vividly portrays the island's pre-tourist life and times. The trip had nothing to do with running, but rather "jogging" as in a leisurely progress. West's book lay forgotten for decades until a BBC radio presenter, Leonard Pearcey, stumbled across it in a secondhand bookshop and subsequently read extracts on air. The programmes were very well received, and the book was reprinted in 1994.

History

David Abulafia *A Mediterranean Emporium: the Catalan Kingdom of Majorca*. Detailed, serious-minded study of medieval Mallorca.

Raymond Carr *Spain 1808–1975* and *Modern Spain 1875–1980*. Two

of the best books available on modern Spanish history – concise and well-considered narratives. Of equal standing are Carr's (shorter) 300-page *Spain: A History*; and *The Spanish Tragedy: the Civil War in Perspective*.

J.H. Elliott *Imperial Spain 1469–1716*. The best introduction to Spain's "golden age" – academically respected as well as being a gripping yarn. Also see his erudite *The Revolt of the Catalans: A Study in the Decline of Spain 1598–1640*.

Desmond Gregory *Minorca, the Illusory Prize: History of the British Occupation of Minorca between 1708 and 1802*. Exhaustive, scholarly and well-composed narrative detailing the British colonial involvement with Menorca. It's only published in hardback, however, and is expensive.

Bruce Laurie *Life of Richard Kane: Britain's First Lieutenant Governor of Minorca*. Detailed historical biogra-phy providing an intriguing insight into eighteenth-century Menorca. Only available in hardback

Geoffrey Parker *The Army of Flanders and the Spanish Road (1567–1659)*. Sounds dry and academic, but this fascinating book gives a marvellous insight into the morals, manners and organization of the Spanish army, then the most feared in Europe.

Hugh Thomas *The Spanish Civil War*. Exhaustively researched, brilliantly detailed account of the war and the complex political manoeuvrings surrounding it, with a section on Mallorca. First published in 1961, it remains the best book on the subject.

General background

Mossèn Antoni Alcover *Folk Tales of Mallorca*. The nineteenth-century priest and academic Mossèn Alcover spent decades collecting Mallorcan folk tales and this is a wide selection – almost 400 pages – of them. They range from the intensely religious through to parable and proverb, but many reveal an unpleasant edge to rural island life, both vindictive and mean-spirited. Makes for intriguing background material, but unfortunately particular places on the island are never mentioned or described.

Anthony Bonner (ed.) *Doctor Illuminatus: A Ramon Llull Reader*. A selection from the lengthy and heavy-going treatises on mysticism and Christian zeal by the thirteenth-century Mallorcan scholar and philosopher (see p.78). His works were some of the first to be written in Catalan, but are not for the faint-hearted. More manageable is *Romancing God: Contemplating the Beloved*, edited by Henry Carrigan Jnr, a 120-page introduction to Llull.

Barbara Catoir *Miró on Mallorca*. Lavishly illustrated book covering Miró's lengthy residence in Cala Major, just outside Palma. There's discussion of the work Miró produced in this period and of his thoughts on the island. Too hagiographical for some tastes.

Carrie B. Douglass *Bulls, Bullfighting & Spanish Identities*. Anthropologist Douglass delves into the symbolism of the bull in the Spanish national psyche, and then goes on to examine the role of the bullfight in some of the many fiestas that encourage it.

Tomás Graves *Bread & Oil: Majorcan Culture's Last Stand*. Written by a son of Robert Graves, this intriguing and entertaining book explores Mallorca via its palate, with sections on what the islanders eat and how the ingredients end up where they do. See p.299 for an extract.

William Graves *Wild Olives*. Another son of Robert Graves, William was born in 1940 and spent much of his childhood in Palma and Deià, sufficient inspiration for these mildly diverting accounts of his Mallorcan contemporaries. The book's real focus, however, is his troubled family life and his difficult relationship with his father.

★ **Gijs van Hensbergen** *Gaudí: the biography*. Thorough, well-written and thought-provoking survey of Gaudí's life and architectural output, including lots of intriguing biographical snippets.

★ **John Hooper** *The New Spaniards: A Portrait of the New Spain*. Well-constructed and extremely perceptive portrait of post-Franco Spain; an excellent general introduction. Highly recommended.

Fiction

Arturo Barea *The Forging of a Rebel*. Autobiographical trilogy, taking in the Spanish war in Morocco in the 1920s and Barea's own part in the civil war. Sometimes reprinted in its component titles: *The Forge*, *The Track* and *The Clash*.

Juan Goytisolo *Marks of Identity, Count Julian, Juan the Landless, The Virtues of the Solitary Bird* and *Makbara*. Born in Barcelona in 1931, Goytisolo became a bitter enemy of the Franco regime and has spent most of his life in exile in Paris and Morocco. Widely acclaimed as one of Spain's leading modern novelists, his most celebrated works (the first three titles listed above) confront the ambivalent idea of Spain and Spanishness. The fourth of the five titles above (from 1988) is a deep and powerful study of pain and repression, the fifth (from 1980) explores the Arab culture of North Africa in sharp and perceptive style.

★ **Lucia Graves** *A Woman Unknown: Voices from a Spanish*

Janis Mink *Miró*. Beautifully illustrated book that tracks through the artist's life and times. The text is rather ponderous, but there are lots of interesting quotations and, at 96 pages, you're not drowned in detail.

George Orwell *Homage to Catalonia*. Stirring account of Orwell's participation in, and early enthusiasm for, leftist revolution in Barcelona, followed by his growing disillusionment with the factional fighting that divided the Republican forces during the ensuing Civil War.

Miranda Seymour *Robert Graves: Life on the Edge*. Lengthy account of Robert Graves's personal life with lacklustre commentary on his poetry and novels. Includes much detail on Graves's residence in Deià.

Life. Robert Graves's children seem determined to make a literary name for themselves. This effort by his daughter Lucia is a thoughtful recollection of life in Mallorca in particular and Spain as a whole – lucid and interesting in equal measure.

Roderic Jeffries *An Enigmatic Disappearance*. This Inspector Alvarez murder mystery is set in Mallorca against a background of arrogant expats and a disapproving boss. The author is a Londoner by birth, but is now resident on the island. Other novels in the Alvarez series are *An Artistic Way to Go* and *A Maze of Murders*.

Juan Masoliver (ed.) *The Origins of Desire: Modern Spanish Short Stories*. Enjoyable selection of short stories from some of Spain's leading contemporary writers, including Mallorca's own Valentí Puig and Carme Riera.

Ana María Matute *School of the Sun*. The loss of childhood innocence on the Balearics, where old enmities are redefined during the Civil War.

★ **Manuel Vázquez Montalbán** *Murder in the Central Committee, The Angst-ridden Executive, Off Side.* Original and wonderfully entertaining tales by Spain's most popular crime thriller writer, a long-time member of the Communist Party and now a well-known journalist resident in Barcelona. Montalbán's great creation is the gourmand private detective Pepe Carvalho. If this trio of titles whets your appetite, move on to *Southern Seas* and a world of disillusioned communists, tawdry sex and nouvelle cuisine – key ingredients of post-Franco Spain.

Arturo Pérez-Reverte *The Fencing Master.* Subtle, heavily symbolic novel set in 1860s Madrid that traces the demise of the fencing master, a man in search of the perfect sword thrust. A journalist by profession, Pérez-Reverte is one of Spain's best-selling contemporary authors.

George Scott *The Bloody Bokhara.* Detective thriller set in modern-day Mallorca, a debut from an American who also runs a hotel on the island – a fairly good yarn, if a bit ponderously written, though it's excellent for background information on the island.

Maruja Torres *Desperately Seeking Julio.* The Julio in question is of course the crooner Iglesias (the original Spanish title – "It's Him!" – had no need for names) in this enjoyable romp of a novel. Torres is quite a name in Spain, writing for gossip columns.

Llorenç Villalonga, *The Dolls' Room.* Subtle if somewhat laboured portrait of nobility in decline in nineteenth-century Mallorca by a Mallorcan writer. First published in 1956. Several works by Villalonga are in print, but only in Catalan or Spanish. The author's old house in Binissalem is now a museum.

Specialist guidebooks

David & Rosamund Brawn The Brawns produce the best hiking books about the islands: directions are almost always easy to follow and each slim booklet detailing the hikes comes with a 1:25,000 map – and they're inexpensive too. Their *Mallorca Mountains Walking Guide* describes nineteen hikes in the Sóller region; the *Mallorca West Walking Guide* focuses on the coast west of Andratx; while the *Mallorca North Walking Guide* covers the Pollença and Alcúdia area. All three are erratically available in Mallorca. Their *Menorca (South East) Walking Guide* is one of the less inspired of the series, featuring fourteen walks in the vicinity of Maó – it's sometimes available Maó bookshops. The Brawns also publish a 1:40,000 *Touring & Walking Map of Menorca* –

cheap and quite useful as a reference, though the spelling is mostly Castilian.

Chris Craggs *Rock Climbs in Mallorca.* Over 300 pages detailing possible rock climbs across the island.

Lindsay Fisher, *A Layman's History of the Steam Railways of Mallorca* (The King's England Press, UK). The only specialist book on the subject – 68 pages to satisfy trainophiles.

Herbert Heinrich *Twelve Classic Hikes through Mallorca* (Editorial Moll, Mallorca). Heinrich has published a number of Mallorcan hiking guides in German. This was his first (and best) English volume, a compilation of some of the most enjoyable and less demanding one-day hikes in the Serra de Tramuntana mountains. The descriptions are a bit patchy, but the topographical sketches are extremely helpful. Widely available in Mallorca.

Gaspar Martí *Walking Tours around the Historical Centre of Palma*

Flora and fauna

Christopher Grey-Wilson, et al *Collins Field Guide: Mediterranean Wild Flowers*. Excellent, comprehensive field guide.

Graham Hearl *A Birdwatching Guide to Mallorca*. First-rate description of where to see what bird – and how to get there – in every part of the island. There is a handy bird checklist at the back of the book and the text is sprinkled with useful local maps. The sketches of various birds are, however, not very illuminating – and you'll still need a field guide.

Lars Jonsson *Birds of Europe*. As good a field guide as the Collins guide by Mullarney et al., but more specialized.

(Ajuntament de Palma, Mallorca). Detailed and enjoyable exploration of Palma's historical nooks and crannies. Quality sketches illuminate the text. Published by Palma city council and available in most leading bookshops in the city.

Killian Mullarney, et al *Collins Bird Guide*. Excellent field guide to birds – nothing better.

Oleg Polunin, et al *Flowers of Europe: a Field Guide*. First-rate field guide.

Enric Ramos *The Birds of Menorca*. Specialist handbook describing all the species of birds recorded in Menorca. It's well illustrated, but you'll still need a field guide.

Ken Stoba *Birdwatching in Mallorca*. First published in 1990, this slim book is a competent introduction to Mallorca's birdlife and major birdwatching sites.

Language

Language

Language

Most of the inhabitants of Mallorca and Menorca are bilingual, speaking Castilian (Spanish) and their local dialect of the Catalan language – *Mallorquín* or *Menorquín* – with equal facility. *Català* (Catalan) has been the islanders' everyday language since the absorption of the Balearics into the medieval Kingdom of Aragón and Catalunya in the thirteenth century following the Reconquista. Castilian, on the other hand, was imposed much later from the mainland as the language of government – and with special rigour by Franco. As a result, Spain's recent move towards regional autonomy has been accompanied by the islanders' assertion of Catalan as their official language. The most obvious sign of this has been the change of all the old Castilian town and street names into Catalan versions.

On paper, **Catalan** looks like a cross between French and Spanish and is generally easy to understand if you know those two, although when spoken it has a very harsh sound and is far harder to come to grips with.

Numerous **Spanish phrasebooks and dictionaries** are available. The most user-friendly is Rough Guide's *Spanish Dictionary Phrasebook*. No **English–Catalan phrasebook** is currently in print and there's only one **dictionary**, published by Routledge.

Some background

When **Franco** came to power in 1939, publishing houses, bookshops and libraries were raided and *Català* books destroyed. There was some relaxation in the mid-1940s, but throughout his dictatorship Franco excluded Catalan from the radio, TV, daily press and, most importantly, the schools, which is why many older people cannot read or write *Català* even if they speak it all the time. The islands' linguistic picture has been further muddied by the emigration of thousands of mainland Spaniards to the island, and nowadays it's estimated that Castilian is the dominant language in around forty percent of island households.

Català is spoken by over six million people in the Balearics, Catalunya, part of Aragón, most of Valencia, Andorra and parts of the French Pyrenees; it is thus much more widely spoken than several better-known languages such as Danish, Finnish and Norwegian. It is a Romance language, stemming from Latin and more directly from medieval Provençal. Spaniards in the rest of the country often belittle it by saying that to get a *Català* word you just cut a Castilian one in half (which is often true!), but in fact the grammar is much more complicated than Castilian and there are eight vowel sounds, three more than in Castilian.

Getting by in Mallorca and Menorca

Although Catalan is the preferred **language** of most islanders, you'll almost always get by perfectly well if you speak Castilian (Spanish), as long as you're aware of the use of Catalan in timetables and so forth. Once you get into it, Castilian is one of the easiest languages there is, the rules of pronunciation pretty straightforward and strictly observed. You'll find some basic pronunciation rules below for both Catalan and Castilian, and a selection of words and phrases in both languages. Castilian is certainly easier to pronounce, but don't be afraid to try Catalan, especially in the more out-of-the-way places – you'll generally get a good reception if you at least try communicating in the local language.

Castilian (Spanish): a few rules

Unless there's an accent, words ending in d, l, r, and z are **stressed** on the last syllable, all others on the second to last. All **vowels** are pure and short; combinations have predictable results.

A somewhere between back and father.

E as in get.

I as in police.

O as in hot.

U as in rule.

C is lisped before E and I, hard otherwise: *cerca* is pronounced "thairka".

CH is pronounced as in English.

G is a guttural H sound (like the *ch* in *loch*) before E or I, a hard G elsewhere: *gigante* is pronounced "higante".

H is always silent.

J is the same sound as a guttural G: *jamón* is pronounced "hamon".

LL sounds like an English Y: *tortilla* is pronounced "torteeya".

N as in English, unless it has a tilde (ñ) over it, when it becomes NY: *mañana* sounds like "man-yaana".

QU is pronounced like an English K.

R is rolled, RR doubly so.

V sounds more like B, *vino* becoming "beano".

X has an S sound before consonants, a KS sound before vowels.

Z is the same as a soft C, so *cerveza* is pronounced "thairvaitha".

Catalan: a few rules

With *Català*, don't be tempted to use the few rules of Castilian pronunciation you may know – in particular the soft Spanish Z and C don't apply, so unlike in the rest of Spain it's not "Barthelona" but "Barcelona", as in English.

A as in hat if stressed, as in alone when unstressed.

E varies, but usually as in get.

I as in police.

IG sounds like the "tch" in the English scratch; *lleig* (ugly) is pronounced "yeah-tch".

O varies, but usually as in hot.

U lies somewhere between put and rule.

Ç sounds like an English S: *plaça* is pronounced "plassa".

C followed by an E or I is soft; otherwise hard.

G followed by E or I is like the "zh" in Zhivago; otherwise hard.

H is always silent.

J as in the French "Jean".

LL sounds like an English Y or LY, like the "yuh" sound in "million".

N as in English, though before F or V it sometimes sounds like an M.

NY replaces the Castilian Ñ.

QU before E or I sounds like K; before A or O as in "quit".

R is rolled, but only at the start of a word; at the end it's often silent.

T is pronounced as in English, though sometimes it sounds like a D, as in *viatge* or *dotze*.

TX is like the English CH.

V at the start of a word sounds like B; in all other positions it's a soft F sound.

W is pronounced like a B/V.

X is like SH in most words, though in some, like *exit*, it sounds like an X.

Z is like the English Z.

Useful words and phrases

Basics

	Castilian	Catalan
Yes, No, OK	Sí, No, Vale	Si, No, Val
Please, Thank you	Por favor, Gracias	Per favor, Gràcies
Where, When	Dónde, Cuándo	On, Quan
What, How much	Qué, Cuánto	Què, Quant
Here, There	Aquí, Allí, Allá	Aquí, Allí, Allà
This, That	Esto, Eso	Això, Allò
Now, Later	Ahora, Más tarde	Ara, Més tard
Open, Closed	Abierto/a, Cerrado/a	Obert, Tancat
With, Without	Con, Sin	Amb, Sense
Good, Bad	Buen(o)/a, Mal(o)/a	Bo(na), Dolent(a)
Big, Small	Gran(de), Pequeño/a	Gran, Petit(a)
Cheap, Expensive	Barato/a, Caro/a	Barat(a), Car(a)
Hot, Cold	Caliente, Frío/a	Calent(a), Fred(a)
More, Less	Más, Menos	Més, Menys
Today, Tomorrow	Hoy, Mañana	Avui, Demà
Yesterday	Ayer	Ahir
Day before yesterday	Anteayer	Abans-d'ahir
Next week	La semana que viene	La setmana que ve
Next month	El mes que viene	El mes que ve

Greetings and responses

English	Castilian	Catalan
Hello, Goodbye	Hola, Adiós	Hola, Adéu
Good morning	Buenos días	Bon dia
Good afternoon/night	Buenas tardes/noches	Bona tarda/nit
See you later	Hasta luego	Fins després
Sorry	Lo siento/discúlpeme	Ho sento
Excuse me	Con permiso/perdón	Perdoni
How are you?	¿Cómo está (usted)?	Com va?
I (don't) understand	(No) Entiendo	(No) Ho entenc
Not at all/You're welcome	De nada	De res

English	Castilian	Catalan
Do you speak English?	¿Habla (usted) inglés?	Parla anglès?
I (don't) speak	(No) Hablo Español	(No) Parlo Català
My name is . . .	Me llamo . . .	Em dic . . .
What's your name?	¿Cómo se llama usted?	Com es diu?
I am English	Soy inglés/esa	Sóc anglès/esa
Scottish	escocés/esa	escocès/esa
Australian	australiano/a	australià/ana
Canadian	canadiense/a	canadenc(a)
American	americano/a	americà/ana
Irish	irlandés/esa	irlandès/esa
Welsh	galés/esa	gallès/esa

Hotels and transport

English	Castilian	Catalan
I want	Quiero	Vull (pronounced "fwee")
I'd like	Quisiera	Voldria
Do you know . . . ?	¿Sabe . . . ?	Vostès saben . . . ?
I don't know	No sé	No sé
There is (is there?)	(¿)Hay(?)	Hi ha(?)
Give me . . .	Deme . . .	Doneu-me . . .
Do you have . . . ?	¿Tiene . . . ?	Té . . . ?
. . . the time	. . . la hora	. . . l'hora
. . . a room	. . . una habitación	. . . alguna habitació
. . . with two beds/	. . . con dos camas/	. . . amb dos llits/
double bed	cama matrimonial	llit per dues persones
. . . with shower/bath	. . . con ducha/baño	. . . amb dutxa/bany
for one person	para una persona	per a una persona
(two people)	(dos personas)	(dues persones)
for one night	para una noche	per una nit
(one week)	(una semana)	(una setmana)
It's fine, how much is it?	Está bien, ¿cuánto es?	Esta bé, quant és?
It's too expensive	Es demasiado caro	És massa car
Don't you have	¿No tiene algo más barato?	En té de més bon preu?
anything cheaper?		
Can one . . . ?	¿Se puede . . . ?	Es pot . . . ?
. . . camp (near) here?	¿ . . . acampar aquí (cerca)?	. . . acampar a la vora?
Is there a hostel nearby?	¿Hay un hostal aquí cerca?	Hi ha un hostal a la vora?
It's not very far	No es muy lejos	No és gaire lluny
How do I get to . . . ?	¿Por dónde se va a . . . ?	Per anar a . . . ?
Left, right, straight on	Izquierda, derecha, todo recto	A l'esquerra, a la dreta, tot recte
Where is . . . ?	¿Dónde está . . . ?	On és . . . ?
. . . the bus station	. . . la estación de autobuses	. . . l'estació de autobuses
. . . the bus stop	. . . la parada	. . . la parada
. . . the railway station	. . . la estación de ferrocarril	. . . l'estació

English	Castilian	Catalan
. . . the nearest bank	. . . el banco más cercano	. . . el banc més a prop
. . . the post office	. . . el correo/ la oficina de correos	. . . l'oficina de correus
. . . the toilet	. . . el baño/aseo/servicio	. . . la toaleta
Where does the bus to . . . leave from?	¿De dónde sale el autobús para . . . ?	De on surt el auto bús a . . .?
Is this the train for Barcelona?	¿Es este el tren para Barcelona?	Aquest tren va a Barcelona?
I'd like a (return) ticket to . . .	Quisiera un billete (de ida y vuelta) para . .	Voldria un bitllet (d'anar i tornar) a . . .
What time does it leave (arrive in . . .)?	¿A qué hora sale (llega a . . .)?	A quina hora surt (arriba a . . .)?
What is there to eat?	¿Qué hay para comer?	Què hi ha per menjar?
What's that?	¿Qué es eso?	Què és això?

Days of the week

English	Castilian	Catalan
Monday	lunes	dilluns
Tuesday	martes	dimarts
Wednesday	miércoles	dimecres
Thursday	jueves	dijous
Friday	viernes	divendres
Saturday	sábado	dissabte
Sunday	domingo	diumenge

Numbers

	Castilian	Catalan
1	un/uno/una	un(a)
2	dos	dos (dues)
3	tres	tres
4	cuatro	quatre
5	cinco	cinc
6	seis	sis
7	siete	set
8	ocho	vuit
9	nueve	nou
10	diez	deu
11	once	onze
12	doce	dotze
13	trece	tretze
14	catorce	catorze
15	quince	quinze
16	dieciséis	setze
17	diecisiete	disset

18	dieciocho	divuit
19	diecinueve	dinou
20	veinte	vint
21	veintiuno	vint-i-un
30	treinta	trenta
40	cuarenta	quaranta
50	cincuenta	cinquanta
60	sesenta	seixanta
70	setenta	setanta
80	ochenta	vuitanta
90	noventa	novanta
100	cien(to)	cent
101	ciento uno	cent un
102	ciento dos	cent dos (dues)
200	doscientos	dos-cents (dues-centes)
500	quinientos	cinc-cents
1000	mil	mil
2000	dos mil	dos mil

Food and drink

In this section, we've generally given the **Catalan** names for food and drink items, since dialects of Catalan are the islanders' first language. Most restaurants, cafés and bars have **multilingual menus**, including English, but out in the countryside in cheaper cafés and restaurants there may only be a Catalan menu or maybe no menu at all, in which case the waiter will rattle off the day's dishes in Catalan. You'll occasionally find menus in **Castilian** (Spanish), which is understood by almost all restaurant staff, and we've given Castilian names alongside Catalan ones wherever useful.

Basics

	Catalan	Castilian
Bread	Pa	Pan
Butter	Mantega	Mantequilla
Cheese	Formatge	Queso
Eggs	Ous	Huevos
Oil	Oli	Aceite
Pepper	Pebre	Pimienta
Salt	Sal	Sal
Sugar	Sucre	Azúcar
Vinegar	Vinagre	Vinagre
Garlic	All	Ajo
Rice	Arròs	Arroz
Fruit	Fruita	Fruta
Vegetables	Verdures/Llegumos	Verduras/Legumbres

To have breakfast	Esmorzar	Desayunar
To have lunch	Dinar	Almorzar
Sopar	Cenar	To have dinner
Menu	Menú	Carta
Bottle	Ampolla	Botella
Glass	Got	Vaso
Fork	Forquilla	Tenedor
Knife	Ganivet	Cuchillo
Spoon	Cullera	Cuchara
Table	Taula	Mesa
The bill/check	El compte	La cuenta
Grilled	A la planxa	A la brasa
Fried	Fregit	Frit
Stuffed/rolled	Farcit	Relleno
Casserole	Guisat	Guisado
Roast	Rostit	Asado

Fruit (fruita) and vegetables (verdures/llegumes)

	Catalan	Castilian
Apple	Poma	Manzana
Asparagus	Espàrrecs	Espárragos
Aubergine/eggplant	Albergínies	Berenjenas
Banana	Plàtan	Plátano
Carrots	Pastanagues	Zanahorias
Cucumber	Concombre	Pepino
Grapes	Raïm	Uvas
Melon	Meló	Melón
Mushrooms	Xampinyons (also *bolets*, *setes*)	Champiñones
Onions	Cebes	Cebollas
Orange	Taronja	Naranja
Potatoes	Patates	Patatas
Pear	Pera	Pera
Peas	Pèsols	Arvejas
Pineapple	Pinya	Piña
Peach	Préssec	Melocotón
Strawberries	Maduixes	Fresas
Tomatoes	Tomàquets	Tomates

Bocadillos fillings

	Catalan	Castilian
Catalan sausage	Butifarra	Butifarra
Cheese	Formatge	Queso

Cooked ham	Cuixot dolç	Jamón York
Cured ham	Pernil salat	Jamón serrano
Loin of pork	Llom	Lomo
Omelette	Truita	Tortilla
Salami	Salami	Salami
Sausage	Salxitxó	Salchichón
Spicy sausage	Xoriç	Chorizo
Tuna	Tonyina	Atún

Tapas and racions

Catalan	Castilian	English
Anxoves	Boquerones	Anchovies
Bollit	Cocido	Stew
Calamars	Calamares	Squid, usually deep-fried in rings
Calamars amb tinta	Calamares en su tinta	Squid in ink
Cargols	Caracoles	Snails, often served in a spicy/curry sauce
Cargols de mar	Berberechos	Cockles (shellfish)
Calamarins	Chipirones	Whole baby squid
Carn amb salsa	Carne en salsa	Meat in tomato sauce
Croqueta	Croqueta	Fish or chicken croquette
Empanada petita	Empanadilla	Fish or meat pasty
Ensalada russa	Ensaladilla	Russian salad (diced vegetables in mayonnaise)
Escalibada	Escalibada	Aubergine (eggplant) and pepper salad
Faves	Habas	Broad beans
Faves amb cuixot	Habas con jamón	Beans with ham
Fetge	Hígado	Liver
Gambes	Gambas	Prawns
Musclos	Mejillones	Mussels (either steamed, or served with diced tomatoes and onion)
Navallas	Navajas	Razor clams
Olives	Aceitunas	Olives
Ou bollit	Huevo cocido	Hard-boiled egg
Pa amb tomàquet	Pan con tomate	Bread, rubbed with tomato and oil
Patates amb all i oli	Patatas alioli	Potatoes in garlic mayonnaise
Patates cohentes	Patatas bravas	Fried potato cubes with spicy sauce and mayonnaise
Pilotes	Albóndigas	Meatballs, usually in sauce
Pinxo	Pincho moruno	Kebab
Pop	Pulpo	Octopus
Prebes	Pimientos	Sweet (bell) peppers
Ronyons amb xeres	Riñones al jerez	Kidneys in sherry
Sardines	Sardinas	Sardines
Sípia	Sepia	Cuttlefish

Tripa	Callos	Tripe
Truita espanyola	Tortilla española	Potato omelette
Truita francesa	Tortilla francesa	Plain omelette
Tumbet	Tumbet	Pepper, potato, pumpkin and aubergine (eggplant) stew with tomato purée
Xampinyons	Champiñones	Mushrooms, usually fried in garlic
Xoriç	Chorizo	Spicy sausage

Balearic dishes and specialities

Many of the specialities that follow come from the Balearics' shared history with Catalunya. The more elaborate fish and meat dishes are usually limited to the fancier restaurants.

Sauces

Salsa mahonesa	Mayonnaise
Allioli	Garlic mayonnaise
Salsa romesco	Spicy tomato and wine sauce to accompany fish (from Tarragona)

Soups (*sopa*), starters and salads (*amanida*)

Amanida catalana	Salad with sliced meat and cheese
Carn d'olla	Mixed meat soup
Entremesos	Starter of mixed meat and cheese
Escalivada	Aubergine/eggplant, pepper and onion salad
Escudella	Mixed vegetable soup
Espinacs a la Catalana	Spinach with raisins and pine nuts
Esqueixada	Dried cod salad with peppers, tomatoes, onions and olives
Fideus a la cassola	Baked vermicelli with meat
Llenties guisades	Stewed lentils
Pa amb oli	Bread rubbed with olive oil, eaten with ham, cheese or fruit
Samfaina	Ratatouille-like stew of onions, peppers, aubergine/eggplant and tomato
Sopa d'all	Garlic soup
Sopas mallorquínas	Vegetable soup, sometimes with meat
	and chickpeas (garbanzos)
Truita (d'alls tendres; de xampinyons; de patates)	Omelette/tortilla (with garlic; with mushrooms; with potato). Be sure you're ordering omelette (*tortilla*), not trout (*truita*).

Rice dishes

Arròs negre	"Black rice", cooked with squid ink
Arròs a banda	Rice with seafood, the rice served separately
Arròs a la marinera	Paella: rice with seafood and saffron
Paella a la Catalana	Mixed meat and seafood paella, sometimes distinguished from a seafood paella by being called *Paella a Valencia*

Meat (*carn*)

Albergínies en es forn	Aubergines/eggplants stuffed with grilled meat
Botifarra amb mongetes	Spicy blood sausage with white beans
Conill (all i oli)	Rabbit (with garlic mayonnaise)
Escaldum	Chicken and potato stew in an almond sauce
Estofat de vedella	Veal stew

319

Fetge	Liver
Fricandó	Veal casserole
Frito mallorquín	Pigs' offal, potatoes and onions cooked with oil
Mandonguilles	Meatballs, usually in a sauce with peas
Perdius a la vinagreta	Partridge in vinegar gravy
Pollastre (farcit; amb gambas; al cava)	Chicken (stuffed; with prawns; cooked in sparkling wine)
Porc (rostit)	Pork (roast)
Sobrasada	Finely minced pork sausage, flavoured with paprika

L

Fish (*peix*) and shellfish (*marisc*)

Bacallà (amb samfaina)	Dried cod (with ratatouille)
Caldereta de llagosta	Lobster stew
Cloïsses	Clams, often steamed
Espinagada de Sa Pobla	Turnover filled with spinach and eel
Greixonera de peix	Menorcan fish stew, cooked in a pottery casserole
Guisat de peix	Fish and shellfish stew
Llagosta (amb pollastre)	Lobster (with chicken in a rich sauce)
Lluç	Hake, either fried or grilled
Musclos al vapor	Steamed mussels

Pop	Octopus
Rap a l'all cremat	Monkfish with creamed garlic sauce
Sarsuela	Fish and shellfish stew
Suquet	Fish casserole
Tonyina	Tuna
Truita	Trout (sometimes stuffed with ham, *a la Navarre*)

Desserts (*postres*) and pastries (*pastas*)

Cocaroll	Pastry containing vegetables and fish
Crema Catalana	Crème caramel, with caramelized sugar topping
Ensaimada	Flaky spiral pastry with fillings such as *cabello de ángel* (sweetened citron rind)
Mel i mató	Curd cheese and honey
Panades sobrasada	Pastry with peas, meat or fish
Postres de músic	Cake of dried fruit and nuts
Turrón	Almond fudge
Xurros	Deep-fried doughnut sticks (served with hot chocolate)

Drinking

	Catalan	Castilian
Water	Aigua	Agua
Mineral water	Aigua mineral	Agua mineral
(sparkling)	(amb gas)	(con gas)
(still)	(sense gas)	(sin gas)
Milk	Llet	Leche
Juice	Suc	Zumo
Tiger nut drink	Orxata	Horchata
Coffee	Café	Café
Espresso	Café sol	Café solo
White coffee	Café amb llet	Café con leche

Decaff	Descafeinat	Descafeinado
Tea	Te	Té
Drinking chocolate	Xocolata	Chocolate
Beer	Cervesa	Cerveza
Wine	Vi	Vino
Champagne/Sparkling wine	Xampan/Cava	Champán/Cava

Glossary

Catalan terms

Ajuntament Town Hall

Albufera Lagoon (and surrounding wetlands)

Altar major High altar

Aparcament Parking

Avinguda (Avgda) Avenue

Badia Bay

Barranc Ravine

Barroc Baroque

Basílica Catholic church with honorific
privileges

Cala Small bay, cove

Camí Way or road

Ca'n At the house of (contraction of *casa*
and *en*)

Capella Chapel

Carrer (c/) Street

Carretera Road, highway

Castell Castle

Celler Cellar, or a bar in a cellar

Claustre Cloister

Coll Col, mountain pass

Convent Convent, nunnery or monastery

Correu Post office

Coves Caves

Església Church

Estany Small lake

Festa Festival

Finca Estate or farmhouse

Font Water fountain or spring

Gòtic Gothic

Illa Island

Jardí Garden

Llac Lake

Mercat Market

Mirador Watchtower or viewpoint

Modernisme Literally "modernism", the
Catalan form of Art Nouveau, whose most
famous exponent was Antoni Gaudí;
adjective *modernista*

Monestir Monastery

Mozarabe A Christian subject of a medieval
Moorish ruler; hence Mozarabic, a
colourful building style that reveals both
Christian and Moorish influences

Mudéjar A Moorish subject of a medieval
Christian ruler. Also a style of architecture
developed by Moorish craftsmen working
for Christians, characterized by painted
woodwork with strong colours and complex
geometrical patterns; revived between the
1890s and 1930s and blended with Art
Nouveau forms.

Museu Museum

Nostra Senyora The Virgin Mary ("Our Lady")

Oficina d'Informació Turística Tourist office

Palau Palace, mansion or manor house

Parc Park

Passeig Boulevard; the evening stroll along it

Pic Summit

Plaça Square

Platja Beach

Pont Bridge

Port Harbour, port

Porta Door, gate

Puig Hill, mountain

Rambla Avenue or boulevard

Reconquista The Christian Reconquest of
Spain from the Moors beginning in the
ninth century and culminating in the
capture of Granada in 1492

Rei King

Reial Royal

Reina Queen

Reixa Iron screen or grille, usually in front of
a window

Renaixença Rebirth, often used to describe
the Catalan cultural revival at the end of the
nineteenth and beginning of the twentieth
centuries. Architecturally, this was
expressed as *modernisme*.

Retaule Retable or reredos, a wooden ornamental panel behind an altar

Riu River

Romeria Pilgrimage or gathering at a shrine

Salinas Saltpans

Salt d'aigua Waterfall

Santuari Sanctuary

Sant/a Saint

Serra Mountain range

Talayot Cone-shaped prehistoric tower

Taula T-shaped prehistoric megalithic structure

Torrent Stream or river (usually dry in summer)

Urbanització Modern estate development

Vall Valley

Art and architectural terms

Ambulatory Covered passage around the outer edge of the choir in the chancel of a church.

Apse Semicircular protrusion at (usually) the east end of a church.

Art Deco Geometrical style of art and architecture popular in the 1930s.

Art Nouveau Style of art, architecture and design based on highly stylised vegetal forms. Popular in the early part of the twentieth century. See also **Modernisme** (p.322).

Baroque The art and architecture of the Counter-Reformation, dating from around 1600 onwards. Distinguished by its ornate exuberance and (at its best) complex but harmonious spatial arrangement of interiors. Some elements – particularly its gaudiness – remained popular in the Balearics well into the twentieth century.

Caryatid A sculptured female figure used as a column.

Chancel The eastern part of a church, often separated from the nave by a screen or by the choir.

Churrigueresque Fancifully ornate form of Baroque art named after its leading exponents, the Spaniard José Churriguera (1650–1723) and his extended family.

Classical Architectural style incorporating Greek and Roman elements – pillars, domes, colonnades, and so on – at its height in the seventeenth century and revived, as Neoclassical, in the nineteenth.

Cyclopean Prehistoric style of dry stone masonry comprising boulders of irregular form.

Gothic Architectural style of the thirteenth to sixteenth centuries, characterized by pointed arches, rib vaulting, flying buttresses and a general emphasis on verticality.

Majolica See p.148.

Nave Main body of a church.

Neoclassical Architectural style derived from Greek and Roman elements – pillars, domes, colonnades, and so on – that was popular in the nineteenth century.

Plateresque Elaborately decorative Renaissance architectural style, named for its resemblance to silversmiths' work (*platería*).

Presbytery The part of the church to the east of the choir and the site of the high altar.

Renaissance Movement in art and architecture developed in fifteenth-century Italy.

Retable Altarpiece.

Romanesque Early medieval architecture distinguished by squat forms, rounded arches and naïve sculpture.

Transept Arms of a cross-shaped church, placed at ninety degrees to nave and chancel.

Triptych Carved or painted work on three panels.

Tympanum Sculpted, usually recessed, panel above a door.

Vault An arched ceiling or roof.

Rough Guides

advertiser

Rough Guides travel...

326

...music & reference

frica & Middle East
ape Town
gypt
he Gambia
erusalem
ordan
enya
Morocco
outh Africa, Lesotho
  & Swaziland
yria
anzania
unisia
est Africa
anzibar
mbabwe

ravel Theme guides
rst-Time Around the
  World
rst-Time Asia
rst-Time Europe
rst-Time Latin
  America
ay & Lesbian
  Australia
kiing & Snowboarding
  in North America
ravel Online
ravel Health
Valks in London & SE
  England
Vomen Travel

estaurant guides
ench Hotels &
  Restaurants
ondon
ew York
an Francisco

Maps
lgarve
msterdam
ndalucia & Costa del Sol
rgentina
thens

Australia
Baja California
Barcelona
Boston
Brittany
Brussels
Chicago
Crete
Croatia
Cuba
Cyprus
Czech Republic
Dominican Republic
Dublin
Egypt
Florence & Siena
Frankfurt
Greece
Guatemala & Belize
Iceland
Ireland
Lisbon
London
Los Angeles
Mexico
Miami & Key West
Morocco
New York City
New Zealand
Northern Spain
Paris
Portugal
Prague
Rome
San Francisco
Sicily
South Africa
Sri Lanka
Tenerife
Thailand
Toronto
Trinidad & Tobago
Tuscany
Venice
Washington DC
Yucatán Peninsula

**Dictionary
Phrasebooks**
Czech
Dutch
Egyptian Arabic
European
French
German
Greek
Hindi & Urdu
Hungarian
Indonesian
Italian
Japanese
Mandarin Chinese
Mexican Spanish
Polish
Portuguese
Russian
Spanish
Swahili
Thai
Turkish
Vietnamese

Music Guides
The Beatles
Cult Pop
Classical Music
Country Music
Cuban Music
Drum'n'bass
Elvis
House
Irish Music
Jazz
Music USA
Opera
Reggae
Rock
Techno
World Music (2 vols)

**100 Essential CDs
series**
Country
Latin

Opera
Rock
Soul
World Music

History Guides
China
Egypt
England
France
Greece
India
Ireland
Islam
Italy
Spain
USA

Reference Guides
Books for Teenagers
Children's Books, 0–5
Children's Books, 5–11
Cult Football
Cult Movies
Cult TV
Digital Stuff
Formula 1
The Internet
Internet Radio
James Bond
Lord of the Rings
Man Utd
Personal Computers
Pregnancy & Birth
Shopping Online
Travel Health
Travel Online
Unexplained
  Phenomena
The Universe
Videogaming
Weather
Website Directory

327

so! More than 120 Rough Guide music CDs are available from all good book
and record stores. Listen in at www.worldmusic.net

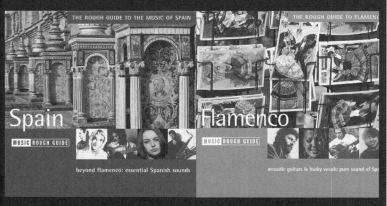

332

PALACIO CA SA GALESA
*****

Palacio Ca Sa Galesa is in the heart of the ancient city, with one of Palma´s famed Renaissance courtyards. Dating to 1571, it is one of the most exquisite establishments on the island. Surrounded by works of art and original stained-glass windows, guests enjoy the sensation of sojourning in their own private palace.

The hotel is a unique lodging choice, its 12 rooms and suites, with 17th- & 18th-century Mallorcan furniture and modern paintings and sculptures, evoking a luxurious atmosphere, yet one that feels like home, with all the most up-to-date services.

Strolling through its halls and lounges, bathing in the Gothic Quarter´s only covered pool (a restored ancient Roman bath), reading by the fireplace, or relaxing to the agreeable splash of the Moorish patio fountain – these are inimitable experiences. The spacious rooftop solarium offers a magnificent panoramic view of the Cathedral and the Bay of Palma, where it becomes impossible to distinguish where the sea ends and the sky begins.

Carrer de Miramar, 8 07001 Palma de Mallorca.
Tel: +34 971 71 54 00   Fax: +34 971 72 15 79   www.palaciocasagalesa.com
E-mail: reservas@palaciocasagalesa.com

SON BRULL

HOTEL & SPA
3|65 Restaurant

Pollença

Index

and small print

A Rough Guide to Rough Guides

In the summer of 1981, Mark Ellingham, a recent graduate from Bristol University, was travelling round Greece and couldn't find a guidebook that really met his needs. On the one hand there were the student guides, insistent on saving every last cent, and on the other the heavyweight cultural tomes whose authors seemed to have spent more time in a research library than lounging away the afternoon at a taverna or on the beach.

In a bid to avoid getting a job, Mark and a small group of writers set about creating their own guidebook. It was a guide to Greece that aimed to combine a journalistic approach to description with a thoroughly practical approach to travellers' needs – a guide that would incorporate culture, history and contemporary insights with a critical edge, together with up-to-date, value-for-money listings. Back in London, Mark and the team finished their Rough Guide, as they called it, and talked Routledge into publishing the book.

That first *Rough Guide to Greece*, published in 1982, was a student scheme that became a publishing phenomenon. The immediate success of the book – with numerous reprints and a Thomas Cook prize shortlisting – spawned a series that rapidly covered dozens of destinations. Rough Guides had a ready market among low-budget backpackers, but soon also acquired a much broader and older readership that relished Rough Guides' wit and inquisitiveness as much as their enthusiastic, critical approach. Everyone wants value for money, but not at any price.

Rough Guides soon began supplementing the "rougher" information about hostels and low-budget listings with the kind of detail on restaurants and quality hotels that independent-minded visitors on any budget might expect, whether on business in New York or trekking in Thailand.

These days the guides – distributed worldwide by the Penguin group – offer recommendations from shoestring to luxury and cover more than 200 destinations around the globe, including almost every country in the Americas and Europe, more than half of Africa and most of Asia and Australasia. Our ever-growing team of authors and photographers is spread all over the world, particularly in Europe, the USA and Australia.

In 1994, we published the *Rough Guide to World Music* and *Rough Guide to Classical Music*; and a year later the *Rough Guide to the Internet*. All three books have become benchmark titles in their fields – which encouraged us to expand into other areas of publishing, mainly around popular culture. Rough Guides now publish:

- Travel guides to more than 200 worldwide destinations
- Dictionary phrasebooks to 22 major languages
- History guides ranging from Ireland to Islam
- Maps printed on rip-proof and waterproof Polyart™ paper
- Music guides running the gamut from Opera to Elvis
- Restaurant guides to London, New York and San Francisco
- Reference books on topics as diverse as the Weather and Shakespeare
- Sports guides from Formula 1 to Man Utd
- Pop culture books from *Lord of the Rings* to Cult TV
- World Music CDs in association with World Music Network

Visit **www.roughguides.com** to see our latest publications.

Rough Guide Credits

Text editor: Gavin Thomas
Layout: Ajay Verma
Cartography: Stratigraphics
Picture research: Joe Mee
Proofreader: Antonia Hebbert
Editorial: London Martin Dunford, Kate Berens, Helena Smith, Claire Saunders, Geoff Howard, Ruth Blackmore, Gavin Thomas, Polly Thomas, Richard Lim, Lucy Ratcliffe, Clifton Wilkinson, Alison Murchie, Fran Sandham, Sally Schafer, Alexander Mark Rogers, Karoline Densley, Andy Turner, Ella O'Donnell, Keith Drew, Andrew Lockett, Joe Staines, Duncan Clark, Peter Buckley, Matthew Milton; **New York** Andrew Rosenberg, Richard Koss, Yuki Takagaki, Hunter Slaton, Chris Barsanti, Thomas Kohnstamm, Steven Horak
Design & Layout: London Dan May, Diana Jarvis; **Delhi** Madhulita Mohapatra, Umesh Aggarwal, Ajay Verma

Production: Julia Bovis, John McKay, Sophie Hewat
Cartography: London Maxine Repath, Ed Wright, Katie Lloyd-Jones, Miles Irving; **Delhi** Manish Chandra, Rajesh Chhibber, Jai Prakesh Mishra, Ashutosh Bharti, Rajesh Mishra, Animesh Pathak
Cover art direction: Louise Boulton
Picture research: Mark Thomas, Jj Luck
Online: New York Jennifer Gold, Cree Lawson, Suzanne Welles, Benjamin Ross; **Delhi** Manik Chauhan, Amarjyoti Dutta, Narender Kumar
Marketing & Publicity: London Richard Trillo, Niki Smith, David Wearn, Chloë Roberts, Demelza Dallow, Kristina Pentland; **New York** Geoff Colquitt, David Wechsler, Megan Kennedy
Finance: Gary Singh
Manager India: Punita Singh
Series editor: Mark Ellingham
PA to Managing Director: Julie Sanderson
Managing Director: Kevin Fitzgerald

Publishing Information

This third edition published May 2004 by **Rough Guides Ltd,**
80 Strand, London WC2R 0RL.
345 Hudson St, 4th Floor,
New York, NY 10014, USA.
Distributed by the Penguin Group
Penguin Books Ltd,
80 Strand, London WC2R 0RL
Penguin Putnam, Inc.
375 Hudson Street, NY 10014, USA
Penguin Books Australia Ltd,
487 Maroondah Highway, PO Box 257,
Ringwood, Victoria 3134, Australia
Penguin Books Canada Ltd,
10 Alcorn Avenue, Toronto, Ontario,
Canada M4V 1E4
Penguin Books (NZ) Ltd,
182–190 Wairau Road, Auckland 10,
New Zealand
Typeset in Bembo and Helvetica to an original design by Henry Iles.

Printed in China

© Phil Lee

No part of this book may be reproduced in any form without permission from the publisher except for the quotation of brief passages in reviews.

352p includes index
A catalogue record for this book is available from the British Library

ISBN 1-84353-252-2

The publishers and authors have done their best to ensure the accuracy and currency of all the information in **The Rough Guide to Mallorca & Menorca**, however, they can accept no responsibility for any loss, injury, or inconvenience sustained by any traveller as a result of information or advice contained in the guide.

3   5   7   9   8   6   4   2

Help us update

We've gone to a lot of effort to ensure that the third edition of **The Rough Guide to Mallorca & Menorca** is accurate and up-to-date. However, things change – places get "discovered", opening hours are notoriously fickle, restaurants and rooms raise prices or lower standards. If you feel we've got it wrong or left something out, we'd like to know, and if you can remember the address, the price, the time, the phone number, so much the better.

We'll credit all contributions, and send a copy of the next edition (or any other Rough Guide if you prefer) for the best letters. Everyone who writes to us and isn't already a subscriber will receive a copy of our full-colour thrice-yearly newsletter. Please mark letters: "**Rough Guide Mallorca & Menorca Update**" and send to: Rough Guides, 80 Strand, London WC2R 0RL, or Rough Guides, 4th Floor, 345 Hudson St, New York, NY 10014. Or send an email to
mail@roughguides.com

Have your questions answered and tell others about your trip at
www.roughguides.atinfopop.com

SMALL PRINT

Acknowledgements

Jeffrey Kennedy thanks: María Andersson, Emilio Balanzó, Maria Casanovas i Codina, Helmut Clemens, Mirella d'Angelo, Tomeu Deyà, Oriol Galgo, Suzanne Hartley, Carlos Baqués Meler, Britta Ploenzke, Anna Skidmore, Ricarda Söhnlein, Mike Suarez, The Suau Family, Davina, et al.

The editor would like to thank Ed Wright and Katie Lloyd-Jones for additional map-making; Joe Mee for prompt assistance in a pictorial crisis; and Umesh Aggarwal for making sense of the mess.

Readers' letters

Many thanks to all the readers who wrote in with their comments and suggestions (and apologies to anyone whose name we've misspelt):

Marek Antoszewski, Wendy Ashworth, Jenny G. Atton, Billy Averall, Jim Barrell, Bridget Beck, K. Behr, Mike Braide, Rod Braxton, Derek Bryce, Stuart Bull, Vivienne Carmichael, John and Midge Cassetton, Fiona Clampin, Sue Coats, V. A. Cooke, I. A. Cowie, Anita Creed, Damon Crawshaw, Alison Ewington, Julian Fenn, John Girdley, John & Valerie Given, Anne Goodchild, Sean Gostage, Annekatrin Grafton, Amanda Grainger, Caroline Hadley, Nick Halstead, Nicola Hambridge, Liz and James Heesom, Karin von Herrath Ross, Liz Heron, Gary Hunt, Pam and John Ireland, Malcolm Jackson, Tim Jenkins, Stuart Johnson, Hugh Kearney, J.A. Ketley, Elizabeth and Geoff Key, Paul Lampard, John Landau, Tim Lang, Beverley B. Lawe, Margaret Leafe, D. Lee, Peter Lloyd, B.R. & C.R. Lumby, James McLeod, Janet Macdonald, Abe Marrache, David Mather, Nicola and Ian Maunders, David McManus, Clare and Richard Morgan, Vera Morris, Chris Peake, Ian Pearson, Tony Robinson, Gordon A. Roe, Carol Saddington, Paul Sherratt, Anthony Schlesinger, Jan Shepherd, R. Sinclair, Debbie Smith, Richard Strutt, Alastair Tainsh, Ann Viera, Mr & Mrs Wallington, Brian Wallis, M. Welch, John Weldon, Selina Westbury, Clive Wilkin, David and Irene Williamson, Stephen Withers, Claire Woodward-Nutt, Lai Mie Wright, Leesa Yeo

Photo Credits

Index

Map entries are in colour.

INDEX

Map symbols

Maps are listed in the full index using coloured text.

– – – – –	Chapter division boundary	▲	Mountain peak
▬▬▬▬	Motorway	ᴸᴬᴸᵁᴸᴬ	Cliff
═══	Main road	ᴧᴧ	Spring
═══	Minor road	⚇	Gardens
▬▬▬▬	Pedestrianized road	⬐	Viewpoint
- - - - - -	Footpath	⚠	Campsite
⊞⊞⊞⊞⊞	Steps	◉	Accommodation
▬•▬•▬	Railway	■	Restaurant
─┼─┼─┼─	Tram line	ⓘ	Information office
— – – –	Ferry route	⊠	Post office
────	Waterway	@	Internet access
▬▬▬▬	Wall	★	Bus stop/taxi stand
♦	Place of interest	🅿	Parking
✈	Airport	🅑	Petrol station
⚲	Church (regional maps)	⊞	Hospital
⚶	Monastery	▬	Building
♖	Castle	⊞	Church (town maps)
⍓	Stately home	◯	Stadium
♖	Tower	▢	Market
∴	Ruins	▨	Park
◒	Cave	▨	Beach
⚓	Lighthouse	⬭	Saltpan